Case Studies
in the
Development of
Close Air Support

Edited
by

Benjamin Franklin Cooling

OFFICE OF AIR FORCE HISTORY
UNITED STATES AIR FORCE
WASHINGTON, DC 1990

Library of Congress Cataloging-in-Publication Data

Case studies in the development of close air support / edited by
  Benjamin Franklin Cooling.
        p.   cm. -- (Special studies)
  Includes bibliographic references and index
  ISBN 0-912799-64-1 (paperbound). -- ISBN 0-912799-65-X (casebound)
  1. Close air support--History. 2. Military history. Modern--20th
  century. I. Cooling, B. Franklin. II. Series: Special studies
  (United States. Air Force. Office of Air Force History)
  UG700.C38 1990
  358.4'142--dc20   90-14399

For sale by the Superintendent of Documents, U.S. Government Printing Office,
Washington, DC 20402

Foreword

The introduction of airplanes to warfare led almost from the first to their application in close support of ground forces. The earliest attempts at influencing the outcome of a ground battle from the air were limited by the fragility of the craft engaged and the lack of coherent ideas on the most effective use of what was still a novelty. What began as an expedient, however, has become over nearly ten decades an essential role for air power. Taken virtually for granted by troops and aviators today, the employment of air power in this way has been controversial from the first instance in which bombs were dropped on ground combatants during the Italo-Turkish war of 1911–1912. Ground and air commanders have differed over the proper use of aviation; preferences and assumptions on doctrine have evolved in both the ground and air communities; technology has changed air systems and defensive ground weaponry; and with time different systems or techniques have developed in various military establishments for the command and control of ground and air forces operating in concert, for liaison and communications, and for delivering aerial firepower in support of land forces locked in combat with an enemy.

In December 1982, Maj. Gen. Perry McCoy Smith, then the Air Force Director of Plans, asked the Office of Air Force History to prepare a number of case-study volumes on various aspects of air warfare. Col. John A. Warden III, in the Office of the Deputy Chief of Staff for Plans and Operations, provided funds from the Air Force's Project Warrior Program. With further generous assistance of Dr. Andrew Marshall, then Director of Net Assessment in the Office of the Secretary of Defense, the Air Force History Program approached some of the foremost historians in the field of military aviation to record their assessments as a resource for planning within the Air Force and the Army for several years to come.

Each author was asked to produce an original case study on a defined period or subject. The essays were to be based on all relevant published literature and on the key archival documents containing the record of how various air forces actually developed and applied their systems of close air support to ground combat. Each author was also asked to cover certain basic topics: initial doctrine, organization of forces, background and courses of the air-ground campaigns, communications systems, command and control arrangements, weaponry and technology, and the decisions and people that determined the course of action and shaped its outcome. A concluding retrospect draws generalizations from the experiences presented.

The Office of Air Force History believes that this volume will be of substantial value not only to the U.S. Air Force and the U.S. Army, but should also appeal to a wider audience interested in all aspects of military history and contribute to informing the American public about the characteristics and the use of air power in all of its aspects.

Richard H. Kohn
Chief, Office of Air Force History

Contents

Photographs

Maps

Introduction

Close air support of ground operations has become a recognized element of modern warfare. Stripped to its barest essentials, its definition proves deceptively simple. As the authoritative Department of Defense *Dictionary of Military and Associated Terms* defines it: close air support comprises "air attacks against hostile targets which are in close proximity to friendly forces and which require detailed integration of each air mission with the fire and movement of those forces." Not only is this U.S. doctrine, but it also has been accepted by the North Atlantic Treaty Organization (NATO), Southeast Asia Treaty Organization (SEATO), Central Treaty Organization (CENTO), and the Inter-American Defense Board (IADB), although these allied bodies prefer the term "air action" to "air attacks." Presumably, other nations and signatories to similar defense agreements—the Warsaw Pact countries, for example—have similar doctrinal positions on this critical function. A more descriptive definition can be found in the now dated 1956 edition of the *United States Air Force Dictionary*, which defines the doctrine as "air support or cooperation provided friendly surface forces, consisting of air attacks with guns, bombs, guided airborne missiles or rockets on hostile surface forces, their installations or vehicles so close to surface operations as to require detailed coordination between air and friendly surface forces." Whatever the precise definition, this aspect of warfare is the modern version of one of the oldest air combat missions, having been derived from the air arm's original function as an air reconnaissance auxiliary of the land force. It is also one of the most controversial. Since aerospace technology and doctrine have long since carried air warfare to more effective methods for aviation to fulfill national strategic military goals, close air support of ground operations has become one of the most divisive topics between soldiers and airmen.[1]

Since the emergence of strategic bombardment during World War I as an operational rationale for aviation's organizational independence from the other services, few airmen have willingly embraced what the British called "army cooperation," in which aviators are merely direct supporters of the foot-slogging "Queen of Battle," the infantry. American and British aviators particularly have made unmistakably clear their desire to perform missions that do not involve complicated liaison with ground forces, subordination of air forces to ground requirements, or attrition of air resources in dangerous and unrewarding missions. They have viewed their proper contribution to victory to be through strategic bombardment, air superiority, and interdiction.

In spite of the fact that close air support has shown that it is often one of the truly pivotal uses of air power in modern warfare, even now no other single issue seems more quickly to lead to outspoken disagreement between professionals charged with coordinating the air-land battle. Through the years, the nature of the prime questions has been both philosophical and practical: whether or not air forces have a duty to provide battlefield aid to land forces at the point of engagement, or whether air action might be more cost-effective through interdiction elsewhere, or in long-range strategic operations against the political, economic, and societal underpinnings of an enemy war effort.[2]

The question of close air support has assumed peculiarities of detail in different nations and in different eras. The issue has been as much organizational and technological as it has been doctrinal. The success or failure of close air support in a given situation has depended as much upon quality, quantity, and type of aircraft and personnel, command and control arrangements, air-ground communication systems, and air-ground training as upon any differences of doctrinal semantics. While discussion between air and ground professionals has been discordant in doctrinal definition, the hands-on experience to be derived from the historical record can be useful for the present and future. It remains important, however, to understand that the major hurdles have always been principally organization, numbers and types of aircraft to be employed, and wise assignment of relative importance of the various ingredients to such support. The story hinges as much upon personalities, institutional politics, and production technology as upon ideology. Such facts of life in wartime led Professor James A. Huston to declare that close air support in World War II displayed a remarkable ambiguity, sometimes meaning "closeness in space, that is, to the air attack of targets close to the lines or columns of troops on the ground," while at other times referring more to "closeness of command, communication, and cooperation." Usually, concluded Huston, it included both.[3]

Huston discerned three categories of close air support of ground troops during World War II. First, were those large-scale operations minutely planned by higher headquarters to concentrate massive firepower at a decisive breakthrough point in the land battle. Such operations included the bombing of Monte Cassino, Cherbourg, and the St. Lo operation. Second, were those special missions extending over a longer period of time for a particular Army, such as the protection afforded Third Army's flank by XIX Tactical Air Command during the summer campaign across Northwest Europe. Third were those unsung and unheralded specific missions, scheduled or on call, flown at the request of ground commanders. Naturally, ground commanders saw the latter as bread-and-butter aspects of their own operational missions. In any event, the separate essays in this volume focus upon key case studies in the development of close air support. Disproportionate attention is given to wartime experience—World War II in particular—since such episodes were the proving ground for doctrine.[4]

The initial essay focuses upon the formative years of air support of ground actions. Lee Kennett briefly notes the developments arising from World War I and then analyzes those pivotal interwar years before World War II. He suggests that the air impact upon ground troops in the first was more psychological than material given, the state of aircraft, type or ordnance, and employment of air power in the close support role. Kennett suggests, however, that the original reconnaissance role for aircraft soon gave way to strafing and bombing of enemy troops and ground positions with initially a spectacularly adverse effect on the morale of the foot soldiers. Then, a counter cycle of ground antiaircraft defenses, indoctrination of infantrymen and artillerymen to overcome their fear of the air weapon, and the introduction of more sophisticated fighter aircraft, appeared to dampen the early effects of close air support. High casualty rates to ground fire also lessened airmen's enthusiasm for this mission, causing their leaders to seek alternatives to ground support in interdiction and long-range bombardment behind the battle lines. Still, ground commanders sought to employ aviation like other arms, directly upon the battlefield. Issues like "bomblines," proper air-ground communication, and technical dimensions of ground-support aircraft were introduced in this period. Later, when the war was over, low peacetime budgets and different military priorities precluded honing the wartime lessons of close air support. As Kennett contends, the lessons of close air support in World War I awaited further clarification until the onset of renewed conflict in the late 1930s. Meanwhile, he suggests, close air support clung to the shadows of phlegmatic peacetime experimentation with technology, techniques, and doctrine. It fared least well during the interwar years in nations where the army produced no new doctrine, and the air force committed itself to the concept of strategic air power. In the United States, for example, the "episodic" history of close air support, says Kennett, resulted from the Army Air Corps attempt, through emphasis upon the importance of the strategic bombardment mission, to gain organizational status independent of the ground army. Only the example of successful use of air power in direct support of ground combat, as witnessed in Spain, China, and the European war after 1939, led military experts in various nations to attempt codification of a close air-support doctrine, with all the modernized tools of proper materiél and improved communication systems to implement that doctrine.

Williamson Murray carries this discussion forward with his examination of the close air-support mission of the German *Luftwaffe* and the spectacular success which that air arm enjoyed in Poland and against the western Allies in 1940. He suggests that doctrinally the *Luftwaffe* was committed less to conventional close air support of ground operations and more to air superiority, interdiction, and, in certain cases, strategic bombardment missions in support of land warfare. The armies of the world followed similar patterns by developing a basic land force of the World War I type, with but little regard for the necessities of modern combat imposed by the advent of air power. The Spanish Civil War changed this, at least for the *Luftwaffe*, says Murray. With only tepid support from Berlin, German volunteer aviators of the Condor Legion developed close air doctrine and capability. Ironically, however, it was at about the level of sophistication it had reached at the end of World War I. Neither within *Luftwaffe* circles nor between air and ground services was there a clearly agreed-upon system of precise close air support when Germany invaded Poland in 1939. Yet, Murray contends that the German air arm was one of the few in the world in the late 1930s that had thought at all about the problems of close air support, and accepted the fact that such air missions could render vital aid to ground troops in critical situations. Poland provided a laboratory in which weaknesses of liaison, communications, and ground recognition of aircraft surfaced. The war in the West, in the spring of 1940, further clarified problems such as incompatible air-ground, and fighter-bomber communication systems, difficult organizational relationships between army and air services, and the challenges posed by fluid mechanized battle. He suggests that German air warfare was quite traditional at this time, with the *Luftwaffe* moving initially to establish air superiority by suppressing enemy aerodromes, and interdicting enemy supply routes, and only when these objectives had been accomplished moving to support the land units directly at critical moments such as the Meuse river crossing. He attributes the progress of the battles as much to Anglo-French weakness in coordination as to German superiority. Finally, he turns to the German-Russian war in the east, concluding that measurably improved close air support and efficiency of execution marked *Luftwaffe* contributions. Nevertheless, contends Murray, no matter what the brilliance of German victory initially in Russia—to which the *Luftwaffe* contributed so much in terms of army support—the air arm, like its ground counterpart, could not overcome strategic and logistical miscalculations of the Hitler regime as to the vastness of Soviet resources and terrain. While German military prowess might rest upon a cooperative spirit at lower and intermediate echelons both within and between the services, the brilliance of short-run tactical success dimmed as the war in the East dragged on for three more years. Attrition, in this case, dramatically affected the *Luftwaffe*'s ability to continue its close air support of the army as Russian arms bled the *Wehrmacht* into ultimate defeat.

Kenneth Whiting explores in some depth the Soviet story of close air support in World War II. He suggests that the lessons learned during Soviet intervention in Spain, and the absence of an effective long-range bomber, led the regime of Josef Stalin to overwhelmingly to embrace air superiority and close air support as twin tenets of Russian air power. By 1944, most Soviet Air Force assets, whether fighter, attack, or bomber aircraft, were committed to the close support of ground forces in a series of major offenses. As perhaps in no other major military power, by both prewar doctrine and wartime experience, the Soviets doted (to use Whiting's verb) on the concept of combined arms in a given battle or operation. Economic as well as military doctrine emphasized the forging of a combined arms war machine, but one in which the air element was to serve only as a support for ground forces, which remained the principal striking arm of the Soviets. Nonetheless, the state of upheaval and transition in Soviet military aviation when the Germans attacked in 1941 produced near disaster, as surprise and superior equipment enabled the *Luftwaffe* to slaughter its Soviet counterpart. As the conflict developed, it was Russian winter, not Russian arms, that contained the initial German invasion by the end of the year. By mid-summer 1943 and the battle of Kursk, Soviet attrition of German air resources, superior factory production of materiel necessary for close air support from "sanctuaries" beyond *Luftwaffe* range, and the perfection of tactics, air-ground communications, organization, and provision of pilot and parts replacement all affected the battle favorably for the Soviets. Locally, the Soviet Air Force wrested air superiority from the Germans, and never relinquished it through the death throes of Nazi Germany in May 1945. In Whiting's view at least, the Soviets' and the Germans' principle air missions on the eastern front related to close air support of ground operations. He contends that the Soviet leadership did the better job through production of appropriate aircraft, the training of sufficient pilots, providing the support infrastructure, and never deviating from the principle that air power's main mission was cooperation with ground forces to win the air-land battle.

The next four essays focus upon American experience with close air support during World War II. David Syrett opens the discussion with an analysis of Operation Torch, and the Allied conquest of Tunisia in 1942–1943. His story is one of Allied unpreparedness for air-ground cooperation, a muddled command and control system, and several months of sorting out both the allied and joint aspects of cooperation in close air support. He discusses the process of trial and error which led U.S. Army Air Forces to acquire control over all air assets, and the American acceptance of British close air-support doctrine learned in the Western Desert as the preferred method of helping land forces on the battlefield. He also shows the relationship between inadequate ground facilities (all-weather airfields), types of aircraft, and proliferation of air missions such as land and sea interdiction, and the Army Air Forces' ability to provide timely and decisive ground support. Particularly revealing in Syrett's essay is the role of personalities in crisis, as well as the persuasive diplomacy of airmen such as General Carl Spaatz and Air Marshall Sir Arthur Coningham in convincing land generals like Field Marshals Harold Alexander and Bernard Law Montgomery or Generals Dwight D. Eisenhower and George Patton, that an employed air force under the command of its own officers could provide more unified and concentrated air power in support of embattled troops on the ground than one whose employment was at the command of Army officers.

Alan F. Wilt provides the sequel to North Africa in coverage of close air support in Sicily and Italy. He suggests that the early attainment of air superiority enabled Allied air forces to concentrate on interdiction and close air-support missions. As a result, they devoted additional time and attention to perfecting techniques and procedures learned in Tunisia. His essay is one of detail; the details of perfecting organizational arrangements, smoothing air-ground teamwork through such forward control devices as the famous Rover, Horsefly, Timothy, and Pineapple arrangements, as well as determining the best close airsupport aircraft from among old and new models. He suggests that the emergence of competent air and ground generals overcame many of the leadership hassles that had arisen in North Africa. Still, lack of air-ground coordination, little participation by air planners in invasion preparations, a yet cumbersome command and control arrangement, slow reaction time to ground requests, and inadequate bombline procedures plagued Allied close air support in Sicily. The lengthy campaign up the Italian peninsula showed a slow but steady improvement in all facets of the problem. Wilt sees the close air-support issue in Italy as one of mainly doctrinal and organizational difficulties. Emergence of an independently controlled air command by this stage of the war often caused American air leaders to remain detached from joint planning and coordination. Furthermore, Wilt feels that air leaders continued to place far too much emphasis upon achievement of air superiority, when the crux of that issue had long since been resolved. Wilt suggests lack of training, distance from airbases to battle line, and poor air-naval cooperation continued to cause concern in Italy. Nevertheless, he feels that close air support had come of age by early 1944. The *Luftwaffe* seldom proved more than an irritant, and implementation rather than conceptualization was the problem by the time the fighting moved north of Rome.

In one of the most provocative conclusions of the book, Wilt contends that by April 1945, the attritional war in a secondary theater like Italy no longer influenced the doctrine and techniques of air warfare. Ironically, the concurrent fighting in Northwest Europe influenced the Italian campaign. Wilt sees the tactics developed for close air support of armored column advances (from Normandy to beyond the Rhine) pervading the Italian scene by the last month of the war in Europe.

W. A. Jacobs explores in similar detail close air support in the battle for France in 1944. Here one might expect to find examples of lessons learned during several years of close air-support experience from North Africa to Rome, from Guadalcanal to the China-Burma-India theater. Jacobs suggests, however, that air-ground cooperation in France evidenced only limited application of wisdom that should have been acquired in earlier campaigns. Anglo-

American ground commanders still sought the ultimate in air support, including even the use of heavy bombardment in a tactical role. Similarly, RAF and USAAF leaders adhered to a doctrine emphasizing air superiority and interdiction as preferred roles for the tactical squadrons, despite the decline of enemy air-fighting strength, non-prohibitive loss rates in close air support, and the obvious need for more such support during the six-week stalemate following the Normandy landings.

Jacobs discusses in great detail the problems of airfield positioning, logistics, and communication equipment—factors seemingly more important than previous issues of command and control, aircraft type, or even doctrine. In covering this campaign, he describes the use of Rover, Armored Column Cover, and Air Alert tactics, advanced communications equipment, and emergence of a distinct fighter-bomber type of aircraft. He suggests the use of heavy bombers in key attempts to relieve the stalemate was marginally effective and concludes that at no time in France did the "miracle weapon" anticipated by air leaders appear on the scene.

Jacobs' essay shows the evolution of close air support from preoperational planning through the lessons learned and applied in combat. He maintains that by mid-August, close air systems, particularly those employed by American forces, became more flexible and more responsive to army needs while still retaining the centralized air allocation control required for efficient employment of air resources. He concludes that while close air support was not the decisive weapon in this campaign, it nevertheless impressed ground commanders with its impact upon enemy morale, communications, cohesion and organization of ground forces. To Jacobs, at least, it set the stage for an even more pivotal role when the war of movement began in late summer. In Jacobs' view, the battle for France in 1944 transformed close air support into a regular component of the Allied combined arms battle team.

Was the close air-support experience in the Pacific Theater similar to that in Europe? Joe Gray Taylor shifts the story to that part of the world and recounts many of the close air-support features in the unique "island-hopping" war. Here, as in Europe, the story was as much one of joint operations of the American army, navy, and air forces as it was a story of joint operations with our Allies. Naval gunfire and attack aviation, Marine aviation, as well as the U.S. Army Air Forces resources, complemented the ground commanders' own artillery and tanks. The same kinds of problems as those facing air-ground cooperation in the European theater, such as inadequacies of radio equipment, problems of rapid airfield construction during offensive operations, lack of replacement parts and trained personnel, target identification, and bomb-line demarcation, were also present in the Pacific. Nevertheless there were features unique to the Southwest Pacific: (1) regular employment of B-24 Liberator heavy bombers in close air-support missions, (2) a top

7

air commander in the theater who willingly embraced close air support as his primary mission, and (3) a time-gap between ground request and air delivery ("day-after strikes") that would have been intolerable in the faster moving campaigns of the European theater. One of the significant features of air war in the Southwest Pacific theatre was the influence of General George C. Kenney, the air commander, whose advocacy of the air-ground mission was well known. Communication of his attitude down the chain of air command assured more willing compliance to ground requests than would have been the normal USAAF wont. There remained, however, the question of whose air support was provided in a more timely and effective manner—that of the Marine Corps or the Army aviator. Taylor pointedly suggests that no one service won that honor, and that, as in Europe, perfection of this mission did not come overnight. He concludes that the air forces in the Southwest Pacific developed probably as effective a system of close air support as was possible, given their problems of aircraft and personnel resupply, the nature of a war of vast distances over water, the intractable weather, the ever dangerous and deceptive enemy, and the earlier, prewar Army Air Corps straightjackets of doctrine and tactics which had necessarily to be modified by combat experience to suit the peculiarities of time and place.

Allan R. Millett attacks the close air-support issue in the context of the first major conflict of the post World War II period. Korea offered air leaders a chance to use the lessons learned in World War II, particularly in Europe. What developed, however, in Millett's view was a major controversy as to whether the now independent U.S. Air Force or Marine aviation could provide the most timely, adequate, and accurate close air support as desired by the ground forces of the United Nations Command. Three factors contributed to a major imbroglio involving the press and the Pentagon: (1) the organizational change of 1947, which gave the Air Force independence from the Army, (2) the fact that the Marine Corps had not had its aviation units, or for that matter many of its ground contingents in the European Theater of Operations where they might have competed with the Army Air Forces style of close air support in World War II, and (3) the frustrations of America's first limited war. Fundamentally, as Millett shows, lack of coordination in close air support was rooted in contrasting perspectives on the nature of warfare itself, and this ultimately transcended mere service intransigence.

Throughout the three-year war, Army, Navy, and Marine Corps leaders stood against those of the Air Force on these close air-support issue. The Air Force, once air superiority was assured, clung to interdiction as its major contribution to the stalemated war; the other three services wanted air power applied right at the battle line. A major post hoc conference on close air support following the armistice in 1953 focused on changes in the air request and air control system. Millett argues that like the war itself, the story of two close air-support systems used by American forces (and by implication the

United Nations Command) ended on an inconclusive note. Nevertheless, he contends that for the men on the ground, close air support did offer tangible results whichever the style of delivery.

All of the services tacitly recognized that bickering among themselves would not win the war and thus accepted reforms and refinements on this issue, within the context of the original "Joint Training Directive for Air-Ground Operations," which the Air Force had promulgated in September 1950. Millett finishes his essay with a somewhat disheartening portrayal of post Korean separatism as the U.S. Army and Air Force voided the Korean war doctrine, with the Air Force focusing almost exclusively upon strategic bombardment and the Army eventually attempting to form its own close air-support aviation.

John T. Sbrega discusses close air support in the Vietnam conflict. He traces the neglect of interservice cooperation to the Massive Retaliation and Flexible Response periods between the Korean and Vietnam wars. He suggests there was virtually no joint Army-Air Force doctrine in this period. Thus, close air-support problems once more arose during America's involvement in Southeast Asia. Here was yet another joint interservice and Allied effort—although U.S. doctrine, men, and weapons predominated in the fighting. Air-ground problems surfaced even during the so-called advisory years, and only escalated with introduction of large American land, sea, and air forces. Absence of defined doctrine, lack of compatible air request systems, and complicated rules of engagement hampered U.S.-Republic of Vietnam efforts and many resurfaced once the war became "Americanized."

Sbrega shows that the issues could be found both in the field and in the Pentagon—defying solution in both places. He suggests, however, that by 1965, Army and Air Force leaders had signed a concept paper for improving close air support, and that, despite even congressional investigations, a joint study group concluded that the command and control systems used by the two services for this task were essentially sound and compatible. In fact, Sbrega shows that the Air Force developed an efficient tactical air control system and effective weapons for the close air-support mission, despite the fact that it still ranked that mission only third on its list of priorities for tactical air. He also notes the sometimes odd circumstances in which B-52 strategic bombers were employed in tactical roles while sophisticated tactical fighters went north to the strategic air war over North Vietnam. He cites the perennial operational problems of night flying, bad weather, poor communications, target marking, short rounds, and strike assessment that interfered with close-air support efficiency in Vietnam, much as they had in previous conflicts. Inadequate numbers of Forward Air Controllers and the search for suitable aircraft for them, the continuous interservice bickering over the concept of a single-manager-for-air assets, and the complicated rules of engagement, all stand out as issues. Sbrega is not sanguine about resolution of these outstanding CAS problems in the years since Vietnam. Nevertheless, he asserts that enjoyment of complete air superiority over the battlefield enabled Air Force, Navy, and Marine Corps aviation to provide almost classic examples of close-air support of the ground battles at Khe Sanh, Bu Dop, and Loc Ninh, to name but a few.

Brereton Greenhous provides the final essay. The succession of Israeli victories in their Middle East wars since 1948 has resulted in large part from combined arms teamwork of the Israeli Army and Air Force. Prominent members of that air force refused to use the term close-air support, preferring to call their role "participating in the ground battle." Doctrinally, as Greenhous shows, their air force espouses but three missions; air superiority, interdiction, and close air support, with interdiction enjoying slightly higher priority than CAS. All of this derives from Israel's need always to execute "blitzkrieg," a type of war that demands speed, maneuver, violence, and firepower. These can best be provided by armored ground forces and tactical air power.

Greenhous shows how the Israeli Air Force enjoys a certain functional autonomy while at the same time being ultimately responsible to the General Staff, headed by a soldier. In describing the hodge-podge air support provided in the 1948 war for independence, through the successes of 1956 and 1967, Greenhous shows how its quality and serviceability offset the Israeli Air Force's numerical inferiority against the Arab coalition. He does not hide the facts that slow response to ground requests and poor communications caused problems, but shows how an adroit combination of tactical air and tanks secured the quick victories for which the Israelis became famous. He also suggests that most air losses came from antiaircraft fire, a theme which acquired even greater significance in the 1973 Yom Kippur war. Here, notes Greenhous, the Israelis encountered an elaborate enemy system of ground-to-air antiaircraft missiles, which denied them local air superiority over the battlefield and hampered interdiction. He notes the countermeasures the Israelis eventually used to gain success. To this day, he also concludes, Israeli airmen prefer the interdiction mission to that of close air support, much as their counterparts do around the world. Despite the Israeli Air Force's use of the term "supporting ground forces" or "participating in the ground battle," Israel's national survival dictates that her military leaders retain flexibility of thought and speed in decisionmaking so that they can seize the opportune moment in battle to pass from interdiction to close air support, and back again to interdiction so as to insure victory.

Finally, I. B. Holley, Jr., provides a conclusion that sets the entire content of this volume in perspective. Though he hopes that the essays will inform and suggest insights from past experience, he insists once more that history also teaches that there are no formulae to be slavishly repeated. Noting that close air support has proven attainable, he questions why so much time has elapsed after the onset of hostilities before reaching the level of air-ground cooperation necessary to affect the battle. Citing fundamental doctrinal mindsets that have come between air and ground leaders, Holley shows how they have been transferred to organizational arrangements, leading in turn, to unconscionable delays in mission accomplishment. Holley sees a pattern in which the slowly evolving air-ground teamwork in each of these examples forgotten with the return of peace. He suggests it is during peacetime that military professionals can use the historical record to prepare themselves for the cooperative tasks that must inevitably reappear in the next conflict. Whether the specifics be those of colocating air and ground headquarters, recognizing the relationship of ground facilities (weather-resistant airstrips, adequate fuel and repair support etc.), to sortie rates, or developing smoothly functioning communications and air-ground liaison arrangements, Holley calls for insight beyond mere doctrinal reaffirmation. Recognition of ever-changing technology, for example, the ceaseless swing back and forth between offensive (aircraft) and defensive (surface antiaircraft) for the ascendancy, and the abiding difficulties of finding adequate numbers of qualified personnel, emerge from the historical record. Thus, he treats both the possibilities and the limitations of close air support among Air Force missions.

In sum, the essays in this volume suggest that more than ever "cooperation" is a crucial necessity of modern warfare. As writers of the 1979 edition of Air Force Manual 1-1 emphasized, both joint and allied cooperation and understanding of doctrine, procedures, and teamwork are necessary to provide for the national security of one and all.[5] U.S. Air Force doctrine writers highlighted this spirit in their 1984 updating of that manual to say "close support can create opportunities, protect maneuver, and defend land forces" by massing aerospace firepower at decisive points.[6] Indeed, cooperation between land and air provides the underpinning of the current so-called "Thirty-One Initiatives" for the Army and Air Force. Still, as Professor Holley notes in his conclusion, the priority accorded close air support remains noticeably subordinated in Air Force thinking—in this case in fifth place behind strategic aerospace offense, strategic aerospace defense, counter air, and air interdiction. Given the indivisibility of modern warfare, the airman cannot overlook what the historical record has to say about close air support of ground operations. To help him meet this necessity is the purpose of this book.

Notes

1. U.S. Joint Chief of Staff, Department of Defense, *Dictionary of Military and Associated Terms—JCS Pub. 1*, (Washington: Government Printing Office, January 3, 1972), p 61; Woodford Agee Heflin, editor. *The United States Air Force Dictionary* (Maxwell AFB: Air University Press, 1956), pp 119–120.

2. One example of the continuing dialogue can be found in Group Captain Ian Madelin, RAF, "The Emperor's Close Clothes Air Support," *Air University Review*, 31, (Nov–Dec 1979), pp 82-86, and subsequent rejoinders in "Commentary" section, *Air University Review*, XXXI, (May–Jun 1980), pp 94–103. The points of unending controversy in U.S. military circles can be followed in Robert Frank Futrell, *Ideas, Concepts, Doctrine: A History of Basic Thinking in the United States Air Force 1907–1964* (Maxwell AFB, 1974 edition), pp 91–93, 152, 155–156, 168, 172, 178, 180–181, 193, 196, 198–199, 206, 221–222, 264, 380, 406–407, 411–412, 414, 416.

3. For illustrations of this point, see James A. Huston, "Tactical Use of Air Power in World War II: The Army Experience," *Military Affairs*, 14, (Winter 1950), pp 166–185; William A. Jacobs, "Tactical Air Doctrine and AAF Close Air Support in the European Theater, 1944–1945," *Aerospace Historian*, 27 (March 1980), pp 35–49; W. A. Jacobs, "Air Support for the British Army, 1939–1943," *Military Affairs*, 56, (December 1982), pp 174–182.

4. *Ibid*, pp 175–177.

5. Air Force Manual 1–1, February 14, 1979, *Basic Aerospace Doctrine of United States Air Force*, p 5–3; also, see Edgar Ulsamer, "Down-to-Earth Concerns About Tactical Air," *Air Force Magazine*, 68 (April 1985), pp 62–66; see especially p 64.

6. Air Force Manual 1–1, January 5, 1984, pp 2–15, and Chapter 3.

1

Developments to 1939

Lee Kennett

The history of close air support during the first four decades of the twentieth century can be divided into three distinct phases. The first was the era of World War I, especially the years 1917 and 1918, characterized by rising interest in air power, its rapid development, and its increasing combat potential. The second phase was the interwar period to about 1935, a decade and a half of only limited doctrinal discussion, restricted development, and a virtual absence of meaningful battlefield application. The final phase, which began about 1935–1936 and continued into the opening campaigns of the Second World War, was marked by renewed interest, considerable experimentation, and operational experience in several minor conflicts. This chapter will trace the evolutionary phases: first in their general or international context, then in American experience; and finally, the chapter will offer some conclusions on this formative era in the history of close air support.

The First World War, 1914–1918

Prior to 1914 military leaders were chiefly interested in air power because of the enhanced possibilities it offered in observation and reconnaissance. First Lt. Benjamin D. Foulois, writing in 1908, foresaw a struggle for control of the air over the battlefield, with the victor of that struggle enjoying an advantage in aerial observation that would be "an important factor in bringing campaigns to a short and decisive end."[1] Nevertheless, well before the outbreak of the First World War, both military and civilian figures in a number of countries spoke of a combat role for the airplane and the airship. In 1893 Count Zeppelin informed the Chief of Staff of the German Army that the airship he was building would be capable of attacking both fortifications and troop concentrations.[2]

Official views on the nascent air weapon were more guarded. At the outbreak of war, the French Army had only the sketchiest doctrinal basis for the use of airplanes as weapons: "They can have a genuine offensive power against dirigibles and potentially against troops in dense formations. . . . Combat between airplanes is not envisaged at present."[3]

The years before 1914 also saw practical efforts to make the airplane and the airship effective weapons as France, Great Britain, Germany, and Italy mounted bombs on aircraft and adapted machineguns for aerial warfare. There were pioneering experiments with two types of projectiles later used in ground attack: rockets and flechettes. In the United States, the Army's Signal Corps conducted flight tests to perfect a bombsight and to use machineguns against ground targets. As a result of these and other experiments, "by the time war came to Europe in 1914, the airplane had been demonstrated in the United States as a valuable weapon."[4]

The air-to-ground offensive potential of the airplane had been tested in several small wars even before World War I. Aerial bombing in support of ground operations was introduced during the Italo-Turkish War of 1911–1912, fought principally in Libya. On November 1, 1911, an Italian

In the first such American experiment, Lt. Myron S. Crissy demonstrates a mechanical arm he devised to drop a 36-pound practice bomb from a Wright aircraft. Crissy hit a 20-foot circle on the Tanforan Racetrack, San Francisco, on January 15, 1911.

pilot dropped three small bombs on Turkish positions, and thereafter the Italians continued bombing from aircraft and airships from time to time.[5] There was also bombing in the Balkan Wars of 1912–1913. In those wars, as well as in the Italo-Turkish conflict, however, such action was random, incidental, and often at the initiative of the individual aviator.[6] During this period, the French Army used aircraft against insurgents in Morocco and gained its first experience in cooperation between air units and advancing columns of ground troops.[7] According to reports, air attacks had an important effect on morale of enemy troops, but there were no procedures for organizing and conducting such attacks before 1914.

In the first part of World War I, military aviation still had only one officially recognized function: to serve as the eyes of the army. During the first weeks of the war, however, when hundreds of thousands of troops swarmed the roads, aviators from both sides often attacked marching columns on their own initiative with whatever weapons they happened to have. By October 1914, officials began to sanction and encourage the offensive use of aircraft. Headquarters of the Royal Flying Corps (RFC) noted: "Several instances have occurred lately in which targets suitable for attack have been passed over without any action being taken. In future all aeroplanes carrying out reconnaissances [sic] will carry bombs and whenever . . . suitable targets present themselves they should be attacked by dropping bombs."[8] But by October the nature of the war had changed, and such lucrative and gratuitous targets became rare. The Western Front became positional, with opposing armies sheltered in an elaborate complex of trenchworks, which soon reached from the Swiss frontier to the Channel.

It was over the Western Front that air power reached its most sophisticated level of development during the Great War, with the evolution of combat aircraft, each with its specific task. The first bombing units appeared in the final months of 1914. The early bombing plane served chiefly as an extension of artillery and made its impact well behind the enemy front. What support it did offer in close air support was indirect.

The fighter had as its chief target enemy aircraft. It could affect the outcome of a battle by shielding land forces from enemy air reconnaissance, though that contribution was also indirect. The only aircraft that "worked" the battlefield in the first year of the war were those in reconnaissance and artillery observation. Increasingly they needed protection from enemy fighters—hence, the introduction of "protective patrols" or *Schutzstaffeln*, as the Germans called them. Reconnaissance craft had less to fear from ground fire. Rifle and machinegun fire, the chief menace in the early months of the war, presented no danger at an altitude of one thousand meters, and only a limited one at half that height.

Early command relationship between air and ground forces sprang largely from the need for air reconnaissance and artillery spotting. The Royal

Flying Corps (RFC) assigned a squadron to each army corps; in the French and German services the various army corps were allotted *Escadrilles* and *Fliegerabteilungen* (flight units) respectively.

Air-ground communications were primitive. Though aircraft used for artillery spotting often carried wireless transmitters, pilots commonly found it more feasible to drop messages to the batteries with which they worked, to be forwarded to corps, division, or even battalion headquarters, if necessary. Ground troops, on the other hand, signalled to aircraft by flares and visual displays, such as arrows laid out on the ground.[9]

As air power developed and adapted itself to positional warfare, its organization became more elaborate. In the British service, for example, squadrons were organized into wings, and wings grouped into brigades. Command relationships also grew more complex when it proved advantageous to place fighter units at the disposal of armies and in some instances to assign control of bombing forces to an even higher level of ground command. More centralized control accorded well with the mobility of air units and facilitated rapid and massive concentrations at critical times and points in a battle.

By 1918 air units were being used to support ground forces to a degree inconceivable four years before. A major offensive such as that launched by the British in August of that year at Amiens was supported by eight hundred aircraft that followed an elaborate air plan. According to a historian of the battle "a mere summary of the air attacks would require many pages."[10] The missions flown in support of the offensive varied widely. Some aircraft were sent to rev engines loudly over the German front lines as a cover for the sound of approaching British tanks, while bombers struck troop billets, depots, and rail facilities miles from the front lines. These operations ordered by general headquarters were conducted on the basis of air reconnaissance as well as other intelligence sources. Much of the air effort called for interdiction—to prevent supplies, reinforcements, and communications from reaching the enemy's front-line units. Accordingly, most air attacks did not take place to British ground forces or in coordination with them.

Beginning in 1915, a new tactical reconnaissance aircraft called the infantry contact patrol plane (sometimes called the infantry liaison plane in the U.S. Air Service) appeared. This aircraft led to air support along the "cutting edge" of the battle, where opposing forces (chiefly infantry) met and fought. The infantry contact patrol plane was charged with following the progress of the friendly infantry in battle, filling the communications gap that often developed when landlines were cut by bombardment and when backup systems of runners, dogs, or pigeons failed. By 1916 infantry contact patrol systems served both the Allied and German armies.

Contact patrol work required front line units and airplanes over the battlefield to communicate in some fashion. It was particularly important that ground units identify themselves on request, so that the pilot could record their positions and report them to battalion or brigade headquarters—often by dropping an appropriately marked map. The pilot might ask, "Where are you?" by revving his motor, trailing a pennant, sounding a klaxon, or firing a flare. Ground forces identified themselves with flares, lights, smoke generators, or most commonly with panels—strips of cloth laid on the ground. At first the procedure was makeshift, varying from one sector of the battlefront to the other, but as early as April 1916, the French Army brought out a unified set of instructions defining techniques of air-infantry cooperation. The British, and eventually the Americans, borrowed the French system. Ultimately, it became possible for ground units to signal such conventional messages as "can't advance" or "request artillery support."[11]

The first attempts at liaison on the battlefield were plagued by a number of difficulties, most of them stemming from the ground troops' hesitation to use their signalling devices. They were fearful that the use of flares and smoke would advertise their position to the enemy artillery. There was less resistance to the use of panels, but even here compliance was far from perfect. Units exhausted from heavy engagement rarely displayed panels; those withdrawing almost never did, despite repeated requests.[12] Contact patrol pilots found that they often had to verify the positions of friendly troops, whom they could generally identify by their uniforms if they flew at 800 feet or less. (During the First World War German troops wore grey uniforms, the French wore light blue, and British, American, and French colonial troops wore khaki.)

As patrol pilots approached the battlefield, they could identify enemy as well as friendly positions, and it was inevitable that they needed to increase their communication with the ground forces they supported. Initially, they signalled the nature and location of enemy resistance points by dropping messages—and soon the contact planes themselves began attacking those resistance points. Records leave a clear impression that this activity was initiated by pilots.

Low-level attacks on targets gained official sanction at the Battle of the Somme, which the British opened in July 1916. For the beginning of the battle the Royal Flying Corps assigned eighteen contact aircraft for low-altitude "trench flights" with the dual purpose of "close reconnaissance and destructive bombardment."[13] After the first day's battle, the British made an encouraging discovery: "The Royal Flying Corps was prepared to take extreme risks to give the infantry a helping hand, but the contact pilots and observers found the German troops were often too distracted to pay serious attention" to hostile air activity.[14] Probably for this reason no contact planes were lost to enemy fire on that day.

The RFC's low-level attacks had considerable effect on German infantry. The chief of the German Air Service later recalled that, while the British attacks were poorly organized and the actual casualties they inflicted were very few, the effect on morale was extraordinarily depressive.[15] To restore morale, the German air service sent its own planes over their positions, flashing recognition signals. They were immediately fired on by their own infantry, who took them for British craft signalling their positions to enemy artillery. On other occasions the soldiers did not fire at enemy planes, but simply tried to conceal themselves.

The use of low-flying aircraft expanded during the battles of 1917. In Flanders that spring the Germans attached as many as nine contact aircraft to a division and charged them with the double mission of close reconnaissance and ground strafing. At Arras, on May 11th, British aircraft worked directly with troops for the first time, attacking obstacles in the path of the advancing infantry.[16] In June, RFC contact aircraft escorted the first wave of British troops "over the top," and then roamed freely over the battlefield and behind it, looking for suitable targets. "Their purpose," said Maj. Gen. Hugh Trenchard, commander of RFC units in France, was "to harass the enemy as much as possible and to spoil the morale of his troops. . . ."[17] In the attack at Cambrai in November, the British released four fighter squadrons for ground attack roles. They struck German artillery batteries previously spotted, then crisscrossed the battle areas looking for other targets.[18] The Germans also combined air and infantry assaults in their counterattacks.

The year 1918 saw further refinements in close air-support techniques. British instructions of February 1918 sanctioned formation flying in ground support, provided that no more than six aircraft participated in each formation. This technique increased the volume of fire and strengthened formations against enemy aircraft attacks.

In the great German offensive of March 1918, ground attack units worked in particularly close coordination with the infantry. On March 21, for example, air attacks were used to "soften up" the village of Roupy for the ground assault.[19] The British, for their part, committed masses of aircraft to hamper the German breakthrough by low-flying attacks on advancing German columns. At Bapaume, later in the summer, the Royal Flying Corps assigned Sopwith Camel aircraft to work in close support of the Royal Tank Corps. Each pilot covered a sector of the front on which tanks were to advance, attacking antitank gun emplacements, thus clearing the path for the advancing armor.[20] The final months of the war also saw greater use of ground attack on other fronts. The Italian Army opened its attack at Vittorio Veneto with waves of low-flying aircraft; at the Second Battle of Gaza, six British aircraft stampeded three thousand Turkish troops that had been massed for a counterattack.[21]

The most ambitious creation in close air support was undoubtedly the German *Schlachtstaffeln* of 1918, organized on the eve of the March offensive. These "battle" units were created from preexisting *Schutzstaffeln* or "protection units" which flew light two-seater aircraft and escorted reconnaissance planes. These battle units could and did revert to their escort roles whenever they were not used in ground attack. The fundamental formation of six aircraft, the *Staffel,* joined several others into a *Geschwader.*[22] These battle units represented the most sophisticated approach in close air support during the Great War and merit examination in some detail.

Battle craft were not released pell-mell to find their own roles in the battle. A German instruction on "The Employment of Battle Flights," dated February 20, 1918, described battle aircraft as "a powerful weapon which should be employed at the *decisive* point of the attack." The instruction continued: "They are not to be distributed singly over the whole front of attack, but should be concentrated at decisive points. Less important sectors must dispense with the support of battle flights."[23] Since battle craft were most effective in close formation, the February instructions provided that the fighting strength of a battle formation should never consist of fewer than four aircraft, and six for effective control. As many as six separate *Staffeln* might operate in the same sector, in which case they would be flying from the same airfield. The German techniques were observed as early as November 1917, near Passchendaele, where the German approach to close air support contrasted markedly to the British small patrols roving freely in search of targets. Canadian ground units in the battle reported that they were steadily harassed by German aircraft attacking in groups of from three to nine. There is no evidence, on the other hand, that British aircraft in similar roles made such impact. A recent study of this battle concluded: "The British efforts contrasted poorly with those of the enemy, whose *Schlachtstaffeln* were employed according to a well-developed tactical doctrine."[24]

In order that the *Schlachtstaffeln* be committed in sufficient concentration when and where their intervention could be decisive, they were controlled by infantry division or corps commanders, who were in the best position to decide on their disposition. To facilitate communications, battle units were placed on airfields near corps or division headquarters, where they could be in close telephone contact. Equipped with a wireless receiver, headquarters received messages from contact patrol machines and dispatched orders, such as: (1) Exact position of friendly and the enemy front lines, (2) Objective and sectors of the attack, (3) Nature of the preparatory phase, (4) Method of attack, (5) Zero hour, and (6) Targets specially allocated to the battle flight.[25]

While tactical techniques differed for various aspects of the battle unit assignments—attacking enemy front lines, artillery batteries, and objectives behind the front, and breaking up enemy counterattacks—it was the *Schlachtstaffel's* assault role on enemy front lines that required the most detailed instructions. These provided a conventional code by which air and ground units could coordinate the time of attack. If the battle planes attacked too soon, they revealed the direction of the coming attack; if they attacked late, they gave no impetus to the infantry. The instructions indicated that "the greatest effect is obtained if the battle flights cross the front line at the same moment that the infantry advances to the attack."[26] The combat aircraft "fly ahead of and carry the infantry along with them, keeping down the fire of the enemy's infantry and barrage batteries."[27] The lower the attack, the greater their effect. Attacks against infantry positions were recommended at a height of thirty to fifty meters; attacks against larger targets—reserves and batteries—four to five hundred meters. Where several *Schlachtstaffeln* were used against the same objective, attacks by succeeding waves were preferred: "The attack will be timed and the targets selected in such a manner that the enemy is continuously threatened at the decisive point of the battlefield."[28]

It was impossible to draw up such detailed instructions when the army was on the defensive. Ideally, low-level air attacks would be most productive if they could be delivered on enemy infantry as they massed in trenches or shell craters, awaiting the signal for assault. In such a situation, the *Schlachtstaffeln* would delay attack until enemy disposition was detected. If the enemy succeeded in launching a surprise attack, battle units would not be dispatched as long as the outcome was pending. They would be held until infantry reserves were committed to counterattack.[29] Here, as on the offensive, the commitment of combat aircraft depended on precise timing for optimum effect.

By the time of Armistice, close air-support experience yielded a number of lessons, offering the belligerents new opportunities in air power, but it also presented them with new problems, many of which reappeared twenty years later. First of all, aircraft had a significant effect on the morale of troops in battle. Aerial tacticians were much struck by this phenomenon and attached considerable importance to it in their thinking. An RFC policy paper drafted in September 1916 noted that appearance of hostile aircraft over the front affected morale "all out of proportion to the damage" which the aircraft can inflict. Each soldier felt that enemy aircraft attacked him personally: "If it dives at him he has no doubt that he is the target." In general, "the mere presence of a hostile machine in the air inspires those on the ground with exaggerated foreboding."[30] An American observer noticed the same phenomenon among troops of the AEF:

> A division of first class troops, that received with equanimity four thousand shells per day in its sector, has been known to be greatly disturbed and harassed by the efforts of one persistently active day bomber. Inquiry showed that almost every man in the division believed himself to have been in danger from this plane.[31]

Occasionally troops became so "intoxicated" by this fear that they came to regard all aircraft as "enemy," refusing cooperation with their own planes and notably refusing to identify themselves. Rumors would spread that the enemy was using captured aircraft or camouflaging his planes as friendly ones. This led troops to fire on their own aircraft. Should the aircraft return fire, thinking it was the enemy below them, the strength of the rumor would be reinforced. Cases of such "intoxication" were not uncommon in campaigns as late as 1939 and 1940.

Not surprisingly, the Germans strived "to shatter the enemy's nerve," and psychological considerations played a role in their tactics.[32] Aircraft in close formation were more intimidating than single planes; and the closer they swarmed over ground forces, the more frightening they became; for proximity heightened fear as did the unfamiliar roar of aerial engines. The emphasis on psychological rather than physical damage to the enemy may have slowed the development of weaponry especially suitable to ground attack. Aircraft on such missions usually carried small bombs, under ten pounds or so, and grenades; they strafed with machineguns in the 30–cal/8–mm range. With such light weapons, the damage that could be inflicted on field fortifications and their defenders was negligible. Against artillery batteries, which were often their targets, they had even less effect. As the official historian of the Royal Flying Corps wrote in this connection: "Bullets, and even light-weight bombs, could not, except by chance, do much harm to a gun. Furthermore, the target was small and the detachment usually had some measure of shelter."[33] While new armament appeared for aircraft by 1918, notably cannon and rockets, there was little effort to exploit their air-to-ground capabilities.

Concerning the positive psychological effect on friendly troops, the German instruction previously cited was very explicit: "In defense, the appearance of battle aeroplanes affords visible proof to heavily engaged troops that the higher command is in close touch with the front and is employing every possible means to support the fighting troops. Confidence in a successful defense is thereby strengthened."[34] It was for the same reason that the French high command sometimes sent low-flying planes over hard-pressed troops to "show the roundels." Both the Germans and the Allies used low-level flights along their own front lines just before launching infantry attacks to assure the troops massed in forward positions that air support was at hand.

As time went on, the purely emotional reaction to aircraft over the battlefield tended to decline, especially to hostile aircraft. This would have occurred in any case, but once military commanders became aware of the morale implications, they quickly trained troops in countermeasures. Such indoctrination sought to diminish fear of enemy aircraft and to show troops the advantages of friendly air power. The U.S. Army Air Service performed exemplary work in this regard. In the Second Army, for example, it opened liaison schools with week-long instruction on air-ground cooperation for ground troops. The Air Service also dropped leaflets over the trenches to help soldiers distinguish friendly from hostile aircraft and to encourage cooperation: "Use us to the limits, show your panels, burn the signal lights, wave a cloth; anything to tell us where you are and what you need."[35]

A German circular of July 1918 also provided its infantrymen with practical instructions for defense against air attacks, informing front-line troops that their own weapons, correctly used, would suffice for antiaircraft defense.[36] There came other measures as well as countermeasures on both sides, as the tremendous firepower of the front lines was increasingly adapted against aircraft, and as antiaircraft guns began to multiply along the front. In October 1918, for example, the U.S. Air Service organized a system for intercepting German planes that crossed American lines, maintaining from seven to nine fighters on patrol between two and eight hundred feet. This tactic was very successful; the patrols claimed ten German planes for each American fighter lost.[37]

American ground crews load bombs at the Aviation Bombing School, Clermont, France.

As a result of such changing nature of aerial warfare, by the end of the war, ground attack aircraft could no longer expect successes they had earlier enjoyed in close air support, and their missions had become more hazardous. Few statistics have survived, save those of the Royal Flying Corps, but if they are indicative of activity at that time, then it would appear that close air support could have indeed been costly. Some forty aircraft of the RFC 46, 64, and 68 Squadrons were committed to ground attack at Cambrai on November 20, 1917; nine failed to return, four were wrecked, and thirteen so heavily damaged from groundfire that they had to be rebuilt. Casualties reached thirty-five percent on that day.

For the whole period of the Cambrai fighting, squadrons engaged in ground attack operations suffered about 30 percent casualties daily.[38] RFC losses during the German offensive of March 1918 and the heavy fighting around Amiens 5 months later were only slightly lower. Sir John Slessor cites the case of No. 80 Squadron, which conducted close air support missions almost continuously from March 1918 until the end of the war: "Their average strength was 22 officers, and in the last 10 months of the war no less than 168 officers were struck off the strength from all causes—an average of about 75 percent per month, of whom little less than half were killed."[39]

The increased danger for aircraft involved in ground attack led to a search for models and types better suited to such combat. Low-flying aircraft enjoyed an advantage over fighters operating above them, since it was more difficult to spot low-flying aircraft against the background of terrain below, while those above formed a silhouette against the sky. Such advantage could be enhanced by camouflage, which was then introduced as additional protection. A two-seater with a well-armed rear gunner offered even more protection from pursuing enemy fighters. Such were the Halberstadts and Hannovers which the Germans used in *Schlachtstaffeln*. Americans seemed to lean toward the two-seater as well. Colonel Frank P. Lahm of the U.S. Air Service described the optimum aircraft as "high speed, protected two-seater fighting planes" (by protected Lahm meant armored).[40] In a memorandum on "Fighting in the Air," the Royal Flying Corps leadership expressed a preference for "fast single-seater machines," but added:

> It is possible that a special type of machine will be evolved in which pilots and some of the most vulnerable parts will be armoured. They will probably be adapted to carrying a few light bombs and will have at least one gun, capable of being fired downward at an angle of 45° to the horizontal, and another firing straight ahead."[41]

Late in 1917, the British Ministry of Munitions sought designs for a specialized aircraft called the E.F. Type No. 2 or armored trench-fighter. Several prototypes were constructed, of which the most impressive was the Sopwith T.F. 2 Salamander, built early in 1918. It had two forward-firing machine-

Col. Frank P. Lahm

guns, with two others projecting through the floor of the cockpit. After field-testing and modifications in France, it was ordered into production; the improved version began to appear in the squadrons in the summer of 1918. The machineguns for trench strafing, originally fixed at 45 degrees, were later only slightly depressed from the horizontal, since that position gave better dispersion and higher lethality.

The Salamander, essentially a modified Sopwith Camel, carried the wings of a Snipe with 640 lbs of armor plate, sheathing the fuselage from the engine bulkhead to the trailing edge of the lower wing. Armor on the underside effectively protected the aircraft against the German armor-piercing bullet at 150 feet, while the side plates would turn bullets striking at more than 15 degrees from the vertical and protect against shrapnel.[42]

There was a similar development in the French air service. A modified Salmson reconnaissance plane, the 4 Ab2 cu 250, appeared in the spring of 1918, modified chiefly by the addition of armor.[43] In May 1918, General Duval, Chief of the French air service, asked for something better, a fast, lightly armored *avion d'assaut* or assault plane. It was on the drawing board with the arrival of Armistice.

The Germans were designing or modifying a variety of aircraft for combat. These ranged from the light Halberstadt CLII and Hanover CL II/III to the heavily armored A.E.G. JI (860 lbs of armor plate), and the all-metal Junkers JI, which was probably the most sophisticated aircraft of this general type built during the war.[44] German air designers tended toward the more heavily armored craft for infantry contact work and toward the faster, more lightly armored types for ground attack, though the Germans as well as the Allies never completely separated the two functions.

The various experiments in design led to the obvious conclusion that in a purely technical sense the belligerents were still groping for the ideal craft for close air support. And there was still considerable disagreement in 1918 over the role itself. In theory and in practice, air support aircraft in 1918 had two categories of targets: objectives along the enemy's heavily defended frontal positions, which some generals called the "crust", and a whole range of targets extending twenty miles and more behind that crust. By the end of the war, a considerable body of opinion held that the chief contribution of aircraft should be against those objectives behind that crust. Enemy reinforcements moving up in column were much more visible and much more vulnerable than front-line troops in field fortifications, and there was less danger of confusing them with friendly ground forces. Then too, objectives behind the front lines tended to be less fiercely defended—no minor consideration, given the losses suffered by ground attack units. Additionally, excellent targets often lay beyond the effective range of friendly artillery, in a zone where only the airplane could reach them. Toward the end of the war, targets such as dense troop columns and convoys of vehicles appeared in great numbers.

The tactical stalemate in ground fighting that had characterized the earlier part of World War I was moderating in the final months of the war. The battlefront moved more readily and more quickly. "Drives" in one direction or the other, such as the great German campaigns in the spring and summer of 1918, exposed armies on the roads, where they offered better targets for air attack. Air activity increased greatly during this period because of mobile warfare. In January and February 1918, the Royal Flying Corps had been logging about 20,000 flying hours each month, but when the Germans launched their offensive in March, the RFC flew 40,000 hours.[45]

The advancing German armies proved extremely vulnerable to air attack. On March 25, 1918, for example, a German regimental column lost 3 officers and 135 men from a single strafing attack which lasted only a few seconds.[46] What is more, the Allied air effort slowed or halted the progress of German ground forces, which had shattered Allied defenses. At one point during the German offensive, a large concentration of German troops preparing to advance was massed in a ravine which shielded them from French artillery. One hundred and twenty French bombers attacked them in repeated sorties from a height of 2,000 feet, dropping a total of 7,000 bombs and disrupting the planned advance. On another occasion, the Germans had thrown bridges across the Marne out of the range of French artillery, but for several days French bombers blocked the passage of German troops, turning the area of the bridges into a "hell."[47] This all-out air offensive against an advancing enemy army was considered an emergency. Accordingly, RFC orders to its units specified: "Very low flying is essential. All risks to be taken."[48]

The role of air power in stemming the great German thrusts of 1918 drove home an important lesson: there were critical times, such as when one's front was ruptured, that required committing all available aircraft to land battle. The great battles of 1918 also demonstrated that centralized control of aviation could be as valuable in defensive warfare as in offensive operations. In the last few weeks of the war, when the German army was forced on the defensive, a system of centralized control enabled the German air service to take advantage of the high mobility of the airplane to concentrate its air force at critical points along a battle line extending over a hundred miles. Thus in the heavy fighting around Cambrai in September, it brought in *Schlachtstaffeln* from the region of Laon, some seventy miles away, then returned them to their home base that evening to face a threat developing there.[49]

While air power could be rapidly shifted and concentrated, it could not easily be used for close air support on a battlefield with which the pilots were unfamiliar, or one on which the battlelines were shifting or fluctuating. A French authority warned that "participation in the fighting on the very front lines is a very delicate matter."[50] It could only be entrusted to pilots familiar with the terrain and thoroughly briefed on the most recent changes in the battlelines; otherwise there was great danger of attacking one's own troops. At Cambrai, the British furnished their pilots maps with bombing lines, hoping that the maps would correspond with the pace of their advance. For the first hour and a half of the attack, the pilots were instructed to attack no targets on the near side of the "brown line."[51] Ground forces, on the other hand, could not follow such a timetable.

Experiments in centralized command encountered opposition in the ground forces, particularly among the corps and army commanders, who wanted to retain direction over "their" aviation. And there were complaints from air units as well. In the fighting at Kemmel in the summer of 1918, German battle units had intervened very effectively at the beginning of the battle. Thereafter, the German High Command held them on their airfields, sending orders from time to time to attack objectives spotted by German reconnaissance. They lost so much time in transmission that the battle units rarely were able to exploit the information they received.[52] As a general rule, the air staff tended to see the benefits of centralized control, while army staff tended to focus on its shortcomings. This fundamental difference of opinion would remain one of the key problems to be resolved in the subsequent history of close air support.

Trends and Developments from 1919 to 1935

The postwar period posed some unique challenges to military aviation. Technological progress generally continued unabated for aviation with the development of all-metal construction and more efficient power plants. As a result, the airplane by 1939 could boast a performance far exceeding that of aircraft two decades before. Yet the major air forces of the world often had difficulty incorporating these innovations. The Russian air force, like most of that country's institutions, was for a time disorganized by revolution and civil war. Germany was barred by the Versailles Treaty from possessing military aircraft, but undercover development continued, and it was not until 1935 that Hitler unveiled the *Luftwaffe*.

Britain's Royal Air Force, created in 1918, was hobbled by the "ten-year rule," which required that all the services estimate their needs on the assumption that there would be no major war for a decade.[53] Accordingly, the twenties and early thirties reflected slender military budgets in many countries; and in democratic ones, the military establishments became targets of pacifist agitation. In Britain and France this agitation labelled the "bomber" so disdainfully that the British and French air forces briefly adopted the terms "Wessex Area" and "Heavy Defense Aviation" for their respective bombing forces.[54]

As the air forces of the 1920s and 1930s changed their equipment and revised their doctrines, they usually had very little to guide them by way of practical lessons from recent combat. For a decade and a half after 1918, air power was chiefly applied in what was called "air control," that is, using aircraft to maintain order in various colonial possessions. The French, for example, called upon aviation extensively to quell rebellion, and the Spanish to maintain order in their African possessions.[55] The steadiest and most capable practitioner of air control, however, was the Royal Air Force. Its principal concentration of air power in the colonies was to attack ground objectives, villages, market places, and sometimes the houses of rebellious chieftains. The main objective was not so much physical destruction as intimidation—in other words, psychological.[56] For such purposes, weaponry from the Great War was adequate. The enemy had no air force, no antiaircraft guns, and generally little firepower. There was little to be learned about the effectiveness of air power in major conflicts during this period.

Quite understandably, air doctrine in the interwar period rested largely on World War I lessons. While there were shades of difference from one country to another, there was general agreement that the air force had at least two fundamental missions: to win air battles and to support ground forces.* While air superiority was desirable for effective intervention in a land battle, it was not an absolute prerequisite. It was the overriding obligation of the air force, nevertheless, to throw its strength into a ground battle at critical times.

The Germans distinguished two basic types of air support: direct and indirect (*unmittelbar* and *mittelbar*), a distinction that was essentially the same as in 1918. Direct support involved intervention against a heavily defended frontal complex of an enemy army; indirect support comprised attacks on objectives to a considerable depth behind the "crust" of frontal positions, including interdiction efforts and strikes at reserves, ammunition dumps, depots, and the like.

While there was general agreement on this distinction, there was some confusion over terminology. In literature of the thirties, the words "direct," "close," and "immediate" are sometimes synonyms and sometimes not. In staff discussions between the Royal Air Force and the British Army late in 1939, the term "close support" did not have the same meaning in the two services. An RAF officer reported that during maneuvers, his army counterparts "thought that close support meant ground strafing of front-line trenches . . . and even asked to have forward batteries put out of action."[57] After considerable discussion, the two services agreed that "with regard to bomber support for the Army, the term 'Direct Support' implies the isolation of the battlefield; and that of the term 'Close Support' implies the intervention by aircraft on the battlefield itself."[58] German literature of the thirties reflected a similar confusion over the meaning of terms.[59]

Training and operations manuals of the time tended generally to emphasize indirect rather than close or direct support. While the Soviet manual of 1941 proclaimed that the chief task of the air force was "assisting the ground forces," it portrayed air power as a supplement to ground weaponry, to be used on objectives that the ground weapons could not reach, essentially those beyond artillery range.[60] The *Luftwaffe*'s Air Manual No. 16 (*Luftkriegführung or Conduct of Air Operations*), drawn up in 1935, stated that "combat action by air forces will generally provide indirect support for the combat of the other military forces."[61] The 1938 *Règlement* for French bombardment aviation stated that operations over the battlefield would be undertaken only "exceptionally."[62] The same term was used by General Amedeo Mecozzi of the Italian Air Force in a manual on air support written in 1934.[63] The air support role which the British Royal Air Force saw for itself was the

---

*The Royal Air Force and the U.S. Army Air Corps had become convinced during the interwar years that strategic bombardment was their most important mission. They believed that it could be decisive in future war.

most restrictive of all. According to an Air Staff memorandum of November 21, 1939, aircraft might be used against artillery and reserves "to make sure of breaking the crust of the defense for the initial break-in," or "in a critical situation when the overriding consideration was to stop a hostile break-through," or "in pursuit of an already beaten enemy." Direct intervention in land battle was to be limited to these exceptional situations.[64]

The tendency to emphasize indirect rather than close or direct support can be traced to two general considerations: the first was the perception of the battlefield and the targets it offered (a perception heavily influenced by the First World War), and the second was the limited offensive capability of air power in the 1930s. The battlefield offered small targets which were "widely dispersed and usually were dug into the ground to protect them against artillery fire."[65] The Soviet aviation authority, A. Lapchinskii, wrote: "The further we go into enemy territory the more we can count on very important and immovable targets; and on the other hand, the nearer we are to the battle, the more we will have to count on what is called 'the emptiness of the battlefield.' "[66] Over such a battlefield, bombers of the mid-1930s could bring only limited destruction. They were incapable of precision bombing, particularly at altitudes of 10,000 feet and above, which would give them some protection from antiaircraft fire. At 12,000 feet, the *Luftwaffe's* best bombing crews could put no more than two percent of their bombs in a rect-angle roughly the size of a football field—a margin of error that effectively ruled out the use of bombers in proximity to friendly ground forces.[67]

Bombers could attack only broad areas, hoping to hit the specific targets within them. This technique would require twenty to twenty-five tons of explosives to neutralize one square kilometer of a modern defensive position; and with bombers capable of carrying perhaps a half-ton payload, several hundred would be needed to neutralize enemy positions along a sector of three or four kilometers—the sector suitable for assault by a reinforced infantry division. A major attack, such as the one the French made at Mal-maison in October 1917, required 80,000 tons of explosives, delivered by artillery fire in a week—12,000 on the first day. This was far beyond the capacity of any existing bomber force.[68] Most authorities concluded that bombers were ineffective in land battles and that artillery could provide more accuracy and efficiency. They conceded perhaps a single exception: because of its extreme mobility, a bomber force was better suited in a surprise offen-sive, since an artillery buildup prior to an offensive was usually detected by the enemy.[69]

Fighter aircraft had greater potential in land battle because of their speed, maneuverability, and the ability to engage in low-level flying, which had proved to be the key to successful air intervention during World War I. Most of the aircraft used for ground attack in the war had in fact been fighter craft. But the use of fighters in air support was challenged in literature of the interwar period on two grounds. First was a problem of adaptation for both pilot and aircraft. The pilot, trained to destroy enemy aircraft in the air, had to learn an entirely different technique, while his aircraft had to be altered to carry light bombs; the result, according to some writers on aerial warfare, was a hybrid not particularly well suited for either air combat or ground support. A second criticism of fighters as ground attack aircraft was that they lacked protection from the rear. Encountering enemy fighters during ground attack missions, they would have to jettison their bomb loads and turn to face their attackers. Many doctrinaires on close air support insisted that a rear gunner was necessary for such protection.[70]

Ultimately, air force leadership faced this basic question: could air support be satisfied by fighter and/or bomber forces in a secondary or subsidiary task, or was it sufficiently important to warrant new, specialized units in the tradition of the German *Schlachtstaffeln*? Advocates of separate ground attack or assault aviation argued that only specially trained pilots flying aircraft designed and armed specifically for low-level attack could offer effective close support for land forces. Opponents argued that such units would suffer prohibitive losses, or that their infrequent employment would not warrant keeping such a force. Between 1919 and 1935 such specialized units were created and maintained in three countries. The first was the 3d Attack Group of the U.S. Air Service, created in 1921. Six years later, the Soviet Air Force created five squadrons of *Shturmovaya Aviatsia*, after several years of informal experimentation with ground attack techniques.[71] Finally, late in 1931, Italy's *Regia Aeronautica* created its first *gruppo* of *aviazione d'assalto*, under the leadership of Colonel Mecozzi.[72]

Whether an air force provided ground forces with air support through special units or whether it employed fighter and bomber aircraft, neither ground nor aviation officers in any nation did much to explore the command relationships for air support until the late 1930s. In part, this neglect stemmed from the peacetime organization of the two services. In most countries this involved identical geographical commands. In Germany, for example, the *Luftkreise* (air districts) corresponded to the *Wehrkreise* (defense districts) of the German Army. In peacetime there was, obviously, liaison between the two commands, but save for maneuvers and joint exercises there was relatively little contact between the two at lower echelons and no day-to-day exchange on problems which would require cooperation. In war everything would change. Upon mobilization, in the French and German systems, an army group would be paired with an *armée aérienne* or a *Luftflotte*. Commanders of air support forces would be placed with or near army group and army headquarters, with liaison officers or teams stationed at army corps and division levels.

The mechanics of arranging air support that were worked out in peacetime often proved cumbersome or impractical once the war had begun. The

French *règlement* of 1940 called for the assignment of air support missions at army group levels. Unfortunately, French field organizations required that all requests for air support and corresponding orders percolate through an elaborate hierarchy. In wartime, this system produced disastrous delays. Air Marshal A. S. Barratt, who commanded British air units in France in 1939-40, reported that "the French system of organizational control seemed suited to the slow and methodical days of trench warfare."[73] As a result, Barratt recalled, it was impossible to arrange for air intervention within less than four hours. French records indicate the delay was often six to eight hours after a request had been initiated.

The schemas and timetables provided in Soviet treatises on air support during the thirties reveal built-in uncertainties. The author of an article on cooperation between *Shturmovik* aircraft and an infantry division described a "closely coordinated" operation: a scout plane spotted an advancing enemy column and twenty minutes later dropped a message to friendly ground troops. It took another twenty minutes for the division commander to receive the message and to request air support, another twenty for instructions to reach the air base situated twenty-five to thirty kilometers to the rear, and forty minutes for the *Shturmoviks* to take off and fly to the target—a total lapse time or "dead time," as the Soviets called it, of one hour and forty minutes. While the author of the article stressed closely coordinated operations, with the *Shturmoviks* an "integral part" of the division, he was obliged to add this proviso:

> The conditions of ongoing battle require allowance of wide initiative to the commander of the *Shturmoviks*. Even with faultless communications with the airdrome, the division commander is not in a position to give firm direction to the work of the *Shturmoviks*. In the majority of cases he can only indicate the general target to the commander of the *Shturmoviks* plus the region and the approximate time of their action.[74]

Tactical doctrine for close air support was rooted in the experience of World War I and updated by field exercises, maneuvers, and limited lessons offered by air control operations. The chief ingredient in ground attack was low-level flying (under 500 meters) or extremely low-level—so-called "shaving" or "grass cutting" flight (under 50 meters). At low altitudes, strafing and small bombs were effective against targets. Moreover, low-level flying accomplished two other tasks: dropping chemical agents and laying smoke screens.[75]

By the late thirties, doctrine in ground attack circles, especially in the United States and in the Soviet Union, held that neither air superiority nor fighter escort was prerequisite to ground attack operations involving rapid, shallow incursions. Low-level flight offered sufficient guarantee that a close air-support plane could carry out its mission and return safely without falling prey to enemy fighters.[76] The basic fact that aircraft were more difficult to spot from above than below, particularly if they flew over variegated country and were suitably camouflaged, led Soviet theorists to conclude that *Shturmovik* craft needed no fighter escort for most missions. Ground attack pilots were taught to avoid flying over broad, flat surfaces, such as lakes or wheatfields, and to plot their courses over broken country. Soviet *Shturmovik* pilots were told to look for "trap doors" through which they could cross enemy lines, such as ravines and swamps, where their passage would be less noticed. Low-level flight also offered some protection against ground fire, since it reduced the period of time the aircraft was exposed to an enemy battery or machinegun emplacement. Typical targets for close air support were those vulnerable to small bombs and machinegun fire, such as personnel, draft animals, and "light" materiel objectives, chiefly carts, trucks, and other unarmored vehicles. In general, the view prevailed that pilots, with machineguns blazing, should make a long run of a kilometer or so up to the target. This approach would neutralize enemy firepower, so that the attackers could then climb to 200 meters or so for the bomb release. Some tacticians favored a preliminary bombing attack, which they felt would distract the enemy and assist penetration of defenses in subsequent attacks.

Diving attacks were also the object of discussion and some experimentation, since tests carried out by naval pilots indicated that greater bombing accuracy was possible. Ernst Udet and others favoring this technique led the *Luftwaffe* to design a dive bomber early in 1935, though generally such planes elicited little interest until the late thirties. Dive bombing was known in the First World War, but airmen generally considered it too dangerous where heavy ground fire would be encountered.[77]

Close air support tactics also included laying smoke screens and chemical agents, but these required very low-level flight and favorable weather. Chemical agents, either in bombs or as spray, incapacitated enemy troops, thereby interdicting portions of the battlefield. Smoke, prescribed in a number of tactical situations, was designed to blind the enemy thereby marking off his position for friendly forces.

Soviet tactical literature of the thirties discussed a wealth of ground attack scenarios, many of them very elaborate, and, one suspects, difficult or impossible to execute under battle conditions. One of the Soviet tactics stressed preliminary reconnaissance. First of all, a target was located by a reconnaissance aircraft. Then a *shturmovik* unit consisting of six to twelve aircraft would move to a "waiting area" a few kilometers from the reported target. There the aircraft would circle while the commander scouted the target, then return to lead the attack. If he failed to return, the second in command would duplicate the reconnaissance. Attacks often included two separate sections, one flying at higher altitudes for bombing, and the other at lower altitudes for strafing. To confuse the enemy, they launched simultaneous attacks from two directions. In one scenario, a single *shturmovik* would cover the target—a troop column or a trench—with a dense, low trail of smoke. Other aircraft could fire into the cloud or bomb with impunity.[78]

The technical evolution of military aviation in the interwar years influenced thinking on close air support in a number of ways. In the immediate aftermath of the war, the first impulse was to follow the technological line of development that led to a highly specialized "trench fighter," heavily armored and equipped with a number of downward firing machineguns. Several of these aircraft, under development at war's end, were completed and tested, but with disappointing results. Interest in heavily armored craft then rapidly declined.[79]

On the basis of war experience, the ground attack airplane needed to be robust and invulnerable to considerable damage. The air-cooled, radial engine was the projected power plant—air-cooled to shed the vulnerable radiator and radial to continue functioning even after heavy damage. (World War I pilots had returned safely with whole cylinders shot from their motors.) The pilot needed a good downward view, and his plane had to operate from makeshift airfields near the front.

Summing up Soviet requirements, Lapchinskii wrote: "The need is for a light plane, quickly moved, near to the command which puts it to work, and so only slightly dependent on aerodrome conditions."[80] These are the qualities of observation aircraft, and several air forces equipped their attack squadrons with suitably modified observation planes. The Soviet Union *shturmovik* units were equipped with the R–5sh version of the R–5. The Japanese Army used the Mitsubishi Ki–51 for reconnaissance and ground attack. This was an extremely versatile plane with a takeoff distance of 540 feet.

Attempts to create a special ground attack airplane were long plagued with ill success. The Soviet Tsh–3, for example, was a short-lived experiment. In Italy, the Breda 65 was a disappointing design, developed in accord with the ideas of Mecozzi, who called for "a fast, maneuverable plane of medium carrying capacity, capable of attacking ground targets, but also of imposing battle on all aircraft other than fighters and of defending itself against fighters."[81] Powered by an unreliable motor, it was difficult to fly, and in 1939 the Italians retired it from service.[82] Perhaps the most successful specialized airplane developed in the thirties was the Ilyushin Il–2 *Shturmovik*, which first flew in 1937. It was a single-engine aircraft with three-quarters of a ton of armor, constituting about fifteen percent of the plane's weight.[83]

The late thirties saw further changes in ground attack aircraft with the switch to high performance, twin-engine planes with greater range and larger carrying capacity. Ground attack began to merge with light bombardment, as twin engine craft replaced the single-engine Breda in the Italian *aviazione d'assalto*. The French chose the two-engine Breguet 691 for their new *aviation de bombardement d'assaut* at the same time that the *Luftwaffe* was developing a similar aircraft, the Focke–Wulf 189, for the ground support role.

The development of specialized aircraft for ground attack was undertaken only in a handful of countries, for in most cases military aviation leaders chose another course. In the 1930s there was much discussion of the multi-purpose plane (*Mehrzweckflugzeug* in German, *avion à tout faire* in French), a concept that was particularly attractive to small countries with very limited military budgets. The basic idea was that a single design could be used for observation and reconnaissance, light bombing, and ground attack. It led to the development of such multi-purpose planes as the Polish P.Z.L. Karas and the Swiss T.C. 35, both of which were single-engine creations of the late thirties. The British view of aircraft construction was similar. An RAF spokesman said: "We try to develop the bulk of our force on a 'general utility' basis."[84] This policy rested on the basic assumption that "given a good basic design, the aircraft could be made to do an infinite variety of jobs in addition to that for which it was originally designed."[85]

There were relatively few technological advances in aviation applied particularly to close air support or that pointed the way to the development of the ideal support plane. Perhaps that is one reason that this aspect of air power tended to lag. In truth, during the interwar period most developmental work and most interest centered on air combat and on what aviation historian Georg Feuchter called the "race" between the fighter and the bomber.[86]

Here and there certain innovations in civil aviation carried a special significance for ground attack. The development of retractable landing gear was viewed as having special importance for aircraft that flew at very low levels;[87] and the techniques of aerial spraying, perfected for commercial and sanitary purposes, had obvious implications for chemical warfare. Higher aircraft speeds enhanced the possibilities of achieving surprise in low-level attacks, and at the very least, gave hostile ground forces less time to prepare for air attack. At the same time, higher speeds and greater wing loadings made low-level flight more challenging and hazardous to those who were not well trained for it. Finally, the development of diving brakes made it possible for the heavier and aerodynamically cleaner aircraft of the thirties to use diving techniques safely.

Technological innovation probably had a greater impact on the weapons employed in close air support than it did on the aircraft that would use them. In 1918, the machinegun was the most effective weapon for ground attack, but its effectiveness diminished, because greater and greater aircraft speeds during the next two decades increased the distance between impact points of successively fired bullets. According to the calculations of one expert, a pilot flying along a trench at 240 miles per hour and firing a single machinegun with a rate of 300 rounds per minute would put a bullet in the trench every twenty-three yards.[88] Sir John Slessor, writing in 1936, claimed that this phenomenon had made the machinegun "a surprisingly innocuous weapon."[89] Greater density of fire could of course be had by increasing the number of guns or their rate of fire, and both of these developments took place in the late thirties, with the advent of eight-gun fighters and the use of machineguns with rates of fire approaching a thousand rounds per minute. The use of the machinegun in close air support posed another problem to the tacticians of the thirties. If guns were slightly depressed from the aircraft's line of flight or axis, say by five degrees, then it would be possible to strafe the target in horizontal flight at very low level, and the rear gunner could also bring his weapon to bear on a ground target. On the other hand, machineguns so depressed would be useless in air combat. After lengthy debates over the question, opinion favored aligning the guns on the plane's longitudinal axis.

In the thirties, airpower leaders assigned greater importance to the bomb. Slessor, for example, maintained that it was "the weapon to use every time."[90] Bombs used in close air support were typically small, weighing about twenty pounds, fragmentation type, each exploding about a thousand fragments. They were effective at a range of forty to fifty yards from point of detonation. Delayed action fuses or parachutes allowed the aircraft to get clear before the bombs exploded. Some air forces developed even smaller fragmentation bombs or grenades, weighing five pounds or less, and these could be dropped in considerable numbers. Since ground attack planes could not bomb with great accuracy, there was a tendency toward saturation bombing. (Many ground attack aircraft of the thirties had no bombsights.)

Both the machinegun and the fragmentation bomb were most effective against "soft" targets, especially against personnel in the open. They could be used to harass enemy artillery, but they could rarely knock out the guns themselves. They were of little value against tanks and armored cars, targets that would be increasingly encountered in future warfare. A French commentator writing in 1938 argued that such "hard" targets were "growing in importance and in number with the motorization and mechanization of modern armies."[91] Such considerations led to a search for new weapons to use in ground attack. A number of these were found, though in most cases they were simply adaptations of air-to-air weapons spawned by the competition between the fighter and the bomber.

Some fighter craft of the 1930s carried a heavy machinegun, firing a projectile in the 50–cal or 13–mm class, notably the Breda 12.6–mm guns, which equipped the Fiat CR 32. The automatic cannon made its appearance in the mid-thirties, when the French Air Force adopted the 20–mm Hispano Suiza 404. The Soviet theorist, B. Teplinskii, recognized its value in air support: "The development of present-day mechanized troops urgently demands the introduction of cannon into the armament of attack planes."[92] By 1939 there were a half dozen types of aerial cannon of 20–, 25–, and 37–mm, firing from 100 to 300 explosive projectiles per minute. Tests soon proved the effectiveness of these armor-piercing projectiles against hard targets. (The horizontal surfaces or deck armor on tanks of the 1930s were typically 5 or 6 millimeters thick, making them especially vulnerable to attacks from above.) There was still another promising air-to-ground weapon on the horizon; the Soviets had been working on rockets from the early thirties. They used air-to-air rockets against the Japanese on the Manchurian border in 1939, and by the time they entered World War II (in 1941), they had developed air-to-ground rockets for their Il–2 *Shturmovik*.[93]

The one weapon more suited for the ground attack plane was the chemical weapon. It was also the least understood. Aircraft during the First World War did not drop chemicals, and after 1918 there was almost no air-delivered, live-agent testing. While a number of agents such as phosgene and mustard were stocked in bomb form, it was generally believed that they could be most effectively sprayed from low flying planes. On a tactical level, they could be used to attack personnel or to poison portions of the battlefield, sealing off an enemy's avenue of retreat or protecting the flanks of a friendly ground force. Spraying chemical agents was hazardous work demanding special skills and equipment. Unless spray nozzles were placed well out on the wings, there was a danger that the aircraft and its crew would both be contaminated.[94]

The most important equipment carried by close air support aircraft, next to armament, was the wireless or radio set. There was considerable progress in this field between the wars, with the radio telephone increasingly used in preference to wireless telegraphy. Still, at the beginning of World War II, radio communications left much to be desired. "Command" sets linking one aircraft to another were generally more efficient than air-ground links. Most air forces, nevertheless, carried visual signals, and in the maneuvers of the 1930s, ground forces still used panels, and airplanes dropped weighted messages to communicate.

Unreliability and limited range posed the basic problems in the unperfected state of radio communications. Moreover, the heavy, bulky sets of the era were especially cumbersome to aircraft, where weight was critical.[95] Low-altitude flight reduced radio efficiency even further, and in very low-level or "grass-cutting" flight, an aircraft often lost its trailing antenna. Pilots of single-seat aircraft also found it difficult in certain phases of flight to manipulate microphones and dials.

Improved equipment was under development before the war. For example, the U.S. Army Air Corps field-tested throat microphones in 1937.[96] Yet the real revolution in radio communications, as in electronics generally, occurred during the war rather than before it.[97] Reequipping aircraft proved a disappointingly slow process, as radio manufacture then did not readily lend itself to the mass-production techniques of vast armament programs.

Furthermore, there was resistance and distrust of radio within the air forces, particularly among flying personnel. The distrust was rooted only partly in the system's technical flaws. Some felt, for example, that radio transmissions would be intercepted by the enemy, thus compromising missions and operations. A U.S. Army Signal Corps officer recalled: "The attitude of most of the flying people was that when war came, the radio equipment would be left out of the plane, and the corresponding weight would be used to carry more machinegun ammunition or more bombs."[98]

Shortcomings in communications showed up very quickly when the U.S. Army Air Corps sought to perfect close air-support techniques at the beginning of the war, but the same problem plagued other belligerents as well in the first campaigns of World War II. The air-support mission of the Russian Air Force, for example, was hamstrung for lack of radios. Observation planes were sometimes reduced to landing at *shturmovik* airfields, picking up a unit of ground attack aircraft, and leading them to a previously spotted target. The ground links of the communications net of the French Air Force were supplied by a telephone system that proved unable to handle the traffic once fighting began. Clogged communications channels were as much to blame as leisurely staff work for the hours that elapsed between a request for air support and the dispatch of aircraft.

The Period from 1935 to 1939

In December 1934, Italian and Ethiopian forces clashed on the ill-defined frontier between Ethiopia and the Italian Somaliland. The "Wal–Wal incident" led to full-scale warfare and ultimately to the Italian conquest of Ethiopia. It was the first of a series of limited conflicts that preceded World War II with a considerable influence on the military policies of the great powers in that global contest. These limited wars led to a reexamination of air power and a growing interest in its tactical application.

In 1935, the Italian Air Force was rated as one of the most modern in the world. As the showpiece of the Fascist regime, it played a prominent role in the war with Ethiopia. On the other hand, the Ethiopian air force consisted of a dozen planes, most of them not airworthy; nor were the Ethiopians well equipped with antiaircraft guns. With uncontested supremacy in the air, the Italian Air Force could use its planes in a variety of ways to support the Italian Army, including air resupply. Because much of the fighting took place on open plateaus, the air force intervened easily in most major engagements. After the Battle of Inderta it pursued the retreating Ethiopian forces relentlessly. On another occasion Italian planes caught a body of 7,000 Ethiopian soldiers massed at a river crossing, killing an estimated 3,000 with repeated bomb and machinegun attacks.[99] A Russian officer serving with the Ethiopians recalled the effects of air attacks on his men: "The morale effect was enormous. . . .They [Italian airplanes] kept us from eating or from warming ourselves after difficult marches because we dared not light fires in our camps. They changed us into moles who scurried to their holes at the slightest alarm."[100]

Even though the Italian air campaign was extremely successful, many observers found that it provided few serious lessons. Detailed information was not easy to obtain from that inaccessible area, and the Italians often mixed propaganda with their facts. But more important, the war was not a real test of air power because it was one-sided. Indeed it was similar to colonial air control operations mounted by the Royal Air Force. One aspect, which most intrigued European analysts, was the Italian use of chemical weapons, especially of mustard gas sprayed by low flying planes. While the Italians did carry out such attacks, they did not publicize them, and very little was learned of their effectiveness.[101] Yet the war was instructive in demonstrating the range of assistance that a modern air force could offer ground forces, as virtually all the operations of the Italian Air Force directly or indirectly supported the army.

In the summer of 1937, fighting broke out between China and Japan. Here too, the contest was one-sided, for the Japanese dominated the air war. Nor was it a conflict easy to follow in detail, being far removed from Europe, in a region where there were few qualified observers. Japan's air forces were modern and virtually unknown, but the war brought them considerable publicity. Both army and navy air forces existed essentially to serve land and sea forces respectively.[102] Japanese aircraft design reflected this support mission, and most planes lacked the range for strategic employment. Reconnaissance was strongly stressed, but army aircraft designated for this role were armed with bombs and machineguns and could also intervene in land battle very effectively. On the other hand, bombing attacks on Chinese cities produced disappointing results. This was notably the conclusion of a study entitled "The Conduct of the Air War in the Japan-China Conflict" prepared by the Fifth *Abteilung* of the *Luftwaffe* in 1938.[103] Here, as in the Ethiopian War, fighting tended to focus attention on the tactical role of air power and away from the strategic concepts of theorists such as General Giulio Douhet.

The Spanish Civil War, which broke out in 1936 and continued until 1939, was by far the most illuminating of the localized conflicts that preceded World War II; though its lessons were read differently from one country to the next, its overall impact on air power was considerable.

The importance of the Spanish Civil War to the development of military aviation outweighed that of other conflicts, because it occurred in the center of the European stage where it could be closely followed. Secondly, the opposing sides, the Loyalists and the Nationalists, both mounted serious efforts in the air on terms of rough equality. Thirdly, the two sides used, in limited quantities, much of the most modern air materiel of the late thirties. Aircraft types that would later figure in the Second World War were combat-tested, as were pilots, and to a limited degree, doctrine as well.

As in the other conflicts, it was the tactical use of air power that most attracted attention. One episode in particular stirred this interest in a spectacular way. In March 1937, Soviet pilots and planes serving the Loyalists came upon two divisions of Italian "volunteers" (who were aiding the Nationalists) moving in on Guadalajara, with a 1,000–vehicle convoy stretching for 10 miles. In two attacks, the 115–plane Soviet force dropped 500 bombs and fired 20,000 rounds of ammunition. The exact number of casualties was never revealed, but the two divisions were shattered.[104] Efforts to regroup were broken up by subsequent air attacks, and ultimately the Nationalists withdrew from the sector and the Loyalists claimed a major victory. Essentially, aviation had won the Battle of Guadalajara.

That same year, German aircraft and pilots of the "Condor Legion," which fought on the Nationalist side, gained considerable attention with close air-support operations in the tradition of the *Schlachtstaffel*. The German government had sent a number of aircraft that proved too slow to serve as fighters, so Wolfram von Richthofen, who commanded the German contingent, converted them to ground attack planes. This conversion was successful, and the German government dispatched aircraft more suited for this purpose, notably the Henschel HS–123 and the celebrated Junkers JU–87 dive bomber.[105] Italian planes and pilots also arrived to help the Nationalists and to test the techniques of *aviazione d'assalto*. By 1938, articles on tactical aviation and air support were appearing in military journals throughout Europe, and many countries sought to learn the lessons of the air war in Spain.

While it was still a rule of thumb in many air forces that bombers were an extension of the artillery, in Spain the airplane was often used as a substitute for the fieldpiece. In mountain fighting, it could strike enemy formations shielded on a reverse slope from artillery fire.[106] The airplane could also "prepare" for an infantry attack in place of the artillery barrage, though ground commanders found it far more difficult to coordinate aircraft than artillery for exact timing.[107]

Ground commanders stressed the psychological impact of air attack on their troops, especially in the early stages of the war. A Loyalist general tried to impress on a French observer the damage that enemy planes were doing in this regard: "Nothing is quite so demoralizing. German aviation is going to be a terrible menace for you French. . . . Your generals are incredibly stupid and shortsighted, and you are going to pay dearly for it. They don't realize that aviation is changing the forms of war."[108] On the other hand, airplanes could not intervene in the battle zone without risk, and as in the First World War, the risk tended to increase as the war progressed. Bombers needed fighter protection. After bombers had recrossed their lines, fighters could return to other missions—half of them to strafing, the other half patrolling.[109]

Tactics in ground attack work tended to be less complicated than those discussed in literature. Probably the best known tactic against strongpoints of resistance on the ground was the "Carousel", as the Soviet pilots called it, or the *Cadena* or "Chain" in Spanish. An Italian pilot described it as follows:

> The aircraft designated for the attack enter the enemy zone line astern, separated by perhaps 200 meters at an altitude of 800 to 1500 meters, which is maintained all during the approach phase. The formation's commander, who is always at its head, then dips down toward the target, machinegunning it down to an altitude of 200 meters. At that point, just as he is pulling up to regain altitude, he releases his bomb or bombs. The firing of the guns is thus followed (by) the fall of the bomb and the first pilot's work is done. The other aircraft follow the formation leader and in turn bring the objective under fire. The "chain," husbanding its projectiles, may return over the objective from two to four times.[110]

Soviet aviators in Spain found that air support in offensive operations generally followed a relatively simple pattern:

> The aircraft of the attacker, prior to launching the offensive, operate in the direction of the main effort against the enemy's rear (against airdromes, supply bases, bridges, and communications). The attack is preceded by an artillery preparation. During the artillery preparation the aviation operates against the same objectives against which the artillery is directing its fire, or else the objectives are divided among them. The serial attacks were here undertaken at intervals of 10 to 15 minutes.

> After the bombers have delivered several attacks, the pursuit craft enter the action, attacking the troops along the front lines and the artillery positions of the defender.

> Meanwhile the infantry of the attacker moves up to within 200 or 300 meters of the enemy trenches. The infantry attacks as soon as the pursuit aviation has delivered its attack. The combined effect of the aviation and artillery on the defender was frequently so great that some of the defender's infantry abandoned their positions even before the infantry of the attacker advanced to the assault. And even steadfast infantry troops when subjected to aerial attack frequently took refuge in individual or collective shelters and were retarded in meeting the hostile forces.[111]

As a rule, procedures for arranging timely and effective air support had to be derived or at least refined under combat conditions, and it was in this connection that the *Luftwaffe* gained invaluable experience during the Spanish Civil War. The recollections of Condor Legion veterans are explicit in this regard:

> Cooperation with ground forces was of the most primitive kind, and there was no ground-to-air R/T [radio contact] or even an effective method of signalling. In the

early days Richthofen himself used to stand on a hill overlooking the battle and lay on sorties by W/T (wireless telephone) or landline to the forward landing grounds.[112]

This procedure was endorsed in the report on military operations submitted to the German High Command early in 1939:

> Close cooperation between ground troops and air forces was made possible by having the commander of the air units, like the artillery commander, take up a combat post which was near that of the ground commander and situated so that it gave a good overview of the battle area. From there he could call in his alerted units by radio or telephone, so that attacks in support of the infantry were successfully carried out in a very short time.[113]

In general, the Spanish experience seemed to validate both diving and low-level attack techniques. While the *Stuka* was especially designed for the first of these tasks, experience in the war confirmed the fact that light bombers and especially fighters could be adapted to ground attack tasks. There was even some testimony that the fighter was superior to a specially designed ground attack plane, as this Soviet report attests:
"The experience in Spain has shown that pursuit craft are more suitable for employment in attacks against ground forces than the previously used two-seater attack planes—because of their maneuverability, fire power, greater speed, etc."[114]

The effectiveness of weapons traditionally used in ground attack—the machinegun and the small fragmentation bomb—was confirmed. Neither chemical agents nor incendiaries were used to any great extent. The French sent two cannon-equipped Morane–Saulnier 405 fighters to Spain, but they had no impact on the air battle. There was some evidence that machineguns in the 50–cal/13–mm class were effective against light tanks.[115] In sum, there were few innovations in weaponry in the Spanish Civil War.

What was the impact of the Spanish Civil War on the air policies of the great powers? It varied considerably, having the most impact on those powers most directly involved, those who had tested their planes, pilots, and doctrines in battle: Germany, Italy, and the Soviet Union. In those countries it led to further work in strengthening air support for the army. In Germany, for example, it brought about the establishment of the *Schlachtflieger* late in 1938. The French, though less directly involved, sent an air mission to Spain and acted on its recommendations, one of which called for the creation of a special close air-support force. The *Groupe de Bombardement d'Assaut* was to be equipped with light bombers, trained in low-level flight for combined operations with the army and for the "destruction of objectives of small dimensions."[116]

But it was possible to argue that the war in Spain was not a prototype for a general European conflict. If the airplane played the role of artillery, it was because both sides lacked artillery. If the airplane intervened in the land battle, it was because both sides lacked antiaircraft weapons. And if the airplane shattered the morale of troops, it was because they were ill-trained, ill-disciplined, and probably ill-led. This line of argument was adopted by the British Air Ministry. An Air Staff memo written two months after the beginning of World War II warned that it was "very dangerous to draw" conclusions from campaigns in China and Spain, which were considered as "almost guerilla affairs in which the air forces were relatively insignificant."[117] Given this viewpoint, it is not surprising that Great Britain had made less progress than any of the belligerents in providing effective air support for her armies when the war broke out.

The American Experience, 1918–1942

The evolution of air support for the U.S. Army in the interwar period sprang from the experience of World War I. The Army Air Service was a late arrival in the fighting in France and was able to play a significant role only in the last battles of the Great War, the first of which was the reduction of the Saint Mihiel salient in September 1918. American and French air forces concentrated 1,500 combat planes to support the ground attack. Colonel William "Billy" Mitchell, Chief of Air Service for the First Army, directed the air operations. Overcast skies interfered with the work of American bombers, but swarms of Allied fighters covered the area, where they found the roads clogged with German troops fleeing their collapsing salient. For three days the fighters bombed and machinegunned the retreating Germans, inflicting heavy casualties and considerable damage to German materiel.[118] Such "ground straffing" [sic] attacks on German ground forces prompted the Air Service to create specialized "battle" squadrons for this work, but the war ended before the squadrons could be organized.[119]

After the Armistice, the Air Service did not forget its successful participation in the land battles of 1918. Lt. Col. William C. Sherman's "Tentative Manual for the Employment of Air Service" and General Mitchell's "Provisional Manual of Operations of Air Units," both written just after the war, sought to distill the experience and served as repositories for ideas that circulated in the postwar Air Service. Implicit in each was the belief, drawn from the great battles of 1918, that at crucial times the whole weight of the air force might have to be committed to the land battle—but that under more usual wartime conditions the bulk of air power would be most profitably employed elsewhere. Mitchell thus listed attacks on ground troops as one of four "special" missions sometimes assigned to pursuit squadrons, whose most attractive targets were reserves massing for major military operations. Mitchell regarded bombing and strafing attacks on well-constructed positions held by seasoned troops as an insignificant effort producing very little effect on either morale or materiel.[120] By the same token, Colonel Sherman's thesis called for low-level bombing raids, to be carried out "at the beginning of an advance, or during an offensive, by either friendly or hostile troops." In both texts there are suggestions for a shift in emphasis from targets on the battlefield proper.[121]

The notion of a specialized branch of aviation for ground attack found its most emphatic champion in General Mitchell. His "Provisional Manual" contained an entire section on the "Organization and Employment of Attack Squadrons."[122] Many of his concepts materialized in due time. He placed great stress on psychological effects of low-flying attack aircraft upon friendly and enemy forces, and he insisted that attack squadrons be committed in "decisive infantry actions" only. To this end he placed them under the command and control of the Chief of Air Service of an Army or Army Group. On many points Mitchell expressed views very similar to those in the German Instruction of February 1918 on "The Employment of Battle Flights." Mitchell no doubt had seen the captured document in translation and may well have consulted it, for a comparison of the texts indicates a number of virtually identical passages.

The creation of attack aviation and its maintenance during the interwar years, as a distinct organizational element specialized in ground attack, led inevitably to a close identity between the attack concept and close air support. The practical result of this interest in battlefield aviation had been the creation in 1921 of the 3d Attack Group. While the idea persisted in the Air Service (which became the Air Corps in 1926) that in certain circumstances all aircraft might have to be committed directly into the land battle, and while the notion also persisted that bombardment, fighter, and attack units might each do the other's work to a limited degree, the tendency was to confirm specialization and to orient training accordingly. Pursuit units were to defeat the enemy in the air, bombers were to sow destruction behind his lines, and attack units were to provide air support.

General Mitchell gave the new branch of aviation its name, derived from the term "ground attack," current at that time, and it was he who set out its role as one of direct and intimate involvement in land battles:

> During offensives, attack squadrons operate over and in front of the infantry and neutralize the fire of the enemy's infantry and barrage batteries. On the defensive, the appearance of attack airplanes affords visible proof to heavily engaged troops that Headquarters is maintaining close touch with the front, and is employing all possible auxiliaries to support the fighting troops.[123]

To carry out such missions, the Air Service sought a heavily armored airplane capable of flying at low altitudes over enemy ground forces and

43

Col. William Mitchell,
portrayed by
artist Linda Nikkelson.

Lt. Col. William C. Sherman,
Chief of Staff,
First U.S. Army Air Service.

44

bringing to bear on them a heavy weight of firepower. The G.A.–1 (Ground attack) aircraft was designed for this purpose by the Engineering Division of the Air Service and built by Boeing in 1921. It was a twin-engine, heavily armored craft bristling with machineguns and a 37–mm cannon that fired through the propeller hub. It was not a success. The aircraft suffered from "a number of aerodynamic deficiencies and power plant problems, and from the excessive weight of its ton of 1/4–inch thick armor plating."[124]

Its successor, the G.A.–2, was also disappointing in performance. By the mid-twenties the heavily armored battle plane was abandoned. In what was undoubtedly an economy move, the 3d Attack Group was equipped with DH–4 observation planes powered by Liberty engines developed during World War I. In 1925 one officer lamented that "there is a total of fourteen DH planes in the attack air force of this country"[125] Training in ground attack techniques was hampered, because the worn-out DH–4s could not carry both bombs and machineguns at the same time.[126]

The new branch of aviation was also having problems with doctrine in further defining its role. In the early 1920s, the 3d Attack Group was the only specialized force in the world, so there was little to be learned from other air forces. Attack aviation, moreover, was a postwar creation with no past, no combat tradition, and no backlog of practical experience. The only operational experience in the 3d Attack Group was as a "surveillance" unit along the Mexican border following World War I, but this mission ended when Mexican bandits stopped their incursions. In the late twenties, the U.S. Marine Corps flew a number of air support missions in Nicaragua. A detailed account of the operations was presented in 1929 by Maj. Ross E. Rowell (USMC) during a lecture at the Army War College on "Experience with the Air Service in Minor Warfare."[127] The Marines' experience in air support was rich and varied. Airplanes served as artillery, in which the Marines were deficient; they intervened in sieges and battles where very little space separated the contending forces; they flew escort missions for columns; and they detected and broke up enemy attempts at ambush. In subsequent campaigns and exercises, the Marines were to build up a sizable fund of expertise on close air support, particularly related to amphibious operations.[128]

Interested in the campaign, the Chief of the Air Corps, in 1928, had asked for information on the fighting, and as late as 1939 a conference on attack aviation at the Command and General Staff School was partly based on a "personal conversation" with a member of the Nicaraguan Force—Capt. L. T. Burke (USMC).[129] Yet the experience in Nicaragua is rarely mentioned in the surviving texts of the Air Corps Tactical School in the late twenties and thirties. Why it should have been largely ignored is not completely clear, but most likely it was because the campaign was considered similar to air control operations and too different from conventional warfare to hold any valuable lessons. We have some evidence of this view in a comment written by General

Mitchell in 1930, four years after he had left the Army. Once a warm partisan of attack aviation, he now felt it had only limited usefulness:

> This branch of aviation will have most of its application in the future against what are termed partisan or irregular troops, and as are found in Asia, Africa, Mexico and Central America, that is those not equipped with large air forces and which do not move in large numbers but in comparatively small mobile detachments.[130]

Maneuvers and joint air-ground exercises might have helped fill the void of experience, but there was very little of this. Coordination of attack aviation operations with fighter action was essential because in the doctrine of the early twenties, air superiority was a precondition to ground attack.[131] Air strikes on the battlefield and in proximity to friendly ground forces called for careful air-ground coordination as well. But occasions for working out such procedures were infrequent. General Earle E. Partridge recalled how 3d Attack Group maneuvers in the late 1920s "were few and far between, . . ." but he could not recall any discussions with his Army counterparts about the role of aviation in land battle: "Socially, we knew a lot of them . . . we ran into these people at parties and so on, but as for getting together to talk tactics, no." Asked where the commander of the 3d Attack Group was getting his doctrine, Partridge replied that "he was manufacturing it."[132]

There was also some interest in air support at the Air Corps Tactical School (ACTS), for in the late twenties the attack aviation instructor, Capt. George C. Kenney, who was drawn to the ground attack role, years later told an interviewer: "The thing that I was interested in more than anything else was attack. I taught attack aviation and wrote the textbook on it and developed the tactics by using the class as a tool to build the tactics in low-altitude work."[133] In sum, doctrine on air support developed in a disjointed and haphazard fashion, and also somewhat in the shadows. In the 1920s, the fighter or pursuit was considered the critical aircraft, so that the 1926 edition of the Training Manual (TR 440–15) stipulated: "The full value of observation, bombardment, and attack aviation can only be obtained with adequate pursuit aviation."[134] In the 1930s the strategic bomber similarly held the spotlight.

For a time, air support doctrine followed the guidelines laid down by General Mitchell in his "Provisional Manual of Operations of 1918." The 1926 edition of TR 440-15 still reflected a strong commitment to direct participation in the land battle. In some cases, bombers could be used to supplement or replace artillery, while fighters might temporarily assume the ground attack function. Attack aviation was to support infantry directly in taking important objectives. Here its role was that of the *Schlachtflieger* of 1918: "It precedes and accompanies the troops in their advance, increasing the fire action when necessary at any section of the line."[135] But subsequently doctrinal emphasis shifted. Less was said about the role of the fighter or the

George C. Kenney as a First Lieutenant.

bomber in land battle. The role of attack aviation was gradually altered to that of more indirect support of ground forces.

By 1930, the doctrinal changes from 1926 were clear. In the ACTS text, "The Air Force," there is a broad assertion that "the air force does not attack objectives on the battlefield or in the immediate proximity thereof, except in most unusual circumstances." Bombing planes would operate over the battlefield "in only the rarest situations." As for attack aviation, suitable objectives were listed as "reserves of armies, corps, and occasionally of divisions, while still massed prior to their engagement in battle. . . ."[136] By 1939, the role of attack aviation was to conduct operations in the zone beyond the reach of friendly artillery. Air attacks were not to be made within artillery range or against deployed troops "except in cases of great emergency."[137]

Shifts in doctrinal emphasis continued in the thirties. The concept of interdiction was popular in the Air Corps at that time, and it had its effect on air support doctrine. An ACTS text of 1937–1938 described "support prior to and during battle of the ground forces" as isolation of hostile troops in the battle zone from their sources of supply, and disruption of enemy troop movements. Following was the rationale for this type of support: "The element most vital to the success of the enemy force is its line of communications. The troops in the forward area cannot long survive if the flow of supplies has been disrupted, and all means of transporting these are vulnerable to a certain degree."[138]

Other aspects of air support were studied as well. The Army—and the

Air Corps—spent considerable time with schemes to repel invasion. While this was an unlikely task, it was an acceptable one to a nation anxious to maintain its neutrality and committed to a narrow concept of self-defense. Attack aviation was to have a role in coastal defense, in which aircraft would destroy small enemy boats and protect against mustard gas contamination of shorelines.[139] The Air Corps was anxious to fit attack aviation into the struggle for air superiority, so studies concentrated on using attack planes against enemy airfields and aircraft on the ground. Then too, as bomber doctrine evolved, Air Corps leadership was attracted to the idea of using attack aircraft to neutralize enemy antiaircraft defenses before the arrival of bomber forces. This idea was tested in Air Corps exercises in California in 1937, when attack and bomber forces struck a target complex representing Los Angeles and its defenses laid out on the bed of Muroc Dry Lake.[140]

The United States learned no clear and indisputable lessons on air support from the limited wars of the late thirties. Though the conflicts were analyzed, notably by the ACTS, views on the fighting in China, Ethiopia, and Spain varied considerably. Major Omer O. Niergarth wrote: "As we read of these instances in which the air force has been of material assistance to the ground forces, we cannot avoid being impressed with the fact that, in all future wars, ground troops are going to demand much more of this close-in cooperation from air forces."[141]

When Brig. Gen. Henry H. Arnold addressed the U.S. Army War College on recent developments in air warfare in the fall of 1937, he praised Japan because "she has not assigned her air force to operate against front-line trenches, as have the Spaniards."[142] As for the Spanish Civil War, Arnold said that high aircraft losses resulted from using aircraft "promiscuously and indiscriminately to supplement artillery actions on a large number of petty, heterogeneous missions. . . ." He drew the following moral from the war in Spain: "Do not detach the air force to small commands where it will be frittered away in petty fighting. Hold it centrally and use it in its proper place, that is, where it can exert its power beyond the influence of your other arms, to influence general action rather than the specific battle."[143]

While the nature and extent of air support to ground forces was the subject of differing viewpoints throughout the thirties, the organizational linkage for that support was never fully developed or tested. This was particularly true of the critical link between ground and air forces. In the United States, as in Europe, coordination would come into existence with mobilization and the constitution of field armies. Until the mid-1930s, each American army formed was to be supplied with a wing of aircraft composed of one attack and one pursuit group. Air Corps officers at army, corps, and division level were to exercise tactical command and to serve as technical staff officers of the army, corps, or division commander. This structure, laid down in the 1926 Training Manual, TR 440–15, contained one notable exception:

> When attack aviation is employed to assist the ground forces in the taking of definite objectives, close cooperation becomes necessary, particularly when such objectives are within the range of artillery fire. In most cases this cooperation is best accomplished by placing the attack aviation units directly under the command of the ground commander charged with the tactical handling of the forces involved.[144]

The Air Corps always resisted such an arrangement. The Air Corps Tactical School was particularly outspoken on this point. It held that "even when a segment of the air force was allotted to the task of close support, it should be retained under centralized control at the theater level in order that its inherent flexibility might be exploited."[145]

The 1926 edition of TR 440–15 also provides some data on ground attack tactics then current: "The approach should be made from different directions and every advantage taken for concealment, utilizing particularly all natural features of terrain, and a concerted diving attack should then be launched with machinegun fire and bombs."[146] Low-level flight was the basic element in ground attack. The commander of the 3d Attack Group wrote in 1934:

> We fly close for concealment, in order to gain the prime requisite of a successful mission—surprise, and to apply our weapons properly. Machineguns must have grazing fire, bombs must be placed accurately without benefit of bombsights, and chemical agents must be placed just where they are required and in the proper concentration. Attack bombs and chemical agents are greatly affected by the wind. Then too, we are frankly apprehensive of rifle fire and to some extent of machinegun fire.

> An attack formation moving at a hundred yards a second, popping over a clump of bushes or a ridge with all machineguns wide open and bombs ready on a hair trigger has some chance. Not everyone can get a shot at it, and if one happens to be in its path the first warning of approach will consist of a hail of machinegun bullets.[147]

For low-level attacks, an assault unit of three planes was common. A flight of nine planes was about maximum size for low-level formation flying. General Partridge recalled: "We flew in three-ship formations, and if we wanted to have a big formation, we sometimes had twelve airplanes. The technique," he related, "was to come in as low as you dared to fly. Just before you got to the target, that initial point, you'd pull up and maybe get 300–400 feet, and then you'd dive on the target, strafe, drop your bombs in pattern as you went along, and then dive for the deck again."[148] The strafing was essentially to intimidate the enemy and interfere with his fire. For ground attack, the planes would customarily carry the 30–lb fragmentation bomb as the chief destructive weapon.

Despite the strong emphasis on indirect support in the 1930s, the Air Corps Tactical School and the 3d Attack Group both conducted a variety of tactical experiments related to close air support. These involved calculating casualties on ground troops in various forms of deployment, represented by pasteboard targets (the results were published and cited in European military journals). General Kenney recalled testing parachute bombs and doing "skip" bombing. The 3d Attack Group experimented with dive-bombing in the interest of greater accuracy. A German flyer named Hans Rohmer, visiting the U.S. in the early thirties, attended maneuvers in Texas where he saw heavy bombers and attack planes testing tactics against tanks. The heavy bombers cratered the earth in the tanks' path, then, when they slowed to negotiate the craters, attack planes strafed and bombed them from a height of ten meters.[149]

Attack aircraft missions were not roving ones, seeking targets of opportunity. Doctrine stipulated that they be carefully prepared beforehand, with the unit commander briefing his men thoroughly before they took off. While the commander might receive further data on the target by radio from an observation plane during the flight to the objective, radio generally was little used. An Army War College text of 1937-38 advised:

> Airplane radio sets are most valuable for training. Their combat employment is prejudicial to security and surprise. If not carefully maintained, they are noisy and conversation is difficult. Voice communication is slow and difficult. The best principle for the use of radio is "Silence is Golden." Let the responsibility for breaking radio silence rest with the senior officer commanding the flight. Airplane radio is used but little in the Spanish War.[150]

Brig. Gen. Henry H. Arnold.

In the post–World War I period, it was customary to prescribe protective fighter "cover" for ground attack missions, though the chances of a low-level attack plane accomplishing its mission and returning safely without cover were rated as considerably better than the chances of conventional bombers. By the 1930s, the tendency was to consider fighter protection unnecessary. The higher speed of attack aircraft of the thirties made it difficult for fighters to be alerted in time to intercept them in their brief incursions. The higher speed of attack aircraft also reduced the chances that the sound of their engines would precede them and warn of their approach.[151] Interest in engine noise reduction devices waned accordingly.

The changing views of the ground attack function in the interwar period made it difficult to fix upon a satisfactory aircraft. The heavily armored "trench fighter" of the early twenties with its twenty-odd machineguns was replaced by a fast, maneuverable, more lightly armed plane. The makeshift DH–4s which the 3d Attack Group had flown were replaced by the A–3, a modified version of the Curtiss 0–1 observation plane. The role and nature of attack aircraft were debated from 1927 to 1930, and in 1928 Maj. Millard F. Harmon urged the abolition of the attack type, whose ground assault role could be taken over by the fighter. Defenders of attack aviation had insisted that a rear gunner was necessary—hence a special aircraft. In 1929, a board of officers was named to determine the best type. (Capt. Kenney was a member.) It recommended a fast, two-seater biplane, but by 1930 a low-winged monoplane was favored.[152] This change of viewpoint resulted in the adoption of the Curtiss A–12 acquired in 1933 and the Northrop A–17 in 1936.

As early as 1934 there was interest in a twin-engine attack plane, and that interest grew in the 1930s. There was, first of all, the view that the per-

Northrop A-17. This aircraft reflected the American philosophy of ground attack planes through the late 1930s. The A-17 did not see combat service in World War II.

formance of twin-engine aircraft, at that stage in their evolution, was superior to those with single engines. Then too, twin engine attack planes would have greater range to hit the enemy's more distant airfields, to escort bombers neutralizing antiaircraft fire, or to strike mechanized and motorized forces. Another consideration was the need for more power to carry heavier armament. In 1937, therefore, the Air Corps began testing the twin-engine Curtiss A–18. The plane's performance was not entirely satisfactory. Nevertheless, its potential reinforced thinking in favor of a heavier plane for ground support. In 1938, the Air Corps sought a new twin-engine attack-bomber, with a high speed (350 mph), a range of 1,200 miles, and armament that included 6 machineguns and a ton of bombs. This specification led to the successful Douglas A–20 and to a line of effective light bombers.[153]

As if to signal the change, at the end of 1939 the Air Corps Tactical School dropped the designation "attack" and substituted "light bombardment." The development of this concept was a considerable gamble, but one which paid off once the war started.

Unfortunately, the renovation in materiel was not accompanied by any updating of methods and procedures for ensuring effective air support of armies in the field. The Air Corps Tactical School's text, *Light Bombardment Aviation*, dated January 15, 1940, contained this *caveat*:

> To use this force on the battlefield to supplement and increase the firepower of ground arms is decidedly an incorrect employment of this class of aviation, since it would neglect the more distant and vital objectives."[154] But "the most amazing thing," one historian has written, "is that despite . . . [the] mutual recognition of the air force's support role, neither the Air Corps nor the General Staff had devised the machinery necessary for executing it. When World War II began in Europe, there still was no consolidated, clear-cut, concrete body of doctrine, nor for that matter even a field manual dealing with air-ground cooperation and direct support of ground troops.[155]

It was not so much the outbreak of war in September 1939 that galvanized the Army and the Air Corps but rather the catastrophic events of the summer of 1940, particularly the fall of France and Hitler's conquest of Western Europe. In a clear reaction to the dazzling tactical successes of the *Luftwaffe*, and especially to the close collaboration of armored forces and *Stukas*, the Air Corps addressed the Navy in June 1940, saying it was "extremely anxious" to obtain information on dive bombers.[156] Within a month, General Arnold decided to create two groups of dive bombers, to be equipped with an Air Corps version of the Navy's SBD. They were designated the A-24 (first one delivered to Wright Field in June 1941). The Air Corps hastened the development of a 37-mm cannon as well as armor protection and self-sealing gas tanks.

Perhaps most important, General Arnold took steps to provide effective air support for the armored units that the Army was rapidly organizing. In a letter to Lt. Gen. Frank Andrews,* he stressed "the vital importance of developing tactics and techniques necessary in rendering close air support to mechanized forces."[157] To this end he ordered two light-bombardment groups for work with armored forces. Then, in December 1940, the War Department ordered extensive tests to develop sound "techniques, methods of cooperation, direction and control of combined operations involving support of ground forces by combat aviation. . . ."[158] In 1941, Headquarters, Army Air Forces (AAF) was established under General Arnold, with responsibility for all Army aviation. AAF Headquarters created the Directorate of Air Support and for the rest of the year ordered tests, prepared training circulars, and issued field manuals.

In April 1941, General Arnold conferred with British military leaders in London, hoping to profit from their recent experiences with close air support. In the aftermath of Dunkirk, the British had embarked on a crash program of tests and exercises conducted in Northern Ireland. This led to the "Directive on Close Support Bombing" issued on December 6, 1940.[159] British capabilities were centered on an organization called Close Support Bomber Control, which was staffed with air and ground officers and placed adjacent to the ground command it served—an army or a corps. This body evaluated and responded to requests for air support, being helped by its own forward subsidiary units called tentacles. Arnold sent a copy of the British plan to Army Chief of Staff General George C. Marshall, recommending "strongly" that the directive be sent to light-bomber commands and armored divisions.[160]

The British scheme was useful, but even more so was the series of tests conducted at Fort Benning, Georgia, between February and June 1941, involving an armored division, two infantry divisions, several pursuit and light bombardment squadrons, a parachute battalion, and cavalry units. Though hampered by equipment shortages, especially radios, the tests sought to determine, among other things, how close to friendly troops bombing should be conducted. This proved to be dependent upon a number of variables, including the skill of the pilots. Further tests indicated that bombing safety was not a serious concern and that "troops rarely can designate or identify targets for air attack," while those they did designate were generally not "profitable."[161] The tests also indicated that aviation support was different from artillery support in that it involved "more centralized control." The tests revolved around "Air Support Control," which received requests for air support, evaluated them, and ordered intervention when appropriate. The average time needed to secure air support was one hour and nine minutes. The key to this system was "simple, prompt communications," which were

---

*Commander of the Air Corps' new consolidated strike force, the General Headquarters Air Force, until mid 1939.

Curtiss A-18s in low-level flight *(above)*. Dissatisfied with the performance of these light, two-place attack craft, the Army Air Forces began purchasing faster, heavier craft with longer range. The Douglas A-24 *(below)*, an Army Air Forces copy of a U.S. Navy dive bomber.

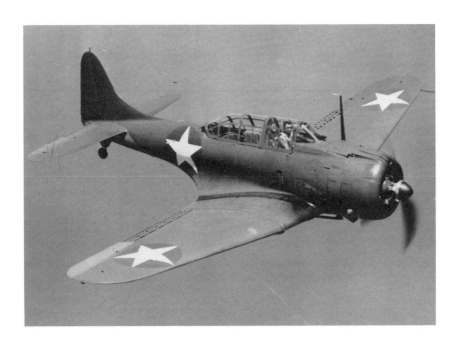

Maj. Gen. Frank M. Andrews, Commander, General Headquarters Air Force, 1936.

not always available.[162] (The SCR 197 radio took ten minutes to set up and could not be operated in motion.)

The year 1941 also saw extensive maneuvers in the southeastern U.S., beginning in Arkansas and Louisiana and ending in the Carolinas. They were the first extensive army-size exercises ever held, and they offered an excellent opportunity to experiment with air support. In the Louisiana maneuvers, the Second Army operated an air task force with its ground units against the Third Army. The air and ground commanders exchanged liaison officers, but their command posts were not contiguous or located near an airfield. A postmortem of the maneuvers cited this as a weakness. Once again "Air Support Control," arranged for air support, which from call to execution averaged seventy minutes. Air reconnaissance seemed to generate more profitable targets than ground reports.[163]

On the basis of tests and maneuvers, the War Department began issuing preliminary instructions on close air support. *Training Circular No. 52*, issued on August 29, 1941, called for the retention of the Air Task Force Commander and an Advanced Air Support Command Post set up near the command post of the unit supported.[164] *Training Circular No. 70* of December 16, 1941, fitted the ground-support role into the general range of air force functions. Finally, FM 31-35, Aviation in Support of Ground Forces, of April 1942, amplified *Training Circular No. 52* concerning organization for combat, general functions, and employment of aviation used in tactical support of ground forces.

Support aviation assigned to an army was under the command of an air support commander, who directed its activities from his air support command post. He was to determine support roles based on several factors, including the need for flexibility, economy of force, and air superiority, without which losses in support missions could be excessive. Linked to the command post proper were subsidiary units called air support controls and air support parties. Paired with subordinate ground units, they relayed and evaluated requests for air support. There were exceptions to the principle of centralized command and control. Air units might be allocated and, in exceptional circumstances, attached to subordinate ground units for air support.[165]

The publication of FM 31–35 was a crash effort to establish a comprehensive system of air support; whether it could be the basis for a viable system remained to be seen. Air and ground units also trained on a crash basis, with top priority given to the air-armor relationship. On July 20, 1942, General Arnold sent General Marshall a memo in which he outlined progress since February 1941. The armored forces had had more training with combat aviation than all other units of the Army combined. The memo came to the attention of Maj. Gen. Jacob L. Devers, who wrote Arnold a personal letter "to let you know that I still stick to my opinion that there is no air-ground support training. We are simply puttering. Cannot something be done?"[166] Devers complained particularly of shortages of serviceable planes at the training sites.

Arnold defended the AAF, adding: "There is just so much aviation available for cooperative training in this country with the Army Ground Forces."[167] This exchange of letters took place in September 1942. Within two months, American land and air forces were heavily engaged in North Africa, where close air support became a much more pressing issue.

Conclusion

When the Second World War broke out in September 1939, the German *Luftwaffe* probably had the most effective close air-support system of any of the great powers. Even so, that system was a recent creation based on very limited combat experience, and it was with some trepidation that the *Luftwaffe*'s leaders committed aircraft to land battles in Poland. For other belligerents, even less well prepared to provide air support for their armies, the first campaigns posed enormous problems. The Chief of Staff of the British Expeditionary Force in France noted in his diary in the spring of 1940: "But really this coordination of air effort of fighters, bombers, and reconnaissance, is enough to drive one quite crazy."[168]

The basic reason for these early difficulties is clear: most air forces entered the conflict armed with doctrine, planes, and pilots untested in battle conditions. Camille Rougeron, a French military analyst of the 1930s, reminded the air leaders of his day that they had been "deprived for the previous fifteen years of a rigorous day-to-day testing of their concepts by an enemy fighter force."[169] This fundamental weakness applied to all aspects of air power, but it had special validity for close air support, which was one of the last of the air missions to emerge during the Great War. By 1918 the role of the fighter had been well defined, as had been the basic requirements of fighter aircraft and the attributes of bombers. On the other hand, the proper task of close air-support aircraft had not been established with certainty, nor had the characteristics of the ideal ground attack plane. Indeed there was not even agreement that close air support was a separate and distinct function of air power. In the French service, for example, it never evolved beyond occasional and secondary activity for fighters and light bombers.

The limited experience of 1917–1918 left other unresolved questions concerning close air support. Centralized command and control committed ground attack units in considerable numbers at critical times and places. On the other hand, effective intervention, which required a familiarity with terrain and disposition of friendly and enemy ground forces by air units would presuppose the attachment of air units to specific sectors and ground units. It was often argued that tactical aviation was similar to artillery, a form of firepower to be placed at the disposal of the ground commander, and in 1941 Soviet *Shturmovik* units were parcelled out in this fashion. Elsewhere air force leaders were generally able to keep their planes from being "frittered away," to use General Arnold's phrase. They argued successfully that the system of command and control should make maximum use of air power's capacity for mobility and concentration. They also insisted that the decision to commit such a specialized means of destruction to the battlefield should be made or reviewed by a competent air authority, who alone could determine that the objective was suitable for air attack and that the attack would not entail prohibitive losses. An RAF memo of 1939 expressed this concern in unequivocal language: "The Air Forces have never been unwilling to face heavy losses; but it must be realized that highly trained pilots cannot by replaced with the same ease as infantry soldiers."[170]

To these concerns, which were the legacy of 1918, we must add the challenges posed by technological changes following the Great War. The performance of aircraft improved dramatically, and this improvement was bound to influence their use in ground attack. At the same time, the increasing mechanization and motorization of armies would inevitably alter the nature and disposition of objectives for ground attack. The enhanced mobility of ground forces could mean rapidly evolving battles with fleeting objectives requiring rapid air intervention and demanding speedy and efficient communications between air and ground.

As a general rule, all these questions were but seldom addressed in the 1920s. Only in the 1930s were there sporadic efforts to draw air power closely into new concepts of land warfare, as with the German *Blitzkrieg* doctrine and the Soviet Deep Battle concept. Most thinking, however, was directed toward improving positional warfare of the previous conflict, a preoccupation best expressed by the term "Maginot mentality." In such a climate there was little meaningful dialogue between air and ground leaders. The army asked little of the air force save the classic functions of observation and reconnaissance, air superiority over the battlefield, and a statement of commitment to ground support to be generally applied "beyond artillery range." Left largely to itself, the air force concentrated on the air and how to control it—and on the "race" between the fighter and the bomber. In Great Britain and the United States, creative thinking among airmen in the 1930s centered upon strategic bombing.

In the years between the wars, exchanges between air and army leaders often tended to be negative in tone, if not acrimonious. In Italy and France, air leaders engaged in a struggle to obtain and affirm independence for their services; in the United States, such conflict was dramatized by the celebrated "Billy Mitchell Affair." In Great Britain, where the RAF fought to maintain its independence in the 1920s, relations between air and land services were also unharmonious. A Royal Air Force officer summed up the British Army's attitude toward air power with these words: "Believe me, it was quite impossible to make the Army believe we could have contributed anything worthwhile to the land battle."[171] Yet, at the same time, a senior officer in the Air Ministry denounced air support operations in Spain as "a prostitution of the Air Force."[172]

The lack of dialogue between air and ground leaders had more serious effects on the evolution of close air support than on any other aspect of air power. With no common interest in resolving the problems inherent in ground support, little effort was expended on joint exercises and manuevers or on the formulation of doctrine. Air leaders showed little interest in the research carried out by naval aviation, in spite of significant accomplishments in the destruction of relatively small, mobile, and defended objectives of the kind encountered in close air-support work. Only in 1940 did the French, British, and U.S. air forces develop a serious interest in the dive bomber. By the same token, the lessons in tactical air power in the conflicts in China and Spain were often ignored or little noted. Even lessons about air control operations that could have been learned from World War I and later conflicts had to be learned on the battlefields of World War II: the psychological impact of air attack on enemy soldiers tended to wear off, and when those soldiers fought back, their concentrated fire posed a serious hazard.

If these factors help explain the limited progress in close air support by the eve of World War II, there are special considerations which affected its evolution in the United States. Endowed with the 3d Attack Group, the oldest unit in any of the post–1918 air forces dedicated to support of ground forces, the U.S. Army Air Corps should have led the world in such techniques. Actually, in 1939 it was among the least advanced. As we have seen, the fate of close air support was bound up with that of attack aviation, and the fate of attack aviation was not a happy one. The U.S. Army asked little of it, while "within the Air Corps a certain amount of official lip service was given to the attack mission in order to escape the wrath of the General Staff, but on the whole very little constructive effort was put into the program."[173]

In some other countries, the ground-support role of aviation found vociferous champions in the interwar period: General Mecozzi in Italy, Camille Rougeron in France, and Turgianskii and other air tacticians in the Soviet Union. No such advocates appeared in the U.S. Air Corps:

> After 1926 attack aviation simply became a mission with few aggressive and vocal supporters. Without the demands of a combat situation or realistic maneuvers, the War Department, with no organization charged with the responsibility for developing and preserving concepts such as the attack mission, allowed that idea to slowly die from a benign sort of neglect.[174]

Nonetheless, the 3d Attack Group made significant strides in air support. In the late thirties, for example, the unit studied the problem of night operations in air support, specifically denying the enemy the nighttime use of roads and railways. But whatever was learned in such studies did not find its way into manuals or official journals; and, according to General Partridge, such findings were passed on "by word of mouth."[175] Years later, in the summer of 1944, the Allies still had no effective means of attacking German road traffic at night.

The limited wars of the late 1930s did little to stimulate interest in the support role in Air Corps circles. Judging from the oral history interviews with Air Corps veterans of the interwar period, there was in the air arm a sense of insularity, or isolation. One veteran of that era recalled: "Air Corps-wise, we were just nowhere near as interested in foreign development and so forth."[176] Another admitted frankly: "I had almost no knowledge of what was going on outside the country."[177] There was no systematic, exhaustive study of the fighting in China and Spain, and no observers were sent to the latter country. Translations of articles in foreign journals only infrequently found their way to the Air Corps Tactical School, judging by the few samples that survive. Lack of complete and first-hand information may explain why General Arnold's analyses of the war in Spain were sometimes contradicted by the facts. There is another consideration that helps explain why the Air Corps generally neglected close air support and tactical aviation, and that is its preoccupation with strategic bombing. In the view of one historian, "the slow development of pursuit and attack aviation in the early and mid–1930s was clearly the result of preoccupation of Air Corps leaders with the heavy bomber."[178] Colonel Paul M. Robinette, attached to the General Staff at the beginning of the war, noted the same phenomenon. Speaking of General Arnold, he noted:

> His faith in heavy long range bombers was unbounded, and this faith carried into action gave the U.S. outstanding position in strategic aviation, and ultimately supremacy in the air. But there was little thought given to the ground troops or to their problems, second place going to pursuit type airplanes.[179]

The colonel concluded that if "we could not be broad-minded enough to appreciate both sides of the question," it was better to have emphasized the strategic air effort.[180] That may be true, but it is no less true that the U.S. Army Air Forces went to war ill-prepared to support the ground forces. The lack of preparation can be imputed to the nation's air and army leaders alike.

Notes

1. Quoted in John Frederick Shiner, "The Army Air Arm in Transition, General Benjamin D. Foulois and the Air Corps, 1931–1935" (Ph D Dissertation, Ohio State University, 2 Vols), I, p 7.
2. Cited in *Kriegswissenschaftliche Abteilung der Luftwaffe, Die Militärluftfahrt bis zum Beginn des Weltkrieges 1914*, 3 Vols (Berlin, 1941), II, p 13.
3. Quoted in Patrick Facon, "l'Armée Francaise et l'Aviation," paper presented at meeting of the Southern Hist Association, Houston, Texas, Nov 14, 1985.
4. I. B. Holley, Jr., *Ideas and Weapons. Exploitation of the Aerial Weapon by the United States during World War I. A Study in the Relationship of Technological Advance, Military Doctrine, and the Development of Weapons* (Camden, Conn, 1971), p 29.
5. On the Italian air activity in Libya see Angelo Lodi, *Storia Delle Origini dell' Aeronautica Militare 1884–1915: Aerostieri, Dirigibilisti, Aviatore dell' Esercito e della Marina in Italia nel Periodico Pionieristico* (Rome, 1961), pp 93–146.
6. For an account of air operations during the Balkan Wars see Henri Mirande and Louis Olivier, *Sur la Bataille. Journal d'un Aviateur Français a l'Armée Bulgare, au siége d'Adrianople* (Paris, 1913), *passim*.
7. Serge Laine, "l'Aeronautique Militaire Française au Maroc (1911–1939)," *Revue Historique des Armées* 5 (Nr 4, 1978), pp 107–19.
8. Quoted in William C. Smith, *Dive Bomber! An Illustrated History* (Annapolis, 1982), p 9.
9. For examples of early signalling techniques see S. F. Wise, *Canadian Airmen and the First World War [The Official History of the Royal Canadian Air Force*, Vol 1] (Toronto, 1980), pp 343–4.
10. H. A. Jones, *The War in the Air: Being the Story of the Part Played in the Great War by the Royal Air Force*, 6 Vols (London, 1922–37), VI, p 437.
11. For extracts of the French *Instruction* on air–infantry liaison transl for use by the U.S. Air Service see "Infantry Liaison, 19 Jun 1918" in Maurer Maurer, ed & comp, *The U.S. Air Service in World War I*, 4 Vols, (Maxwell AFB and Washington, D.C., 1978), II, pp 199–203.
12. Georg P. Neumann, *Die Deutschen Luftstreitkräfte im Weltkrieg* (Berlin, 1920), p 425.
13. Jones, *War*, II, 200, 210.
14. *Ibid*, p 233.
15. Ernst von Hoeppner, *Deutschlands Krieg in der Luft; Ein Rückblick auf die Entwicklung und die Leistungen unserer Heeresluftstreitkräfte im Weltkrieg* (Leipzig, 1921), p 73.
16. Jones, *War*, III, p 378.
17. Quoted in *Ibid*, IV, p 129, note 2.
18. *Ibid*, pp 129–130.
19. Neumann, *Luftstreitkräfte*, p 485
20. See on this subject Brereton Greenhous, "Close Support Aircraft in World War I. The Counter Anti-tank Role," *Aerospace Historian* 21 (Jun 1874), pp 87–93.
21. Wing Commander J. C. Slessor, *Air Power and Armies* (London, 1936), p 90.
22. On the development of this aviation see Neumann, *Luftstreitkräfte*, pp 453–5.
23. This document is reproduced as App XII in Jones, *War*, IV, pp 433–8.
24. Wise, *Airmen*, p 440.
25. Jones, *War*, IV, p 436.
26. *Ibid*, p 435.
27. *Ibid*, p 433.
28. *Ibid*, p 437.
29. *Ibid*, p 436.
30. "Future Policy in the Air," in *Ibid*, II, p 473.
31. Lt Col William C. Sherman, "Tentative Manual for the Employment of Air Service," in Maurer, *Air Service*, II, p 316.

32. Jones, *War*, IV, p 434.
33. *Ibid*, IV, p 238.
34. *Ibid*, pp 433–4.
35. General William Mitchell, *Memoirs of the World War I: From Start to Finish of our Greatest War* (Westport, Conn, 1979), p 263.
36. "Protection against Enemy Aeroplanes. Transl from a German Document, July, 1918," Jones, *War*, App Vol, App XXII, pp 113–4.
37. H. A. J. Toulmin, *Air Service American Expeditionary Force 1918* (New York, 1927), p 377.
38. Jones, *War*, IV, pp 234, 247.
39. Slessor, *Air Power*, p 100.
40. Report, Col Frank P. Lahm, Chief of Air Service, Second Army, nd, in Maurer, *Air Service*, IV, p 20.
41. "Fighting in the Air," Jones, *War*, App Vol, App XX, pp 94–5.
42. Harald Penrose, *British Aviation. The Great War and Armistice 1915–1918* (New York, 1969), p 416.
43. Albert Etévé, *La Victoire des Cocardes. l'Aviation Francçise Avant et Pendant la Premiere Guerre Mondiale* (Paris, 1970), p 289.
44. Peter Gray and Owen Thetford, *German Aircraft of the First World War*, 2d revised ed (Garden City, N.Y., 1978), pp 154–7.
45. Jones, *War*, App Vol, App XXXVII, p 161.
46. General Charles Christienne, Gen Pierre Lissarague, Alain Degardin, Patrick Facon, Patrice Buffotot, and Marcellin Hodeir, *Histoire de l'Aviation Militaire Francaise* (Paris & Limoges, 1980), p 154.
47. Bruce Robertson, *Sopwith, the Man and his Aircraft* (Letchworth, England, 1970), p 108.
48. Order to the 9th Wing, Mar 25, 1918, quoted in Jones, *War*, IV, p 320.
49. Hoeppner, *Krieg*, pp 172–3.
50. Capitaine Canonne, "l'Avion d'Infanterie," *Revue de l'aéronautique Militaire* II (May–Jun 22), 80.
51. III Brigade Royal Flying Corps Special Ops Order Nr 370, Nov 16, 1917, in Jones, *War*, App Vol, App IX, p 432.
52. Hoeppner, *Krieg*, p 158.
53. On the ten year rule, see H. Montgomery Hyde, *British Air Policy Between the Wars 1918–1931* (London, 1976), p 59.
54. Lee Kennett, *A History of Strategic Bombing* (New York, 1982), p 74.
55. For a contemporary account of operations in Morocco see *Los Ailes*, Jul 23, 1925, pp 1–2. See also fn 7.
56. Air Commodore C. F. A. Portal, "British Air Control in Underdeveloped Areas," in Eugene Emme, ed, *The Impact of Air Power* (New York, 1959), pp 351–62.
57. Ltr, Air Vice Marshal N.D.K. McEwen, RAF to Air Commodore R.P. Willoch, RAF, Dec 9, 1939, W0 106/5162, PRO (Public Record Office, Kew).
58. Army Air Requirements. Summary of Decisions made at a Meeting Held at the Air Ministry on 2 Aug 1940, *Ibid*.
59. Major Gottfried Hufenbach, "*Die Unterstützung des Heeres in der Aufassung der Deutschen Luftwaffe bis zum Vorabend des Zweiten Weltkrieges. Ein Beitrag zum Problem der Führungskoordination von Teilstreitkräften*" (Jahresarbeit, Führungsakademie der Bundeswehr, Sep 1975), pp 7–9.
60. I. V. Timokhovich, *Operativnoie Iskusstvo Sovietskikh VVS v Velikoi Otechestvennoi Voine* (Moscow, 1976), p 102.
61. Quoted in Paul Deichmann, *German Air Force Operations in Support of the Army* (New York, 1962), p 93.
62. Quoted in Gen J. Hébrard, *Vingt-cinq Années de l'Aviation Militaire*, 2 Vols (Paris, 1946) II, p 27.
63. General Amedeo Mecozzi, *Quel che l'Aviatore d'Assalto deve Sapere* (Rome, 1936), p 102.
64. Bmbr Support for the Army, memo by the Air Staff, 21.11.1939, Air 35/214, PRO.
65. Deichmann, *Air Force*, p 92.
66. *Tactics of Aviation*, typescript translation of *Taktika Aviatsii* (Moscow, 1926) in the library of the National Air and Space Museum, p 105.

67. Kennett, *Bombing*, p 93.
68. Camille Rougeron, *l'Aviation de Bombardement*, 2d ed, 2 Vols (Paris, 1937), II, p 178.
69. *Ibid.*
70. On this subject see Robert 0. Purtee, Development of Light and Medium Bombers, prepared by Hist Section, Air Materiel Command, Wright Field, Dec 1946, typescript in USAFHRC, p 21.
71. See on this subject "Shturmovaia Aviatsia," in *Sovetskaia Voennaia Entsiklopedia*, 8 Vols (Moscow, 1978–80) Vol VIII, pp 540–41.
72. On the development of this aviation see Amedeo Mecozzi, "Origini e Svilupo dell' avazione d'Assalto," *Rivista Aeronautica*, X (Feb 35) pp 193–201.
73. Memo, Air Marshal A.S. Barratt, RAF, nd, in Air Hist Branch, Ministry of Defense.
74. A. Tsiemgal, "Boevaia Rabota Shturmovikov s Divisiei v Nastupatelnuyu Boyu," *Vestnik Vozdushnovo Flota* (Apr 30), pp 9, 11.
75. On the use of chemical weapons by aircraft see Alden H. Waitt, *Gas Warfare, the Chemical Weapon, Its Uses and Protection against It* (New York, 1943), especially Chap IX, "Air Chemical Weapons," pp 118–36.
76. "The two-seater attack formation, through its defensive fire from the rear cockpits, will be able to continue on its mission unless opposed by greatly superior numbers of hostile pursuit aviation." Attack Aviation, 1935–1936, Air Corps Tactical School text, sec 3, p 2, USAFHRC.
77. For a discussion of this viewpoint in *Luftwaffe* circles see Smith, *Dive Bomber*, pp 71–2.
78. Tsiemgal, "Rabota," pp 10–11.
79. "The heavy, partly armored airplane . . . is now regarded everywhere as inexpedient." Capt A. Ilver, "Attack Aircraft, Particularly from the Soviet Viewpoint," Sep 28, 1934, *U.S. Military Intelligence Reports. The Soviet Union, 1919–1941* (University Publications microfilm, reel 7), p 2.
80. Lapchinskiy, *Tactics*, pp 105–6
81. Mecozzi, *Quel che*, p 22
82. On the development of this aircraft see Giancarlo Garello, *Il Breda 65 e l'Aviazione d'Assalto* (Rome, 1980), *passim.*
83. Jean Alexander, *Russian Aircraft since 1940* (London, 1975), pp 94–9.
84. Air Vice Marshal E. L. Gossage, "Air Power and Its Employment, Pt. 1," *The Aeroplane*, 32 (Mar 1937), p 249.
85. M. M. Poston, D. Hay and J. D. Scott, *The Design and Development of Weapons: Studies in Government and Industrial Organization* (London, 1965), p 17.
86. See in this connection George Feuchter's chapter entitled "Die Technische Entwicklung des Flugzeuges als Kriegsmittel bis zum Ausbruch des Zweiten Weltkrieges," in his *Geschichte des Luftkrieges, Entwicklung und Zukunft* (Bonn, 1954), pp 47–65.
87. See for example the discussion in the folder "Attack Plane Directives," RG 18, Central Decimal Files 1917–1938, Box 1005, NA.
88. Ltr, "Fusilier" to ed, Apr 12, 1938, *Royal United Service Institution Journal* 83 (1938), p 856.
89. Slessor, *Air Power*, p 95.
90. *Ibid.*
91. *Etude sur l'Aviation d'Aassaut et sur le Bombardement en piqué*, nd, box K16701, SHAA (Service Historique de l'Armée de l'Air, Vincennes).
92. B. Teplinskiy, "Some Questions with Reference to Combat Employment of Modern Attack Aviation," transl of article in *Krasnaya Zvezda* (Dec. 1, 1939), USAFHRC, p 8.
93. A survey of the weaponry for ground support will be found in N. Shaurov, *Razvitie Voennykh Tipov Sukhoputnykh Samoletov* (Moscow, 1939, pp 54, 61–6, 82–9.
94. For details of gas use in the Army Air Corps see Omer O. Niergarth, The Attack Plane in Support of Ground Forces, ACTS text, 1937–8, USAFHRC, pp 30–32.
95. See in this connection the discussion in Dulaney Terret, *The Signal Corps: The Emergency (to Dec 1941)* [*U.S. Army in World War II: The Technical Series*] (Washington, 1956), pp 116–21.
96. "The G.H.Q. Maneuvers on the West Coast," Air Corps News Letter 20 (Jun 15, 1937), p 5.
97. David L. Woods, *A History of Tactical Communication Techniques* (New York, 1974), p 209.

98. Quoted in Terret, *Signal Corps*, p 119.
99. Wing Commander H. P. Lloyd, "The Italo–Abyssinian War, 1935–1936," *Royal Air Force Quarterly* 8 (Oct, 1937), 562–3.
100. Quoted in Fleury Seive, *l'Aviation de'Assaut dans la Bataille de 1940* (Paris, 1948), p 42.
101. See in this connection Lloyd, *Italo–Abyssinian War*, p 363.
102. *The Japanese Air Forces in World War II. The Organization of the Japanese Army & Naval Air Forces, 1945* (New York & London, 1979), pp 5–7, 82–8; M. Rudloff, "Le Conflit Sino–Japonais," *Revue Militaire Generale II* (Dec 1938), pp 761–92.
103. Cited in Horst Boog, *Die Deutsche Luftwaffenführung 1935–1945. Führungsprobleme, Spitzengliederung, Generalstabsausbildung* (Beiträge zur Militär-und Kriegsgeschichte, Vol 21) (Stuttgart, 1982), p 176.
104. Lt Jack W. Randolf, USA, "Guadalajara: An Aerial Counterattack," *Infantry Journal* 45 (Mar–Apr 1938), 109–14.
105. Raymond L. Proctor, *Hitler's Luftwaffe in the Spanish Civil War* (Westport, Conn, 1983), pp 46–7, 182–3.
106. Captain Didier Poulain, "The Role of Aircraft in the Spanish Civil War," *Royal United Service Institution Journal*, 83 (Aug 1938), 585; Oberst Dr. Gustav Daniker, "Betrachtungen über die Bewertung von Erfahrungen mit Kriegsmaterial in Spanien," Wissen und Wehr 10 (1937), pp 573–9.
107. Wolfgang Kern Erhard Moritz, "Lehren des Faschistischen Deutschen Oberkommandos des Heeres aus der Bewaffneten Intervention in Spanien 1936–1939," *Militärgeschichte* XV (1976), 329.
108. General Paul Armengaud, "La Guerre d'Espagne, Technique et Tactique des Forces de l'Air," *Revue Militaire Generale II* (Apr 1938), 435.
109. *Ibid*, p 434.
110. Pierro Incerpi, "l'Attaco al Suolo Nella Guerra di Spagna," *Rivista Aeronautica* 14 (Aug 1938), 260.
111. G. Gagarin, "Aviation in Modern Combat," Transl of article in *Krasnaya Zvezda*, Apr 26, 1938, USAFHRC, p 3.
112. The GAF *Schlachtflieger* —I. An Hist Account of the Ground Attack Organization from Gen Maj Hetschold, Gen Lt Galland and Maj Bruecker, Jun 23, 1945, typescript, USAFHRC.
113. Moritz, *"Lehren,"* pp 328–9.
114. Gagarin. "Aviation," p 4.
115. General M. Velpry, "Tactique d'Hier et de Demain," *Revue Militaire Generale II* (Feb 1938), 171.
116. Seive, *Aviation*, p 1.
117. Memo 21–11–1939, Air 35/214, PRO.
118. For a brief account of air action in the Saint Mihiel Battle see Maurer, *Air Service* I, pp 301–11.
119. Ronald R. Fogleman, "The Development of Ground Attack Aviation in the U.S. Army Air Arm. Evolution of a Doctrine, 1908–1926" (thesis, Duke University, 1971), p 81.
120. Brig Gen William Mitchell, USA, Provisional Manual of Ops, Dec 23, 1918," in Maurer, *Air Service*, II, p 399.
121. Sherman, "Tentative Manual," in Maurer, *Air Service*, II, p 399.
122. In Maurer, *Air Service*, II, pp 290–5.
123. *Ibid*, p 290.
124. Kenneth Munsen and Gordon Swanboro, *Boeing. An Aircraft Album* (New York, 1972), p 21.
125. Quoted in Fogleman, "Development," p 81.
126. *Ibid*, p 82.
127. "Experiences with the Air Service in Minor Warfare," lecture delivered at the Army War College, Jan 12, 1929, text in U.S. Army Military History Institute, Carlisle Barracks, Pa.
128. Captain Charles W. Boggs, Jr., USMC, "Marine Aviation: Origins and Growth," *Marine Corps Gazette* 34 (Nov, 1950), pp 68–75.
129. Conference, Attack Aviation, Doctrine, Sep 27, 1939, typescript in USAFHRC, p 3.

130. General William Mitchell, *Skyways. A Book on Modern Aeronautics* (Philadelphia, 1930), p 280.
131. Fogleman, "Development," p 52.
132. Intv, Thomas A. Sturm and Hugh N. Ahmann with Gen Earle E. Partridge, Apr 23–25, 1974, USAFHRC transcript K239.–512 –729, pp 68–9.
133. Intv, Col Marvin M. Stanley with Gen George C. Kenney, Jan 25, 1967, USAFHRC transcript K239–512–747, p 8.
134. Training Manual TR 440–15, 1926, p 8.
135. *Ibid*, p 12.
136. The Air Force, ACTS text, 1930, pp 70, 82.
137. Air Force, the Employment of Combat Aviation, Tentative ACTS text, Apr, 1939, p 25.
138. Niergarth, Attack Airplane, p 27.
139. *Ibid*, pp 7–8.
140. "G.H.Q.A.F. Exercises," *Air Corps News Letter* 20 (Jun, 1937), pp 1–3.
141. Niergarth, Attack Airplane, p 18.
142. "The Air Corps", address to the Army War College, Oct 8, 37, text in U.S. Army Center of Military History, Carlisle Barracks, Pa; p 10.
143. *Ibid*, p 4; see also the judgement of Gen Carl A. Spaatz, "Ethiopia, China, and the Spanish Civil War," in Emme, *Impact*, pp 362–7.
144. TR 440–15, 1926, p 6.
145. Robert T. Finney, History of the Air Corps Tactical School, 1920–1940 (USAF Hist Study 100, Maxwell AFB, Ala., 1955), p 36.
146. TR 440–15, 1926, p 6.
147. Lt Col Horace Hickham, "Why Attack Aviation?" U.S. Air *Services* 19 (Feb, 1934), p 17.
148. Intv, Partridge, p 61.
149. Hans Rohmer, *Mit den amerikanischen Luftflotte in Kriegsmanoever* (Salzburg, 1935), pp 81–3.
150. *Air Forces and War*, text for Army War College Course, 1937–1938, U.S. Military History Institute, Carlisle Barracks, Pa., p 44.
151. On this subject see Purtee, "Development," p 21.
152. Proceedings of a Bd of Officers for the Purpose of Determining the General Requirements for an Attack Airplane at Langley Field, Virginia, on Apr 8, 1929, typescript in USAFHRC: see also Purtee "Development," p 21.
153. On these aircraft see Purtee, "Development," pp 31–6.
154. Light Bombardment Aviation, Jan 15, 1940, p 2.
155. Robert T. Finney, *The Development of Tactical Air Doctrine in the U.S. Air Force, 1917–1951* (Maxwell AFB, Ala., n.d.), p 157.
156. Ltr, Gen George H. Britt to Chief of Aeronautics Bureau, USN, Jun 8, 1940, RG 18, Central Decimal Files, 1938–42, Box 741, NA.
157. Ltr, Aug 9, 1940, in *Ibid*.
158. Quoted in Finney, *Air Doctrine*, p 16.
159. Directive on Close Support Bombing, Dec 6, 1940, WO 106/5162, PRO.
160. Notation on Brief of Meeting, Apr 17, 1941, Reel 32, Item 1344, George C. Marshall Papers, George C. Marshall Research Library.
161. Report on Combined Tests to Develop Doctrine and Methods for Aviation Support of Ground Troops, Jul 19, 1941, USAFHRC, p 14.
162. *Ibid*, pp 6, 35.
163. Comments for Critique, Second-Third Army Maneuvers, Louisiana, September, 1941, 30 Sep 1941, File "Maneuvers," Box 224, H. H. Arnold Papers, Library of Congress, *passim*.
164. TC 52, Employment of Aviation in Close Support of Ground troops, Aug 29, 1941, p 9.
165. FM 31–35, Aviation in Support of Ground Forces, Apr 9, 1942, p 9.
166. Ltr, Sep 5, 1942, RG 18, box 410
167. Ltr, Sep 23, 1942, in *Ibid*.
168. Brian Bond, ed, *Chief of Staff. The Diaries of Lieutenant-General Sir Henry Pownall*, Vol 1, *1933–1940* (London, 1972), I, p 301.
169. Rougeron, *Bombardment*, I, p 5.

170. Memo, 21.11.1939 Air 35/214, PRO.
171. Sir Maurice Dean, *The R.A.F. and two World Wars* (London, 1979), p 205.
172. Maj Gen Sir John Kennedy, *The Business of War* (London, 1957), p 107.
173. Fogleman, "Development," p 90.
174. *Ibid*, 84.
175. Intv, Partridge, p 55.
176. Intv, Hugh N. Ahmann with Lt Gen Lawrence C. Craigie, Dec 6, 1973, USAFHRC transcript K239.512–695, p 63.
177. Intv, Partridge, p 63.
178. A Part of the Story. The Diary of Col Paul M. Robinette, WDGS and GHq, typescript in the George C. Marshall Research Library, p 21.
179. *Ibid*.
180. *Ibid*.

Bibliographical Essay

The scope of the chapter being very broad and the sources both exten-
sive and varied, the survey of relevant literature might best begin with bibliographies. One of the best and most recent is that produced by the Office of
Air Force History and compiled by Samuel Duncan Miller: *An Aerospace
Bibliography* (Washington: Office of Air Force History, 1978). Another compilation, international in scope and covering works appearing up to 1961, is
Karl Köhler's *Bibliographie zur Luftkriegsgeschichte* (Frankfurt a.M.:
Biblothek für Zeitgeschichte, 1966). For the period of the First World War,
researchers can profitably consult Myron J. Smith, *World War I in the Air: A
Bibliography* (Metuchen, N.J.: Scarecrow Press, 1977). A valuable guide to
the great mass of periodical literature that appeared before World War II is
the series of volumes entitled *Bibliography of Aeronautics* issued by the
National Advisory Committee for Aeronautics (Washington: Government
Printing Office, 1909–1937).

Close air support during World War I, having been considered a secondary function of air power, tends to be treated only incidentally in broader
works on the air war. The air support functions of the Royal Flying Corps and
Royal Air Force are covered in Sir Walter Raleigh and H. A. Jones, *War in the
Air: Being the Story of the Part Played in the Great War by the Royal Air Force*
(6 vols. plus appendices, Oxford: The Clarendon Press, 1922–37). The last
volume of this work contains a number of important documents relating to
both British and German techniques of air support. A more recent account of
the British experience is contained in S. F. Wise, *Canadian Airmen and the
First World War* [*The Official History of the Royal Canadian Air Force, Volume
I*] (Toronto: University of Toronto Press, 1982). The German experience is
treated *passim* in Ernst von Hoeppner, *Deutschlands Krieg in der Luft. Ein
Rückblick auf die Entwicklung und die Leistungen unserer Heeres–Luftstreitkräften im Weltkrieg* (Leipzig: K.F. Koehler, 1921). Attack against
ground targets evolved more slowly in the French air service than in its counterparts in the forces of other participants, hence it is best seen as an aspect
of more general tactical operations. These are covered by Charles
Christienne, Pierre Lissarrague, *et al*, in their *Histoire de l'aviation militaire
franôaise* (Paris and Limoges: Charles Lavauzelle, 1980). Also useful is an
article by Captain Canonne, entitled "L'Avion d'infanterie," in the *Revue de
l'aéronautique militaire* II (May-Jun 1922, pp. 77-82). The story of the U.S.
Army Air Service in World War I has been told briefly by James J. Hudson in
Hostile Skies: The Combat History of the Army Air Service in World War I (Syracuse, N.Y.: Syracuse University Press, 1968). More recent and more valuable for air support materials is the four-volume documentary compilation by

Maurer Maurer: *The U.S. Air Service in World War I* (Washington: U. S. Government Printing Office, 1976–78).

During the interwar period, a number of air power theorists speculated on the role of aircraft in future land battles. Perhaps the best known of these was the French engineer Camille Rougeron, whose two-volume *L'Aviation de bombardement* (Paris: Berger–Levrault, 1936) had a German translation and numerous excerpts published in English language journals. Sir John Slessor devoted an entire book to the subject of *Air Power and Armies* (London: Oxford University Press, 1936), while Georg Feuchter chose a similar theme in a slim volume entitled *Flieger als Hilfswaffe. Die Zusammenarbeit zwischen Luftstreitkräften und den drei Wehrmachtteilen* (Potsdam: L. Fogenreiter, 1938). Journals specializing in military aviation included a number of articles on the employment of aircraft in land battles, especially in the 1930s. Some of the more useful in this regard are the *Rivista Aeronautica*, the *Revue de l'Armée de l'Air, Deutsche Luftwacht, Die Luftwaffe*, and *Vestnik Vozdushnovo Flota*.

The military impact of the wars in China, Ethiopia, and Spain has yet to be treated in general fashion, though Camille Rougeron summed up the lessons from Spain in *Les enseignements aériens de la guerre d'Espagne* (Paris: Berger Levrault, 1939). There was extensive analysis in the journals of the day, and three articles might be cited in this connection: Captain Didier Poulain, "The Role of Aircraft in the Spanish Civil War," *Royal United Service Institution Journal* 83. (Aug 1938), pp. 581–6; Piero Incerpi, "L'attaco al suolo nella guerra di Spagna," *Rivista Aeronautica* (Aug 1938). pp. 257–65; and "Lehren des Spanischen Krieges im Spiegel ausländischen Schriftums," *Wissen und Wehr* 10 (1938), pp. 719–734. For two modern assessments see Madeleine Astorkia, "Les Leçons aériennes de la guerre d'Espagne," *Revue Historique des Armées*, special number (1977), pp. 145–75; and Wolfgang Kern Erhard Moritz, "Lehren des fascistischen deutschen Oberkommandos des Heeres aus der bewaffneten Intervention in Spanien 1936–1939," *Militärgeschichte*, (1976), pp. 321–330. For air support techniques of the Italian Air Force in Ethiopia see H. Scheuttel, "Die Mitwirkung der italienischen Luftwaffe im Niederbruch Abissiniens," *Militärwissenschaftliche Rundschau*, 1936, pp. 541–54.

The experience of each of the great powers in the formulation of close air-support doctrine and its implementation can be followed in monographic literature, save possibly in the case of Great Britain, where printed sources are few. While H. Montgomery Hyde's *British Air Policy Between the Wars, 1918–1939* (London: Heinemann, 1976), is valuable for the general evolution of policy, it has disappointingly little on the tactical use of aircraft. The volume entitled *Air Support* (Air Publication 3235, London: H.M.S.O. 1955), produced by the Air Historical Branch of the Ministry of Defence, scarcely touches prewar activity. The best point of departure is W. A. Jacobs, "Air

Support for the British Army, 1939–1943" *Military Affairs* (Dec 1982), pp 174–82. This can be supplemented with materials in the Public Record Office, notably Bomber Support for the Army, Memo by the Air Staff, 21 11. 1939 (Air 35/214), Aircraft for the Field Force, 29.10.35–24.4.39 (WO 93/685), and especially the Draft Report of Air Support for the Army 1939–1945 (WO 233/60), which is the most extensive treatment of the subject, though emphatically from the point of view of the British Army.

The French experience in close air support was limited for most of the interwar period, save for operations in colonial areas. See in that connection Serge Lainé, "L'Aeronantique militaire francaise au Maroc, (1911–1939)," *Revue Historique des Armées* 5 (no. 4 1978), pp. 107–19. The development of assault aviation in the late 1930s is chronicled by Fleury Seive, *L'Aviation francçise au combat. L'Aviation d'assaut dans la bataille de 1940.* (Paris: Berger-Levrault, 1948).

For developments in Germany the fundamental work is that of Horst Boog, *Die deutsche Luftwaffenführung 1935–1945. Führungsprobleme, Spitzengliederung, Generalstabsausbildung* (Stuttgart: Deutsche Verlags–Anstalt, 1982). Air-ground cooperation is the subject of two extensive studies: Gottfried Hufenbach, *"Die Unterstützung des Heeres in der Auffassung der Deutschen Luftwaffe bis zum Vorabend des Zweiten Weltkrieges. Ein Beitrag Zur Problem der Führungskoordination von Teilstreitkräften"* (Jahresarbeit: Führungsakademie der Bundeswehr, 1976); and Paul Deichmann, *German Air Force Operations in Support of the Army* (Maxwell AFB: 1962). Wartime and postwar evaluations by *Luftwaffe* officers can be found in typescript at the U.S. Air Force Historical Research Center (USAFHRC), Maxwell AFB, among them: "Development of the German Ground Attack Arm and Principles Governing its Operations up to the End of 1944" prepared by the *Luftwaffe*'s Eighth *Abteilung* (512.621–VII/14); and the G.A.F. *Schlachtflieger–I.* An Historical Survey of the Ground Attack Organization, prepared by Generalmajor Hetschold, Generalleutnant Galland, and Major Bruecker and dated June 23, 1945 (142.042–16).

The evolution of the concept of close air support and its application by the Italian Air Force can be seen in broader context in Rosario Abate, *Storia della aeronautica italiana* (Milan: Bietti, 1974). General Amedeo Mecozzi, creator of the *Aviazione d'Assalto*, was a frequent contributor to the *Rivista Aeronautica*, though the most complete repository of his ideas on tactical aviation is his *Quel che l'aviatore d'assalto deve sapere* (Rome: Comminus 1936). The history of the Italian air support units before and during World War II is to be found in Giancarlo Garello, *Il Breda 65 e l'aviazione d'assalto* (Rome: Edizori dell'ateno & Rizzarri, 1980).

The Soviet literature on ground support is very copious for the interwar period, reflecting two decades of theoretical and developmental work. A general background and very useful bibliography will be found in Von Hardesty, *Red Phoenix* (Washington: Smithsonian Institution Press, 1983). The evolution of Soviet ground attack aviation also figures prominently in Kenneth A. Steadman, *A Comparative Look at Air Ground Support Doctrine and Practice in World War II* [Combat Studies Institute Report No. 2], Fort Leavenworth: U.S. Army Command and General Staff College, September 1, 1982. Soviet military journals of the interwar period dealt frequently with close air support; *Vestnik Vozdushnovo Flota*, the official publication of the Soviet Air Force, gave particularly good coverage to the subject. (USAFHRC has a number of typescript translations of articles from Soviet Journals of the 1930s). The doctrinal basis for *Shturmovik* operations on the eve of World War II is provided in I.V. Timokhovich, *Operativnoie Iskusstvo Sovetskikh VVS V Velikoi Otechestvennoy Voine* (Moscow: Voenizdat, 1976). A particularly full treatise on tactics is provided in A. Mednis, *Taktika Shturmovoi Aviatsii* (Moscow: Gosudarstvennoe Voenne Izdatel'stvo Narkonata Oborony Soyuza SSR, 1936); while transformations in tactics under the impress of war are treated in S. Chepelyuk, "Razvitie Taktiki Shturmovoy Aviatsiy v Velikoy Otechestvennoy Voine," *Voyenno–Istoricheskiy Zhurnal*, (January, 1970), pp. 23-33. The development of specialized aircraft for close air support is covered by R.I. Vinogradov and A.V. Minaev in their *Samolëti SSSR. Kratkiy Ocherk Razvitiye* (2nd Edition, Moscow, Voenizdat, 1961).

The U.S. Army's Air Service developed its interest in air support during the First World War. That interest was reflected in a number of documents reproduced in Maurer Maurer's compilation *The U.S. Air Service*, previously cited. The Air Service–Air Corps views on tactical aviation in the interwar period found expression in the successive editions of various texts prepared by the Air Corps Tactical School, particularly *Air Force, Bombardment Aviation* and *Attack Aviation* (various dates). Other sources from the era are the articles and notices that appeared in the *U.S. Air Services*, among others the article by Lt. Col. Horace M. Hickam, "Why Attack Aviation?" (February 1934, pp. 15–17). Archival sources include the papers of General H.H. Arnold and Lt. Gen. Frank M. Andrews and the records of the U.S. Army Air Corps for the period 1938–1942 (National Archives and Records Administration Record Group 18, Central Decimal Files, especially 452.1—aircraft and 470–72—armament). Of special interest are the oral history interviews with Generals George C. Kenney and Earle E. Partridge, both of whom were associated with attack aviation (USAFHRC K239.0512–747 and K239.0512–729).

2

The Luftwaffe Experience, 1939–1941

Williamson Murray

Since the appearance of aircraft as a weapon of war in the early 20th Century, close air support has performed a major role in air power. This essay reviews how the Germans initiated a close air support doctrine and developed capability in the years immediately before the Second World War, and then how they refined those concepts as operations and battlefield conditions suggested employment possibilities. Air–ground cooperation on the immediate battlefield has never been an easy matter to orchestrate. Not surprisingly neither the *Luftwaffe* nor the *Heer* found it easy to work out operational concepts. What should be of interest to the historian and current Air Force officer was the relatively open mind with which German ground and air officers approached the problem, and the relative lack of rancorous debate that accompanied the evolution of common doctrine and concepts. When the war began in September 1939, the *Luftwaffe* had not worked out fully satisfactory methods for aiding the *Heer* with direct, close air support. Moreover, most air force commanders were not convinced that this role represented the best employment for air power. Nevertheless, they were willing to approach the problem with an open mind.

The traditional picture of German victories in the 1939–1941 period depicts a combination of tanks, infantry, and *Stuka*s working in close and explosive cooperation to overwhelm the cowering hordes of World War I type infantry that the other European powers placed on the battlefield to oppose the Reich's advance. As with much of military history, there is exaggeration as well as truth in the traditional picture. While it is clear that at certain critical moments, especially along the Meuse between May 13–14, 1940, close air support contributed enormously to the German success, the evidence suggests that at least in the early war years, close air support for the *Heer*'s advance played a relatively small role in the *Luftwaffe*'s operations. As with most other air forces in the 1930s, the *Luftwaffe* was only beginning to evolve a system of army-air force cooperation that could be called sophisticated.[1]

As this evolution proceeded in the late 1930s, the Germans had considerable experience from World War I on which to draw. In the trench stalemate of the 1914–1917 period, the aircraft contributed photo reconnaissance, interdiction, and even close support to front-line troops. That stalemate, with its clearly defined opposing trench systems, provided a relatively stationary and well-defined area within which reconnaissance, fighter, and ground support aircraft could render significant and important help. By 1917, during the Flanders battles, the Germans had evolved a system of air liaison, employing officers serving with front-line divisions, and even the radio technology, to communicate between air observers and front-line artillery batteries.[2]

As the system of air-ground cooperation was evolving, changes in German offensive doctrine at the end of 1917 introduced a major problem in the support of ground forces from the air: the area being supported became fluid. In effect, the German General Staff managed to design and implement an infantry doctrine that returned maneuver to the battlefield.[3] That revolution in operational concepts and capabilities meant, however, that once German armies had broken through the enemy front lines and had reached the exploitation phase, communication and coordination between air units and advancing ground forces would become more and more difficult. The Germans recognized this, and the great German ace and operational commander, Manfred von Richthofen, devoted a section of his lessons of the air war to air support for the army in "breakthrough battles and maneuver warfare (*Bei Durchbruchsschlachten und Bewegungskrieg*)."[4] Complicating the transition was the fact that a major reorganization of signal troops worked to the disadvantage of air units supporting the spring offensives.[5] Although the Germans were moving towards a more effective system of air-ground cooperation in 1918, it was still in a most primitive stage. Several factors were clear: along with effective communications, air-ground cooperation depended on general air superiority. Overwhelming number of Allied aircraft made it increasingly more difficult for German air units to intervene in the ground battle as the year progressed.[6]

The Treaty of Versailles in 1919 successfully removed aircraft from the German inventory of weapons for the next fourteen years. Admittedly, there was some experimentation in Russia between the military of the Weimar Republic and the Soviet Union. Moreover Hans von Seeckt, creator of the postwar German Army, insured that a small but significant number of officers with flying experience remained in the tiny postwar officer corps. These factors could, however, only mitigate a situation in which most officers had virtually no experience with aircraft. When Hitler took power in January 1933, the Germans underwent a rapid military expansion that pulled them from the depths of disarmament to heights of military power that by 1940 had destroyed the equilibrium in Europe.[7] During that process of rearmament, the creation of an effective and powerful air force was critical to German success in the early years of the war.

The traditional picture that the *Luftwaffe* was "in effect the handmaiden of the army"[8] largely misrepresents the intentions of those who created the German air force. At the beginning of the war, the majority of the *Luftwaffe's* high command and officer corps believed in the importance of strategic bombing. Moreover, they believed that the *Luftwaffe* was creating the force structure required to make it an effective strategic bombing force, certainly within the confines of Central Europe.[9] In the late 1930s, other air forces and most European statesmen (as well as Germany's leaders) agreed.

Nevertheless, if the *Luftwaffe's* leaders were pushing for a strategic bombing capability, they also placed the *Luftwaffe's* strategic conceptions within a broad framework of national strategy and interservice cooperation. Such attitudes distinctly contrasted with most air power theorists (military as well as civilian) in Great Britain and the United States. But then, the Germans faced quite different circumstances. Unlike the British and Americans, the Germans faced significant ground operations from the opening of hostilities. Consequently, no matter what successes German air power might achieve, if the ground battle were lost, Germany lost.

The *Luftwaffe's* first chief of staff, Gen. Walther Wever, played a critical role in the development of German prewar air doctrine. Wever possessed one of the best operational minds among his generation of officers (the Defense Minister offered Goering the choice between Wever or the future Field Marshal Erich von Manstein for the position of the *Luftwaffe's* first chief of staff).[10] Unlike many of his German army colleagues, Wever possessed a generally realistic understanding of the relationship between operations and strategy.[11] This understanding gave him a keener appreciation of the political and strategic context within which the *Luftwaffe* might fight than that of other theorists such as Douhet, Trenchard, or most of those at the American Air Corps Tactical School. Thus, Wever was anything but an unabashed champion of strategic bombing. As he made clear in a speech in 1935 at the *Luftkriegsakademie* (Air War College), the *Luftwaffe's* status as a separate service did *not* mean that its employment would be independent of the army or the navy. Rather, depending on circumstances, its contribution could involve missions as varied as attacks on the enemy air force, army, fleet, and industrial base. The goals and purposes of national strategy would play the critical role in determining air power employment.[12]

The clearest statement of Wever's conception of air war came with the publication of the *Luftwaffe's* doctrinal manual in 1936 (*Die Luftkriegführung*, the Conduct of the Air War)."[13] In it Wever and his co-authors showed a ready grasp of the political and strategic complexities of Twentieth Century warfare. They clearly understood that air war would be inseparable from the conduct of campaigns in other dimensions. First of all, they recognized that air superiority would be a critical but difficult goal. Strategic bombing, while a major factor, represented an unknown quantity and might well take too long to be decisive.

With respect to air-ground cooperation, "Conduct of the Air War" was explicit in its argument that the *Luftwaffe* could and should aid the Reich's ground forces. It warned that close cooperation would be difficult for the type of targets "against which [bomber units] could bring their full attack potential to bear."[14] Nevertheless, the manual suggested that the *Luftwaffe* should be committed to support the *Heer* in critical moments of the land battle. As to when and where that would be justified, the manual argued that the basic requirement would depend upon most productive results for successful ground operations: "The closer the contesting armies are locked in combat and the closer the decision in battle comes, the greater will be the effectiveness of bomber attacks in the battle area." It pointed out, however, that close air attacks against well-camouflaged enemy forces in good tactical positions were "unlikely to produce results commensurate with the effort." Moreover, air attacks against enemy forces within the range of friendly artillery fire should only occur where the weight and capabilities of artillery were insufficient for the mission.[15]

The impression created by the "Conduct of the Air War" was that, while close air support was an important mission, it was subsidiary to missions such as interdiction, air superiority, and, in certain cases, strategic bombardment aimed at enemy industrial or economic resources. There was an important attitudinal point, however: unlike the RAF, which generally rejected the close air support mission except in the most desperate of circumstances, the *Luftwaffe* was willing to consider close air support on a sustained basis. Close air support did not necessarily represent the best employment of air power in general terms, but it was a mission in which air power could and should render significant help to the ground forces when the overall battlefield situation demanded it.

The development of the *Luftwaffe* in the 1933–1939 period followed priorities established by Wever and "The Conduct of the Air War," which emphasized interdiction and strategic bombing. To that end the Germans created the largest bomber force in the world. Admittedly, their aircraft consisted of twin-engine bombers, but the *Luftwaffe* viewed the aircraft available in the late 1930s as sufficient for strategic bombing attacks within the confines of Central Europe. Meanwhile, its engineers were hard at work on a four-engine aircraft, the He–177, with the range and payload to attack targets far removed from Central Europe.[16]

The German post–1933 rearmament effort in aircraft faced considerable obstacles. To begin with, the Reich's aircraft industry numbered approximately 4,000 workers scattered among a number of underutilized and undercapitalized firms.[17] Nevertheless, from the start the chief priority was to establish a strategic bomber force; the second priority was to create an air superiority fighter force; and the third priority, to develop an antiaircraft artillery capability that could defend German industry from the depredations of enemy bombing attacks.[18]

While the *Luftwaffe* did believe that air support for the Army could be a major role in a future war, little was done in early rearmament years to prepare for such a mission. The individual problems confronting the services during rapid expansion were daunting enough. The Army's emphasis through 1938 remained on creating a well-trained World War I infantry force. Hitler did not interfere in the build-up, and while armor advocates such as Guderian and Lutz were creating the kernel of the future *panzer* force, their efforts remained a side show in the overall rearmament picture.[19] There were some contacts between the new *Luftwaffe* and the new *panzer* divisions. One former *Luftwaffe* officer remembers participating, in 1936, in a joint *Heer-Luftwaffe* command post exercise in which Guderian also participated. He remembers the *panzer* general as generally unrealistic and unknowledgeable as to the capabilities and limitations of aircraft support.[20]

The Spanish Civil War played a critical role in pushing the *Luftwaffe* towards a more accurate assessment of its equipment, as well as in providing a modicum of air combat experience. At least in air-to-air tactics, that experience played an important role in preparing the *Luftwaffe* for World War II. Unlike the Italians, in all areas the Germans limited their commitment in Spain to a small and manageable size.[21] The initial contribution to Franco's cause came when Ju–52s ferried Nationalist troops from Morocco to Spain. The German combat aircraft first deployed to Spain, the bomber version of the Ju–52 and the He–51 fighter (both aircraft representing the first generation of aircraft production) quickly proved inferior to Russian aircraft on the Loyalist side.[22] In fact, this clear inferiority may have been *the* major contribution of the Spanish Civil War to German rearmament. It forced the Germans to deploy their new prototype fighters and bombers and quickly shifted German production to second-generation aircraft.

At its height in the autumn of 1938, the Condor Legion (cover name for German air aid to Franco) consisted of only 40 He–111s, 5 Do–17s, 3 Ju–87s, 45 Bf–109s, 4 He–45s, and 8 He–59s.[23] But from that force the Germans learned important doctrinal and technological lessons. By late 1938, the fighter ace Werner Mölders had developed the finger four formation that all air forces would eventually adopt but which gave the *Luftwaffe* a considerable edge in World War II's first encounters.[24] On the other hand, the Condor Legion took the first steps in developing a close air support doctrine. The critical figure in this area, Wolfram von Richthofen, recognized that theoretical musings on strategic bombing and the political and military realities of the Spanish Civil War had little in common. Thus the stalemate on the ground, the lack of suitable targets for strategic bombing attacks, the weakness of Nationalist artillery, and the combat deficiencies of the first German aircraft led Richthofen to push for available air power in direct support of Franco's offensive against Bilbao.[25]

With little encouragement from Berlin, Richthofen developed a primitive, but for its time, effective close air support doctrine and capability.[26] Before the Bilbao offensive launched by Franco in 1937 against the northern Spanish port, few of the tactical or support elements required for close air support existed in the German air force. Within a year, the Condor Legion evolved a system that insured close coordination between ground and air units and detailed *Luftwaffe* officers to serve directly with front-line units. What in fact had evolved was a system that was close to the air-ground practices and coordination at the end of World War I. Significantly, there was not much enthusiasm in Berlin for the system developed in Spain.[27]

In retrospect, Richthofen managed to reintroduce German close air doctrine as it existed at the end of World War I. Recognition devices, liaison officers, telephone and radio communications had all been used during the 1918 spring offensives. One of Richthofen's close associates in Spain, Maj. Gen. Hans W. Asmus, suggested that Richthofen had drawn largely from his own wartime experience and those of others to establish the procedures for air-ground cooperation on the battlefield. In some respects, the Condor Legion's system was even more primitive than that of World War I; German pilots sometimes identified Spanish infantry by the flags they carried.[28] In other cases Nationalists infantry wore large pieces of white cloth on their backs, making it easy to spot advancing troops from the air and at the same time discouraging thoughts of retreat.[29]

What Richthofen could not solve was the problem of coordinating close air support strikes with rapid exploitation drives of motorized and mechanized formations. That experience was not attainable in Spain, because military operations closely resembled those of World War I—with infantry breakthrough operations against static defense lines providing the basis of combat. The tactical and operational concepts of Nationalist military leaders, as well as the capability of their armies, simply did not allow for rapid mobile operations. Moreover, the Spanish forces possessed primitive communication links, especially radios, so that telephone links represented the most advanced communications available.

Interestingly, the Ju–87, the famed *Stuka*, flew few close air support missions in Spain. Some *Stuka*s were sent to Spain (there were only three there in autumn 1938), but those that did go were sent for combat evaluation against precision targets such as bridges, railyards, and other choke points. The air staff in Berlin regarded close air support missions as too dangerous for the few *Stuka*s that had arrived in Spain for evaluation.[30] In fact, the *Stuka* proved both survivable against interdiction targets as well as superior bombing accuracy compared to conventional horizontal bombers such as the He–111 or the Do–17. Thus, given the constraints on ammunition production in Germany in the late 1930s (lack of industrial capacity), it was the *Stuka's* accuracy that made it such an attractive aircraft, prompting Ernst Udet, director of the *Luftwaffe's* design bureau, to push for a dive-bombing capability for future German bombers no matter how disastrous a design error.[31]

By 1938, Richthofen's experiments in Spain had created a place for close air support in the *Luftwaffe's* preparations—one that was, nevertheless, still relatively low in terms of the *Luftwaffe's* other missions. It is worth underlining the relative lack of stress that the close air support mission received in overall force structure planning. At the outbreak of war against Poland in September 1939, the *Luftwaffe* possessed the following numbers and types of aircraft: 1,180 bombers, 771 fighters, and 366 dive bombers. Only the bombers could perform close air support missions. The *Stukas* could also support air interdiction missions and attack enemy air bases.[32] Moreover, the one wing dedicated exclusively to the close air support mission possessed obsolete fighters and was assigned the mission, because its aircraft could not undertake any other role. Significantly, the Germans were making no effort to design an aircraft with the primary mission of supporting the *Heer* in the battle zone.[33]

As the Spanish Civil War drew to a close in 1938 and 1939, the Germans began final preparations for what turned into World War II. While interservice cooperation generally was good, particularly at lower command levels, there were considerable conceptual differences as to the extent to which the *Luftwaffe* would directly support the Army. At a May 1938 war game, one participating *Luftwaffe* officer underlined those important differences in a memorandum.[34] He attempted to explain to the participating army officers that the *Luftwaffe's* primary goal in war would be the destruction of opposing air forces. In the case of *"Fall Grün"* ("Case Green," war with Czechoslovakia only), that period of time would probably last four days; in the case of *"Fall Rot"* ("Case Red," war with France), at the minimum, four weeks. Only then could the *Luftwaffe* support the Army with its bomber squadrons (in interdiction as well as close air support missions). The army officers' reply, irrelevant on the issue of air superiority, was that Spain had shown that air support for ground operations was more important than any effects gained by strategic bombing. The *Luftwaffe's* representative reported that "army officers again and again uttered the desire to employ the air force on the battlefield and for this purpose to support each army with a bomber *Geschwader* (squadron)."

In May 1939 the major *Wehrmacht* General Staff exercise again suggested considerable differences between the views of *Luftwaffe* and the ground forces. A *Luftwaffe* staff paper stressed that in no case would bomber units be placed directly under Army control.[35] Rather the *Heer* must state its priorities, requirements, and requested time for support to the appropriate *Luftwaffe* command level. Only then would the *Luftwaffe* determine what it would and could support. There would be *no* employment of bomber units in the immediate battle zone. Major General Hans Jeschonnek, *Luftwaffe* Chief of Staff in 1939 (Wever had died in a plane crash in 1936), underlined the *Luftwaffe's* position, emphasizing the destruction of enemy air forces and air superiority.[36] On close air support for the *Heer*, General Jeschonnek suggested difficulties and compared it to a cavalry charge: "It could bring great success when it achieved surprise, but only then. When it did not possess surprise and met an enemy who was prepared, then such an attack had little success and that at a disproportionately high cost." Jeschonnek questioned the effectiveness of close air support materially as well as morally, especially against a first-class enemy.

Before turning to the evolution of close air support doctrine in the first years of World War II, it is important to examine the organizational and communication links between the *Heer* and *Luftwaffe* that, in the late 1930s, coordinated employment of air power in support of ground operations. At the highest level, Goering assigned a *General der Luftwaffe beim Oberbefehlshaber des Heeres* (*Luftwaffe* [liaison] general to the Commander in Chief of the Army).[37] Unfortunately for the Germans and typical of Goering's brand of leadership, this liaison officer possessed no authority to discuss common *Heer-Luftwaffe* problems. Rather he served two distinct functions: (1) He was Goering's messenger boy to the *Heer* high command, and (2) He commanded the close and long range reconnaissance aircraft assigned directly to *Heer* support (approximately 450 aircraft at the beginning of the war).[38] Thus, doctrinal differences and tactical problems between the *Heer* and *Luftwaffe* were not funneled through one liaison office but when faced, if at all, were addressed on an *ad hoc* basis at different levels of command.

The reconnaissance squadrons, directly assigned to the *Heer*, while not strictly falling under the rubric of close air support, did pose interesting questions about the system of air-ground cooperation and suggested considerable systemic weaknesses on the outbreak of war. Under the *General der Luftwaffe beim Oberbefehlshaber des Heeres* (Luftwaffe [liaison] general to the Commander in Chief of the *Heer*) were *Kommandeure der Luftwaffe* (*Kolufts*) (commanders [or officers] of the *Luftwaffe*) assigned to *Heer* groups who in turn commanded *Kolufts* at army level. These *Kolufts* were responsible for reconnaissance squadrons assigned at corps level (infantry as well as mechanized and motorized). Thus, the chain of command for close air reconnaissance ran down to the army corps level (through the French campaign close air reconnaissance squadrons were only rarely assigned to *panzer* divisions.[39] There was some organizational confusion, because the *Kolufts* at the various levels could order reconnaissance squadrons to support other army groups or armies without *Heer* knowledge of what was going on.[40] Nevertheless, the system was generally effective, although costly in terms of aircraft and crews. Radio communications ran directly from He–126s to artillery batteries on the ground (in morse code transmissions through the end of 1939 and by voice at the opening of the French campaign).[41]

There was a second system of coordination between *Heer* and *Luftwaffe* through liaison officers (*Fliegerverbindungoffiziere* [air liaison officer] or *Flivo* for short). These officers were assigned by the numbered air forces (*Luftflotten*) to *Heer* ground, by *Fliegerkorps* to armies, and by air divisions and *Geschwaders* (squadrons) to corps. The *Flivos* played a critical role in coordinating operational air and ground units of *Heer* requirement and of *Luftwaffe* capabilities. Surprisingly, there was no direct relationship between the *Kolufts* and the *Flivos* except on the personal level—a major weakness. Thus, coordination between the *Luftwaffe* officers with the *Heer* had to be informal. Moreover, and here lay the greatest weakness in the system, there were no means to communicate directly between the close reconnaissance squadrons and *Luftwaffe* fighter, bomber, or dive bomber units.[42] Moreover, there were no common radio frequencies between the *Heer* and *Luftwaffe* units. Cooperation in fact worked somewhat better than the organizational outline might suggest—largely because of a general willingness of those at different levels of command and service to pull together despite organizational differences or limitations.[43] But it does seem surprising that the *Kolufts* were virtually excluded from the coordination process. The only satisfactory explanation appears to have been Goering's desire to keep the entire decision-making process within the *Luftwaffe* under his personal control.

In assessing the prewar system, one must stress several points. The system possessed serious weaknesses in organization, coordination, and tactics. The close air reconnaissance squadrons were excluded from the close air support loop despite the fact that they could have helped directly and effectively in coordinating and directing close air support strikes. Nevertheless, despite such systemic weaknesses, the *Luftwaffe* was one of the few air forces in the late 1930s that had even considered the problems of close air support and had recognized that an air force could render important help to ground troops in critical situations. The system was best at supporting the *Heer* when it assaulted well-defined enemy defensive lines. It was *not* effective at supplying close air support once *panzer* units were in the open and moving with the rapidity that caused such surprise and consternation among other European armies.

For the attack on Poland, the *Luftwaffe* set for itself three basic missions: (1) Destruction of the Polish air forces, their ground service organization, and the Polish air armament industries; (2) Support of *Heer* operations in order to insure a quick breakthrough on the ground and a speedy advance by the ground forces; and (3) Attacks against Polish military installations and armament industries in Warsaw.[44]

POLAND
1939

0   50   100   150 Statute Miles

BALTIC SEA

LITHUANIA

Danzig

EAST PRUSSIA

Pomorze Army

Modlin Army

Vistula   River

Poznan Army

Modlin

Lodz

WARSAW

Bug

Lodz Army

Deblin

River

Krakow Army

GERMANY

Lublin

Krakow

SOVIET
UNION

CZECHOSLOVAKIA
(German Protectorate)

AUSTRIA

HUNGARY

There is an important point to be made here in how the *Luftwaffe* executed these three missions in the Polish campaign. According to one observer: "The *Luftwaffe* did not go in for the 'tidy priorities' beloved of the American Army Air Corps and the RAF, both of which were following policies that were political [and ideological] rather than operational."[45] Rather, the *Luftwaffe* set a general mission framework for itself and then executed its air campaign in accordance with the realities of combat, the conduct of the war on the ground, and its logistics and operational capabilities. In other words, it adapted to the real conditions of combat as fast as it could. In its plans the *Luftwaffe* scheduled a major raid on Warsaw for the early morning hours of September 1 for the opening move of the air war. Weather conditions, however, prevented execution of this operation (clearly an effort at strategic bombing).[46] Consequently, *Luftwaffe* operations in Poland emphasized the first two elements.

As prewar doctrine had suggested, the *Luftwaffe* high command regarded air superiority as its major operational goal. In the first days of the campaign the *Luftwaffe* emphasized strikes against the Polish Air Force. At the same time, ground support He–123s with some *Stuka* support helped the Army break through Polish defenses and achieve the operational freedom that *panzer* and motorized units required in order to execute deep penetration, exploitation drives. By the fourth day, German mechanized forces were loose and rampaging through Polish rear areas. The *Luftwaffe* did render some direct support to these units, but the bulk of its sorties were interdiction strikes against the transportation system and direct strikes against a crumbling Polish army. Particularly along the Bzura River, the *Luftwaffe* struck so effectively against Polish army units attempting to regroup and counterattack German breakthroughs that some Polish troops simply threw away their weapons.[47]

The devastating nature of the *Wehrmacht*'s success evoked an interesting response within the German military. The *Heer* high command, despite having destroyed enemy armed forces of 30 plus divisions and having captured in excess of 700,000 prisoners in less than 3 weeks, found the performance of its units, regular as well as reserve, most unsatisfactory. The General Staff immediately instituted a massive program to collect the lessons and experiences of the campaign and to pass those lessons on to its divisions through a massive training program. That effort in effect turned the *Wehrmacht* into the formidable instrument that broke the back of Allied ground power in the spring of 1940.[48] The lessons for the *Luftwaffe*, however, were less clear. In general, tactical execution of missions had been outstanding, and *Luftwaffe* crews and aircraft had proven generally superior to their opponents. Poland had also been useful in indicating that the *Luftwaffe*'s approach to air war—emphasis on gaining air superiority—was on the right track.[49]

In terms of close air support a number of important lessons had either been learned or confirmed. On return from Spain in the early summer of 1939, Richthofen had been appointed as *Fliegerführer zur besonderen Verwendung* (air commander for special purposes). As such, he received the mission of directing close air support at the critical points of the *Heer*'s effort. Richthofen had then taken the first steps towards establishing support *panzer* forces in a fluid battle situation. He organized 4 teams, designated Air Signal Detachments, 2 of which possessed armored reconnaissance cars and radio equipment, to accompany the mechanized forces with lead units.[50] The strengths of Richthofen's special force suggests the relative priority that the air superiority, interdiction, and close air support missions enjoyed within the *Luftwaffe*. Richthofen commanded 3 *Stuka* squadrons, 1 close air support aircraft squadron, 1 Bf–110 squadron, and 1 Reconnaissance flight (approximately 114 *Stukas*, 30 Bf–110s, 20 He–123s, and 9 He–126s). Interestingly, nearly 130 *Stukas* served with other units to provide other than close air support missions.[51]

Overall, Richthofen controlled a small portion of the *Luftwaffe*'s force structure for the close air support mission. Richthofen's forces supported the Tenth Army's advance. There they performed yeoman service in supporting the breakthrough of Gen. Walther von Reichenau's armored forces.[52] Once the mechanized forces had achieved operational freedom, however, the rapid collapse of the Polish defenses and military forces did not provide an ideal laboratory for delineating and defining close air support tactics in fluid battle situations. It took the more complex military operations against Allied forces in the west in the spring of 1940 to refine close air support doctrine for armored formations.

Nevertheless, much had been learned. By November 1939, Gen. Franz Halder, Chief of Staff of the *Heer*, had signed a new directive establishing a framework within which he hoped *Heer–Luftwaffe* cooperation would take place.[53] In particular, Halder suggested that the *Kolufts*'* foremost responsibility was to coordinate air reconnaissance assigned to the *Heer* with those flying reconnaissance missions for the *Luftwaffe*. Moreover the *Wehrmacht* clearly hoped to have the *Kolufts* more directly included and informed as to operational air force intentions and objectives. This was prompted by the fact that the *Kolufts* had the most recent reconnaissance information. Thus they were in the best position to keep *Luftwaffe* commanders informed of where the *Heer* needed help. The *Luftwaffe*, however, successfully resisted such a change. As the French campaign showed, Goering had no intention of allowing the *Kolufts*, who were clearly tied to the *Heer*, to replace the *Flivos*, who were directly within the *Luftwaffe*'s chain of command.

---

*See page 94 for a discussion of the *Koluft*'s position in the German system.

Henschel 123s were still in use as ground-support aircraft when the German Army overran western Poland in September 1939.

For *Luftwaffe* formations, the Polish campaign provided a number of lessons. Above all, reported First Air Force (*Luftflotte* 1), the communications between ground forces and supporting *Luftwaffe* units would have to be considerably improved. In high-speed, mobile warfare it had proven difficult to keep command authorities informed of movements on the ground.[54] In the

Courtesy Bundesarchiv/Militärarchiv

Field Marshal Wolfram von Richthofen *(above)* **greeting Italian Marshal Rudolfo Graziani. Messerschmitt Me-110** *(below)*.

Courtesy Bundesarchiv/Militärarchiv

case of breakthrough operations through prepared fortification systems and defensive lines, First Air Force had found it relatively easy to coordinate with the *Heer* as to time, place, target selection, and close air support. Interestingly, the *Luftwaffe* commentators were willing to admit that the material effects of such attacks were not impressive; rather it was the impact on the enemy morale that resulted in significant accomplishments.[55]

First Air Force's "after-action" report suggested that the *Luftwaffe* had an impression of events fundamentally different from that of the *Heer*. It argued that the *Kolufts* should *not* be more closely included in cooperation between *Luftwaffe* operational units and the *Heer* (outside of the directly assigned close recce squadrons). The *Kolufts*, argued First Air Force, simply did not possess the ties to *Luftwaffe* command and control networks necessary to effective cooperation. It added that the critical element in cooperation would have to be liaison officers possessing good communications, including radio and liaison aircraft, in order to keep up a steady flow of information between air and ground. The after-action report admitted, that in mobile warfare, a major problem was that the *Heer*'s command authorities as well as the *Luftwaffe* possessed only sketchy information of the front-line situation possessed by the *Heer* as well as the *Luftwaffe* command. Advancing troops would have to use smoke and clearly marked recognition devices to indicate who they were (obviously a situation demanding complete air superiority). Fluid situations would also demand security zones within which the *Luftwaffe* would attack only those ground formations that it could identify with certainty as enemy.[56]

Under First Air Force, the 1st Air Division reported in a similar vein. In particular it singled out the general lack of signal troops within its organization as a major weakness in coordinating the rapid advance. It suggested major changes in its TO&E (Table of Organization and Equipment) to repair this deficiency. The importance of good communications emerged in *Heer* requests for close air support forwarded so late that 1st Air Division units could not meet their obligations. Finally, its experience in Poland suggested that it would be difficult to keep air commanders informed of the rapidly changing ground situation.[57]

Heer after-action reports from front-line units displayed even less satisfaction with the existing level of *Heer–Luftwaffe* cooperation. Some units had nothing to say, suggesting that there had been little cooperation.[58] The 10th *Panzer* Division, which had played an important part in Guderian's movements, was most dissatisfied. It noted that air reconnaissance had been either late or inaccurate. In one incident, the *Luftwaffe* had reported that fortifications and defensive positions near the Polish town of Lomza were free of Polish troops, whereas 10th *Panzer* Division's reconnaissance units discovered the Polish defenses occupied by Polish cavalry and other units.

More distressing was the fact that throughout the campaign 10th *Panzer*

Division's units were constantly machinegunned and bombed from the air by German aircraft. One of its units received a particularly graphic demonstration of *Luftwaffe* effectiveness that left thirteen dead and twenty-five badly wounded Germans. This incident had occurred despite the use of prearranged recognition devices by the ground troops.[59]

One of the factors that made the Germans such imposing opponents in both world wars was their ability to absorb and learn from their combat experience at operational and tactical levels. The *Luftwaffe* possessed this quality along with its sister services. In February 1939, the *Luftwaffe* high command had established a Tactical Experience Group as part of its Operations Division. The new department had the job of examining tactical combat lessons, preparing them in clear, understandable form, and then passing them along to front-line units.[60] Under its control, the air staff passed along the tactical and operational lessons of Poland to the flying schools, to the operational training units, and to those who were preparing for the next campaign, the great offensive against the west. Consequently, largely as a result of its ability to absorb the "lessons" of Spain and Poland, the *Luftwaffe* would prove superior to its opponents in the coming battles.[61]

For the Germans, even victory over Poland raised serious strategic problems. Not only had difficulties appeared in the *Heer*'s performance, but the imposition of an Allied blockade had resulted in a ruinous drop in imports, with severe implications for the Reich's ability to pursue the war.[62] As a result of the tension created by these factors, German strategy in late 1939 led in two separate directions. On the one hand, the *Heer* pushed for a delay in offensive operations against the West until the spring of 1940. Hitler on the other hand desired an immediate ground offensive to seize the Low Countries and northern France as a strategic base to strike at Great Britain.[63] Consequently, the planning for a fall campaign did not aim to replay the Schlieffen plan of World War I,* or to overthrow Allied military power on the continent.[64] Rather it hoped to achieve limited geographic goals.

Not until January did Hitler finally postpone the western offensive to the spring. By then a new issue had appeared in strategic discussions. Led by Manstein, at that time Chief of Staff of Army Group A, a number of officers approached Hitler with an alternative. They suggested that the weight of the offensive be moved from the north to the center to break through French forces deployed along the Meuse River. This breakthrough would be carried out by the bulk of Germany's *panzer* forces. Once in the open, the German armed forces were to race for the English Channel and bottle up Allied forces

---

*The Schlieffen plan had aimed to overthrow France in a rapid campaign by a massive wheeling movement through Belgium and into northwestern France. It failed in the opening campaign movements of 1914.

that had driven into the Low Countries to defend the Dutch and the Belgians against Army Group B's advance. This proposal met considerable opposition in the highest command levels, in particular from the *Heer*'s Chief of Staff, Franz Halder. Only in mid-March of 1940 did a major wargame on the operational prospects of the Manstein plan finally cause the Germans to decide in favor of the new alternative. Even then it was obvious that Hitler and several senior generals still felt apprehensive. Guderians's memoirs recorded the scene at the conclusion of the exercise:

> Hitler asked: "And then what are you going to do [after you break through]?" He was the first person who had thought to ask me this vital question. I replied: "Unless I receive orders to the contrary, I intend on the next day to continue my advance westward. The supreme leadership must decide whether my objective is to be Amiens or Paris. In my opinion the correct course is to drive past Amiens to the English Channel." Hitler nodded and said nothing more. Only General Busch, who commanded the Sixteenth Army on my left, cried out: "Well, I don't think you'll cross the river in the first place!" Hitler, the tension visible in his face, looked at me to see what I would reply. I said: "There's no need for you [Busch] to do so in any case."[65]

The critical element in Manstein's plan was not how quickly the Germans could get to the Meuse, but whether they would cross that river and how quickly they could exploit that crossing with their armored mobility. In the war gaming of the Ardennes proposal, it had been clear that mechanized forces would come up on the Meuse by the third or fourth day. Halder had argued that the armor should wait for the infantry divisions to arrive (on the ninth or tenth day) before crossing—precisely what the French expected if the Germans came through the Ardennes.[66] In the end, Halder was persuaded, and by April the final plans were set for the mechanized forces to cross the Meuse as soon as they came upon it.

Within the overall plan, the *Luftwaffe* would play an important role. Its first and most important task was to win air superiority over western Europe by defeating Allied air forces. The achievement of air superiority by a series of major air strikes would place enemy air forces on the defensive and allow the *Heer* to execute its operations without serious interference from enemy air attacks. The subsidiary task in the early days would be to support the attack on Holland through airborne drops and, if necessary, bombing attacks to eliminate the Dutch as quickly as possible. Third, close air support missions would be laid on during critical moments in the ground battle. The *Stuka* force and not the twin-engine bombers would support ground forces directly as part of an overall air superiority strategy. In the early days of the offensive even the *Stuka*s were to launch strikes against enemy air installations.

The strength of the two numbered air forces (Second and Third) deployed to support "*Fall Gelb*" ("Case Yellow"—code name for the offensive) was approximately 1,300 bombers, 860 single-engine fighters, 350 twin-engine fighters, and 380 dive bombers. Thus, the dive-bomber force, the only air units specifically trained to support the ground advance directly, numbered less than 15 percent of combat aircraft assigned to the offensive.[67]

Second Air Force would support Fedor von Bock's Army Group B's advance with Richthofen's VIII Air Corps (*Fliegerkorps* VIII) for short-range targets, and IV Air Corps (*Fliegerkorps* IV) for longer-range objectives. Third Air Force had V Air Corps (*Fliegerkorps* I and V) for longer-range objectives and II Air Corps (*Fliegerkorps* II) to provide close air support at critical moments.[68] Surprisingly, VIII Air Corps (*Fliegerkorps* VIII), the *Luftwaffe*'s most experienced close air support corps, was not assigned directly to the Ardennes drive—a fact that underlined the importance the

The Junkers Ju-87, shown in its B-model, was the classic dive bomber of the early years of World War II.

Germans placed on destroying the Belgian airfields. The flexibility of air power did, of course, allow the *Luftwaffe* to switch VIII Air Corps (*Fliegerkorps* VIII) to support Third Air Force efforts to expedite the crossing of the Meuse on May 14.

Right up to the beginning of the offensive, the Germans were hard at work attempting to iron out the problems of *Heer–Luftwaffe* cooperation. In late April, they conducted experiments to see whether the *panzer* units could communicate directly with close support aircraft.[69] Nevertheless, the problems of coordinating *panzer* units with *Stuka*s by means of radio proved too intractable to solve at such short notice.[70] What the *Luftwaffe* and *Heer* had to fall back on were a set of clearly defined bomb lines drawn across the proposed line of operations in France and Belgium.[71] Moreover, for the early days of the campaign a set of carefully delineated ground targets (mostly fortified positions) lying in the path of the advancing *panzer* forces were selected to receive a pounding from the *Luftwaffe*, but only *after* its forces had accomplished their air superiority strikes.[72] The communication problems generally reflected the rather sloppy approach that both services took towards supply, and the lack of commonality between communications is thus not surprising. It is worth noting that as late as the Battle of Britain, the *Luftwaffe*'s own fighter and bomber forces were unable to communicate with each other—the former using voice radio, the latter Morse radio transmissions.[73]

On May 10 the offensive began. In a series of major strikes against enemy airfields, the *Luftwaffe* virtually eliminated the Dutch and Belgian air forces. Attacks on British and French air bases in northern France were not as successful, but they placed Allied air forces in a defensive posture from which they never fully recovered.[74] Significantly the *Luftwaffe* did nothing to interfere with the move to the Dyle in Belgium, which in effect placed Allied troops within a great trap, since their advance practically guaranteed the effect of Manstein's plan. The *Luftwaffe* did make a major effort to screen Army Group A's deployment into and through the Ardennes. The first four days of the campaign proceeded as the Germans had hoped. The *Luftwaffe* had achieved a measure of air superiority over its opponents; Holland was almost out of the war; *panzer* forces of Army Group A had come up on the Meuse; and the *Luftwaffe* had already given significant indirect help to troops on the ground by screening the move through the Ardennes from the prying eyes of Allied aircraft.

The key moments in the Battle of France occurred on the Meuse between the 13th and 16th of May. By the evening of May 12, German armored forces had arrived on the banks of the Meuse, Guderian's XIX *Panzer* Corps on both sides of Sedan, Reinhardt's XLI to the north of Charleville, and Hoth's XV by Dinant. The decision for an immediate crossing was implicit in the nature of the final "Case Yellow" (*Fall Gelb*) plans. By late evening May 12, opera-

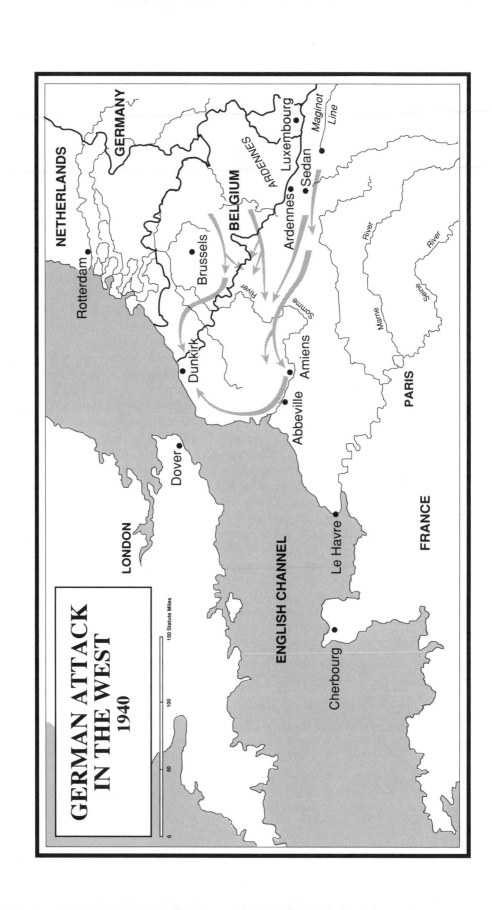

GERMAN ATTACK IN THE WEST
1940

tional plans containing mission objectives and specific times for attacking units had been drawn up and passed down the chain of command. *Panzer* Group Kleist issued its third major order of the campaign at 2330 hours on the 12th. First *Panzer* Division of Guderian's XIX *Panzer* Corps extended and clarified the order at 1200 hours on May 13 in its Divisional Order Number 5. Both orders set the time for the start of the infantry assault across the Meuse as 1600 hours (German time) on the 13th.[75] Both orders made clear the support framework with which the crossings would occur. While the artillery attached to the *panzer* divisions bombarded French positions, II Air Corps (*Fliegerkorps* II) would hammer French positions immediately across the Meuse from *Panzer* Corps XIX. Units attached to VIII Air Corps (*Fliegerkorps* VIII) would support the crossing of *Panzer* Group Kleist's other *panzer* corps to the north of Charleville.[76]

These attacks would begin at 0800 (German time) and last until 1600 when the crossing began. At that moment bomber forces would shift back away from front-line areas to attack French rear area positions. The *Stukas* from II Air Corps (*Fliegerkorps* II) would support Guderian's crossing, and VIII Air Corps (*Fliegerkorps* VIII's) *Stukas* would aid the crossing above Charleville from 1600 to 1730 hours. After that the *Stukas* also would shift to interdicting French movement and reinforcements in the rear areas.

If one can describe any combat action executed like clockwork, then the *Luftwaffe* support rendered along the banks of the Meuse came as close to that description as possible. A German sergeant with the 1st Armored Division recalled:

> Three, six, nine, oh, behind still more, and further to the right aircraft, and still more aircraft, a quick look in the binoculars—*Stukas*!. . .Squadron upon squadron rise to a great height, break into line ahead [formation] . . .and there, there the first machines hurtle perpendicularly down, followed by the second, their—ten, twelve aeroplanes are there. Simultaneously like birds of prey, they fall upon their victims and then release their load of bombs on the target. . . . It becomes a regular rain of bombs, that whistle down on Sedan and the bunker positions. Each time the explosion is overwhelming, the noise deafening. Everything becomes blended together, along with the howling sirens of the *Stukas* in their dives, the bombs whistle and crack and burst.[77]

The devastating nature of continuous pounding by *Luftwaffe* aircraft began the rout that led to a general collapse of French defenses along the Meuse. By the evening the rear areas of the French X Corps facing Guderian had become clogged with fleeing troops. In addition, the corps artillery commander panicked and pulled his supporting guns out.[78] The collapse on the Meuse might not have been decisive had not French doctrine been so faulty. Once the Germans had achieved a breakthrough and crossed with their tanks, the French high command, possessing no strategic reserve, had no chance to plug up the hole.

Consequently, the *Luftwaffe's* employment, in helping the *panzer* divisions cross the Meuse and break through French positions, played a major role in one of the 20th Century's most decisive strategic victories. Still it is interesting to note that Hoth's *panzer* corps, which crossed the Meuse to the north at Dinant, received little air support, while Rommel's account suggests that his 7th *Panzer* Division (part of Hoth's corps) saw no supporting *Luftwaffe* aircraft on the 13th and thus crossed the Meuse entirely on its own effort. Not until the 15th, when he was rolling towards Philippeville and beyond, did Rommel receive significant air support.[79] The evidence does suggest, however, that the heavy *Stuka* attacks played a major role in the rapid collapse of the French X Corps, that unhinged the entire Allied position.

The support missions along the Meuse did not represent a revolutionary employment of air power. They were an outgrowth and extension of previous experience, going back to World War I. The effort on May 13, as with the close air support of the German offensive in March 1918, involved the use of aircraft to support infantry that were attacking prepared defensive positions. Consequently, the coordinated *Heer–Luftwaffe* support plan for crossing the Meuse, drawn up in outline the night before, targeted known enemy positions. It aimed to achieve a breakthrough of a defensive system about which the Germans already possessed considerable knowledge. It did not involve the coordination and communication difficulties present when the panzers plunged into Allied rear areas at a pace that surprised their own high command almost as much as the rest of the world.

A second point needs emphasis: General air superiority played a critical role in (1) the successful intervention of the *Luftwaffe* in the ground battle and (2) the disastrous failure that met Allied efforts in their attack on the logistic links across the Meuse on May 15.

On May 12, five French Curtiss fighters had caught twelve *Stukas* returning from a raid over the Ardennes and shot down all of the German aircraft.[80] Unfortunately, such occurrences were the exception. On the other hand, Allied air attacks on May 15 against the Meuse bridges to isolate German spearheads resulted in such catastrophic losses (the British lost fifty-six percent of their attacking bombers on that day) that the RAF's shattered formations were not able to resume such attacks.[81] The contrast between Allied air forces and *Luftwaffe* on the outcome of the ground battle was directly proportional to German air superiority as well as German doctrine.

The German advance now rolled to the English Channel despite increasing nervousness within the German high command. By Monday, May 20, elements of Guderian's XIX *Panzer* Corps had reached beyond Amiens to the channel coast. The rapidity caused a mad scramble of Allied air units to bases south of the Somme, and Allied air forces played little role in the unfolding events. The German's uncontested air power could smash the Allied rear and aid in the ground battle. Generally *Luftwaffe* missions involved the former rather than the latter. The rapidity of the mechanized advance often rendered strikes for direct ground support pointless.

The victory certainly owed much to air support. The *Luftwaffe* gained air superiority and suppressed allied reconnaissance missions, blinding Allied armies; helped win the breakthrough battles along the Meuse; and interdicted Allied logistic and reserve movements. The close air support for mobile warfare had been less distinguished, as after-action reports soon made clear. The most glaring deficiency was the inability of ground units (or even *Luftwaffe* close reconnaissance units allocated to the *Heer*) to communicate with airborne operational units. To put it simply, the *Luftwaffe* and *Heer* still did not possess common radio frequencies.[82] Generally, the *Wehrmacht* could overcome this handicap where sufficient time existed to coordinate common airground operations (such as crossing the Meuse). Such coordination, however, required constant courier flights between *Luftwaffe* and *Heer* headquarters.[83]

When sufficient time did not exist to coordinate, or when army units moved so fast as to make coordination difficult, serious problems arose. The traditional means of identifying ground units from the air all presented problems. Bomb lines proved difficult to enforce or to coordinate, especially in the face of rampaging *panzer* units through northern France. Once mechanized forces reached bomb lines, they faced the disagreeable choice either of stopping, thus losing what might prove an important opportunity, or of advancing and putting themselves under the threat of air attack by their own air force.[84] Though ground recognition devices worked, they also presented difficulties. Advancing front-line units did not use their cloth markers to indicate front-line positions often enough. Where used, they presented German aircraft with a clear mark of front line positions. Nevertheless, they were small and hard to see from rapidly moving aircraft. Markers for vehicles and convoys were adequate, but many formations did not mark their columns in the prescribed manner. The use of swastika flags as marking devices was less satisfactory because the red blended in with the color of vehicles, while the white circle was too small for ready identification from higher altitudes.[85]

A major problem, implicit before the offensive, was the organizational relationship between *Heer* and *Luftwaffe*. Only the rapid French collapse had diminished the seriousness of the deficient organizational coordination. Manstein's infantry corps reported that while cooperation with close reconnaissance air units had functioned satisfactorily, the assignment of such units shortly before the start of operations had not made sense. To function effectively in combat, the corps' after-action report suggested, close reconnaissance squadrons should be constantly exercised with the units they would support prior to battle operations.[86] Following the army doctrinal position enunciated after the Polish campaign, Sixth Army argued that it was bad policy to exclude *Koluft* from input into and coordination of *Luftwaffe* operations, for it was the *Koluft*, who possessed the most recent reconnaissance information. Thus, it suggested, the *Koluft* should not only serve as the *Luft-waffe* adviser in all air matters to the chief of staff at army level, but he should also coordinate the air strikes and supporting missions that lay within the army's sphere of interest. Such a responsibility would be added to his reconnaissance duties. Under this proposal the *Flivos* (liaison officers) from the *Fliegerkorps* would work directly for the *Koluft*, and liaison officers from the *Koluft*'s staff would be assigned to *Luftwaffe* units supporting the army.[87]

Such a solution was unsatisfactory to the *Luftwaffe* and particularly to Hermann Goering. The *Luftwaffe* had no intention of providing input to the *Koluft*s, who were directly assigned to the *Heer*. Whatever the outcome of *Heer–Luftwaffe* differences, ambiguities in the functioning of the *Flivo* system existed throughout the campaign—particularly in the ability to communicate up the chain of command. A request from *Panzer* Group Kleist to VIII Air Corps (*Fliegerkorps* VIII) met the response that such requests must be passed up to army level and then across to the air corps (*Fliegerkorps*) by the air liaison officer (*Flivo*) at that level. At the same time Army Group A indicated that such requests could be passed directly to the air corps (*Fliegerkorps*).[88] Nevertheless, what made the *Wehrmacht* so effective despite such organizational difficulties was the penchant of the officer corps in both services to take matters into their own hands and to cooperate informally, ignoring whatever command or organizational difficulties existed.

Overall, the *Luftwaffe* was satisfied with the campaign's operational results and remained silent on the organizational difficulties. As a September 1940 training directive from VIII Air Corps (*Fliegerkorps* VIII) reported, "the earlier combat lessons that had been learned in various campaigns had been confirmed" in the campaign in France and Flanders."[89] Close air support of ground troops in critical situations had been decisive. For future close air support operations, the VIII Air Corps' (*Fliegerkorps* VIII) chief of staff underlined the importance of fighter support for dive-bomber missions, especially where enemy fighter forces were still operating (undoubtedly a lesson reinforced by the hammering the *Stuka*s took in the Battle of Britain). Finally, in discussing experiences in rapid mobile operations in France, he stressed that, in the swift movements of mobile warfare, difficulties in gaining a clear picture of the ground situation would continue. Therefore, pilots operating over the battle zone must accurately and immediately report their observations.[90] What was not mentioned was the fact that closer coordination between ground and air signal units might have presented a clearer picture of the situation on the ground.

It is worth contrasting the *Luftwaffe*'s contribution to the ground battle with Allied air strategy and capabilities during the same events. As the diary of Guderian's *panzer* corps made clear, Allied air attacks on advancing German columns early in the campaign caused his troops considerable discomfort. As a result of heavy RAF attacks on the bridges across the Meuse on

May 14, XIX *Panzer* Corps noted in its diary: "The completion of the military bridge at Donchery had not yet been carried out owing to heavy flanking artillery fire and long bombing attacks on the bridging point. . . . Throughout the day all these divisions have had to endure constant air attacks—especially at the crossing and bridging points."[91] But the losses suffered by the attacking British units were so catastrophic as to render them unfit for further combat. In the largest sense the Allied air forces did not possess a strategy or a doctrine that placed significant emphasis on helping the hard-pressed ground forces. The RAF Bomber Command attacked the Ruhr in a series of

Flanked by *Luftwaffe* senior officers, Reich Marshal Hermann Goering interviews a German airman in France, 1940.

ill-coordinated and futile attacks; Fighter Command in Britain was removed from the struggle; RAF fighters and light bombers in France were assigned tasks all over northern France; and the French had only recently awakened to the threat of air power and were ineffective throughout the short campaign.

Moreover, neither the British nor the French had thought through the problem of close air support. A November 1939 RAF memorandum summed up the British attitude toward close air support: "Neither in attack nor in defense should bombers be used on the battlefield itself, save in exceptional circumstances."[92]

The result was that on one hand the *Luftwaffe* was able to render significant help to its *Heer*; while on the other side, Allied air forces possessed neither the doctrine nor the desire to give the disastrous ground battle the attention needed.

Between victory in the west and the onset of operation *"Barbarossa"* (invasion of the Soviet Union) on June 22, 1941, the *Wehrmacht* was involved in two major campaigns: the Battle of Britain (only the *Luftwaffe*) and the Balkan campaign of spring 1941. Neither was of particular importance to this study of close air support. The first was almost entirely a *Luftwaffe* affair, while the latter possessed not only similarities to the French campaign but came so close in time to the invasion of Russia that it had little doctrinal or organizational impact.

Preparations and thinking about the invasion of the Soviet Union began on July 3, 1940, within the *Heer* High Command—even before Hitler turned to that possibility.[93] By December 1940, Hitler had committed the Reich to a massive campaign to conquer the Soviet Union before the onset of the next winter. To execute such an undertaking, the *Heer* could carry out the bulk of the fighting. Close air support would obviously form an integral part of the effort. The Germans were now on the way toward a coordinated system that would respond more and that could function with greater effectiveness in a fluid environment.

Before addressing those improvements, it is necessary to describe several factors that in the long run would impinge on the effectiveness of military preparations. Recognizing that the victory in France had rested largely on the power and combat capabilities of the ten *panzer* divisions (less than 10 percent of deployed forces), Hitler ordered that the number of such divisions be doubled.[94] At the same time, he recognized the implications of that decision and requested that tank production increase from approximately 120 per month to a level of 800 per month. The Army's ordnance department simply rejected the *Führer*'s suggestion with the casual and inaccurate observation that such production would ruin the German economy.[95]

Fortunately for her enemies, such attitudes were common in the *Wehrmacht* after victory over France. As a result, for the next year and a half the Germans made few substantive efforts to mobilize the economic and productive resources of the continent now at their disposal. Instead, despite the looming campaign against the Soviet Union, German industry continued its prewar production levels—a result of overconfidence and arrogance rather than of any so-called Blitzkrieg strategy.[96] In a similar vein of muddleheaded overconfidence, Jeschonnek turned away from the frustrations of the Battle of Britain and the failure of the night strategic bombing of the British Isles with the remark: "At last, a proper war [the attack on Russia]!"[97]

The doubling of the *panzer* divisions coupled with the replacement of obsolete tanks by newer models forced the *Heer* to cut the tank Tables of Organization and Equipment (TO&E) of the armored divisions in half— hardly a recipe to increase effectiveness and striking power.[98] Similarly, *Luftwaffe* forces available for the invasion indicated not just a leveling off of German combat power but an actual decrease from the levels attained for the offensive against France. For the French campaign, the *Luftwaffe* had possessed 1,300 bombers, for the Russian (*Barbarossa*), 775; for France, 380 *Stuka*s, for *Barbarossa*, 310; for France, 860 single-engine fighters, for Russia, 830; for France 350 twin-engine fighters, for Russia, 90; for France 300 long-range reconnaissance aircraft, for *Barbarossa*, 340; for France 340 tactical reconnaissance, for Russia 370.[99] Overall, even including aircraft committed to other theaters, the *Luftwaffe* actually possessed 200 fewer bombers than it had at the beginning of May 1940.[100] This decrease resulted from the fact that, unlike the Army, the *Luftwaffe* had sustained heavy losses from the summer of 1940 right through to the start of the Russian campaign. The following table indicates the level of *Luftwaffe* losses in the bomber and dive-bomber forces from May 1940 through May 1941.[101]

	Losses in Percentages of Aircraft assigned to Units	
	Dive Bombers *(percent)*	*Bombers* *(percent)*
May 1940	6.8	27.4
June 1940	7.3	12.6
July 1940	2.7	6.0
August 1940	13.7	19.6
September 1940	1.7	18.9
October 1940	1.6	12.3
November 1940	2.4	9.2
December 1940	0.6	5.2
January 1941	2.1	4.8
February 1941	3.0	5.5
March 1941	3.7	8.6
April 1941	10.0	10.6
May 1941	7.2	12.0

Thus, the *Wehrmacht* invaded the vast spaces of the Soviet Union with little change in the force structure that it had possessed the previous year for the invasion of Western Europe.[102] What is particularly surprising, given the German reputation for a high level of military competence, is that few in the high commands of either the *Heer* or *Luftwaffe* found this worrisome. German plans resembled the strategic conceptions that had destroyed France the previous year. The *Luftwaffe* aimed to destroy the Red Air Force in a massive surprise attack and subsequent operations in the campaign's early days. Similarly the Army hoped to surround and liquidate so much of the Red Army in the border areas by its mobile deep penetration thrusts that the Russians would not recover.

In support of the Army's operational goal to destroy the Red Army in the border areas, the *Luftwaffe* was again prepared to render sustained and important help. Close air reconnaissance squadrons were now detailed to each *panzer* division as well as to the *panzer* and army corps, as had been the case during the previous year. But this improvement had only been achieved by cutting the number of reconnaissance aircraft allocated to each squadron.[103] In addition, air liaison officers (*Flivos*) had now been established down to the *panzer* division level. The *Luftwaffe* also established Air Signal Liaison Detachments with a driver and four radio operators. These detachments were assigned to critical areas of the front where mobile operations were taking place. They received armor-plated vehicles in order to allow them to operate right up with the mobile spearheads.[104] The result was a considerable increase in the *Luftwaffe's* ability to coordinate air strikes with the Army in a mobile environment. Provided that the Signal Detachments and *Flivos* were up front, the *Luftwaffe* could now talk to the lead elements of the Army's advance on the ground. There is, however, a considerable irony here. Because these detachments reported to their *Luftwaffe* headquarters by radio, transmissions were intercepted by the British and, with the help of their "enigma" deception device, they were eventually deciphered, providing much material on German Army operations.[105] These reports would play a major role in giving the British a view of what was going on behind German lines in Russia, the Mediterranean, and northwest Europe.[106]

One other major organizational change was made before *Barbarossa*. Because several *Fliegerkorps*, in particular II and VIII Air Corps (Fliegerkorps II and VIII), were responsible for close air support missions, regular interdiction, and air superiority strikes, the *Luftwaffe* established a permanent *Nahkampfführer* (close air support leader) to control the close air support missions between the air corps (*Fliegerkorps*). This individual was responsible for the movement forward of close air support units, for coordination with the army in the ground battle, and for the communications between the *Fliegerkorps* (air corps) and the *panzer* groups (later *panzer* armies).[107]

The administrative change reflected several factors. First of all, the distances involved in Russia were going to make it likely that the squadrons assigned to the *Fliegerkorps* were going to be widely dispersed. Thus, it was going to be difficult for the *Fliegerkorps* commander to keep up with the close air support units that would have to move rapidly forward with the *Heer*. Moreover, this move may have reflected a desire to meet the *Heer* half way and to provide a means of defusing *Heer* efforts to have close air support assets directly under the control of army commanders.

At the start of the invasion, the Germans had already begun moving away from bomb lines as recognition devices. In view of the consistently fluid state that had marked operations, by late summer the *Luftwaffe* abandoned their use entirely. In their place came a heavier reliance on marking devices, light signals, or pyrotechnics.[108]

The *Wehrmacht*'s operations, air as well as ground, lived up to expectations in the campaign's first days. Across the length and breadth of the front, the *Luftwaffe* caught its opponent by surprise with his aircraft parked in nice neat rows. On the first day, IV Air Corps (*Fliegerkorps* IV) reported destroying 142 enemy aircraft on the ground and only 16 in the air.[109] By noon on June 22d the Soviets had lost 528 aircraft on the ground and 210 in the air in the western district alone. Along the entire front on that day the Red Air Force was to lose 1,200 aircraft in the first 8 hours.[110] Moreover, the rapidly disintegrating situation on the ground forced the Soviets to commit what was left of their air assets in desperate attempts to stem the German tide. Ill-trained, ill-equipped, and badly led Soviet aircrews floundered in impossible formations from which they were shot out of the skies in huge numbers.[111] Within 2 weeks of *Barbarossa*'s beginning, as 2 great *panzer* armies were swinging east towards Smolensk, Halder recorded in his diary:

> On the whole, one can already say that the task of destroying the mass of the Russian army in front of the Dvina and Dnepr has been fulfilled. I believe the assertion of a captured Russian general to be correct that we can calculate on meeting east of the Dvina and Dnepr only disjointed forces which alone do not possess the strength to hinder German operations substantially. It is, therefore, truly not claiming too much when I assert that the campaign against Russia has been won in fourteen days.[112]

These enormous successes carried the Germans to Smolensk within a month, placed them three-quarters of the distance to Moscow, and pulled their forces almost to the gates of Leningrad. The *Luftwaffe* as usual had played a most helpful role. It had gained general air superiority, and it had supported the *Heer* directly. Its close air support enormously helped the *Heer*'s mobile columns driving into the Soviet Union. The new system of mobile liaison proved particularly helpful in aiding the advance of Second and Third *Panzer* Groups (Armies) towards Minsk and Smolensk. *Luftwaffe* strikes also considerably damaged Soviet military forces in rear areas, and finally, air attacks had broken up numerous Soviet units desperately attempting to escape from German encirclements.

Nevertheless, shortly after their arrival at Smolensk, the Germans discovered the enormity of their miscalculations. What had worked in France did *not* work in Russia. Halder, almost despairingly, noted in his diary on August 11:

> The whole situation shows more and more clearly that we have underestimated the colossus of Russia—a Russia that had consciously prepared for the coming war with the whole unrestrained power of which a totalitarian state is capable. This conclusion is shown both on the organization as well as the economic levels, in the transportation, and above all, clearly in infantry divisions. We have already identified 360. These divisions are admittedly not armed and equipped in our sense, and tactically they are badly led. But there they are; and when we destroy a dozen, the Russians simply establish another dozen.[113]

Quite simply, the Soviets possessed the strategic depth to absorb the catastrophic defeats on the frontier, while calling up the reserves of manpower and production to continue the struggle. The Red Air Force was in a more difficult situation than its army in that the numbers of aircraft lost in the early days were harder to replace. Nevertheless, Soviet aircraft production facilities were either outside the range of German offensive operations or were moved as the Germans approached, and a steady and noticeable recovery of the Red Air Force took place by the end of the summer. At the same time, the vastness of Russia began to exert its influence. German forces were quite literally fanning out across the mouth of a great funnel, and as they did so they became more and more thinly spread out on the ground. Thus, the number of German troops and guns per kilometer steadily declined, and the logistic difficulties of supporting the advance increased.

The same factors affected *Luftwaffe* forces committed to the theater. As early as July 5, VIII Air Corps (*Fliegerkorps* VIII) reported fuel shortages in the face of the severely limited number of missions flown. Richthofen noted accurately: "Supply is for us the greatest difficulty in this war."[114] Like the *Heer*, the *Luftwaffe* faced almost unsurmountable supply problems for its forward units. The flexibility of German air power was powerless in concentrating aircraft on threatened sectors of the front, and the very extent of the front meant that there had to be areas where the *Luftwaffe* could bring nothing to bear. Moreover, declining operational ready rates, due to supply and maintenance problems as well as fuel shortages, cut further into the *Luftwaffe's* effectiveness. While the *Luftwaffe* could still achieve local air superiority wherever it committed sufficient forces, it could not be everywhere. Where it was not, the Red Air Force could operate with impunity. By late summer, ground troops had stopped displaying recognition devices, because their visibility was as likely to draw Red Air Force attacks as it was to warn off the *Luftwaffe*.[115] The Soviets, moreover, produced armored ground attack aircraft that took advantage of the devices and proved difficult to shoot down.[116] Unlike the *Stuka* and earlier German close air support aircraft, these Soviet aircraft had been designed solely for operations over the main battlefield and represented a distinct improvement in survivability. Like the T–34 tank, they came as a nasty shock to the Germans.

The dispersal of forces on the ground as well as the rising pressure of Soviet ground counterattacks led to a drastic increase in army requests for close air support by the end of July 1941. With scantier resources at its disposal, organizational and administrative improvements in the *Luftwaffe* could not meet growing operational demands. As the *Heer* spread throughout the theater, it increasingly depended upon and demanded close air support for offensive operations. As one infantry regimental commander noted: "Tanks in the lead, artillery in the rear, and aircraft overhead—only then will the infantry advance to the attack."[117] By late summer 1941, Hitler as Commander-in-Chief of the *Wehrmacht* ruled that "large-scale offensive operations by the army will only be allowed to commence after extensive support by the *Luftwaffe*."[118]

Constant combat also exerted great pressure on *Luftwaffe* capabilities. *Fliegerkorps* VIII (VIII Air Corps), during a 12–day period (August 10 to 21), supported I Army Corps in its effort to cut the major Moscow–Leningrad railroad, and in supporting just this one army corps, lost 10.3 percent of its aircraft (destroyed or written off as the result of operations), with 54.5 percent damaged but repairable. Additionally, Richthofen's corps also lost 3.9 percent of its flying personnel killed, 5.7 percent wounded, and 2.9 percent listed as missing (for an overall casualty rate of 12.5 percent).[119] For the first 4 months of the Russian campaign, 20.5 percent of the front-line strength of the *Stuka* force was destroyed or damaged each month. Crew losses over that 4-month period amounted to nearly 28 percent.[120]

Overall, the Russian campaign drastically increased the attrition of the force structure (a factor that would not end until May 1945). The following table[121] underlines the extent of the losses in the bomber and dive-bomber fleets.

Considering the deterioration of battle, the *Luftwaffe* now had to commit its regular bomber squadrons to support the *Heer*'s desperate bid to punch through to Moscow and Rostov. The shortage of aircraft in the east was aggravated by the removal of much of Second Air Force in November to redress Rommel's critical supply situation in North Africa. Finally, in December of 1941 the *Heer*'s advance halted in front of Moscow in the middle of the Russian winter. When the Soviets counterattacked, the entire Ger-

	Losses in Percentage of Aircraft Assigned to Units	
	Dive Bombers (percent)	Bombers (percent)
June 1941	8.1	12.3
July 1941	12.7	18.4
August 1941	8.8	9.7
September 1941	8.5	8.6
October 1941	7.0	10.3
November 1941	Not available	Not available
December 1941	13.8	15.3

man situation in the east trembled on the brink of a complete collapse. In these circumstances the *Luftwaffe* had no choice but to throw in all available resources to prevent catastrophe.

After the 1941 campaign, the failure in Russia resulted from a fatal overconfidence that had led the Germans to invade with inadequate resources. Close air support undoubtedly contributed to a series of impressive operational victories—Minsk, Smolensk, Kiev, Bryansk, and Vyazma—but even in combination with the Army's mobile spearheads it was not enough to solve the strategic problem posed by the size and magnitude of the resources possessed by the Soviet Union. The system generally functioned more effectively than in France. For the first time there was continuous and effective close air support in a mobile environment. That is not to say that the system worked flawlessly. In fact, Richthofen's diary was replete with references to a lack of the *Heer*'s understanding of close air support. There were times where the army did not fully utilize the *Luftwaffe*'s capabilities. Moreover, the speed of the *Heer*'s early advance made it difficult for the divisional and corps level commanders to estimate exactly where their advance elements were. And finally, as Richthofen once noted in frustration and the eternal spirit of interservice conflict, the *Heer* was "unteachable."[122] Nevertheless, the system on the whole worked as well as one could expect, given the technology and experience.

The situation in the late fall of 1941 represented more than a temporary failure in front of Moscow.[123] In effect it represented the defeat of Germany's effort to gain world hegemony. Now the *Wehrmacht* was deployed deep within the boundaries of European Russia. Its opponent possessed extraordinary recuperative powers in the military as well as the industrial sectors. With limited firepower and almost no reserves, the Reich's ground forces were spread thinly across the breadth of theater. Thus, the *Luftwaffe* had to supply a substantial portion of the missing firepower to provide a bulwark for a *Heer* that was in serious straits, even during the summer 1942 offensive. The drive to Stalingrad and the Caucasus represented a desperate gamble with inadequate resources on the ground and in the air. The *Luftwaffe* had to make up the army's deficiencies in artillery, and as a source of firepower support, for which the *Luftwaffe* was a most inadequate instrument. Only a small proportion of the *Luftwaffe*, the *Stukas*, were trained and dedicated to close air support. The *Stuka* itself was a vulnerable target with no special protection against ground fire. Consequently, while it could drop its ordnance far more accurately than Soviet ground support aircraft, it became more and more vulnerable—especially as Soviet forward antiaircraft defenses began to improve after 1941. Ironically the Germans in 1941 were not working on a replacement aircraft for the *Stuka*.

German ground and air forces in the depths of Russia faced a gloomy prospect. Because of the constantly recurring crises on the ground, the *Luftwaffe* had to throw in anything that was available to help the thinly stretched ground forces hold out. Oftentimes the only forces available were long-range bombers; and as one *Luftwaffe* report in December 1942 indicated, such aircraft were unsuitable for the mission. Moreover, most bomber crews did not possess the requisite tactical knowledge or training for the close air support mission. Finally, the report emphasized, considering the resources devoted to producing bomber aircraft in terms of engines, size of aircraft, and number of aircrew, such aircraft were cost ineffective compared to aircraft specifically designed for close air support.[124]

As the situation in Russia deteriorated, the *Luftwaffe* found it increasingly difficult to provide the degree of support that the Army needed. The specialized antitank, close air support forces were rushed from one sector of the front to another, reducing their operational ready rate, while the constant use of pilots and aircraft seriously drained their capabilities. One *Luftwaffe* pilot in an antitank squadron in Russia noted that his unit lost as many aircraft as the number of tanks that it destroyed—hardly a cost-effective employment of aircraft.[125] Outnumbered in the air, facing heavy antiaircraft defense on the ground, with its best pilots siphoned off to fight the Allied air forces over the *Reich*, the *Luftwaffe* faced an impossible situation on the Eastern Front.

The picture that emerged from German close air support operations in the first years of World War II was that of a system undergoing considerable development, rather than that of a clear-cut recipe for operational and tactical employment of the *Luftwaffe* in support of the *Heer*. Close air support did not rank among the top missions that *Luftwaffe* planners foresaw for air power employment before the war. Even in terms of support for the army, *Luftwaffe* commanders and planners had a clear preference for the interdiction mission over the close air support mission.[126] There was, moreover, a sense, quite correct as World War II proved, that close air support missions against well-defended targets were a costly means of employing air power.

But what the *Luftwaffe* was willing to recognize, unlike the RAF, was the fact that there would be moments in both offensive and defensive battles on the ground, where air power could provide the margin on which victory or defeat turned. Admittedly, the *Luftwaffe*'s approach was tailored for a break-through of prepared enemy positions. It was less capable of handling the problems associated with close air support of army formations in a mobile environment. Again, one should not be surprised that this was so. Even the *Heer* had conceptual problems with mobile operations, as the various stop orders and command nervousness indicated in the French campaign. Having taken the first steps towards a close air support capability, the *Luftwaffe* was able to refine that capability for the Russian campaign. Nevertheless, what-ever contribution the *Luftwaffe* made in advancing ground forces, no matter what operational brilliance the *Heer* might show in executing its orders to destroy the Red Army, the *Wehrmacht* could not overcome the handicaps of a high command (not just Hitler) drunk with victory, of a logistical system that functioned badly because of command negligence, and of the vastness of Soviet resources and space.

Two subsidiary points should be made. As with so much of German mil-itary history in the 20th Century, one comes away with a sense that, in the operational sphere, the *Heer* and *Luftwaffe* represented military organizations that willingly grappled with difficult problems in a realistic, rational fashion. They could and *did* learn lessons from combat experience, and then applied those lessons in preparing for the next battles. One also has a sense that Ger-man military effectiveness rested on a spirit of cooperation at the lower and intermediate levels both within and between services. Consequently, opera-tions tended to run more smoothly and with less bickering over roles and mis-sions between the services than did those of the Allies. Most German officers seem to have felt that the lives of aircrews and ground troops, and the suc-cessful completion of military operations, were more important than the nar-row concerns of their own service.

Notes

1. This statement is based on research done at the *Militärarchiv* and the *Militärgeschichtliches Forschungsamt* in Freiburg in June, 1984.
2. General der Kavallerie von Hoeppner, *Deutschlands Krieg in der Luft* (Leipzig, 1921), pp 114, 117–118, 149–150.
3. See Timothy Lupfer, *The Dynamics of Doctrine: The Changes in German Tactical Doctrine During the First World War* (Leavenworth, 1982).
4. *Rittermeister Manfred Frhr von Richthofen, Sein Militärisches Vermächtnis, Das Testament, Die Erfahrungen im Luftkampf,* ed by the *Luftwaffe* historical section (Berlin, 1938); copy provided by Gen Hans Asmus, Baden-Baden, Jun 23, 1984.
5. Hoeppner, *Deutschlands Krieg in der Luft*, pp 149–150.
6. Reichsarchiv, *Der Weltkrieg, 1914 bis 1918*, Vol 14, *Die Kriegführung an der Westfront im Jahre 1918* (Berlin, 1944), pp 720–721.
7. For a discussion of how this process worked see: Williamson Murray, *The Change in the European Balance of Power, 1938–1939, The Path to Ruin* (Princeton, 1984).
8. Denis Richards, *The Royal Air Force, 1939–1945*, Vol I (London, 1953), p 29.
9. For the first statement of this revisionist position see Klaus Maier's discussion in Klaus A. Maier, Horst Rohde, Bernd Stegemann, and Hans Umbreit, *Das Deutsche Reich und der Zweite Weltkrieg*, Vol II, *Die Errichtung der Hegemonie auf dem europäischen Kontinent* (Stuttgart, 1979). For a more detailed English discussion of this point see: Williamson Murray, *Luftwaffe* (Baltimore, 1985), and "The *Luftwaffe* before the Second World War: A Mission, A Strategy?": *Journal of Strategic Studies* (Sep 1981).
10. Edward L. Homze, *Arming the Luftwaffe*, The Reich Air Ministry and the German Aircraft Industry, 1919–1939 (Lincoln, 1976), pp 40–41.
11. For the general unwillingness of the senior German leadership to think on the strategic level see Williamson Murray, "JCS Reform, A German Example?" *JCS Reform*, ed by Steven Ross (Newport, 1985).
12. I am indebted to Oberstleutnant Kr. Klaus A. Maier for drawing my attention to Wever's lecture. See: "*Vortrag des Generalmajors Wever bei Eröffnung der Luftkriegsakademie und Lufttechnischen Akademie in Berlin-Gatow am 1 Nov 1935*," *Die Luftwaffe* (1936).
13. Again I am indebted to Oberstleutnant Klaus Maier for providing me a copy. See: "*Die Luftkriegführung*," Berlin, 1935.
14. *Ibid*, pp 21.
15. *Ibid*, pp 125–132.
16. For the difficulties involved in developing the He–177 see: Edward R. Homze, "The *Luftwaffe*'s Failure to Develop a Heavy Bomber Before World War II," *Aerospace Historian* (Mar 1977).
17. Wilhelm Deist, Manfred Messerschmidt, Hans-Erich Volkmann, Wolfram Wette, *Das Deutsche Reich und der Zweite Weltkrieg*, Vol I (Stuttgart, 1979), pp 480–481.
18. There were some in the Air Ministry in 1933 who went so far as to argue that the *whole* emphasis in Germany's air rearmament should be on the creation of a four-engine strategic bombing force. The technical capabilities of Germany's aircraft industry at the time made such a proposal completely unrealistic. See: Bernard Heimann and Joachim Schunke, "Eine geheime Denkschrift zur Luftkriegskonzeption Hitler-Deutschlands vom Mai 1933," *Zeitschrift für Militärgeschichte* 3 (1964), pp 72–86.
19. For the inadequacies of the theories of a "Blitzkrieg strategy" in the prewar period see Murray, *The Change in the European Balance of Power, 1938–1939*, Chap I.
20. Conversation with Gen Hans W. Asmus, Baden Baden, Jun 23, 1984. In fairness to Guderian, he reported that the *panzer*general did at least see that aircraft could play an important role in furthering the exploitation drive of tank forces. See: Heinz Guderian, *Schnelle Truppen Einst und Jetzt* (Berlin, 1936), p 236.
21. Hitler understood that it was to Germany's advantage that the war in Spain serve as a distraction from the growing threat posed by German rearmament, and that, beyond its ability

to distract the European powers, Spain had little strategic significance for the immediate future of the Reich. See: Gerhard Weinberg, *The Foreign Policy of Hitler's Germany, 1933–1936*, Vol I (Chicago, 1970), p 298.

22. Matthew Cooper, *The German Air Force, 1933–1945, An Anatomy of Failure* (New York, 1981), p 59.

23. *Ibid*, p 59.

24. Derek Wood and Derek Dempster, *The Narrow Margin* (London, 1961), pp 49–50. The finger-four formation involved the combination of two-ship formations in which the second pilot was responsible for covering the tail of the lead aircraft and in which all four pilots had designated areas of the sky to cover to insure that the formation was not taken by surprise.

25. Conversation with Gen Asmus, Baden Baden, Nov 7 and 8, 1980 and letter from Gen Asmus, Feb 6, 1981.

26. Air Ministry, *The Rise and Fall of the German Air Force, 1933–1945* (London, 1948), pp 16–17. For the considerable difficulties that Richthofen faced and had to overcome see the entries in his *Tagebuch* for Mar and Apr 1937 referring to the shortcomings and misunderstandings that stood in the way of establishing even a relatively primitive system.

27. Air Ministry, *The Rise and Fall of the German Air Force*, pp 16–17; and "Lehren aus dem Feldzug in Spanien, Einsatz von Schlachtfliegern," aus einer Studie der 8. Abt des Generalstabes aus dem Jahre 1944; Hans Hennig Freiherr von Beust, "Die Deutsche Luftwaffe im Spanischen Krieg," 2.10.56., p 162, USAFHRC: K 113.302.

28. Conversation with Gen Asmus on Jun 23, 1984, Baden Baden, Federal Republic of Germany. Gen Asmus indicated that the flags were carried by advancing infantry as well as spread out as recognition devices.

29. Bundesarchiv/Militärarchiv (BA/MA) RL/57, Auswertung "Rügen," Anlage 2 zu LwGr.Kdo.3, 7179/38g.Kdos, Heft 2, a Führung Abschnitt IV bis VI, p 50.

30. Conversation with Gen Asmus on Jun 23, 1984, Baden Baden, Federal Republic of Germany.

31. For a fuller discussion of Germany's economic difficulties in the late 1930s and the constraints that this placed on German rearmament see Murray, *The Change in the European Balance of Power, 1938–1939*, Chap I.

32. Air Hist Branch, Air Ministry, Vol VII, Translations: "*Luftwaffe* Strength and Serviceability Statistics," G302694/AR/9/51/50.

33. BA/MA, Za 3/109, "*Studie zum Schlachtfliegereinsatz*," Oberst ing Cornelius and Maj Bruker, 8.Abt, XII, 1944.

34. BA/MA, RL 7/155, Lw Gruppenkommando 3, Abt Ic, 23 Mai 1938, "Bericht über die Reise für Führer oberer Dienststellen, Thüringen 15–22.5.38," Section IV Zusammenarbeit mit der Luftwaffe, pp 9–10.

35. BA/MA RL 7/158, Luftflottenkommando 3, Führ. Abt/Ia op/Nr 93/39, 17.5.39, "Bericht über die Heeresgeneralstabsreise 1939," Anlage 1, "Beitrag für Schlussbesprechung (Luftwaffe)," p 2.

36. BA/MA, RL7/159 Verlauf der Generalstabsreise Luftwaffe 1939, Lft. Kdo 3, Fähr. Abt Nr 2778/39, pp 6–17.

37. BA/MA, Lw 106/15, *Der Einsatz der dem Heer taktisch unterstellten Verbände der Luftwaffe*.

38. Unpublished paper by Hauptmann v. Gyldenfeldt, "Die Beurteilung des Luftwaffeneinsatzes während des Norwegen und Frankreich-Feldzuges 1940 durch die Heeresführung," Führungsakademie der Bundeswehr, Hamburg 1970; copy made available to me by Dr. Horst Boog, Militärgeschichtliches Forschungsamt, Freiburg, Federal Republic of Germany.

39. Conversation with Gen Asmus, Baden-Baden, Federal Republic of Germany, Jun 24, 1984. Gen Asmus stated that the *Luftwaffe* close reconnaissance squadron commander worked directly for the Army corps commander and had virtually nothing to do with the division commanders. Rommel's comments on the campaign hardly suggest the assignment of a close reconnaissance squadron to his *panzer* division (see Erwin Rommel, *The Rommel Papers*, ed by B.H. Liddell Hart (London, 1953), Chap I. But BA/MA RH 19 III/152, "Taktische Erfahrungen im Westfeldzug," Oberkommando des Heeres, GenStdH/Ausb.

Abt (Ia), Nr 2400/40, 20.11.40 does, however, suggest that close reconnaissance squadrons were at times assigned directly to *panzer* division in special circumstances.

40. Gyldenfeldt, "Die Beurteilung des Luftwaffeneinsatzes während des Norwegen und Frankreich-Feldzuges 1940 durch die Heeresführung."

41. Conversation with Gen Asmus, Baden Baden, Federal Republic of Germany, Jun 24, 1984.

42. *Ibid.*

43. *Ibid.*

44. General der Flieger Paul Deichmann, *German Air Force Ops in Support of the Army*, USAF Hist Study Nr 163 (Montgomery, 1962), p 153.

45. I am indebted to Dominic Graham for this point and quotation. His trenchant, carefully thought-out comments on an earlier draft were enormously helpful in the reworking of this piece.

46. "The *Luftwaffe* in Poland," a study produced by the German Hist Branch (8th Abteilung), 11.7.44, AHB, Transl Nr VII/33.

47. For an account of German *Stukas* along the Bzura see: Rolf Elbe, *Die Schlacht an der Bzura im Sep 1939 aus Deutscher und Polnischer Sicht* (Freiburg, 1975).

48. For a fuller discussion of this process see: Williamson Murray, "The German Response to Victory in Poland: A Case Study in Professionalism," *Armed Forces and Society* (Winter, 1981).

49. For a fuller discussion of Germany's air superiority strategy see Williamson Murray, "Poland and the West" in the Air Superiority sister volume to be published by the Office of Air Force History.

50. Deichmann, *German Air Force Ops in Support of the Army*, p 131. Deichmann implies they accompanied *panzer*divisions in the Polish campaign. It is more likely that they were assigned to corps level as the campaign evolved.

51. BA/MA, Lw 106/14, "Die Unterstützung des Heeres durch die Deutsche Luftwaffe im zweiten Weltkrieg (Versuchsweise Aufstellung einer Stoffgliederung mit Erläuterungen) von Gen d Fl: Paul Deichmann," pp 40–52.

52. BA/MA, RL7/340 Luftflotte 4. Divisionsbefehle, Flieg Div 2., Ia Nr 70/39, 1.9.39., Befehl für den Einsatz am 2.9.39.

53. BA/MA, H35/88, *Oberkommando des Heeres*, GenStdH/Ausb. Abt (Ia) Nr 750/39, Richtlinien für die Zusammenarbeit Heer-Luftwaffe auf Grund der Erfahrungen im Polnishchen Feldzuge.

54. BA/MA, RL7/2, Abschrift, Erfahrungsbericht der Luftflotte 1 über den Polnischen Feldzug, p 1.

55. *Ibid*, pp 9–10.

56. *Ibid*, pp 11–12.

57. BA/MA, RL 7/2 Anlage zu Fliegerdivision 1, Br. B. 3185/39, "Vorläufiger Erfahrungsbericht über den Einsatz während des poln. Feldzuges."

58. 20. Div, Abt Ia Nr 510/39, Betr.: Erfahrungen, 4.10.1939, National Archives and Records Service, NARS T–314/614/000656.

59. 10. *Panzer* Div, Abt Ia Nr 26/39, Erfahrungsbericht, 3.10.1939, NARS, T–314/614/000632.

60. Deichmann, *German Air Force Ops in Support of the Army*, p 56.

61. Because virtually all of the *Luftwaffe*'s records were destroyed at the end of the Second World War, it is difficult to evaluate how this process worked. The records of the army are more complete and thus one can more fully evaluate how vigorously combat experience was worked into the training programs and preparations for the next campaign. See Murray, "The German Response to Victory in Poland: A Case Study in Professionalism."

62. For a fuller discussion of the strategic and economic factors involved in the first six months of the war see: Murray, *The Change in the European Balance of Power, 1938–1939*, Chap X.

63. For a fuller discussion see Murray, *Luftwaffe*, Chap II.

64. On the Schlieffen plan and other provocative aspects of German strategy, see Michael Geyer, "German Strategy in the Age of Machine Warfare, 1914–1915," in Peter Paret, ed., *Makers of Modern Stategy from Machiavelli to the Nuclear Age*, (Princeton, 1986), chapter 19.

65. Heinz Guderian, *Panzer* Leader (New York, 1953), p 92.

66. Telford Taylor, *March of Conquest* (New York, 1958), p 168–171.

67. Air Ministry, *The Rise and Fall of the German Air Force*, p 66.
68. Taylor, *The March of Conquest*, p 183.
69. 1 *Panzer Div*, Ia Nr 232/40, 24 Apr 1940, "Zusammenarbeit Panzer–Stuka," NARS, T–314/615/00393.
70. Generalkommando XIX.A.K., Ia/NaKa Nr 362/40, 6.5.1940, "Zusammenarbeit Panzer-Stuka," NARS, T-314/615/00396.
71. Nahkampfführer II, Ia Nr 58/40, "Sicherheit der eigenen Truppe vor eigenen Luftangriffen," 4.4.40, NARS, T–314/615/00358.
72. Nahkampfführer II, Ia Nr 145/40, 30.4.40, Befehl .2, Befehl Für die Kampfführung des Nahkampfführers II am A-Tag Ausser dem Ersten Einsatz Gegen die Französische Luftwaffe, NARS, T–314/615/00377.
73. Francis K. Mason, *Battle over Britain* (London, 1969), p 237.
74. BA/MA, Lw 106/15, "Überblick über den Einsatz der Luftwaffe bei den Operationen in den Niederlanden, in Belgien, und Nordfrankreich," D.Ob.d.Lftw. Führungsstab Ic Nr 10641/40, 3 Juni 1940.
75. For the 1st *Panzer* Div order see: BA/MA Lw 106/15, "Befehl der 1. Panzer Div zum übergang Über die Maas am 13.5.40 mit Gemeinsamen Feuerplan für Luftwaffe und Heer," Ia, 13.5.40, 12 Uhr. For the *Panzer* Group see v. Gyldenfeldt, "Die Beurteilung des Luftwaffeneinsatzes während des Norwegen und Frankreich-Feldzuges durch die Heeres Führung," Anlage 9.
76. BA/MA RL 8/45 Gen Kdo VIII Fliegerkorps. "Einsatz im Feldzug gegen Frankreich (Fragment eines Tägliches-Abschrift)."
77. Quoted in Alistair Horne, *To Lose a Battle, France 1940* (Boston, 1969), p 289.
78. Jeffery A. Gunsburg, *Divided and Conquered, The French High Command and the Defeat in the West, 1940* (Westport, Conn., 1979), p 190.
79. Erwin Rommel, *The Rommel Papers*, ed by B. H. Liddell Hart (New York, 1953), pp 7–15. Rommel's account on how he was informed of air support for the 15th by a *Luftwaffe* major, clearly not familiar to him, suggests that the *Flivos* were not yet assigned below corps level.
80. Horne, *To Lose a Battle*, p 253.
81. Calculation based on mission reports in Maj L. F. Ellis, *The War in France and Flanders* (London, 1953), pp 55–56.
82. Conversation with Gen Asmus on Jun 23, 1984, Baden Baden, Federal Republic of Germany.
83. See BA/MA, RL 8/45, *Fliegerkorps VIII*, War Diary, pp 5–6, 15–16, 5.40 for the constant comings and goings of commanders and liaison officers.
84. BA/MA, Lw 106/4, "Die Unterstützung des Heeres durch die Deutsche Lw im zweiten Weltkrieg (Versuchsweise Aufstellung einer Stoffgliederung mit Erläuterungen)" von Gen. d.Fl. Paul Deichmann.
85. BA/MA, RH12–5/v.246, Armeé-Oberkommando 6, Ia Az 2 3104/40, 10 Aug 1940, Betr. Erfahrungsbericht.
86. v. Gyldenfeldt, "Die Beurteilung des Luftwaffeneinsatzes wírend des Norwegen und Frankreich-Feldzuges 1940 durch die Heeresführung," p 11.
87. BA/MA, RH 12–5/v.246, Armeé-Oberkommando 6, Ia Az 2 Na. 3104/40, 10.Aug 1940, Betr. Erfahrungsbericht.
88. v. Gyldenfeldt, "Die Beurteilung des Luftwaffeneinsatzes während des Norwegen und Frankreich-Feldzuges 1940 durch die Heeresführung," p 12.
89. BA/MA, RL 8/250, Generalkommando des VIII. Fliegerkorps, Abt Ia, 21.9.1940, "Richtlinien für Ausbildung und Einsatz der zur Unterstützung des Heeres Eingesetzten Fliegerverbände des VIII Fliegerkorps."
90. *Ibid*, p 11.
91. Quoted in Maj L. F. Ellis, *The War in France and Flanders, 1939–1940* (London, 1953), p 56.
92. Public Record Office, CAB 21/903, 18.11.39., "Bmbr Support for the Army," memo by the Air Staff; see also the letter from Adm Lord Chatfield to Prime Minister Chamberlain, 15.11.39. on the air force arguments against training special units to cooperate with the army.

93. Horst Boog, Jürgen Förster, Joachim Hoffmann, Ernst Klink, Rolf-Dieter Muller, Gerd R. Ueberschär, *Das Deutsche Reich und der Zweite Weltskrieg*, Vol IV, *Der Angriff auf die Sowjetunion* (Stuttgart, 1983), p 9.

94. *Ibid*, pp 168–189.

95. Guderian, *Panzer* Leader, p 114.

96. For a full discussion see Murray, *Luftwaffe*, pp 92–106.

97. David Irving, *The Rise and Fall of the Luftwaffe* (Boston, 1973), p 123.

98. For a more complete discussion of the deficiencies in German equipment preparations for *Barbarossa* see: Boog, *et al, Das Deutsche Reich und der Zweite Weltkrieg*, pp 186–187.

99. Air Ministry, *The Rise and Fall of the German Air Force*, pp 66, 165.

100. Comparative figures available in: "*Luftwaffe* Strength and Serviceability Tables, Aug 1938–Apr 1945," AHB, Transl VII/107.

101. BA/MA, RL 2 III/1025, Genst 6 Abt: (III A), Front-Flugzeugverluste.

102. The German preinvasion war games had indicated most clearly the implication of Russia's vastness. See: George Blau, *The German Campaign in Russia—Planning and Ops 1940–1942* (Washington, 1955), p 20.

103. Deichmann, *German Air Force Ops in Support of the Army*, p 70.

104. *Ibid*, p 132.

105. See Ralph Bennett, *Ultra in the West* (New York, 1980).

106. One of the ironies of the "alliance" with the Soviet Union is the fact that the British garnered more information about what was going on in military operations in the east from enigma decrypts than from our Soviet "allies."

107. BA/MA, RH 27–18/14, Oberkommando des Heeres, Gen StdH/Ausb Abt (Ia), H Qu Okh, 26.5.41, Nr 1161/41, "Taktisches Merkblatt für die Führung von Nahkampf-Verbänden."

108. Deichmann, *German Air Force Ops in Support of the Army*, pp 134–35.

109. BA/MA, RL 8/31, Generalkommando des IV. Fliegerkorps, Abt IC, "Lagebericht v 22.6.41."

110. John Erickson, *The Road to Stalingrad* (New York, 1975), pp 118–119.

111. Albert Kesselring, *A Soldier's Record* (New York, 1953), p 90.

112. Franz Halder, *Kriegstagebuch*, Vol III, (Stuttgart, 1964), p 38.

113. *Ibid*, p 170.

114. BA/MA, RL 8/49, Russland-Feldzug 1941, VIII Fliegerkorps.

115. Boog, *Das Deutsche Reich und der Zweite Weltkrieg*, Vol IV, p 658.

116. *Ibid* , p 661.

117. Deichmann, *German Air Force Ops in Support of the Army*, p 126.

118. *Ibid*, p 126.

119. BA/MA RL 8/47, Generalkommando I.A.K., Abt Ia 545/41, 16.9.41, "Einsatz des Fliegerkorps VIII vom 10.–21.8.41,": Anlage 1, Tätigkeit des VIII. Fliegerkorps bei der Unterstützung des Durchbruchs des I.A.K. bis zur Eisenbahnlinie Leningrad-Moskau vom 10.8.41–21.8.31.

120. Based on figures in BA/MA, RL 2 III/715, *Gen Qu 6 Abt (I)*, "Übersicht über Soll, Ist-bestand, Verluste und Reserven der Fliegenden Verbände, 1.11.41.

121. BA/MA RL 2III/1025, Genst. 6.Abt (IIIA), Front-Flugzeugverluste.

122. BA/MA, RL 8/47, VIII, Fliegerkorps, zusammengestellt von H. W. Deichmann . . . von Aufzeichnungen, Umfragen, und Tagebuch G.F.Frhr. von Richthofen. See entries for 25.6, 26.6.41 in particular.

123. For a full examination of the reason for the German failure see: Klaus Reinhardt, *Die Wende vor Moskau* (Stuttgart, 1977).

124. BA/MA, RL 7/8, Luftwaffenkommando 1, 5585, 21 Dec 1942, An den Oberbefehlshaber der Luftwaffe Führungstab Ia.

125. Murray, *Luftwaffe*, p 236.

126. Deichmann, *German Air Force Ops in Support of the Army*.

Bibliographical Essay

Original Sources

Unfortunately, at the end of the Second World War virtually all of the *Luftwaffe*'s records were burned by its archivist at the express orders of the Chief of the Historical Division. Those materials that do exist are heavily weighted toward the supply and production side of the *Luftwaffe*, and few records remain that deal with the operational units. Those few records that survived the war were captured by the Anglo-American allies and have been returned to the Germans. They are now at the military archive in Freiburg in the Federal Republic of Germany. Microfilms of a portion of those records are available at the National Archives in Washington and at the Imperial War Museum in London. In addition, the records of the team that worked on *Luftwaffe* histories for the United States Air Force in Karlsruhe in the 1950s are available in both the Freiburg military archives and in the USAF Historical Research Center at Maxwell Air Force Base. Fortunately for this study, the surviving records of the *Heer* are in considerably better shape. Though there was intermittent loss due to the war, the great bulk of those records surviving the war were captured by the Americans and are presently available at two locations: on microfilm at the U.S. National Archives in Washington, D.C., and at the military archives in Freiburg. The records of the *OKH*, the armies, and the corps were the most useful, and the correspondence between *Luftwaffe* and *Heer* over close air support were most illuminating.

These archival sources can be fleshed out by reference to published documentary sources such as those dealing with the war crimes trials of the Nazi political and military leadership after the war. The most obvious and important is the International Military Tribunal, *The Trial of Major War Criminals*. The collection of German diplomatic papers, published both in original and in translation (*Akten zur deutschen auswärtigen Politik*) contains many important military documents. Karl-Heinz Volker, *Dokumente und Dokumentarfotos zur Geschichte der Deutschen Luftwaffe* (Stuttgart: Deutsche Verlags, 1968) contains many important documents on the prewar development of the German Air Force. On the overall conduct of German strategy and operations see H. R. Trevor Roper, *Blitzkrieg to Defeat, Hitler's War Directives* (New York: Holt, Rinehart and Winston, 1965), and Franz Halder, *Kriegstagebuch*, ed. by Hans Adolf Jacobsen (Stuttgart: Deutsche Verlags, 1964). The statistical materials on German production contained in the United States Strategic Bombing Survey, *The Effects of Strategic Bombing on the German War Economy* (Washington: Government Printing Office, 1945) and in Sir Charles Webster and Noble Frankland, *The Strategic Air Offensive Against Germany*, Vol. IV (London: HMSO, 1961), are also useful.

Memoir Sources

As with the other German military services, an extensive collection of autobiographic works exists on the *Luftwaffe*—some good, some dreadful. At the highest level, Walter Warlimont's *Inside Hitler's Headquarters* (New York: Praeger, 1964) provides insights on the inner workings of the high command, while Nicholas von Below's *Als Hitlers Adjutant 1937–1945* (Mainz: Hase and Koehler, 1980) covers Hitler's working relations with the *Luftwaffe*. Of the direct war literature, Adolf Galland's *The First and the Last* (New York: Holt, 1954) is by far the best memoir on the fighter force. On the bomber side Werner Baumbach's *The Life and Death of the Luftwaffe* (New York: Coward-Mac-Cann, 1960) is the best.

Secondary Sources

The first years of the Second World War have come in for a general reevaluation over the past ten years and a number of important works have appeared that have added substantially to our knowledge of the *Luftwaffe*. The first two volumes of the semiofficial, on-going history of Germany's part in World War II have particular applicability to this study and have synthesized as well as expanded our knowledge of the 1933–1940 period. They are Wilhelm Deist, Manfred Messerschmidt, Hans-Erich Volkmann, and Wolfram Wette, *Das Deutsche Reich und der Zweite Weltkrieg*, Vol. I, *Ursachen und Voraussetzung der Deutschen Kriegspolitik* (Stuttgart: Deutsche Verlags, 1979); and Klaus Maier, Horst Rohde, Bernd Stegmann, and Hans Umbreit, *Das Deutsche Reich und der Zweite Weltkrieg*, Vol II, *Die Errichtung der Hegemonie auf dem Europaischen Kontinent* (Stuttgart: Deutsche Verlags, 1979). Our understanding of the intellectual and organizational framework within which the *Luftwaffe* was born, organized, and died has been enormously expanded by Horst Boog's *Die Deutsche Luftwaffenführung, 1933–1945, Führungsprobleme, Spitzengliederung, Generalstabsausbildung* (Stuttgart: Deutsche Verlags, 1982). His views in condensed fashion appear in an article in English, "Higher Command and Leadership in the German *Luftwaffe*, 1935–1945," in *Air Power and Warfare, Proceedings of the Eighth Military History Symposium, USAF Academy*, ed. by Colonel Alfred F. Hurley and Major Robert C. Ehrhart, (Washington: Government Printing Office, 1979). Two recent works on the *Luftwaffe* from different perspectives have appeared in English and are important sources for their coverage of the early war years: Williamson Murray, *Luftwaffe* (Baltimore, Md: Nautical and Aviation Press, 1985); and Matthew Cooper, *The German Air Force, 1933–1945, An Anatomy of Failure* (New York: Jane's, 1981). Richard Overy's *The Air War, 1939–1945* (London: Europa Publications, 1980) represents a significant departure point. While it contains several small errors, it puts the air war into a much larger perspective than is generally true of airpower histories. For a general background on the military, political, and strategic history of the late 1930s, see Williamson Murray, *The Change in the European Balance of Power, 1938–1939* (Princeton: Princeton University Press, 1984). On the development of German air doctrine before World War II see Williamson Murray, "The *Luftwaffe* before the Second World War: A Mission, A Strategy?" *Journal of Strategic Studies* (September, 1981). The most important work on the prewar plans and development of an industrial base is Edward L. Homze's *Arming the Luftwaffe, The Reich Air Ministry and the German Aircraft Industry, 1919–1939* (Lincoln: University of Nebraska Press, 1976). Homze's excellent article: "The Luftwaffe's Failure to Develop a Heavy Bomber Before World War II," *Aerospace Historian* (March, 1977) makes clear the technological and conceptual failures in the German attempt to design a four-engine bomber.

There are a number of histories that are still of considerable importance and that have not been dated by newer work. The best general work on the air conflict during the Second World War is the brilliant and careful examination of Bomber Command's operations: Sir Charles Webster and Noble Frankland, *The Strategic Air Offensive Against Germany*, Vols. I–III (London: HMSO, 1981). While their story is obviously that of the Bomber Command, their discussion of doctrinal, technological, and strategic issues is of enormous importance to any airpower historian. David Irving's *The Rise and Fall of the Luftwaffe, The Life of Field Marshal Erhard Milch* (Boston: Little Brown, 1973) is overly favorable to its subject but contains interesting points of view on the *Luftwaffe*. Denis Richards, *The Royal Air Force, 1939–1945* (London, 1953) is somewhat dated but still useful. An early in-house study of the *Luftwaffe* by the RAF's Air Historical Branch, *The Rise and Fall of the German Air Force* (London: HMSO, 1948) has just been issued publicly by the Air Historical Branch and is most valuable. Cajus Bekker, *The Luftwaffe War Diaries* (New York: MacDonald & Co., 1968) adds little to our understanding of the subject. Richard Suchenwirth's *Historical Turning Points in the German Air Force War Effort*, USAF Historical Study No. 189 (Montgomery: Air University, 1968) contains some interesting information as does that author's *Command and Leadership in the German Air Force*, USAF Historical Study No. 174 (Montgomery: Air University, 1969).

There are numerous works on the *Luftwaffe*'s preparations for the coming war. The best of these in German are Karl Heinz Volker, "Die Entwicklung der militärischen Luftfahrt in Deutschland, 1920–1933," in *Beiträge zur Militär-und Kriegsgeschichte*, Vol. III (Stuttgart: Deutsche Verlags, 1962) and that author's *Die deutsche Luftwaffe, 1933–1939: Aufbau, Führung and Rüstung der Luftwaffe sowie die Entwicklung der deutschen Luftkriegsführung*. For the early development of the Nazi rearmament effort, see

Edward W. Bennett's *German Rearmament and the West, 1932–1933* (Princeton: Princeton University Press, 1979). Wilhelm Deist's *The Wehrmacht and German Rearmament* (Toronto: University of Toronto Press, 1981) has an excellent section on the *Luftwaffe*'s place in Germany's preparations for war. On early strategic thinking in the *Luftwaffe* see particularly Bernard Heimann and Joachim Schunke, "Eine geheime Denkschrift zur Luftkriegskonzeption Hitler-Deutschlands vom Mai 1933," *Zeitschrift für Militärgeschichte*, Vol. III (1964). Richard Overy's "The German Pre-War Aircraft Production Plans: November 1936-April 1939," *English Historical Review* (1975) represents an important account of the muddle in prewar planning. On the Spanish Civil War, Klaus Maier's *Guernica* (Freiburg: Militärgeschichtliches Forschungsamt, 1975) is the best account of that controversial incident.

A number of important works exist that deal with the *Luftwaffe*'s role in the early campaigns of World War II. On the Polish campaign, Robert M. Kennedy's *The German Campaign in Poland, 1939* (Washington: Government Printing Office, 1956) remains the best account of operations in English. On the western campaigns the most interesting and authoritative in English remains Telford Taylor, *The March of Conquest* (New York: Simon and Schuster, 1958). Alistair Horne's, *To Lose a Battle, France 1940* (London: Little, Brown, and Company, 1960) is of considerable importance. For obvious reasons these campaigns do not concentrate on the air battle and its significant losses but rather on the course of the decisive land conflict. Hans-Adolf Jacobsen's *Fall Gelb, Der Kampf um den deutschen Operationsplan zur Westoffensive 1940* (Wiesbaden, 1957) is the best work in German. Patrice Buffotat and Jacques Ogier, "L'armée de l'air francaise dans la campagne de France (10 Mai–25 Juin 1940)," *Revue historique des Armées*, Vol. II, No. 3 offers a unique look at the problems that the French air force faced in 1940 as well as its contributions. Major L.F. Ellis, *The War in France and Flanders, 1939–1940* (London: HMSO, 1953) contains invaluable information on air operations. On the Battle of Britain, the most authoritative work on the conduct of operations is Francis K. Mason, *Battle over Britain* (London: McWhirter Twins Ltd, 1968). Telford Taylor's *The Breaking Wave* (New York: Simon and Schuster, 1967) is outstanding on the strategic framework within which the battle was fought. The official history by Basil Collier, *The Defense of the United Kingdom* (London: HMSO, 1957) is also important on various aspects of the battle. On the subject of close air support *General der Flieger* Paul Deichmann's *German Air Force Operations in Support of the Army*, USAF Historical Study, No. 163 (Montgomery: Air University, 1962) is very useful.

3

Soviet Air–Ground Coordination, 1941–1945

Kenneth R. Whiting

In the prewar period and all during the war with Germany, the Soviets regarded air power much in the same manner as they did artillery, as an instrument for facilitating ground force operations. Some commentators have even characterized the role of the Soviet Air Force in the war as flying artillery. Neither Germany nor the Soviet Union made other than token efforts in using air power as a strategic weapon; neither had an effective long-range, strategic bomber. Air power was used almost exclusively in direct support of ground forces on or near the battlefield. The Soviets were able to do this in part because their Anglo-American allies took care of strategic bombing, and the widespread activities of their partisans behind the German lines eventually crippled Nazi communications.

Throughout the war, *front** commanders exercised control over the air forces assigned to them. This was the standard prewar Soviet military organization, and it seemed logical, since the main mission of aviation was to support land forces. Stalin, imbued with the "combined arms" concept, and having been disillusioned with the efficacy of bombers during the Soviet intervention in Spain, opted for a predominantly tactical air force in which even the bombers were used mostly for missions not far beyond the front lines.

The main objectives of Soviet air power, as enumerated repeatedly in field regulations and in historical accounts, were air supremacy and close support for ground troops. Control of the air was needed to make close air support feasible; somebody had to keep the German fighters from interfering with ground-attack and light-bomber aircraft as they bombed and strafed ground targets.

---

* The Russian term *front* denotes an army group. It was the largest formation in World War II, except when two or more fronts were merged in some of the later offensives.

115

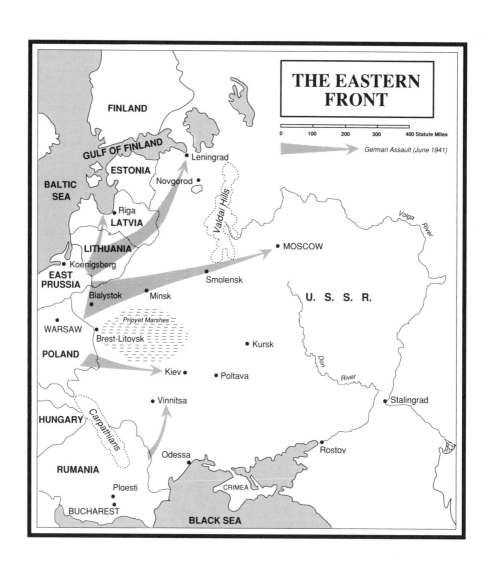

THE EASTERN FRONT

0	100	200	300	400 Statute Miles

→ *German Assault (June 1941)*

FINLAND

GULF OF FINLAND

ESTONIA

BALTIC SEA

Leningrad

Novgorod

Riga

LATVIA

Valdai Hills

Volga River

LITHUANIA

Koenigsberg

EAST PRUSSIA

Bialystok

Minsk

Smolensk

MOSCOW

U. S. S. R.

WARSAW

Pripyet Marshes

Brest-Litovsk

POLAND

Kiev

Kursk

Poltava

Don River

Vinnitsa

Stalingrad

HUNGARY

Carpathians

Odessa

Rostov

RUMANIA

Ploesti

CRIMEA

BUCHAREST

BLACK SEA

After a disastrous beginning, the Soviet *VVS** was reinforced by a steady flow of new aircraft, and it benefited from organizational changes, including the formation of large reserves that ensured flexibility. As a result, in early 1943 it was able to contribute effectively in turning the tide at Stalingrad, in gaining air superiority at Kursk in mid–1943, and in playing an important role in the drive to force the Germans out of Russia in the great offensives of 1944 and 1945. By 1944, most of the *VVS* assets were committed to close support of ground forces during a series of major offensives. The air force, however, did have its role early in the operation, when the *VVS* contribution was termed an "air offensive."

Soviet military theorists have long concentrated upon the concept of "combined arms" or *obshchevoyskoy* [usually linked with the "battle" (*voy*) or "operation" (*operatsiya*) or some other noun].[1] Soviet writers push the origins of the concept back to the Civil War of 1917, although there was little aviation to "combine" in that conflict. It was not until the forced tempo of the industrialized expansion in the Five-Year Plans that the wherewithal to implement the "combined-arms" concept became available.

Notwithstanding the accelerated output of aircraft in the First and Second Five-Year plans (1929–38), the Soviet aviation industry continued to lag behind those of the most developed countries, largely because of relatively poor engines, shortages of aluminum, substandard armament, and underdeveloped radio technology.[2] Nevertheless, the Soviet aircraft designers, especially Polikarpov and Tupolev, turned out some respectable planes for their day. The Polikarpov I–15 and I–16 fighters and the Tupolev TB–3 and SB–2 bombers were good aircraft for the middle thirties and remained the main staple for the *VVS* up to the very eve of the German invasion in June 1941.** But, as one Soviet writer has pointed out, all four dated from the period 1935 to 1936 and were obsolescent by 1941. The German aircraft, on the other hand, coming from a 1937–1938 vintage, benefited from the rapid advances in aeronautical science and technology in those two years.[3]

Some Soviet theorists flirted with the Douhet doctrine, which put all emphasis on the heavy bomber, the weapon system for smashing and terroriz-

---

*In 1941 the Soviet Air Force (*Voenno-Vozdushnye Sily*), or *VVS*, came in five varieties: (1) long-range aviation (*Dal'ne Bombardirovochnaya Aviatsiya*), or *DBA*; (2) frontal aviation (*VVS Fronta*); (3) army aviation (*VVS Armii*); (4) corps aviation (*Korpusnye Aviaeskadril'i*); and (5) reserve aviation (*Aviatsionnie Armii Reserva*). *DBA* was controlled by the high command, frontal aviation by the front commander, *VVS* of the army units were attached to each army, while both corps and reserve aviation were controlled directly by the high command and could be shifted about as needed. Most writers refer to all of these as the *VVS*. In addition, Soviet air power included the interceptor component of *PVO Strany* (the national air defense force), naval aviation, and the civil air fleet.

**The "I" stands for the Russian *istrebitel'* (fighter), the "TB" for *tyazhelyy bombardirovshchik* (heavy bomber), and the "SB" for *skorostroy bombardirovshchik* (fast bomber).

ing the enemy by massively attacking his industry and cities. The heavy bomber appealed to many Soviet strategists who visualized (or fantasized) reducing the Japanese and German industrial centers to rubble. An outstanding theorist of the 1930s, A. Lapchinskiy, conceded the importance of independent bomber operations, but he still stressed aviation's role in "combined-arms" doctrine.[4] Unsatisfactory Soviet experience with bombers in Spain from 1936 to 1938 lowered enthusiasm for strategic bombing and reinforced the tactical concept for the role in aviation, namely the support of ground forces, an idea already summarized in the Red Army Provisional Field Regulations of 1936, or PU–36.[5] These field regulations stated that aviation was to destroy "those targets that cannot be neutralized by infantry or artillery fire or that of other arms." For maximum success, the *VVS* must be used en masse, and it must cooperate with ground forces. On the eve of the German invasion, the Field Regulations issued in June 1941 stated that the basic task of aviation was to assist ground forces in combat operations and to ensure control of the air.[6]

In a sense, air superiority was considered the most important task of the *VVS*, as successful close support depended to a large extent upon air control. The struggle for such control could be carried out by destroying enemy aircraft either on the ground or in the air. Experience in Spain, however, led Soviet planners to favor air combat as the best method, thus giving the main role to fighter aviation. In the Combat Regulations for Fighter Aviation of 1940, it was clearly stated that fighter aviation was the chief means for gaining control of the air.[7] Thus by the end of the 1930s, Soviet aircraft production heavily emphasized fighters. Although ground-attack planes, light bombers, and even heavy bombers were assigned a role in air control, fighters predominated by 1941.

Soviets, moreover, adopted a "semi-isolationist" foreign policy in the early thirties, as Stalin's main attention focused on the fulfillment of the Five-Year Plans. But Japanese expansion into Manchuria in the East and the rise of Hitler in the West (the leadership in both powers imbued with hatred for communism) made it mandatory for the Soviets to seek allies to offset the threat. In 1935, Stalin shifted to a "united-front" policy that sought good relations with anyone not Fascist, regardless of his other leanings. Hardly had he launched his new policy when the outbreak of the Spanish Civil War (1936) put him on the horns of a dilemma. Either he had to let down his new leftwing supporters, such as the Popular Front in France, or support the Loyalist forces in Spain against Franco, an intervention that could alarm the democratic but pacifist British and French governments about the spread of communism. As cautiously as possible, in October 1936 he began to slip aircraft, tanks, and artillery, along with specialists into Spain. Inasmuch as Italy and Germany were providing Franco with similar "volunteers" and equipment, Spain became a testing ground for fascist versus communist weapon systems (especially aircraft), doctrine, and personnel.

In mid–1936, the German *Luftwaffe* sent an air contingent known as the Condor Legion to Spain, where its Ju–52 bombers and He–51 fighters were not very impressive against the Soviet I–15 and I–16 fighters, probably the best machines in Spain in late 1936 and much of 1937. Then the Condor Legion was reequipped with Messerschmitt Bf–109s, and the Soviet fighters were clearly outclassed.

It was in the Spanish conflict that the Ju–87 *Stuka* dive bomber made its combat debut. The accuracy achieved by the *Stuka*s in contrast to the poor performance of the Soviet SB–2 or German He–111 bombers impressed both air forces.[8] Additionally, the German Bf–109 pilots worked out a new fighter tactic. They began flying as a pair (*Rotte*) or as a pair of pairs (*Schwarm*), in other words as a leader and his wingman, a formation that was emulated widely during World War II.[9] More important, both the Germans and the Russians extracted the lesson from Spain that air power was most effective when used in close support of ground forces, rather than independently, and that there should be a close liaison between air and ground commanders.

While still engaged in Spain, the *VVS* was also tested in the Far East. In July 1937, the Japanese began an all-out assault on China. In order to keep the Japanese busy in China rather than in Outer Mongolia or Siberia, Stalin sent aid to Chiang Kai-shek, supplying him with aircraft, setting up assembly and repair facilities, and even providing pilots. This indirect opposition to the Japanese became a face-to-face confrontation at the end of July 1938, when the two sides clashed in the battle of Lake Khasan or Changkufeng, in Manchuria. The fighting escalated for two weeks, until the Japanese decided that the stakes were getting too high. According to one authority, where the enemy was strongly entrenched and had his guns dug in, Soviet air strikes proved ineffective when supporting artillery was lacking.[10]

The Soviet–Japanese confrontation of the 1930s culminated in a miniwar on the Outer Mongolian–Manchurian border in the Khalkhin–Gol (or Nomonhan) incident (the Russian and Japanese names). The conflict lasted four months (May to September 1939). Between May and the end of July, they waged a see-saw battle as both sides augmented their forces in the area, but in August the Soviets decided to go all out, assigned Georgiy K. Zhukov as commander of the Khalkhin–Gol front, and sent him massive reinforcements.

When Zhukov launched a counteroffensive on August 20, he had a 1.5 to 1 superiority over the Japanese in infantry and cavalry, 1.7 to 1 in machineguns, 2 to 1 in aircraft, and 4 to 1 in tanks.[11] Zhukov insisted on very close air-ground coordination, which he developed by having pilots as well as infantry and armored forces study the terrain and by creating special reconnaissance groups. His handling of mechanized forces in deep penetrations and his use of almost 500 aircraft for all missions to prevent enemy reinforcements from reaching the battlefield were early indicators of the strategy and tactics that he would employ so successfully in the German-Soviet war two years later.[12]

On the home front, meanwhile, Stalin purged his senior military commanders in a move that wiped out four-fifths of the top leaders in the armed forces. Soviet aviation was especially hard hit, as three-quarters of its senior officers were eliminated from 1936 to 1939. The *Yezhovshchina**—the worst period of the purge—extended to managers of the aircraft industry as well as to some aircraft designers such as Petlyakov and Tupolev. It even pervaded various research organizations and design bureaus.[13] The massiveness of the purges directly affected the performance of the Soviet Air Force in the Winter War with Finland (1939–1940) and in the early phase of what the Russians styled the Great Patriotic War against Germany.

The euphoria engendered by the victory over the Japanese at Khalkin–Gol and the easily attained territorial gains from the Soviet–German Non-Aggression Pact of August 1939 (when Hitler and Stalin divided Eastern Europe into spheres of influence) was dashed two months later by the fiasco of the Winter War with Finland. The Red Army vastly outnumbered the Finns in manpower, guns, armor, and especially aircraft. The Soviet Air Force numbered 2,500 airplanes to a mere 200 for the Finns, only half of which were serviceable.[14] The Soviet command underestimated Finnish resistance and assigned only 900 planes to the Finnish front, but exceedingly heavy loses in I–15s, I–16s, and SB–2s forced it to double the commitment.[15] Furthermore, in the early part of the war the *VVS* proved incapable of coordinating its operations with the ground forces, impairing the effectiveness of both. Soviet pilots learned their trade as the fighting progressed, but the commander of the Finnish forces, Field Marshal Mannerheim, claimed later that Russian air power was not a factor of decisive importance.[16] By May 13, 1940, the Finns were so swamped by Russian numbers of troops and machines that they could no longer resist. Even the most generous assessment of the Winter War would have to conclude that it was hardly a glorious feat of arms for either the Red Army as a whole or the *VVS* in particular.

The extremely poor performance of Soviet arms mandated some fairly radical changes in organization, strategy, and tactics. Reorganization was in midstream when the Germans abrogated the Non-Aggression Pact and attacked the Soviets in June 1941 with tremendous success. As early as 1937, the Committee for Defense of the USSR had been created to centralize further control of the

---

*Yezhovshchina, or "the bad times of Yezhov," referred to the worst period of the Stalinist purges when Yezhov headed the NKVD.

armed forces, and in May 1941 Stalin himself assumed the chairmanship of *Sovnarkom* (Council of People's Commissars), the executive arm of the government, thus combining party and government under his control.

On the eve of the war, the High Command controlled long-range aviation (*DBA*). Frontal commanders directed frontal aviation, and army aviation operated under ground force commanders at army level or below. In addition to these components, the *VVS* contained the national air defense (*PVO*) and the Navy air arm (VMF).*

PVO interceptors commanded by the air defense commander had four fleets, each with its own air component. In 1940, a reorganization of the *VVS* did away with brigades and instituted a divisional structure with three to five regiments in each air division. Some divisions had only one type of aircraft (fighter, attack, or bomber); others were composite, made up of regiments with different types of planes.[17]

The Soviet seizure of vast new territories in Eastern Europe led Stalin to order new airfields in those regions. With construction scheduled to peak in the late summer and early fall of 1941, many airfields were either partially or completely unusable when the *Luftwaffe* struck on June 22. Crowded on inadequate runways and unable to operate efficiently, Soviet aircraft were sitting ducks for German pilots.[18] Deployment to new air bases plus a rapidly increasing inventory of aircraft, beginning in February 1941, led to restructuring the supply, repair, and maintenance system (*Tyl*), which had been set up on a regional basis to support air regiments. Airfield service battalions, which were more mobile than the air base units, were also created at this time. But, like the airfield construction plan, the restructuring of aviation logistics was just getting under way when the war began.[19]

Consequently, at the beginning of hostilities with Germany, Soviet aviation was in a state of confusion; command and control was not centralized but fragmented among ground commanders of fronts and armies, air defense commanders, and naval commanders. By late June, the Germans had deployed their armed forces along the western borders of the USSR in accordance with the *Barbarossa* plan for the invasion of Russia, which called for a three-pronged advance toward Leningrad, Moscow, and Kiev—army groups North, Center, and South respectively. Each army group had an air fleet (*Luftflotte*) assigned. The Germans controlled a total of about 2,000 combat aircraft, supplemented by 1,270 transports and liaison planes and 1,000 Finnish and Rumanian planes, for a grand total of 4,300 aircraft. Russian estimates put the total number of enemy aircraft at nearly 5,000.[20]

---

*The abbreviations *DBA* stood for the Russian *Dal'ne Bombardirovochnaya Aviatsiya* or long-range aviation, while *PVO strany* stands for *protivovozdushnaya oborona strany*, or air defense of the nation. *VMF* stands for *voenno-morskoy flot*, or naval fleet.

The strength of Soviet aviation in the western regions remains more elusive than that of the *Luftwaffe*. Soviet expert Raymond Garthoff, after totaling the losses in the summer of 1941 and the number of airplanes still flying at the end of the year, estimated that there were about 10,000 aircraft facing the *Luftwaffe* in June 1941.[21] The quality of the machines was probably more important than the quantity. Only 22 percent of the Soviet fighters were new types; the rest were obsolescent.[22] The German Bf–109 against the Soviet I–15 or I–16 was not a fair match, and even the Ju–87 *Stuka* was a superior weapon system in the summer of 1941.

Using the element of surprise and possessing superior aircraft, the *Luftwaffe* "slaughtered" the Soviet Air Force in the first days of the war. The carnage on Soviet airfields was almost beyond belief, and those aircraft that did become airborne were soon shot down.[23] *Luftwaffe* bombers flew up to six missions a day, while dive bombers and fighters flew up to eight. One Soviet account states that on the first day, the *Luftwaffe* attacked 66 airfields and destroyed 1,500 newest types of Soviet fighters and other aircraft parked or flying along the frontier.[24] The Soviet and German figures for kills and losses on the ground throughout the entire war are unreliable and often vary considerably, but even Soviet historians admit that their losses on the opening days of the war were catastrophic.

A poorly organized antiaircraft defense, inferior planes, inexperienced pilots, and utter confusion in the upper echelons of command, all combined to make Soviet efforts to oppose the initial Nazi onslaught almost futile. Within a few days, the German airmen almost demolished the Soviet Air Force. Field Marshal Albert Kesselring, Commander of the Second Air Fleet, claimed that German pilots achieved "air superiority" two days after the opening of hostilities.[25] Lt. General V. Gorbachev claimed that the Soviet pilots continued their opposition a little longer, but he admitted that by early July the enemy controlled the air. He argued, however, that the Germans did not accomplish their objective to destroy the Soviet Air Force.[26] The very fact that so many Soviet aircraft were destroyed on the ground meant that the pilots were alive and able to fly new machines being turned out by the Soviet aviation industry. As one historian claimed: "Whenever it was essential, the Germans could always achieve air superiority over any sector of the Eastern Front they chose; it was only superiority over all sectors simultaneously which eluded them for the lack of aircraft."[27]

Soviet airmen attempted unsuccessfully to recover air superiority during the first six months of the defensive. Deep penetration strikes against German airfields, fuel and ammunition dumps, as well as transportation in general (one of the objectives set forth in the 1940 tactical regulations and part of accepted doctrine), failed catastrophically. Soviet medium bombers were shot down with ridiculous ease by German fighters or by antiaircraft fire, largely because they flew unescorted over their targets. Long-range bombers of *DBA* were no more effective, and the heavy losses suffered in the first few weeks crippled Soviet bombardment efforts for much of the war.[28] Thus, the combination of heavy losses in carrying out strikes against the German rear, strikes flown without fighter escort, and the dire straits of the ground forces, all resulted in the transfer of *VVS* army aviation from support corps and divisions to the operational control of front commanders for close air support.[29] In describing the ineptness of Soviet bombardment, V. Roimistrov succinctly stated that experience in Spain had resulted in "a limitation of air operations to a tactical framework over the battlefield."[30]

By the end of June, the *Luftwaffe* became so confident in its air supremacy that the bulk of its planes were shifted to close support for advancing ground forces. Some 60 percent of its sorties flew in direct support with a concomitant reduction of indirect support missions. The Ju–88s, He–111s, and Do–17s designed for attacking objectives behind the front lines were used over the battlefield itself.[31]

As the Soviets began trading space for the time required to regroup and rebuild, they shifted their limited air resources from air superiority to close air support. Deficient leadership and aircrew abilities, obsolescent aircraft, and the continuing heavy losses generally plagued Soviet air efforts until autumn. On the positive side, however, there were the reorganization and recovery efforts at higher levels, where *Stavka* reorganized the *VVS* command structure shattered by the initial attacks. Formation of the State Defense Committee led to total reorganization of Soviet defense, including the appointment of new air force commanders. New air and ground reserve forces, as well as creation of improved *VVS* rear services all pointed toward stabilizing Soviet air and regaining initiative both on the ground and in the air.

As the *Luftwaffe* concentrated upon tactical support, Soviet leaders moved their vital industrial base east of the Ural Mountains to enable aircraft plants to produce vast quantities of new aircraft types without interruption. The remarkably speedy recovery, arrival of aid from the West by the fall of 1941, and the ability of the nation to absorb huge equipment and personnel losses permitted Russian defenders to hold out until autumn rains turned roads and terrain in the USSR into quagmires that slowed or halted the *Panzer* forces.[32]

Aided by mud and then by frigid weather, the Soviets finally checked the enemy advance on Moscow. In late November and early December, the *Luftwaffe* was reduced to a semimobile force trying to operate off primitive air strips with an overextended logistical system. The *VVS* now had two great advantages: accustomed to cold weather, it had developed techniques for operating under extreme weather conditions, and as the Russians retreated, it was falling back on relatively well-equipped air bases. Interceptors of the Moscow

PVO could now supplement the *VVS*, and between mid-November and December 5, the Russians claimed 15,000 sorties to the *Luftwaffe*'s 3,500 in the battle for the capital city.[33]

The Soviet counteroffensive in the Moscow area began on December 5, and by the 25th, the Soviets not only stopped the Germans, they turned them back. The Soviet Air Force concentrated about 1,200 planes, pulling in those from the east and utilizing *PVO* interceptors and long-range bombers. At this point Hitler withdrew a large number of planes from the eastern front to send to the Mediterranean theater, and the *Luftwaffe*'s losses in bombers used for close support in the USSR were very severe. In December and January, the *VVS* for the first time in the war was able to gain a temporary air superiority, having about twice as many aircraft as the *Luftwaffe*.

The resuscitation of the *VVS* late in 1941 resulted from meteorological factors, from the influx of new aircraft types, and from much needed organizational changes. Although Lt. Gen. P. Zhigarev assumed command of the Red Army Air Forces soon after the start of the war, his new position seemed to have little authority for centralizing control of the components of the *VVS*.

Because the *VVS* was shredded into a number of semiautonomous forces under diverse commands, it was impossible during the first months of the war to organize massive air strikes in crucial situations. According to official Soviet accounts, unified control of army, frontal, and long-range aviation in the battle for Moscow demonstrated the need for centralized control over these elements everywhere.[34]

In April 1942, General A. Novikov replaced General Zhigarev, and on May 5 the air forces under the Western Front were united into the First Air Army; army aviation was completely abolished as a separate entity, and long-range aviation remained under *Stavka*. This grouping of air assets into air armies proved so effective that by 1945 there were 17 of them with a combined total of 175 divisions.[35]

Another problem facing the High Command was the lack of air reserves that could be used to bolster air support for tottering fronts—forces that could be moved swiftly from one front to another. In the summer of 1941, a few new formations of reserve aviation groups, or RAGs, each consisting of three to five air regiments, were placed at the disposal of *Stavka* to reinforce crucial sectors. For example, at the end of August, Number One RAG was sent to Bryansk to attack the German 2d Tank Group, while the other five RAGs went to other fronts during the next three months.[36] This precedent led to the formation, in the summer of 1942, of aviation corps of the High Command Reserve that served to strengthen the air armies. These aviation corps could be shifted as needed from front to front at distances of hundreds of kilometers. Altogether the Soviets formed thirty aviation reserve corps (seven bomber, eleven ground-attack, and twelve fighter corps).[37]

When the Red Army first desperately tried to stem the Nazi onslaught, there was no time to adhere to doctrine, and almost anything that could be flown was devoted to close support. In 1941, according to Col. Gen. A. V. Reshetnikov, even long-range aviation flew 74.3 percent of its missions "for the destruction of troops and combat equipment in operations close to the front." In the following year, more than 50 percent flew such missions.[38] But this tactic was costly.

By the end of 1941, *DBA* was down to only seven divisions of two regiments, each of which had sixty aircraft assigned, and they mustered only twenty planes per regiment. By July 3, 1941, the slaughter had become so great that *Stavka* restricted bombing to higher altitudes at night. Reshetnikov concluded: "The decision to shift to night bombing was correct, but, unfortunately, belated."[39]

Initially, there were few organized procedures for combined air-ground operations. Each front headquarters worked out its own signals designating friendly forces and indicating targets, most of which were close to the forward edge of the battle area (FEBA). The Soviets did not seriously analyze the problem of close air support until defensive operations neared Moscow.[40]

Because of shortages of aircraft designed for close air support, the Soviets diverted the whole spectrum of aviation to this role during the hectic months of 1941 and the first half of 1942. Soviet experience with close air support in combat operations in Spain and the Far East in the late 1930s disclosed the disastrous vulnerability of the Polikarpov R–5Sh attack plane and prompted efforts to develop a better *Shturmovik*. The aircraft that would figure so prominently in close support later in the war, the Il–2 *Shturmovik*, was not produced in sufficient quantities in 1941 to affect materially the course of combat at that time. The number of attack planes came to only two percent of the total aircraft available in June 1941.[41] Designed by Ilyushin in 1939, the heavily armored Il–2 could carry up to 600 kilograms of bombs plus 8 rockets, and it sported 2 *ShVAK* 20–mm cannon and 2 *ShKAS* 7.62–mm machineguns.[42] As a single-seater, it was extremely vulnerable coming out of a dive, so in the second half of 1942 it was converted into a two-seat aircraft which accommodated a gunner manning a *UBT* 12.7–mm machinegun.[43] With its armor and powerful armament, the Il–2 became the main attack plane of the *VVS*, and some 35,000 of them were built during the war. The Soviet troops referred to it as the "flying tank," and the Germans called it the "black death." Its main drawback was the large amount of wood used in fabricating the fuselage, and it was not until nearly the end of 1944 that an all-metal version appeared as the Il–10.[44] By 1942, increasing numbers of Il–2s had begun to outmatch the German *Stuka* as a superior close-support aircraft. To catch up, the Germans designed and produced the Henschel–129, a plane that never came up to expectations and was not produced in large numbers.[45]

Soviet fighter aircraft also found employment in ground support roles. The Commissar of Defense issued an order on June 18, 1942, decreeing that fighters could be used as daylight bombers for attacks on the enemy rear within twenty or thirty kilometers of the front lines. After dropping their bombs, they would revert to their basic mission of air superiority and support for Soviet ground troops. They were equipped with high-explosive, incendiary, and fragmentation bombs of fifty to one hundred kilograms. Either at the front or in the rear, all fighter regiments were supposed to teach daytime bombing techniques to their aviators.[46] The Soviets did not distinguish clearly between interdiction and close-support missions, referring to both as "support of the ground forces."[47]

The Soviets attained air superiority in the Moscow region at the very end of 1941 and maintained it during the first few months of 1942. But it turned out to be transitory. The colossal losses of the summer of 1941 plus the hiatus in aircraft production from the transfer of most of the aircraft industry to the east enabled the Germans to regain air superiority in the campaigns at Kharkov and in the Crimea during the spring of 1942. Soviet aviation would not play an important role again until the end of the defensive period in the battle for Stalingrad (the three months before the launching of the counteroffensive on November 19, 1942). Nevertheless, by August one air division, the 287th of the Eighth Air Army, was reequipped with new La–5 fighters, which proved capable of matching the German Bf–109.[48] In slightly less than a month, according to an official Soviet version, this division engaged in 299 air battles and destroyed 97 enemy aircraft.[49] In early November 1942, the two-seater Il–2 *Shturmovik* went into action, as the *VVS* began to benefit from the rapidly increasing production of the Soviet aircraft industry. Some 25,240 planes were produced in 1942, of which 21,342 were combat aircraft.[50] This combination of more and better aircraft plus better command and control seemed to instill more confidence in Soviet pilots.

Soviet forces, after fighting a retreat, entrenched in the city of Stalingrad by September to wage the cellar-to-cellar defense that the Germans termed *Rattenkrieg*, or "war of the rats."[51] Zhukov, by then Deputy Supreme Commander, along with Marshal A. M. Vasilevsky, Chief of the General Staff, prepared a counteroffensive. Their plan called for a two-month buildup of the fronts adjacent to Stalingrad and then for launching a gigantic pincer movement with the Southwest and the Stalingrad fronts meeting at Kalach, the only feasible Don River crossing over which General F. von Paulus could get his Sixth Army out of the Russian trap. Zhukov saw that time was on the side of the Soviets, as Paulus's Army was burning itself out in Stalingrad. The Red Army was beginning to get a steady flow of T–34 tanks and new types of aircraft, including the La–5 and the Yak–9, a modified Yak–7 with a top speed of 360 mph, armed with a 37–mm cannon and two 12.7 machineguns.[52] The success of the plan depended upon General V. I. Chuikov's forces in Stalingrad holding out until the counteroffensive could be mounted. And they did.

The main task of *VVS* in the defense of Stalingrad was close air support, reconnaissance, and very short-range bombing. As the authors of the official history stated:

> Ground-attack planes and fighters operating with infantry and artillery attacked the enemy right on the front line, and aircraft of the front and long-range bombers struck against reserves, artillery, and troops located two to five kilometers from the front line.[53]

The Commander-in-Chief of the *VVS*, General A. A. Novikov, remained at Stalingrad to insure success (as did also the *aviatsiya dal'nago deystviya* [long-range aviation] Commander, General A. Ye. Golovanov). As the *Stavka* representative to coordinate air at Stalingrad, Novikov participated in planning the counteroffensive. When Novikov informed Zhukov that his aviation was not yet ready, the latter informed *Stavka*. On November 12, Zhukov

The Ilyushin Il-2 *(top)* **and the improved Il-10** *(below)* **were among the most successful** *sturmovik*, **or ground assault, aircraft in use by the Red Air Force during World War II.**

received a reply informing him that it would be better to postpone operations until air support was ready. *Stavka* stated: "The experience of the war shows that operations against the Germans can be successful only if carried out with superiority in the air."[54]

The Stalingrad counteroffensive marking the end of the first period of the Great Patriotic War began on November 19, 1942. By then, the *VVS* occasionally enjoyed the edge in numbers and even air superiority. Increased aircraft production made it possible to augment the inventory of the individual fighter regiments from 22 to 32 airplanes. Furthermore, experience gained during 1941 and most of 1942 had shown the desirability of making the basic unit the *zveno*, or flight of four aircraft, subdivided into two *para* (pair) to function as offensive and defensive partners. Actually, the Soviets learned from their German enemy, modifying the latter's *Rotte*, *Schwarm*, and *Staffel* arrangements to fit particular Russian needs. By the end of this period in the war, the *VVS* claimed to have flown more than 850,000 sorties, 66 percent of which could be termed close support of ground forces. The vast rebirth of Soviet air power could be seen in production figures indicating that 41,000 aircraft were built since the onset of the conflict. Of these, 34,000 had reached the front. During the first 18 months of the war, 90,000 new aviators and 41,224 flight personnel had been trained, which meant that 570 units had been manned, trained, equipped, and sent to the battle lines. One commentator concluded: "The *VVS* recovery during these months of trial was almost as remarkable as the 1941 disasters."

The Stalingrad counteroffensive succeeded in surrounding Paulus's Sixth Army within a week. Much of this success could be attributed to newly developed cooperation between air and ground elements of the Red Army. A planned "air offensive" required a concentration of air resources in predetermined areas around Stalingrad to prepare special breakthrough zones for the attacking Soviet ground units and to harass Axis forces trying to regroup. Two Soviet air armies were directed against German airfields in order to suppress the *Luftwaffe* and to gain air superiority. Even so, the Soviets enjoyed a two- or even three-to-one superiority in inventory of operational aircraft over the Germans at this time.

At first, poor weather conditions hampered all aviation in the area. But later, with the return of better flying weather, it was still necessary for Soviet ground forces to complete their encirclement of the Germans before the full impact of tactical air power could be brought into the battle. During the week of November 24 to November 30, improved weather conditions allowed the Soviets to fly 5,760 sorties against a mere tenth of that figure for the Germans. Soviet fighters severely hampered German air resupply destined for Paulus's entrapped forces—despite optimistic prognostications for success from Hermann Goering and Adolf Hitler.[55]

The Soviets claimed that during the period of November 19, 1942 through February 2, 1943, *Luftwaffe* losses totalled an astronomical 3,000 planes destroyed in addition to some 2,100 planes lost at Stalingrad.[56] Such claims rested upon massive attacks of *shturmovik* formations against the German airfields to destroy transports on the ground. One such raid hitting the Sal'sk airfield on January 9, 1943, destroyed 72 aircraft.[57] Between November 24, 1942 and January 31, 1943, the Germans admitted losing 266 Ju–52s, 165 He–111s, 42 Ju–86s, 9 FW–200s, and a Ju–290—some 483 transport planes.[58] Even worse, the image of the *Luftwaffe* as an indestructible force was shattered.

The qualitative character of the *VVS* during the battle of Stalingrad was possibly more important than the quantitative increase. According to Air Marshal S. I. Rudenko, less than a third of the Soviet aircraft were new types at the beginning of the defensive phase of the struggle for Stalingrad in July 1942. By the beginning of the counteroffensive on November 19, however, almost 74 percent were new types, and fighter aviation had more than 97 percent new aircraft. For example, of the 125 fighters of the Sixteenth Air Army, only 9 were obsolete LaGG–3s.[59] Air operations during the counteroffensive were coordinated closely with the ground forces command, virtually a necessity, since more than 80 percent of the combat missions had been flown for close support in some form. Few fighters were employed in this task from 1941 to 1943. They provided the air cover necessary for the *shturmoviks* to operate at their preferred altitudes of 300 feet above the ground action.[60]

Soviet pilots increasingly displayed audacity in the air battles in the spring of 1943, and by midsummer the Battle of Kursk proved to be the last hurrah for *Luftwaffe* air on the Eastern Front. From then on, German air power stood on the defensive. An extensive protrusion of the Soviet front, the Kursk salient provided a tempting target for a victory-starved Hitler, as his generals attempted to repeat one of those great encirclements so prevalent two summers before. Russian intelligence discerned the German plan, Operation *Zitadelle* (Citadel). Soviet leaders filled the bulge with artillery and tanks, and they heavily reinforced their air capability from *Stavka* reserves. *Stavka*, in fact, assigned several air armies, 2 *PVO* fighter divisions, and a sizeable segment of its long-range aviation to the Kursk area—about 3,000 aircraft in total. Two-thirds of the German planes on the Eastern Front (2,000 aircraft) were similarly allotted to the battle, including 1,200 bombers, 600 fighters, 100 dive bombers, and 150 reconnaissance aircraft.[61]

The German offensive started on July 5, 1943, and lasted until the early days of August. Though Kursk was famous for the largest tank battle of the war, it also witnessed an air battle of monumental proportions, with both sides committing all of their resources to gain air control, hoping thereby for effective close air support. The Russian counterattack at Kursk concentrated air power on a very narrow sector against tanks and artillery that blocked penetration deep into the German rear. Radio communications greatly improved air-ground coordination and even included a separate network for control of close air support. The command posts for attack aircraft were located close to those of ground commanders to ensure close cooperation.[62] Soviet attack and bombardment aircraft began to operate in larger formations (thirty to forty aircraft), to which the Russians attributed lower losses and easier escort for accompanying fighters to defend them.[63] The Il–2 *Shturmoviks*, often referred to as "Ilyushas" by the Soviets, were much improved close-support aircraft by the summer of 1943, with their 37–mm cannon, RS–82 missiles, and *PTAB* antitank bombs.[64]*

Although German Bf–109G and FW–190 fighters held their own against Soviet La–5Fn and Yak–9 aircraft, Soviet air power literally smothered the *Luftwaffe* with numbers. German ground forces at Kursk were forced to rely increasingly on obsolescent fighters, bombers, and the Ju–87 for close air support. After the last German attacks in the Kursk salient failed in the autumn, "the Russians definitely ruled the air," and found it ever easier to provide overwhelming close air support for their own ground operations.[65]

Steady improvements in tactics accompanied the Soviet technological and industrial recovery. After 1943, Soviet groundsupport operations became diversified and quite sophisticated. In the preparatory period of an air offensive, *VVS* formations conducted concentrated strikes against individual targets. Formations of twenty-five to sixty aircraft participated in sorties over the battlefield. They would arrive from different angles in closely spaced waves, attack the German positions, and retire behind Soviet lines before German fighters could appear. Attack elements operated either in "support" (emphasizing central control of air units), or "assignment" where attack units operated while attached to specific ground formations (mainly armored and mechanized units). "Assignment" allowed individual air commanders more freedom in choosing targets.

The widespread use of patrols and roving fighters to close off an entire battle sector, with each air regiment committed to a specified zone of operations, became a trademark of Soviet ground support. The Soviets also introduced radar detection and radio communications to their air operations. As these tactics improved and new equipment was introduced, the *Luftwaffe* was swept from the skies.

Eventually, however, continuous patrols over the battle area lost favor. By 1945, the perimeter of the target area expanded beyond the immediate battle to include interdiction targets in the rear. Yet Soviet aviation always

---

*RS (*reaktivnyy snaryad*) is a rocket projectile, while *PTAB* is the abbreviation for *protivotankovaya aviatsionnaya bomba*, or antitank aerial bomb.

functioned best with close ties to a clearly delineated ground battle zone. Even in Soviet air support for offensive operations, when bombardment as well as attack aviation functioned as long-range artillery to reach targets beyond the range of ground guns, everything depended on careful coordination of front and air army commanders. Some problems arose in coordinating the functions of attack aviation with those of mobile armored and mechanized groups. Nevertheless, Soviet aviation successfully played the role for which it was uniquely suited: containing the encircled German formations after their envelopment by the mobile ground units, especially in the deep penetration offensives of 1944–1945. These victories came only with the experience and steady buildup of men and machines that followed the initial two years of disaster and defeat from 1941 to 1943.[66]

After the Kursk campaign, when the German *Wehrmacht* retreated across the Dnepr River, the everdiminishing *Luftwaffe* made largely futile efforts to provide air cover for ground forces. The air war involving the Allied land operations in the Mediterranean and northwest Europe, and the combined bomber offensive drew off resources desperately needed to support German ground forces in the East. By June 1944, the *VVS* operated 13,500 aircraft (up from an 8,500 average in 1943), and by January 1945, the total had risen to 15,000.[67] Furthermore, the Soviet air arm not only rose in numbers but its aircraft also steadily improved in quality. For example, the Yak–9 had been so improved by 1944 that it could function not only as an interceptor, but also as a low-level fighter-bomber for close air support, while the Petlyakov Pe–2 was refitted with an M–105PF 1,200-hp engine which enabled it to confront the Me–109G.[68] The Yak–3, a 400-mph fighter replacing the Yak–1 on the production lines in mid–1943, was a match for either the Me–109 or the FW–190. In addition, the La–7, with a top speed of 420 mph, went into series production in mid-1944. It was specifically designed to counter the FW–190.[69]

In January 1945, the Red Army smashed into Poland and began its march on Berlin at the rate of twelve to fourteen miles a day. Due to shortages in aircraft and trained pilots and because of inadequate supplies of fuel and lubricants over the next five months, the *Luftwaffe* could do little to challenge *VVS* control of the air. The culmination came in April, when 7,500 Russian aircraft overwhelmed the remnants of the *Luftwaffe* in the attack on Berlin.[70] The Soviet claim of 1,132 German planes shot down in this battle may be dubious, but there is little doubt who could boast of air control over the city.[71] The importance of close air support in the triumphant march from Stalingrad to Berlin would be hard to exaggerate. Wisely, the *VVS* accepted close air support as its main mission in the last three years of the war and used every branch of the air force in that effort—fighters, bombers, and attack planes. Both sides, for that matter, used bombers for close support during the entire war, but the Russians were especially prodigal in their use in the third and fourth period "air offensives." This apparent extravagance was found to be cost-effective, for it shattered the German lines, thereby enabling armor and infantry to penetrate deeply on its way to victory. Even the *ADD* (*aviatsia dalnego deistvia*), although entitled "long-range aviation," was used mostly for close-support operations and did very little that could be termed strategic bombing, even if one were to stretch that term outrageously.[72] Actually, "strategic bombing" for the Soviets usually referred to attacks a few miles beyond the FEBA.

The dive bomber, however, was the air weapon *par excellence* in close-support operations. As early as 1936, the Germans emphasized the Ju–87 *Stuka*, and after the Spanish adventure, all German bombers were supposed to have a dive-bombing capability, a requirement that precluded effective strategic bomber design. As long as the *Luftwaffe* was carrying out *Blitzkrieg* operations against relatively feeble opposition in restricted areas such as Poland and the Low Countries, the slow and lumbering *Stuka*s were effective, especially against armored forces, communications, and even streams of fleeing refugees. However, when the enemy achieved air superiority, as in Russia after mid-1943, the Ju–87 became an easy target for the faster Soviet aircraft, particularly when the *Stuka* was coming out of its dive. But the Soviets were just as enthusiastic about dive-bombing as the Germans, an enthusiasm that clearly manifested itself in production of 35,000 Il–2 *Shturmoviks* during the war. Once the Il–2 was redesigned to accommodate a rear-gunner, it was probably the best assault aircraft on the Eastern Front.[73]

Naval, air defense, and fighter aviation often assisted assault aircraft, and Soviet writers attributed 46.5 percent of fighter aviation missions to close support over the course of the war.[74] These same writers claim that the "shallow operational area" covered by bombers and assault aircraft "was the result of the type of conflict on the Soviet–German front." Troops were never deployed to any depth but were concentrated on the battlefield, and the preferred targets were the enemy formations along the FEBA and their reinforcements near the front lines.[75] In short, the titanic struggle between the Soviet and Nazi ground forces, a struggle involving enormous numbers of men, guns, and tanks, almost compelled Soviet strategists to tailor their air assets to the needs of the ground forces, and in many cases to serve simply as a substitute for artillery.

By early 1944, the *VVS* had more or less won command of the air, and since there were few highly lucrative targets within range of their short-legged bombers, the overwhelming effort went into supporting infantry and armor in the continuous offensive along the battleline stretching from the Kola Peninsula to the Black Sea.

Ground forces, according to Marshal V. D. Sokolovsky, represented more than eighty percent of the armed services during the Great Patriotic War. Though this branch accomplished the most important tasks in the war, the Air Force, next in importance, was indispensable. Its "main efforts . . . were directed at supporting the operations of the ground forces and destroying enemy troops and equipment directly on the field of battle."[76] Direct support on the battlefield necessarily meant that air and ground commanders had to devote much time and meticulous effort to coordinating activities, as the assigned targets for air support were dangerously close to their own troops.

Coordination was poor during the first period of the war. As the war went into the second, then the third period, improvement accelerated, as accumulated experience provided more and more indications of needed changes. These included improvements in command and control of ground-air cooperation, human and technological advances for perfecting the best possible team of man and aircraft, increased availability of radio and radar, and the growing skill and experience of commanders. Between May and November 1942, the creation of air armies and the formation of *Stavka* reserves (the air corps of the *RVGK*)* made it possible to shift air support rapidly from one region to another, to increase air support for ground forces and, because of the increasing centralized command, to attain closer coordination of ground and air operations.[77] Air representatives from *Stavka* participated in planning combat operations and in some cases called upon neighboring air armies for help. By late 1942, *Stavka* representatives, generals, and high-ranking staff officers joined air army command posts at the front, where they served as liaison officers to front commanders. *Stavka* also devised plans, transmitting them to representatives, both air and ground. They, in turn, coordinated efforts, by radio or wire communications.[78]

Command and control of air operations was ensured through a system of command posts (CPs). During the early period of the war, an air army usually established two CPs, a main one and one for the rear. The commander of the air army, or his deputy, was in charge of the main CP. Established fifty to eighty kilometers from the front line in the first and second periods of the war, they were gradually moved up to a distance of twenty-five to forty kilometers from the front in the last period.[79]

In addition to the main and rear CPs, later in the war the Soviets created auxiliary command posts, or *VPU*s.† In the Stalingrad counteroffensive, the Eighth Air Army *VPU*s were placed close to those of the front commander, and because of the proximity to the front line, command and control of air operations directly over the battlefield improved greatly. In May 1943, orders called for *VPU*s in all air armies. They required manning of six to ten offi-

---

RVGK is the acronym for the Russian *reserv verkhovnogo glavnokomandovaniya* (Reserve of the Supreme High Command).

†*VPU*, the abbreviation for *vspomogatel'nyy punkt Upravleniya* (auxiliary command post).

cers skilled in reconnaissance, communication, cryptographic, and meteorological services. In the event of ground force operations on a very wide front, one or two forward observation posts (*PNP*)* were set up to observe the battlefield more closely and to feed information into the *VPU*s.

By mid–1943, the radio served as the prevalent method of command and control in air operations.[80] In the battle for Kursk, the increased number of radio networks helped enormously in coordinating ground forces and air units, and it ensured better control over aircraft. As a matter of fact, accounts reveal that: ". . . a separate radio network was organized for controlling ground-attack aircraft on the battlefield."[81]

Throughout the Great Patriotic War, however, the Soviets lagged behind their Allies and the Germans in radio and radar communications. It was not until late 1941 that radio control of airborne fighter and ground-attack aircraft was in use, but on the whole, the system proved inadequate, because it lacked equipment and skilled operators with radio discipline.[82] During the defense of Stalingrad, Air Marshal A.A. Novikov, Commander-in-Chief of *VVS*, ordered the Sixteenth Air Army to install a radio network consisting of a main station near the Air Army headquarters, with substations at divisional and regimental airfields and transmitters along the front for direct contact with pilots. According to the Soviets, the installations had the following tasks: "Inform fliers in the air concerning the situation in the air, warning against enemy aircraft that might appear; summon fighter planes from airfields and reassign them new targets."[83] In the struggle over Kuban in May 1943, all Russian fighter and ground-attack aircraft had radios and "were systematically and consistently directed by control stations established along advanced positions at the points of main effort."[84]

Soviet radar, or *RLS*,† was primitive at the outset of the war and developed slowly. Soviet sources claim an important role for it in the defense of Leningrad and Moscow in 1941, a claim whose validity seems to depend upon how "important role" is defined. It was not until the autumn of 1943 that most authorities describe radar as a valuable tool for command and control of aircraft over the battlefield. One source declared that even for the *PVO*, it was not until after 1943 that "visual observation posts virtually lost their importance as a means of detection. . . ."[85] Marshal D. S. Kutakhov, Commander of *VVS* until his death in 1944, wrote that "with the acquisition of radar by the *VVS* (from September 1943), there began a wider use of a more economical method of operations—interceptions of enemy aircraft from 'airfield alert.' "[86] By the spring of 1944, radar was used extensively for

---

*PNP is the abbreviation for *peredovoy nabluydetel'nyy punkt* (forward observation post).
†*RLS* is the abbreviation for *radiolokatsionnaya stantsiya*.

vectoring interceptors against enemy aircraft, but just how effectively this was done is difficult to ascertain with any accuracy.

Most Westerners agree that the Soviets improved their radio-radar capabilities considerably during the war, especially in the latter half of the conflict, i.e. from Kuban to Berlin. *Luftwaffe* General Klaus Vebe, however, disagreed. He found little improvement in Soviet air operations resulting from radio and radar installations.[87] Even those who agree on the considerable improvement in Soviet radio-radar capabilities maintain that Russian electronics were vastly inferior to those of the Allies and the Germans.[88] Although crude in some respects, by late 1943 the fairly well-organized Soviet electronic industry was meeting the basic needs of the Soviet air forces.

The close air support tactics of Soviet fighters, *shturmoviks*, and bombers were in many ways quite similar. Fighter aviation flew almost half of its sorties against ground targets on the battlefield or close to it, but the fighters also afforded escort for bombers or assault aircraft. With such widely differing missions demanded of the same aircraft, it was almost inevitable that the advantages of a multi-purpose plane designed to destroy both air and ground targets would become obvious to Stalin and his *Stavka*. The prototype of such a plane was the Yak–9B fighter-bomber, which went into action with the 130th Fighter Aviation Division of the First Air Army in early 1944 with great success.[89] The fighter-bombers employed the same tactics as the fighters namely: (1) bomb the selected target, (2) cover the *shturmoviks* and bombers during their strike,and (3) strafe ground targets with machinegun and cannon fire, reserving enough ammunition to cope with any enemy aircraft that might be encountered en route home. The advantage of the fighter-bomber over a pure fighter was the 400–kilogram bomb that it carried internally, which made the initial bombing strike more effective—especially in suppressing hostile ground-based air defenses in the target area. Attacking antiaircraft batteries, the aircraft would dive-bomb the target, and succeeding aircraft would strafe it from an altitude of 400 to 600 meters.[90]

Although *shturmovik* fighter tactics did not differ considerably from other ground-attack tactics, fighter pilots could not devote enough time for extensive training in complicated ground-attack maneuvers to improve their skills. On the plus side, however, the speed and maneuverability of other fighters in comparison with *shturmoviks* gave the former a decided advantage in evading hostile antiaircraft fire.[91] Inasmuch as the combat formations of fighters in the third period of the war were larger than in the first two periods, often squadron-size, they could be divided into strike and cover groups, which in turn could alternate with each other.

In describing fighter tactics against ground targets, Col. N. Zavgorodniy even designated the number of fighters needed to isolate the battlefield. According to his estimates, one squadron could inflict enough damage to disorganize and to hold up an infantry battalion for about an hour. A fighter aviation regiment could do the same to a hostile infantry regiment, while a *zveno* of fighters could stop an artillery battery of four to six guns with six to eight trucks.[92]

The Soviets attached an increasing importance to the *shturmovik* during the course of war, as is evident in its steady numerical growth relative to the numbers of fighters and bombers in the *VVS*. In mid–1941, fighter aviation comprised 56.2 percent of the total *VVS* inventory, and bombers made up 38.8 percent. By mid-1944, fighters were down to 42 percent and bombers to 25 percent. These changes resulted from the emphasis put on the production of *shturmoviks*—which made up nearly 30 percent of *VVS* aircraft strength by the end of 1943.[93] The *shturmovik* became the weapon system par excellence for hitting targets just out of artillery range.

In the initial period of the war, the Soviets used a basic method of attacking small and large targets, on or near the battlefield, at an altitude of 2,000 to 3,000 meters. Later, when tanks and motorized columns became the most crucial targets, the bombing altitude was dropped to 600 to 1,000 meters.[94]

Various other methods were tried, including dive- and glidebombing. Combat group formations then used a wedge or snake with flights at intervals of 200 to 300 meters. The favorite formation for mutual protection against those enemy fighters that managed to get through the friendly fighter cover was a circle. On reaching the start of the bombing run, each aircraft zeroed in on the target, bombing independently for one or two passes, then rejoined the circle. It was found that dive-bombing achieved the best results. For example, before it adopted dive-bombing, one air division had a circular error probable (CEP)* of 200 meters or more. After converting to dive-bombing, the CEP was reduced to 18 meters.[95]

At the beginning of the war, the Soviet inventory of bombers, with the exception of the Petlyakov Pe–2, included a conglomeration of obsolete and obsolescent aircraft notable for their slowness, inadequate armament, and antiquated avionics. The Pe–2, produced by Petlyakov in 1939 as a twin-engine, high-altitude fighter, was quickly converted into a dive bomber and entered production in June 1940, as the basic tactical bomber of the *VVS*. It could accelerate to 337.5 mph, carry a maximum bomb load of 2,200 pounds, and shoot with four 7.62–mm machineguns, later replaced by two 12.7–mm guns. (As early as the Soviet intervention in the Sino-Japanese War in the late 1930s, Soviet pilots realized that the 7.62–mm machinegun was relatively ineffective against Japanese bombers. Additional impetus for a

---

*CEP: The radius of a circle within which half of the bombs would fall.

change to a heavier caliber arose when they came up against the cannon carried by the German Me/Bf–109). Some 11,400 Pe–2s were produced, but only 458 before the *Luftwaffe* struck the *VVS* in June 1941.[96] As production picked up during the war, the Pe–2 became the workhorse of tactical bomber aviation, a fitting stable-mate for attack aviation's Il–2 *Shturmovik*.

Because of catastrophic bomber losses in the summer of 1941 (SB,

The Yakovlev Yak-1 *(bottom)*, **was used in close-support roles. The basic airframe also appeared in the superb Yak-3** *(top)*, **the B-model of which had an internal bomb bay. The T-model featured a heavy antitank cannon firing forward.**

137

DB–3, and Il–4 types), all except the Pe–2 were restricted to night bombing. In 1942, medium-bomber aviation consisted mainly of Pe–2s, and the increased production with better equipment reflected a change in its tactics. Combat missions with *zveno*s and squadrons were increased to regimental and divisional size for ground force operations. Furthermore, Pe–2s began dive- bombing at 50– to 60–degree angles, which improved accuracy on small targets by two or three times.[97] Better bomb sights, which automatically took into account altitude and speed, augmented the effectiveness of Soviet tactical bombers in 1943.

The Tu–2, a twin-engine bomber, like the Pe–2, was initially produced in 1940. Greatly improved during the course of the conflict, it could fly at 341 mph, carry a maximum bomb load of 4,400 pounds (increased to 6,600 in 1944), and it was equipped with three 7.62–mm machineguns (later exchanged for three 12.7–mm) and two 20–mm cannons. According to one Soviet historian, the Tu–2 was the best tactical bomber of the Second World War,[98] an evaluation that would probably be contested by many. The fact that only 764 Tu–2s were produced during the war would seem to call this statement into question.

Improvements in the capabilities of Soviet tactical bombers between 1941 and the end of the war considerably enhanced the role of tactical bomber aviation in combined operations with the ground forces. According to Novikov, ". . . Soviet bomber aviation consisted basically of tactical bombers, because the outcome of the war was decided directly on the battlefield."[99] That judgment is echoed in an official history that claims the "combat use of bomber formations of tactical aviation was characterized by massive operations in the sectors of the ground forces' main blows."[100]

In addition to the increases in the quantities of men and matériel involved in successive counteroffensives and offenses, the depth and duration of the operations were also greater. For example, the Moscow counteroffensive at the end of 1941 ranged in depth from 100 to 250 kilometers, lasting 33 days. The Byelorussian offensive in 1944 was 600 kilometers, taking 68 days. The following table demonstrates the increases in areas with the concomitant commitment of men, guns, and machines.

The enormous areas involved in the later offensives and the speed of the breakthroughs made close air support by all types of aviation invaluable. As can be seen from the table, the Soviets involved more than six times the number of aircraft and more than four times the number of men in Berlin operations than in the Moscow counteroffensive.

Soviet World War II historians devote a great deal of attention to the effectiveness of "combined arms" in defeating the Germans. The more honest ones confess that the concept worked out in the prewar period did not yield very good results in the early days of the war. They attribute these failures to the lack of good communications, the difficulty of discerning any

The Petlyakov Pe-2, a medium bomber, served as a dive-bomber early in the war.

clearly designated front, the remoteness of the command posts of the air and ground commanders from each other, and the delays in transmitting plans and operational orders to each other. With such drawbacks, they write, it was little wonder that any successful coordination of air support with the ground operations could be achieved.[101] By the second and third periods of the war, "combined arms" operations worked well, largely because air armies were created, the *Stavka* reserves were formed, and an "air offensive" was instituted as an integral segment of the general offensive operation. Furthermore, the widespread use of radio for command and control, the vast improvements

Men and Weapons Used in Ground Force Operations

Operation	No. of Fronts	No. of men (1000s)	No. of Guns and Mortars	No. tanks & Self-Prop Guns	No. of Aircraft
Moscow (counter-offensive)	3	600	5,700	720	1,170
Stalingrad (counter-offensive)	3	1,100	15,500	1,460	1,350
Byelorussian	4	1,400	31,000	5,200	5,000
Berlin	3	2,500	42,000	6,250	7,500

*Derived from Table 3 in Karpov and Zubkov, *"O Nektorykh Tendentsiyakh Razvitiya Teorii i Praktiki Nastupatel'nykh Operatsiy Grupp Frontov"* (Some Tendencies in the Development and Practice of Offensive Operations of Groups of Fronts), *Voenno-Istoricheskiy Zhurnal*, no. 10 (October 1983), p 19.

in air-ground communications, and the cooperation between air and ground officers in coordinating operational timing and targets, all greatly enhanced the performance of "combined arms" offensives.[102]

The tactical coordination of air support for ground operations had to be worked out in detail, as the air units were very likely to be assigned targets as close as 500 to 800 meters to their ground forces. In August 1943, *Stavka* established a unified set of identification signals (panels, rockets, colored smoke) as well as radio codes, which greatly improved target designation and identification and at the same time diminished casualties to Soviet troops caused by their own aircraft. The main branch of the *VVS* that had been affected by growing use of radio and the unified code signals was the *shturmovaya aviatsiya*, ground-attack aviation, since more than eighty percent of its sorties struck targets on the immediate battlefield. It was not until late in the war that the *shturmovik*s were widely used in "free hunting" (*svobodnaya okhota*). On such missions, generally flown by a pair (*zveno*), the ground-attack aircraft, usually Il–2s, searched out targets independently, attacking targets such as trucks, trains, artillery on the move, and reserve forces of the enemy.[103]

Staff work in aviation units at all levels also improved considerably during the course of the war. As previously described, staff work at the front and on the air army level was closely tied into that of *Stavka*, largely through the latter's representatives with the combat forces: representatives of the caliber of Zhukov, Vasilevsky, and Novikov, Commander-in-Chief of the *VVS*. Operational plans worked out at the *Stavka*-front-air army level dealt with overall objectives in major offensives. The details for attaining those objectives devolved upon regimental and squadron staffs.

One Soviet historian pointed out that a squadron had the strength to carry out complicated tasks independently and that it was the optimal group for a commander to control successfully in complex operations. Even if the formation had to break up into *zveno*s, advanced planning plus good ground control could help considerably in conducting the squadron's operations. Each *zveno* had a designated target, but if conditions during the mission should change radically, the *zveno* leader had latitude to attack an alternate target.[104] Once the squadron was airborne, it was controlled by radio and radar control. The RUS–1 *Reven* (Rhubarb) and the later RUS–2 *Redut* (Redoubt) radars could detect aerial targets well over a hundred kilometers away. Radio information for pilots came from transmitters located on all airstrips, at CPs, and at auxiliary CPs. By the third period of the war, tactical aircraft carried *RSI*–3, *RSI*–4, and *RSI*–6* radios, which could receive and

---

RSI is the acronym for *radiostantsiya istrebitelya*, or fighter radio set.

transmit. Ground transmitters were often located near the front line at 10 to 15 kilometer intervals.[105] General Mikryukov stated that the number of sorties per enemy plane shot down decreased from 155 in 1943 to 53 in 1945, indicating the steady improvement of the system.[106] He does not point out, however, that better Russian aircraft and the declining quality of the German pilots also probably had a lot to do with that statistic.

Staff work at and, in particular, below the regimental level, improved. The system worked as follows: Receiving operational orders from higher commands, the regimental commander and his staff proceeded to work out the details of their share of the offensive. The staff of the air regiment was made up of several elements, such as reconnaissance, communications and the important operations section, which was commanded by the deputy chief of staff. Operations analyzed inputs from air reconnaissance, visual sightings, and radar scans; then drew up the operational orders for regimental units and transmitted them to the squadron commanders, and even to *zveno* leaders.[107] In the early period of the war, the air regimental staff had little time to plan and execute combat operations because of the rapidly changing conditions. In the later periods of the war, better intelligence and communications resulted in a better understanding of the battlefield situation, enabling the staffs to plan and carry out well-designed and coordinated operations.[108]

Another ingredient in the increased efficiency of close air support in the second and third periods of the war was the vastly improved aviation in rear services. The *BAO*s,* or air base maintenance battalions, each supporting either a regiment of twin-engine aircraft or two regiments of single-engine planes, were the basic units for the many services the air formations needed to operate effectively.[109] The *BAO*s were supplied by truck, air transport, or rail, as the air units they were responsible for moved across Russia at a constantly accelerating pace during the later periods of the war. Repair and maintenance of aircraft were accomplished by the mobile aircraft repair base, or *PARB*,† or the mobile aircraft repair shop, or *PARM*,‡ the latter following its assigned air unit right up to the front.

By mid-1943 the care and feeding of the air units was fairly well organized, considering the prevailing combat conditions. In 1943, a new manual which defined the role of aviation repair units in some detail was issued for the Engineering–Aviation Services. They were to follow standard procedures in coping with climate, aircraft camouflage, and the evacuation of air units from one airfield to another. They were also instructed in maintenance of armament and specialized equipment under combat conditions.[110]

BAO is the acronym for *batal'on aerodromnovo obsluzhivaniya.*
†*PARB* stands for the Russian *podvizhnaya aviaremontnaya baza.*
‡*PARM* is the acronym for *podvizhnaya aviaremontnaya masterskaya.*

Repair methods differed with circumstances. Units repaired insignificant damage on the spot, at operational airfields; but they transported seriously damaged planes to rear areas or even to aircraft plants for reconditioning. By mid-1943, in spite of numerous difficulties, various repair echelons succeeded in reducing the number of grounded aircraft in the *VVS* to 14.8 percent. In the air armies, the score was even better—from 22 percent in March to only 9.6 percent in July 1943. The *PARBs* and *PARMs* in the field reconditioned 12,352 planes in March, 13,594 in April, and 17,277 in May. At the same time, they reconditioned 62,867 engines and 6,829 props in the first nine months of 1943.[111]

All was not as promising, however, as the those figures suggest. Some of the quality was very low, partly because the officers in charge were not technologically qualified. Only 9.6 percent of the *PARB* commanders had received higher engineering training; and those in charge of *PARMs*, less than 3 percent. Technical courses were set up, and by July 1945 more than 1,000 commanders and specialists had completed the courses, and the quality of repair work rose dramatically.[112]

During the third period of the war, mechanics needed utmost initiative and endurance to keep their charges flying, as the tempo of operations accelerated to the point where air formations were transferring their air bases as many as four to six times a month, and regiments up to ten times. The result was that some new airfields were so short of manpower that a single mechanic had to take care of two or three aircraft, each flying several missions a day.[113] Adding to the mechanics' adversities, new airfields were extremely primitive. Of the 8,545 airfields constructed during the war, 5,531, or 65 percent, were dirt strips, often built in two or three days, largely with unskilled labor.[114]

In summary, under difficult combat and climatic conditions, the aviation technical services of the *VVS* managed to keep a surprisingly large number of planes available for close air support. General E. F. Longinov points out that their work ensured 3,808,136 combat sorties for which they supplied 696,268 tons of bombs and 1,628,059 tons of POL.[115]

Although many statistics cited in this study may be suspect, the magnitude of the overall accomplishment is not in doubt. Inasmuch as the Soviet–German War involved overwhelming masses of men and armor, close air support remained the principal role of the air forces for both belligerents. The *VVS* still produced massed of aircraft, trained enough pilots, and erected the support structure that helped exhaust its opponent.

The *VVS* was a tactical air force, operating in close coordination with artillery, mechanized units, and tank armies as a combined arms team. It performed a variety of roles in preparing air strikes, supporting tank armies in offensives, and engaging enemy reserves and retreating troops. It provided air cover for frontal troops; two fighter divisions usually supported a tank army. By the end of the war, an aggressive *VVS* took on a failing *Luftwaffe* with far more confidence than it had in 1941, leading one historian, Von Hardesty, to liken the Soviet Air Force in World War II to that of a phoenix, rising from the ashes of early defeat in the war.[116]

The Soviet Union parleyed its vast geographical distances, adapted its tactics of attrition, relocated its aviation industry east of the Ural Mountains, and lavishly employed its men and machines to achieve a combined arms victory. Moreover, Soviet air leaders like Alexander Novikov tied air power to Red Army ground operations in a way unequaled by the Allies. The *VVS* was not used as a separate strategic weapon. Instead, it localized air superiority to its advantage by massing aircraft to provide air cover for other distinctive Soviet tactics. These were styled by Von Hardesty as an "air offensive" (the application of enormous concentrated firepower of armor, artillery, rockets, and aircraft for land assault) or an "air blockade" (similar applications of aircraft to isolate enemy resupply operations such as at Stalingrad).[117]

The picture of the war in the East emerges, as two antagonists vying for air superiority but only to aid ultimately in a ground-oriented, combined arms operation. What matured for the *VVS* during the course of four, hard-fought years was teamwork with the Red Army. Together, air and ground power of the Soviet Union steamrollered over a steadily weakening Axis force fighting a multi-front war on land, sea, and in the air against a coalition of enemies.

Notes

1. A thorough discussion of the term "combined-arms" can be found in John Erickson's chapter, "Theory and Practice," in *Soviet Combined Arms*, College Station, Texas, Center for Strategic Technology, 1981, pp 1–26.

2. P. Avdeyenko, "*Sovetskoe Samoletstroenie v Gody Predvoennykh Pyatiletok (1929–40) gg.*" (Soviet Aircraft Construction in the Years of the Prewar Five-Year Plans, 1929–1940), *Voenno-Istoricheskiy Zhurnal*, Nr 7 (Jul 1974), p 86.

3. *Ibid*, pp 87–88.

4. John Erickson, *The Soviet High Command*, London, St. Martin's Press, 1962, pp 382–83.

5. *Ibid*, App III, pp 800-803 in which Erickson provides a translation of some excerpts from the *PU 36 (Vremennyy Polevoy Ustav RKKA 1936)*, Moscow, People's Commissariat of Defense, 1937.

6. *Polevoy Ustav Krasnoy Armii (proekt 1941 g)* [Field Regulations of the Red Army (draft 1941)], Moscow, Voenizdat', 1941, p 17 as cited in *Istoriya Velikoy Otechestvennoy Voyny Sovetskogo Soyuza 1941–1945* (The History of the Great Patriotic War 1941–1945), 6 Vols, Moscow, Voennoe Izdatel'stvo Ministerstva Oborony Soyuza SSR, 1960–65, Vol I, p 90. Will be referred to hereafter as *Ist. Velik. Otech. Voyn.*

7. *Boevoy Ustav Istrebitel'noy Aviatsii 1940 g.* as cited in *Ist. Velik. Otech. Voyn.*, Vol I, p 444.

8. Matthew Cooper, *The German Air Force: 1933–1945*, New York, Jane's, 1981, pp 59–60.

9. Mike Spick, *Fighter Pilot Tactics*, New York, Stein and Day, 1983, pp 43–44.

10. Erickson, *Soviet High Command*, pp 498–499.

11. *Ist. Velik. Otech. Voyn.*, Vol I, p 240.

12. Erickson, *Soviet High Command*, pp 532–537.

13. *Ibid*, pp 505–506.

14. Richard Ward and Christopher Shores, *Finnish Air Force, 1918–1968*, New York, Arco, 1969 (no pagination).

15. *Ibid*.

16. *The Memoirs of Marshal Mannerheim*, transl by Count Eric Lewenhaupt, London, Cassell, 1953, p 346.

17. Kutakhov, P., "Manevr' Silami Aviatsii" (Maneuvering Aviation Forces), *Voenno-istoricheskiy zhurnal*, Nr 8 (Aug 1972), p 11.

18. *Ist. Velik. Otech. Voyn.*, Vol I, pp 476–77; V. Gorbachev, "Primenenie Sovetskikh VVS v Nachal'nom Periode Velikoy Otechestvennoy Voyny," (Employment of the Soviet VVS in the initial period of the Great Patriotic War), *Voenno-istoricheskiy zhurnal*, Nr 11 (Nov 1983), p 31. Lt Gen Gorbachev also points out that the size of the regiment in that period (60 to 64 planes) made it necessary in some cases to occupy more than one airfield or to crowd them excessively on a single field.

19. P. Kutakhov, "*Manevr Silami Aviatsii*," p 12; the Soviet term *tyl* (literally "rear") covers all kinds of rear services and logistics.

20. *The Soviet Air Force in World War II*, ed by Ray Wagner and transl by L. Fetzer, New York, Doubleday, 1973, p 26; P. A. Roimistrov in his *Istoriya Voennogo Iskusstva* (A History of Military Art), 2 Vols, Moscow, *Voennoe Izdatel'stvo Ministerstva Oborony SSR*, 1963, Vol II, p 43, gives a total of 4,040 aircraft with the three main army groups, with the inclusion of the Rumanian contribution, plus the Finns with 900 aircraft for a grand total of 4,940 planes; Gorbachev, "Employment of the Soviet VVS in the Initial Period," p 25, gives a figure very close to Roimistrov's, viz. 4,980.

21. Raymond Garthoff, *Soviet Military Doctrine*, Glencoe, Ill, Free Press, 1953, p 563.

22. *Ist. Velik. Otech. Voyn.*, Vol I, p 476.

23. H. Plocher, *The German Air Force versus Russia, 1941*, (ed) Harry R. Fletcher, USAF Hist Div, ASI, Air University, Maxwell AFB, 1965, p 41.

24. *Ist. Velik. Otech. Voyn.*, Vol II, p 16; Erickson, *Soviet High Command*, p 593, estimates 2,000 Soviet aircraft destroyed in the first 48 hours.

25. Plocher, *German Air Force Versus Russia, 1941*, p 42.
26. Gorbachev, "Employment of Soviet *VVS* . . .," p 28.
27. Cooper, *The German Air Force*, p 224.
28. Up to Mar 1942, the Soviet long-range bombing force was called *Dal'nyaya Bombar-dirovochnaya Aviatsiya*, or *DBA*. From Mar 1942 until Dec 1944 it was named *Aviatsiya Dal'nego Deystviya*, or *ADD*, and for the rest of the war was called the Eighteenth Air Army. Under any of the above designations, the "long-range" was a relative term since the inventory had more medium- and short-range bombers than really long-range ones. See A. Tyskin, "Taktika Dal'ney Bombardirovshnoy Aviatsii v Letne-Osenney Kampanii (1941 goda)," [Tactics of Long-range Bombardment Aviation in the Summer and Fall Campaign (1941)], *Voenno-Istoricheskiy Zhurnal*, Nr 12 (Dec 1971), p 65.
29. V. Reshetnikov, "Primenenie Aviatsiya Dal'nego Deystviya," (Employment of Long-Range Aviation), *Voenno- Istoricheskiy Zhurnal*, Nr 2 (Feb 1978), p 36.
30. Roimistrov, *Istoriya Voennogo Iskusstva*, Vol II, p 49.
31. Cooper, *German Air Force*, pp 225-226.
32. John T. Greenwood, "The Great Patriotic War, 1941-1945," in Robin Higham and Jacob W. Kipp, eds, *Soviet Aviation and Air Power; A Historical View* (Boulder, 1977), 76-80.
33. R. Wagner, *The Soviet Air Force in World War II*, pp 78-79; this is an English transl of the Soviet official history of the Russo-German air war. The title in Russian: S. Rudenko, et al., *Sovietskie Voenno-Vozdushnye Sily v Velikoy Otechestvennoy Voinye 1941-1945*, Moscow, 1968
34. *Ibid*.
35. *Sovetskaya Voennaya Entskilopediya* (The Soviet Military Encyclopedia), Moscow, Voenizdat, 1976-1980, Vol 2, p 292. Will be referred to as *SVE* hereafter. See also M. Kozhevnikov, "Rozhdenie Vozdushnykh Armiy," (Birth of the Air Armies), *Voenno-Istoricheskiy Zhurnal*, Nr 9 (Sep 1972), pp 68-72 for details. A translation of this article by James Waddell can be found in *Aerospace Historian*, Jun 1975, pp 73-76.
36. Kutakhov, "Maneuvering Aviation Forces," p 12.
37. *Ibid*, pp 12-13.
38. Gen Col Avn V. Reshetnikov, "Is Opyta Boevykh Deystviy Dal'ney Aviatsii v Operatsiyakh Sukhoputnyukh Voysk," (From the Experience of Combat Activities of Long-Range Aviation in Ground Force Operations), *Voenno-Istoricheskiy Zhurnal*, Nr 7 (Jul 1984), pp 36-37.
39. *Ibid*, p 38.
40. *Ibid*.
41. Col N. Zavgorodniy, "Is Opyta Boevogo Primeneniya Istrebitel'noy Aviatsii po Nazemnym Tselyam v Gody Velikoi Otechennoy Voinye," (From Experience in the Combat Use of Fighter Aviation during the Great Patriotic War), *Voenno- Istoricheskiy Zhurnal*, Nr 12 (Dec 1983), p 18.
42. *SVE*, Vol 8, p 541; ShVAK stands for the designers: Shpital'nyy and Volkov and ShKAS for Shpital'nyy and Komarmitskiy.
43. *Ibid*; UBT stands for Berezin all-purpose turret machinegun.
44. *Ibid*, pp 541-542.
45. *Ibid*; Cooper, *German Air Force*, p 265, describes the Hs-129 as not having a strong enough fuselage to accommodate powerful engines, thus a maximum speed of only 253 mph and a radius of action of just 174 miles. The plane also had severe serviceability problems.
46. Zavgorodnyy, "Combat Use of Fighter Aviation," p 19.
47. Garthoff, *Soviet Military Doctrine*, p 333.
48. Alexander, *Russian Aircraft Since 1940*, pp 168-70.
49. Wagner (ed), *Soviet Air Force in World War II*, p 99.
50. *Ibid*, p 91.
51. The best account of the fierce struggle within the city is in Marshal V. I. Chuikov, *Nachalo Puti (The Beginning of the Road)*. Moscow, 1959. The English translation by Harold Silver is entitled *The Battle for Stalingrad*, New York: Holt, Rinehart, and Winston, 1964. Marshal A. I. Yeremenko, Chuikov's commander of the Stalingrad Front, describes the battle viewed from headquarters in *Stalingrad*, Moscow, 1961.

52. Alexander, *Russian Aircraft Since 1940*, pp 426–29; A. Novikov and M. Kozhevnikov, "Bor'ba za Strategicheskoe Gospodstvo v Vozdukhe," (The Struggle for Strategic Command of the Air), *Voenno-Istoricheskiy Zhurnal*, Nr 3 (Mar 1972), p 26.

53. *Soviet Air Force in World War II*, pp 103–4.

54. Novikov and Kozhevnikov, "Struggle for Strategic Command of the Air," p 26.

55. On German and Soviet uses of air power at Stalingrad, see, Greenwood, "Great Patriotic War, p 93; Cajus Bekker, *The Luftwaffe War Diaries* (transl by F. Ziegler), (London, 1964), pp 278, 283–285.

56. On losses, see *Ibid*, App 14, p 377; Murray, *Strategy for Defeat*, pp 89 and 114; Wagner (ed.), *Soviet Air Force in World War II*, pp 110, 146, and 114.

57. Novikov and Kozhevnikov, "Struggle for Strategic Command of the Air," p 28.

58. Bekker, *Luftwaffe* Diaries, p 294.

59. S. Rudenko, "Aviatsiya v kontrnastuplenniy" (Aviation in the Counterattack), *Voenno-Istoricheskiy Zhurnal*, Nr 11 (Nov 1972), p 48.

60. *Ibid*, p 51; also Greenwood, "Great Patriotic War, 107–108.

61. *Soviet Air Force in World War II*, pp 164–65; Novikov and Kozhevnikov, "Struggle for Strategic Command of the Air," p 29; Plocher, *German Air Force Versus Russia, 1943*, pp 75–83. Plocher gives 1,830 operational aircraft as the total used by the *Luftwaffe* in *Zitadelle*

62. *Soviet Air Force in World War II*, pp 185–86.

63. *Ibid*, pp 173–74.

64. "Struggle for Strategic Command of the Air," p 26. *The German Air Force Versus Russia, 1943*, p 105.

65. Schwabedissen, *The Russian Air Force in the Eyes of German Commanders*, p 168.

66. Greenwood, "Great Patriotic War," 107–111.

67. Alexander Boyd, *The Soviet Air Force Since 1918* (New York: Stein and Day, 1977) p 180; "The Great Patriotic War, 1941–1945," pp 118–119.

68. Alexander, *Russian Aircraft Since 1940*, pp 299–300 and 426–29.

69. *Ibid*, pp 430–33 and 172–73.

70. *Soviet Air Force in World War II*, p 361.

71. Greenwood, "The Great Patriotic War, 1941–19455," pp 118–119.

72. Oleg Hoeffding, *Soviet Interdiction Ops, 1941–1945*, RAND, R–556–PR 1970, p 5; Greenwood, "The Great Patriotic War," pp 130–1.

73. Greenwood, "The Great Patriotic War," p 130; Von Hardesty, *Red Phoenix; The Rise of Soviet Air Power, 1941–1945*, Washington: Smithsonian Institution Press, 1982, pp 169–76.

74. *Soviet Air Force in World War II*, p 383.

75. *Ibid*, p 384.

76. *Soviet Military Strategy* (Transl and ed by Dinnerstein, Goure, and Wolfe), Englewood Cliffs, New Jersey, Prentice-Hall, 1963, pp 258–60.

77. A. Silyant'yev, "Upravlenie aviatsiey v nastupatel'nykh deystviyakh voysk," (Command of Aviation in Offensive Ops of Troops), *Voenno-istoricheskiy zhurnal*, Nr 4 (Apr 1976), p 30.

78. *Ibid*, pp 32 and 34.

79. *Ibid*.

80. *Ibid*, p 33.

81. *Soviet Air Force in World War II*, p 185.

82. Schwabedissen, *Russian Air Force in the Eyes of the German Commanders*, pp 54–55.

83. *Soviet Air Force in World War II*, p 103.

84. *Ibid*, p 163; Schwabedissen, *Russian Air Force in the Eyes of German Commanders*, p 255.

85. *SVE*, Vol 2, p 164.

86. P Kutakhov, "Voenno-Vozdushnye Sily," (The Air Forces), *Voenno-Istoricheskiy Zhurnal*, Nr 10 (Oct 1977), p 41.

87. Lt Gen D. Klaus Uebe, *Russian Reactions to German Airpower in World War II*, USAF Hist Div, ASI, Maxwell AFB, 1964, pp 99–100.

88. R. J. Overy, *The Air War*, New York, Stein and Day, 1980, p 200.

89. Zavgorodniy, "Combat Use of Fighter Aviation," p 20.

90. *Ibid.*
91. *Ibid*, p 23.
92. *Ibid*, p 22.
93. *Ist. Velik. Otech. Voyn.*, Vol 6, p 210.
94. V. Babich, "Osnovnye Napravleniya Razvitiya Taktiki Frontovoy Bombardirovochnoy Aviatsii" (Basic Trends in the Development of Tactics of Frontal Bmbr Aviation), *Voenno-Istoricheskiy Zhurnal*, Nr 5 (May 1978), p 20.
95. *Ibid*, p 22.
96. M. Novikov, "Razvitiya tekniki bombarirovovochnoy aviatsii v gody voyny" (Development of Technical Equipment of Bomber Aviation during the War) *Voenno-Istoricheskiy Zhurnal*, Nr 4 (Apr 1978), pp 35–36.
97. *Ibid*, p 38.
98. *Ibid*, p 39.
99. *Ibid*, p 40.
100. *Ist. Velik. Otech. Voyn.*, Vol 6, p 210.
101. M. Kozhevnikov, "Vzaimodeystvie Voenno-Vozhdushnykh Sil s Sukhoputnymi Voyskami v Nastuplenii" (Coordination of Military Air Forces with Ground Forces in Offensives.), *Voenno-Istoricheskiy Zhurnal*, Nr 5 (May 1976), p 34.
102. *Ibid*, pp 34–36.
103. *Ibid*, pp 36–37.
104. L. Mikryukov, "Upravleniye Istrebitelyami v Vozdushnom Boyu" (Control of Fighters in Air Combat), *Voenno-Istoricheskiy Zhurnal*, Nr 9 (Sep 1977), pp 43–44.
105. *Ibid*, p 42.
106. *Ibid*, p 43.
107. Yu. Khramov, "Shtab Aviapolka pri Vedenii Boevykh Deystviy" (The Aviation Regimental Staff in Conducting Ops), *Morskoy Sbornik*, Nr 8 (Aug 1983), p 25.
108. *Ibid*, pp 21–22.
109. V. Longinov, "Tyl Voenno-Vozdushnykh Sil v Velikoy Otechestvennoy Voyny" (The Air Force Rear in the Great Patriotic War), *Voenno-Istoricheskiy Zhurnal*, Nr 5 (May 1973), p 27.
110. V. Filippov, "Sovershenstvovanie Inzhenernogo Obespecheniya Boevykh Deystviy Aviatsii, 1941–1945" (The Improvement of Engineering Maintenance in the Combat Ops of Aviation), *Voenno-istroicheskiy zhurnal*, Nr 1 (Jan 1975), p 24.
111. *Ibid*, p 25.
112. *Ibid*, p 26.
113. *Ibid*, p 27.
114. Longinov, "Air Force Rear in the Great Patriotic War," p 30.
115. *Ibid*, p 32.
116. Hardesty, *Red Phoenix,* chap 8.
117. *Ibid*, pp 223–223.

Bibliographical Essay

The Soviet use of aviation in World War II, like the German employment of the *Luftwaffe*, was in large part an extension of artillery, and once air superiority was attained by the *VVS* in late 1943, close air support became the main job of the Soviet Air Force. Soviet historians praise attack aviation, especially the role of the Il–2 *Shturmovik*, and see little that could have been gained by a more effective strategic component. As a consequence of that view of air warfare, Soviet literature is plentiful although somewhat biased.

German historians, many of them participants in the air war on the Eastern Front, are more prone to find rationalizations for the *Luftwaffe*'s defeat rather than to seek historical accuracy. The defeat is variously blamed on the Russian climate and terrain, Hitler's strategic peculiarities, partisan interference with logistics, and, above all, Hermann Goering's inadequacies as leader of the *Luftwaffe*. Soviet writers, on the contrary, suffer from a severe case of braggadocio; statistics of German losses are prominent in Soviet accounts and usually exaggerated, while their own are either ridiculously low or not even mentioned. The net result for the outsider is a never-never land of conflicting claims and assertions.

Bibliographies specifically devoted to the air war on the Eastern Front are scarce, and the researcher-writer has to make do with pertinent sections of works dealing with the *Luftwaffe* on all fronts or the *VVS*'s role as a relatively minor part of the Great Patriotic War. Michael Parrish's *The USSR in World War II: An Annotated Bibliography of Books Published in the Soviet Union, 1945–1975*, 2 vols. (New York: Garland Publishing, 1981); Myron J. Smith, Jr.'s *The Soviet Air and Strategic Rocket Forces, 1939–80: A Guide to Sources in English* (Santa Barbara, Calif.: ABC–Clio, 1981); the extensive bibliography in Von Hardesty's *Red Phoenix: The Rise of Soviet Air Power, 1941–1945* (Washington, D.C.: Smithsonian Institution Press, 1982); and the excellent bibliography of works available on the *Luftwaffe* in World War II to be found in Williamson Murray's *Strategy for Defeat: The Luftwaffe 1933–1945* (Washington, D.C.: USGPO, 1982), are some of the more valuable bibliographical sources.

Thanks to a project conceived and developed by the Air Force Historical Division at Air University, the German side of the conflict is copiously, if not entirely satisfactorily, covered in a series of monographs written by senior German officers who had participated in the war. This project, which got under way in 1953, enlisted the aid of many *Luftwaffe* generals and some historians who were able to refresh their memories (and, one hopes, check them) through the use of a collection of *Luftwaffe* documents known as the Karlsruhe Document Collection. Some of the outstanding products of the project were General Paul Deichman's *German Air Force Operations in support of the*

Army, General Hermann Plocher's three volumes entitled *The German Air Force versus Russia*, General Walter Schwabediessen's *The Russian Air Force in the Eyes of German Commanders*, General Klaus Uebe's *Russian Reaction to German Airpower in World War II*, and Richard Suchenwirth's *Historical Turning Points in the German Air Force War Effort*. All of these were published by the USAF Historical Division, Research Studies Institute, Air University, in the 1950s and early 1960s.

There are also a few eye-witness accounts written by German pilots, including fighter-pilot Adolf Galland's *The First and Last* (New York: Ballantine, 1957); Hans Rudel's *Stuka Pilot* (New York: Ballantine, 1958); and bomber pilot Werner Baumbach's *Broken Swastika: The Defeat of the Luftwaffe* (London: Robert Hale, 1960). Altogether, these sources give the reader some insight into the details of *Luftwaffe* operations but have only a "tunnel-vision" of the war as a whole. All in all, spotty as the German accounts may be, there are enough solid works to help counterbalance the unbridled Soviet outpouring of histories, memoirs, and analyses; a veritable deluge of literature concerning the Soviet Air Force in World War II.

In spite of that "deluge" there are still practically no original sources open to Westerners. Foreign scholars, therefore, have to do the best they can with secondary works (histories and memoirs), many of which are studded with references to archival materials, but impossible to check for accuracy and context. Fortunately for those stubborn enough to try to get a fairly accurate picture of the Soviet performance in the air war, the war has become "big business" in the USSR. Every anniversary of an important battle, and some not so important, elicit a torrent of speeches, articles, and books depicting the event, usually with an admixture of patriotic exhortations. Of course, the Soviet military historian must tailor his recitation to conform with whatever political line is in the ascendancy, but this is not surprising since custom-made history has been *de rigeur* ever since Stalin achieved political control in the 1930s. Nevertheless, much of the material may be good history. Descriptions of the *VVS*'s activities in the war are less likely to run athwart the censor than such larger questions as Stalin's role as supreme commander.

In lieu of access to documentary collections, major sources include the official histories of the Second World War. The *Istoriya Velikoy Otechestvennoy Voyny Sovetskogo Soyuza, 1941–1945 gg* (History of the Great Patriotic War of the Soviet Union), a six-volume work edited by a staff headed by P. N. Pospelov, is rich in detail, but the *VVS* gets rather sparse coverage. This work has been dwarfed recently by the *Istoriya Vtoroy Mirovoy Voyny, 1939–1945 gg* (History of the Second World War), a twelve-volume history published between 1973 and 1982. It was a joint effort of several institutes under the direction of an editorial commission headed first by Marshal of the Soviet Union and Minister of Defense A. A. Grechko and upon his death, by Marshal of the Soviet Union and Minister of Defense D.F. Ustinov. The official history of the air war, *Sovetskie Voenno–Vozdushnye Sily v Velikoy Otechest-vennoy Voyne, 1941–1945 gg* (The Soviet Air Forces in the Great Patriotic War) (Moscow: Voyenizdat, 1968), is an especially blatant, one-sided version and a relatively useless, self-serving publication. It has been translated by Leland Fetzer and edited by Ray Wagner under the title of *The Soviet Air Force in World War II* (New York: Doubleday, 1973).

The best source for studying the Soviet activities in World War II, including the air war, are articles in periodical literature, especially those in the *Voenno–Istoricheskiy Zhurnal* (Military Historical Journal), one of the Ministry of Defense's more prestigious journals. The articles in this journal cover a wide spectrum, from detailed descriptions of specific actions to broad analyses of extensive periods of the war. Since it has been published continuously since January 1959, nearly every senior commander who survived the conflict, and some not so senior, have published their perceptions of some aspect of the struggle. John Erickson, *The Road to Berlin* (Boulder Colo.: Westview Press, 1983) lists all the articles devoted to World War II on pp. 816–22, in his superlative bibliography. Fugitive pieces pertaining to the fortunes of the *VVS* in World War II occur in a number of other military journals. For example, there are the Air Force's own journals, *Aviatsiya i Kosmonavtika* (Aviation and Astronautics), *Kryl'ya Rodina* (Wings of the Motherland), *Morskoy Sbornik* (Naval collection), *Kommunist Vooruzhennykh Sil* (Communist of the Armed Forces), and *Voprosy Istorii* (Problems of History), as well as some interesting sketches and articles in the Ministry of Defense's daily newspaper, *Krasnaya Zvezda* (Red Star). A judicious reading of this voluminous output in periodicals and newspapers is probably the best way to acquire an approximate picture of the Great Patriotic War and the *VVS*'s role in it.

Some major Soviet books dealing with the Great Patriotic War have been translated into English. Among these are the *Memoirs of Marshal Zhukov* (New York: Delacorte Press, 1971); V.I. Chuikov, *The Battle for Stalingrad* and his *The Fall of Berlin* (New York: Holt, Rinehart, and Winston, 1968), S. M. Shtemenko, *The Soviet General Staff at War, 1941–1945* (Moscow: Progress Publishers, 1975) and his *The Last Six Months* (New York: Doubleday, 1977). There is, however, a paucity of information about aviation's role in these books—the authors seem to have kept their eyes firmly on the ground. Aleksandr S. Yakovlev, designer of the famous Yak fighters and also the Deputy Minister of the Aviation Industry during the war, has written rather extensively about both planes and his part in the arcane activities in the Kremlin in his *The Aim of a Lifetime* (Moscow: Progress Publishers, 1972), and *Fifty Years of Soviet Aircraft Construction* (Washington, D.C.: NASA, 1970). A good sampling of memoir literature apropos the war can be found in Seweryn Bialer (ed.), *Stalin and His Generals* (New York: Pegasus, 1969) and an overall analysis of the conflict in V. D. Sokolvsky (ed.), *Soviet Military*

Strategy (New York: Crane, Russak, 1975) on pp. 136–166 in the third edition edited by Harriet Scott.

Finally, mention should be made of books written by American and British air historians of the *VVS*'s role in World War II. Surprisingly enough there are relatively few good ones, especially in view of the voluminous output devoted to air combat in the ETO, North African, and Pacific theaters. Probably the definitive work in English on the Great Patriotic War is John Erickson's two volumes: *The Road to Stalingrad* (New York: Harper & Row, 1975) and *The Road to Berlin* (Boulder, Colo.: Westview Press, 1983). Alexander Boyd's *The Soviet Air Force Since 1918* (New York: Stein and Day, 1977), which, in spite of its title, concentrates largely on World War II. Von Hardesty, *Red Phoenix* (Washington, D.C.: Smithsonian Institution Press, 1982) is devoted to World War II and has a very extensive bibliography. John T. Greenwood's chapter entitled "The Great Patriotic War, 1941–1945," in Robin Higham and Jacob Kipp (eds.), *Soviet Aviation and Air Power* (Boulder, Colo.: Westview Press, 1977) is a good summary of the air war over Russia. Raymond Garthoff, *Soviet Military Doctrine* (Glencoe, Ill.: Free Press, 1953) has stood the test of time and is still one of the best analyses of how Russia fought the war, while R.J. Overy, *The Air War, 1939–1945* (New York: Stein and Day, 1981) has some very perceptive observations about the air war in general and the Soviet participation in particular.

Lest we forget that essential ingredient of air warfare, the aircraft, let us note a few of the better works. Jean Alexander, *Russian Aircraft Since 1940* (London: Putnam, 1975); Henry Nowarra and G. Duval, *Russian Civil and Military Aircraft, 1884–1969* (London: Mountain Press, 1971); and William Green and Gordon Swanborough, *Soviet Air Force Fighters*, 2 parts (New York: Arco, 1978). The Soviet journal *Aviatsiya i Kosmonavtika* has over the years published numerous articles about both the Soviet aircraft in the war as well as information on the designers of both aircraft and engines.

4

The Tunisian Campaign, 1942-43

David Syrett

On November 8, 1942, American and British forces landed in French Northwest Africa and quickly seized Algeria and Morocco from the Vichy French government. By the narrowest of margins, the Allies failed to capture Tunisia before it was occupied by Axis forces. This led to a protracted campaign to clear all of North Africa of the enemy and provided the first major testing ground of American air and land power against German and Italian forces in World War II. Eventually, the Allies achieved victory in Tunisia, in part because American, British, and Free French forces combined operations with minimal inter-Allied and interservice friction. Solutions for problems of command and control, logistics, and doctrine worked out during the Tunisian campaign proved useful in later Allied campaigns in Sicily, Italy, Northwest Europe, and Southern France. This was especially true for the employment of tactical aircraft in close air support as well as in other forms of air support for ground operations, including land and maritime interdiction. The principles of command, control, and doctrine for close air support learned in Tunisia became a part of United States Army Air Forces (AAF) field regulations for wartime operations.

Background—The American Experience

In the years before the United States entered World War II, the major mission of the Army Air Corps (AAC) was the support of ground forces. However, in the 1930s, while officially paying lip-service to ground support operations, the AAC became preoccupied with strategic bombardment. This strategy called for long-range bomber aircraft to attack and destroy an enemy's capability to wage war by attacking industrial targets, deep within enemy homeland. The virtually simultaneous development of aircraft (XB–15, and XB–17) and of an organization to implement the doctrine for strategic bombardment (GHQ Air Force) in 1935 pointed toward a role for air power less closely tied to conventional ground support tasks. In 1937, GHQ

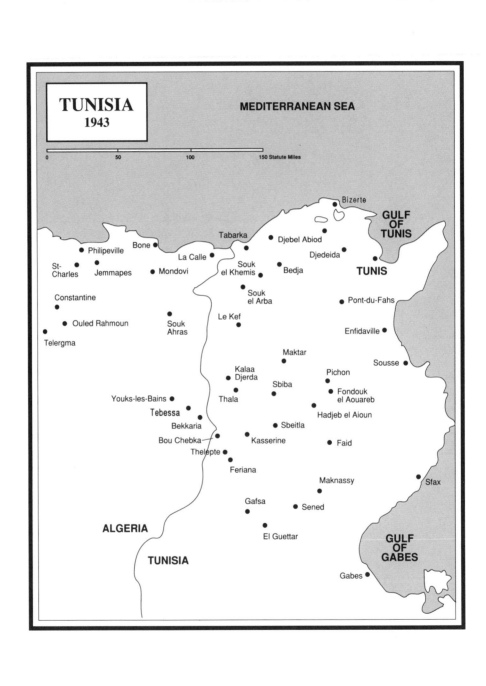

Air Force received its first B–17. By 1941, United States was committed to strategic bombardment, as both the B–17 and another workhorse long-range bomber, the B–24, entered large-scale production. An even more powerful bomber, the B–29, would soon undergo testing. No other nation entered World War II with the range, defensive firepower, and armored protection of these aircraft, thereby underscoring U.S. commitment to a strategy of heavy bombardment by the AAC and its successor, the AAF, established on June 20, 1941.[1]

Given the emphasis on strategic bombardment by the AAC before the war, it is hardly surprising that the methods and techniques for conducting more traditional missions, such as close air support of ground forces, remained undeveloped before American entry into the conflict in 1941. The plan for conducting the air war, drawn up at the end of the summer of 1941, was called AWPD–1. This scheme emphasized strategic bombardment of the German homeland as the way to achieve victory. The main objective of American air power, according to AWPD–1, would be to launch mass attacks on German industry with the goal of destroying key portions of Germany's war economy. There was also an "intermediate objective" of defeating the German air force as a prerequisite for the large-scale attacks.[2]

No subject produces more disagreement between soldiers and aviators than the employment of tactical aircraft in close air support. The basis for this continuing controversy is that the aviator and the soldier view warfare on the battlefield and in the skies differently. Most soldiers in 1941, as today, thought that some aircraft should be controlled by ground force commanders, to be used to protect their units from enemy air attack by maintaining patrols over the battlefield, and to attack ground targets immediately in front of ground units. Ground force commanders viewed tactical problems as those requiring immediate solutions, and they were not particularly interested in the longer term effects of interdiction or strategic bombardment. By comparison, the airman viewed the ground battle more expansively and considered the battlefield to be any place within range of his aircraft. The best—if not the only—way to defend against enemy air attack was to secure air superiority by destroying the enemy's air force. Then support of ground operations could be more properly rendered by attacking an enemy's tactical and strategic rear, including communications, transportation, and logistical facilities as well as home front industries. Aviators considered flying defensive patrols over ground forces and parceling out small groups of aircraft to attack lesser targets in enemy front-line positions a misuse of air power and a waste of heavy striking power.

Recognizing that such different views of the battlefield and the role of air power were held by air and ground officers is a prerequisite to understanding the doctrinal disagreements over the use of tactical air power.

In 1942, both the AAF and Royal Air Force (RAF) asssigned top priority to strategic bombardment of Germany. Army manuals like FM 1–10, "Tactics and Technique of Air Attack," and FM 1–5, Tactics and Technique of Air Fighting, reflected aviator preference for the strategic mission. On April 9, 1942, however, the War Department published FM 31–35, "Aviation in Support of Ground Forces," largely in response to what seemed to be lessons from the first two years of the war in Europe, prior to American involvement. This manual set forth the doctrine employed by the AAF in support of ground units at the beginning of the fighting in Northwest Africa. Targets to be attacked from the air were to be selected by ground force commanders, but other features of the manual reflected AAF doctrine. For example, neither dive-bombing nor employment of fighter-bombers formed part of American doctrine.[3]

Because both American air and ground commanders knew that air superiority over the battlefield was essential, AAF organization called for all fighter or pursuit aircraft to be assigned to an Interceptor Command in an air force, such as the Twelfth Air Force, which would be deployed in Northwest Africa. The War Department formed special organizations, the air support commands, to handle the function of air support for ground forces.[4] Various types of aircraft units were assigned to the air support commands to carry out interdiction, air defense, and observation, as well as close-in strafing and bombing missions. By November 1942, fighter and light-bomber groups were assigned to the XII Air Support Command for support of the invasion of Northwest Africa.[5]

According to FM 31–35, Army requests for air support were to be transmitted via the ground forces' chain of command until they reached headquarters, which contained an "air support party." Such parties were usually attached to a divisional headquarters, commanded by an Army Air Forces "air support officer," and consisted of men and equipment necessary for maintaining communications with a higher air support level, usually a corps. The air support party officer would advise the division commander and forward "only such air support requests as have been approved by the commander." Approved requests would be retransmitted by air force radio to the next echelon, usually the corps level, to another AAF communications unit, the "Air Support Control."

These "Air Support Control" units were located at the corps headquarters. The AAF officer in charge of "Air Support Control" evaluated the air support party request and consulted with the corps commander as to the practicability and the execution of the mission. Whether or not an air support mission would be ordered still rested with the corps commander. When a decision was reached, the requesting ground unit was notified through the air support party. An "attack order" was then issued by the air support control to a bomber unit, which ordered the mission.

Meanwhile, at the higher field army level, an air support command, situated next to the army commander, would listen in on the radio or wire net to provide centralized guidance. Under this system of command and control, the ground force commander, at division, corps, or army level, almost totally controlled supporting aircraft. Not surprisingly, this procedure was anathema to air officers who thought it to be based on faulty doctrine.[6]

Actually, the actions of the AAC before the invasion of Northwest Africa provide a much clearer view of the situation than do the field manuals. In virtually all the joint air-ground maneuvers during 1940, the AAC seemed incapable of undertaking ground support missions assigned to it. This weakness resulted from the AAC's commitment to strategic bombardment, its rapid expansion, and a shortage of aircraft. However, during the large maneuvers held the following year in the Carolinas, Tennessee, and Arkansas–Louisiana, the AAF, the U.S. Navy, and the U.S. Marine Corps deployed a large number of aircraft for ground support. The conflict in Europe ultimately suggested a pivotal role for air support for ground forces in modern warfare.

By ground force standards, however, most of the missions undertaken during the maneuvers had little to do with close air support. Rather, they comprised interdiction operations, or traditional reconnaissance and observation. By the end of 1941, it had become clear that the AAF conducted operations according to its own concept of air power, without regard for the needs of ground forces. Basically, it remained AAF doctrine not to attack targets within the range of friendly artillery.[7] As a result, at the beginning of the campaign in Northwest Africa, a large number of U.S. Army ground officers believed that the AAF lacked the will, the ability, and the means to conduct a sustained campaign employing aircraft in close support of land units.[8]

The rapid assembly of the U.S. Twelfth Air Force for the invasion of Northwest Africa (Operation Torch) affected the composition of the air support to be provided ground operations in that campaign. The decision to invade Northwest Africa was made on June 30, 1942.[9] The Twelfth Air Force was activated at Bolling Field, Washington, D.C., sent to Great Britain on September 12, and assigned as part of the Allied invasion forces which would land on November 8. Most of the air units had never trained or operated together as a unified force before being sent overseas. In most cases, the air and ground support units came directly from the United States or from the Eighth Air Force in Great Britain. They arrived in no particular order, but rather in bits and pieces.[10] Furthermore, because of the pace of the buildup, little thought beyond what was contained in the manuals, could be given to doctrinal problems of aircraft supporting ground forces.

Background—The RAF Experience

Experiences of the British Royal Air Force (RAF) were different from those of the AAF. American ground commanders had the power to control air units deployed in support of ground forces. The RAF was an independent service, and with the exception of the Fleet Air Arm[11] and aircraft used by the Royal Artillery,[12] the RAF controlled all aviation in the British armed forces. After Dunkirk, the RAF in the United Kingdom had, according to its own thinking, three major missions. One was to protect the home island from air attack, using the Fighter Command. The second was to mount a strategic bombardment offensive against Germany with the Bomber Command. The third mission, with as little expenditure of men and aircraft as possible, required Coastal Command to support the Royal Navy in the Battle of the Atlantic. After the disasters of 1940, most of the ranking officers of the RAF looked upon the British Army in the United Kingdom as a force to defend against invasion and to move into Europe as an occupation force after the Bomber Command had won the war by strategic bombardment. RAF commanders thought that the Army would be incapable of mounting major offensive operations in Northwest Europe.[13] The RAF did establish the Army Cooperation Command in the British Isles, but almost as an afterthought. Army Cooperation Command was an unwanted stepchild of the RAF, and at times had more staff officers than aircraft. The few aircraft assigned to this activity were constantly shuffled to conduct operations, such as antishipping missions in the English Channel.[14] Thus, because of a lack of proper types of aircraft and, more important, the RAF's concept of how the war should be fought, virtually no training or planning was devoted to joint air–ground operations from 1940 to 1942.

The British Army thought that it had been "let down" by the RAF, since it had fought with inadequate air cover in Norway, the Low Countries, France, Greece, Crete, East Africa, the Eastern Mediterranean, Malaya, and Burma. No Army officer was more bitter about the lack of air support than General Sir Alan Brooke.[15] It was he who had commanded in the withdrawal from Dunkirk, reconstituted the shattered British Expeditionary Force, and for most of the war served as Chief of the Imperial General Staff. Brooke maintained that during the Dunkirk operation he had never seen a British aircraft, and he and other ground officers believed that the Army should have aircraft placed under the local ground force commander to operate in direct support of the Army and to protect it from enemy air attack.

Until the end of 1941, the RAF could, and generally did, ignore the Army. But with the threat of invasion of Great Britain gone, and the refusal of the Germans to respond to the fighter sweeps over northern France and the Low Countries, RAF Fighter Command became a force without a mission.[16]

In an attempt to regain a meaningful role, it began to take interest in fighter-bombers and ground attack operations. The entry of the United States into the war, and shifts in grand strategy that envisioned a return to the continent of Europe, forced the RAF to consider how it would support such land operations.[17]

The British Army and RAF in England failed to agree on what form such support might take. Brooke, however, wanted to enlarge the Army Cooperation Command, subordinating it to the ground forces commander, while the Air Staff sought to use Fighter Command units for support of ground operations.[18] The whole question of air support for the Army dragged on for months, and nothing was resolved, simply because the airmen and soldiers could not agree. Finally, on October 5, 1942, just days before the invasion of Northwest Africa, Prime Minister Winston S. Churchill forced a settlement by decreeing that air support for ground forces "should be organized on the Libyan model [the Western Desert Air Force experience], which was admitted on all sides to be extremely effective."[19] Western Desert doctrine called for as many fighter-bomber and light-bombardment aircraft as possible to undertake mass air strikes on ground targets of the greatest tactical and strategic importance.

Actually, the years between Dunkirk and the Tunisian campaign had not been completely wasted. Despite disagreement between the RAF and the British Army, the aviators and the Royal Artillery had negotiated problems and procedures for using aircraft as artillery spotters. In fact, Royal Artillery officers flew aircraft to direct fire for the British First Army as early as the Tunisian campaign.[20] Then, too, a number of Army and RAF staff officers in England worked out procedures for aircraft employed in close air support operations. Regrettably, due to poor communications between staff and field units in Great Britain and between the Western Desert Air Force and Air Ministry, RAF units in the United Kingdom had little or no knowledge of the evolving methods. The result was that RAF sent units to Tunisia supposedly versed in Western Desert Air Force doctrine, but nobody really understood how that doctrine worked. Thus both the RAF and the AAF participated in the invasion of Northwest Africa with little knowledge of Churchill's decreed procedures for providing close support to ground forces in battle.[21]

In many respects, the lack of knowledge of proper doctrine and techniques for close air support was surprising. The British, for example, had been repeatedly defeated by enemy land forces closely supported by tactical aircraft. American observers furthermore, followed these campaigns very closely and understood to some extent the role of tactical aircraft in Axis operations. In addition to the nascent planning for close air support in Great Britain,[22] the British Eighth Army and the Western Desert Air Force displayed an extremely effective system for such support during the Battle of

Alam el Halfa (August 19–September 6, 1942), in which massed airborne firepower stopped an Axis ground attack dead in its tracks.[23] There were also units of the AAF serving in the Western Desert Air Force.[24] It remains unclear, therefore, why both the American and the British forces in Northwest Africa had so little understanding of close air support and its utility for ground forces. The only apparent causes were the basic naiveté and overconfidence of an expedition untested by battle and the failure to transfer close air support concepts between theaters of operation.

Only the harsh realities of combat against Axis forces would cause the Allies in Tunisia to acknowledge that neither the AAF's Twelfth Air Force nor RAF's Eastern Air Command understood the proper role of aircraft in direct support of ground forces. Not only would they have to change doctrine, but they would also have to reassess methods of command and control of aircraft used by both Allied air forces. These changes would take place because the men who had learned the hard way in the Western Desert—by trial and error—would insist upon them. Above all, victory in Tunisia would demand them.

These American P-40D Warhawks were redubbed Kittyhawks by the British, who used them in close support of ground forces in North Africa.

Initial Lessons in North Africa

The first objective of the Allied Air Forces in Northwest Africa was to gain air superiority over Tunisia and the Central Mediterranean. Just after the Allies had landed in Northwest Africa, however, Axis forces entered Tunisia and, facing no opposition from the Vichy French administration, quickly developed all-weather airfields and the supporting ground organization required by a modern air force. Thus the Axis powers were "in the remarkable position of fighting on an equality, if not actually possessing tactical air superiority, since Allied ground organization was faced by immeasurably greater problems, which were only gradually overcome."[25] The lack of Allied allweather airfields within operational range of eastern Tunisia permitted the enemy to have *de facto* aerial superiority over all of Tunisia.

Allied knowledge of conditions in Tunisia was remarkably poor. The region was mountainous, the roads were poor, and only one "inefficient" railroad moved supplies eastward from Algiers. Rain and mud confronted the Allies, and even Lt. Gen. K.A.N. Anderson, commanding the British First Army, had thought of North Africa as a "dry country." Although he was aware that winter was the wet season, he soon discovered that "rains began in early December and continued until early April," with March as the wettest month. He concluded after the war that rain, mist, and "a peculiar glutinous mud" formed the backdrop for all operations during the period.[26] During the winter of 1942–43, Allied airfields in western Tunisia were "liable to become unserviceable at very short notice after heavy rain."[27] Obviously, without all-weather airfields, Allied aircraft could not provide dependable close air support and could not successfully challenge the Axis air forces operating from the Tunisian coastal plain for air superiority.

When the Allies landed in Northwest Africa, they captured only five all-weather airfields. By the end of the campaign in Tunisia, however, 9,000 AAF aviation engineers had constructed more than 100 additional airstrips. With the arrival of heavy construction equipment for the aviation engineers at the beginning of March 1943, the Americans began to construct airfields with increased skill and speed. Then too, the Allied command issued a realistic set of specifications for airfield construction. In forward areas, they would comprise one runway with loop taxiways and dispersed hardstands. There would be no buildings, while munitions as well as fuel dumps would be located just off the existing roads. Simple accommodations and the extensive use of heavy construction machinery, nevertheless, enabled AAF aviation engineers to construct all the airfields required to support the rapid movement of Allied forces in the final months of the campaign.[28]

The lack of all-weather airfields was just one of the logistical and administrative problems confronting the Allies at the beginning of the Tunisian campaign. At the American airfield at Thelepte, for example, there were no spare parts to repair aircraft, and they could only be obtained from wrecks. Strips cut out of British gasoline cans served to patch up holes in aircraft because no aluminum could be found. Propeller blades were interchanged between aircraft. Hand pumps had to be used to fuel aircraft from makeshift tanks mounted on trucks.[29] Before the Allied air forces could properly undertake close air support for ground units, the logistical apparatus necessary for supporting such operations had to be moved into eastern Tunisia and western Algeria.

Command and control presented one of the most troublesome problems in the North African campaign. Lt. Gen. Dwight D. Eisenhower, Supreme Allied Commander for the Torch operation, knew by the end of November 1942 that the air forces were not effective. He realized that the rush to get to Tunisia had resulted in a waste of equipment, especially aircraft, since it had been impossible to defend bases and lines of communication. Furthermore, he realized that little coordination existed between Maj. Gen. James H. Doolittle, commander of Twelfth Air Force, and Air Marshal Sir William Welsh, commander of Eastern Air Command, and that neither officer had an overall picture of what was happening.[30] The chain of command between British and American forces was awkward.

For the November 8, 1942, invasion, Eisenhower had direct command over the British in Anderson's Eastern Task Force; the Americans in Maj. Gen. Lloyd Fredendall's Central Task Force; and the Americans in Maj. Gen. George S. Patton, Jr.'s Western Task Force. The American ground commanders had direct control over their air resources. Patton had the XII Air Support Command, and Fredendall had portions of the XII Bomber Command and XII Fighter Command. On the other hand, Air Marshal Welsh controlled the air resources supporting Anderson's Eastern Task Force, while Doolittle at Twelfth Air Force had advisory or indirect control over the air forces supporting Fredendall and Patton. More important was the fact that Doolittle and Welsh did not communicate with each other, then or later, as forces reformed for the push eastward into Tunisia.

Other than landing supplies, bringing in paratroops, and gaining air superiority over the small French Air Force, Allied air forces did not play a significant role in the short campaign against the French in Northwest Africa. As Eisenhower turned eastward, however, Welsh's Eastern Air Command was asked to provide close air support for Anderson's First Army drive against the Axis buildup in Tunisia, while Doolittle reorganized the Twelfth Air Force to conduct interdiction strikes and to provide close support to the Fifth Army, formed in Morocco to protect lines of communication against potential Spanish involvement.

As Anderson's drive stalled, the use of American air and ground forces increased. Through November and December, Doolittle's C–47 transports

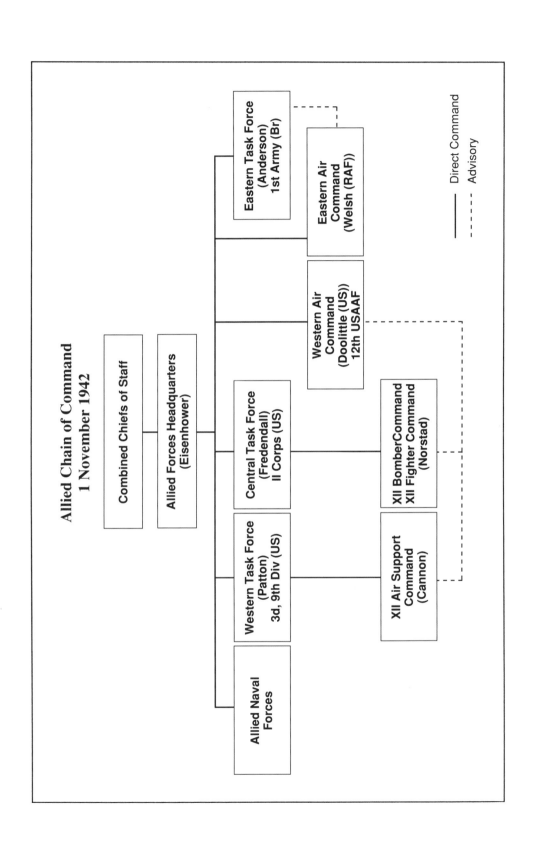

**Allied Chain of Command
1 November 1942**

Combined Chiefs of Staff

Allied Forces Headquarters
(Eisenhower)

Allied Naval Forces

Western Task Force
(Patton)
3d, 9th Div (US)

Central Task Force
(Fredendall)
II Corps (US)

Western Air Command
(Doolittle (US))
12th USAAF

Eastern Task Force
(Anderson)
1st Army (Br)

Eastern Air Command
(Welsh (RAF))

XII Air Support Command
(Cannon)

XII BomberCommand
XII Fighter Command
(Norstad)

——— Direct Command
- - - - - Advisory

ferried supplies to forward air bases, and P–38 fighters flew strafing missions against enemy columns.

British air units generally responded to the demands of Anderson's subordinate ground commanders. But in one celebrated case, British airmen pointed to mismanagement of air resources under the ground command. On December 4, a ground commander demanded that a light-bomber squadron attack an Axis landing field. Under protest from the British airmen, who said the aircraft could not protect themselves in daylight, ten light Bisley bombers went on the mission—none returned.

Even by the first of December, it was clear that the campaign failed partially because of poor organization and poor coordination of resources. Anderson also placed some of the blame on enemy air action, and his ground commanders complained that they were not receiving RAF protection from air attack nor close air support for bombing and strafing of the forces in front of them. The Allies obviously failed to win the necessary air superiority, but the ground commanders did not appreciate the large effort given to the bombing and strafing of enemy forces behind the lines.

Doolittle, among others, saw the need for a new organizational arrangement and suggested that all air resources be placed under an air force commander. Air Chief Marshal Sir Arthur Tedder, Air Officer Commander in Chief, Middle East, visiting Eisenhower's command in Northwest Africa, also suggested centralizing air resources. He told Eisenhower on November 27 that virtually no communication existed between the various Allied commands, and, in fact, the main means for communicating came from "the archaic French telephone system." Since Doolittle had a separate headquarters in Algiers and since the RAF's Eastern Air Command headquarters lay outside the city, Tedder thought that the Commander of the Twelfth Air Force was running his own private air war. Tedder further told Air Chief Marshal Sir Charles Portal, Chief of the Air Staff in London, that he "was frankly concerned at the situation" in Algiers. He cited a lack of drive among the air commanders as well as the faulty communications and recommended that the whole Allied command structure for air operations in the Mediterranean should be overhauled.[31] Tedder was an aviator who spoke with authority, for he commanded an air force that had defeated Axis air forces in the Western Desert, and he had helped organize an effective joint service team.

Following a series of communiques between London, Washington, and North Africa about the need for centralized control of air resources, Eisenhower appointed Maj. Gen. Carl A. Spaatz to command all-Allied air force in Algeria and Tunisia, effective January 5, 1943. Though Eisenhower hoped that Spaatz could better apportion the limited air resources for the campaign, the centralization of air forces suggested that close air support and other air missions would be defined more from the air than from the ground point of view.[32] Despite British opposition to a man of relatively little experience in

Maj. Gen. Carl Spaatz and Air Vice Marshal Arthur W. Tedder in conversation during the Casablanca Conference, January 1943.

senior command, they too agreed that "any system of unified Air Command of Torch cannot fail to be better than the present chaos" and agreed that Eisenhower should be free to choose his own subordinates.[33] The chaos resulted from confusion in command and control, lack of all-weather airfields, and the penny-parceling of air units for ground support at the whim of ground commanders. Moreover, there was no concerted drive to establish air superiority. Actually, the command and control problem would not be resolved fully until the Combined Chiefs of Staff conference at Casablanca in January and the establishment of the Northwest African Air Forces the following month.[34]

In late 1942, a number of Allied ground and air force commanders thought that Allied air forces in Tunisia did not have the correct close air support doctrine. On December 8, 1942, for example, Brig. Gen. Paul Robinett, of Combat Command B, First U.S. Armored Division, wrote to the U.S. Army's Chief of Staff, Gen. George C. Marshall, describing a "perfect" German combined-arms attack on a British position in Tunisia. He claimed that the Allies had not been able to achieve the same degree of air-ground coordination, noting "there are many gadgets and liaison setups here to achieve it, but they have not worked." Robinett then stated that he was sure that "men cannot stand the mental and physical strain of constant aerial bombing without feeling that all possible is being done to beat back the enemy air effect." What was needed were not reports or photographs of ships being sunk, ports being smashed, or cities being bombed to ashes, but seeing Allied aircraft over their front-line positions and attacking targets in the path of Allied oper-

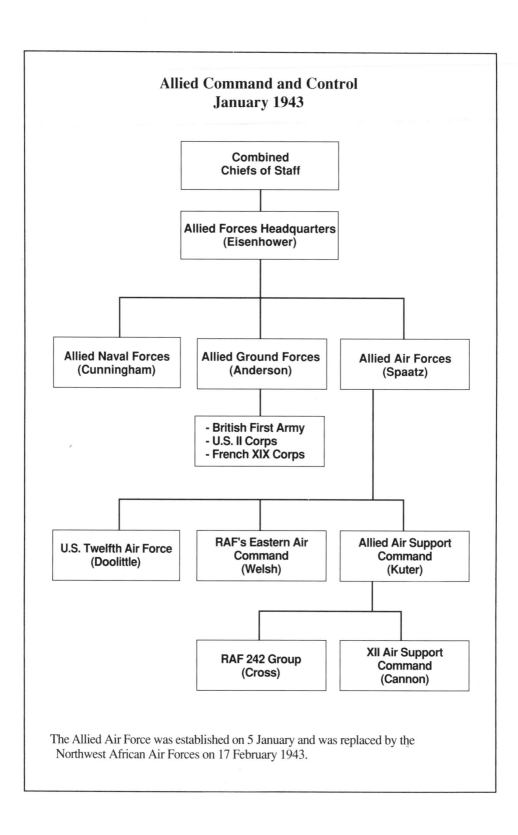

Allied Command and Control
January 1943

Combined Chiefs of Staff

Allied Forces Headquarters (Eisenhower)

Allied Naval Forces (Cunningham)

Allied Ground Forces (Anderson)

Allied Air Forces (Spaatz)

- British First Army
- U.S. II Corps
- French XIX Corps

U.S. Twelfth Air Force (Doolittle)

RAF's Eastern Air Command (Welsh)

Allied Air Support Command (Kuter)

RAF 242 Group (Cross)

XII Air Support Command (Cannon)

The Allied Air Force was established on 5 January and was replaced by the Northwest African Air Forces on 17 February 1943.

ations.[35] Robinett simply stated the position held by most Allied ground force commanders in Tunisia at this time. To them, the only way to achieve such results was by placing aircraft under ground force command.

Most Allied air force leaders saw the problem somewhat differently, even though the XII Air Support Command on January 9 consisted of only two understrength squadrons of the 33d Fighter Group and the 47th Light Bombardment Group. Furthermore during most of January the XII Air Support Command "remained relatively inactive," according to one RAF staff study. Tedder felt that aircraft "have been frittered away in penny packets" by "attacking targets all on the orders of local Army Commanders."[36] Doolittle perhaps suggested on Christmas Day 1942 the most radical position held by any Allied aviator. He wanted to "abandon our present 100 percent bitched-up organization, stop trying to win the Tunisian War in a day" and to place all Allied ground forces and the Eastern Air Command on the defensive. He would have given the bulk of the logistical support to the Twelfth Air Force, which was the only force, in Doolittle's view, "that can win the Tunisian War." After the Twelfth Air Force bombed the Axis forces into a state of demoralization, the ground forces could mop up what was left of the enemy. Doolittle obviously overstated his case. He did however, express the general frustration of aviators in northwest Africa over what they considered to be the misuse of air power.[37]

Spaatz then attempted to solve problems of close air support in early 1943. He removed a number of aircraft from the Twelfth Air Force's XII Fighter and Bomber Commands and placed them in the XII Air Support Command, whose function was to provide air support to ground forces. When put to the test, however, the XII Air Support Command proved wanting in combat due to command and control failures.[38] On January 17, Spaatz learned that Maj. Gen. Lloyd R. Fredendall, U.S. II Corps Commander with *de facto* control of the aircraft in XII Air Support Command, had denied a request for air support from the French XIX Corps, because an American battalion G–2 thought that his unit required this support. In consequence, while the French came under heavy Axis assault, aircraft from the XII Air Support Command flew air cover for the U.S. 509th Parachute Regiment, with no enemy air or ground forces to attack in front of the Americans. Spaatz resolved that henceforth no Allied ground commanders would interfere with air operations, and he briefed Fredendall personally on the matter. The airman also stated that II Corps headquarters should be collocated with XII Air Support Command headquarters so that Col. Howard A. Craig, the air force commander, could prevent Fredendall from "making damned fool decisions" about the use of aircraft.[39] Apparently this had little impact on Fredendall, who continued to deny American close air support to Free French ground units.[40]

Eisenhower and Spaatz met on January 21 to discuss the cooperation problems of Allied ground and air forces and how they might aid in stopping German assaults on the Free French XIX Corps. Eisenhower told Spaatz that he had designated General Anderson as his deputy in command over all Allied ground forces and instructed Spaatz to collocate an army support command headquarters with Anderson's headquarters to coordinate air-ground operations. Spaatz ordered Brig. Gen. Laurence S. Kuter to help centralize air support by setting up an Allied Support Command, consisting of the XII Air Support Command and the RAF's 242 Group.[41] Even before formal establishment of the Allied Support Command, aircraft from the Command and the Group had been supporting the British II and French XIX Corps.[42]

The establishment of the Allied Air Support Command was really the first step toward a "centralized theater control of air" resources.[43] Such control, however, still left many unresolved problems of doctrine, command, and control. Spaatz maintained that air power should attack with greatest possible force against constantly shifting target priorities to prevent the enemy from massing against Allied air strikes. Another tactic that Spaatz considered essential to victory was to attack enemy aircraft on the ground. Above all, Spaatz thought that it was a mistake to engage in indecisive operations on the battlefield itself, contending that the role of air power *was* to hit the enemy's "soft part . . . and in return, protect the soft parts of one's own force . . ."[44] The doctrine that Spaatz was advocating was very similar to that of the Western Desert Air Force and the one that would be adopted by the Northwest African Tactical Air Force. Disarm enemy air power, then switch to massive interdiction against targets whose loss will cripple enemy ground forces to the point where their ability, or will, to fight is destroyed.

Spaatz actively discussed air force problems with his fighter group commanders, such as Maj. Philip Cochran of the 58th Fighter Squadron, 33d Fighter Group, in order to determine shortcomings in American ground support tactics. The 33d Fighter Group had sustained heavy casualties in flying continuous air cover over battle areas and in providing fighter escort for A–20 and P–39 strikes.[45] German air strength in Tunisia had been reinforced by units driven out of Libya by the British, and enemy counterair operations against the Allies in Northwest Africa became acutely effective. According to Cochran, American losses in close-support missions had resulted from "sending up flights of a few planes in attacks on gun positions and on patrol over troops, and no protection of P–39's and A–20's when it was known that they would meet enemy aircraft in superior numbers." Cochran also told Spaatz that P–40 fighters should be used only when they enjoyed a three-to-one superiority over the opposing forces. Cochran was obviously thinking of concentration or massing force at the point of contact with the enemy.[46]

Spaatz also discussed air problems with Kuter and Anderson's chief of staff, Brigadier V. C. McNabb. The British officer reported that the U.S. II Corps had recently lost "seven hundred men from attacks of dive bombers," and then told Spaatz that Anderson "wanted the whole air effort put on ground positions immediately in front of our troops in the coming offensive." Kuter interjected that Anderson had told him that support of Allied ground forces remained the main task of Allied air power, and that he, Anderson, "was not interested in the bombing of enemy airdromes such as that at Gabes." The discussion ended with McNabb saying that he "hardly thought" that his superior "had intended to go that far."

Spaatz and Kuter then traveled to Fredendall's headquarters to learn of his theories on air support. The U.S. II Corps Commander wanted aircraft flying over his troops for a forty-eight hour period preceding an offensive, to protect them from German air and artillery activity. Putting it bluntly, Fredendall "wanted his men to see some bombs dropped on the positions immediately in from of them, and if possible, some dive bombers brought down in sight of his troops so that their morale would be bolstered."[47]

Fredendall told Spaatz that he had lost 300 men to dive bombers, and that this was unacceptable. Spaatz replied that he had "worn out" two fighter groups and a light-bombardment squadron supporting ground troops. He could not continue such operations, for "the rate of replacement would not allow extravagant dissipation of available air force."

Spaatz wanted to give all the help he could but noted that the correct use of air power was not really close air support, but rather air superiority and interdiction operations, hitting enemy airfields, tank parks, motor pools, and troop convoys—in effect, interdicting enemy supplies, equipment, and troops *before* they reached the battlefield. If he maintained a constant umbrella over one small portion of the front, then his available force would be dissipated without any lasting effect. The airman thought "that the hard core of any army should be able to take care of itself when it came to dive bombers." Fredendall replied that he had lost two artillery batteries to German dive bombers, and that he could not take the offensive without direct air support. The two Americans remained widely separated on their approach to proper use of air assets in support of ground operations.[48]

Spaatz later conferred with Fredendall's chief of staff, who flatly contradicted his commander saying that very few men had been lost to enemy dive bombers, with the exception of one infantry convoy that had been caught in open country because of the "stupidity on the part of the Battalion Commander." The ground staff officer declared emphatically that soldiers in forward positions should be able to take care of themselves and would be able to do so when they learned to open fire at enemy aircraft, keep proper dispersion, and have sufficient antiaircraft weapons. Fredendall's chief of staff claimed that "a defensive fear complex was being built up" in the II Corps.[49] The views of Spaatz, Anderson, Fredendall, Kuter, and McNabb reflected the classic conflict between ground and air officers over the proper use of air power.

By 1943, the problem remained complex because the AAF, while operating semiindependently, was still organizationally a part of the U.S. Army. Thus ground officers thought that they retained the right to order aviation squadrons around in much the same way they could task an infantry, tank, or artillery unit. Before Allied ground and air commanders could come to any consensus on doctrine, command and control, or communications for aircraft in close air support, the Axis counterattacked in the famous Kasserine Pass battle (February 14–22, 1943), throwing into doubt the future success of both Allied air and ground operations.

The Aftermath of Kasserine

At the beginning of February, Field Marshal Erwin Rommel had withdrawn his forces behind the old French-built Mareth Line in Tunisia. Planning a bold counterattack against the Allies' southern flank, he intended to catch Eisenhower's inexperienced forces off-guard before they could be joined by battle-seasoned British Eighth Army units from Libya. At midmonth, German armor, supported by aircraft, attacked the U.S. First Armored Division between Faid and Gafsa. A large tank battle in the Sidi Bou Zid region resulted in a resounding defeat of the First Armored Division, with the loss of fifty percent of its tanks. The rapid advance of German armor and infantry threatened to collapse the whole Allied position in Tunisia, and British and American reserves were thrown into the breach in the Allied line. By February 25, the combination of exhaustion and a stiffened Allied resistance (mainly artillery) stopped Rommel. Hampered by bad weather and crippled by the loss of key airfields in the Sbeitla, Gafsa, Thelepte, and Tebessa regions, Allied air power played a minor role. On an average day during the height of the battle, the Allied Air Support command flew only about 365 sorties of all types (excluding antishipping missions). As the author of the RAF staff history portrayed the role of air power during this battle: "It is apparent that air action in the Kasserine battle was not decisive."[50]

The Kasserine fiasco caught the Allies in the midst of wide-reaching command and control changes designed to remedy chaotic conditions, especially air-ground cooperation. On January 20, at Casablanca, Prime Minister Winston S. Churchill and President Franklin D. Roosevelt, the Combined Chiefs of Staff, and numerous advisers rearranged the command structure of Allied forces in the Mediterranean.

General Sir Harold Alexander became Deputy Commander in Chief to Eisenhower and took direct charge of the 15th Army Group comprising the British First and Eighth Armies, the French XIX Corps, and the U.S. II

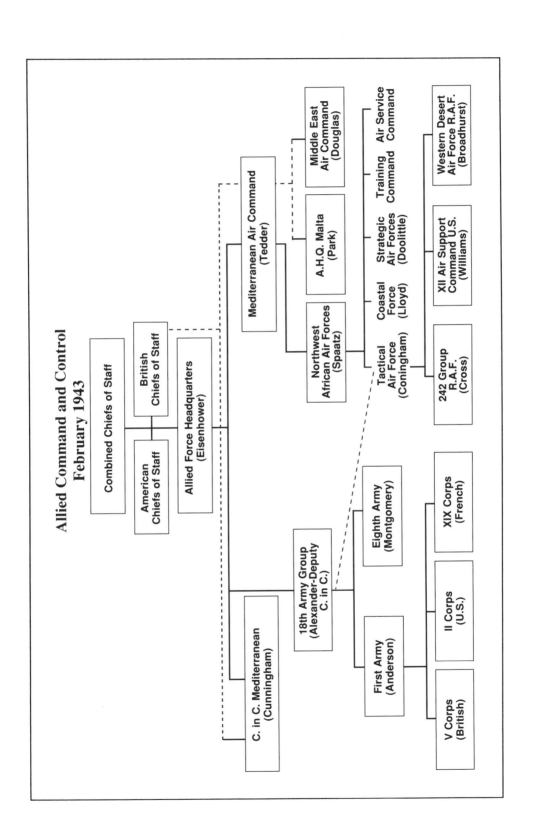

Allied Command and Control
February 1943

Combined Chiefs of Staff

British Chiefs of Staff

American Chiefs of Staff

Allied Force Headquarters (Eisenhower)

C. in C. Mediterranean (Cunningham)

Mediterranean Air Command (Tedder)

18th Army Group (Alexander-Deputy C. in C.)

First Army (Anderson)

Eighth Army (Montgomery)

V Corps (British)

II Corps (U.S.)

XIX Corps (French)

Northwest African Air Forces (Spaatz)

A.H.Q. Malta (Park)

Middle East Air Command (Douglas)

Tactical Air Force (Coningham)

Coastal Force (Lloyd)

Strategic Air Forces (Doolittle)

Training Command

Air Service Command

242 Group R.A.F. (Cross)

XII Air Support Command U.S. (Williams)

Western Desert Air Force R.A.F. (Broadhurst)

Corps. Tedder assumed command of all Allied air forces in the Mediterranean.[51] Spaatz took over the Northwest African Air Forces (NAAF) for operations against the Axis in Tunisia. The NAAF would comprise three major commands: the Northwest African Strategic Air Forces (NASAF) for strategic bombardment, the Northwest African Coastal Air Force (NACAF) for maritime operations and protection of North African ports, and the Northwest African Tactical Air Force (NATAF), which would support Allied ground operations. Spaatz would be subordinate to Alexander for Tunisian operations.[52]

NATAF was activated on February 18—during the Battle for Kasserine Pass. At this time, it would only begin its shakedown period under Air Vice Marshal Sir Arthur Coningham, the former Commander of the Western Desert Air Force, who had many definite ideas from his experience in Egypt and Libya. Kuter became Coningham's deputy, and the force consisted of 242 Group (Air Commodore K.B. Cross); the XII Air Support Command (Col. Paul L. Williams, who had replaced Craig because of illness); and the Western Desert Air Force, now commanded by Air Vice Marshal Harry Broadhurst.[53]

The infusion of British experience from the Western Desert into the unified theater command also had considerable impact on subsequent Allied operations. On February 16, the commander of the British Eighth Army, Gen. Sir Bernard Law Montgomery, met with American and British officers in Tripoli to discuss lessons learned during the Libyan campaign. In anticipation, he prepared and circulated a pamphlet entitled "Some Notes on High Command in War," (which Tedder styled "a gospel according to Montgomery"). No one could miss his bluntly stated opinion: "Any officer who aspired to high command in war must understand clearly certain basic principles regarding the use of air power." Montgomery contended that aircraft should be centralized under the command of an air force officer who worked in conjunction with the commander of the ground forces, just as had been done under his command at the battle of El Alamein.[54]

Montgomery suggested that the great value of air power was its "flexibility," since it could mass attacks on one target and then concentrate on a completely different target. To ensure the full measure of such attacks, it was vital to coordinate air and ground operations. If aircraft were commanded by ground force commanders, however, air power would lose its flexibility and would be unable to conduct large-scale attacks.

To obtain the greatest possible air assistance, said Montgomery, commanders of both the air and ground units should not only plan together, but their staffs should work together from the same headquarters. More specifically, the general stated that the army commander should have an air headquarters with him that would have direct command and control over squadrons allocated for operations in his army. Such resources, however, would

172

Brig. Gen. Laurence S. Kuter　　　　**Air Vice Marshal Arthur Coningham**

both be under his command. The army commander could on occasion obtain the support of the whole air striking force in the theater through this air headquarters, thanks to the flexibility of air power. Were this flexibility destroyed or negated, the success of the battle would be endangered.[55]

Amplifying Montgomery's remarks at the conference, Coningham simplified the picture, suggesting that: "The Soldier commands the land forces, the Airman commands the air forces, both commanders work together and operate their respective forces in accordance with the combined Army–Air plan, the whole operation being directed by the Army Commander."

Coningham acknowledged "fundamental" differences between ground and air operations. The army fights the land battle while the air force has to fight two battles—destruction of the enemy air force either in the air or on the ground to secure air superiority, and then the subsequent ground support battle. The two were sequential. He considered that "in this technical age" no single person had the knowledge to master the skills required to command both army and air forces at the same time. It took a lifetime of study "for a sailor, a soldier, or airman to learn his profession."[56]

To make certain that everybody knew about the doctrine and methods of the Western Desert Air Force for employing tactical air power, Coningham sent copies of his speech to every ranking officer in Tunisia.[57] Eisenhower, after reading the speech and discussing it with Spaatz and Tedder, agreed that this doctrine would be used for the remainder of the campaign.[58] The Tripoli speech as well as Coningham's subsequent direction of air operations became the charter for the Army Air Force and, after 1947, United States Air Force tactical air doctrine.[59]

After the war, Coningham would restate the basic principles of 1943: (1) air superiority is the first requirement for any major land operation; (2) the strength of air power lies in its flexibility and capacity for rapid concentration; (3) it follows that control must be concentrated; (4) air forces must be concentrated in use and not dispersed in penny packets; (5) the [ground and air] commanders and their staffs must work together; and (6) the plan of operation should be mutually adjusted and combined from the start.[60]

In practice, close air support of ground forces during the Tunisian campaign would receive third priority behind air superiority acquired by destroying enemy air power supply lines on the ground and in the air; and interdiction by cutting enemy supply lines. Tactical air doctrine expressed by Montgomery and Coningham at Tripoli did not call for any headlong assault on enemy front-line positions by Allied tactical aircraft. Third priority notwithstanding, the Allies did use tactical aircraft in massed air attacks to destroy enemy front-line positions, tanks on the battlefield, and artillery in battles such as Alam Halfa and El Alamein before Torch, and El Hamma during the Tunisian campaign.

On February 20, Coningham issued his first "General Operational Directive" to NATAF, in which he emphasized that the first objective was to gain air superiority by a continual offensive against enemy airfields in Tunisia.[61] When the New Zealander issued this directive, Tedder thought that "Coningham is not going to have any easy time to get rid of the fantastic ideas of soldiers controlling aircraft."[62] But Tedder was wrong, for Alexander, who understood the doctrine of the Western Desert Air Force, simply removed control of aircraft from ground commanders. On February 22, at a meeting with Eisenhower, Coningham, Kuter, and several American and British staff officers, Alexander authorized Kuter (mainly for American consumption), to quote him saying: "I shall never issue any orders on air matters. The Airman must be the final authority on air matters. . . ."[63] The next day, Kuter reported to Spaatz that Alexander had overruled Anderson and Fredendall on the question of air umbrellas over the ground troops, and that the aircraft of NATAF were going to be deployed offensively, in accord with Coningham's directive.[64]

After the Kasserine crisis has passed on March 8, Coningham's headquarters issued an outline of the NATAF air plan for the overall Allied campaign to conquer Tunisia in three phases. The plan had been carefully coordinated with Alexander and the staff of 18th Army Group. Phase A was the support of an attack eastward by the U.S. II Corps to take Gafsa and to "operate towards Maknassy," which is located about fifty miles from Mahares on the Golfe de Gabes. The object of Phase A was to threaten the Axis forces facing the British Eighth Army poised before the Mareth Line. Phase B called for the British Eighth Army and U.S. II Corps to clear the enemy out of Tunisia south of Gabes. Phase C was to be the final assault on northern Tunisia. Air power in support of these objectives would be paramount.[65]

During Phases A and B, NATAF's principal mission was to gain air superiority over the battlefield as the Allies cleared Axis forces from southern Tunisia. The first step would be the construction of radar early-warning and fighter control systems on high ground to cover the region over which the ground forces would fight. Radar and fighter control networks would enable the Allies to detect and plot the location of all enemy aircraft that entered the battle area and to direct Allied aircraft to engage these enemy aircraft. The second step would be the construction of a number of all-weather airfields in the Thelepte region and others in central Tunisia. The third step was to plan for and amass the necessary supplies for units of 242 Group, thereby reinforcing the XII Air Support Command supplying the Western Desert Air Force when it would move into central Tunisia. The mission of 242 Group and the XII Air Support Command was to attack enemy aircraft in the air and continually raid enemy airfields in Tunisia to pin down or destroy the Axis air force. At the same time, the British Eighth Army, supported by the Western Desert Air Force, would break through the Mareth Line, and advance northward to the Gabes region.[66]

On March 17, the U.S. II Corps, under the command of Maj. Gen. George S. Patton, who had replaced Fredendall, began Operation Wop, which called for a series of limited attacks against enemy communications in southern Tunisia. The Americans attacking south and then east met slight opposition, and while the weather was inclement, units of II U.S. Corps captured Gafsa and El Guetter by the next day. By March 21, other elements of U.S. II Corps had driven east to take Maknassy.[67] During the week of March 13–19, aircraft of the XII Air Support Command had bombed and strafed enemy ground positions and supplies to support U.S. II Corps, but because of bad weather, the effect proved marginal. Both NATAF and NASAF flew more than 700 sorties, dropping 241,680 pounds of bombs, mostly upon shipping targets.[68]

Details for the air plan of Phase B, breaking through the Mareth Line, were ironed out at the meeting on March 12. Coningham directed the XII Air Support Command and 242 Group to attack enemy airfields by day and night in an "endeavor to neutralize and divert the attention of the enemy air forces from the Eighth Army front. . . ." This would permit the Western Desert Air Force to commit its support to the British Eighth Army against the Mareth Line.[69] Coningham also requested NASAF aircraft to attack enemy airfields before and during the assault.[70] Allied strikes on enemy airfields throughout

Tunisia proved so successful that only five Axis aircraft appeared over the battlefield during the British attack.[71]

On March 20, Montgomery's forces attacked the Mareth Line, formed by a system of interconnected strong points running from the sea in the east to the almost impassable, steep-sided Matmata Mountains in the west. Rommel knew that the line could be outflanked by a force moving northward across the desert west of the Matmata Mountains toward El Hamma, and then attacking in a northeast direction between Chott El Fedjadj and the sea. This would cut off the Mareth Line defenders, and this is precisely what Montgomery did by mounting a frontal assault on the fortifications on his right flank. At the same time the II New Zealand Corps marched 150 miles north along the east side of the Matmata Mountains, arriving before El Hamma on March 21. Attacking the eastern side of the Mareth Line on the night of March 20–21, the British 50th Division, at considerable cost, occupied the edge of the enemy position. Still, it became clear by March 23 that the British Eighth Army, even with strong air support, could not smash its way through enemy defenses. Montgomery ordered the British First Armored Division to join the II New Zealand Corps for the forthcoming attack on the Axis defenses at El Hamma.[72]

With several days of inconclusive fighting on the ground and numerous attacks by the Western Desert Air Force against the enemy rear and front lines, the British turned to air power to win victory at the Mareth Line.[73] Broadhurst of the Western Desert Air Force developed the plan which called for the air assault two nights before the ground offensive, punishing the enemy through saturation bombing of targets that included vehicles, telephonic communications in the El Hamma region, and launching morale raids against the ground forces. In these two nights, aircraft flew 300 sorties and dropped 800,000 pounds of bombs.[74]

In the late afternoon of March 26, the Western Desert Air Force began to attack enemy lines before El Hamma. The British and New Zealand forward elements were marked by yellow smoke, while British artillery fired smoke shells into important enemy positions. Behind the Allied front line "a large land-mark [was] cut into the ground against which red and blue smoke was burned . . . . Lorries were also arranged in the form of letters to act as ground strips at selected pinpoints."[75] At 1530 hrs, fifty-four bombers—Bostons and Mitchells of the AAF and the South African Air Force—conducted "pattern bombing" on targets near El Hamma. On the heels of the bombers came the first group of fighter-bombers—P–40s, Spitfires, and Hurricanes—which machine-gunned and bombed enemy positions from the lowest possible height at fifteen-minute intervals. The pilots, including some in the AAF, were ordered to attack preset targets and shoot-up enemy gun crews to knock out enemy artillery and antitank guns. Twenty-six fighter-bomber squadrons provided effective close air support, strafing and bombing the enemy for two-and-a-half hours, while a squadron of Spitfires flew top cover for the fighter-bombers.

At 1600, half an hour after the fighter-bomber attacks had begun, British and New Zealand forces attacked behind an artillery barrage. The offensive moved at a rate of one hundred yards every three minutes, thus automatically defining the bomb-line." Allied fighter-bombers continued to work in front of the barrage. This combined air-artillery fire proved too much for the Axis defenders, and by the time the moon rose, British armor and New Zealand infantry broke through the enemy line. Within two days, the New Zealanders took Gabes, and the British Eighth Army marched north through the gap between the sea and Chott El Fedjadj.[76]

The Allied use of aircraft during the Mareth Line battles provided a classic example of great flexibility. While the XII Air Support Command and 242 Group pinned down the enemy air force by attacking airfields, the Western Desert Air Force worked with ground artillery to blast a path through the defenses at El Hamma for the ground troops. Broadhurst thought that the battle fought on March 26 at El Hamma was "an example of the proper use of air power in accordance with the principle of concentration."[77] The Allied breakthrough at El Hamma and the capture of Gabes forced the retreat of Axis forces from southern Tunisia.

After Axis forces lost Gabes, they retreated north along the coast to Wadi Akarit. During the first few days of the retreat, bad weather greatly reduced Allied air operations. But on March 29 the weather cleared, and the fighterbombers of the Western Desert Air Force conducted a series of heavy attacks on retreating enemy vehicles. On April 6, the British Eighth Army forced the enemy to abandon the Wadi Akarit position and retreat north to Enfidaville. There was good flying weather on April 7, and all available aircraft from XII Air Support Command and the Western Desert Air Force attacked the retreating enemy columns: more than 200 enemy vehicles were destroyed. Such attacks continued by night and day until April 11, when the enemy set up defensive positions Enfidaville.[78] The break through at El Hamma, the capture of Gabes, and the forced Axis retreat northward to Enfidaville cleared the enemy from southern and central Tunisia.

During the following months, several incidents underscored the importance of harmonious personal relations, common sense, and good will among British and American leaders in achieving air-ground cooperation and effectiveness. For example, on April 1, a flight of Ju–88s attacked an American position killing three men and wounding several others. Among the dead was a young officer, Richard Jenson, Patton's favorite aide. His untimely death enraged Patton, who reflected his displeasure with air support in the U.S. II Corps situation report.[79] When Coningham read the report the New Zealander took it as an insult to NATAF. Angered, he sent a cable to the U.S. II Corps Commander, with copies to every possible major command, including, according to Tedder, "even the official historian in the Pentagon."[80] Coningham listed all missions flown in support of the U.S. II Corps and pointed out that enemy air attacks caused only six casualties. Then he criticized the U.S. II Corps in turn.[81]

Both Spaatz and Kuter read Patton's situation report which as Spaatz wrote, "caused great concern as to its inaccuracy and unjustness of its accusation plus the wide distribution given to it by Patton."[82] Learning of the affair, Tedder at once saw that "this was dynamite with a short-burning fuse . . . [a] situation [that] could well have led to a major crisis in Anglo-American relations." Tedder told Coningham to withdraw his cable and to apologize personally to Patton. Next, Tedder requested Eisenhower to do nothing about the Patton–Coningham messages until Tedder could make peace between the soldier and airman.[83]

On April 3, Kuter, Spaatz, and Williams met at the Thelepte airfield to discuss Patton's problem with air support. Williams claimed that Patton's complaint was mainly about lack of fighter cover and failure of the XII Air Support Command to attack a tank concentration. This had occurred because weather prevented aircraft of Williams's XII Air Support Command from flying. Broadhurst's Western Desert Air Force also had planned to attack the armor concentration with 160 sorties, but the mission was called off when it was learned that Patton's artillery was shelling the tanks. After analyzing the situation, the three American airmen accompanied Tedder to Patton's headquarters. At the meeting, Patton acted like "a small boy who knew that he'd been bad but believed he would get away with it," recalled Kuter.[84] Patton confessed that he was getting "good air support and that he was satisfied." Spaatz felt that the problem was caused by lack of Allied radar coverage east of Gafsa and the fact that Patton had moved his headquarters away from that of XII Air Support Command. The next day, Spaatz took Williams and Patton's chief of staff to the British Eighth Army and the Western Desert Air Force to show how an effective combined headquarters worked.[85]

Accounts of the meeting between these senior army and air leaders differ. Coningham, nevertheless, sent a message of regret to Patton, and the incident closed with Eisenhower's letter of reprimand to Patton.[86] But the seriousness of the Patton-Coningham affair for Allied relations should not be underestimated, for it almost led to Eisenhower's relief from command on grounds that he could not control his commanders.[87]

The campaigns in Northwest Africa from November 1942 to May 1943 did not lend themselves to important close air support operations. Coningham directed the weight of the Northwest African Tactical Air Force's attacks against enemy air forces and supply lines. Almost no close air support operations were undertaken, with the exception of such actions as the Battle of El Hamma, from April 3–9, when the Northwest African Air Forces (NAAF) flew more than 3,000 sorties and dropped a total of 1,549,780 pounds of bombs in the course of 28 major attacks. Twelve of these attacks were directed against enemy airfields and another twelve attacks against targets such as ships, marshalling yards, and docks. Only four major attacks were undertaken against "targets of opportunity, enemy troop concentrations, etc."[88] NATAF's daily operational summaries, listing objectives for every sortie, further illustrate the very small number of attacks carried out in direct support of ground forces.[89]

Close air support operations remained a minor objective, and it is clear that NAAF aircraft were employed in accordance with doctrine held by air force commanders and not in direct support of Allied ground forces.[90]

NATAF concentrated on gaining air superiority over the enemy. As early as March 22, 1943, despite the fact that the Allies thought the Axis still had some 435 combat aircraft in Tunisia, the NAAF weekly intelligence summary proclaimed: "One fact stands out from all reports, this being that the NAAF has air superiority in North Africa to present."[91] To the author of this summary, "air superiority" meant that the enemy lacked the ability to prevent the Allies from employing aircraft and ground forces at a time and place of their choice, and not that the Axis did not have some combat aircraft. This was clearly shown when the British Eighth Army, supported by the Western Desert Air Force, assaulted the Mareth Line and on 27 March broke through at El Ḥamma. The defeat of Axis air forces in Tunisia must be viewed not only in the context of NATAF's operations in Tunisia but also as part of the greater effort throughout the theater against Axis air power.

Allied air forces in North Africa forced opponents in the Mediterranean to operate defensively during the early months of 1943 through attacks on airfields in Tunisia, Sicily, Italy, and Sardinia, and by counterair operations. From early February to mid-April, Allied aircraft attacked Sardinian airfields 14 times, those in Sicily 16 times, and airfields in Tunisia approximately 13 times, destroying an estimated 180 enemy aircraft. These attacks significantly reduced the ability of the enemy to undertake offensive air operations either in support of Axis ground forces or in an effort to provide air cover for logistical lifelines.[92]

The defeat of enemy air forces in Tunisia and the central Mediterranean was a slow process—similar to grinding down a metal object with a file.[93] Raids on Axis airfields might be dramatic, but their effect on enemy air operations was not immediately apparent. In November 1942, Axis aircraft attacked Allied convoys in the central and western Mediterranean with an average of forty sorties per day. By January 1943, the number was reduced to fifteen or twenty per day; while in February and March the Axis could mount only ten or twelve, and that was further reduced to only about six sorties per day by April. The weight of Allied air attacks forced many Axis planes into defensive roles protecting convoys, airfields, and communications.[94]

By mid-April 1943, some 3,241 Allied combat aircraft opposed about

1,800 German and Italian planes. However, in terms of serviceable combat aircraft, the ratio was more like 3 to 1 in favor of the Allies, with a serviceability rate of 80 percent for the Mediterranean Allied Air Force compared to a rate of 58 percent for the Germans and 50 percent for the Italians. Approximately 2,590 Allied combat aircraft could therefore be arrayed against about 900 Axis warplanes.[95]

There are other factors in the equation that are important but difficult to evaluate—equipment, skill, training of aircrews and leaders, command and control, state of technology, intelligence, logistics, strategy, and tactics. While the Axis employed no aircraft comparable to the Allied B–17 and B–24 heavy bombers, only the Germans used dive bombers and possessed superior fighter planes. The British employed such obsolete aircraft as Fleet

American pilot checks maps on the wing of his F-5, a photo-reconnaissance version of the Lockheed P-38 Lightning.

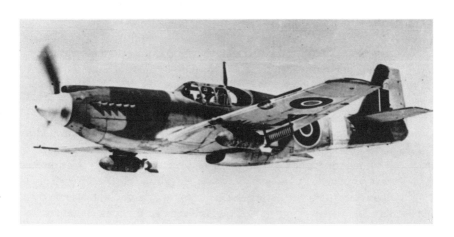

This North American A-36, a ground attack configuration of the P-51 Mustang fighter, has the dive brake beneath its port wing deployed. Two 500-pound bombs complete its ordnance load for a mission against North African targets.

Air Arm Albacores of the Western Desert Air Force, but these proved indispensable in marking targets for medium and heavy night bombers.[96] By mid-April 1943, Allied air forces were superior in the Mediterranean, for they had more, if not necessarily better, aircraft, and their aircrews were improving daily. The Axis lagged badly in some intelligence areas and in the use of some new technology such as radar. Drained by a three-front war, moreover, it could not match the strong and ever-growing allied logistics capability. Still, Axis air and ground elements proved tenacious opponents, fighting desperately to the last aircraft and the last rifle to preserve the tenuous Axis hold in North Africa as long as possible.[97]

While Allied air power in the Mediterranean cannot be compared with the massive numbers used over Northwest Europe a year later, the 1943 operations were unprecedented in size and scope. During the period March 29 through the night of April 21–22, bombers of NASAF and the Middle East Air Command averaged 997 sorties daily against enemy airfields, communication networks, and tactical ground targets, in addition to attacks on ports and ships. The estimated daily sortie average for all types of aircraft was 1,171.[98] During the period 1800 hrs April 4 to 1800 hrs April 5, NATAF flew more than 800 sorties over Tunisia, while the NASAF flew some 178 sorties.[99] Between April 10 and April 16, aircraft of the NAAF not only carried out 51 strikes, dropping 2,421,520 pounds of bombs on a variety of enemy targets in the central Mediterranean and Tunisia, but claimed to have shot down 134 enemy aircraft.[100] By the eve of the final Allied offensive in Tunisia, the enemy air forces in the central Mediterranean were beaten.

The Final Operations

Issuing a directive on April 14, 1943, Coningham started preparation for the offensive, code-named Vulcan, which would destroy the remaining forces in Tunisia. Operative orders came two days later. By his directive, Tunisia was divided into two regions for controlling Allied air power. One was placed under the command of the Western Desert Air Force, the other under 242 Group, with the aircraft from the XII Air Support Command controlled by 242 Group's operations room, for the area of operations was too small for three operations rooms and too large for one. Further, the U.S. II Corps had been moved from central Tunisia across the rear of the British First Army to a position on the Allied northern flank in northern Tunisia. At the same time, the Western Desert Air Force moved into airfields on the coastal plain of east central Tunisia, while the XII Air Support Command airfields remained for the most part in west central Tunisia.[101]

Allied radar was situated on high ground to cover the air space over both Allied- and Axis-held areas of Tunisia. Information on enemy aircraft movements obtained by this radar network was sent to the operations rooms of 242 Group and the Western Desert Air Force in order to monitor the movement of enemy aircraft and control those of the Allies.[102]

Between April 17 and 23, Allied aircraft flew more than 5,000 sorties against enemy airfields, shipping, troop concentrations, supply dumps, and vehicles. There were 24 major attacks on enemy airfields in which Allied aircraft dropped 727,168 pounds of bombs. Almost half of the Allied air effort was directed against airfields during the week of April 17–23.[103] The enemy, because of the great weight of Allied air attacks, withdrew a majority of their aircraft from Tunisia to Sicily and Italy. The fighters that remained in Africa were deployed to defend Tunis and Bizerte.[104]

The main Allied ground attack began on April 22, when the British V Corps attacked enemy positions north of Medjez el Bab. Opposing them, according to Allied intelligence estimates, were 157,900 troops supported by approximately 100 aircraft.[105] The NATAF flew 716 daylight sorties at the beginning of this offensive, conducting interdiction operations in support of Allied ground forces and carrying out offensive fighter sweeps. These latter were, for the most part unsuccessful, as the *Luftwaffe* was "not conspicuous and was unwilling and difficult to engage."[106]

As the British First Army and the U.S. II Corps slowly advanced towards Tunis and Bizerte, they met with strong resistance from enemy ground forces and had to fight for each hill and ridge. Concurrently, during the last week in April, the NATAF attacked enemy airfields and maritime targets, while fighters and fighter-bombers carried out extensive interdiction operations, meeting almost no resistance from the enemy air forces. During this period,

Allied aircraft dropped 1,410,956 pounds of bombs, even though there were several days of bad flying weather.[107]

In the first week of May, the enemy air forces in Tunisia flew between 70 and 200 sorties a day, mostly defensive. An Allied intelligence summary described enemy air activity as attempting "to hold back the tide with a thimble." On May 6, the Allies flew 200 sorties against enemy shipping and targets in Sicily while at the same time flying about 1,200 other sorties, for the most part against enemy airfields and interdiction targets in Tunisia. In an operation similar to the battle of El Hamma, on March 26 a number of these sorties were directed against the Madjerda Valley in front of the attacking British First Army, where in an area 1,000 yards deep and 4 miles long Allied aircraft "literally pounded the enemy into submission."[108]

On May 7, enemy defenses before Tunis and Bizerte cracked, and in the afternoon, units of the British First Army reached the center of Tunis. The U.S. First Armored Division captured Ferryville, and the U.S. 9th Division seized Bizerte.[109] The capture of Bizerta and Tunis split the Axis forces in half, but the fighting continued until May 13 when the last pocket of enemy ground forces surrendered. At the time, it was estimated that fewer than 1,000 enemy troops escaped from Tunisia. The last air operation in Tunisia was an attack by NATAF aircraft against a group of enemy troops pinned north of Enfidaville.[110]

The annihilation of Axis forces in Tunisia was the first great victory for the western Allies in the European theater during World War II. Superior air power, which permitted the Allies to smash enemy air forces and then to attack enemy rear positions and supply lines, was of great assistance in this victory. It is true, however, that Allied tactical aircraft did not systematically strafe and bomb enemy front-line positions during the campaign. Not until Allied ground forces overran northern Tunisia did the great effect of Allied air power on enemy operations become apparent. Only then could the Allied ground forces see smashed warehouses and docks, Tunisian ports filled with sunken enemy ships, and hundreds of destroyed enemy vehicles and aircraft. Between April 22 and May 16, the Allies shot down 273 aircraft and forced more than 600 German and Italian aircraft to be abandoned around Tunis, Bizerte, and on Cape Bon.[111]

During the campaign in Tunisia, NATAF doctrine called for a continuous series of attacks on the enemy's air force both in the air and on the ground until air superiority was achieved. Then while still attacking the enemy's air force to maintain air superiority, strikes would be directed at what Spaatz called the "soft parts" of the enemy ground forces—motor pools, supply dumps, truck convoys, docks, bridges, ships, and the like. Lastly, special missions were flown in direct support of ground forces for occasions such as the Battle of El Hamma and during the last phase of the campaign in Tunisia.

In later campaigns, in the Mediterranean and northwest Europe, the techniques of close air support of ground forces would be further developed. But this would not have been possible without the doctrinal foundations laid down by the NATAF in 1943.

The Tunisian campaign proved the worth of the Western Desert Air Force's tactical air doctrine, but it also had a profound effect on the tactical doctrine and organization of the AAF as well as its relations with the U.S. Army Ground Forces. Establishment of the NAAF during the campaign totally removed the aircraft from ground force commanders and placed them under RAF and AAF control. Furthermore, the commander of NATAF, with Spaatz's approval, imposed the doctrine of the Western Desert Air Force on all American tactical air units in Tunisia. Although, Alexander technically commanded NATAF, he would not issue orders to that organization, but he established the doctrine of coequality between the commanders of ground and air forces. According to Spaatz, "Alexander very clearly stated that air could not be considered as artillery, but was a force that could only be operated and controlled by airmen."[112]

Obviously, the end of the Tunisian operation did not mean that AAF commanders would relinquish the concept of coequality between air and ground force commanders, or allow the disappearance of Western Desert Air Force doctrine from AAF tactical units. Their views were supported by their reports and letters. Several AAF officers wrote higher headquarters, both in North Africa and Washington, praising doctrine and command arrangements employed by NATAF.[113]

Impact on Doctrine—FM 100–20

On April 24, 1943, Gen. George C. Marshall, the Army's Chief of Staff, ordered a new manual on the command and employment of air power. His directives for the manual delineate concepts of air power and the relationship between air and ground commanders.

On June 9, under the direction of the G–3 Division of the U.S. Army General Staff, a committee drafted FM 100–20, "Command and Employment of Air Power," first published on July 21, 1943. Committee members included Col. Martin H. McKinnon, Commandant of the Air Support Department of the School of Applied Tactics; Col. Ralph F. Stearley, Commander of the I Air Support Command; and Lieut. Col. Orin H. Moore, Armored Forces liaison officer at AAF Headquarters. The manual established the doctrine, organization, command requirements, and strategy of a tactical air force as outlined in Marshall's memorandum of April 24, and in the Coningham and Montgomery talks of February 16 at Tripoli. FM 100–20 spelled out the following points: The principal of coequality for air and ground force commanders must be maintained; centralized command of tactical aircraft is necessary to obtain "the inherent flexibility of air power" which "is its greatest asset;" and, finally, the commander of a tactical air force must have the ability to mass his aircraft to attack the decisive targets and to fully exploit the striking power of tactical aircraft.

According to the manual, the command of air and ground forces would be the responsibility of a theater commander, who would be responsible for all operations. It also stated that the first priority for successful ground operations was the attainment of air superiority over the battlefield. The second priority was interdiction, followed by close air support. FM 100–20 would shape the way the AAF employed its tactical air forces for the remainder of the war.[114]

The publication of FM 100–20 caused a mixed reaction among the American military. Arnold ordered a copy sent to every AAF officer for his future guidance. U.S. Army ground forces generally took it to be an "AAF Declaration of Independence," and showed varying degrees of "dismay" about its contents. Some other officers thought that the doctrine expressed in the manual to be too British in content.[115] Yet, as Lt. Gen. Elwood R. "Pete" Quesada, commander of the XII Figher Command for most of the African campaigns, stated years later: "Coningham was the first senior air force guy who established tactical air doctrine as supportable doctrine that almost everybody accepted. Coningham is the architect of it."[116] But whatever the opinions surrounding FM 100–20, this manual formed the core of formally stated tactical air doctrine. It was the product of personalities and experiences gained in Tunisia and the Western Desert by the Allied air forces.

Notes

1. Wesley Frank Craven and James Lea Cate, *The Army Air Forces in World War II* (Washington, 1983 reprint) Vol I, pp 66–69, 109–110.
2. *Ibid*, Vol I, pp 146–150; Richard Kohn and Joseph P. Harahan, eds., *Air Superiority in World War II and Korea* (Washington, 1983), pp 38–40.
3. FM 1–15, *Tactics and Techniques of Air Fighting* (Washington, 1942), pp 3840.
4. FM 31–35, *Aviation in Support of Ground Forces* (Washington, 1932), pp 1, 6.
5. FM 1–5, *Employment of Aviation of the Army* (Washington, 1943), pp 23, 38–39.
6. FM 31–35, *Aviation in Support of Ground Forces*, pp 2, 12–13.
7. Christopher R. Gabel, "The US Army GHq Maneuvers of 1941" (Unpublished Ohio State University Ph D Dissertation, 1981), pp 65–67, 70–71, 97–99, 310–313.
8. Kent R. Greenfield, *Army and Ground Forces and the Air-Ground Battle Team Including Organic Light Aviation* (np, 1948), pp 1–22.
9. Maurice Matloff and Edwin M. Snell, *Strategic Planning for Coalition Warfare, 1941–1942* (Washington, 1953), p 283.
10. AAF, Hist Div, *The Twelfth Air Force in the North African Winter Campaign: 11 Nov 1942 to the Reorganization of February 1943* (Washington, 1946), pp 44, 49–50, 74.
11. S. W. Roskill, *The War at Sea* (London, 1983), Vol I, p 26.
12. Peter Mead, *The Eye in the Air* (London, 1983), p 163.
13. Public Record Office, CAB/80/58, The Air Program, 21 May 1940. Hereafter this archive will be cited as PRO.
14. W.A. Jacobs, "Air Support for the British Army, 1939–1943," *Military Affairs* (Dec 1982), Vol XLVI, pp 175–76.
15. Arthur Bryant, ed, *The Turn of the Tide* (New York, 1957), pp 188–90.
16. John Terraine, *A Time for Courage: The Royal Air Force in the European War, 1939–1945* (New York, 1985), pp 282–88.
17. Jacobs, "Air Support," p 177.
18. *Ibid*, p 188.
19. AAF, Hist Div, *The Twelfth Air Force*, p 30.
20. Mead, *The Eye*, pp 175–77.
21. Shelford Bidwell and Dominick Graham, *Fire-Power: British Army Weapons and Theories of War, 1904–1945* (London, 1982), pp 264–67.
22. For a full account of the British Army's and the RAF's views in Britain during 1940–1943 on close air support, see Jacobs, "Air Support," pp 174–82; Bidwell and Graham, *Fire-Power*, pp 260–75; Air Ministry, *Air Support* (np, 1955), pp 7–45; C.E. Carrington, "Army/Air Cooperation, 1939–1943," *Journal of the Royal United Service Institution* (Dec 1970), Vol 115, pp 3741.
23. Terraine, *Courage*, pp 375–83.
24. Harry C. Coles, "Ninth Air Force in the Western Desert Campaign to 23 Jan 1943," unpublished Army Air Forces Hist Study #30, Washington: Ass't Chief of Staff for Intel, Hist Div, Feb 1945.
25. PRO, AIR/20/2107, Axis Air Ops: North Africa and Mediterranean: The Last Phase in North Africa, 1st Jan 1943–12 May 1943.
26. *Supplement to the London Gazette*, Nov 6, 1946.
27. PRO, AIR/41/33, p 57; AAF, Hist Div, *The Twelfth Air Force*, pp 40, 44, 46, 51.
28. Alfred M. Beck, Abe Bortz, Charles W. Lynch, Lida Mayo, and Ralph F. Weld, *The Corps of Engineers: The War against Germany* (Washington, 1985), pp 85–90.
29. AAF, Hist Div, *The Twelfth Air Force*, pp 40, 44, 46, 51.
30. Memo by Spaatz, Nov 30, 1942, Box 97, Spaatz Papers, Library of Congress. Hereafter this archive will be cited as LC.
31. Arthur Tedder, *With Prejudice: The War Memoirs of Marshal of the Royal Air Force Lord Tedder G.C.B.* (Boston, 1966), p 370.

32. Constitution and Activities of the Allied Air Force, Jan 5, 1943, Box 10, Spaatz Papers, LC.
33. PRO, AIR/8/1035, Portal to Churchill, Jan 1, 1943; Portal to Sec of State for Air, Jan 1, 1943.
34. Craven and Cate, *Army Air Forces*, Vol II, pp 161–65.
35. Robinett to Marshall, Dec 8, 1942, Box 103, Arnold Papers, LC.
36. PRO, AIR/20/2568, Mediterranean Air Command to Air Ministry, Feb 28, 1943; AIR/41/33, pp 12022.
37. Doolittle to Spaatz, Dec 25, 1942, Box 19, Doolittle Papers, LC; Kohn and Harahan, *Air Superiority*, pp 3032.
38. Craven and Cate, *Army Air Forces*, Vol II, pp 134–40; Kenn C. Rust, *Twelfth Air Force Story* (Temple City, Calif, 1975), pp 5–7.
39. Memo by Spaatz, Jan 17, 1943, Box 10, Spaatz Papers, LC.
40. PRO AIR/41/33, ff 7273.
41. Memo by Spaatz, Jan 21, 1943, Box 10, Spaatz Papers, LC.
42. PRO AIR/41/33, f 77.
43. Dan Mortensen and Alexander Cochran, "Joint Ops, An Examination of Close Air Support in the European Theater of Ops" (unpubl paper produced for CMH and OAFH, nd), pp 26–27, 30.
44. Some Principles of Air Support Employment Followed in the Tunisian Campaign, Feb 3, 1943, Box 10, Spaatz Papers, LC.
45. Craven and Cate, *Army Air Forces*, Vol II, pp 138–39; Memo by Spaatz, Feb 4, 1943, Box 10, Spaatz Papers, LC; PRO AIR/41/33, ff 77–78.
46. Memo by Spaatz, Feb 5, 1943, Box 10, Spaatz Papers, LC.
47. *Ibid.*
48. *Ibid.*
49. *Ibid.*
50. I.S.O. Playfair and C. J. C. Molony, *The Mediterranean and Middle East* (London, 1966), p 303; PRO AIR/41/33, f 80.
51. George F. Howe, *Northwest Africa: Seizing the Initiative in the West* (Washington, 1957), pp 35455.
52. PRO AIR/8/1035, Combined Chiefs of Staff, System of Air Command in the Mediterranean, Jan 20, 1943.
53. Craven and Cate, *Army Air Forces*, Vol II, pp 162–63.
54. Tedder, pp 369–67; B. L. Montgomery, *Some Notes on High Command in War* (Tripoli, 1943), p 2.
55. Montgomery, *Notes*, p 2.
56. Talk given by Vice Air Marshal Sir A. Coningham. [Tripoli, Feb 16, 1943], Box 12, Spaatz Papers, LC.
57. Coningham to Spaatz, Mar 1, 1943, Box 11, Spaatz Papers, LC.
58. Memo by Spaatz, Feb 17, 1943, Box 11, Spaatz Papers, LC.
59. Riley Sunderland, *Evolution of Command and Control Doctrine for Close Air Support* (Washington, 1973), pp 13–14; Kohn and Harahan, *Air Superiority*, pp 2944.
60. Arthur Coningham, "Development of Tactical Air Forces," *Journal of the Royal United Service Institution* (May 1946), Vol 91, p 215.
61. General Operation Directive issued by Coningham, Feb 20, 1943, Kuter Papers, USAF Academy Libr.
62. Tedder, p 398.
63. Laurence S. Kuter, "Goddammit Georgie: North Africa, 1943: The Birth of TAC Doctrine," *Air Force Magazine* (Feb 1973), Vol 56, p 55.
64. Memo by Spaatz, Feb 23, 1943, Box 10, Spaatz Papers, LC.
65. 614.201–1, Outline of Operational Plan by Coningham, Mar 6, 1943. The Office of Air Force History at Bolling AFB holds a large collection of AAF World War II records on microfilm. Each document is numbered, and hereafter documents from this collection will be cited by their number and title.
66. *Ibid.*

67. Howe, *Northwest Africa*, pp 543551.
68. 612.606–1, Weekly Intelligence Summary Nr 18, Period from 0001 Hours Mar 13 to 2400 Hours Mar 19, 1943.
69. PRO AIR/41/50, ff 489–500.
70. NATAF to NAAF, Mar 17, 1943, Box 12, Spaatz Papers, LC.
71. PRO AIR/41/33, ff 104105.
72. Playfair and Molony, *Mediterranean*, Vol IV, pp 338–43.
73. PRO AIR/41/50, ff 500–503.
74. PRO AIR/41/50, f 506.
75. PRO AIR/41/50, f 508.
76. PRO AIR/41/50, ff 506–509; Playfair and Molony, *Mediterranean*, Vol IV, pp 3435–55; 614.4501–1, The Eighth Army Break Through at El Hamma on Mar 26 1943.
77. PRO AIR/23/1708, The Eighth Army Break Through at El Hamma on Mar 26, 1943: Comment by A.O.C. Tactical Air Force.
78. PRO AIR/23/7111, pp 26, 29.
79. Martin Blumenson, ed, *The Patton Papers, 1940–1945* (Boston, 1974), pp 203–205; Kuter, p 53.
80. Tedder, p 401.
81. Kuter, p 53.
82. Memo by Spaatz, Apr 2, 1943, Box 11, Spaatz Papers, LC.
83. Tedder, p 411.
84. Blumenson, p 207; Kuter, p 54.
85. Memos by Spaatz, Apr 3, 4, 5, 1943, Box 11, Spaatz Papers, LC.
86. Tedder to Eisenhower, Apr 3, 1943, Box 11, Spaatz Papers, LC; Blumenson, pp 108–109; Kuter, p 54; Memo by Spaatz, Apr 5, 1943, Box 11, Spaatz Papers, LC; Alfred D. Chandlier, Jr., ed, *The Papers of Dwight David Eisenhower: The War Years* (London, 1970), Vol II, pp 1073–74.
87. Tedder, p 411.
88. 612.606.1, Weekly Intelligence Summary Nr 21, Period from 0001 Hours Apr 3 to 2400 Hours Apr 9, 1943.
89. 613–307, Operational Summaries, Nos 1–70.
90. Cf Coningham, "Development of Tactical Air Forces," p 215.
91. 612.606–1, Weekly Intelligence Summary Nr 19, Period from 0001 Hours Mar 20 to 2400 Hours Mar 26, 1943.
92. [Air Ministry], *The Rise and Fall of the German Air Force, 1933–194545* (New York, 1983 reprint), pp 219–21, 249–54.
93. Cf Williamson Murray, *Strategy for Defeat: The Luftwaffe, 1933–1945* (Maxwell AFB, Ala, 1983), pp 159–63.
94. PRO AIR/20/5796, Appreciation of the efforts of Allied Air Force Attacks on Axis Airfields in Sardinia, Sicily, and Tunisia, 1943.
95. Playfair and Moloney, *Mediterranean*, Vol IV, p 400.
96. Cf *Janes' All the World's Aircraft, 1943–1944* (New York, 1945).
97. [Air Ministry], *The German Air Force*, pp 249–54.
98. Playfair and Moloney, *Mediterranean*, Vol IV, pp 391, 401.
99. 612.307, Operational Summary Nr 44, Period ends 1800 Hours Apr 7, 1943.
100. 616.606–1, Weekly Intelligence Summary Nr 22, Period from 0001 Hours Apr 10 to 2400 Hours Apr 16, 1943.
101. Craven and Cate, *Army Air Forces*, Vol II, pp 199–200.
102. Control of Fighters in the Final Phase of the Tunisian Campaign, Apr 14, 1943, Box 11, Spaatz Papers, LC.
103. 612.606–1, Weekly Intelligence Summary Nr 23, Period from 0001 Hours Apr 17 to 2400 Hours Apr 23, 1943.
104. PRO AIR/41/33, f 111.
105. 612.606–1, Weekly Intelligence Summary Nr 24, Period from 0001 Hours Apr 24 to 2400 Hours Apr 30, 1943.
106. 612.307, Operational and Intelligence Summary Nr 61, For the Period ended 1800 Hours Apr 22, 1943.

107. 612.606–1, Weekly Intelligence Summary Nr 24, Period from 0001 Hours Apr 24 to 2400 Hours Apr 30, 1943.
108. 612.606–1, Weekly Intelligence Summary Nr 25, Period from 0001 Hours May 1 to 2400 Hours May 6, 1943; Craven and Cate, *Army Air Forces*, Vol II pp 203–204.
109. Playfair and Moloney, *Mediterranean*, Vol IV, p 460.
110. PRO AIR/41/33, ff 112–13.
111. Playfair and Moloney, *Mediterranean*, Vol IV, p 460.
112. Memos by Spaatz, May 3, 4, 1943, Box 11, Spaatz Papers, LC.
113. Eg, Stratemeyer to Arnold, May 7, 1943, Box 11, Spaatz Papers, LC.
114. Robert Frank Futrell, *Ideas, Concepts, Doctrine: A History of Basic Thinking in the United States Air Force* (Maxwell AFB, Ala, 1974), p 69.
115. *Ibid,* pp 69–70.
116. Kohn and Harahan, *Air Superiority*, p 34.

Bibliographical Essay

There is a large amount of manuscript and printed materials on the campaign in Tunisia. In the United States the logical place to begin is the National Archives, but in response to inquiries at the Suitland depository, archivists declared that the records of the AAF during the Tunisian campaign were closed, since they were intermixed with intelligence records concerning the Balkans. This situation was not as great a setback as it would first appear, for four major collections of manuscripts on the operations of the AAF during World War II in Tunisia exist in Washington. There is a large collection of AAF records on microfilm containing orders, reports, and intelligence summaries on the AAF in Tunisia deposited in the Office of Air Force History at Bolling AFB. The papers of Generals Arnold, Doolittle, and Spaatz can be found in the Library of Congress. The Spaatz papers are the most useful for Tunisia. There is also a small collection of Kuter papers in the library of the U.S. Air Force Academy in Colorado; the U.S. Army's Military History Institute at Carlisle Barracks, Pennsylvania, holds a number of AAF field manuals.

In Great Britain, the largest, and perhaps the only collection of manuscripts on the Tunisian campaign, is held by the Public Record Office at Kew. AIR/8/1035; AIR/20/2107, 2568, 25796; and AIR/23/1708, 1711 contain numerous reports, correspondence, and other documents relating to the air war in Tunisia. AIR/41/33 and 50 are two unpublished staff studies of air operations in Tunisia.

Over the years, the Americans and British have produced a number of printed, mimeographed, and typed works that relate to the Tunisian campaign. For example, there is B. L. Montgomery, *Some Notes on High Command in War* (Tripoli: British Eighth Army, 1943). There is a staff study that deals with air operations in Northwest Africa: AAF Historical Division, *The Twelfth Air Force in the North African Winter Campaign: 11 November to the Reorganization of February 1943* (Washington, D.C., 1945). See also Harry L. Coles, *Ninth Air Force in the Western Desert Campaign to 23 January 1943* (Washington, D.C., 1945). See also Harry L. Coles, *Ninth Air Force in the Western Desert Campaign to 23 January 1943* (Washington, D.C.: AAF Historical Division, 1945). There are a number of government publications that deal with problems such as tactics, command, and control. For example, the RAF produced *Air Support* (n.p.: Air Ministry, 1955), and [Air Ministry], *The Rise and Fall of the German Air Force, 1933–1945*, (New York: St. Martin's, 1983 reprint). The American Armed Forces have produced works such as Robert Frank Futrell, *Ideas, Concepts, Doctrine: A History of Basic Thinking in the United States Air Force* (Maxwell AFB, Ala.: Air University, 1971); Williamson Murray, *Strategy for Defeat: The Luftwaffe, 1933–1945* (Maxwell

AFB, Ala.: Air University, 1983); Kent Roberts Greenfield, *Army Ground Forces and the Air-Ground Battle Team Including Organic Light Aviation* (n.p.: Historical Section: Army Ground Forces, 1948); Riley Sunderland, *Evolution of Command and Control Doctrine for Close Air Support* (Washington, D.C.: Office of Air Force History, Headquarters U.S. Air Force, 1973); Shelford Bildwell and Dominick Graham, *Fire-Power: British Army Weapons and Theories of War* (London, 1982); Richard Kohn and Joseph P. Harahan, eds., *Air Superiority in World War II and Korea* (Washington, D.C.: Office of Air Force History, Headquarters U.S. Air Force, 1983); and *Close Air Support Joint Operations: North Africa*, Research and Analysis Division Special Studies Series, U.S. Army Center of Military History, Washington, D.C., 1987.

There are a number of official histories of World War II that cover the air campaign in Tunisia. For a view of strategic planning of the beginning of the campaign, see Maurice Matloff and Edwin M. Snell, *Strategic Planning for Coalition Warfare, 1941–1942* [The United States Army in World War II: The War Department] (Washington, D.C.: Office of the Chief of Military History, Department of the Army, 1953). For air operations the most important is volume two of Wesley Frank Craven and James Lea Cate, *The Army Air Forces in World War Two* (Washington, D.C., 1983). American ground operations are covered in George F. Howe, *Northwest Africa: Seizing the Initiative in the West* [The United States Army in World War II: The Mediterranean Theater of Operations] (Washington, D.C.: Office of the Chief Military History, Department of the Army, 1957). For the building of airfields one should consult Alfred M. Beck, Abe Bortz, Charles W. Lynch, Lida Mayo, and Ralph F. Weld, *The Corps of Engineers: The War Against Germany* [The United States Army in World War II: The Technical Services] (Washington, D.C.: Center for Military History, Department of Army, 1984). The British official history of the Tunisian campaign is Vol. 4 of I.S.O. Playfair and C. J. C. Molony's *The Mediterranean and Middle East* (London: HMSO, 1954–1988). See also Peter Mead, *The Eye in the Air*, (London: HMSO, 1983) and S.W. Roskill, *The War at Sea* (London: HMSO, 1954–1961).

The Tunisian campaign may also be studied in a number of nonofficial works such as memoirs, books, printed documents, and articles. The air war in Tunisia cannot be understood without consulting the memoirs of Arthur Tedder, *With Prejudice: The War Memoirs of Marshal of the Royal Air Force Lord Tedder G.C.B.* (Boston: Little Brown and Company, 1966). See also, Arthur Bryant, ed., *The Turn of the Tide* (New York: Doubleday, 1957). Two sets of printed documents were consulted: Martin Blumenson, ed., *The Patton Papers, 1940–1945* (Boston: Houghton Mifflin, 1972) and volume two of *The Papers of Dwight David Eisenhower: The War Years* (Baltimore: Johns Hopkins University Press, 1970) edited by Alfred D. Chandler, Jr. Also see John Terraine, *A Time for Courage: The Royal Air Force in the European War, 1939–1945* (New York: Macmillan, 1985). In addition, several articles should be consulted for an understanding of the air war in Tunisia. Laurence S. Kuter, "Goddammit, Georgie! North Africa 1943: The Birth of TAC Air Doctrine, "*Air Force Magazine* (February 1973) vol. 55; W.A.Jacobs, "Air Support for the British Army, 1939–1943," *Military Affairs* (December 1982) vol. XLV; Sir Arthur Coningham, "The Development of Tactical Air Forces," *Journal of the Royal United Service Institution* (May, 1946) vol. 91; and C.E. Carrington, "Army/Air Cooperation, 1939–1943," *Journal of the Royal United Service Institution* (Dec. 1970) vol. 114. One must also consult Christopher R. Gable, "The U.S. Army GHQ Maneuvers of 1941" (Unpublished Ohio State University Ph.D. Dissertation, 1981).

Information about various types of aircraft used in the Tunisian campaign can be found in *Jane's All the World's Aircraft, 1943–44* (New York: The Macmillan Company, 1945).

5

Allied Cooperation in Sicily and Italy 1943–1945

Alan F. Wilt

The frustrations of the ground war in Italy did not carry over into close air support, where the Allies achieved considerable success. This can be attributed to gaining air superiority at the outset of the Sicilian campaign and never being seriously challenged in the air thereafter. This made it possible to concentrate on close air support and interdiction, and to refine the techniques and principles so laboriously worked out earlier during exercises in Great Britain and under combat conditions in North Africa.

While RAF experience had a strong influence over Americans, British attitudes toward close air support differed substantially.[1] The British had suffered numerous setbacks early in the conflict and realized that they had to improve close air support tactics if they were ever to meet the Germans on an equal footing, let alone to defeat them. They came to realize that extensive cooperation among the army, navy, and air force at all levels was required.

Having entered the war quite late, the Americans, though aware of the British setbacks, had not undergone the same experience. Despite the fact that the U.S. air units were a part of the U.S. Army, the Americans were slow in achieving the necessary cooperative spirit between air and ground units. By mid-1943, the various American services had only started to appreciate each others' problems. In the end, nevertheless, the air forces of both, RAF and AAF, contributed significantly to the close air support mission in Sicily and Italy.

The ground war can be divided into five phases: the Sicilian campaign of July and August 1943; the takeover of southern Italy during the fall; the ensuing stalemate south of Rome and along the Adriatic Coast, which continued into the spring of 1944; the capture of Rome in June, followed by the advance northward; the winter bivouac in the northern Apennine Mountains; and finally, the buildup and execution of the April 1945 offensive, which carried Allied forces across the Po River to the Alps. The emphasis here will cover the following aspects of close air support during each phase: (1) doctri-

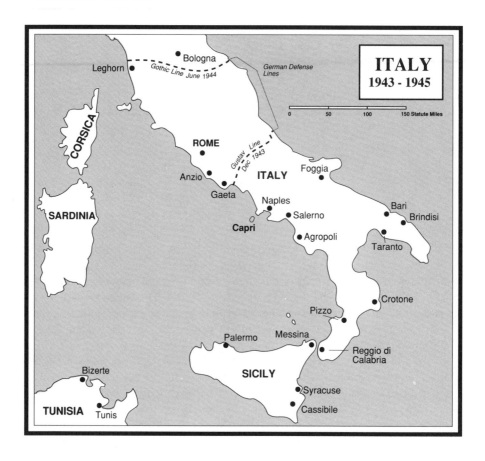

nal issues, (2) the close air support control system, (3) air-ground support techniques, (4) aircraft and armament, (5) operational research, (6) *Luftwaffe* activity, (7) airfield location, (8) other Allied flying missions, (9) bomb safety line and identification difficulties, and (10) interservice and interallied relations. In conclusion, there will be an assessment of close air support in Sicily and Italy, as well as of the significance of air power in relation to the operations as a whole. Greatest emphasis will be on observations that remove all doubt as to the primary importance of cooperation in conducting effective close air support in the Sicilian and Italian campaigns.

Overview

The Sicilian and Italian campaigns featured five Allied amphibious assaults and at least eleven major offensives involving upwards of a million men on each side at all times and resulting in nearly a million casualties.[2] For the Axis powers, it was primarily a war of defensive lines in which Allied movement was accomplished in small increments. A breakthrough in one line of defense led only to another. In Sicily, southern Italy, around Rome, and in crossing the Po River, British and American forces achieved a war of movement, but for relatively short periods. Most of the time during the twenty-two-month offensive, ground was gained slowly against a stubborn foe who gave up territory only when overwhelmed.

Allied military leaders never considered Italy to be the principal land objective. It was always subsidiary to Overlord and the struggle for northwest Europe, even when it was the only active Anglo-American ground front on the continent. At times, the British wanted to nourish it more, especially after the mid-1944 capture of Rome. But the Americans demanded an invasion of southern France instead, as they thought that too much strength might be siphoned off into Italy, and that the British might undertake large-scale operations in the Balkans as well. As a result, the United States insisted that western Europe continue to have first call on resources; Italy was to receive what was left. While this situation did not mean that manpower and equipment sent to Italy were second-rate, they were never sufficient to be decisive. With the United States by 1944 definitely the dominant military partner, the Italian front was destined to receive a secondary emphasis.

Organization

At the top of the Allied organization was the Mediterranean Theater commander, who was ultimately responsible to the Combined Chiefs of Staff (though executive authority was vested in the British Chiefs). During the Casablanca Conference in January 1943, Gen. Dwight D. Eisenhower was named the first combined commander. When he was selected Supreme Allied Commander for Overlord at the end of the year, Field Marshal Sir Henry Maitland Wilson (nicknamed "Jumbo" for his girth) replaced him. Wilson, in turn, was followed in November 1944 by Field Marshal Sir Harold Alexander, when Wilson was designated head of the British Staff Mission in Washington.

Since the British form of organization was used in the theater, Eisenhower and his successors had coequal land, sea, and air leaders under them.[3] The first air commander was the highly respected Air Marshal Sir Arthur Tedder. In December 1943, his command, the Mediterranean Air Command, was redesignated Mediterranean Allied Air Forces, a name which it retained until the end. When Tedder was recalled to the United Kingdom to be Eisenhower's deputy for Overlord, his successor was Lt. Gen. Ira C. Eaker. General Eaker's most recent assignment had been head of U.S. Eighth Air Force in England, which he disliked leaving, as the strategic bomber offensive was beginning to hit its stride. Nevertheless, General Eaker filled the Mediterranean position admirably. During the last two months of the war, he was replaced by Maj. Gen. John K. Cannon. Throughout Eaker's tenure, his deputy was the experienced and capable Air Marshal Sir John Slessor. Cannon's deputy at the end was Air Marshal Sir Guy Garrod.

Because of the changing nature of the Mediterranean Theater, organizational structure of the armed forces there was constantly changing, too. Though always complicated, the structure became less so as the Italian campaign unfolded. Essentially, it consisted of three principal operational air arms—strategic, tactical, and coastal—with an appropriate force structure under each.[4] The tactical forces (Mediterranean Allied Tactical Air Forces) were under Air Marshal Sir Arthur Coningham until December 1943. Called "Mary," or more properly "Maori" because of his New Zealand background, Coningham has been heralded as the father of World War II tactical air doctrine. It was mainly through his efforts during the North African campaigns that American air (rather than Army commanders) were given control over their own aircraft, and air superiority was accorded top priority among tactical air missions.

Coningham was a staunch defender of tactical interests. Just before his leaving for England, other Allied air leaders proposed shifting fighters from tactical units in the Mediterranean to support directly the strategic bombing effort, which was coming on-line in the area. In a masterful response, Coningham and his staff emphasized the necessity of keeping the fighter-bomber groups intact:

> The fighter-bomber force in T.A.F. [Tactical Air Forces] has long experience and is highly specialized. The present standard is due to continuity and the inculcation of fighter-bomber mentality born of more than two years offensive trial and error with armies. It is a difficult task which has to grow on a unit. . . to take these units away from their specialized role and convert them into defensive escorts to long range bombers is unthinkable.
>
> It is appreciated that the heavy bomber forces must have adequate fighter protection, but this can surely be assured without breaking up this unique force.[5]

The transfers did not take place.

Coningham's replacement was the well-liked American Gen. John K. Cannon, who administered the American Twelfth Air Force at the same time. His tactical air forces had three primary components—the Tactical Bomber Force of light and medium bombers, the Desert Air Force (DAF), and the XII Air Support Command (XII ASC). The latter two formed the basis of the tactical air effort.[6]

The DAF was a mixed force of bomber and fighter wings. Its fighter wings were usually divided into four, but might reach six, squadrons of six-

Lt. Gen. Ira C. Eaker as commander of the Mediterranean Allied Air Forces. *(right)* Maj. Gen. John K. Cannon, Twelfth Air Force commander *(below).*

teen aircraft each. It had both advanced and rear headquarters, and the advanced headquarters was, whenever possible, collocated with the army it supported (in this case the British Eighth Army). This collocation made possible continuous contact and coordination between army and air force commanders and their staffs, and became a cardinal feature of tactical air operations.

Like its British counterpart, the American XII Air Support Command had rear and advanced headquarters, the latter being collocated with that of the U.S. Fifth Army. But XII ASC was truly a tactical command in that it had only fighters and fighter bombers assigned to its units. Under it were one or two wings, used mainly for administrative and communications purposes. Its combat flying component centered in the fighter groups. Each group had three squadrons with twenty-five aircraft per squadron, of which between sixty-five and eighty percent were in commission on any given day. A group had about two hundred officers and eight hundred enlisted men, while a squadron had sixty officers and two hundred fifty enlisted. The proportion of ready pilots to operational aircraft was around four to three, but at times, particularly toward the end, it went as high as two to one.

In April 1944, partly because AAF leaders desired to excise the word "support" from their vocabulary, XII ASC became XII Tactical Air Command (XII TAC). After "cooperating" with Allied land forces in Southern France in August, XII TAC's headquarters and a number of its fighter groups remained in France. Those returning to Italy, plus various other units, including British, South African, and Brazilian formations and a U.S. fighter group formerly of the Coastal Air Force, were reconstituted into a new command, XXII TAC, which quickly developed into a top-flight outfit, as evidenced by its operations in the final 1945 offensive.

The Allied air leaders in war theaters were constantly concerned about organizational problems—and the Mediterranean Theater was no exception, especially at the highest levels. Organizational difficulties did have an adverse effect on close air support during the Sicilian and southern Italian operations, but once the Allies were firmly established on the peninsula by the spring of 1944, an effective close air support system had been developed. Its successful development was due in part to the fact that close air support was handled at the army/tactical air command level, where by this time most organizational problems had been ironed out. Capable air force leadership also contributed to the success. In spite of numerous changes in command, the leadership of both the Desert Air Force and the American tactical commands understood well the nature of their missions.[7]

The Sicilian Campaign

By mid-1943, the war turned in favor of the Allies. American and Commonwealth forces stopped the enemy and won substantial victories in the Pacific. So did the Soviets on the Eastern Front, though at great cost. North Africa was finally cleared, the Battle of the Atlantic won, and the strategic bombing offensive beginning to show results. The invasion of Sicily was launched in this atmosphere of increased confidence.

On July 10, 1943, the U.S. Seventh and British Eighth Armies, supported by overwhelming naval and air superiority, assaulted Sicily's southeastern shores.[8] While the Eighth Army advanced north, the Americans fanned out to the west and quickly liberated that portion of the island. Both armies then converged on the Axis forces around Messina, and by August 17 Sicily was in Allied hands.

The air battle also appeared to be highly successful. Prior to the landings, strategic and tactical air forces repeatedly bombed airfields and lines of communications. They effectively supported the invasion by providing air cover for the fleet and over the beaches and assisted the land operations by attempts to isolate the battle area. Though unsuccessful in stopping the evacuation of German forces to the mainland (primarily because of intense enemy flak and a limited night-flying capability), they did help make possible the capture of large amounts of equipment, including 1,100 Axis aircraft left behind by the enemy. On the whole, Allied commanders were pleased with the results.

But beneath the surface, the Sicilian operation had revealed deficiencies particularly in close air support.[9] At the time of the invasion, a rudimentary close air support "system" consisting essentially of two components was devised: (1) Fighter Control Centers (in British parlance, Fighter Directing Ships) to control the air forces from aboard ships; and (2) Air Support Parties (Forward Fighter Controls), equipped with radars and radios, to come ashore on the heels of the armies to assist and eventually take over directing the close air effort. However, due to inexperienced operators, crowded conditions, and poor communications, the Fighter Control Centers did not function well. Although four of the five Air Support Parties landed on the first day, they were hampered by mountainous terrain that masked their radars and by inadequate communications with the land and air components. In fact during the first forty-eight hours there was no close air support at all as fighter and fighter-bomber efforts were devoted to beach and shipping patrols. Even after the beachhead was secured, close support continued to play almost no role. Missions were flown mainly against transportation and communications targets behind the battlefield.

As the campaign progressed, close air support sorties, primarily by North American A–36s and Spitfires, were initiated but were often ineffective. British support for their ground forces was better than that of the Americans, even though it often consisted merely of attacks on enemy motor vehicles near the front. A report prepared in January 1945 by the U.S. Army Air Forces Evaluation Board dealing with the Mediterranean was especially critical, mentioning numerous problems:[10]

> The swift movement of the Sicilian campaign disclosed forcefully the lack of coordination between the American ground and air forces. The Ground forces often failed to keep the Air Support Command posted on the current location of Bomb Safety Lines. Frequently targets for which air support had been requested were overtaken by our own rapid advance before aid from the skies arrived. From an airman's point of view, much of the Sicilian campaign must be classed as an example of inefficient and uneconomical employment of air power, due, in part, to imperfect filtering of air support requests. . . .

Not only was there a lack of coordination, but U.S. Army historians noted a related problem: unwillingness on the part of Army Air Forces staffs to cooperate with other Army elements or with the Navy during the planning stages.[11] In an AAF study after the war, historian Harry Coles is somewhat equivocal on the subject. While noting that air support had improved greatly over its performance in Tunis, he indicates that "it is [still] obvious that at the time of the Sicilian campaign much remained to be done in the improvement and coordination and techniques of air operations in close support of ground forces."[12]

There were doctrinal and operational reasons for the cumbersome command and control, slow reaction time, and inadequate bomb line procedures. The doctrinal issue had two aspects: (1) This was the first campaign in which American air commanders exercised centralized control of air operations, and this newly gained prerogative more than any other factor discouraged AAF leaders from becoming involved in joint planning and coordination at all levels; (2) There was an overemphasis on air superiority. Like centralized control, air superiority was basic for prosecuting successful close air support for a ground campaign. But in Sicily it was overdone. The Germans and Italians could muster only 275–300 sorties during the first few days of the campaign, and about half of these were at night.[13] After that, the Axis' air effort was reduced even further due to heavy losses, and because those aircraft still in commission were being removed to the mainland.

The Allies not only flew fewer and fewer patrol missions, but tactical aircraft were increasingly assigned to interdiction (second priority) rather than to close air support (third priority).

Close air support suffered also from two operational shortcomings: (1) a lack of training and (2) the distances of airfields from the battle area. The distance problem was soon overcome, as Allied progress on the ground allowed Allied air forces to use Sicilian airfields instead of flying from

Malta, Gozo, Pantelleria, or Tunisia. There were twenty-five tactical squadrons in operation in Sicily by D + 9.[14] Insufficient training could also be remedied, but the extensive experience required to develop effective air-ground coordination had to be solved over the longer term.

Capture of Southern Italy

The Allies did not take time to assimilate the lessons of the Sicilian campaign, for on September 3, the British 5th and Canadian 1st Divisions crossed the narrow Strait of Messina that separates Sicily from the mainland and soon were moving north against light opposition.[15]

On the 8th, the new Italian government under Marshal Pietro Badoglio announced an armistice with the Allies, taking Italy out of the war, and the next day the U.S. VI and British X Corps made the first attempt to outflank the Germans by undertaking an amphibious assault at Salerno Bay, one hundred seventy land miles north of the Italian toe. Though the landing was a success, Allied troops withstood with some difficulty a determined *Wehrmacht* counterattack four days later. Only on the 16th did the German Tenth Army give way and start to withdraw. That same evening American Fifth Army formations in the beachhead contacted British soldiers from the south, and Anglo-American units began moving toward Naples, capturing it on October 2. By the 6th, they had reached the Volturno River about twenty-five miles north of the city.

Naples was only one of the major objectives. Another was the Foggia airfields on the eastern side of the peninsula. Consequently on September 9 the British 1st Airborne Division landed at Taranto unopposed and two days later took Bari on the Adriatic. Reinforced by Canadian and British divisions, they advanced north, on the 27th seizing Foggia, which had been abandoned by the Germans. Two weeks later, the forces cleared the area to the north, thereby securing the airfields.

At the same time, the Germans and some Italian troops who remained loyal to the Axis decided to evacuate the major islands of Sardinia and Corsica west of Italy. American paratroopers had no opposition in liberating Sardinia by September 18. Free French and Resistance fighters were able to take Corsica by October 4, but not before the German forces escaped to the mainland. The western flank was now secure, and the islands could serve as staging areas for further Allied operations against northern Italy or southern France.

The Allies also achieved other goals.[16] Despite the German ability to move substantial forces down the peninsula, a major objective—the surrender of Italy—had been achieved. Three excellent harbors—Taranto, Bari, and Naples—and two airfield complexes near Naples and Foggia were now in

Allied hands, and the Fifth and Eighth Armies supported by the U.S. XII Air Support Command and the Desert Air Force were in position to advance northward.

Close air support had not yielded the desired results during the initial operations in Italy, especially at Salerno.[17] Providing adequate air cover from Sicilian airfields at least 150 miles away posed the major problem during the landing phase. The problem was solved in part, however, when the A–36s, P–38 Lightnings, and Spitfires providing patrol extended their coverage in the assault area from 30 minutes to 1 hour by attaching long-range fuel tanks. British Seafires from carriers offshore also supplemented the Sicily-based aircraft.

Using air force and naval planes for patrol duties was one thing; using them for close air support proved to be another. It was necessary to have airfields nearby to carry out effective support of the ground forces. Airfields in the beachhead were under enemy fire and could not be used for a number of days; hence, Allied fighter-bombers were not able to offer strong resistence to German troops when they began their counteroffensive on September 12. Only by invoking all available air power, including medium and heavy bombers, and through the tenacity of some of the army units were the Allies able to avert evacuation. These difficulties eventually prompted General Eisenhower to write:

> . . .[O]ne major lesson should never be lost sight of in future planning . . . that during the critical stages of a landing operation, every item of available force including land, sea, and air, must be wholly concentrated in support of the landing until troops are in position to take care of themselves . . . .

In a remark directed at the air leaders, he ended the memorandum by stating that "this [support for landings] most emphatically includes the so-called Strategic Air Force."

The possibility of developing joint doctrine—at least between the navies and air forces—also was neglected at Salerno.[18] In part this was because land-based aircraft had to fly a long distance to the assault beaches before they could offer close air support.

For the first several days, control of fighter aircraft was better executed from ships and LSTs than on land. As in Sicily, it was found that after Air Support Parties had established themselves ashore, they were generally ineffective. On one occasion, for example, three patrolling squadrons dispatched to investigate an unidentified raid by two or more aircraft some thirty miles north of Salerno left Allied ships virtually without protection. During their absence, low-flying, unopposed enemy planes attacked the ships and beaches causing great damage.

But even though air force-naval doctrine did not develop, cooperation between the navies and the air forces on the operational level did.[19] The 108 carrier-based Seafires flew a total of 713 sorties during the first four days of the operation, thereby augmenting the 2,400 sorties flown by the fighters from Sicily. Even after the force of five carriers departed, "the twenty-six Seafires still serviceable flew back to Paestum airstrip in the U.S. beachhead to continue patrolling until relieved by Spitfires."[20]

While air-ground cooperation showed continuing troubles, it also exhibited some improvement.[21] At Salerno, General Clark, the U.S. Fifth Army Commander, became so dissatisfied with the lack of air support, especially during the German counteroffensive, that he complained to Field Marshal Alexander. His complaint resulted in the maximum Allied air effort of September 14–15, which greatly assisted in turning back the German thrust. Later in September and into October, still further improvement in cooperation became apparent. Centralized control of air assets, close liaison between armies and tactical air commands, and daily meetings of air and ground leaders to choose targets for the following day, all contributed to increased efficiency. There were also experiments with forward air controllers operating from jeeps or other vehicles. As a result, though still in need of much refinement, a close air support system was beginning to take shape.

A further problem, airfield location, was also being addressed. It was particularly difficult to have airfields sufficiently near the battle area during fast-moving operations or before amphibious assaults had established themselves ashore. Although the rapid advances of the early phase were seldom repeated in Italy, the frequency of moving still presented a problem for organizing air support.[22] This should not be surprising, considering that the Allies eventually drove from southern Sicily to the Swiss border, a distance of 1,100 miles. Existing German and Italian airfields, like those around Foggia and Naples, were naturally useful, but many others had to be constructed from scratch. At Salerno, for instance, the Allies hoped to put the Paestum airfield in the beachhead area to immediate use. Though captured soon after the landing, it remained under enemy artillery fire and proved to be of only limited value during the initial stages. Improvised airfields had to be built.

Landing strips and facilities constructed in Italy differed widely. Runways varied in length from 3,200 to 6,000 feet and consisted of packed earth, pierced steel plank, or concrete construction.[23] Fighter-bombers needed 5,000 feet of runway, but shorter runways were normally adequate for fighters.

Living conditions also varied considerably. Two entries in the headquarters war diary of the American 31st Fighter Group, which was flying Spitfires, described some of these conditions.[24] On September 20, 1943, the war diarist noted,

> We moved out to Monte Corvino [on Salerno Bay] last night and this morning. The airdrome shows signs of the battle that raged here; the hangars and buildings on the north side of the field are battered, and scores of German and Italian aircraft are scattered over the entire airdrome.

> . . . it was decided to set up Group Headquarters in a house approximately 1/4 mile from the airdrome. This latter house is a great improvement over the one first selected. We are to live on an estate across the road from the Headquarters building. A large villa on the estate is to be used for the mess, the officers' living quarters, dispensary, and the command and personnel sections' offices. The enlisted men will live in another house near the villa. The 308th Squadron pilots and aircraft are now here with us. The rest of the Group will be here soon. (The airdrome was bombed and strafed this morning with no damage.)

September 21, 1943:

> The Headquarters and 308th air echelon came in . . . in C–47's. We are setting up our offices now. . . . We had a lot of cleaning to do in our living quarters, but they are very pleasant now. Most of the men have been able to get some kind of bed to sleep on, for the first time in many months. This is the first time we have lived and slept in buildings since early in February. . . .

A little more than three weeks later, on October 14, the 31st Fighter Group moved again. The situation was even better for the airmen:

> We moved from Monte Corvino airdrome to Pomigliano [east of Naples] today. Our Group HQ is to be set up in the firehouse on the airdrome and living quarters will be in apartments near the airdrome. Pomigliano d'Arco was the scene of the Alfa–Romeo aircraft engine plant, but all the factory buildings are completely destroyed . . . [from Liberator raids]. Our apartments are pleasant and much more modern than we expected to find here. We have running water, and electric lights in some of the apartments. The electricity for the lights is furnished by gasoline engine driven generators from the factory. There are about 120 blocks of apartments in the area with an average of eight apartments in each block, and we are pretty well-scattered, with civilians occupying apartments in [many of] these blocks.

The living conditions at Monte Corvino and Pomigliano were not duplicated everywhere, especially with the fighter wings and groups constantly on the move.

First Winter of Stalemate

During the fall of 1943, the Allied attempt to push rapidly up the peninsula floundered.[25] Bad weather and a stubborn, formidable enemy played an important role in the slowdown. One German defensive barrier after another gave way—from Victor to Barbara to Bernhard to Gustav—but Allied progress was painstakingly slow. Finally, along the Gustav line—from the

Garigliano River in the west through Cassino to north of the Sangro River on the east coast—the Germans held fast. One historian wrote that the campaign now turned into a "slow, dreary battle up the Italian peninsula."

The stalemate continued throughout the spring and into May 1944. On January 12, 1944, the Allies started an offensive in the west. One of the battles, an attempt to cross the Rapido River, was particularly bloody. The U.S. 36th Infantry Division was decimated. The entire operation was designed to break through the Gustav Line and advance up the Liri Valley, while the British and American soldiers under the U.S. VI Corps attempted an amphibious end run at Anzio, thirty-five miles south of Rome. The assault on January 22 achieved tactical surprise, but the Allies did not seize the high ground beyond the beachhead to prevent German divisions from being rushed to the area before the Allies were ready to advance eight days later. The Germans could not be dislodged. *Wehrmacht* forces even undertook several counteroffensives. One of them in mid-February almost forced the Allies to evacuate. The beachhead was held, but continuing efforts by British, French, New Zealand, and Indian units to reach Anzio and to drive on Rome ran into stout opposition.

Farther east, Allied attempts to take Cassino—both the town and the monastery—failed repeatedly and led to numerous mistakes, the most salient in February being the unnecessary bombing of the famed abbey. The impasse on the ground at Cassino and elsewhere was not broken until late that spring. Ironically, at the same time Allied ground forces were facing heavy resistance, close air support was developing into a highly respected, much appreciated system. By the spring of 1944, it matured to the point where command and control, ground forward air controllers, aircraft and armament, and air-land doctrines required only refinement. In addition, problems associated with close air support, such as *Luftwaffe* air activity, other air priorities, bomb safety lines and identification markers, and interallied relations, were recognized and effectively dealt with. Close air support in Italy came of age.

Of all the changes leading to effective close air support in Italy, none was more significant than the air control process. This process had been used in North Africa and Sicily, but was not fully developed until Allied forces were established on the peninsula in a relatively stable situation.[26] At its heart was a well-defined though intricate procedure for command and control, which was governed by a requirement for extensive air-ground cooperation at all levels.[27] (Liaison with the navies was also important during the amphibious undertakings; but timely close air support missions were limited, since pilots were not dispatched specifically for close air support but were diverted from air patrol and received their briefings during flight.)[28] This meant that requests for air support continued to originate with the armies, but the final decision rested with the tactical air commanders, whose headquarters were collocated with the numbered army command. For Americans, the headquarters of XII Air Support Command, renamed XII Tactical Air Command in April 1944, was located next to that of Fifth Army. Later that year, XXII TAC assumed this responsibility when XII TAC was shifted to southern and then eastern France. For the British, Desert Air Force headquarters was normally adjacent to that of Eighth Army.

The Army's close air support requests were for "prearranged" and "call" missions. Both types were subject to a "filtering" process, which worked as follows: Requests for "prearranged missions" (within 24 hours) could initiate as low as division level; for the British at brigade level. After taking into account enemy as well as their own capabilities, selected division officers (air force liaison personnel acted as advisors) decided on certain targets for close air support attacks that would assist their operations. At approximately 3 p.m. their requests were communicated to corps, which weighed the various division requests against its own plans, and about an hour later proposed to army the mission or series of missions that best fit its requirements. Army then conferred and proposed to a joint army–air force group an air targeting program that conformed with the army's overall tactical plan.

This nightly conference—at 5:30 for Eighth Army, 7 p.m. for Fifth Army—brought together members of the commanders' army and air force staffs. The intelligence and operations officers reviewed the day's activities, and the armies then gave to the air representatives the targets they wanted to have attacked the next day. The air officers accepted as many of the requests as their own resources and commitments would allow. Their commitments were determined by their commanders in consultation with General Eaker's staff at Mediterranean Allied Air Forces headquarters. If the Army's requests were considered of sufficient priority but the air forces had inadequate resources to meet them, the tactical commanders might turn to General Eaker for assistance.[29]

By the time the conference was finished, the air staff was busy preparing a detailed directive for the next day's operations. It assigned each mission to a particular wing or group, gave the number of aircraft to be employed, the time of attack, and available target information. A mission allotted to the RAF's 239 Wing on September 30, 1944, provides a typical example:[30]

Mission # 1 With 6 aircraft within the area L8926, L9726, L9820, L8920 [map coordinates]. Aiming point will be indicated by Red artillery smoke. Time over target 0800 hours.

Information such as this was passed through the army communications net to all subordinate units, including the tactical groups that were to carry out the missions and the army divisions or corps that initiated the requests. The teletyped directive reached the ground units within two hours, followed by mimeographed copies and pertinent photographs delivered that same night by courier to the air groups directly involved.[31]

206

Before take-off, pilots participating in the attacks were carefully briefed on the enemy defenses, call signs, weather, and the latest bomb safety line. In addition, from large-scale maps and aerial photos that they carried on their missions they studied the type of target, its location, and identifying features. After the attack, they assessed the results—often with the aid of photo and visual reconnaissance—and the cycle started again for the next day.

The second type of mission, designated "call missions" because they originated with a radio call, took into account changes in the battle situation that favored attacks against targets of opportunity. In this case, the request came directly to division from units along the front. Division then immediately radioed the joint air–army control center at army headquarters. Even though this procedure bypassed corps, corps would intercede if it did not want the mission flown, as it monitored the division's request. If corps did not intervene, it gave its tacit assent to performing the mission.

The officer at the control center showed or telephoned the request to the army and air force operations officers. If either officer disapproved, a refusal message was immediately sent to the division initiating the request. If approved, the necessary information was sent to the appropriate airfields, whose personnel had already been alerted from the impending mission. Pilots "on call"—certain squadrons were designated alert units in the daily directive—were then briefed and sent to the target. The goal, was to have aircraft over the target within an hour and a half after the request was initiated. "Call missions" often achieved this goal.

Numerous variations in this procedure could be tolerated. For instance, if tactical air did not have enough squadrons on call, or if the targets requested were of sufficient priority, pilots scheduled to undertake lower priority "prearranged" missions might be shifted to the "call" target.

Another variation, devised to cut down aircraft response time—thus gaining wide acceptance—made use of forward ground or air controllers. These controllers, who often had a view of the battlefield, were requested by frontline units to have fighter-bombers attack particularly troublesome enemy targets, such as gun positions or tank formations in their vicinity. If the controller accepted the request—he was linked to the air-army control center for information on problems unknown to him—he radioed aircraft flying overhead to strike the target. (As with normal "call missions," the daily directive had already specified squadrons for this duty.) Often marking the area by colored artillery smoke, the controller then directed pilots to the specific target. After the bombing or strafing run, which could be within 1,000 yards of friendly troops, the forward controller and observers with the army formations recorded the results. Using this method, a flight of aircraft might be able to hit an enemy target within 10 minutes from the time a controller received the request.

Whether "preplanned" or "call missions," effective communication was essential to the success of the entire system. In its final form, the system was linked at three different levels.[32] The highest level, or focal point, was the joint army–air control center, also called a tactical air control center, or in the British lexicon, a Mobile Operations Room Unit. Here the operator communicated command decisions to airfields for implementation. Because the control center kept current information on all air operations in the area, operators also maintained contact with subordinate air and ground units and with friendly aircraft in flight, alerting the pilots to problems and vectoring them to target areas or to other controllers. The intermediate level organizations, termed "forward director posts" or "tactical air direction centers," were located at or near corps headquarters. They too had radars, wireless, telephone and teletype links to warn of hostile aircraft and at times to direct aircraft all the way to the target.

During the final stages of the mission, the direction center would usually turn over control of the aircraft to the forward ground or air controller. The ground controller, generally in a vehicle with a good view of the target area, would be able to guide the pilot to the target by radio. The controller also maintained radio communications with nearby airfields and laid wire for telephone links to the airfields as well as to local ground command posts, artillery-fire direction centers, and to the control center at army headquarters. The air controller flying a two-seater, light, L–5 liaison aircraft near the front lines might have an even better view of the target. He could therefore take over radio control of the fighter-bomber and direct it to the target, while maintaining contact with the forward ground controller, leading elements of the land forces, and artillery observers.

Crossbreeding the liaison personnel bound the system together: army officers serving with air groups and air force officers with army units. Forward air controllers were almost always experienced pilots. The Army also attempted to fill its liaison positions with combat officers. Both land and air force units realized that cooperation was imperative under the unifying principle observed by both: while the armies request support, the ultimate decision rests with the air commander.

As the tactical air command and control system was regularized, forward controller techniques, which were to become an integral part of the system, also became routine. The most widely known of the techniques, Rover, was developed at this time. The British first used it in North Africa, and the Americans worked with it at Salerno; but only late in 1943 did both air forces begin to use it extensively. The United States called it Rover Joe, after GI Joe, the popular nickname for the U.S. Army soldier. The British called theirs Rover David and Rover Paddy, after Group Captains David Haysom, a legendary fighter pilot and originator of the idea, and Paddy Green, who was equally famous for his exploits.[33]

Although the equipment and manning requirements differed,* the technique, already described in part, was virtually the same for both allies.[34] The forward controllers—at least one combat pilot and one army officer—took positions in a well-concealed observation post, preferably on a hilltop with a good view of the front lines. Their radio equipment, behind the hill out of sight of enemy observers and protected from enemy fire, was operated by enlisted personnel who communicated by telephone to the observation post. The air and ground officers were supplied with all the necessary maps and photos of the terrain they were covering.

When ground forces encountered a target that was causing them trouble and that required an air strike, they radioed the Rover unit for support. If the ground and air officers at the army-air control center accepted the request, the Rover controller contacted four (six for Britain) fighter-bombers that were circling overhead out of range of enemy antiaircraft guns. The fighters were part of a procedure known as Cabrank, which consisted of flights of aircraft scheduled to arrive in the area at thirty minute intervals. Before taking off, they were assigned and briefed on alternate targets, and if they received no call from Rover after orbiting for twenty minutes, they were to attack these alternates. If Rover had a suitable target, he would "talk" the flight onto the target by using specially gridded maps and aerial photographs, describing prominent terrain features, and providing colored smoke markers fired by army artillery. When both the flight leader and the controller were satisfied that the target had been positively identified, the flight leader would initiate the attack. A typical example of the Rovers' effectiveness is shown by excerpts of the Fifth Army target diary of October 1, 1944:[35]

Time	Aircraft	Requests	Results
0730	4 Spitfires	Rover Joe occupied;	Bombed strongpoint L8617; 1 direct hit house; strafed house L880267—no movement seen
0900	4 Spitfires	Rover Joe Farm L872253	Bombed and strafed target L745183; 4 direct hits building; much black smoke
1415	4 P–47s	Rover Joe	Bombed 6 houses L7218; 4 buildings hit; no results observed
1715	4 P–47s	Rover Joe	Troop concentration and guns—woods L6519; all bombs target area no results observed; intense small arms target area; target area well-strafed

*The U.S. used more personnel, approximately nine vs. six British, and more vehicles, two trucks and three jeeps vs. one or two armored cars for the British.

Of the four missions described, Rover controllers played an important role in three of them.

A 1944 theater report also praised the technique when it says that 'Rover Joe' has become something of a tradition with our front line troops, who take an active interest in its use. The rapid response to their requests for air support is often a source of elation to them. 'Rover Joe' has definite value in maintaining the morale of our troops. Conversely, it has a shattering effect on enemy morale, a fact substantiated by many PW interrogations.[36]

The Rovers were not always praised. It was a difficult technique to master, and the British contended that it was more effective in static than in fluid situations, where the bombing and strafing of friendly troops was more likely to occur. American land and air personnel claimed it could be effective in either case (the British also eventually came around to this view), but a XXII TAC memorandum of October 1944 noting a number of discrepancies casts some doubt on this optimistic viewpoint. Flights were late hitting their targets, and in many instances flight leaders did not know their assigned mission number or did not have proper maps of the target area. Also, radio pro-

A Rover Joe team in action near Bologna during the latter stages of the Italian campaign. Air officers were detailed to ground units to control air strikes in support of engaged infantry.

P-47 Thunderbolt unloads two 500-pound bombs on a target identified by ground controllers.

cedures proved inadequate, with entirely too much "chatter" on the Rover channels. Some missions had not received alternate targets prior to take-off, and, finally, "the unit tactics in most cases have been poor." It would appear that many flights had no plan for attacking various targets. Bombing runs were frequently too shallow, resulting in extreme cases of inaccuracy. While this memo did not describe the extent of the discrepancies, it did show that the Rover technique was not without its difficulties.[37]

During the relatively static phase from November 1943 to April 1944, the types of aircraft and armament also began to change appreciably, an evo-

211

lution that continued through 1944 and into 1945. Here the results were mixed, for while the Americans found an excellent close air support aircraft, the Desert Air Force never developed a superior fighter-bomber in combat.

The United States did not always have an optimal plane for close air support either. First in Sicily and then in Italy throughout 1943, XII Air Support Command utilized a number of aircraft: A–36s, a version of the P–51 Mustang fitted with bomb racks and dive brakes; P–38 Lightnings; British Spitfires; and especially P–40 Warhawks.[38] The A–36s and P–38s were good bombers but relatively vulnerable to flak with their liquid-cooled, inline engines. The Warhawk was considered better. Though relatively slow with a speed of 300 mph at 10,000 feet, the P–40N could absorb a good deal of punishment and was considered an excellent strafer and dive bomber with a bomb load normally of 500 to 1,000 pounds.

During 1944, however, the Americans turned almost exclusively to the P–47 for close air support needs. It proved to be an outstanding choice. After testing the Thunderbolt in December 1943, Maj. Gilbert O. Wynand, Jr. and other test pilots were convinced that it would "prove to be the most successful dive bomber we have today."[39] They were especially impressed with its "tremendous diving speed" and "wonderful diving characteristics" and thought it better than the P–40 on a number of counts. In their view, it was easier to control during a bombing run, had twice the radius of action, exhibited much better zoom climb characteristics, carried a bigger bomb load, and could withstand flak as well as the P–40. Only in strafing did they find it deficient, since poor downward visibility limited its ability to fly on the deck for extended periods.

The P–47D, the model most used, had a top speed of 425 mph at 20,000 feet, eight .50–cal machineguns on the wings, a radius of action of 250 miles when loaded with two 1,000–pound bombs (extended to 350 miles when wing tanks were substituted for the bombs).[40] Later on, in 1944, it carried 4.5–inch rockets, 100–pound phosphorus bombs, and 260–pound napalm incendiaries, which added to its lethality. It was also easily maintained and durable, because its radial air-cooled engine was not as susceptible to antiaircraft fire as the liquid-cooled engines. Although it could execute level bombing, its bombing run usually began at 6,000 to 8,000 feet, diving at an angle between 25 and 40 degrees, with the release at about 2,500 feet.

The British, for their part, essentially used 3 fighter-bomber types in Italy: A–36s, which were eventually replaced by the faster P–51s; Kittyhawks, Britain's version of the P–40; and Spitfires. Of the 3, the Spitfires were by far the largest in number, with 256 operational in mid-July 1943 as compared with 97 Kittyhawks and A–36s. The proportion was equally great in June 1944, when there were 312 Spitfires operational and only 127 of the others.[41] (A small number of P–47s were also in the Desert Air Force inventory later in the war but did not appear in the combat squadrons.)

Although Spitfire proponents will no doubt disagree, an operational research study in the fall of 1944 casts doubt on its effectiveness as a fighter-bomber.[42] The study concluded that the Spitfire IX had a relatively small bomb load (500 pounds), limited range when loaded (only 95 miles), and less stability in a dive than the Kittyhawk or Mustang. Despite its excellent versatility, durability, speed (404 mph at 21,000 feet), and armament (two 20–mm cannons and two .50–cal machine guns), the study went so far as to recommend keeping the Kittyhawks, which were being phased out in favor of the P–51 Mustang, and using the latter to replace the Spitfire. Nothing came of the recommendation, probably because it came too late in the war. But even though the Spitfire remained a famous fighter aircraft and achieved a number of successes in Italy, its suitability for bombing, if not strafing, was open to question.

The close air support system advanced in another area as well: air-land doctrine. As emphasized earlier, land forces requested air strikes on specific targets, but air commanders controlled the aircraft. This concept was accepted—though reluctantly by some American ground force commanders—before the Sicilian and Italian campaigns ever began.[43] By 1944, the main problems were (1) to decrease the response time for aircraft to reach a target and (2) to determine the extent of air support to be allotted to the army. With respect to the first problem, a solution was reached by creating the fast, coordinated, comprehensive air control system, the procedure for "call" as well as "prearranged" targets, and the expanded use of forward controllers, all described above. The results, though far from perfect, did speed up tactical air's ability to strike army-requested targets in a timely fashion.

The second problem—the extent of air support—was to be determined by joint air–ground planning. General Eaker, head of Mediterranean Allied Air Forces, wrote to the Commanding General, U.S. Army Air Forces, General Arnold, "Army and air force commanders must work in closest consultation throughout all stages of the formulation and execution of the plan, to ensure that the land and air operations interact to the best advantage. . . ."[44]

On occasion, ground operations might be adapted to air concerns, particularly when air superiority or interdiction were accorded a high priority. Other occasions might require air support, in addition to normal tactical air. Still, as Eaker pointed out, "Heavy and medium bombers should rarely be used on the battlefield. Exceptions include a critical situation in defense, as at Salerno, or to precede a large-scale amphibious landing against beach defenses. It is emphasized that these are rare exceptions." Eaker also affirmed another principle, namely, that "fighter-bombers will usually afford more valuable assistance to the advance of land forces if they are used in the enemy's back area, beyond the range of our artillery."

While planners still adhere to this idea today, there were deviations during the later stages of the campaign, for air support at times could be more rapid and effective than artillery gunfire, especially in fast-moving situations. The difficulty, of course, was to find the precise location of targets and to maintain effective control; hence the need for forward controllers *with mobility*, a condition seldom achieved in Italy. In all of this, constant contact among the army and air elements was fundamental for obtaining desired objectives.

Although concern about *Luftwaffe* activity in Italy was never far from the minds of Allied air commanders, *Luftflotte* 2, the German air force responsible for the area, was seldom more than an irritant, and after early 1944 was almost nonexistent.[45] In only two instances—in Sicily and during the Anzio–Gustav Line fighting—did the Axis have more than 400 aircraft operational, and most of the combat sorties were what historian Karl Gundelach calls of the "cat and mouse" variety, or against Allied shipping. In contrast to the Allies' 3,000 to 4,000 combat aircraft in service at all times, *Luftflotte* 2 had only 147 planes (including transports) operational on December 31, 1943. Of these, 88 were fighters and fighter-bombers, and there were no bombers at all.

For the Anzio counterattacks in February 1944, the Air Fleet was built up to 459 operational aircraft, including 163 fighters and fighter-bombers and 103 bombers. Thereafter, its numbers again declined, some aircraft being lost in combat, others being shifted to the west. On the 10th of May 1944, the eve of the Allied Rome offensive, the Germans had 329 planes in commission. From there the situation for the *Luftwaffe* and the small Italian air force continued to deteriorate. All German fighter aircraft were removed to the Reich by the end of July 1944. There was a gasoline crisis in September and October. The Axis had 100 operational aircraft in December (63 Italian), 92 in January 1945, and 120 in April. In short, the Axis' ability to fly combat was negligible for the rest of the campaign.

Even though *Luftflotte* 2 was a negligible factor, Allied air forces lost an average of more than 200 aircraft per month in combat, primarily the result of extensive enemy antiaircraft fire.[46] Throughout the 22 months, as might be expected, losses exceeded victories over Axis planes, even though Allied pilots often claimed more victories than were actually achieved.

British and American air leaders also had to conduct other types of missions and operations.[47] Close air support at this time gave way to an emphasis on interdiction, as between March and May 1944, when Allied pilots did have some "strangling" effect on German supply links to their front-line troops.[48] There were also numerous tactical and strategic bombing missions in which tactical aircraft were called upon to provide additional escort. On occasion, ground situations—such as at Anzio and Cassino—called for bombers to assist the fighters. While their attacks were often effective before an offensive, the use of bombers in close proximity to friendly ground troops brought disastrous results. Fighter-bombers were also diverted to operations outside Italy, such as in the French Riviera in August 1944, and to missions into the Balkans. In these instances, fighter-bombers exhibited one of their most vital capabilities: the versatility to undertake a variety of tasks.

One problem not completely solved during this static period was bomb safety lines, which were set by indentification markers.[49] A bomb safety line (BSL), placed about 1,000 feet in front of the forward line of troops, was usually based on some physical feature easily identifiable from the air, beyond which it was safe to attack enemy targets. But in a fluid situation, problems such as bomb creep and pilots having to fly at right angles rather than parallel to the bomb line (which was preferable) made it exceedingly difficult to establish and maintain. The most infamous violation occurred at Cassino in March 1944, when 30 U.S. bombers dropped their bombs short of the town, killing 57 and wounding 179 soldiers and civilians. But there were many other ground-to-air as well as air-to-ground incidents.

The British and Americans undertook various measures to overcome the problem. Experience indicated that in certain instances the bomb safety line could be moved even closer to the forward positions, and by April 1944, XII TAC had introduced a close support line (around 500 feet) inside the BSL. Allied personnel also worked hard to develop proper identification markings. On individual soldiers, the use of red fluorescent panels proved superior to luminous triangles. White stars and stripes and pennants were attached to vehicles, but none of the markings was foolproof. Nor was red smoke, though it was better than yellow smoke, which blended in too closely with the terrain. Some pilots felt that smoke was the only reliable method, but to be effective even it (or antiaircraft bursts above the target) had to be laid immediately before the attack. Whatever the method, still far from reassuring is a postwar British Air Ministry report indicating that during the later stages of the campaign "instances of bombing of friendly troops were due to human error rather than any intrinsic fault in the [identification] system."[50]

A final issue evolving satisfactorily at this time was cooperation among the Allied nations.[51] Canadian, South African, Australian, Polish, Greek, and French squadrons were integral parts of the Mediterranean air forces almost from the beginning of the campaigns. By the end of 1943 a Yugoslav unit was being phased in, and Italian pilots flying Maachi–205s were undertaking missions for the Allies rather than for the Axis. Many times these units were used for missions other than close air support, but in whatever capacity, they generally proved their worth. By April 1944, therefore, despite the problems—and there were others such as limited night-flying and inclement weather capabilities—the Allies developed a sound close air support system. Refinements to the basic system were added during the coming operations.

Rome and Beyond

On May 11, 1944, the Allies once again made an all-out attempt to break through the Gustav Line.[52] The forces in Italy on both sides were about equal—twenty-three Allied divisions against twenty-three German. But the British and Americans could not be stopped. Their armies and air forces were rested and concentrated west of the Apennines. French troops advanced through the mountains to high ground overlooking the Liri Valley, forcing the Germans to start withdrawing from the southern corridor toward Rome. Although it was no longer a decisive sector, the Allies were further cheered when Polish troops captured Monte Cassino on the 18th. The Gustav Line collapsed, and the British Eighth Army drove forward in the Liri Valley, while the U.S. Fifth Army advanced along the west coast, linking up with the Anzio formations on the 25th. In spite of conflicts between American and British commanders over the honor of liberating Rome, the push on the "Eternal City" began in earnest, and by June 4, it was in Allied hands.

The celebration accompanying Rome's liberation was soon eclipsed by the news of Overlord landings, but the Allied advance in central Italy continued along a broad front. Despite the removal of 3 American and 4 French divisions for the invasion of southern France, U.S. troops reached the Arno River, 175 miles north of Rome, on July 23.

Then Allied progress slowed noticeably. Supply lines were stretched to the limit, the troops exhausted, and the Germans digging in. Florence was liberated on August 13, but by this time Field Marshal Albert Kesselring's forces were giving ground grudgingly if at all. British and American, along with Canadian, South African, and Polish divisions were able to cross the Arno in force, but this brought them up against the Gothic Line, which stretched 180 miles from Massa on the Ligurian coast through the Apennines north of Florence to Pesaro on the Adriatic.

The Canadians and Poles broke the Gothic Line in the east on September 1, 1944, but the Canadians were then held up on the Rimini Line behind it. On the 21st, Eighth Army finally captured Rimini on the east coast and reached the Lombardy Plain, only to become bogged down by autumn rains. In the meantime, the Americans undertook a secondary thrust and pierced the Gothic Line near Firenzuola. During October they were, however, unable to take Bologna, and eventually settled into the northern Apennines for a second winter of discontent. Even a turn-of-the-year plan to seize Bologna had to be postponed. A late December German offensive, to coincide with the desperate Ardennes "gamble" known as "The Battle of the Bulge," this one code-named Thunderstorm, had to be checked instead.

Throughout the summer advance and the fall slowdown, tactical air operations remained quite effective.[53] During the push toward Rome, the AAF emphasized interdiction, but flew a number of close air support sorties as well. In one instance this included the outstanding performance of a forward controller on the top of Mt. Trocchio on the Gustav Line, who directed nine different fighter-bomber missions on a single day. After the fall of Rome, both close air support and interdiction sorties continued. In September, during the British Eighth Army's attempt to force the Rimini Line at San Fortunato, tactical air played an especially prominent role. On the 17th, for example, 132 fighter-bombers supported Canadian troops by directing a well-timed attack against the entrenched enemy, hitting first the forward slopes, then the summit, and finally the reverse slopes. When this operation failed to dislodge the Germans, the next day, between 0600 and 0700 hrs, three DAF wings struck both the forward and reverse slopes with six aircraft attacking every five minutes, each of the bombing and strafing attacks lasting four minutes. During phase two, between 0700 and 0745, red smoke at the top of the hill served as a bomb line, while Canadian infantry assaulted the forward slopes, and fighter-bombers continued to soften the other side of the hill. Measures such as this successfully ruptured the line. On September 30, the following comment appeared in the Desert Air Force Operations Book: "Never before in the history of the D.A.F. has so much effort been concentrated so consistently upon targets immediately in front of ground forces." In November, when the offensive thrust came virtually to a halt, the emphasis returned to road and rail targets.

Between May and the end of 1944, tactical air leaders continued to refine and embellish the existing close air support system, most notably in forward controller techniques. A variation of the "Rover" developed by the British and called "Rover Frank" became operational in late 1944. It was designed to overcome a particularly devastating effect enemy artillery batteries were having on front-line troops.[54] Prearranged air strikes based on information from the day before had been meeting with little success because the guns were constantly being moved to new locations.

Every night the army–air control provided the tactical groups with the latest list of enemy heavy batteries—data used for pilot briefing. On the way to the target, pilots would call Rover Frank to inform him on the status, and if the guns were active, the mission was carried out. If not, or if some other battery had become especially troublesome, Rover Frank cancelled the initial target and rebriefed the flight to attack a new objective. The missions apparently achieved favorable results, as indicated by a considerable reduction in the amount of shelling along the front.

At times Rovers had trouble finding ground locations from which they could oversee the battle area. The problem was partially overcome by the introduction of the Horsefly technique.[55] Begun during the advance on Rome, the Horsefly consisted of an L–5 aircraft hovering near the front lines with a pilot and an army observer aboard. Following a procedure similar to that of the ground-based controller, this team was in contact with him at all times. The basic difference was that they, rather than the Rover, directed the fighter-bomber attack. At first the British were skeptical of the method because they considered control from the ground superior to airborne briefing. But the Americans thought that the Horsefly procedure was definitely a help, especially against moving enemy targets. They further insisted that the plane could operate safely at 6,000 feet and to a depth of about five miles behind enemy lines. As long as air superiority was assured, Horsefly was a valuable addition.

Another technique, Timothy, was first executed in Italy on November 12, 1944, when Desert Air Force pilots provided close support for a British brigade offensive.[56] An Eighth Army history states:

> [It] took the form of a 'blitz' in a limited area on either side of the brigade's axis of advance, to a depth of about 1,000 yards, in front of a smoke bomb line. Three attacks had been prearranged (at 0730, 0830, and 0930) each consisting of 24 aircraft. Results were so good that the attacks were repeated. . . .

By the end of the day, the brigade had advanced 2,000 yards and taken 106 prisoners at a cost of 13 casualties. Timothy was undertaken again the next day with both British Spitfires and American P–47 Thunderbolts participating, and it continued to be used for the remainder of the campaign.

Timothy's essential prerequisite was that it had to be tied in with a ground offensive whose forces had to take immediate advantage of the air attack. The land formations had to furnish precise information on positions, targets, and timing. It was also imperative that two safety factors be observed: (1) the local Rover must control the operation, ordering the smoke bomb line only after pilots had announced they were in the area, and then giving the orders to attack and to cease; and (2) pilots must be briefed not to attack unless both the smoke bomb line had been laid according to plan and Rover had expressly given his permission. This type of operation could degenerate into "area bombing" rather than for an advance in a specific, heavily defended sector, but it did prove effective on a number of occasions.

A variety of Timothy was employed a month later when the 1st Canadian Division requested such an attack, but weather conditions did not permit bombing. Three Desert Air Force squadrons agreed to undertake a strafing operation instead. Code-named Pig, it was similar in all details to a Timothy, except that the aircraft did not carry bombs.

Another widely used technique, called Pineapple, was designed to strike lucrative moving targets discovered by tactical aircraft on reconnaissance missions.[57] Most often, the reconnaissance pilot radioed the army–air control center in the clear, indicating the target location, direction of movement, and composition. If the air force representative could accept the request for attack, the control center immediately passed it on to Pineapple-designated

Stinson L-5 Sentinel shepherds a flight of bomb-laden P-40 Warhawks to a ground target. The airborne controllers supplemented the work of the Rover teams on the ground.

aircraft on alert, which at times were able to reach the target area within 15 minutes of receiving the order. The reconnaissance pilot would assist fighter-bomber pilots in locating the target. If the target were not clearly visible, the reconnaissance pilot might even lead the attacking flight to it. Occasionally, in addition to the control center, the reconnaissance pilot might contact a Rover for support. If the control center gave permission, Rover selected a rendezvous point from which the reconnaissance pilot picked up the fighter-bombers to lead them to the target. Since enemy ground or antiaircraft fire could make an attack on the target too dangerous, the leader of the Pineapple flight could still about the operation by using the code-word Nuts.

A variation, Pineapple Sundae, featured a flight of fighter-bombers orbiting at prearranged positions and waiting for a target at the same time that a tactical reconnaissance mission (usually at last light) was being flown. As with the Pineapple technique overall, though relatively uncomplicated, it did add another dimension to the close air support arsenal.

Besides additional forward controller techniques, another valuable adjunct for conducting aerial warfare—operational research—was begun in Italy. Operational research was initiated in North Africa under Professor Solly Zuckerman and others, and the staff eventually became known as the

British Bombing Survey Unit most closely associated with "surveying" aspects of the RAF's strategic bombing effort. By 1944, British commanders were asking the civilian experts to examine problems on a variety of topics. At least five of them, besides the previously discussed evaluation of the Desert Air Force's fighter-bombers, were related to close air support. A report of December 21, 1944, looked into the "Ability of [Fighter-Bomber] Aircraft to Withstand Punishment." It concluded that while only a direct hit by enemy 88–mm or 20–mm antiaircraft guns would seriously damage Spitfires, Kittyhawks, or Mustangs, 40–mm weapons fired in the form of a barrage would damage Allied aircraft up to 8,000 feet.[58] With regard to the vulnerability of aircraft, the report recommended that a light armored plate fitted around the entire cockpit up to the canopy would reduce losses considerably.

After the war, the Survey unit published another report, entitled "The Reduction of Enemy Artillery Activity, and the Resultant Saving of Army Casualties, by Fighter-Bomber Attacks on Hostile Batteries."[59] It analyzed air strikes on German gun batteries in the British V Corps sector between October and December 1944, and found that, on the average, one battery was hit for every twelve missions flown (seventy-two Spitfire bomber sorties) and that in about one out of two attacks (twelve sorties) a bomb would land within twenty yards of the battery. In the opinion of the research team these attacks helped reduce army casualties appreciably along the front. The team also calculated that for every 500 fighter-bomber sorties undertaken, 60–90 soldiers who would otherwise have been killed were saved as well as 200–300 who would have been wounded. This was at an estimated cost of 2.6 pilots killed or missing, .3 injured, and 4.5 aircraft lost per 500 sorties. Studies such as these obviously benefited armed forces in war or peace. Slide-rule warfare was here to stay.

During the fighting for Rome and the advance beyond, many XII TAC and Desert Air Force squadrons moved three times.[60] A number of U.S. fighter groups were switched to Corsica for the invasion of southern France, then to Italy in September 1944. Others continued to support the U.S.-French northern advance and never did return. These moves, despite some use of existing airfields, constantly required new construction. By now these moves took on the average only five days to complete, and as a result, tactical air was able to maintain pressure on German troops throughout the period.

German air activity remained negligible. Extensive reconnaissance and other intelligence, including Ultra intercepts, assisted the Allies in neutralizing the *Luftwaffe*. Though intercepts were seldom deciphered in time to be of immediate tactical use in Italy, Ultra was especially valuable in confirming Germany's weakness in the air.[61] It indicated, for example, that *Luftflotte* 2 provided only a total of twelve sorties on the night of 27/28 July 1944, of which three were reconnaissance flights. On the 28th, it mounted six sorties;

on the 29th, seven; and on the 30th, again seven. Thus, besides providing targeting information, Ultra helped keep track of enemy air activity.

Interallied cooperation flourished during the campaign.[62] Early in the North African and Sicilian fighting, two U.S. fighter groups were under the Desert Air Force, though eventually transferred to the U.S. command structure. British units reciprocated and often assisted the Americans. During the Rome offensive, the RAF placed entire wings under XII TAC while the stripped-down Desert Air Force looked after the front east of the Apennines. During the fighting in the French Riviera, the opposite occurred. A detachment from DAF was collocated with the U.S. Fifth Army headquarters to help control tactical missions in Italy, and XII TAC concentrated on southern France. Unlike ground commanders, American and British airmen did not complain about direct command by men from a foreign service.

Not only did close cooperation develop between Great Britain and the United States, but extensive cooperation with the other allies also continued. By this time, with Brazilian forces now participating, all of the eighteen Allied nations eventually involved in Italy had been in combat. Moreover, all of the air forces that engaged in close air support had assisted troops of nations besides their own, including New Zealanders, Indians, and a Jewish brigade from Palestine that had no air contingents in the theater.

Only in the area of bomb lines did problems persist.[63] During the breakout toward Rome, five P–40s bombed and strafed a 3d Division column, killing or wounding more than one hundred troops. Other Allied aircraft bombed the town of Cori, which had already been captured by Americans. Gen. Mark Clark, the Fifth Army Commander, became so incensed at one point he ordered General Saville, the head of XII TAC, to stop American pilots from attacking their own troops. Saville responded stating that should the bomb safety line be set too far forward, close air support would cease. The controversy was resolved, and close air support continued, but it did reveal the intensity of the issue.

The April 1945 Offensive

During the three months before the final offensive, the Desert Air Force and XXII TAC flew few close air support sorties and concentrated on interdiction targets. Nevertheless, close air support was not forgotten. A number of ground controllers were trained and experiments with ordnance and air-ground techniques conducted. The most important of these involved the use of contact tanks and contact cars.[64] In this case, the usual situation was reversed. Instead of the close air support concepts developed in North Africa and Italy influencing the western European theater, there was a successful

Lt. Gen. Mark W. Clark, commander of Fifth Army in Italy, late 1943.

technique developed in western Europe having an influence in Italy. The technique, called armored column cover, was used extensively to increase the mobility of the air–ground team, especially during the 1944 dash across France. It consisted of a fighter pilot in the lead tank of a fast-moving column maintaining radio contact with pilots overhead, directing them in strikes on difficult enemy targets that were in the way. It was a substitute for an artillery forward.

In Italy, the Allies demonstrated as well as tested the technique under combat conditions, but instead of one, they used two Sherman tanks within fifty to hundred yards of each other. One, a control tank with a pilot and two army operators, was to direct the aircraft to the target and to maintain contact with the armored force at the same time. The other, a tentacle tank, supported the control tank, linked to the army–air control center and also to air observation and ground units in the vicinity.

Contact cars consisted of two white, half-tracked British vehicles attached to a Rover (though they could operate separately). The controllers in the cars were in contact with forward army elements and with fighter-bombers in the air. They could direct aircraft to targets, but their role was generally limited (like the jeeps in the American Rover setup) to service as forward observation posts. Although never thoroughly tested, both techniques were considered improvements in supporting mobile operations.

The buildup for the final offensive started in March 1945.[65] While one might question the advisability of an offensive with German military force already collapsing on the eastern and western fronts, Allied leaders in Italy were not to be deterred—they wanted a role in the final defeat of German forces. On April 9, at 7:20 p.m., the long-awaited Eighth Army offensive began. On the 14th, the Fifth Army followed suit. After meeting initial resistance, rested and well-prepared Allied forces pushed through dispirited German and Italian lines (there were Italians on both sides) and finally captured Bologna on the 21st. Thereafter the operation became a rout. The Allies were across the Po River by the 22d and began moving rapidly everywhere toward the Alps. Italian partisans were also extremely active, liberating some cities before Allied units arrived. Facing an impossible situation, the German commanders decided to surrender. By the 29th they had contacted the Allies and signed the necessary documents for surrender, which took effect on May 2. The Italian campaign was over.

During the final push, Allied air power continued its vital role.[66] The preliminary air attack on the afternoon before the ground offensive began was particularly devastating. Between 1:50 and 3:20 p.m., 800 heavy bombers in 42 waves, with 18 to 20 aircraft per wave, hit a variety of battlefield targets. Thirty minutes before the heavy bombers ended their attack, 268 mediums started their bomb runs, hitting 180 enemy gun positions, designated "Tom," "Dick," and "Harry," that had been marked with white smoke and strips of tape. This was followed by 656 fighter-bombers on 114 targets pinpointed by the army. These attacks were closely coordinated with intermittent artillery barrages.

When the war of movement began, the close air support system functioned effectively with extensive air–ground communications at all levels and Rover and Horsefly controllers much in evidence. Aircraft reaction time for targets identified by ground units or by controllers was short and brought desired results. Aircraft were successfully moved to new airfields as the front moved forward, and only the persistent bomb safety line problem remained. Despite the use of smoke and other markers, heavy bombers dropped their bombs short on at least two occasions, causing 205 casualties among Polish and New Zealand troops. Nonetheless, for all intents and purposes, excellent cooperation between air and ground forces was achieved.

Extent of Close Air Support

One additional factor needs to be addressed to complete the picture of close air support in Sicily and Italy: its extent as related to the total air effort.

Given the air forces' penchant for statistics, the answer should be readily available. But lamentably it is not. Part of the problem is that the Mediterranean command directed many air operations, not merely those in Sicily and Italy, making it difficult to separate the relevant statistics. Another problem is that while sorties were classified by the type of mission, the classification changed throughout the twenty-two month campaign, and none of them was specifically labelled close air support. At the time of the Sicilian invasion, for instance, fighter missions were separated into categories, with those most closely related to army support called "offensive sweeps" and "ground attacks." Even so, it is still unclear how many of them were actually close air support. The same difficulty applies to the offensive on Rome, where the categories "fighter-bomber" and "strafing and sweep" missions were used, but it is impossible to determine how many of these were for close air support. It is possible, however, to develop general statistics relating to close air support and to describe selected operations. This provides some idea of close air support activity throughout the period.

In general, the two most meaningful figures are the number of operational aircraft per day and the total number of sorties per month.[67] The number of operational aircraft in the theater in 1944 and 1945 varied from an average daily low of 3,933 in January 1944 to a high of 5,671 the following September. The lowest monthly figure for total sorties (not effective sorties) was 27,536 in October 1943. The highest was 71,732 in May 1944, (although 71,716 in April 1945 was a very close second). Even though figures for the number of fighter and fighter-bomber sorties for each month are incomplete, there are adequate statistics for eight months in 1944 (including reconnaissance and night flights).

Sortie Rates

	Total Sorties	*Ftrs & Ftr-Bombers*	*%*
January	46,370	29,287	63
February	34,855	21,621	62
March	42,180	27,061	64
April	48,043	29,148	61
May	71,732	44,326	62
June	56,071	33,738	60
July	58,495	34,399	59
August	66,180	38,426	58

In Sicily, between July 9 and August 17, 1943, over 4,000 aircraft flew 45,173 sorties, of which 13,309 were offensive sweeps and ground attacks.[68] But from what is known from memoirs and other sources, most of the sweeps and attacks reflected interdiction missions and not close air support. During December 1943, the situation along the front was relatively static, but the British Eighth Army did make some gains in the east. The RAF flew a total of 10,947 sorties, 5,938 of which were tactical and 5,695 fighter-bomber, strafing, and sweep sorties. Many of them reflected close air support, but statistics did not cover this category.[69] From what is known about this period, it can be assumed that many of them were close air support.

In 1944, between January 22 and February 15, a total of 2,700 aircraft flew 29,323 Anzio-related sorties: 16,567 fighter sorties and 4,262 strafing and sweep sorties.[70] A substantial portion were undoubtedly close air support, with others classified as escort, patrol, and reconnaissance missions.

During the Rome operation (Diadem), from May 12 to June 22, there were 72,946 effective sorties.[71] Fighter-bomber sorties numbered 20,888 and strafing attacks and sweeps 11,403. About half of the 32,291 fighter-bomber and stafing sorties were probably aimed at interdiction targets, but the other half, or 24 percent of the Diadem total, were for close air support. At the group level, in October, the U.S. 57th Fighter Group flew 134 missions* (as differentiated from sorties).[72] Ninety-eight of them, or 73 percent, were specifically designated as close air support. In December, during a relatively static month, the emphasis was on dive-bombing and interdiction, and close air support made up only 50 of the 275 missions flown, or 18 percent.

In 1945, close air support played a minor role during the first three months, because no major land operations were undertaken. But during the final offensive (Buckland), between April 8 and 28, close air support again came into its own.[73] The 4,393 available aircraft were involved in approximately 60,000 sorties, and 14,133 of them were flown in direct support of Fifth and Eighth Armies. In other words, around 23.5 percent of the total were close air support. These figures show that close air support was used in a variety of situations, that its use was more extensive as the Italian campaign progressed, and that ground troops relied upon air support especially during preplanned land operations, as in the Rome and Buckland offensives.

Conclusion

Brig. Gen. Lauris Norstad, Director of Operations, Mediterranean Allied Air Forces, commented after the war that in his view there were three noteworthy aspects of air operations in the Mediterranean.[74] First, air forces carried through a wide variety of tasks. Second, they maintained a combined command that assigned aircraft by function rather than by nationality. And third, and most significant for our purposes, "the Air Forces in this theater

---

*In military aviation, a mission is the assignment of any number of aircraft to attack a defined objective. A sortie is a single flight undertaken by a single aircraft.

pioneered tactical operations, establishing methods and principles that were of value in all the theaters of war."

In many ways General Norstad's statement summed up the importance of close air support in Sicily and Italy. Allied air leaders who watched close air support evolve throughout the campaigns dealt with a number of problems related to it and instituted important innovations. While the organization of air forces in the Mediterranean was complicated, reflecting the far-flung nature of the theater, Allied commanders through give-and-take overcame most of the difficulties. By the spring of 1944, an effective control system between air and ground elements at all levels—from the battlefield to army-tactical air control centers—had been developed. It was based on the use of prearranged and call missions, interconnected communications nets, and numerous liaison personnel. The keys were coordination and flexibility, both necessary to carry out the variety of close air support tasks in the most efficient way possible.

The most heralded but difficult new close air support techniques involved Rovers, pilots in ground-based forward positions who guided aircraft to close support targets. Others were Horseflies, involving guidance from liaison planes in the air. Fighter aircraft normally called on to carry out close air support sorties changed for the Americans mainly from P–40s to the more effective and equally durable P–47s. The British fought predominantly with Spitfires and achieved considerable success despite their lack of punch as fighter-bombers. Doctrine was refined during the period by the willingness of army to accept air control and to develop close cooperation between the armies and air forces, though not between the air forces and naval components. Although it brought about minimal substantive changes, another new procedure in aerial warfare—operational research—was introduced in an attempt to solve tactical as well as strategic problems.

Other problems affecting close air support that were of constant concern included *Luftwaffe* activity, additional Allied air commitments, airfield location, bomb safety lines and identification markers, and interallied relations. Except for bomb line problems, they were generally handled with efficiency and tact. While it has proved impossible to gauge precisely the proportion of close air support to the total number of sorties in the area, there is no doubt that the percentage was considerable, and increasingly effective as the campaigns continued.

Yet this effective close air support, like the entire air effort, was not the decisive factor in Sicily and Italy.[75] It gave a great boost to ground troop morale, obviously helped undermine that of the opposition, and paved the way for sizeable advances and the ability to exploit them. But it (along with interdiction) did not defeat the enemy. This had to be accomplished by soldiers in painstaking, at times hill-by-hill, river-by-river, fighting.

Close air support operations in Italy clearly demonstrated the necessity for close cooperation among allies and among the services. The Americans did not achieve success in close air support as soon as the British did, but by the spring of 1944, both Allies had worked out an effective system that continued to improve.

Cooperation between land and air components was not achieved without difficulties at first but when army and air commanders realized what close air support could accomplish, these were finally overcome. The impressive close air support system developed in Italy obviously provides an outstanding example of effective joint and combined operations.

Notes

1. Lucian K. Truscott, *Command Decisions* (New York: E. P. Dutton, 1959), p 554; Air Marshal Sir Arthur Coningham to Maj Gen Lawrence Kuter, Jul 22, 1943, AIR 23/7439, Public Record Office (hereafter cited as PRO); and [British] Air Ministry, *Air Support, Air Publication 3235 (The Second World War 1939–1945: Royal Air Force)*, 1955, Ch 3 and 4, K512.041-3235, 1939–1945, United States Air Force Hist Research Center (hereafter cited as USAFHRC).

2. The overview is based on Alfred N. Garland and Howard M. Smyth, *Sicily and the Surrender of Italy [U.S. Army in World War II: Mediterranean Theater of Ops*, Vol 2] (Washington, 1965); Martin Blumenson, *Salerno to Cassino [U.S. Army in World War II: Mediterranean Theater of Ops*, Vol 3] (Washington, 1969); Ernest F. Fisher, *Cassino to the Alps [U.S. Army in World War II: Mediterranean Theater of Ops*, Vol 4], (Washington, 1977]; and C. J. C. Molony, *et al, The Campaign in Sicily 1943, and the Campaign in Italy, 3d Sep 1943 to 31st Mar 1944* [Vol V: *The Mediterranean and the Middle East, United Kingdom Military Series*], (London, 1973).

3. *Ibid*, pp 862–866; and Wesley F. Craven and James L. Cate, eds, *Europe: Argument to V–E Day, Jan 1944 to May 1945 [The Army Air Forces in World War II*, Vol III], (Chicago 1951), pp 482–483.

4. *Ibid*, *passim*; and Mediterranean Air Command, "Order of Battle," Jul 10, 1943, AIR 23/1526, PRO.

5. Hq, NATAF to Hq, MAAF, "Memo on the Effect of Withdrawing Fighter-Bombers from Tactical Air Force," Dec 29, 1943, AIR 23/1529, PRO.

6. Molony, *The Campaign*, pp 874–878; Craven and Cate, *Europe: Argument to V–E Day*, III, pp 448–451; XII TAC, "XII TAC Fights Two Simultaneous Campaigns; The Invasion of Southern France and the Conclusion of the Rome–Arno (July–Sep 1944,)," 655.04–1, USAFHRC, Jul–Sep 1944; Hq MAAF, "Close Air Support of the Fifth Army," Tab R, Dec 6, 1945, 626.4501–1, 1944, USAFHRC; 27th Ftr Gp, "Hist Records, Jun 1944," GP-27–HI(Ftr), Jun 1944, USAFHRC; and XXII TAC, "History: Jan 1–May 9, 1945," I, 658.01, Jan–May 1945, USAFHRC.

7. Coningham to Kuter, Jul 22, 1943, AIR 23/7439, PRO: Cannon to House, May 15, 1944, 168.6007–1, Sep 7, 43–Mar 22, 1945, USAFHRC; Gordon P. Saville Papers, 168.7044–1, Nov 1923–Jul 1951, USAFHRC; Cannon to Giles, Mar 9, 1945, 168.6007-2, Sep 43–Mar 11, 1945, USAFHRC; "History of the Air Material Command," Jul 1–Dec 31, 1949, 200–9, Vol II, Jul–Dec 1949; Truscott, *Command Decisions*, p 482; and *Royal Air Force Lists*, 1943–1945, PRO.

8. Molony, *The Campaign*, pp 33–34; Garland and Smyth, *Sicily and the Surrender, passim*; Craven and Cate, *Europe: Argument to V–E Day*, III, pp 484–485; and Wesley F. Craven and James L. Cate, *eds, Europe: Torch to Pointblank, Aug 1942 to Dec 1943 [The Army Air Forces in World War II*, Vol II] (Chicago, 1949), p 484.

9. Harry L. Coles, "Participation of the Ninth and Twelfth Air Forces in the Sicilian Campaign," *USAF Hist Study #37*, 1945, pp 128, 101–37, July–Aug 1943, USAFHRC; [Mediterranean Allied Air Forces], "Preliminary Report on 'Husky' (Jul 9 to Jul 17, 1943)," AIR 23/1702, PRO: [MAAF], "Summary of Ops Against Sicily and Italy, July–Oct 1943," AIR 23/1509, PRO; and [British] Air Ministry, *Air Support*, pp 94–98.

10. Army Air Force Eval Bd, "Report: Mediterranean Theater of Ops," Vol I, Part VI, Jan 31, 1945, 6, 632.310, 1944–1945, USAFHRC.

11. Garland and Smyth, *Sicily and the Surrender*, p 421.

12. Coles, "Participation," p 185.

13. Karl Gundelach, *Die Deutsche Luftwaffe im Mittelmeer, 1940–1945* (Frankfurt, 1981), p 622.

14. Craven and Cate, *Europe: Torch to Pointblank*, II, p 458.

15. Molony, *The Campaign*, pp 234–242, 287; Blumenson, *Salerno to Cassino*, pp 170–171; and

Samuel Eliot Morison, *Sicily–Salerno–Anzio, Jan 1943–Jun 1944*, [*History of United States Naval Ops in World War II*, Vol IX] (Boston, 1954), pp 304–307.

16. Albert F. Simpson, "Air Phase of the Italian Campaign to Jan 1, 1944," *USAF Hist Study #115*, 1946, pp 174, 101–115, USAFHRC.

17. Molony, *The Campaign*, pp 326–327; Blumenson, *Salerno to Cassino*, pp 147–148; Simpson, "Air Phase," pp 133–137; and [MAAF], "Air Support in the Salerno Area: Report," Oct 1943, AIR 23/1573, PRO. The Eisenhower quote is from Molony, p 327.

18. Squadron Leader H. E. Newton Nicholls, HMS Hilary, "Report on Operation 'Avalanche,'" AIR 23/6635, PRO; [MAAF], "Summary of Ops against Italy and Sicily"; and MAAF, "Operation Avalanche," [Hewitt Report] p 199, 626.430–1, Aug–Sep 1943, USAFHRC.

19. [MAAF], "Operation Avalanche—Report of Proceedings of Force 'V,'" AIR 23/6635, PRO; and Molony, *The Campaign*, pp 261–263.

20. [British] Air Ministry, *Air Support*, p 101.

21. Craven and Cate, *Europe: Torch to Pointblank*, II, p 545, and comments by Dominick Graham to author, Sep 1985.

22. AHq, DAF, "Location of Units List," Jan 19, 1945, AIR 24/457, PRO; [DAF], "Order of Battle," Mar 31, 1945, AIR 24/457, PRO; 86th Ftr Gp, "Hist Records, Sep 1944," GP–86–HI, Sep 1944, USAFHRC; and [MAAF], "Summary of Ops Against Sicily and Italy."

23. XXII TAC, "History: Sep 20, 1944–Dec 31, 1944," I, pp 31–34, 658.01, Sep–Dec 44, USAFHRC.

24. 31st Ftr Gp, "Hist Records, Sep–Dec 31, 1943," GP–31–HI, Sep-Dec 43, USAFHRC.

25. Molony, *The Campaign*, pp 429–430; 785–786; Blumenson, *Salerno to Cassino*, *passim*; Simpson, "Air Phase," p 286.

26. Riley Sunderland, *Evolution of Command and Control Doctrine for Close Air Support*, (Washington, 1973), pp 16–18, K168.01–42, 1916–1969, USAFHRC.

27. AAF Eval Bd, "Report: MTO," I, Part VI, *passim*; Hq, First U.S. Army Gp, "Air–Ground Collaboration in Italy," Jan 18, 1944, pp 4–12, 580.4501–2, Dec 1943–Jan 1944, USAFHRC; and Hq, MAAF, "Ops in Support of Diadem, May 12–Jul 21, 1944," Vol VII, pp 5–1O, 622.430–3, USAFHRC.

28. Hq MAAF, "The History of MAAF, Dec 1943–Sep 1, 1944," Vol IX, Ops Bulletin #7, 622.01–09, Dec 43–Sep 1, 44, USAFHRC.

29. [MAAF], "Ops in Support of 'Shingle,' Jan 1 to Feb 15, 1944," 13, AIR 23/6333, PRO.

30. Hq, MAAF, "Close Air Support of the Fifth Army," Tab Q.

31. XXII TAC, "History: Sep 20, 1944–Dec 31, 1944," I, pp 37–39.

32. Sunderland, *Evolution of Command and Control Doctrine*, pp 23–24; AAF Eval Bd, "Air–Ground Cooperation: Comments by U.S. Army Commanders for AAF Eval Bd, Hq USSTAF (Main)," 138.4–36A, 1945, USAFHRC; U.S. Army Forces, European Theater, General Bd, "The Control of Tactical Aircraft in the European Theater of Ops,' Study Number 55, United States Army Military History Institute (hereafter cited as USAMHI); and [MAAF] "AFHq Army/Air Cooperation Notes Nr 2,": App C, AIR 23/7481, PRO.

33. Rover Paddy was originally called Rover Jimmy until it was found that Jimmy conflicted with a South African wing call sign. MAAF, "An Official Account of Air Ops in the Mediterranean, Jan 1943–May 1945," AIR 23/6337, PRO.

34. XXII TAC, "History: Sep 20–Dec 31, 1944," AAF Eval Bd, "Report: MTO," I, Part VI, 13–16, 42–44; [British] Air Ministry, *Air Support*, 115; [MAAF] "G–Air/8 Army History, Aug 1944 to May 1945," AIR 23/1684, PRO: and [MAAF] "Fighter-Bombing," AIR 23/1826, App C, PRO.

35. Hq, MAAF, "Close Air Support of the Fifth Army," Tab P.

36. "AF Eval Bd, "Report: MTO," I, Part VI, 17.

37. Hq, Mediterranean Theater of Ops, "Training Memo #2: Lessons from the Italian Campaign," 51–52, 632.549–3, Mar 15, 1945, USAFHRC; XXII TAC, "History: Sep 20–Dec 31, 1944," and [British] Air Ministry, *Air Support*, p 115.

38. Hq, MAAF, "The History of MAAF, Dec 1943–Sep 1, 1944," Vol IX, Ops Bulletin #5, 622.01–09, Dec 43–Sep 1, 44, USAFHRC.

39. 57th Ftr Gp, "Report on P-47 Aircraft," Jan 25, 1944, 168.6007–23, Jan 25, 1944, USAFHRC.

40. AAF Eval Bd, European Theater of Ops, *The Effectiveness of Third Phase Tactical Air Ops in the European Theater, May 5, 1944–May 8, 1945*, Aug 1945, 307–308, 138.4–365, May 1944–May 8, 1945, USAFHRC; Lloyd S. Jones, *U.S. Fighters* (Fallbrook, CA, 1975), pp 113–117; [MAAF], "AFHq Army/Air Cooperation Notes Nr 2"; and AAF Eval Bd, "Report: MTO," I, Part VI, p 12.

41. RAF (MAAF), "Monthly Statistical Summaries," AIR 23/1697, PRO: and Northwest African Tactical Air Forces, "Number of Aircraft On Hand and Serviceable," Jul 2–Jul 16, 1943," AIR 23/1574, PRO.

42. Hq MAAF, Operational Research Section, 17.9, "Observations of the Strength and Balance of Desert Air Forces," January, 1945, AIR 23/7513, PRO.

43. Truscott, *Command Decisions*, p 205; and Mark W. Clark, *Calculated Risk* (New York: Harper, 1950), p 186.

44. [MAAF], "Report from Gen. Eaker to Gen. Arnold—Doctrine, Mediterranean Theater of Ops," May 18, 1944, 621.549–1, May 18, 1944, USAFHRC.

45. Gundelach, *Die Deutsche Luftwaffe im Mittelmeer, passim.*

46. MAAF, "Monthly Statistical Summary of Mediterranean Allied Air Forces," 622.3083, Dec 1943–Apr 1945, USAFHRC; and Air Ministry War Room, "War Room Monthly Summary of Ops," 512.308G, Jan–Aug 1944, USAFHRC.

47. [MAAF], "G–Air/8 Army History"; Hq MAAF, "The History of MAAF," X; 31st Ftr Gp, "History for Apr 1945," GP–31–HI, Apr 1945, USAFHRC; and Alan F. Wilt, *The French Riviera Campaign of Aug 1944* (Carbondale, Ill, 1981), *passim.*

48. F. M. Sallager and Eduard Mark have shown that Operation Strangle, once thought to be a failure, did in fact slow down the arrival of supplies at the front and tied down large quantities of troops for other than combat duties. See Eduard Mark, "Aerial Interdiction: A Summary Hist Analysis," Washington: Office of Air Force History, 1984, pp 16–18.

49. Shelford Bidwell and Dominick Graham, *Fire-Power: British Army Weapons and Theories of War 1904–1945* (London, 1982), p 265; MAAF, "Bombing of Cassino," 622.310.4, Pt. 1, Mar 1944, USAFHRC; Cannon to Eaker, May 8, 1944, and Cannon to Slessor, Dec 12, 1944, 168.6007–1, Sep 7, 43–Mar 22, 45, USAFHRC; and [British] Air Ministry, *Air Support*, p 98.

50. *Ibid*, p 122.

51. Molony, *The Campaign, passim*; G. W. L. Nicholson, *The Canadians in Italy, 1943–45 (Official History of the Canadian Army in the Second World War, Vol II)* (Ottawa, 1956), *passim*; and Pierre Le Goyet, *La Participation Francaise 'a la Campagne d'Italie (1943–1944)* (Paris, 1969), p 343.

52. Fisher, *Cassino to the Alps, passim*, and Graham to author, September, 1985.

53. Craven and Cate, III, 388–389; Hq MAAF, "Ops in Support of Diadem," *VII*, Tab FF; [MAAF], "G–Air/8 Army History"; Advanced Hq, Desert Air Force, "Ops Record Book," AIR 24/443, PRO; and Hq MAAF, "Close Air Support of the Fifth Army," Tab R.

54. [MAAF], "G–Air/8 Army History."

55. U.S. Army Forces, European Theater, General Bd, "Liaison Aircraft with Ground Force Units," Study Nr 20, Aug 1945, 14–15, USAMHI; [British] Air Ministry, *Air Support*, p 117; and Hq, MTO, "Training Memo #2," 53–55.

56. [MAAF], "G–Air/8 Army History"; and [British] Air Ministry, *Air Support*, pp 120–121.

57. [MAAF], "G–Air/8 Army History"; Hq MAAF, "Close Air Support of the Fifth Army," Tab D; XII TAC, "XII TAC Policy and Accomplishments," Ops Memo #1, 655.116, Apr–Aug 1944, USAFHRC; and 79th Ftr Gp, "Hist Records, May, 1944," GP–79–HI, May 1944, USAFHRC.

58. MAAF, Operational Research Section, 14.2.3, "Ability of Aircraft to Withstand Punishment," Dec 21, 1944, AIR 23/7465, PRO.

59. Hq, MAAF, CMF, Operational Research Section, 14.2.9, "The Reduction of Enemy Artillery Activity, and the Resultant Saving of Army Casualties, by Ftr-Bmbr Attacks on Hostile Batteries," Jul 4, 1945, AIR 23/7455, PRO.

60. Hq MAAF, "Ops in Support of Diadem," VII, Tab DD.

61. XL 3970, 29/1904Z/7/44, DEFE 3/63, PRO; XL 4206, 31/1931Z/7/44, DEFE 3/64, PRO; and XL 5951, 13/0426Z/8/44, DEFE 3/117, PRO.

62. Simpson, "Air Phase," 43–45; [MAAF], "Desert Air Force Operation Instruction Nr 19," Apr 30, 1944, AIR 23/1822, PRO; XII TAC, "XII TAC Fights," 32; 79th Ftr Gp, "History, Jan 1, 1943–Jan 1, 1944," HI–79–Ftr, Jan–Dec 1943, USAFHRC; and Dhram Pal, *The Campaign in Italy, 1943–45* [*Indian Armed Forces in World War II*] (Calcutta, 1960), pp 15–17.
63. Fisher, *Cassino to the Alps*, pp 166–167; and Truscott, *Command Decisions*, pp 355–356.
64. [MAAF], "G–Air/8 Army History"; [MAAF], "AF Hq Army/Air Cooperation Notes Nr 2"; [British] Air Ministry, *Air Support*, pp 116–117; and [DAF], "Operation Wowser," AIR 24/456, PRO. Operation Wowser was the code-name for the air portion of the final offensive.
65. Craven and Cate, *Europe: Agreement to V–E Day*, III, pp 485–589; and Fisher, *Cassino to the Alps*, p 447.
66. XXII TAC, "History: 1 January–9 May 1945," I, *passim*, 658.01, Jan–May 1945, USAFHRC; [DAF], "Operation Wowser"; Advanced Hq, Desert Air Force, "Ops Record Book," AIR 24/444, PRO; [MAAF], "AF Hq Army/Air Cooperation Notes Nr 2"; [MAAF], "G–Air/8 Army History," App T; and Truscott, *Command Decisions*, p 483.
67. MAAF, "Monthly Statistical Summary"; Simpson, "Air Phase," 387; Air Ministry War Room, "War Room Monthly Summary"; and MAAF, "History of MAAF," LI.
68. JS(Q)16, "Strategic Concept for the Defeat of the Axis in Europe," 14 Aug 1943, CAB 80/73, PRO: and [MAAF], "Ops by Ftr and Ftr-Bmbr Aircraft," 3/4 July–17 Aug 1943, AIR 23/918, PRO.
69. [MAAF], "Monthly Statistical Summary, 1st–31st Dec 1943," AIR 23/1697, PRO.
70. [MAAF], "Ops in Support of 'Shingle'"; and Molony, *The Campaign*, p 653.
71. Hq MAAF, "Ops in Support of Diadem," VII
72. 57th Ftr Gp, "Hist Records, Jul 1944–May 1945," GP–57–HI, Jul–Dec 1944, USAFHRC; Desert Air Force, "Ftr-Bmbr Effort," Mar 2, 1945, 616.198, Dec 1944–May 1945, USAFHRC.
73. Hq, MAAF, "The History of MAAF," II, 413–416; Desert Air Force, "Ftr-Bmbr Effort;" and Hq, MATAF, "Operation Wowser,"Apr 1945, 626.430–17, Apr 45, USAFHRC.
74. "Air Power in the Mediterranean," 622.310–1, 1942–1945, USAFHRC.
75. Fisher, *Cassino to the Alps*, p 543; AAF Eval Bd, "Report: MTO," Part VI, App #3; and AHqDAF/13/AIR, "Effect of Allied Air Attacks on Apr 9, 10, 11—Comacchio Area," 22.4.1945, AIR 24/456, PRO.

Bibliographical Essay

As the Sicilian and Italian campaigns unfolded, American and British leaders increasingly began to appreciate the numerous roles that tactical air power could fulfill. Since air superiority was assured, tactical air commanders could turn their attention to interdiction and close air support missions. Extensive records at the Public Record Office (PRO) in London and at the U.S. Air Force Historical Research Center (USAFHRC), Maxwell AFB, Alabama, provide basic research material on close air support operations.

One rich source for evaluating the effectiveness of close air support in the theater were reports issued by various boards and by Mediterranean air components during and right after the war. Most important of these are two extensive Army Air Force Evaluation Board reports—"Report: MTO," Vol. I, Part VI, 632.310, 1944–1945, USAFHRC; and *The Evaluation of Third Phase Tactical Air Operations in the European Theater, May 5, 1944–May 8, 1945*, August 1945, 138.3–36, 5 May 1944–8 May 1945, USAFHRC. Other helpful reports include Air–Ground Cooperation, "Comments by U.S. Army Commanders for AAF Evaluation Board, Hq USSTAF (Main)," 138.4–36A, 1945, USAFHRC; "Italy: Report on the Great Effect of Close Air Support," 168.6007–22A, Dec 1943, USAFHRC; "Report on P–47 Aircraft, Jan 26, 1944," USAFHRC; and 57th Fighter Group, "Report on P–47 Aircraft, Jan 25, 1944," 168.6007–23, Jan 25, 1944, USAFHRC.

Unit histories especially at the higher theater command levels are useful. The Mediterranean Allied Air Force (MAAF) history is divided into two chronological parts: *The History of MAAF: December 1943–September 1, 1944*, 20 Vols, 622.01, Dec 1943–Sep 1, 1944, USAFHRC: and *The History of MAAF: 1 September 1944–9 May 1945*, 51 Vols, 622.01, Sep 1, 1944–May 9, 1945, USAFHRC. The U.S. XII Tactical Air Command did not leave an actual unit history, but that of its successor, XXII Tactical Air Command, "History: September 20, 1944–December 31, 1944," 4 Vols, 658.01, Sep–Dec 1944, USAFHRC; and "History: January 1–May 9, 1945," 5 Vols, 658.01, Jan–May 1945, USAFHRC, is very complete. Though uneven, various fighter group histories, such as 27th Fighter Group "Historical Records, June 1944," GP–27–HI (FTR), June 1944, USAFHRC; 31st Fighter Group, "Historical Records, June 1944," GP–27–HI (FTR), June 1944, USAFHRC; "31st Fighter Group, Historical Records, Sep–31 Dec," GP–31–HI, Sep–Dec 31, 43, USAFHRC; and 31 Fighter Group, "History for April 1945," GP–31–HI, April 1945, USAFHRC, add to the flavor of life in combat units.

Interviews and personal papers of the air commanders were also of assistance in understanding the Mediterranean air effort. Most of General Eaker's papers are located at the Library of Congress, but there are also additional materials, including Lt. Gen. Ira C. Eaker, US Air Force Oral History

Interview, 1970, K239.0512–868, USAFHRC; and Eaker, "Correspondence, 1944–45," 622.161–2, Apr 1944–Feb 1945, USAFHRC. The Center also has the papers of the head of the Mediterranean Allied Tactical Air Forces (MATAF) after 1943, Major General John K. Cannon, 168.6007, USAFHRC; and of the XII TAC commander, Brig. Gen. Gordon P. Saville, 168.7044, USAFHRC, and biographical material on Brig. Gen. Edwin J. House of XII Air Air Support Command (K141.2421 HOUSE, 1942, USAFHRC), and on Brig. Gen. Benjamin W. Childlaw of XXII TAC ("History of the Air Material Command, 1 July–31 December 1949," 200–9, V.2, Jul–Dec 1949, USAFHRC). Besides the *Royal Air Force Lists, 1943–1945*, PRO, information and views of the top RAF commanders in the theater can be gleaned from MAAF files.

Of all command files, those of the MAAF are most voluminous and exceedingly valuable for the study of close air support in Sicily and Italy. They are scattered among the AIR 23: Overseas Commands holdings at the Public Record Office and mainly under 622: Mediterranean Allied Air Forces and 626: Mediterranean Allied Tactical Air Forces at the USAFHRC. The many records include "G–Air/8 Army History, August 1944 to May 1945," AIR/1684; "An Official Account of Air Operations in the Mediterranean, Jan 1943–May 1945," AIR 23/6337; "AFHQ Army/Air Cooperation Notes No. 2," AIR 23/7481; "Monthly Statistical Summary: 1st–31st December 1943," AIR 23/1697; "Operations by Fighter and Fighter-Bomber Aircraft," 3/4 Jul–17 Aug 1943, AIR 23/918; "Fighter-Bombing," AIR 23/1826; "Summary of Operations Against Sicily and Italy, July–October, 1943," AIR 23/1509; "Preliminary Report on 'Husky,' July 9th to July 17 1943," AIR 23/1702; "Operation Avalanche—Report on Proceedings of Force 'V,'" AIR 23/6635; "Operations in Support of 'Shingle' [Anzio], 1 Jan to 15 Feb, 1944," AIR 23/6333; "Desert Air Force Operation Instruction No. 19," Apr 30, 44, AIR 23/1822; Sqn Leader H.E. Newton Nicholls, "Report on Operation 'Avalanche," AIR 23/6635; Northwest African Tactical Air Force (NATAF), "Memorandum on the Effect of Withdrawing Fighter-Bombers from Tactical Air Force," Dec 29, 1943, AIR 23/1529; NATAF, "Number of Aircraft on Hand and Serviceable, 2nd July–16th July 1943," AIR 23/1574; "Monthly Statistical Summary of Mediterranean Allied Air Forces," 622.3083, Dec 1943–April 1945; "Close Air Support of the Fifth Army, Dec. 6, 1944," 626.4501–1, 1944; "Operations in Support of DIADEM, 12 May–21 Jul 1944," 7 vols., 622.430–3; "Operation Avalanche," 626.430–1, Aug–Sep 1943; "Bombing of Cassino," 622.310–4, Pt. 1, Mar 1944; and "TAF Files, 1943–44," [Microfilm] 622.011. Especially interesting are the operational research studies undertaken to evaluate the effectiveness of various aspects of close air support. Three pertinent studies are MAAF/ORS/14.2.9, "The Reduction of Enemy Artillery Activity and the Resultant Saving of Army Casualties, by Fighter-Bomber Attacks on Hostile Batteries," 4 Jul 1945, AIR

23/7455; MAAF/ORS/14.2.3, "Ability of Aircraft to Withstand Punishment," Dec 21, 1944, AIR 23/7465; and MAAF/ORS/17.9, "Observations on the Strength and Balance of Desert Air Force," Jan 1945, AIR 23/7513.

Though not as extensive, the files of other British and American air elements provide information on specific aspects of the fighting in Sicily and Italy and include the following: MATAF, "Operation WOWSER," April 1945, 626.430–17, Apr 1945, USAFHRC; Advanced HA, Desert Air Force, "Operations Record Book," AIR 24/444, PRO: AHQ, DAF, "Effect of Allied Air Attacks on 9th, 10th, 11th April—Comacchio Area," Apr 22, 45, AIR 24/456, PRO; [DAF] "Operation WOWSER," AIR 24/456, PRO: AHQ, [DAF], "Location of Units List," Jan 19, 1945, AIR 24/457, PRO; [DAF], "Order of Battle," Mar 31, 45, AIR 24/457, PRO; DAF, "Memoranda—Dec 44–May 45," 616.198, Dec 1944–May 1945, USAFHRC; DA, "Order of Battle, Oct 1944–Feb 1945," 616.6318, Oct 1944–Feb 1945, USAFHRC; XII TAC, "XII TAC Fights Two Simultaneous Campaigns: The Invasion of Southern France and the Conclusion of Rome–Arno (July–September 1944)," 655–04–1, Jul–Sep 1944, USAFHRC; XII TAC, "XII TAC Policy and Accomplishments," 655.116, Apr–Aug, USAFHRC; and XXII TAC, "Summary of XXII Tactical Air Command Operations," 658.307, 1944–1945, USAFHRC. Other files which proved helpful are British Air Ministry, "War Room Monthly Summary of Operations, MAAF, 144," 512.308G, Jan–Aug 1944, USAFHRC; British Air Ministry, *Air Support, Air Publication 3235 (The Second World War 1939–1945: Royal Air Force)*, 1955, K512.041–3235, 1939–1945, USAFHRC; JS(Q)16, "Strategic Concept for the Defeat of the Axis in Europe," Aug 14, 43, CAB 80/73, PRO; HQ, First U.S. Army Group, "Air-Ground Collaboration in Italy," Jan 18, 1944, 580.4501–2, Dec 1943–Jan 1944, USAFHRC; HQ, MTO, "Training Memorandum #2: Lessons from the Italian Campaign," 632.549–3, Mar 15, 45, USAFHRC; and Ultra decrypts XL 3970, 29/1904Z/7/44, DEFE 3/63, PRO; XL 4206, 31/1931Z/7/44, DEFE 3/64, PRO; and XL 5951, 13/0426Z/8/44, DEFE 3/117, PRO.

A number of U.S. Air Force and Army studies further add to an understanding of operations and an appreciation of the necessity of army–air cooperation for executing close air support. Those studies used are Harry L. Coles, "Participation of the Ninth and Twelfth Air Forces in the Sicilian Campaign, USAF Historical Study #37," 1945, 101–37, Jul–Aug 1943, USAFHRC; Albert F. Simpson, "Air Phase of the Italian Campaign to 1 January 1944, USAF Historical Study #115," 1946, 101–115, USAFHRC; Riley Sunderland, *Evolution of Command and Control Doctrine for Close Air Support* (Bolling AFB, DC: Office of Air Force History, 1973); US Army Forces, European Theater, General Board, "Liaison Aircraft with Ground Force Units, Study Number 20," 1945, United States Army Military History Institute (USAMHI); and US Army Forces, European Theater of Operations, Study Number 55, USAMHI.

Official histories are basic to any study of modern warfare, and again proved their worth in assessing close air support in the theater. Though occasionally inaccurate, the U.S. Army Air Force histories edited by Wesley F. Craven and James L. Cate remain a monument to historical scholarship and continue to provide details and interpretations unavailable elsewhere. *Europe: Torch to Pointblank, August 1942 to December 1943*, (*The Army Air Forces in World War II, Vol. II*) (Chicago: University of Chicago Press, 1949); and *Europe: Argument to V–E Day, January 1944 to May 1945* (*The Army Air Forces in World War II, Vol. III*) (Chicago: University of Chicago Press, 1951) are the pertinent volumes. Also of great assistance are the U.S. Navy and U.S. Army official histories of Samuel Eliot Morison, *Sicily–Salerno–Anzio, January 1943–June 1944*, (*History of United States Naval Operations in World War II, Vol. IX*) (Boston: Little, Brown, Co., 1954); Albert N. Garland and Howard M. Smyth, *Sicily and the Surrender of Italy* (*U.S. Army in World War II, Mediterranean Theater of Operations, Vol. 2*) (Washington: USGPO, 1965); Martin Blumenson, *Salerno to Cassino* (*U.S. Army in World War II, Mediterranean Theater of Operations, Vol. 4*) (Washington: USGPO, 1977). Though better as a reference than a narrative of events, the British official history, C.J.C. Molony, *et al.*, *The Campaign in Sicily 1943 and the Campaign in Italy, 3rd September to 31st March 1944* (*The Mediterranean and the Middle East, Vol. V, United Kingdom Military Series*) (London: HMSO, 1973) contains significant data. Other official histories that helped fill in the picture of other Allied that participated are Pierre Le Goyet, *La Participation Française a la Campagne d'Italie (1943–1944)* (Paris: Imprimerie Nationale, 1969); G. W. L. Nicholson, *The Canadians in Italy, 1943–45* (*Official History of the Canadian Army in the Second World War, Vol. II*) (Ottawa: Queen's Printer, 1956); and Dharm Pal, *The Campaign in Italy, 1944–45* (*Indian Armed Forces in World War II*) (Calcutta: Sree Saraswaty Press, 1960).

While there is no completely satisfactory single-volume history of the Sicilian and Italian campaigns, a number of important memoirs, biographies, campaign histories, monographs, and articles have been published. Memories of U.S. Army Generals Mark W. Clark, *Calculated Risk* (New York: Harper & Brothers, 1950), and Lucian K. Truscott, *Command Decisions* (New York: E.P. Dutton, 1959), bring out the Army's reluctance to give air force leaders control over tactical air assets. The recollections of the commander of Allied air forces in the Mediterranean through 1943, Air Marshal Sir Arthur W. Tedder, *With Prejudice: The War Memoirs of Marshal of the Royal Air Force, Lord Tedder* (London: Cassell, 1966), and of the deputy commander during 1944–1945, Air Marshal Sir John C. Slessor, *The Central Blue: Recollections and Reflections* (London: Cassell, 1956) are disappointingly thin on close air support activity during their tenures. Biographies of key generals in the theater include Martin Blumenson's *Mark Clark: The Last of the Great World War II Commanders* (New York: Congdon & Weed, 1984); Nigel Hamilton's *Master of the Battlefield: Monty's War Years, 1942–1944* (New York: McGraw-Hill, 1984); and Nigel Nicholson's *Alex: The Life of Field-Marshal Alexander of Tunis* (London: Weidenfeld & Nicholson, 1973).

Among recent campaign histories, the best are Raleigh Trevelyan, *Rome '44* (New York: Viking Press, 1981); David Hapgood and David Richardson, *Monte Cassino* (New York: Congdon & Weed, 1984); John Ellis, *Cassino: The Hollow Victory: The Battle for Rome, January–June 1944* (New York: McGraw-Hill, 1984); Des Hickey and Gus Smith, *Operation Avalanche: The Salerno Landings, 1943* (New York: McGraw-Hill, 1984); and Alan F. Wilt, *The French Riviera Campaign of August 1944* (Carbondale, Ill.: Southern Illinois University Press, 1981). Significant monographs that shed light on additional aspects of the Italian air war are Lloyd S. Jones. *U.S. Fighters* (Fallbrook, Conn.: Aero Publisher, 1975), a description of American fighters and fighter-bombers; Shelford Bidwell and Dominick Graham, *Fire-Power: British Army Weapons and Theories of War 1904–1945* (London: Allen & Unwin, 1982); Karl Gundelach, *Die deutsche Luftwaffe im Mittelmeer, 1940–1945* (Frankfurt a.M.: Lang, 1981), an outstanding study of the *Luftwaffe's* demise in the Mediterranean. Articles by three British air commanders, Air Marshal Sir Arthur Coningham, "The Development of Tactical Air Forces," *Journal of the United Services Institute*, 9 (1946): 21–227; Air Marshal Sir Guy Garrod, "The Part Played by the Allied Air Forces in the Final Defeat of the Enemy in the Mediterranean Theater, March to May 1945, Special Supplement 39367," *London Gazette*, October 29, 1951; and Air Vice-Marshal J. H. d'Albiac, "Air Campaigns in Italy and the Balkans," *Journal of the Royal United Services Institution*, 100 (Aug 1945): pp. 323–345, are too general to be of much help. But historian William A. Jacobs's "Tactical Air Doctrine and AAF Air Support in the European Theater, 1944–1945," *Aerospace Historian*, 27 (March 1980): pp. 35–49, adds a good deal to our knowledge of tactical air doctrine.

6

The Battle for France, 1944

W. A. Jacobs

In the early morning of the June 6, 1944, British and American armies began their landings on the Normandy beaches with the immediate objective of securing a foothold on the coast of France. Over the next three weeks, the Allies built up their strength on the far shore, expanding the beachhead by hard and costly fighting. From mid-June to late July, Allied forces fought to prevent the Germans from consolidating defenses or concentrating for a counterattack. They also fought to secure a position for launching a breakout. During this period, the British Second Army fought to gain the city of Caen and the open ground beyond it, while the American First Army struggled in the hedgerows of the *bocage*.

The nature of fighting changed dramatically on July 25, when the American First Army broke through the German defenses in a major frontal assault known as Operation Cobra. Exploitation of the American breakthrough, combined with a renewed British and Canadian offensive, culminated in a battle of annihilation in the Falaise pocket that proved decisive. The Allies followed this victory with a ruthless pursuit of what appeared to be a thoroughly defeated German army. By mid-September, the Allies pushed the Germans back to the Moselle River in the east, and elsewhere, out of France altogether. The Battle for France was won, but it did not lead to an early collapse of German fighting power, as many in the Allied high command had hoped. It was, however, one of the most significant Allied victories of the Second World War.

Allied air forces contributed significantly to this victory, providing close air support on a scale and with an effectiveness not experienced until this time. The campaign in France presented close air support aviation with the challenge of performing a great variety of operations—landings on hostile and well- defended shores, fierce static or positional fighting, breakthrough attempts, pursuits, sieges, and river crossings. This study examines the functions and development of close air support under the demands generated by so many different kinds of combat situations.

The American Ninth and the British Second Tactical Air Forces were primarily responsible for providing air support to the Allied armies.[1] (See Chart) The Ninth Air Force, commanded by Maj. Gen. Lewis Brereton, was made up of fighters, fighter-bombers, light and medium bombers, and transport aircraft. Operationally it was divided into a fighter command, an air defense command, a bomber command, and a service command. The Fighter Command, under Maj. Gen. Elwood Quesada, organized and trained the tactical air commands, which were the fighter-bomber mobile air forces directly supporting the American armies. In the initial phases of the battle in France, the IX Tactical Air Command (also commanded by General Quesada) operated with Lt. Gen. Omar Bradley's American First Army. When the First Army broke out of the beachhead in late July, the Supreme Allied Commander, Gen. Dwight Eisenhower, activated the American Third Army under Lt. Gen. George Patton. The Ninth Air Force promptly activated a second Tactical Air Command (TAC)—the XIX, under Brig. Gen. O.P. Weyland—to support this force. In mid-August, Lt. Gen. Alexander Patch's American Seventh Army landed in southern France, bringing with it the XII TAC, under Brig. Gen. Gordon Saville, from Italy. The picture was completed in late August with the creation of the American Ninth Army, commanded by Lt. Gen. William Simpson, accompanied by the establishment of the XXIX Tactical Air Command under Brig. Gen. Richard Nugent. Throughout the campaign, the American light and medium bombers were controlled by Maj. Gen. Samuel Anderson's IX Bomber Command, which reported directly to Ninth Air Force.

On the British side, the RAF Second Tactical Air Force, under Air Marshal Sir Arthur Coningham, contained the forces for supporting the British armies. The fighter-bombers were organized into two composite groups—the 83d, under Air Vice-Marshal H. Broadhurst, and the 84th, under Air Vice-Marshal L.O. Brown—which supported the British Second Army, under Lt. Gen. Sir Miles Dempsey, and the Canadian First Army, under Lt. Gen. H. Crerar, respectively. Air Vice-Marshal B. Embry's No. 2 Group controlled the operations of the light and medium bombers.

Both the American Ninth Air Force and the RAF Second Tactical Air Force were under the direction of Allied Expeditionary Air Force Headquarters (AEAF), commanded by Air Chief Marshal Sir Trafford Leigh-Mallory. In the early weeks of the battle in France, Leigh-Mallory delegated the actual control of AEAF operations to an advanced headquarters, AEAF (Adv), commanded by Coningham to ensure the proper employment of the air force in the relatively small area of the ground battle. In August, after the breakout and the disintegration of the German position in Normandy, AEAF (Adv) was dissolved. In early September, AEAF itself was disbanded and replaced with an enlarged air staff at the Supreme Allied Commander's headquarters to coordinate the work of the two tactical air forces.[2]

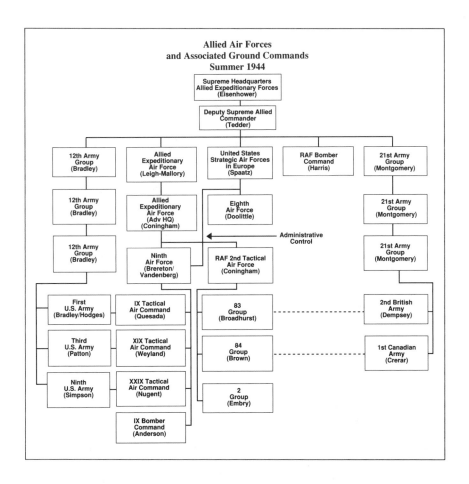

In the summer of 1944, on several occasions Allied heavy bomber forces were also used in close air support. The Eighth Air Force, commanded by Lt. Gen. James Doolittle, included the American heavy bombers as well as a sizeable number of long-range escort fighters. United States Strategic Air Forces in Europe (USSTAF), under the command of Lt. Gen. Carl Spaatz, the senior United States airman in the European theater, directed the operations of the Eighth. USSTAF also exercised operational control over the strategic forces of the American Fifteenth Air Force based in Italy, as well as administrative authority over the American Ninth Air Force. That is, the strategic air force headquarters controlled the flow of supplies and personnel to the tactical air force. RAF Bomber Command, under Air Chief Marshal Sir Arthur Harris, had the heavy bombers of the Royal Air Force. Under the terms of a Combined Chiefs of Staff directive issued in March 1944, General

Eisenhower provided "strategic direction" for both USSTAF and Bomber Command, an authority he chose to exercise chiefly through his deputy, Air Chief Marshal Sir Arthur Tedder.[3]

For a variety of reasons, including personality conflicts, quarrels over strategy, and organizational politics, the Allies never created a single overall air command in northwest Europe. Even Sir Arthur Tedder did not act as Air Commander-in-Chief. He arbitrated in case of conflict between the three senior air commanders, and he conveyed Eisenhower's wishes with respect to the employment of the heavy bomber forces on "strategic" targets.[4] Ground and naval forces were to make their needs known to Leigh-Mallory. If he could not meet them out of the resources of Ninth Air Force and RAF Second Tactical Air Force, he could call upon the USSTAF and Bomber Command. The exact nature of Leigh-Mallory's authority in this respect was murky. According to one document, Leigh-Mallory was "to act for the Supreme Commander" in the operation of Strategic Air Forces in tactical support for Overlord and also in the coordination of these operations with those of the tactical air forces.[5] In practice, this meant that his requests for heavy bomber support were underwritten by General Eisenhower's authority, except where Tedder overrode them or Harris or Spaatz did not concur.

As a result, up to May 23, 1944, the allocation of the heavy bomber

Maj. Gen. Lewis Brereton, Ninth Air Force commander, *(left)* **conferring with Supreme Allied Commander General Dwight D. Eisenhower and Lt. Gen. Carl A. Spaatz** *(rear).*

forces to the close support program for the landing was in the hands of several staff committees who reported to the senior commanders they were representing. This was complicated and awkward, and the final list of targets to be attacked in the prearranged program of close support was not settled until late in May. Whether this delay was due to the messy air command situation or poor staff work by ground and naval forces, or both, continues to be a matter of dispute.[6] After May 23, the senior air commanders met each morning at Leigh-Mallory's headquarters at Stanmore to allocate air effort, the key decision being the employment of the heavy bombers, and in the case of the Eighth Air Force, the large force of long-range escort fighters.[7] In September, the Combined Chiefs of Staff removed the heavy bombers from Eisen-

Ground crewman mounts a field-expedient rocket launcher on the wing of a P-47J Thunderbolt.

hower's "strategic direction." Thereafter, their allocation to the support of ground forces was a matter of lateral "coordination," not command.

The lack of effective centralization did not prove to be the handicap it might have been in other circumstances. Relationships were good enough at lower levels to ensure proper coordination in most instances where the tactical air commands, composite groups, and their associated medium bomber commands operated together. On several occasions during the summer, the RAF Second Tactical Air Force operated with IX TAC to support American ground units and vice versa. Additionally, overwhelming Allied air superiority, overcoming any inefficiency, prevented embarrassment that might otherwise have been inflicted by the *Luftwaffe*. Still it is hard to escape the conclusion that the Allied air forces would have been more effectively employed had a common plan been developed by a single staff and implemented by the authority of a single commander.

The partial independence of the strategic air forces, particularly the Eighth Air Force, was a frequent source of problems. Whenever the Eighth attacked targets in Germany, it took its huge fighter force with it. At full strength, this meant that more than 1,000 fighters were unavailable for regular air superiority and interdiction missions. The AEAF was therefore compelled to rearrange the employment of fighters in the tactical air forces to cover those missions otherwise assigned to the Eighth's fighters. These kinds of operational gymnastics required coordination between no fewer than five separate headquarters: AEAF, USSTAF, Ninth Air Force, Eighth Air Force, and Second Tactical Air Force. Whenever the heavy bombers were called in to operate as close support forces, similar difficulties arose.[8]

Many of the Allied air commanders could point to considerable experience with air support in the Middle East, in northwest Africa, and in Sicily and Italy. In 1944, this proved to be valuable in organizing, training and directing their commands. Shared experience, however, did not produce a close-knit and harmonious organization. In fact, relations between many airmen were bad and got worse as the campaign progressed.

Air Marshal Sir Arthur Coningham, probably the Allied airman most responsible for developing the modern tactical air force, was also a difficult man, and by the summer of 1944, he was alienated from key airmen and soldiers alike. For reasons that are not clear, he did not get on well with one of his most seasoned tactical commanders, Air Vice-Marshal Harry Broadhurst at 83 Group.[9] Toward the end of the summer, he tried to sack Air Vice-Marshal L.O. Brown from 84 Group, on the grounds of "his subservience" to the Army.[10] Relations between Coningham and his immediate superior, Leigh-Mallory, were anything but cordial. Coningham tried to deal directly with Tedder and was active in efforts to eliminate AEAF altogether.[11] Worse still, Coningham was on bad terms with General Sir Bernard Montgomery, with whom he had to work if air support were to be provided effectively.[12]

Air Chief Marshal Sir Trafford Leigh-Mallory *(right)*. Lt. Gen. James Doolittle, commander of Eighth Air Force, *(below)* discussing the details of a mission with bomber crewmen.

Marshal Tedder had a good reputation as an airman who understood how to apply air power in effective support of ground and naval operations. But Tedder lacked sympathy with the problems of the British Army and shared Coningham's antipathy toward Montgomery. He openly criticized the Army's leadership in the summer of 1944. He also clashed frequently with Leigh-Mallory, especially over proposals to use heavy bombers in close support.[13]

Leigh-Mallory has been much maligned. While not a great commander, he deserves a more sympathetic assessment than he has been given in the literature to date. He began his military career as a soldier and was wounded in 1915. Transferring to the Royal Flying Corps, be specialized in reconnaissance and close air support—what the British called "Army Cooperation."[14] In the late thirties, he assumed command of a group in Fighter Command, becoming Commander-in-Chief in November 1942. He presided over the early development of what was to become the RAF Second Tactical Air Force. Instead of sending a staff officer to the Mediterranean to observe air support there, he went himself to study current organization and technique.[15] Above all, Leigh-Mallory was probably the most passionate believer in using all the resources of the Allied air forces, including heavy bombers, to support the Allied armies. This attitude led him into conflict with virtually all of his senior colleagues in the British and American air forces.

Unfortunately, he was not politically skilled nor did he possess the kind of winning personality necessary to disarm the petty hostilities found in the Allied high command. Worse still, he had no personal allies, either in the British or American forces. Tedder openly challenged him, on one occasion going so far as to criticize him in front of subordinates. Coningham sought to by-pass him and work directly with Tedder.[16] General Spaatz, the commander of the American strategic air forces and the administrative commander of all American air forces, including those operating under Leigh-Mallory, reminded American officers serving under the AEAF Commander that their first allegiance was to the U.S. Army Air Forces (AAF)[17]

On the American side, General Brereton was a very experienced senior commander. Before coming to England, he had held responsible commands in the Philippines, in India, and in North Africa. Subsequently, he had learned air support organization and technique in the Libyan desert while operating with Coningham. Brereton got along well with the RAF officers and was on good terms with most of the senior American ground officers, with the possible exception of General Bradley.[18] In August 1944, Brereton left the Ninth Air Force to assume command of the newly formed First Allied Airborne Army. Maj. Gen. Hoyt Vandenberg, formerly Leigh-Mallory's Deputy at AEAF, took over the Ninth and commanded it to the end of the war. General Vandenberg, too, had Mediterranean experience, but had come directly from a staff appointment in Washington.

The lack of harmony in the high command was largely offset by the competence of the commanders who bore the day-to-day operational burden of air support and the excellent relations they enjoyed with their counterparts in the ground forces. The most experienced of these officers was Air Vice Marshal Broadhurst, who had been Coningham's Senior Air Staff Officer in North Africa and succeeded him as commander of the Western Desert Air Force. In Italy, relations between Broadhurst and his Army counterpart, Lt. Gen. Sir Miles Dempsey, were not good. In a happy contrast to the petty quarreling found elsewhere, however, the two patched up their differences and made an excellent team in Normandy.[19]

General Quesada soon came to enjoy a reputation equal to Broadhurst's. With Mediterranean experience, he was innovative and undogmatic about doctrine and organization and regarded air support as his chosen field of expertise, not an assignment of last resort. Quesada was on the very best of terms with his army counterparts; General Bradley once called him a "jewel."[20] While less well known than Quesada, Generals Weyland and Nugent were also very effective tactical air commanders, and they formed equally solid relationships with the commanders of the armies they supported, Generals Patton and Simpson respectively.

Mediterranean experience demonstrated the necessity of close and stable counterpart relationships between air and ground commanders at all levels from theater down to tactical air command or composite group. This relationship was reinforced by the collocation of headquarters whenever possible. At

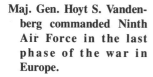

Maj. Gen. Hoyt S. Vandenberg commanded Ninth Air Force in the last phase of the war in Europe.

the higher levels in northwest Europe, there was little possibility of developing and maintaining such relationships because of all the temporary dual commands created by General Eisenhower's decision to assign overall ground command to Montgomery for the early phases of the campaign and to assume that role himself at a later date. General Montgomery thus was both temporary commander of Allied ground forces and a permanent commander of the British ground forces.

Air Marshal Coningham was, at the same time, temporary commander of AEAF (Adv) and the permanent commander of the British tactical air forces committed to the battle. Theoretically, Montgomery should have gone to Coningham as AOC, Second Tactical Air Force for support of British forces, and also to Coningham as AOC, Advanced AEAF, for support of both American and British forces. But Montgomery's bad relations with Coningham led him to consult Broadhurst in the first instance and Leigh-Mallory in the second, especially when the mediums and the heavies were required.[21] At lower levels, there were fewer problems. If Dempsey wanted air support, he always went to Broadhurst. The same was true of Bradley and Quesada. While there were occasional differences of opinion, the good relationship between these officers serves as a model for the conduct of combined air and ground operations.

British and American experience in the Mediterranean led to the adoption of the fighter-bomber as the primary weapon for close air support. Early in the war, that burden had been carried principally by the light bomber—the American A–20 and the British Blenheim. The fighter was used chiefly in defensive roles—to protect rear areas and to provide air cover over the front lines. Offensively, fighters provided escort for light bombers and occasionally used machineguns and cannons in strafing attacks. Ground attack, however, was strictly a secondary function of the fighter arm.[22] The *Luftwaffe* had, of course, used dive bombers to great effect in 1939–40. But neither the AAF or the RAF was very enthusiastic about this type of aircraft, thinking it too slow and vulnerable both to ground fire and to hostile fighters.[23]

RAF operations in France in 1940, and later in north Africa, demonstrated that the light bomber was extremely vulnerable to flak and fighters when flying at the low altitudes required in close support.[24] Accordingly, these aircraft were employed more and more on heavily escorted attacks against airfields and the enemy's lines of communications. At the same time, fighters were increasingly used for ground attack, and in the Middle East the RAF began to fit Hurricanes with bomb racks in late 1941.[25]

Parallel developments occurred in the Metropolitan Air Force, where Fighter Command's search for an offensive mission had led it to carry out large-scale fighter sweeps over northwest France and Belgium. As the *Luftwaffe* largely ignored challenges that contained no bombing forces, Fighter Command's No. 11 Group asked to modify some of its Hurricanes to carry bombs.[26] At one point, Bomber Command even sought to have "Hurribomber" squadrons attached to it for attacking coastal shipping.[27] Over the course of the next two years, the fighter-bomber became the main RAF weapon for close air support.

By the summer of 1944, the primary strength of the RAF 2nd Tactical Air Force was its squadrons of Mustangs, Spitfires, and Typhoons, all equipped to carry bombs, and some fitted for rockets. The Typhoon, a sturdy fighter-bomber capable of carrying bombloads of up to 2,000 pounds, proved to be a particularly effective close support weapon. More than twenty squadrons of this type were equipped with air-to-ground rockets.[28]

American developments proceeded along the same lines. In late 1942, when XII Air Support Command (ASC) began to operate in northwest Africa, the plan was to give its A–20s responsibility for all close air support bombing. Its P–39s were to handle some reconnaissance tasks and to strafe with their cannons. Other reconnaissance and air combat fell principally on P–40s. Changes in theater air organization and strategy forced the command to give up the A–20s, which, along with the British light and medium bombers, were now organized as the Tactical Bomber Force under the control of the Northwest African Tactical Air Force headquarters. This force was used primarily for attacks on airfields and enemy concentrations in the rear areas. For a brief time, these changes limited the XII ASC's offensive role to ground strafing and bomber escort. Then, in late March 1943, XII ASC began to experiment by installing bomb racks on one P–40 group to carry fragmentation clusters. The P–39 could still be used for strafing, but losses tended to be high, and difficulties with bomb mountings meant that it could not successfully be converted to a successful fighter-bomber.[29]

Other work also continued on the development of the fighter-bomber in the Army Air Forces. The American forces based in England in the summer of 1944 employed three of the newer fighter types for this role—the P–51, the P–38, and the P–47.[30] Each was designed as a high-altitude fighter, not as a ground-attack aircraft, and it was fortunate that they all could be modified for their new role. The P–51 had the greatest range, but its liquid-cooled engine made it more vulnerable to ground fire. As a result, it was used more on escort duties and armed reconnaissance in the back areas than on close air support. The P–38 had problems with mechanical reliability, and if supplies of P–47s and P–51 had been adequate, it might have been replaced altogether in the European theater. It also was liquid-cooled and vulnerable to ground fire, a disadvantage somewhat offset by its twin-engine configuration. It was comparatively quiet in low-level approach, which improved possibilities for achieving surprise. Also, its distinctive silhouette made it very useful for certain kinds of work, such as channel cover during the invasion, where nervous Allied antiaircraft gunners were prone to fire on anything that flew over them.

Ground-attack aircraft of the war in northwest Europe *(clockwise from above)*: **the Hawker 1-B Typhoon, the North American P-51D Mustang, the obsolescent Bell P-39 Airacobra, and the Lockheed P-38 Lightning.**

All authorities agreed that the P–47 was the best fighter-bomber, and it was the most widely used of the three. The P–47 combined several attractive qualities—a sturdy airframe able to absorb battle damage and a powerful air-cooled engine that allowed it to carry bombloads of up to 2,000 pounds. The resistance to battle damage was particularly appreciated by pilots:

> Well, for instance in the P–51, Me–109, and the Spitfire, your radiators were all underneath the airplane. At any time you were hit with ground fire you were apt to get hit in a coolant line or radiator. And you've only got about ten minutes—then. Whereas with a P–47 and a radial engine, there's no coolant to worry about . . . they've flown them all the way back [after being hit by flak]. . . . Or they get somewhere where they can make a controlled crash. This is why I like it for the low-altitude area support work.[31]

If the designers had set out to make a multipurpose, high-performance aircraft that could be used for close support, they could hardly have done better within the existing technology. The chief disadvantage of the Thunderbolt was its notorious thirst for fuel. When airfields were too far back, as in the early days after the Normandy landings and during part of the pursuit in August, high fuel consumption always cut into endurance over the battlefield. The time over target could be extended, however, by attaching a drop tank.[32]

Close support weapons included machineguns, cannons, bombs, and rockets. Machineguns and cannons proved to be very effective against personnel and "soft" vehicles. Various sizes of general-purpose, high-explosive, fragmentation, white phosphorous, and napalm bombs were also used.

The standard white phosphorous bomb contained 98 pounds of phosphorous with an instantaneous fuse to ensure the widest possible coverage. One aircraft load could cover an area 90 x 60 yards. The explosion of the bomb produced a shower of particles of various sizes that inflicted serious burns on troops caught in the open. Napalm was also used, though not extensively, to attack fixed fortifications.

The first fragmentation bombs used in France—the M–4 parafrag cluster—were simply not safe when mounted on fighter-bombers. In several instances, bombs worked loose, became armed, dropped prematurely, and worst of all, exploded during takeoffs and landings. The M–4 was replaced first by the 260–pound M–81 and later by the 585–pound M–27, which became particularly effective when it burst in the air or detonated in trees.

A very high percentage of missions was flown with the standard 500–pound general purpose (GP) bomb. Most plentiful type in stock, on some airfields it may have been the only type available. Useful against a variety of targets, it was commonly loaded on armed reconnaissance flights and on aircraft held back to respond to immediate requests for close support. By August 1944, armed reconnaissance and armored column cover flights often carried a mixed load of 500–pound GP and a variety of fragmentation bombs to attack columns on the move. The Ninth Air Force made little use of rockets during the course of the summer campaign. Although Typhoon squadrons of Second Tactical Air Force carried rockets as standard armament from the beginning of the invasion, it was not until the latter part of July that the first squadron of P–47s in IX TAC was similarly equipped.[33]

The prevailing operational doctrine in both the American and British air forces emphasized air superiority as the most important contribution to surface operations of any kind.[34] It freed the attacking armies and their naval support from the threat of effective interference by the enemy air force. Air superiority also allowed the air forces to turn to their second priority task, the attack on the enemy's lines of communications and his concentrations of men and materiel in the rear areas. The principal object was to delay the arrival of enemy reserves, to force the enemy command to commit them piecemeal, and to deprive them of the necessary supplies to fight effectively. Most senior American and British airmen considered close air support the least effective and most costly use of aircraft. Accordingly, it stood third on the list of air priorities. The governing American doctrinal manual—FM 100–20, The Command and Employment of Air Power—asserted:

> . . . in the zone of contact, missions against hostile units are most difficult to control, are most expensive, and are, in general, least effective. Targets are small, well-dispersed, and difficult to locate . . . only at critical times are contact zone missions profitable.[35]

During the summer of 1944, the actual practice of the AAF and the RAF conformed to this doctrine in some respects and deviated in others. In general, both services observed the hierarchy of priorities, although the declining strength of the *Luftwaffe* meant that the Allies rarely, if ever, had to make hard decisions concerning priorities. The most significant aspect of the doctrine—the third priority, close air support—became a relatively normal feature of military operations on the continent. Movement toward this state of affairs had begun in the Mediterranean and reached its fullest development in France and Italy in 1944 and 1945. Command, control, and operation of close air support in the summer of 1944 was a complicated affair. To understand the basic problems, it is helpful to keep in mind the separate "control" functions involved in close support operations: (1) the apportionment of air effort between air superiority, interdiction and close support (allocation control); (2) the collection and evaluation of requests for air support from ground units (the request system); (3) the selection of targets; (4) the assignment of specific aircraft to attack approved targets (mission control); (5) the navigational guidance of aircraft in flight between bases and targets (flying control); and (6) the control of the actual attack on the target (attack control).

The allocation of tactical air force effort was centralized within AEAF. For D–Day operations, the AEAF Advanced Headquarters at Uxbridge with

"All authorities agree that the P-47 was the best
   fighter- bomber, and it was the most widely
   used . . . "

"The P-47 combined several attractive qualities—
a sturdy airframe able to absorb battle damage and
a powerful air-cooled engine that allowed it
to carry bombloads of up to 2,000 pounds."

its command echelons served as the center of command and control. This included the Ninth Air Force, IX Fighter Command, IX Tactical Air Command, RAF Second Tactical Air Force, and RAF 83 Gp. "Senior Air Representatives" from Ninth Air Force were on board each of the flagships and their backup command ships.[36] The Combined Control Center at Uxbridge exercised all mission control. Flying control was in the hands of the static sector organizations of Air Defence of Great Britain (ex-RAF Fighter Command). With the exception of those squadrons detailed for air alert, the combined Control Center exercised final authority over the selection of targets for close support. From command ships, the Senior Air Representatives conducted rebriefing for new targets. Attack control was largely in the hands of the pilots, who depended on the quality of their briefing and map-reading. No provision was made for forward control in the British sectors, as the air parties that landed with British units did not possess VHF radio.[37]

The American Air Support Parties landing with each of the Regimental Combat Teams did have VHF radios, but they were enjoined from contacting aircraft overhead unless specifically authorized to do so. Nor were they allowed to intervene in stopping attacks on friendly troops or the wrong targets.[38] This writer has been unable to find reasons for such inhibitions. Possibly responsible air commanders feared that forward attack control could quickly expand into target control, a development that would undermine the centralized system.

By far the bulk of the air support on D–Day was prearranged against targets that had been designed days and weeks in advance. Provisions were also made to deal with targets of opportunity. The Ninth Air Force Tactical Air Plan put at least one squadron on constant air alert over each of the American assault beaches to attack targets of opportunity that were seen to be hindering the advance of the assault forces.[39] A similar arrangement was made in the British sector. The squadrons flying these missions checked in with the Senior Air Representatives on board the headquarters ships to receive their targets, which had been identified either by aerial reconnaissance or had been radioed from shore by the forward air parties.

The plans provided for target requests appearing in the course of battle. These were to be radioed directly from the forward air parties to the Combined Control Center at Uxbridge. The Senior Air Representatives and their ground commanders were to maintain a listening watch on a prearranged channel and to countermand requests if necessary. They could relay requests from the shore if the direct link failed, and they could originate requests themselves on the basis of reconnaissance information.[40]

As it turned out, on D–Day the American Air Support Parties (ASPs) could not communicate directly with Uxbridge, because their radios lacked the necessary range. Apparently it had been originally intended to give the SCR-399 HF radio to the ASPs for their point-to-point communications. This

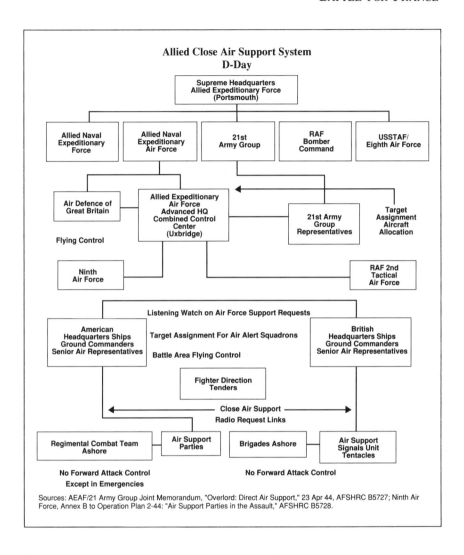

Allied Close Air Support System
D-Day

Supreme Headquarters
Allied Expeditionary Force
(Portsmouth)

Allied Naval
Expeditionary
Force

Allied Naval
Expeditionary
Air Force

21st
Army Group

RAF
Bomber
Command

USSTAF/
Eighth Air Force

Air Defence of
Great Britain

Allied Expeditionary
Air Force
Advanced HQ
Combined Control
Center
(Uxbridge)

21st Army
Group
Representatives

Target
Assignment
Aircraft
Allocation

Flying Control

Ninth
Air Force

RAF 2nd
Tactical
Air Force

Listening Watch on Air Force Support Requests

American
Headquarters Ships
Ground Commanders
Senior Air Representatives

Target Assignment For Air Alert Squadrons

Battle Area Flying Control

British
Headquarters Ships
Ground Commanders
Senior Air Representatives

Fighter Direction
Tenders

Close Air Support
Radio Request Links

Regimental Combat Team
Ashore

Air Support
Parties

Brigades Ashore

Air Support
Signals Unit
Tentacles

No Forward Attack Control
Except in Emergencies

No Forward Attack Control

Sources: AEAF/21 Army Group Joint Memorandum, "Overlord: Direct Air Support," 23 Apr 44, AFSHRC B5727; Ninth Air Force, Annex B to Operation Plan 2-44: "Air Support Parties in the Assault," AFSHRC B5728.

instrument had a good voice (R/T) range of up to 100 miles and a much greater range in Morse (W/T), but it had to be mounted in a 2½–ton truck. Someone apparently decided that this cumbersome equipment could not be landed quickly enough and substituted the SCR–284. Unfortunately its maximum range was only 25 miles, utterly inadequate to reach England from the Normandy beaches. All requests from Normandy had to be relayed by headquarters ships.[41]

There was one major difference between the British and the American request systems. By the summer of 1944, the British manned their system entirely with Army officers and used Army communications exclusively. The forward parties, known as Army Air Support Tentacles, radioed their requests to the joint Army–RAF Composite Group headquarters, who exercised Mission and target control.[42] On D–Day these request went directly to AEAF (Adv) at Uxbridge. In the Mediterranean, this system had been adopted by the American Fifth Army and XII Air Support Command in 1943, and Seventh Army and XII TAC brought it with them in the invasion of southern France in mid-August 1944 in Operation Dragoon.[43] Some evidence indicates that the Ninth Air Force would have preferred to establish the same system for Overlord but could not because it lacked the necessary equipment and trained personnel on the ground.[44] The American air support parties were manned by AAF officers and enlisted men under the control of Ninth Air Force.

Large-scale amphibious assaults of the kind staged on the Normandy beaches were among the most dangerous of all the operations of the war. The unsubtle frontal attacks afforded little opportunity for maneuver. When the moment arrived, even if the enemy could be deceived as to the time and place of the landings (as the Germans were), the troops still had to face direct fire from automatic weapons, mortars, and artillery of the defenders operating from cover. The price of failure was a forced retreat into the sea. Once ashore, the assaulting forces faced a second hazard. While they depended on sea communications for continuing their buildup of troops and materiel, the enemy could rely on the quicker and more efficient road and rail communications. The German army was rightly feared for its ability to organize fierce and extremely dangerous counterattacks of the kind that could inflict a severe defeat on the invaders.

Ideally, supporting fire from naval artillery and air support would incapacitate most defenders and at the same time destroy their weapons and communications. As a practical matter, however, such result could not be expected. Modern in-depth defense systems of the kind found on and behind the Normandy beaches featured well-dispersed personnel fighting from mutually supporting positions. Therefore, the central objects of any competent fire plan were (1) to attack artillery positions that presented the greatest danger, (2) to force defending troops to keep their heads down until the last possible moment while assaulting troops were landing, and (3) to shift to targets farther back. Three basic qualities were required: accuracy, continuity, and the ability to adjust to new targets quickly. The last two were especially important, for without them, the enemy would have a brief spell to organize resistance against the assault and to direct movements from his immediate reserves in local counterattacks.

The prearranged air support for Overlord began during the night before the landings. RAF Bomber Command used the bulk of its force against ten coastal batteries, which, it was feared, would be able to fire on the landing craft if left undisturbed. Air commanders did not expect to destroy the emplacements or to kill very many gun crews, but they did anticipate damage to communications, disorientation of crews, and the reduction of enemy effectiveness. In keeping with this objective and with the principle of continuity, Bomber Command attacks were scheduled to end just before daylight, when bombardment by the American heavy and medium bombers would take over.[45] Heavy bombers of the Eighth Air Force, after a very difficult predawn assembly, arrived in their target areas to find weather conditions unsuitable for visual aiming. Radar, radio, and other aids could not ensure accurate navigation, and there is little evidence that the bombing inflicted more than minor damage to forward defensive positions. Inaccuracy was compounded by the decision to delay the bomb release of the last attacking formations in order to avoid hitting troops in the assault boats. This shows how difficult it was to reconcile the requirement for sustained fire with the need to avoid casualties in the assault force caused by close bombing from heavy bombers. The medium bomber force fared somewhat better. Its efforts were aimed at Utah beach, where much the same overcast conditions existed. Force commanders brought the mediums under 7,000 feet for most of the runs, apparently with better results.[46]

Most of the fighter-bomber force was dedicated to interdiction, which would hinder counterattacks. Some missions were aimed at gun battery targets; a sizeable force was also held back either for air alert or to respond to immediate requests from the ground forces.[47]

American records show modest activity on the immediate request link.[48] Uxbridge received thirteen requests on D–Day. Three came from V Corps and three more from *Ancon*, the headquarters ship for that corps. It is not clear whether the latter originated with the 1st Division or were relayed by the Senior Air Representative on shore. Two requests came from the 4th Division. *Bayfield*, the headquarters ship for that division and for VII Corps, sent two requests, the origins of which were not recorded. No requests can be traced to the VII Corps. Most significantly, no request could be identified with an ASP accompanying an assault regiment. The first of these appeared on D + 1, originating in 8 RCT, one of the Utah formations. Over the entire first week of operations, 8 RCT was the only such unit to be identified in the request records.

There are several possible explanations for the dearth of requests. The RCT requests very likely came from divisions, corps, or headquarters ships, because ASP radios had an inadequate range, and all such requests had to be relayed. Also, some air support needs may have been met by the air alert squadrons who received their targets directly from headquarters ships, and in some cases the breakdown in communications may have thrown the whole system out of order. According to one account, only one air support party with an assaulting regiment made it ashore with working radio equipment. This unit, from the 8th Tactical Air Communication Squadron, could not contact its associated regiment. Its small pack radio and two of its jeeps were put out of action by enemy fire. Nevertheless, at some point it managed to process requests for several units. According to another source, some ASPs managed to make unauthorized VHF contact with aircraft and, "by entreaty" to divert them to urgent targets.[49] Such requests would not have shown up in records kept at Ninth Air Force headquarters.

After one day's operation, V Corps asked for and received an increase in "air alert" squadrons whose target assignments were to be provided not by Uxbridge, but by the Senior Air Representative on board *Ancon*.[50] This change foreshadowed a more substantial move toward decentralization of target selection later in the campaign in both the RAF and the AAF.

The contribution of close air support in the success of landings was difficult to measure. As already noted, with the exception of the medium bombers on Utah beach, the best that could be said for the "beach drenching" exercise was that it forced the defenders to keep their heads down for a while and sometimes disrupted their communications. Fighter-bomber close support was more effective and probably made its most significant contribution against German artillery firing on Omaha beach.

By June 19, the operational headquarters of First U.S. Army and its divisions and corps were ashore, and with them, the advanced headquarters of IX Tactical Air Command and its air support parties.[51] Also, an increasing number of fighter-bomber squadrons arrived at bases on the continent and were more readily available to headquarters. As these command and control echelons arrived, the close air support system began to develop into the basic form it was to take for the rest of the campaign in France. At the top, a Combined Operations Center made up of representatives from IX TAC and First Army exercised allocation (for fighter-bombers) and mission control. Air Support Parties were attached to the headquarters divisions, corps, and combat commands of armored divisions. Finally, the assault system under which ASPs accompanied infantry regiments was ended. Similar developments occurred on the British side.[52]

In the days and weeks that followed D–Day, the military problem facing the Allies was at least as difficult as the assault landing itself. German defenses consisting of mutually supporting fire positions were thickened and deepened. The Allies had to widen and deepen the beachhead to secure themselves in France, and they had to push back or break through German defenses to inflict a major defeat. Allied infantry and armor were therefore condemned to frontal assaults, which required the utmost in fire support from artillery and air. Attacking troops had to be supported both by prearranged and adjusted fire on new targets. Without continuity of such fire support, it would be extremely difficult to penetrate the German defensive system to any depth and to break through. This was especially important for Americans because of the lack of sustained combat power in their infantry

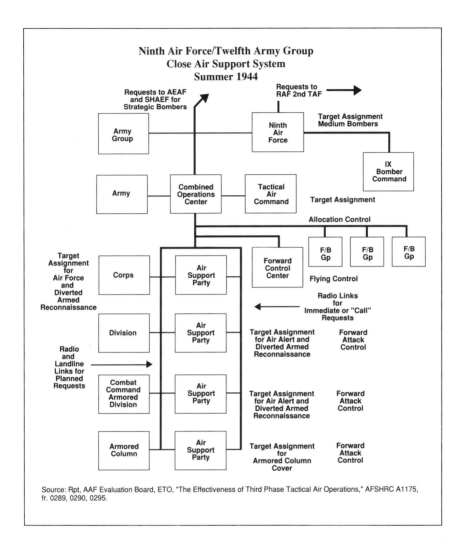

Ninth Air Force/Twelfth Army Group
Close Air Support System
Summer 1944

Source: Rpt, AAF Evaluation Board, ETO, "The Effectiveness of Third Phase Tactical Air Operations," AFSHRC A1175, fr. 0289, 0290, 0295.

divisions, and for the British because of the severe manpower constraints under which they had to operate in the last year of the war. Accurate, quickly delivered air support was a vital ingredient of success in this situation.

Under the reorganized American air support system, requests for attacks on the following day worked their way from the originating unit up to the Combined Operations Center by a prearranged period early in the evening (1800–2100 hrs) to allow time to allocate air efforts.[53] (See chart). At each level, the ASP officer and his ground force counterpart, usually a G–3 (Air) or Ass't. G–3, evaluated target suitability and place in the fire and maneuver plans. If approved, they forwarded it to the next echelon. At a regular evening conference at the Combined Operations Center, the Army G–3 (Air), G–2 (Air), and the TAC A–3 and A–2 discussed the following day's operations and agreed to the basic allocation of air effort for mediums and heavies required by the Ninth Air Force headquarters for air superiority missions, attacks on communications, armed reconnaissance, or for close air support.

When a support request arrived at the Combined Operations Center, this committee of officers determined if the target were suitable for air attack and if it conformed to the general plan of operations. If approved, it was assigned to the pool of aircraft set aside for close air support. Requests that could not be met by TAC, such as those for heavy or medium bombers, were forwarded to Ninth Air Force headquarters. Following approval of a request, TAC A–3 issued an operations order to a fighter-bomber group. When the order arrived at the airfield, the Ground Liaison Officer (GLO) briefed pilots for the attack. The operations center also arranged for the requesting unit to be notified of the rejection or acceptance of its request and of the estimated time over target.

"Immediate" or "call" requests could be radioed from the division or combat command ASP directly to the Combined Operations Center. The ASPs increasingly used the SCR-399 radio, a much more reliable long-range set. Urgent missions were assigned either to aircraft that had been held on the ground or to aircraft already dispatched on armed reconnaissance missions. Corps ASPs maintained a listening watch on these requests and could intervene to deny them—something apparently seldom done. From the time aircraft took off on a closesupport mission, they received flying control from the Fighter Control Center (later Tactical Control Center).[54] Prior to an attack, the flight or squadron commander checked with the Corps or Division ASP to receive final guidance—about five minutes before arrival over the target. The ASP officer would radio the pilot to keep him abreast of any special characteristics of the target, the location of friendly troops, and provisions to mark the target with artillery smoke.[55] In some cases, ASP officers observing the target could actually control the attack. Aside from these changes, the air support system functioned much as it had in the assault landings. Allocation, mission, and target control all remained centralized.

The British do not seem to have developed forward attack control as extensively or as quickly as the Americans. This is puzzling, as they had pioneered the concept in the Mediterranean. The primary AEAF memorandum on air support, which probably reflected Coningham's ideas, stipulated that his form of control would best work only with a prearranged plan and would be employed only at the direction of Coningham himself. And, according to that document, forward attack control by what the British called Visual Control Posts was to be provided on a limited scale—one post per Corps.[56] By contrast, each American ASP was potentially a forward control post, on an equivalent scale of one per division (two or three in armored divisions).

Just how the American system worked can be seen more clearly by examining the records of what the Army official history called a "typical" day—July 18, 1944.[57] On the evening of the 17th, the Combined Operations Headquarters of IX TAC and First Army allocated the air effort for the following day as follows: (1) forty percent dedicated to close support of First Army, then engaged in heavy fighting in the *bocage* country; (2) thirty percent assigned to direct support of the British Second Army, which was to open Operation Goodwood the next day; (3) twenty percent for offensive fighter sweeps and defensive assault area cover; and (4) ten percent for attacks on rail lines and other communications targets.

The Combined Operations Center processed fifty-three requests, either during the evening of the 17th or at various times during the 18th. Twenty-seven of these originated at the TAC/Army echelon, thirteen were from corps, and the balance came either from divisions or were unspecified. Twenty-one of the TAC/Army requests were aimed at rear areas—twelve bridge attacks and nine armed reconnaissance. The remainder of the TAC/Army requests were directed at a variety of targets ranging from supply dumps to "horse artillery" that turned out to be French evacuees. Fortunately, the pilots discovered the error and attacked enemy tanks in the area.

Six of the thirteen Corps requests were rejected for a variety of reasons. In three cases, no aircraft were available; in the other three, an "improper target" was involved. Among the latter were two "CRs" (crossroads) and one town. Accepted targets included supply dumps, a command post, a corps headquarters, and some gun positions.

Two requests from the 83d Division for attacks on an observation post and on some self-propelled guns were also accepted, but the missions were aborted due to weather. A third was rejected, as it had been covered in an early request from a higher echelon. The remaining requests came from unspecified origin for fighter sweeps or cover in the assault area.

Ordnance for the missions consisted of 500–lb GP bombs, with variation only in fuzing. Most attacks were dispatched in formations of twelve aircraft one flight of four provided top cover while the other two bombed.

There often was an unfortunate time lapse in notifying ground units when targets had been refused. In one case, more than nine hours elapsed between the time of request and notification that an attack was scrubbed. In other instances, the elapsed time varied between four and six hours.

Average response times for all missions cannot be calculated from the available records. The vast majority of requests came late in the evening or very early in the morning and were not graded urgent. Some requests for immediate action probably were diverted from armed reconnaissance.

The effectiveness of close air support between D–Day and the Allied breakout at the end of July cannot be measured precisely. On some days, aircraft attacked the right targets on time and rendered important, even crucial

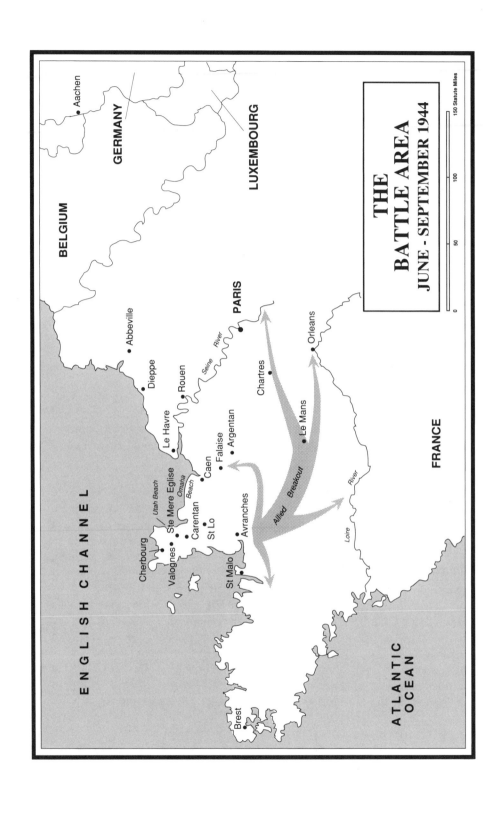

ENGLISH CHANNEL

THE
BATTLE AREA
JUNE - SEPTEMBER 1944

150 Statute Miles
100
50
0

BELGIUM

GERMANY

• Aachen

LUXEMBOURG

PARIS

• Abbeville

Seine River

• Dieppe

• Rouen

Chartres

• Le Havre

• Orleans

• Caen

• Falaise

• Argentan

• Le Mans

Utah Beach

Ste Mere Eglise

Omaha Beach

Cherbourg •

• Valognes

• Carentan

• St Lo

• Avranches

Allied Breakout

River

Loire

FRANCE

• St Malo

Brest

ATLANTIC
OCEAN

fire support. On other days, they hit the wrong targets (sometimes friendly troops). Evidence indicates that both, air and ground forces, were feeling their way on close air support procedures.

The state of development of air support in this early phase is best illustrated by events on the opening day of VII Corps' drive on Cherbourg, which took place on June 22. Generals Bradley and Collins formulated requests on the continent in consultation with Brereton and Quesada. On June 21, Brereton flew back to Uxbridge, where staffs of Second Tactical Air Force and Ninth Air Force worked out a combined plan. The next day the attack began. Artillery fired on known flak positions and, at eighty minutes before the beginning of the ground assault, RAF 83 Group Typhoons and Mustangs began to pepper the target areas with cannon and rocket fire. They were followed by IX TAC fighter-bombers and by some eleven groups of IX Bomber Command medium bombers.[58]

In some respects the results were disappointing. By June 23, Allied forces had taken only a small fraction of the area attacked by air, although the seized positions included some key points on high ground. Many enemy positions in the areas attacked remained active and effective, and there were incidents of short bombing and strafing. Information from POW interrogation, however, indicated that the air attacks disrupted communications and undermined morale.[59]

The mixed record of close air support in the early weeks of the campaign raises the question of how effective the training program had been before D–Day. The Tactical Air Communications Squadrons brought from United States to Britain in late 1943 to form the nucleus of the Ninth Air Force Air Support Parties had been well trained. Their training, however, was limited only to HF radio equipment, while their procedures and organization were dated to the prewar period. However important the Mediterranean experience, it apparently had not been disseminated to training camps in the United States. The first time that ASPs used VHF equipment to communicated with aircraft overhead was in the two months preceding the landing. Some apparently did not work with VHF until their imminent departure for the continent.[60]

In Great Britain, the requirement to support the Eighth Air Force's long-range attacks against German targets hampered Ninth Air Force training. Most fighter-bomber units arrived in the theater seriously ill-trained in strafing and dive-bombing techniques. The excellent RAF "Army Cooperation" School at Old Sarum was put to use to remedy these difficulties somewhat. Communications Squadrons participated in field exercises, and senior officers received "indoctrination" on the principles and procedures of air support. Teams of officers went to the Mediterranean to observe the system there, and some officers from that theater returned to aid in organization and training.[61]

Apparently there were not many large-scale regimental or divisional exercises with aircraft. General Bradley points to this in his memoirs, claiming that the U.S. Army and the Army Air Forces assaulted Normandy unprepared for effective close air support because of such deficiencies. He relates an incident when Brereton came to him in early May with the news that the Ninth Air Force was now ready for combined training, he (Bradley) told him it was too late. The troops were already being sealed into pre-embarkation marshalling areas (the so-called "sausages") and would not be available for such exercises.[62]

Even if the training program had been more extensive, it is hard to escape the conclusion that all systems of this kind require battle experience to become effective. It takes such experience to identify weak personnel, to pinpoint poor procedures, and to create those human bonds necessary to superior performance. No training can realistically simulate the rush and urgency of demands flooding an operational system as it enters combat. It probably was unreasonable to expect the air support system to work very well at the outset. But it was not unreasonable to expect improvement.

Two problems stood out. The first and perhaps most important was weather. Neither Second Tactical Air Force nor Ninth Air Force was an all-weather organization. For missions to be successful, there had to be suitable weather at the bases, enroute to the target, and over the target. Unfortunately, in the summer of 1944, especially in June and July, these conditions rarely existed. On many days in the first six or seven weeks of the campaign, the Allied air effort was either greatly reduced or nonexistent owing to bad weather. Equally frustrating was the problem of weather differential between bases in England and targets on the continent. No matter how good the weather over the targets might be, pilots could not take off, fly, or assemble in formation without adequate visual conditions. This problem diminished somewhat as the number of airfields on the continent expanded, but it reappeared in a new form when warfare became mobile in late July and early August. The rapid advance of the armies greatly increased the average distance between targets and airfields and thereby brought back the more severe weather limitation on flight operations that a weather differential between air base and target can effect. Even if conditions allowed flight to and from the target, for aircraft equipped with visual aiming, flying below a cloud base lower than 12,000 feet would expose the aircraft to enemy medium flak. Any base below 3,000 feet would bring the attacking aircraft within range of the ever-present German light flak.[63]

The second problem that bedeviled all close air support in Normandy was the difficulty in identifying targets, both from the ground and in the air. German ground units used camouflage effectively, and when personnel, guns, or vehicles were under cover and dispersed, they were very hard to spot. Target identification was relatively easy only if they were moving in daylight. In the North African desert, there had been too few terrain features. Both ground and air forces had a hard time figuring out where they were. In Normandy, there were too many features, and they all looked alike. For American troops, the hedgerow country presented an environment in which it was incredibly easy to become disoriented.[64]

There were other important but less fundamental difficulties. Handling requests for prearranged support was a problem. During the summer of 1944, requests for air strikes for the following day had to be delivered to the Combined Operations Center well before darkness set in and before fighting ceased. This meant that often there was a change in front-line positions that had not been anticipated in the original request. As the campaign developed, arrangements for adjustments allowed the corps to accommodate its requests according to the progress of fighting late in the day.[65]

There were some complaints about delays in notifying units about the disposition of their requests. Corps and division fire plans had to be kept flexible to the last moment while awaiting the outcome of the request. In addition, immediate requests to attack targets of opportunity were often delayed in the communications system, because they had to be encoded, transmitted by HF radio to the Combined Operations Center, decoded, and then evaluated. To overcome this problem, some divisions began sending their immediate requests to Corps first, from which they usually could be forwarded by landline.[66] Difficulties of this kind were greatly reduced when air alert, armored column cover (discussed below), or diversions from armed reconnaissance were employed.

Communications equipment used in 1944 occasionally lacked reliability. This was especially true of the standard VHF radio used by air support parties—the SCR 522. Originally developed for use in aircraft, this set was not designed to withstand the abuse to which it was subjected and the extensive service that it received on the ground. Gradually it was replaced with the sturdier SCR 624. The vacuum tubes in the radios of that day made the sets vulnerable to overheating, dust, and vibration. And shortages of spare parts were common. A sergeant in one air support party graphically described the situation:

> We had no spare sets or parts to repair our VHF. . . . We spent a lot of time salvaging parts and complete sets from cracked up planes, both friendly and enemy. Several British planes provided 12 volt dynamotors for our 522s. This was a very critical item, and we acquired them just in time to replace unrepairable units only days before the breakout in Normandy.[67]

Close air support in the most effective manner required close integration of corps and division plans for fire and maneuver. The combination of the ASP and the G–3 (Air) was intended to achieve this, and for the most part it functioned moderately well. But a 12th Army Group study of October 1944

265

pointed out that the G–3 (Air) staff at the various echelons was too small to keep in touch adequately with both ground and air operations.[68]

There were shortages of qualified personnel, both for ASPs and ground force G–3 sections. When Quesada moved to transform the air support party into a forward attack control in mid- to late July, he also decided to employ as ASP officers veteran fighter-bomber pilots who had completed their tours of flying duty. It was hoped that ground controllers with experience in close support missions would direct attacks more effectively. Pilots, however, were not enthusiastic for this duty when fellow aviators were being returned to the States upon completion of their tours. As an incentive, Ninth Air Force limited an ASP tour to ninety days.[69] Ground forces also had problems finding suitable G–3 (Air) personnel. Less than two weeks after D–Day, three of the four American Corps Commanders had relieved their G–3 (Air). The best kind of replacement could be usually found in the small group of ground officers who served as liaison officers at IX TAC airfields.[70]

The problem of mistaken attacks against friendly ground forces was never entirely solved. It was particularly troublesome in the early weeks of the campaign. From June 8 to 17, for example, IX TAC attacked American troops no fewer than nine times.[71] The most notorious incidents of this kind, however, occurred in July and August when the heavy bombers were providing close support.

In part, the solution to the problem of short bombing depended on a good system for marking forward troop positions. At one time or another, ground troops used colored panels, smoke, and flares. The panels were the most successful, but much depended on the discipline of the ground forces using them. Many units, in order to ensure their immunity from friendly air attack, displayed their panels when they were not in the front line. One First Army report stated that pilots had spotted panels all the way back to the corps headquarters areas,[72] which only made the forward units more vulnerable, because troops ahead of the panels were assumed to be the enemy.

The situation became more complicated by the uneven quality of the ground forces' recognition skills. Some units had a tendency to fire at anything in the air.[73] In part this could be traced to defects in the training program in the U.S., but the failure of ground commanders in the theater to take the matter seriously enough also contributed.[74] Even if the ground troops did their best, inadequate briefing at the airfields or pilot error could still produce a tragedy. Smoke and dust raised by earlier artillery fire and air attack and confusion in a fluid situation on the ground could lead to major errors. Under stressful combat conditions, the requirement for action occasionally overpowered the need for adequate preparation. One observer who visited an RAF airfield in Normandy asked a pilot what target he was attacking. The pilot replied: "Haven't a clue, sir. When Bill, there, peels off and goes down I follow and then let my bombs go."[75]

There were also problems with the "bomb line," the imaginary line identified by terrain features that served as a boundary beyond which aircraft were free to attack any military target. Bomb lines were difficult to recognize in the *bocage* country, and they provided inadequate protection, as forward positions lost their linear character in fluid operations. The rule in both the RAF and the AAF was that the bomb line should be set where friendly troops were expected to arrive two hours hence.[76] On at least one occasion, Air Marshal Coningham complained bitterly that the Canadian Army had been too optimistic about its rate of advance, had set its bomb line too far ahead, and thereby deprived Second Tactical Air Force of many profitable targets.[77] An RAF study of close support in this period suggests that this practice was less the product of unwarranted optimism about the rate of advance than an overconservative reaction to incidents of short bombing and strafing by Second Tactical Air Force.[78]

Contributions of close air support to success of ground forces increased considerably in late July and early August. Fighting to expand the beachhead had been fierce, casualties were high, especially among the infantry, and progress frustratingly slow. A breakthrough finally came on July 25, when the American First Army launched Operation Cobra, supported by a massive close air support effort including American heavy bombers. This breakthrough created a war of movement, forcing the Germans out of their positions into open fields and onto roads in daylight, where they were much more vulnerable to fighter-bomber attack.

To support Cobra, the Americans employed the Eighth Air Force. The use of heavy bombers as a close-support weapon was a matter of considerable controversy. All of the senior British and American air commanders were opposed to it with the exception of Leigh-Mallory, who in mid-June had proposed to use heavy bombers in support of the British Second Army.[79] General Spaatz's response to this suggestion is noted in his Daily Journal:

> . . . complete lack of imagination exists in the minds of Army Command, particularly Leigh-Mallory, who visualize best use of tremendous air potential lies in plowing up several square miles of terrain in front of ground forces to obtain a few miles of advance. Our forces now are far superior to the Germans opposing us, both in men and materiel. The only thing necessary to move forward is sufficient guts on the part of the ground commanders.[80]

Two days later, Spaatz told Tedder that the American people "would greatly resent tying up of the tremendous air power provided to plow up fields in front of an Army reluctant to advance." He complained that "all the power of the Americans and the British is being contained in a narrow beachhead by fourteen half-baked German divisions."[81]

Spaatz believed that his bomber forces would be better used against targets in Germany. In a letter to the Supreme Commander, Spaatz introduced a plan to limit his heavy bomber forces for direct support of the invasion force to a short, definite period. After that time, the bombers should be allowed to return to strategic missions, with a small force held back to handle urgent requirements for close air support. The use of the heavy bombers in close support en masse must be restricted to a "grave emergency," for to employ them in this fashion on a regular basis would constitute "uneconomical use of such a force."[82] Spaatz's views were, in general, shared by Tedder and Harris.[83]

Leigh-Mallory's perspective was different. He too was concerned about the lack of progress in Normandy, but he differed from his colleagues in his belief that the air forces could do more to help the ground forces extricate themselves from the stalemate.

> I have always taken the view that the Army should be given all the air support it desires. After all, it is a citizen Army, composed from the most part of men belonging to every walk of life, to whom soldiering is neither natural nor easily learned. . . . What I have been up against more or less since D-Day is the school of thought which takes the view that the air support given to the Army should be the minimum rather than the maximum, on the principle that if you give an inch, it will take a mile.[84]

Leigh-Mallory was in the stronger position: for however much Spaatz and other senior airmen opposed the use of heavy bombers in the battle area, a request from the ground commanders for the support of the heavies in a major offensive operation simply could not be refused without exposing the air forces to the charge of failure to cooperate at a vital moment.

There were a number of problems involved in the use of heavy bomber force to support troops. For all of the emphasis on "precision" daylight bombing in the AAF, the Eighth Air Force was poorly prepared to operate under the exacting requirements for close air support. With the exception of preparing for the D–Day assault, none of the Eighth Air Force heavy units had worked on the problems associated with close air support. Great reliance was placed on good briefings at the fields, good formation-keeping, excellent visual conditions for aiming, and, of course, the right wind and weather over the target.[85]

Ironically, RAF Bomber Command, the "blunt instrument" of the Allied air forces, was somewhat more adaptable to close air support than the Eighth Air Force. This was not because Harris was more interested or because Bomber Command had made deliberate preparations. The requirements of night operations had forced the command to develop a high state of training in the use of radio navigation aids, pyrotechnics for target-marking, and an airborne controller (the "Master Bomber" or "Master of Ceremonies") to adjust target-marking and to direct bombing. Because Bomber Command could not fly in formation at night, each bombardier was responsible for aiming and dropping his bombs. Some elements of the command, particularly

No. 5 Group, had shown that they could achieve accurate and concentrated bombing. Elements of the RAF Air Staff were also interested in seeing the Bomber Command develop as much as possible as a close air support force.[86]

The first experiments with heavy bombers had taken place on D–Day, when at best, the record was mixed. In two major operations following the landings, the British were the first to employ heavy bomber close support. On the first occasion—Charnwood in early July—the desire to ensure that friendly troops were not hit led the planners at British Second Army to select a target area that was too far to the rear. Ground observers found that the area contained very few enemy positions, personnel, or guns.[87] Attacking targets so far back, and in this case several hours before the main ground attack, also violated the principle of continuity so essential to the success of a fire plan supporting an attempt to break into a deep defensive system.

In the second operation—Goodwood in mid-July—Bomber Command heavies attacked positions on the flanks of a corridor through which Allied armored forces were to attack. Attacks in the corridor were assigned to American mediums from the Ninth Air Force and fighter-bombers from the Second Tactical Air Force. American heavy bombers were also to attack positions on the right flank and deep in the corridor. After initial successes, the ground attack foundered and halted when British armor ran up against a relatively undisturbed antitank gun line which had not been a major target in the preliminary air support plan.[88]

Goodwood revealed that while both Bomber Command and Eighth Air Force were less than entirely suitable close-support weapons, Bomber Command could achieve a much greater bombing density, and hence could attack prepared positions more effectively than the Eighth. Reviewing evidence from Goodwood, the AAF Air Evaluation Board found that Bomber Command achieved concentrations of one ton of bombs per acre, while the best performance of the Eighth in this attack was .23 tons per acre.[89]

Goodwood also demonstrated again that it was one thing to break into a German defensive system; it was quite another to sustain enough momentum to break through it. Continuity of fire and air support was essential. And that continuity required further development in control techniques, especially the use of forward air control from the ground. Two controllers served Goodwood on an experimental basis. Unfortunately, the first was wounded early, and the second was hit while coming up to replace him.[90] Apparently the enemy had evaluated the forward controller as a worthwhile target.

The American plan—Operation Cobra—to break through German defenses in mid-July had two main features: concentrated fire support at the outset and continuity of air support as the attack progressed. The attack was to be delivered on a very narrow front of some 7,000 yards, supported by a large-scale preliminary bombardment by heavy and medium bombers. Fighter-bombers of IX TAC were to begin by attacking a strip some 250 yards deep behind the St. Lo–Periers road, which ran along the front of the German positions. The Eighth Air Force heavies were then to expand the bombing area along the front of the German defenses to a depth of some 2,000 yards. After the last bombs had fallen, the infantry were to attack while medium bombers worked over the southern half of the bombardment area.[91]

After an abortive start on July 24, Cobra was successfully launched the next day. On both days, there were serious incidents of short bombing, in which American troops were killed, wounded, and disorganized. The heavy bombing did not make for a "walkover," and initial progress against the surviving German defenses was disappointing. Within forty-eight hours, however, the American VII Corps had committed its armor, and the German positions began to disintegrate. The war became one of movement that was not to end until the German forces in France were badly defeated.[92]

Charnwood, Goodwood, Cobra, and two subsequent operations using heavy bombers as close support disclosed a number of problems. The first was the choice of the right bombs and fuzes. Instantaneous fuzing was effective against personnel in the open, and it made few craters that hampered the advancing forces; but it was more or less useless against troops properly dug in or sheltered in fortifications. Delay fuzing worked better against protected troops, but the cratering that resulted created obstacles to the advance.[93]

Weather was also a major problem. A heavy bomber attack required good visual conditions for bomb placement, not only to ensure that the targets were hit, but also that friendly positions were not. Because weather conditions could not be accurately predicted, and since the heavy bomber attack was a vital part of the whole assault plan, the plans for ground forces were held hostage to the fortunes of weather to a far greater extent than if they depended exclusively on their own artillery or on fighter-bombers.

During a heavy bomber attack, even in good weather, visibility for bombing could rapidly deteriorate, as the smoke and dust from bomb detonations obscured landmarks and aiming points. This was more of a problem for the Eighth Air Force than for the RAF Bomber Command, whose airborne controller could call off the attack or adjust the target markers.

The serious problem affecting heavy bomber close support was safety distance. It was widely accepted as a general principle that to take maximum advantage of artillery fire or close air support, it was necessary for the ground forces to attack as quickly as possible after the last bombs fell. This meant that the infantry had to be as close as possible to the front when the attack began. Unfortunately, the quality of precision-bombing, the chances of mechanical mishaps, and the deterioration of visual conditions combined to create the possibility of bombing friendly troops.

RAF Bomber Command attacked friendly troops on one occasion in the summer campaign—Operation Tractable. The accident seems to have been the result of an unfortunate combination of errors. Bomber Command on that day used the same color of smoke for marker bombs as did the Canadian forces to mark their forward positions. Some crews who had been instructed to make a timed run from the coast as a safety measure failed to do so. As a result, bombs fell short, killing and wounding some 400 men.[94]

Eighth Air Force bombed short on three occasions in the summer of 1944. The first occurred on July 24, when some units did not get the message to abort the attack and dropped on friendly troops. The following day, in the massive attack supporting Cobra, bombs again fell short, killing and wounding several hundred troops, including Lt. Gen. Lesley J. McNair. On the 8th of August, Eighth Air Force joined the Bomber Command in Operation Totalise to support Canadian troops toward Falaise. Again short bombing resulted in casualties.[95]

On August 24, a lead bombardier had difficulty with his bomb-release mechanism, and his load salvoed prematurely. The other fifteen aircraft in his group followed suit. On the 25th, a lead bombardier had problems with his bombsight, another failed to identify appropriate landmarks, and another aircraft commander failed to observe the agreement to bomb by groups. In Totalise, the Eighth had to fly parallel to the front with greater exposure to enemy antiaircraft fire. A lead aircraft was hit, its bombs were dropped prematurely, and the rest of the formation dropped with it.[96] These tragedies illustrated that air forces could only be as flexible as their equipment, training, and experience permitted them to be. The narrow operational focus and training of the Eighth Air Force virtually ensured that, even with the best will in the world, serious mistakes would be made.

Whatever its shortcomings, the massive heavy bomber support for Cobra helped carry the attacking troops deep into the German defensive system. The task was now to sustain the momentum of advance by committing armor and providing continuous air support. General Quesada, a genuine air support enthusiast, introduced a new wrinkle to the IX TAC air support system. Taking advantage of the declining strength of the *Luftwaffe* and the corresponding diminution of the need to commit large forces to air superiority, he decided to experiment with a lavish form of the air alert system. Building on the success that had been achieved with the use of ASPs as attack controls, he decentralized the IX TAC target assignment function as well.

Quesada arranged for the installation of a VHF radio operated by an ASP officer in the tank leading the column in each combat command of each armored division committed to the breakthrough. He also had IX TAC allocate sufficient aircraft for a constant relay of four-plane flights over each column. When a flight arrived, the ASP officer could give it an urgent target or request that it patrol ahead of the column to provide instant reconnaissance information and attack targets of opportunity. This combination of forward attack and target assignment with a prearranged schedule of aircraft, known as "armored column cover," proved to be an instant success and was consistently rated by ground commanders as the most effective form of close air support. When mobile operations began on the British and Canadian front, the RAF introduced a similar system on a smaller scale, using a forward controller in a scout car and an air alert system.[97] The combination of an air alert with a forward controller had been tried earlier in the Mediterranean, but it was relatively novel to place the controller at the front of a moving column.

At IX TAC, allocation plans for operation Cobra were somewhat different from those for the "typical" day of close support described earlier.[98] A full seventy-nine percent of IX TAC air effort was for close support of the First Army, twelve percent for fighter sweeps, and nine percent for defensive air cover. If weather forced cancellation or delay of Cobra past 1500 hrs, the allocation for close air support was to be reduced to forty-one percent, with the remainder going to a wide variety of missions, mostly air cover over the assault area and fighter sweeps.

In support of the attack, the Combined Operations Center processed some sixty-six requests, forty-five from the TAC/Army level, the remainder from corps echelon. No divisional requests were recorded, although it can be assumed that some divisional emergencies were satisfied by diverting aircraft from the thirteen armed reconnaissance missions laid on for the day. The twenty-one corps targets were a mixed bag, including a barracks, a communications center, a "Gestapo headquarters," troop positions, an observation post, a variety of supply dumps, and troops in fixed positions.

The principal difference between the plans and those of the "typical" day was the provision for attacks by large formations of fighter-bombers on troops in prepared positions in the forward part of the enemy's defensive zone. Eleven missions using formations ranging between thirty-five and forty aircraft carrying mixed ordnance loads of 500–pound GP, 360–pound fragmentation, and 100–pound white phosphorus bombs were detailed to this task. It appears that this day's effort also marked the first operational use of a rocket-equipped P–47 squadron.

On the day after Cobra, the pattern of close air support operations changed dramatically with the beginning of a battle of movement and the first employment of armored column cover.[99] Of 155 preplanned missions processed on August 26, no fewer than 74 were assigned to that task. Each column cover mission was flown by a flight of 4 aircraft armed largely with 500–pound general purpose bombs. A few missions used rockets.

Operation Dragoon—the American and French landings in the south of France in early August 1944—introduced the Mediterranean system of close air support into the European theater.[100] This system was closely modeled on the RAF arrangements and differed in some key respects from that employed in the Ninth Air Force. In its original form, as worked out by XII Air Support Command and Fifth Army, the ground forces were responsible for transmission and evaluation of requests, which were handled by G–3 (Air) staff sec-

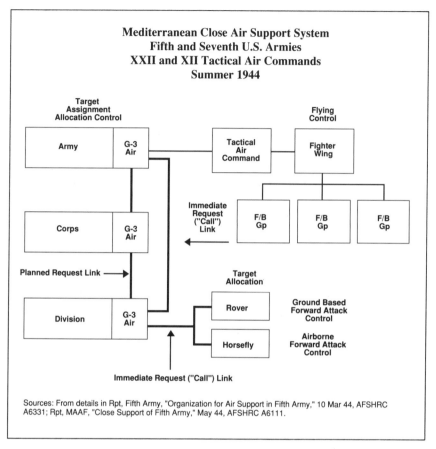

**Mediterranean Close Air Support System
Fifth and Seventh U.S. Armies
XXII and XII Tactical Air Commands
Summer 1944**

Sources: From details in Rpt, Fifth Army, "Organization for Air Support in Fifth Army," 10 Mar 44, AFSHRC A6331; Rpt, MAAF, "Close Support of Fifth Army," May 44, AFSHRC A6111.

tions at division, corps, and army. The Air Support Command provided no liaison officers to either of the two lower echelons. The first an air officer heard of the request was when it was presented by the G–3 at army to the TAC A–3. If the A–3 accepted the request, he relayed the orders to the 64 Wing Fighter Control Center, which handled TAC navigation control. Pilots would already have been briefed by the ground liaison officer before the orders reached the airfields.

This system depended heavily on airfield briefing. Most targets attacked were far removed from forward positions held by friendly troops. The need to attack closer to the front lines led the XII Air Support Command to experiment with what came to be known as the "Rover" forward control system.[101] The Rovers, who travelled with the ground forces, were used in two ways. They could provide more precise control for attacks laid on in the regular fashion, or they could receive emergency requests directly from divisions. Flights arrived at prearranged intervals; if no targets were available, the

Rover could release the aircraft to fly armed reconnaissance. Once divisions began to realize how quickly Rovers could deliver an air strike, they tended to pass all urgent requests to that controller. This tended to overload the team and to force upon it some target evaluation, work normally accomplished by corps or army G–3 (Air) sections.

Fifth Army and XII Air Support Command developed a second innovation that was brought to France with Operation Dragoon: a forward air controller—or "Horsefly"—flying L–5 liaison aircraft. The first experiments with Horseflies were conducted north of Rome in June 1944.[102] They were attempts to solve the problem of locating forward elements of rapidly moving friendly columns and of exploiting the tactical information provided by low-flying aircraft in forward areas. The little liaison aircraft was equipped with a VHF radio for air-to-air communication with fighter-bombers. The airborne controller directed fighter-bomber to a rendezvous point at predetermined intervals. At first the Horseflies operated only over friendly lines, but as the *Luftwaffe* virtually disappeared and the L–5 pilots became bolder, they flew as deep as twenty miles into enemy territory to find targets. The Horsefly was extremely useful in uncovering targets otherwise difficult to see and sometimes in helping control attacks by providing the controller a view similar to that of the attacking aircraft.[103]

Throughout the month of August, the effectiveness of Allied air effort increased dramatically, both in interdiction and close air support. Allied ground advances in northwestern and southern France forced German defenders to move in daylight, which greatly increased their exposure to various types of air attack. Close air support helped maintain the momentum of the Allied advance. A good example of its contribution at a critical time occurred during the Battle of Mortain on August 7, 1944. The American 30th Division, newly arrived in its positions, was compelled to bear the brunt of a German counterattack aimed at cutting the American line of communications. Both the RAF No. 83 Group and the IX TAC provided support by attacking the concentrations of armor and other vehicles that the Germans had assembled for the assault. The two forces did so much damage that the German commanders believed them chiefly responsible for halting the attack. This incident demonstrated again that, whatever the deficiencies in high command, coordination at lower levels was sufficient to provide combined support from both tactical air forces at a critical area on short notice.

The onset of mobile warfare created a host of new problems in communications, airfield position, and logistics. Each tactical air command had to keep in close touch with the most recent developments in operations and plans of the army commander; it had to maintain quick and reliable communications with its airfields and operating groups; and it had to keep serviceability and overall combat power at a high level. This was especially difficult after the war of movement developed in August.

The XIX TAC, formed to operate with the new Third Army commanded by General Patton, had the greatest problems in this regard. The Third moved very rapidly to the east while a portion of its command—VIII Corps—remained behind to besiege the fortress of Brest. At various times, VIII Corps' front lines were more than 300 miles away from the advancing spearheads of the rest of the army. To keep up, XIX TAC spun off an advanced communications unit called X–Ray to accompany Third Army advanced headquarters. XIX TAC (Adv) exercised operational control from a location farther to the rear where communication with airfields could be more reliable. Still farther back was XIX TAC (rear), responsible for administration.

When the pace of the advance slowed in September and October, these various headquarters recombined. IX and XXIX (operating with Ninth Army) TACs never faced quite the same set of movement problems. Even when obliged to move forward rapidly, they were able to handle these advances by creating two echelons, one for contact with army headquarters, the other for operational control and administration.[104]

The success of tactical air operations depended heavily on the number of serviceable airfields within effective operating range of the front lines. Airfield position directly affected response times, weight of support, and endurance in the battle area.[105] To provide effective support in rapidly changing conditions, it soon became apparent that tactical air forces had to be mobile. New airfields had to be developed quickly, and facilities abandoned by the enemy had to be rehabilitated for use as rapidly as possible to accommodate the operations, service, and logistics organizations pushed forward.

At the outset, while the problems of constructing airfields in the constricted area of the beachhead were considerable, requirements for construction were less than anticipated, because the ground forces failed to capture airfield sites as rapidly as anticipated. Aircraft operated from bases in the UK longer than planned. The result was to prevent the scale of air support from rising as rapidly as it otherwise could have. This was less of a problem for the American air forces than for the British, as American fighter aircraft generally had greater range and endurance.[106] Both forces benefited greatly from the declining strength of the *Luftwaffe*. Had it been more active and effective, the shortage of airfields on the continent in the early stages might well have been more damaging to the whole effort, both air and ground.

The whole picture changed when the breakout occurred in late July 1944. The air forces faced a new major problem: not only build and rehabilitate airfields at a rapid rate, but also keep up with rapidly moving armies. Inevitably, the effort fell short. Toward the end of August, some airfields were as much as 200 miles behind the leading columns of the troops they were supporting.

From early July, almost all fields under construction had to support fighter-bombers as well as fighters. That meant that 5,000– rather than

3,600–ft runways had to be built. The decision in early August to begin air-field construction for medium bombers in Brittany aggravated the situation. These fields with 6,000–ft runways surfaced with pierced steel plank (PSP), a material much heavier than either wire mesh or asphalt-impregnated jute sur-facing, placed considerable strain on an overtaxed transportation system. During the delay in airfield site development in June and early July, the ton-nage intended for special airfield materials was diverted to other special tasks. As a result, nowhere on the continent were to be found major stock-piles of standard materials for dry-weather surfacing of hastily prepared fields. Even if large stocks had been built up, it would have been difficult to get them forward because of a truck shortage. By late August, engineers faced distances of 150–200 miles between supply dumps and airfields under construction. To give some measure of the problem, at least 750 tons of sur-face material were required to prepare a 5,000–ft runway. Some surfacing was always required, even on an old German sod airfield, as the heavier American fighter aircraft exerted significantly more surface pressure than their German counterparts. Under the circumstances, it was fortunate for the Allies that a large number of hard-surfaced airfields in France had been built previously either by the French or Germans.

In the retreat, German demolition of buildings and other vertical facili-ties on these fields was thorough, but it proved nearly impossible for them to put a runway out of action for an extended period of time. The experience of IX Engineer Command proved that, with only a few exceptions, it required

P-47 roars over an American tank column in central Europe.

less effort and significantly less material to repair a hard-surfaced runway than to build a temporary dry-weather strip. Work on the first captured field started in early July and, thereafter, the restoration of such sites occupied an increasing portion of the Command's work.[107]

Because of increasingly mobile operations in August, logistical support for the Tactical Air Commands also became a major problem. In the early days of the campaign, it was difficult to supply the few airfields in the beachhead. Later, when TACs were on the move with the armies, Ninth Air Force's overworked transport had to move airfield construction material, as well as operational supplies, to an increasing number of sites located at greater distance from the beaches, where the bulk of this materiel was still being landed. Accomplishing this feat without any serious impairment of air support in the key month of August, when a decisive defeat was inflicted on the enemy, was a major achievement by the Ninth Air Force's Service Command.[108]

When Allies invaded Normandy, intelligence expected that the *Luftwaffe* would mount a major effort.[109] It did not. For a brief period, however, *Luftwaffe* activity increased, then declined steadily during the last half of June. The Germans were increasingly limited to the harassment of Allied artillery spotting planes and to the protection of lines of communication against Allied armed reconnaissance. The German air effort picked up again in July, especially in "tip and run" raids at dusk, but declined rapidly again in August.[110] At no time could the *Luftwaffe* interfere effectively against close air support operations. It was a nuisance force, keeping alive the threat of high-speed "bounces" against fighter-bombers and thereby forcing a continuous Allied investment in air superiority missions and air cover for close support tasks.[111]

The declining strength of the *Luftwaffe* did not spare the Ninth Air Force from significant aircraft losses in the battle for France. During the four months beginning on June 1, the monthly average number of bombers and fighters on hand in the Ninth's tactical units ranged from a low of 1,927 to a high of 2,254. The Ninth lost 295 fighters in June, 218 in July, 271 in August, and 123 in September. Expressed as a percentage of unit equipment strength, these losses in fighters were 25.1, 24.3, 26.7, and 13.3 percent respectively.[112] Precampaign planning allowed for an average of 20 percent per month losses to unit equipment. This was clearly not enough, for while the monthly average number of fighters on hand in tactical units varied between 1,462 and 1,591 for the 4 summer months of the campaign, it fell to 1,315 in December, a month in which the Ninth lost a full 28.6 of its fighter strength. The flow of aircraft from the United States fell off in the fall and winter; by January the strength of some P–47 groups had fallen from a standard establishment of 75 aircraft to 48 aircraft, and some P–38 groups to 35.[113]

Significant as these losses were, they did not seem exceptionally severe in comparison to other operations. In fact, they indicate that prewar fears about the exorbitant cost of close air support were mistaken. It is also important to recognize just how much close air support operations benefited from Allied air superiority. In the six months beginning in June 1944, the Ninth's fighters never lost more than 1.3 percent of sorties in any single month. By comparison, in October 1943, the Eighth Air Force's heavy bombers suffered a loss rate of 9.2 percent sorties in their operations over Germany, a figure that fell to 3.5 percent during February 1944, the month of the Big Week battles. By June, heavy bomber losses were down to about 1.1 percent of sorties.[114]

Over the entire period from November 1943 to May 1945, almost 70 percent of Ninth Air Force's fighter sorties were fighter-bomber missions on which the average loss rate was just under 1 percent of sorties. Close air support accounted for 20.55 percent of all sorties with a loss rate of 1.02 percent.[115]

The combination of high losses per month with a relatively low rate of loss per sorties was principally the result of a high rate of operations, often in difficult weather, in an environment where air superiority had been firmly established and constantly maintained. To put it another way, the relatively lower risk of a sortie over occupied France was offset by the high number of such sorties likely to fly in a given period.

Force sizes used in close air support missions varied considerably. Armored column cover or air alert employed four-plane flights on a twenty- to forty-minute schedule between arrivals over the rendezvous areas. Other types of missions used forces of squadron or group strength. Larger forces usually assembled beneath a ceiling of 1,000 feet. To save time and fuel, aircraft flights reassembled above the cloud deck on course to the assigned target. With lower cloud bases, individual planes made their way up through the overcast and then circled during assembly.[116]

Enroute to the target, pilots normally flew at 8,000 feet or above in order to avoid the ubiquitous German light flak. Ninth Air Force practice resisted breaking up a formation in order to avoid heavier flak; evasion or the temporary use of "war emergency power" to get out of the area were the preferred techniques. In a dive-bombing attack, the formation usually approached the target with planes in loose echelon and flights (if more than one) in trail at an angle of 90 degrees to the direction of attack. The force usually made frequent altitude changes between 7,000 and 10,000 ft in order to frustrate flak aiming.

Normally, Ninth Air Force fighter-bombers preferred to make their bombing runs either up or down wind (to reduce deflection errors) and out of the sun (to counter flak gunners). Planes peeled off to the attack in string and dived at an angle of from 45 to 60 degrees. Bombing technique tended to be

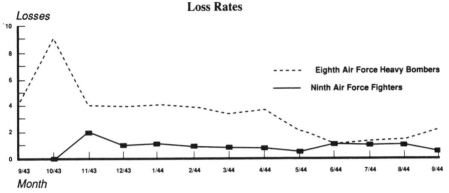

**Comparison of Eighth Air Force Heavy Bomber
and
Ninth Air Force Fighter
Loss Rates**

	Ninth Air Force Fighters		Eighth Air Force Heavy Bombers	
Month	Percent of Strength		Month	Percent of Strength
9/43	0		9/43	3.9
10/43	0		10/43	9.2
11/43	0		11/43	3.9
12/43	1.93		12/43	3.6
1/44	1.23		1/44	3.8
2/44	0.89		2/44	3.5
3/44	0.84		3/44	3.3
4/44	0.77		4/44	3.6
5/44	0.49		5/44	2.2
6/44	1.01		6/44	1.1
7/44	0.9		7/44	1.5
8/44	1.06		8/44	1.5
9/44	0.6		9/44	2.2

Sources: Computed from Rpt, "Statistical Summary of Ninth Air Force Operations, 16 October 1943 to 8 May 1945, "AFSHRC 85587, fr. 1627; Rpt, "Statistical Summary of Eighth Air Force Operations," AFSHRC A5871, fr. 0855.

highly individualistic, but on average, pilots attempted to release between 2,000 and 3,000 feet, so that they could recover at about 1,000 feet.

There were two standard methods of escape. One was to pull out in a climbing turn in order to gain altitude as quickly as possible. This was especially desirable in rough terrain. When flak was in the immediate area of the attack, many pilots preferred to break away on the deck at full power. In either case, severe slipping or skidding were recommended to avoid flak.[117]

Antiaircraft fire was a constant problem. Flak accounted for more than half of the casualties on close air support missions and almost ninety-five percent of the battle damage during the summer. At various times in the campaign, battle damage significantly reduced the air effort available for support. Apart from evasive action, two methods were commonly employed for dealing with flak. In many cases where the standard of cooperation between the supporting air forces and the ground units was high, the air support party could arrange with division artillery for counterbattery fire against known flak positions just prior to the air attack. In other cases, where formations of squadron strength or larger were involved, one flight would be detailed to suppress flak batteries by strafing.[118] One pilot recalled an encounter with a flak battery on an airfield:

> . . . they were good gunners. They were experts, and they stayed with that gun. I tried a gun position one time. Our squadron was strafing Fürth Airport and I was leading the second section . . . I hit that gun emplacement. He had probably quad 20s. I made four passes on it and he was back there at those guns every time. If I'd have been there myself I'd have said: "Let those boys go."[119]

In some circumstances, fighter-bomber pilots preferred glide-bombing attacks, especially if deflection errors had to be minimized and range errors were relatively unimportant. This technique was used also in cloud cover under 7,000 feet, the condition which most often prevented accurate dive-bombing. A most important prerequisite for glide-bombing was relative absence of ground fire and flak, because the attacking aircraft had to

Enemy fire caught the port wing of this Thunderbolt supporting the U.S. 12th Armored Division outside Würzburg in March 1945.

approach at the much lower altitude of between 3,000 and 5,000 feet. To prevent the bomb from actually skipping along the surface of the ground, the pilot dropped into a shallow dive of about 30 degrees, releasing preferably at the lowest altitude that would allow a safe recovery, normally about 800 ft. There was no worry about excessive speed in these attacks; the pilots used full throttle and then broke away as in a dive-bombing mission.[120]

Other techniques were employed for strafing attacks. When surprise was important, the fighter-bombers approached at high speed on the deck. After rising to an altitude of about 500 feet the pilot made his strafing run, taking care not to make his approach too flat or too steep. If too steep, the pilot began firing too early and pulled out too soon. If too flat, the pilot tended to focus on avoiding obstacles rather than on hitting the target. Targets without flak protection could be worked over carefully, the only danger being from small arms fire.[121]

It is difficult to measure precisely the contribution of close air support to the success of a battle or campaign, largely because in most cases it is almost impossible to separate the impact of specific weapons from the total effect of various combinations of fire and maneuver. It is possible, however, to generalize. The best evaluation is available in responses of army, corps, and division commanders to two questionnaires administered by the American 12th Army Group in 1945, one on behalf of the AAF Evaluation Board, European Theater of Operations,[122] and the other in support of General Bradley's report to the United States Strategic Bombing Survey.[123]

All commanders who had worked under armored column cover or air alert regarded those systems superior to any other employed in the theater. The support was predictable. The strength and the schedule of support relays were known, and the air effort could be easily integrated into the ground plan. There was no significant time lag in processing urgent requests, and lower echelon commanders at corps and below had authority to allocate targets (assuming their ASP officer would agree).[124] It should be kept in mind that when this system was employed on any scale, it required a large number of aircraft and a high degree of air superiority.

It was also painfully clear that the medium and heavy were the least responsive. A medium bomber attack required a lead-time of at least forty-eight hours. This was not especially troubling to army group and army commanders, whose planning perspective almost always involved similar lead-time. The delays, however, discouraged the use of these forces by corps and division commanders and prevented the exploitation of many opportunities. Higher commanders were frustrated more by what they called the "inflexible" commitment of mediums and heavies to other bombing programs. To remedy this, General Bradley went so far as to call for temporary attachment of some mediums to the TACs, a reversion to something resembling the structure of the old air support command.[125]

Almost all officers interviewed agreed that visible close air support raised the morale of their troops.[126] It also contributed greatly to the reduction of enemy artillery fire,[127] and generally undercut the organization and cohesion of enemy forces.[128] Air support was most effective and profitable against concentrations of "soft" targets—personnel and vehicles in the open. Where personnel were dispersed and dug-in, deployed in strong-points, or where armor was dispersed and camouflaged, air support was less effective. Generally, ground commanders agreed that the effects of air support on enemy morale, communications, cohesion, and organization were more important than the physical destruction.[129]

At no time during the summer campaign did heavy bomber close support prove to be a miracle weapon. It should have come as no surprise that heavy concentrations of high explosive, even when accurately delivered, could not entirely destroy resistance in modern, properly prepared defensive systems. These attacks did, however, create havoc in those areas where bombs fell. Units became badly disorganized and disoriented by a scale of fire beyond their experience or expectation. Bomb attacks cut communications, and craters often immobilized equipment. POW testimony also indicated depressing effects on morale caused by a constant parade of heavy bomber formations uninterrupted by the *Luftwaffe*. As in most other instances of close air support, the usefulness of a heavy bomber attack depended, in large measure, on the speed with which it was followed-up by ground attack.[130]

Most, but not all commanders, believed that they generally received satisfactory support over the entire campaign in France and Germany. On occasion, however, the distance of airfields from the front and the failure to concentrate air effort in support of attacking divisions lessened the weight of attack and undermined effectiveness.[131] Ineffective attacks were also caused by poor description of targets by the requesting ground units and by failure to mark targets accurately with smoke.[132]

Another frequently mentioned source of inefficiency was the failure of ground forces to follow up an air attack promptly. Sometimes this was the fault of poor planning or poor communications, as was the case with the assault on Brest, where ground forces did not know either the time-on-target (TOT) of the medium bomber assault or when the last bombs were scheduled to fall.[133] In other cases, it was due to the safety distance established to protect forward troops from short bombing.[134] This was not a problem in fighter-bomber attacks, but it was always a difficulty when mediums or heavies were employed. Another version of this problem occurred in the Normandy assault when safety considerations (and bad visual conditions for bombing) resulted in a largely ineffective attack against the beach defenses.[135]

Contemporary German sources also provided useful evaluation of close air support. Some German officers rated Allied artillery fire, especially naval fire in the early days of the invasion, as more dangerous than air support.[136] Overall, however, the preponderance of German evidence pointed to the damaging effects of Allied air action on their operations. For one thing, all German strategic movements were seriously hampered by Allied interdiction effort. As units approached the battle zone, they came under more frequent and heavier attack from the Allied fighter-bomber force, a great part of which was engaged in armed reconnaissance. In a document prepared in June 1944, von Rundstedt reported that a zone from 150 to 200 kilometers behind the main line of resistance (MLR) was entirely dominated by the Allied air forces. Movements within 20 kilometers of the MLR were subjected to especially heavy attack, a substantial part of which should be classified as close air support.[137]

German sources seemed to have been impressed by two factors—speed of attack and Allied willingness to commit resources to strike anything that moved, even the smallest units. Rundstedt reported that, once detected, assembly areas were attacked "without delay."[138] Reports from Army Group B declared that widespread Allied aerial reconnaissance was transformed into attack "almost immediately."[139] The same source noted that even the movement of the smallest formations came under Allied air and artillery attack.[140] An antiaircraft unit reported with some dismay that "even motor cyclists and isolated soldiers are attacked."[141] As a result, German commanders feared to move either troops or supplies during the day. They were forced to deploy at night, a factor which contributed to general disorganization and to piecemeal commitment.

With the exception of commanders whose units had been hit by "bomb carpets" dropped by heavies and mediums, few German sources were impressed by the sheer destructive effects of close air support. The effects on morale were even more severe, especially from saturation bombing. As Field Marshal von Kluge reported to Hitler after a visit to the front:

> The psychological effect on the fighting forces, especially the infantry, of such a mass of bombs raining down on them with all the force of elemental nature, is a factor which must be given serious consideration. It is not in the least important whether such a carpet of bombs is dropped on good or bad troops. . . .[142]

The shock effect of fighter-bomber attacks was undoubtedly less severe, but there can be little doubt that air domination and Allied aircraft attacks on even insignificant individual soldiers had some impact on morale. This is not to say that discipline broke down or that whole units ran away under the impact of air attack. They did not. Allied ground officers, nevertheless, noted that effective air attacks almost always made it easier to take a position, and such attacks usually increased the surrender rate.[143]

In sum, it cannot be said that close air support played a decisive role in the Battle of France in the sense that an Allied victory was inconceivable without it. It nevertheless contributed significantly by complementing fire-power of Allied artillery and was only marginally effective in attacks on forward positions during the set-piece beach assault. It did not play a significant role in *bocage* fighting, because the Allies decided to interdict German movements to the battlefield and because no serious commitment had been made to decentralize target selection to corps or division. The contribution of close air support increased significantly when the war of movement broke out in late July 1944. The breakout and pursuit saw a combination of the most flexible and responsive form of close air support—armored column cover—with a substantial increase in the number of targets that could be effectively attacked from the air, particularly troops and vehicles concentrated in open daylight. It was in that portion of the Battle for France that close air support finally became a regular component of the American combined-arms battle team.

Notes

Quotations in this chapter from Crown Copyright documents in the Public Record Office appear by kind permission of the Controller of Her Majesty's Stationery Office.

1. See the order of battle of the Allied air forces in L. F. Ellis, *Victory in the West*, Vol I, (London, 1962), App VI, pp 556–63.

2. The evolution of these command arrangements may be found in "Hist Record, AEAF, Jun to Aug 1944," Public Record Office London (hereafter cited as PRO-AIR 37/1057. See also W. F. Craven and J. L. Cate, *The Army Air Forces in World War II, Europe: Argument to V–E Day, Jan 1944 to May 1945*, Vol III, (Chicago, 1951, reprinted by the Office of Air Force History, 1984), pp 110–13, 620–2.

3. See the order of battle cited in n. 1. For an introduction to the difficulties involved in Allied air command from the perspective of the American official historians, see Craven and Cate, *Europe: Argument to V–E Day*, p 5–7, 79–83.

4. Tedder insisted that he was not the "Air Commander-in-Chief." VCAS to CAS, Aug 24, 1944, PRO-AIR 20/5308; Introduction to "SHAEF (Air) Hist Record," PRO-AIR 37/1436.

5. Memo, "Command and Control of Air Forces," nd Spaatz Papers, Manuscript Div, LC) Box 15. According to a typewritten annotation on the paper, the original had been initialled by Tedder.

6. Max Hastings, *Overlord: D-Day and the Battle for Normandy* (New York, 1984), p 45. Hastings maintains, on the basis of a 21 Army Gp report, that the delays were the product of bad organization on the air side. For the opposite view see British Air Ministry, Air Hist Branch (AHB) Narrative, "The Liberation of Northwest Europe," I, p 135, n. 2, United States Air Force Hist Research Center (USAFHRC) Microfilm Reel 23357, fr 0429. This source asserts that the delay was the result of frequent changes in targets made by 21 Army Gp.

7. The minutes of these meetings are at PRO-AIR 37/563.

8. Air Chief Marshal Sir Trafford Leigh-Mallory, "Daily Reflections on the Course of the Battle," Entry for Jun 29, 1944, PRO-AIR 37/784.

9. Carlo D'Este, *Decision in Normandy* (New York, 1983), p 219.

10. Ltr, Coningham to AVM J. Breen (Air Ministry), Aug 30, 1944, PRO-AIR 37/2.

11. Memo, Coningham, "Reorganization for Future Ops," Jul 6, 1944. This memo has no addressee in PRO-AIR 37/1012. Another copy in AIR 37/1032 is initialled by W.G. Scarman, Tedder's personal assistant.

12. D'Este, *Decision in Normandy*, pp 218–19. Who or what was responsible for the bad relations between Montgomery and Coningham is a matter of dispute. For arguments critical of Coningham see Rprt, BGS (Air), 21 Army Gp, "History of Air Support Procedure, Northwest Europe, Jun 1944 to May 1945," PRO-AIR 37/881. Coningham's own views are best represented in his Despatch, "Report on Ops Carried Out by Second Tactical Air Force, Jun 6, 1944 to May 9, 1945," PRO-AIR 37/876.

13. For Tedder's view of Leigh-Mallory, see his memoir *With Prejudice* (London, 1967), pp 564-5. See also D'Este, *Decision in Normandy*, pp 216–7.

14. There is no biography or memoir. Leigh-Mallory died in an air crash on his way to Southeast Asia Command. See the entry in the *Dictionary of National Biography*.

15. "Report by Sir Trafford Leigh-Mallory on his Visit to North Africa, Mar 27 to Apr 4, 1943" PRO-AIR 20/6130.

16. "Hist Record, AEAF, Jun to Aug 1944," p 2, PRO-AIR 37/1057.

17. Vandenberg Diary, Mar 24, 1944, Box 1, LC. The relevant entry is partially quoted in Hastings, p 45.

18. Bradley apparently held Brereton partly responsible for what he believed to be inadequate air-ground training prior to the invasion. Bradley, *A Soldier's Story* (New York, 1951), p 249.

19. D'Este, p 220.

20. Russell Weigley, *Eisenhower's Lieutenants* (Bloomington, 1981), p 166.
21. D'Este, *Decision in Normandy*, p 219. On the problem of coordination between staffs and the co-location of headquarters see Coningham Despatch, pp 14, 175. For the view from 21 Army Gp, see "History of Air Support Procedure . . . ," Chap 1.
22. See the discussion of these ideas in W.A. Jacobs, "Tactical Air Doctrine and AAF Close Air Support in the European Theater, 1944–45," *Aerospace Historian*, (Spring, 1980), pp 36–8. In 1941, The Plans Div of the OCAC did not concur in a proposal to install bomb racks on the P–39 as bomb carrying and "excessive range" would lead to "opportunities for improper use of pursuit types." Memorandum, Plans Div, OCAC, "Disapproval of Change Order," (Mar 10, 1941), USAFHRC A1422, fr 1779.
23. Robert F. Futrell, *Ideas, Concepts, Doctrine: A History of Basic Thinking in the United States Air Force, 1907-64* (Maxwell AFB, 1971), p 52, 55. For RAF views see Air Staff "Bmbr Support for the Army," n.d., probably Nov 1939, PRO-AIR 20/37–5.
24. British Air Ministry, Air Hist Branch (AHB), *Air Support, 1939–45* (A.P. 3235) (London, 1954), p 32.
25. *Ibid*, pp 80–1.
26. Ltr, AOC, 11 GP, (Leigh-Mallory) to Hq, Ftr Command, (Apr 15, 1941) PRO-AIR 16/517.
27. Ltrs, AOC in C, Ftr Command (Douglas) to Air Ministry, (24 and 28 Jul 1941) PRO-AIR 16/517.
28. AHB, "Liberation of Northwest Europe," Vol II, p 137.
29. Rprt, "XII Air Support Command in the Tunisian Campaign, Jan to May, 1943," USAFHRC A6331, fr 1508–10.
30. The description of relative aircraft capabilities in this and succeeding paragraphs is drawn from material in Rprt, AAF Eval Bd, ETO, "The Effectiveness of Third Phase Tactical Air Ops. . .," USAFHRC A1175, fr 0315–17.
31. Intvw of Mr. Wm. C. Jarvis by Frank Jordan, Oct 7, 1977, USAFHRC 33836.
32. AAF Evaluation Board, ETO, "The Effectiveness . . .," fr. 0315–17.
33. *Ibid*, fr 0321-9; and Rprt, AAF Eval Bd, ETO, "The Relative Effectiveness of Various Types of Bombs and Fuzes," (Jun 1, 45), USAFHRC A1173, fr 0383 ff.
34. FM 100–20, *Command and Employment of Air Power*, (1943). United States Air Force Hist Research Center (USAFHRC) R1. B1717, fr 1052 ff; War Office/RAF Air Staff, *Army Air Ops Pamphlet #1*, *"General Principles and Organization* (Mar, 1944) (26/GS Publications/1127).
35. FM 100–20.
36. Craven and Cate, *Europe: Argument to V–E Day*, Vol III, pp 139-40; AHB Narrative, "The Liberation of Northwest Europe," pp 17, 50, 52, USAFHRC 23357, fr 0799, 0836, 0838.
37. AEAF/21 Army Gp Joint Memorandum, "Overlord: Direct Air Support," Apr 23, 44, USAFHRC B5727, fr 0714 ff.
38. Ninth Air Force, "Annex B to Operation Plan Nr 2–44," USAFHRC B5728, fr 0136.
39. AFHS #36, *Ninth Air Force,Apr to Nov 1944* (1945) USAFHRC K1005, p 14.
40. AEAF/21 Army Gp Joint Memorandum, Apr 23, 1944.
41. For a description of the characteristics and capabilities of these radio sets, see Dulany Terrett, *The U.S. Army in World War II: The Signal Corps: The Emergency* (Washington, 1956), pp 312, 314. The substitution is noted on a chart contained in a report dated 16 Jul 1944 which was prepared by the First Army G–3 (Air) (Col. E.L. Johnson) for Army Ground Forces Bd. USAFHRC B5724, fr 1447. (Hereafter cited as Johnson Report, Jul 16, 1944). The fact that the ASPs were equipped with the short-range SCR 284 is corroborated in IX Tactical Air Command, "Plan Neptune," Annex 5, USAFHRC B5893, fr 1281.
42. AHB Narrative, "The Liberation of Northwest Europe," III, p 54, USAFHRC 23357, fr 0840.
43. The best description of the fully developed Seventh Army/XII TAC system is found in "A Report on the Phase 3 Ops of the XII TAC for AAF Eval Bd, ETO," (Apr 1945) USAFHRC A6356.
44. "Notes of Meeting Held at Cannes on 25–6 November, 1944," Spaatz Papers, Box 16, MD, LC; Minutes of Meeting Held at Ninth Air Force Hq, Feb 24, 1944, USAFHRC B5602, fr 0888–9.

45. AHB Narrative, "The Liberation of Northwest Europe," Vol III, pp 39–43.

46. Craven and Cate, *Europe: Argument to V–E Day*, p 190.

47. *Ibid*, pp 190–1; AHB Narrative, "The Liberation of Northwest Europe," III, pp 68–9, USAFHRC 23357, fr 0859–0861.

48. Record of Requests, Ninth AF Jun 6–20, 1944, (in the handwriting of the Ninth AF historian, Lt Col Robert George). USAFHRC B5725, fr 0921–0926.

49. Rprt, 12th Army Gp, "The Effect of Air Power on Military Ops, European Theater of Ops," (1945) USAFHRC C5169, p 91.

50. AFHS #36, p 80.

51. *Ibid*, p 98.

52. First Army G–3 (Air), "Air Support Report," (Aug 6, 44) USAFHRC B5724, fr 1401–9. The Johnson Report of 16 Jul cited above is attached to this report.

53. This description of the Ninth AF system as it functioned in the summer of 1944 in this and succeeding paragraphs is based on the following sources: First Army G–3, "Air Support Report," (Aug 6, 44) USAFHRC B5724; AAF Eval Bd, ETO, "Report of Tactical Committee on the Subject of Doctrine, Organization, Tactics and Techniques of AAF in the ETO," (Sep 26, 44), USAFHRC A1175; Rprt, 12th Army Gp G–3, "Close Support within 12th Army Gp," (Nov 20, 44), USAFHRC A5060, fr 0327–0335. For a picture of the system as it had evolved by the end of the campaign see Rprt, AAF Eval Bd, ETO, "Effectiveness of Third Phase Tactical Air Ops in the ETO, May 4, 44 to May 8, 45," USAFHRC A1175.

54. The system for navigational control in the Ninth AF as it existed in Sep 1944 is described in AAF Eval Bd, ETO, "Report of Tactical Committee on the Subject of Doctrine, Organization, Tactics, and Technique of the AAF in the ETO," (Sep 26, 44) USAFHRC A1175, fr 0857–0868.

55. First Army G–3 (Air) "Air Support Report," USAFHRC B5724, fr 1402.

56. AEAF/21 Army Gp Joint Memorandum, "Direct Air Support," Apr 23, 1944. The first use of forward control appears to have been in Operation Goodwood, Jul 18, 1944. 83d Gp "Ops Record Book" at PRO–AIR 25/698 refers to the use of a "Visual Control Post" on that date as a "trial."

57. Martin Blumenson, *Breakout and Pursuit* (Washington, 1961), p 207. This analysis is based on "First Army and IX TAC Air Ops Summary for 18 Jul 1944," USAFHRC B5860, fr 1500–1509.

58. Craven and Cate, *Europe: Argument to V–E Day*, pp 199-200.

59. Gordon Harrison, *Cross-Channel Attack* (Washington, 1951), 428–29.

60. History, 4th Tactical Air Communication Squadron, 5 Jun 1942 to 31 May 1945, USAFHRC A0503, fr 0975–83; History, 11th Tactical Air Communication Squadron, Sep 8, 1942 to May 31, 1945, USAFHRC A0504, fr 0069–0070.

61. Craven and Cate, *Europe: Argument to V–E Day*, pp 134–36.

62. Bradley, *A Soldier's Story*, p 249.

63. Ninth AF, "Weather and Air Ops, 6 Jun to 23 June, 1944," USAFHRC B5745, fr 0498–519. This is a collection of weather summaries put together by the Ninth AF historian, Col Robert George.

64. See the description of the *bocage* terrain in Blumenson, pp 10-12.

65. 12th Army Gp, "Answers to Questionnaire for Key Commanders on the Effects of Strategic and Tactical Air Power on Military Ops, ETO," p 142, USAFHRC C5169. 21 Army Gp's study of air support identified the same problem, "History of Air Support Procedure. . . ," Chap 1, PRO–AIR 37/881.

66. VII Corps, "Study on Air–Ground Cooperation," (Jun 6, 45), USAFHRC C5131, fr 0811–0812.

67. History, "11th Tactical Air Communications Squadron, 8 Sep 1942 to 31 May 1945," USAFHRC A0504, fr 0074. XIX TAC, "Signals: The Story of Communications in XIX TAC up to VE–Day," USAFHRC, B5939, fr 0848 ff, esp pp 24–31, 39–40. On the problem of spare parts on the British side, see "History of Air Support Procedure. . . ," Chap 3, p 18, PRO–AIR 37/881.

68. Rprt, 12th Army Gp G-3, "Close Support within 12th Army Gp," USAFHRC A5060, fr 0329.

69. Jacobs, "Tactical Air Doctrine," p 45.
70. Johnson Report, (Jul 16, 1944), fr 1446.
71. "Attacks on Friendly Troops," USAFHRC B5725, 0718–19. This is a typed list of extracts from signals.
72. Johnson Report, fr 1436.
73. *Ibid*, fr 1442–3.
74. *Ibid*.
75. Solly Zuckerman, *From Apes to Warlords, 1904–46* (London, 1978), p 278.
76. AEAF/21 Army Gp Joint Memorandum, "Direct Air Support," Apr 23, 1944.
77. Coningham to AVM J. M. Robb (DCAS, Air at SHAEF), Aug 29, 1944, PRO–AIR 37/1132.
78. AHB, *Close Air Support*, pp 163–64.
79. Leigh-Mallory proposed the use of the heavy bombers to Montgomery on 14 June. "AEAF Hist Record," p 13. PRO–AIR 37/1057. Next day, Leigh-Mallory presented the plan to the conference of senior air commanders and represented it as having come from the army, a subterfuge which, no doubt, was a tactical necessity. Minutes, Allied Air Commanders' Mtg, (Jun 15, 1944), PRO–AIR 37/563.
80. Daily Journal, Jun 15, 1944, Spaatz Papers, Box 15, MD, LC.
81. *Ibid*, entry for Jun 17, 1944.
82. Ltr, Spaatz to Eisenhower, Jun 28, 1944, Spaatz Papers, Box 143, MD, LC.
83. Tedder successfully forestalled Leigh-Mallory's proposal by flying to the continent to break up a meeting between British Second Army and AEAF staff. See the description of the events in D'Este, *Decision in Normandy*, pp 224–8. Harris was said to have referred to heavy bomber close support as "bombing between the Army's legs." Ltr, Broadhurst (AOC, 83 Gp) to Coningham Jul 29, 1944, PRO–AIR 37/762.
84. Leigh-Mallory, "Daily Reflections on the Course of the Battle," entry for Jul 10, 1944, PRO–AIR 37/784.
85. For an account of Eighth AF's preparations for D–Day operations, see "Hist Study of Air Support by Eighth AF for the Land Invasion of Continental Europe, Jun 2 to Jun 16, 1944," USAFHRC A1715, fr 1544–53.
86. RAF developments in this area can be followed in these papers: B.Ops 1, "Memo on the Development of Air Cooperation with the Army by the bombing of Enemy Positions at Night," 17 Mar 1943, PRO–AIR 20/6166; D.B. Ops. "Density of Attack in Relation to Air Support for Overlord," nd (probably early May, 1944), PRO–AIR 37/723; S. Zuckerman (Scientific Advisor, AEAF) to Leigh-Mallory, Jun 24, 1944, PRO–AIR 37/723. A negative view can be found in DAT (Director of Air Tactics) to AVM J. M. Robb, May 22, 1944, PRO–AIR 37/1120.
87. S. Zuckerman and E. J. Kingston-McCloughry, "Observations on RAF Bmbr Command's Attack on Caen, 7 Jul 44," PRO–AIR 37/1255.
88. See the description of the Goodwood attack in D'Este, *Decision in Normandy*, 370–90.
89. AAF Eval Bd, "The Effectiveness of Third Phase Ops, ETO," USAFHRC A1175, fr 0095.
90. AHB, "The Liberation of Northwest Europe," Vol IV, p 47; Memorandum, "Discussion between Air Commodore Geddes (D/SASO 2d TAF and 2d Lt P. M. Roberts, RAC," nd, in PRO–AIR 37/858. Roberts was the tank driver for the first RAF forward controller.
91. Craven and Cate, *Europe: Argument to V–E Day*, pp 228–232.
92. The most extensive account of these events is in Blumenson, *Breakout and Pursuit*, 224–338. See also Weigley, *Eisenhower's Lieutenants*, pp 136–188.
93. This general description of the problems involved in heavy bomber close support is based on the following sources: Rprt, Eighth AF, ORS, "Survey of the Effectiveness of Bombing on Coastal Defenses," USAFHRC B5049, fr 0119–21; Rprt, RAF Second TAF, "Examination of Operation Goodwood," Jul 26, 1944, PRO–AIR 37/762 (Coningham marked this "not for distribution"); Ltr, Broadhurst (83 Gp) to Geddes (RAF Second TAF), Jul 29, 1944, PRO–AIR 37/762; 2d Army, "Report on Air Ops in Support of Operation Goodwood, Aug 3, 1944, PRO–WO 205/556; Rprt, Lt Col C. E. Carrington, (ALO, Bmbr Command), "Overlord, Attacks by Bmbr Command on Tactical Targets" Aug 3, 1944, PRO–AIR 37/535; Rprt, S. Zuckerman, "Preliminary Analysis of Air Ops, Goodwood," Aug 4, 1944, PRO–AIR 37/762; Lt Col C. E. Carrington, "Notes on the Use of Heavy Bombers in Oper-

ation Totalise," Aug 12, 1944, PRO–WO 205/556; and 21 Army Gp, "The Use of Heavy Bombers in a Tactical Role," nd PRO–AIR 37/759.

94. "Proceedings of a Court of Inquiry Held at Nr 1 Gp." 16–18 August, 1944. PRO–AIR 14/861; Harris to Leigh-Mallory, Coningham and Tedder, Aug 25, 1944, with attached "Report on the Bombing of our own Troops during Operation Tractable," PRO–AIR 37/1033. L. F. Ellis, *Victory in the West*, Vol I, (London, 1962), 429–31.

95. See the description from the Canadian point of view in Reginald H. Roy, *The Canadians in Normandy: 1944* (Ottawa, 1984), pp 193–97.

96. Daily Journal, Jul 26, 1944, Spaatz Papers, Box 15, MD, LC; Craven and Cate, *Europe: Argument to V–E Day*, Vol III, pp 233–4, 251.

97. See, for example, Rprt, 12th Army Gp, "The Effect of Air Power on Military Ops, European Theater of Ops," USAFHRC C5169, pp 41–2.

98. "First Army and IX TAC Air Ops Summary for 25 July," USAFHRC B5860, fr 1457–1464.

99. "First Army and IX TAC Air Ops Summary for 26 July," USAFHRC B5860, fr 1442–1456.

100. The original Fifth Army–XII ASC system is detailed in Rprt, Fifth Army, "Organization for Air Support in Fifth Army," (Mar 10, 1944), USAFHRC A6331, fr 1534 ff; Rprt, AEAF, "Notes on Air Support Taken During a Visit to Fifth Army Front between 5th and 20th Feb 1944," USAFHRC A6331, fr 1544–6.

101. Memo, MAAF, "Rover Joe: Forward Ftr-Bmbr Control" (May 1944), USAFHRC A6111, fr 1132–37.

102. IV Corps G–3, "Report on Close Support of 1st Armored Div, Jun 26, to Jul 3, 1944," USAFHRC A6111, fr 1374–8.

103. A detailed evaluation of "Horsefly" may be found in Rprt, General Bd, ETO, "Air Liaison with Ground Force Units," (1945), USAFHRC A5046, fr 0243–7.

104. Ninth AF, "Report on Tactical Air Cooperation, Organization, Methods and Procedures," (1945), USAFHRC A1174, fr 0696–0702.

105. The analysis in this and succeeding paragraphs on airfields is based on: Report, Ninth AF, "IX Engineer Command in the European Theater of Ops," USAFHRC B5587, fr. 005–0032; Ninth AF, "Report on Tactical Air Cooperation, Organization, Method and Procedures," 1945. USAFHRC A1174, fr 0921–68. Rprt, AAF Eval Bd ETO, "The Effectiveness of Third Phase Ops in the European Theater," USAFHRC A1175, Fr 0331–38; Craven and Cate, *Europe: Argument to V–E Day*, pp 562–573.

106. A.H.B. 3235, *Air Support, 1939–45*, p 149.

107. Rprt. AAF Eval Bd, ETO, "Effectiveness of Third Phase Tactical Air Ops . . ." A1175, fr 337–8.

108. See the extended discussion of logistics in Craven and Cate, *Europe: Argument to V–E Day*, Vol III, Chap 16.

109. Memo, Ninth AF, A–2, "Estimated Scale of Efforts of GAF Against Operation Overlord," USAFHRC B5728, fr 0175–8.

110. Rprt, AAF Eval board, ETO, "Effectiveness of Third Phase Ops . . ." USAFHRC A1175, fr 0035. For a contemporary account from the German side, see 8th Abt, *Luftwaffe* General Staff, "Some Aspects of the German Ftr Effort During the Initial Stages of the Invasion of Northwest Europe," Nov 18, 1944, British Air Ministry AHB translation, USAFHRC A5421, fr 1017–22.

111. In the initial stages of Operation Cobra, it was standard practice to devote one flight of a twelve plane squadron to a covering role to guard against surprise attacks by small *Luftwaffe* forces. See sources cited in notes, pp 98–99.

112. "Statistical Summary of Ninth Air Force Ops, 16 Oct 1943 to 8 May 1945." USAFHRC B5587, fr 1624.

113. Ninth AF, "Rprt on Tactical Air Cooperation, Organization, Methods, and Procedures," 1945. USAFHRC A1174, fr 0914.

114. "Statistical Summary of Ninth Air Force Ops, 16 Oct 1943 to 8 May 1945." USAFHRC B5587, fr 1627 and "Statistical Summary of Eighth AF Ops," USAFHRC A5871, fr 0855.

115. "Statistical Summary of Ninth Air Force Ops," USAFHRC B5587, fr 1635.

116. Rprt, AAF Eval Bd, ETO, "Effectiveness of Third Phase Ops in the ETO," USAFHRC A1175, fr 0387.

117. *Ibid*, fr 0388.
118. *Ibid*, fr 0365–6.
119. Intvw of Mr. William Jarvis by Frank Jordan, Oct 7, 1977, USAFHRC 33836.
120. AAF Evaluation Board, ETO, "Effectiveness of Third Phase . . . , fr 0388.
121. *Ibid*, fr 0391.
122. 12th Army Gp (comp), "Answers to AAF Eval Bd Guide Questions on Air Ground Cooperation." (1945) USAFHRC C5169.
123. 12th Army Gp., "Answers to Questionnaire for Key Commanders on the Effects of Strategic and Tactical Air Power on Military Ops, ETO," (1945), USAFHRC C5169.
124. 12th Army Gp, "Answers to the AAF Eval Bd. . . ," pp 48–52.
125. *Ibid*, pp 67–70; Rprt, 12th Army Gp, "Effects of Air Power on Military Ops, ETO," USAFHRC C5169.
126. 12th Army Gp, "Answers to AAF Eval Bd. . . ," pp 37–8.
127. *Ibid*, pp 34–6.
128. *Ibid*, pp 28–31.
129. *Ibid*, pp 1–23; 12th Army Gp, "Answers to Questionnaire for Key Commanders," pp 1–50. The first part of this questionnaire asked each of the officers surveyed to assess the contribution made by each type of aircraft in support of a long list of types of operations.
130. For contemporary assessments of heavy bomber close support, see the sources cited in note 71.
131. 12th Army Gp "Answers to AAF Eval Bd. . . ," pp 1–5.
132. *Ibid*, p 3.
133. VIII Corps, "Study on Air–Ground Cooperations," 31 May 45, USAFHRC, C5131, fr 0820.
134. 12th Army Gp., "Answers to AAF Eval Bd. . . ," pp 73–4.
135. Craven and Cate, *Europe: Argument to V–E Day*, Vol III, pp 190–3.
136. Interrogation of Oberst Hans Linger, Ia of 10 SS *Panzer* Div. USAFHRC C5169, fr 0953.
137. "Extract from a Captured Document containing an Appreciation by Field Marshal Rundstedt," USAFHRC A5687, fr 0497.
138. *Ibid*.
139. British Air Ministry, A.H.B., "Situation Reports by German Army Commanders," entries for Jun 11, 22 to Jul 2, Jul 3 to 9, Jul 10 to 16 all 1944. USAFHRC A5422, fr 0334 ff.
140. *Ibid*.
141. *Luftflottenkommando 3, Führungsabt, Ia, Flak.* "Rprt Nr 5," Jul 13, 1944. USAFHRC B5725, fr 0663.
142. Von Kluge to Hitler, Jul 21, 1944, in A.H.B. "Situation Reports . . ." A5422, fr 0353–4. Similar testimony to the effects of bomb carpets was given by *Generalleutnant* Fritz Bayerlein, CG, *Panzerlehr* Div. See 12th Army Gp, Air Effects Committee, USAFHRC C5169, fr 0950.
143. 12th Army Gp, "Answers to AAF Eval Bd. . . ," pp 27–31.

Bibliographical Essay

The European theater was the showcase for large-scale American air and ground operations in the Second World War. There was a tendency in both the air and the ground forces to regard operations there as a guide to future doctrine and organization. As a result, there are numerous printed sources for one writing a history of close air support as it was during the last year of the Second World War in Europe. The best among these are two reports prepared by the AAF Evaluation Board for the European Theater of Operations (ETO) in 1945: "Tactics and Techniques Developed by the U.S. Tactical Air Commands in the ETO," (USAFHRC A1174) and "The Effectiveness of Third Phase Tactical Air Operations in the ETO, May 5, 1944 to May 8, 1945." (USAFHRC A1175). Largely from the perspective of the Army Air Forces, these reports are very detailed, with thorough coverage of the subject. The latter report is particularly valuable. It should be reprinted for general circulation. A study written from the perspective of the ground forces and prepared by 12th Army Group for the U.S. Strategic Bombing Survey, "The Effects of Air Power on Military Operations, European Theater of Operations," (USAFHRC C5169) is also of great value. A report of the General Board, ETO, on "Organization, Operations, and Equipment of Air Ground Liaison in all Echelons from Divisions Upwards" (USAFHRC A5046) provides additional important detail. In preparing these studies, the AAF Evaluation Board and 12th Army Group circulated two questionnaires to army, corps, and division commanders. The replies to these questionnaires (USAFHRC C5169) comprise a valuable source for ground force opinion at the end of the war.

The major difficulty with the above sources is that, for the most part, they present a picture of the American close air support system as it existed in the last few months of the campaign against Germany. They do not provide detailed information on covering the first weeks of the battle in Normandy. Fortunately, such information can be gleaned from a substantial number of manuscripts in Ninth Air Force, First U.S. Army, and 12th Army Group files, all of which are available on microfilm in the USAF Historical Research Center at Maxwell Air Force Base. Duplicates of the microfilm files are also on deposit at the Office of Air Force History, Bolling Air Force Base, Washington, D.C. One of the most important of such sources to survive is a relatively complete set of air support request records for IX TAC and First Army during most of the Battle for France (USAFHRC B5860 and B5861). These identify the originating unit, the time of receipt, the target, the TOT, the time the requesting unit was notified of the disposition of its request, the size of the attacking force, and the ordnance loadings. Among the other important sources for the early period are two reports prepared by the U.S. First Army

G–3 (Air), Col. E. L. Johnson: "Report to Army Ground Forces Board" July 16, 1944, and "Air Support Report," August 6, 1944, both on USAFHRC B5724.

On the British side, Coningham's Despatch, "Report on Operations Carried Out by Second Tactical Air Force, June 6, 1944 to May 9, 1945," (PRO–AIR 37/876) is a major source. It reflects Coningham's perspective on the subject of command relationships with Leigh-Mallory and Montgomery but contains little useful detail on the close air support system. A better source for details is a report prepared by the BGS (Air) at 21st Army Group, Brigadier C.C. Oxborrow, one of the four or five British Army officers most expert in close air support. This document, "History of Air Support Procedure: Northwest Europe, June 1944 to May 1945" may be found at PRO–AIR 37/881.

Important manuscript material on the use of heavy bombers in close support may be found in the files of AEAF (AIR 37), RAF Bomber Command (AIR 14), RAF Second TAF (AIR 37), and SHAEF (Air) (also AIR 37) preserved in the Public Record Office, London. Of considerable importance in any discussion of organization and policy are the Leigh-Mallory Office Diary ("Daily Reflections on the Course of the Battle") in PRO–AIR 37, the Vandenberg Diary (Vol. I) in the Vandenberg Papers, Library of Congress Manuscript Division, and the Official Diaries kept in General Spaatz's Headquarters in the Spaatz Papers, also held in the Library of Congress.

One disappointment is that the Quesada papers (also in the Library of Congress) do not contain much on close air support that is helpful. Quesada, as CG, IX TAC, was one of the few AAF officers (along with John Cannon, Richard Nugent, and Otto Weyland) to make close air support his primary career interest in the latter part of the war.

The subject has received some treatment in the secondary literature. Col. Robert George's *Ninth Air Force, April to November, 1944* (Air Force Historical Study #36) was the earliest survey and is still a good place to start. George was the Ninth Air Force historian, and it is to him that we are indebted for the preservation of so much primary material from that organization. He also wrote the relevant chapter in W. F. Craven and J. L. Cate, *The Army Air Forces in World War II* Vol. III, (Chicago, 1951, Office of Air Force History Reprint, 1983). His work is good narrative history, especially the Craven and Cate material, but some of it labors under the necessity of portraying the summer campaign as the manifestation of the truth contained in FM 100–20. One early article also provides a good introduction to the subject: James A. Huston, "Tactical Use of Air Power in World War II: The Army Experience," *Military Affairs*, Winter 1950, Vol. 14, No. 4, pp. 166–185. For an examination of the relationship between prewar doctrine and the way the close air support system actually worked see W.A. Jacobs, "Tactical Air Doctrine and AAF Close Air Support in the European Theater,

1944–45," *Aerospace Historian* (Spring, 1980), pp. 35–49. In order to see the development (or lack thereof) of close air support from the perspective of the ground forces, one should consult Kent Roberts Greenfield, *Army Ground Forces and the Air–Ground Battle Team* (Study #35, 1948). This study is particularly critical of the shortcomings of training in the Zone of Interior.

A good introduction to the history of RAF close air support in the Second World War is provided in the British Air Ministry publication, *Air Support, 1939–45*, which has just recently been declassified. The author is indebted to Air Commodore Henry Probert of the Air Historical Branch for providing a copy of this study. The British Army began to prepare a similar study but failed to finish the task. The papers collected for the manuscript are in the Public Record Office, Kew at WO–233/60. These materials provide useful comparisons and contrasts of British and American experience in the European theater.

Air support has been discussed briefly in two important recent works: Russell Weigley, *Eisenhower's Lieutenants: The Campaigns of France and Germany, 1944–45* (Bloomington: Indiana University Press, 1981); Carlo D'Este, *Decision in Normandy* (New York: Dutton, 1983). To one degree or another, both draw attention to the conflicts of interest and personality that reigned in the senior circles of the British and American air forces. These books also emphasize the major contributions of lesser known commanders, such as Broadhurst, AOC 83 Gp, and Quesada, CG, IX TAC. Max Hastings's recent work, *Overlord: D–Day, June 6, 1944* (New York: Simon and Schuster, 1984), is highly critical of the attitudes of senior airmen and of the shortcomings experienced in close support. John Terraine's *The Right of the Line: The Royal Air Force in the European War, 1939–45* (London: Hodder and Stoughton, 1985) is a very good comprehensive history with much material on close air support.

Among the official histories, Gordon Harrison's *Cross-Channel Attack* (Washington: GPO, 1951) and Martin Blumenson's *Breakout and Pursuit* (Washington: GPO, 1961) are indispensable as are L. F. Ellis's two volumes in the British official histories published under the title *Victory in the West* (London: H.M.S.O., 1962 and 1968). They treat air support only in an incidental fashion but are important for their detailed description of ground operations.

7

American Experience in the Southwest Pacific

Joe Gray Taylor

This essay deals with close air support in the Southwest Pacific Area during the Second World War, with some reference to the adjoining South Pacific Theater, including Guadalcanal and Bougainville. There were two other Pacific theaters of operations: the North Pacific, which included Alaska and the Aleutian Islands, and the tremendously important Central Pacific Theater. While Allied forces in the south and southwest Pacific were isolating Rabaul and moving westward along the north coast of New Guinea, then north into the Philippine Islands, Central Pacific forces under Adm. Chester W. Nimitz, USN, were driving toward Japan by way of the Gilbert Islands, the Marshall Islands, the Marianas, Iwo Jima, and Okinawa. The Pacific Ocean was more than large enough to hold those four operational theaters of war. Indeed, three more areas the size of the European Theater of Operations could have been added with room to spare. One of the central facts of the entire war in the Pacific was the tremendous distance involved, creating logistical difficulties that in 1942 and 1943 slowed the pace of operations. On December 7, 1941, when the Japanese attack on Pearl Harbor plunged the United States into open belligerence in the Second World War, the United States Army Air Forces had had no experience whatsoever with close support of ground troops. In fact, the term close support had no official existence; it was not to be defined completely until after the war had ended.[1] "Close air support" applied to air missions in support of ground forces, directed at targets so near to friendly ground force positions that special precautions were necessary to prevent harm to friendly forces. By the end of World War II this always included, in the Southwest Pacific Area, some element of immediate ground-based communication with, and control of, the aircraft making the attack, but this was often not the case in the early years of the war.

For various reasons American air officers after the First World War had come to believe that air components of the armed forces should not be under ground force command. Not all air officers went so far as to advocate a com-

KOREA

JAPAN

CHINA

INDIA

RYUKYU IS

BONIN IS

Marcus Is

BURMA

FRENCH INDOCHINA

Formosa

THAILAND

Luzon

MARIANA IS

PHILIPPINE IS

Samar

Guam

Leyte

Yap

Ulithi Is

Mindanao

Palau Is

MALAYA

Talaud Is

Morotai Is

CAROLINE ISLANDS

BORNEO

Biak Is

NETHERLANDS

INDIES

NEW GUINEA

Bismarck Arch

Solomon Is

SOUTHWEST PACIFIC AREA

0   100   200   300   400 Statute Miles

AUSTRALIA

pletely separate service, like the British Royal Air Force, but air arm senti-
ment against any command system that destroyed the unity of air power was
almost unanimous. The idea of parcelling out air units to divisions, corps,
and armies was particularly offensive.

Certainly there was cause for concern. As a result of experience in the
First World War, nearly everyone agreed that the first task of the air arm was
to win air superiority over the battlefield. Once that was accomplished, however, no less an authority than Gen. John J. Pershing maintained that the role
of air power was to attack enemy artillery and ground troops. Captain Claire
Chennault found that the ground commander for the 1934 maneuvers would
forbid air attacks on lines of communication and even restrict heavy bombers
to bombing trenches. A paper produced by the Air Corps Tactical School at
Maxwell Field, Alabama, assumed as late as 1936 that air squadrons would
be allocated to ground units.[2]

The infant Army Air Corps accepted the tactical task of winning air
superiority without question. Once this task was accomplished, however, its
leaders argued that interdiction of enemy supplies and reinforcements and

attacks upon lines of communication targets should take priority over action in direct support of the ground forces. No one can say how much a belief in the greater effectiveness of attacks on line of communication targets influenced Air Corps opinion and how much it was formed by fear of air units coming under ground command. After the Louisiana and Carolina maneuvers of 1941, General Arnold reported that air-ground cooperation had been largely ineffective, and this was certainly true. On the other hand, as late as May 1943, Assistant Secretary of War John McCloy was convinced that Army Air Forces officers opposed close support primarily because they feared that it would bring about control of air units by ground force commanders.[3]

Without question, the most important factor affecting Air Corps disregard of and distaste for close support was the development of the doctrine of strategic bombardment. Influenced by the Italian, Giulio Douhet, British Air Marshal H. M. Trenchard, and American Brig. Gen. William Mitchell, and encouraged by improvement in bomber aircraft, more and more Air Corps officers became convinced that bombardment from the air would become the decisive element of the next war. There was some confusion as to whether wars would be won by destroying enemy morale or his vital centers of military production. But in any case, explosives dropped from the air would either destroy an enemy's will to resist or make it impossible for him to resist. By the mid-1930s the Air Corps Tactical School was advocating an idea prevalent before the mid-1930s, the destruction of production centers, and the development of the Boeing B–17 (Flying Fortress) heavy bomber made the idea much more feasible.

When it came off the production lines, the B–17 was as fast, or almost as fast, as any existing fighter aircraft. It thus seemed safe from defensive pursuit aircraft. As luck would have it, the development of the B–17 coincided with the appearance of the Norden bombsight, which was supposedly so accurate that small targets could be destroyed from high altitudes. One press release asserted that with the Norden, a B–17 bombardier could hit a pickle barrel from 20,000 feet. The speed of the B–17, its defensive firepower, and the accuracy of the Norden sight led to the belief in the Air Corps that a war against an industrial nation could be won by daylight precision bombing, and the Air Corps turned this concept into a crusade. The idea had much appeal, from its identification with the steady eye of the frontier marksman to the promise of victory without the mud and blood of the Civil War and World War I or to wholesale destruction of civilians. Daylight precision strategic bombing became an article of faith. Speaking of the strategic bombing offensive against Germany, General Arnold said in his memoirs: "We didn't know quite how we were going to make that offensive work at first. . . . All we knew was that we *would* make it work."[4]

Thus, in the ten years preceding the outbreak of the Second World War, the Air Corps paid little attention to tactical aviation as a whole. The development of more advanced pursuit aircraft received a high priority during the 1930s; but since it was assumed that bombers could make their way unescorted to enemy targets, long-range fighters were not needed. "Attack aviation," aircraft envisioned for low-altitude bombing and strafing attacks, received minor attention when Capt. (later General) George C. Kenney was on the faculty of the Tactical School in the late 1920s. Fighter-bomber tactics were neglected in the United States before Pearl Harbor and for some time thereafter. Bomber escort, fighter bombing, low-altitude attack, observation, and reconnaissance were all neglected, but close air support of ground forces was most neglected of all.[5] Army Field Manual 1–5, Employment of Aviation of the Army, on April 15, 1940, gave no answers to questions of air-ground cooperation, making it necessary after Pearl Harbor to work out the answers in combat zones. In 1942, Field Manual 31–35 attempted a solution, creating air support commands, the commanders of which were to act as air advisors to ground commanders, but these played no role in the southwest Pacific. As late as 1943 Field Manual 100–20, Command and Employment of Air Power, which remained in force throughout the war, stated that combined actions with the ground forces were the most difficult air actions to control and were the least effective. Close air support retained the lowest priority of all air operations. Fortunately ground and air commanders in the Southwest Pacific looked pragmatically at problems that arose and worked out solutions.[6]

Marine aircraft and the Navy's air arm were to play a significant role in the southwest Pacific. Marine pilots gained some experience with close support during the intervention in Nicaragua, and apparently these officers considered Marine aviation solely as a supporting arm of Marine Corps ground troops. Before the war, however, the Marines had not developed any particular techniques, organization, or communications for close support work. It would be late 1943 before Marine units began to train specifically for such operations, and 1945 before they would undertake close support as a primary mission. In the Pacific they performed exceptionally well in the role.[7]

Naval air had done even less than the Marine and the Army Air Forces to prepare for close support missions, yet such missions would become a major task in Pacific amphibious operations. In fact, the Navy before the war had not thought through the role of its air arm other than in terms of operations in support of fleet action. During that period, however, it learned to operate aircraft from carriers (no mean feat in itself) developed dive-bombing and torpedo-bombing tactics, and with the Marines, practiced amphibious operations. For the Navy, the question was never whether close support should be undertaken, but rather when and how it was to be accomplished.[8]

In the south and southwest Pacific, aircraft of all three services would have an opportunity to develop techniques for supporting ground troops in contact with the enemy. More quickly than thought possible, the Japanese drove Allied forces from the Philippine Islands and from Indonesia (then the

Dutch East Indies). They occupied the Port of Rabaul in northern New Britain and began extending their power to the southeast, down the Solomon Islands. The ease of this victorious expansion persuaded the Japanese to extend their conquests to Port Moresby on the south coast of New Guinea and to Midway Island in the central Pacific.

Japanese naval forces moving toward Port Moresby were turned back in the Battle of the Coral Sea, and the Imperial Japanese Navy suffered a decisive defeat in the Battle of Midway. The new offensive had come to naught on the seas, but the Japanese were not ready to go on the defensive. The push down the Solomons continued to Guadalcanal, where construction of an airfield began, posing a definite threat to sea routes between the United States and Australia. Japanese troops also landed at Buna, on the north coast of New Guinea, from whence they began pushing southward across the Owen Stanley Ranges, again putting Port Moresby in peril.

Remnants of Allied air units defeated in the Philippines and the East Indies had gathered in Australia, where reinforcements from the United States arrived with agonizing slowness. The aircrews available were either battle-weary or inexperienced, but it was necessary to throw them into the struggle against the Japanese Army and Navy Air Forces on the one hand and against the equally threatening ground advance against Port Moresby on the other. The ground threat was the most acute in August and September 1942. The Japanese drove inexperienced Australian militia defending the Kokoda Trail back until, on September 25, they reached Imita Ridge, less than twenty five miles from their objective. Here they were stopped, as much by disease and starvation as by military opposition, and the Australians began a counteroffensive that would take them to the north coast of the island.

In both defensive and offensive phases, Allied aircraft assisted the Australians. Nearly all the fighting, however, took place under dense jungle canopy, and pilots had great difficulty identifying targets. For this reason the Curtis Wright P–40s (Warhawks), P–400s (an export version of the Bell P–39 Aircobra), and Douglas A–20s (Havocs) struck at targets well removed from friendly troops. Some attempts were made to mark friendly lines with panels, and on at least one occasion Australian troops wore white markings on their helmets, but these attempt were unsuccessful. The lines were not static along the Kokoda Trail, and pilots did not have an opportunity to become familiar with the terrain.[9]

It is difficult to assess the effect of air support on this fighting, but at Milne Bay air support played a critical role at a crucial time. At the southeast tip of New Guinea, Milne Bay was occupied by Allied forces in July, and by mid-August one airstrip was in operation and another near completion. The Japanese launched an amphibious operation that was repulsed, after hard fighting, with the support of Australian P–40s based at Milne Bay and other Allied planes from Port Moresby. Effective air support was possible, because the area was not jungle but rather a huge, somewhat open coconut plantation and because during the important phase of the fighting, Allied ground forces were clearly identified on one side of an airstrip, the Japanese clearly on the other. Also, the RAAF P–40 pilots were very familiar with the terrain.[10]

While the Japanese were being driven back along the Kokoda Trail to the Buna-Gona area on Holnicote Bay, the southeast coast of Papua, New Guinea Island, a major battle was being fought on Guadalcanal, in the Solomons. Fearing disruption of supply lines to Australia, the Joint Chiefs of Staff ordered the seizure of the airfield then being constructed by the Japanese. The August 7, 1942, landing on Guadalcanal was the first significant Allied amphibious operation of the war, and the hurried plans included provisions for air support of the Marines who made the landing. The transport *McCawley* served as headquarters for the amphibious phase of the operation. An air support group was attached to the staff of the amphibious force commander, and an Air Support Director Group, working through the senior Carrier Air Group commander, controlled air units in the area. The senior commander of the *Saratoga* air group, Comdr. H. D. Felt, USN, spent most of August 7 in the air over the invasion areas. Controllers aboard the *McCawley* maintained radio communication with the carriers, with the airborne controller, and with the ground forces ashore. No support missions were needed on Guadalcanal, but help was needed at Tulagi and small islands adjacent to Tulagi. These attacks were poorly executed, and on Gavutu several Marines were killed by "friendly" bombs. The events of D–day and the next two days

Douglas A-20 Havoc.

demonstrated that more frequencies were needed for air support communications, that all participants should be within voice radio range, and that above all, ground forces needed direct radio communication with the aircraft giving them support.[11]

Japanese air reaction to the invasion of Guadalcanal was delayed until August 9, but then it came in such strength that the carriers had to withdraw from the Solomons. This left the Marines defending Henderson Field, as the strip was named, without any air support whatsoever for ten days. On August 20, Navy and Marine Grumman F4F (Wildcat) fighters and Douglas SBD (Dauntless) dive-bombers arrived, followed a few days later by some Army Air Forces P–400s.

From August 20 until December, 1942, Guadalcanal and adjacent waters were the scene of a violent battle for air and naval superiority between Japanese and Americans even as the Marines desperately struggled to hold Henderson Field against Japanese ground attacks. Marine and Navy F4F fighters bore the brunt of this air battle, aided toward the end of the period by AAF P–38s (Lightnings). The SBDs of necessity concentrated mainly on local search operations and attacked on shipping, but they did expend some effort on close support. The P–400s, lacking oxygen equipment, proved useless against Japanese fighters and were in fact a death trap for their pilots. After this had been discovered, and it took only a few engagements, the P–400s and some P–39s that eventually arrived at Henderson Field were used almost entirely for strafing and bombing in support of ground troops. If these airplanes had been effective as air-to-air fighters, the ground forces might have had no direct support at all.[12]

The pilots on Guadalcanal did practically everything that was possible with the equipment they had to provide air support for the ground forces. Some unsuccessful efforts with panels were attempted to point out targets. Though far from perfect, designating and outlining targets by mortar smoke shells was much more successful. Pilots sometimes served on the front lines to familiarize themselves with targets. Returning to Henderson Field, they flew missions against the Japanese, who were constantly strafed and hit with bombs up to 500 pounds. When the airmen had nothing else, they used depth charges against ground troops. The blast effect, they found, could be devastating in confined areas. In a few instances, successful air-ground radio communication was maintained during a strike, but this was not common. The available maps of Guadalcanal were practically useless, but gridded photomosaics became available before the end of 1942, and these were of great help to pilots in identifying targets. During the defense of Henderson Field and the offensive that followed in early 1943, strikes were made sometimes no more than 100 yards from friendly positions, a very real demonstration of rapport between air and ground units.[13]

Air support of ground forces in the fighting along the Kokoda Trail was

The Grumman F4F Wildcat, a Navy carrier fighter that figured prominently in the American defense of Guadalcanal.

not a complete failure, and support on Guadalcanal was modestly successful. Unfortunately, in the battles that followed in late 1942 and early 1943 at Buna in New Guinea and on New Georgia in the Solomons, air support proved to be much less effective. By the time the Japanese defenders were pinned into Buna and Gona, American, Australian, and Dutch air units achieved a degree of air superiority that should have permitted heavier and more effective ground support, particularly in view of the fact that the fighting lasted long enough for airmen to have become familiar with the terrain.

The Fifth Air Force and the Royal Australian Air Force were eager to help, and when Maj. Gen. Robert L. Eichelberger, USA, left Australia to take command of the floundering American troops at Buna, Gen. George C. Kenney, Commander of Fifth Air Force and Allied Air Forces, assured him somewhat optimistically that he would have bombs on any target Eichelberger designated within three hours of receiving the request.[14]

Though somewhat complicated and clumsy, a workable system of requesting air support was in operation. A battalion commander who needed air support at Buna sent his encoded request upward through channels to ground force headquarters in New Guinea (Alamo Force for Americans, New Guinea Force for the Australians). An Allied Air Forces officer attached to ground force headquarters would then forward the request to Advanced Echelon Fifth Air Force at Port Moresby. It had to reach Advanced Echelon Fifth Air Force by 1700 hrs of the day preceding the mission, but in the slow-moving jungle war of New Guinea this was no great handicap. In practice, the "day before" remained the rule in the southwest Pacific for the remainder of the war, though there were exceptions.

The request could be rejected at any point along the line, but generally only division headquarters or Advanced Echelon Fifth Air Force did so. The

302

Gen. George C. Kenney.

air headquarters decided what armament would be used, but a ground officer attached to the air unit making the strike assisted in briefing the crews.[15]

Certainly the troops at Buna needed all the air support they could get. Southwest Pacific troops were for the first time encountering Japanese infantry dug into well-prepared positions and ready to fight to the death. Furthermore, the artillery available was made up mainly of flat-trajectory guns, when high-trajectory howitzers would have been much more effective against the Japanese dugouts. Unfortunately, the A–20s and occasional North American B–25s (Mitchells) of the Fifth Air Force had great difficulty in finding their targets. When they did find them, they had difficulty hitting them; when they did hit them, their machinegun bullets and fragmentation bombs did little harm to the Japanese.

They did do damage to friendly troops. The very first day the 127th Infantry Regiment was on the battleline, it suffered a dozen casualties from Allied bombers. To add insult to injury, captured Japanese diaries indicated that the enemy at Buna feared mortar fire most, artillery next, and strafing and bombing least; close air support played a small role. Buna was taken on January 18–20, 1943.[16]

After the Japanese evacuation of Guadalcanal in February 1943 and the

Allied occupation of the undefended Russell Islands in the same month, American forces moved against New Georgia, the next important island group to the northwest. This was a full-fledged amphibious operation, although most of the air support came from Guadalcanal rather than from the three escort carriers available. Brig. Gen. Francis R. Mulcahy, USMC, designated Commander Air, New Georgia, with an air support group, was stationed aboard the command ship *McCawley* until he could move ashore with the occupation force commander. This movement may have come earlier than intended, as the *McCawley* was sunk during this operation. Japanese ground forces offered only slight opposition to the landings, and the planes on ground alert for support missions were never needed, although the Japanese Naval Air Force did keep Allied fighters busy during the early stages of the operation. Eight hastily created air liaison parties, apparently Marine personnel, served with various ground units, but their function was to advise the ground forces and to transmit requests for support, not to direct air strikes.[17]

The main Allied objective was the Japanese airfield at Munda, on the northwest end of New Georgia I in the central Solomons. The Japanese there were as well prepared and as determined to defend Munda as they had been to defend Buna. What the Allies had hoped would be a quick campaign of maneuver degenerated into a siege. Land-based aircraft, mainly Marine SBDs and TBFs (Avenger torpedo bombers), flew hundreds of missions in support of the embattled infantry. They turned Japanese rear areas into a shambles, but made little attempt to give ground forces close support. When they did attempt to hit targets near friendly lines, they sometimes inflicted casualties on Allied ground forces but apparently did little damage to the Japanese.[18]

Thus close air support had been a negligible factor in the hard-won Allied victories at Buna and at New Georgia. Whatever was responsible for the poor showing of air support, it was not the pilots or the planes. American pilots of 1943 were at least as skillful as those of 1945, and the aircraft used at New Georgia were used for ground support for the remaining part of the war. The SBD was technologically outmoded, underarmed for defense against enemy aircraft, and slow; but these qualities did not make it less suitable for close support bombing. This Douglas dive bomber would, in fact, prove to be a superb close support vehicle over the Philippines in 1945. The A–20s and B–25s of the Thirteenth Air Force had already been modified to give them far greater forward firepower than they had at the beginning of the war. P–39s and especially P–40s were being used more and more as fighter-bombers, and the F4U, which would arrive in the South Pacific before the end of 1943, was a superb fighter-bomber. Napalm had not yet become available as a weapon against enemy personnel, but there is no reason to suppose that it could have been dropped any more accurately than demolition bombs in New Guinea and New Georgia.

The Navy's F4U Corsair, produced by Chance Vought, was one of the outstanding close air-support aircraft of the Pacific war.

Certainly the air arm had to overcome handicaps. Tropical weather was always uncertain, and weather was an especially acute problem in New Guinea so long as aircraft had to cross the Owen Stanley Range from their base at Port Moresby. Likewise, the distances were great when compared with missions flown against targets on the Kokoda Trail or on Guadalcanal, but they were not insuperable. There were no adequate maps here either, but as before, gridded photomosaics did become available. In an area without definite distinguishing physical features, however, a photogrammetric map was no magical solution to target location; the cameras then in use could see no more than the human eye could see. Basically it was the jungle cover that made close air support so difficult. Panels, bed sheets, reflecting surfaces, smoke shells, and even rockets were tried as a means of identifying friendly positions or enemy targets, but to little avail. Some jeep-mounted high-frequency radio sets were available to the air liaison parties, but the jungle, the terrain, and the humidity seem to have interfered with short-range radio communications. Even had the radios worked well, it is difficult to see how an air liaison officer could have directed close support aircraft against targets that he himself could not see.[19]

There can be no doubt that the Buna and New Georgia campaigns reduced whatever confidence the ground forces had had in the ability of support aircraft to blast away Japanese who were shooting at them. Indeed, some air officers who really wanted to aid ground troops by close support missions were beginning to doubt their ability to do so. General Kenney was himself discouraged. He wrote General Arnold that attaining local air superiority and isolating the battlefield "goes through quite rapidly. Eventually, however, the troops get in close contact in an area so restricted that if we bomb, we will hit both our troops and the Japs."[20]

During the last half of 1943 and the first months of 1944, the pace of the offensive in the south and southwest Pacific accelerated (The South Pacific was soon to be absorbed by the Southwest Pacific Area). In mid-July the Japanese still had strong air bases at Wewak in New Guinea and at Rabaul in New Britain, but Wewak was crippled by a series of Fifth Air Force missions in August of 1943. Rabaul would remain strong until after the first of the year, but the Allies had local air superiority over the Solomon Islands and eastern New Guinea. American factories were beginning to supply not only the aircraft but also the ships, tanks, and other equipment needed for an offensive, and more men were arriving.

It had taken more than a year from the time of Pearl Harbor and more than six months from the Battles of the Coral Sea and Midway to establish the Allies in Buna and New Georgia. These objectives had to be accomplished before an offensive could begin, and it would take several months more to accumulate the necessary men and material. Once the offensive started, the occupation of part of Bougainville and some lesser islands in the Solomons, the Huon Peninsula in New Guinea, the tip of New Britain, and the Admiralty Islands left Rabaul isolated and neutralized. Southwest Pacific forces were then ready to move rapidly westward along the north coast of New Guinea, thence northward to the Philippines. Air support of amphibious operations and of ground forces played a major part in these activities.

For the Bougainville campaign, ComAirSols, made up of the Thirteenth Air Force, Marine and Navy air units in the Solomons, and New Zealand squadrons, provided a detachment known as ComAirNorSols to control all aircraft in the beachhead area during the amphibious phase and to exercise the same function ashore when the amphibious phase was ended. Two fast carrier task forces supported the invasion, but the carrier aircraft were kept clear of the beachhead area. Requests for air support would be sent to ComAirNorSols by air liaison parties located with the troops ashore and relayed to ComAirSols. Radio communication with planes over the beachhead was possible but was not used to guide attacking aircraft to targets.[21]

Fifth Air Force, now a part of Far East Air Force that included Australian and Dutch units, used procedures for supporting amphibious operations that differed more in nomenclature than in purpose from those followed by

ComAirSols. Advanced Echelon Fifth Air Force at Port Moresby was the main air headquarters north of Australia, but the establishment of Dobodura and other bases in the Buna area led to the creation of the First Air Task Force, a more advanced headquarters with some autonomy. Before the western New Guinea campaign was completed, a Second and a Third Air Task Force had come into being. It is uncertain whether air liaison parties (officially, "support air parties") went ashore with landing forces at Woodlark and Kiriwana Islands earlier in June or at Nassau Bay on June 30, 1943. Such a party definitely did accompany the landings near Lae on September 4 and at Finschhafen on September 22, 1943. It was in the assault on New Britain in late December, though, that the southwest Pacific system of air support of amphibious landings appeared in mature form.[22]

In order to control the Vitiaz Strait, Southwest Pacific Area Headquarters believed that it needed airfields on the northern New Britain side of the strait as well as those already established in New Guinea on the south side. Two objectives were chosen, Arawe on the south coast, and Cape Gloucester on the tip of that peninsula, the assaults to be mounted on December 15 and 26, respectively. The amphibious phase followed the procedure developed by the Navy, as might be expected, but Far East Air Forces refused to use Navy personnel for fighter direction or for the control of support aircraft. Instead, Fifth Air Force personnel boarded Navy ships and remained there until the amphibious phase of the operation was over, when they returned ashore to resume normal air support.

During the landings at Arawe, an air alert of B-25s flew over the beachhead, and practically all the bombers under First Air Task Force at Dobodura were on ground alert. Following Navy practice, the ranking officer of the air alert planes was designated "control officer" or "air controller" of the support aircraft. He received instructions from the support air party aboard the command ship and then led or directed strikes by the air alert planes. In practice, only one flight of air support planes had a target assigned by the support air party; all others bombed secondary targets on which they had been briefed before takeoff. No targets were struck in the vicinity of friendly ground troops.[23]

The invasion of Cape Gloucester on December 26, 1943 was a much more elaborate operation. During the amphibious phase, one support air party was assigned to the flagship to act as commander; support aircraft and parties were attached to each of the two Marine regimental combat teams assigned to carry out the landings. A fourth support air party remained in reserve at Finschhafen. The First Air Task Force officers from Dobodura would carry out the air phase of planning, and the Task Force would then mount most of the D–day strikes. They already had been bombing Cape Gloucester intensively for some weeks, and aircrews were in large measure familiar with the terrain in the target area. Assigned missions, including bombing and strafing of the landing beaches, were carried out by no less than eleven squadrons of B–24s and nine squadrons of B–25s—and four of the B–25 squadrons flew two missions during that first day. Three squadrons of A–20s provided air alert over the landing beaches, striking previously assigned targets if not called upon by the air alert controller. Bombers returning from these missions were rearmed upon landing, to go on ground alert for subsequent missions if needed.[24]

In spite of Japanese aerial reaction to the invasion of Cape Gloucester, it was almost a textbook operation. Consolidated B–24 heavy bombers (Liberators) plastered their targets with 1,000–pound bombs and B–25s strafed and bombed the beaches ahead of the landings, dropping white phosphorus bombs on Target Hill, which would otherwise have afforded the Japanese observation of the landings. B–25s also bombed likely Japanese defense positions. The air alert A–20s were not needed, so they added the weight of their bombs and strafing to predetermined targets. No close support missions were flown. The day went nearly perfectly until after noon when the 345th Bombardment Group, flying its second mission of the day in support of the landings, swept over the area just as Japanese dive bombers launched an attack. Our naval gunners fired at every aircraft in sight, shooting down two B–25s and seriously damaging two others.[25]

Three more amphibious landings completed the physical isolation of Rabaul. Saidor, on the New Guinea coast, was assaulted on January 2, 1944, Los Negros in the Admiralty Islands on February 29, and Emirau Island, near New Ireland, on March 20. Techniques that proved successful were repeated, and adequate air support for the landings was available in each case. February 19 was the last day that Rabaul-based Japanese aircraft rose to fight Allied bombers. Rabaul remained a strong fortress, and thousands of tons of bombs were still to be dropped to prevent its recovery, but it ceased to count as a naval and air base. It could be safely bypassed and left to surrender at the end of the war.

Successful landings on enemy-held shores did not mean that fighting was at an end in those places. In New Guinea, Australian forces engaged Japanese troops in the valleys of the interior even as landings were made on the coast. At Bougainville, American assault forces expanded the beachhead only enough to permit the construction of airfields out of range of enemy artillery. They then waited for the subsequent bitter Japanese counterattacks. On Bougainville, at Cape Gloucester, in New Guinea, and especially in the Admiralty Islands, air support of the Allied ground forces was a major factor in eventual victory.

Once ComAirNorSols landed at Bougainville, it opened communications with ComAirSols at Munda. Many requests for bombing and strafing to aid the Third Marine Division's advance were received and acted on, but most of them were for attacks on positions well away from friendly lines. Some

North American B-25 Mitchell bombers often went into action in support of troops landing on hostile beaches.

strikes, however, were close support missions in every sense of the word. On D–day the Japanese were strongly entrenched in Piva Village, against which Marines requested an air strike. The next morning seventeen SBDs and twelve TBFs reported to ComAirSols and then received directions from an air liaison party. Upon securing an "execute" signal, infantry marked its front lines with colored smoke grenades and fired white phosphorus shells into the targets. After the bombing, the infantry attacked and took the village.

Four days later, with targets and friendly lines marked the same way, TBFs dropped 100–pound bombs within 100 yards of friendly troops at Piva Village No. 2. The hardest nut to crack at Bougainville was a sharp rise. Named "Hellzapoppin Ridge" by the Marines, it overlooked the airfields that engineers had already made operational. The ridge was easily identified, and planes attacked almost immediately after takeoff from the new airfield. First attacks were not successful, however, and for reasons unknown one pilot dropped a bomb 600 yards from the target inflicting eight Marine casualties. Eventually, while friendly infantry crouched on one side of the ridge, 11 TBFs attacked the reverse slope with delayed action bombs. Some of the bombs struck within 50 yards of the Marine positions, but the ridge gave them more protection than the distance alone would indicate. After this strike, Marines charged over the ridge with fixed bayonets and eliminated the remaining Japanese soldiers.[26]

After the beachhead at Bougainville was established, most Marines withdrew, and XIV Corps, composed primarily of two Army divisions, took over the defense of the airfields that were now bases for planes attacking Rabaul. Each division received an air support party from the Seventh Support Communications Squadron, which had arrived in the theater. There was little for them to do until March 1944, when the Japanese launched a counterattack. The XIV Corps then made extensive use of air support. The Japanese had deployed a large number of guns, most of them on reverse slopes, where they were protected against artillery fire from within the perimeter; most air strikes, therefore, were directed at gun emplacements. SBDs and TBFs flew most missions; the rest were flown by B–25s. The decline of Japanese air strength at Rabaul was indicated by the fact that fighter planes were used for dive-bombing enemy positions during the defensive phase of the Battle of Bougainville. Very few of the strikes could be considered close support, although one air liaison officer was wounded by a sniper while directing a strike, and at least one target was marked by a smoke grenade dropped from a small liaison aircraft. During the height of the battle, two SBDs orbited over the perimeter during daylight hours, directing allied artillery and attacking targets assigned to them by liaison officers of the ground forces.[27]

Despite the fact that XIV Corps used close support almost exclusively against artillery emplacements, the Battle of Bougainville was a significant step forward in close support techniques. With ComAirSols as an air support headquarters for the operation, liaison parties with the infantry (or "air support parties" after XIV Corps took over), jeep-mounted SCR–193 air-ground radios, and pyrotechnic bomb line and target marking, nearly all the elements needed were in place. During the invasion phase, the Marines, providing both aircraft and infantry, demonstrated that well-aimed bombs could be dropped successfully far closer to friendly troops than previously believed. Most of these bombs were 100–pounders; but late in the war bombs ten times as large would be dropped almost as close.

It was also demonstrated that close support could not perform miracles. On occasion it took days of bombing and artillery fire, to destroy enemy artillery, and even after the most accurate bombing many Japanese who were well dug in survived. As demonstrated at Hellzapoppin Ridge, it did immobilize them temporarily, however, leaving them vulnerable to an infantry attack that followed immediately. Probably not until the Lingayen landings on Luzon in January 1945, would close air support again be as effective as it had been on Bougainville. One probable reason was the fact that the Allied Air Forces in the southwest Pacific were never fully aware of what had been accomplished on Bougainville in early 1944.

In New Guinea the Allied Air Forces of General Kenney developed techniques based on principles later set forth in FM 100–20, "Command and

Employment of Air Power," well before that manual was released in July of 1943. Kenney saw his command as basically a tactical air force with the primary function of defeating the enemy air force. When this had been accomplished, and while it was being accomplished, attacks on Japanese shipping would isolate any battlefield. In fact, the Battle of the Bismarck Sea in February 1943 largely isolated the Huon Peninsula, the next objective of southwest Pacific forces after the fall of Buna. General Kenney felt that once the battlefield was isolated, the strength of the air force could be devoted to direct cooperation with the ground forces.[28]

Kenney did not believe in unified command, but rather in cooperation between services. In early 1943, when officers arrived in Australia from Washington to form an air support command within the Allied Air Forces, Kenney decided against such a headquarters, believing that it would lessen the flexibility of his Far East Air Forces. He therefore sent the higher ranking officers back to the United States but kept those of lesser rank as intelligence officers. The Fifth Air Support Communications Squadron, however, was welcomed when it arrived. His A–3 operations officers were sent to Australian courses so that American and Australian concepts of air support could be coordinated, and some American air officers gained combat experience with Australian forces in New Guinea. Originally, the officers of these support air parties were not aviators. There was no uniformity. A party at this stage of the war, normally consisting of five or six men and a jeep equipped with an SCR–193 radio, might be attached to a division, brigade, or regimental headquarters of the ground forces. In practice some probably functioned temporarily with battalions.[29]

The standard operating procedure (SOP) was for a ground force commander to request assistance through the support air party. Presumably the ground force commander would seek the advice of the air officer, ideally a pilot who had close support experience. The support air party would forward the coded request by radio to Advanced Fifth Air Force Headquarters at Port Moresby, with a copy to Alamo Force (Sixth U.S. Army) if the requesting unit were American or to New Guinea Force if the unit were Australian. The message also went to the Air Task Force that would actually mount the attack. Alamo Force or New Guinea Force could disapprove the request, and Advanced Echelon Fifth Air Force had to approve it.

The request would specify whether bombing or strafing was desired, the object of the attack, whether it would be coordinated with infantry or artillery action, the nature of the target, and, above all, the location and description of the target. Usually the coordinates of the target were given on gridded aerial photographs, including the increasingly used oblique, low-level photographs. It was especially important that the target and friendly lines be identifiable by some natural feature if at all possible, and also that the request include information about target indication by smoke, mortar, or artillery fire. If the target were moving, the time last seen and the direction of movement were needed, but this rarely happened with a close support target.

The request also included the exact time when the attack was desired—not before a certain time, and not after a certain time. Air headquarters frowned on exact timing and preferred that it be left to the air arm.

A suggested approach based on the advice of the air support officer with the ground troops was expected. The request, however, was not to include the type of plane needed to make the attack nor the armament that should be used. That was a matter that could best be determined by the air headquarters ordering the strike.[30] Even as air officers advised the ground units who had requested air support strikes, ground officers advised the air units making those strikes and contributed greatly to the briefing of pilots and crews. The latter, primarily Australians in 1943, were stationed at Advanced Echelon Fifth Air Force headquarters at Port Moresby and at First, Second, and Third Air Task Force Headquarters in northern New Guinea.

The procedure of encoding and decoding messages and getting decisions on them took time—from five to eight hours. In a situation involving rapid ground movement, this could have been disastrous, because in actuality it meant that the request was made one day, the strike delivered the next. In jungle fighting against the Japanese, however, movement over terrain was so slow that "next day" support was not a particular handicap. Occasionally, however, the support strike arrived overhead before the ground commander knew that his request had been approved.[31]

All accounts agree that the Allied Air Forces were generous in their response to air support requests. Very few were turned down. Sometimes weather interfered with strikes that had been laid on, but since most were flown in the morning before tropical clouds built up, this did not happen as often as might have been anticipated under continental climatic conditions. On the other hand, very few, perhaps only two, of the New Guinea strikes during the last half of 1943 and the first quarter of 1944 were what a purist would term close support. The bombing and strafing was carried out in the contested area, and often the Allied infantry had its morale raised by its ability to see the explosion of the bombs raining down on the Japanese; but the bombs usually were not aimed at Japanese directly in contact with the American or Australian soldiers.[32]

Two examples of true close support can be cited, both strikes in support of the Australians fighting in the interior of northern New Guinea in late 1943 and early 1944. Unlike American infantry, the Australians had "army cooperation squadrons," equipped with Boomerangs and Wirraways—light Australian-built aircraft more or less equivalent to the American AT–6 advanced trainer, but armed with two machineguns. Their primary function was tactical reconnaissance and artillery spotting for the ground forces. The pilot of one of these planes saw the Japanese hastily preparing positions at a new place in the line, flew back to the Third Air Task Force area, landed, and returned, leading in a strike by Australian P–40 fighter bombers. In this case the tactical reconnaissance pilot briefed the P–40s as they flew toward the target. "It was one of the few times pilots actually saw Japs when they were attacking."[33]

In December 1943, the Australian Seventh Division found itself held up by a group of determined Japanese occupying a ridge, soon known as Shaggy Ridge, which could be approached only by another ridge three feet wide with a sheer drop on either side. On December 19, four P–40s, guided by a Boomerang, bombed and strafed the ridge, but friendly troops less than one hundred fifty yards away were not hurt. Encouraged by this, a coordinated air, artillery, and infantry attack was delivered on December 27, when seventeen P–40s took part. This enabled the Australians to capture the key to the position, but the remaining Japanese decided to die where they were rather than retreat. A major strike helped them achieve this desire. On January 18, 1944, forty-eight B–25s struck the ridge from low altitude, and on the next day sixty-five B–25s, twelve Australian Beaufighters, and twelve Australian Vengeance dive bombers struck. Sixty-three B–25s returned on January 20, and for three more days the P-40s and Vengeances dive-bombed the enemy position. When the 7th Division resumed its advance, it met little opposition. Pilots in the attacking planes maintained radio contact with the support party during these strikes, but the air support officer did not attempt to direct the attacks. Friendly lines were marked with smoke grenades and rockets. Some targets were identified by mortar smoke. In one instance the Australians combined all their panels to make a huge arrow pointing at the target. Probably the most effective innovation, however, was the use of the tactical reconnaissance plane to lead bombers to the target.[34]

As noted earlier, a total of five support air parties was assigned to the Arawe and Cape Gloucester operations of December 1943. Once the troops were ashore, these parties played an important role in the operation, at one time providing the only communication between the ground forces and headquarters in rear areas. Their main function was to call for air strikes, and this they did. Only one true close support mission was recorded, however. In this case the target, near the airfield, was five hundred yards from friendly troops. On the other hand, this distance accorded to generally observed procedure, for the strike was delivered by B–26s (Marauders), B–25s, and even B–24s, thus involving considerable risk even with that separation.

Undoubtedly more close support would have been called for, but the jungle cover on New Britain was at least as thick as it had been on New Georgia. This cover, combined with inadequate maps, made it difficult for pilots and bombardiers to identify targets, and sometimes ground commanders were highly uncertain of the exact location of their troops. Fortunately easily identifiable features—Target Hill, Mount Talawe, Razorback Hill, and the airfield—played a significant role in the Japanese defenses, so support aircraft could often bomb profitably, even if not closely.[35]

The last southwest Pacific campaign aimed at isolating Rabaul, took place in February 1944 against Los Negros and Manus in the Admiralty Islands. All the experience that the Allied Air Forces in the southwest Pacific had acquired was applied in this fighting. The attack was launched earlier than initially planned. After a carrier strike against the great Japanese base of Truk in the Caroline Islands forced the withdrawal of most Japanese planes from bases near the Bismarck Sea, and after Allied B–25s flew over Los Negros Island at low altitude without provoking any Japanese fire, General MacArthur decided to carry out a reconnaissance in force with approximately 1,000 men of the 1st Cavalry Division.

Actually, the Japanese garrisons on Manus and Los Negros were much stronger than expected. On Los Negros, an inferior force attacked a superior one. The cavalrymen were supported by destroyers and Allied air power that went far to balance the scales, but the first few days in the Admiralties were precarious. Had it not been for naval gunfire and air support, the ground forces probably could not have held their positions.

Elaborate plans were made for air support for the landings, but weather prevented their execution on the scale expected. Nevertheless, an air support party led by a very able officer, Capt. George Frederick, went into action soon after the troops waded ashore. The initial landing came very close to the Japanese airfield at Momote, Los Negros, and the airstrip gave pilots easily determined points of reference for aiming bombs and making strafing runs. During the first few days there were several instances of B–25s and B–17s dropping supplies to the attackers and then strafing to keep the Japanese from firing as the supplies were collected. Before the airfield was opened to normal use, courier B–25s landed, then took off and strafed nearby Japanese positions before returning to New Guinea. Finally, in early March, a detachment of RAAF P–40s was stationed at Momote. These fighter-bombers performed admirably, blasting Japanese strong points uncovered by advancing infantry on Manus and outlying islands.

Captain Frederick was personally responsible for much of this success. He made the best possible use of his radio equipment and was usually in radio communication with strike planes. He assured marking friendly front lines by smoke, and he stationed himself in advance of the front lines to see exactly where bombs were falling. When he could not get his radio equipment near enough to targets, he relayed instructions back to his party by telephone so that they could be broadcast to the planes overhead. Frederick was a true believer in close air support and was convinced that Maj. Gen. Verne D. Mudge, Commander of the 2d Cavalry Brigade, was overcautious and uncertain of the support that air could accomplish. Unfortunately, the captain was killed near the end of the battle, and his experience and enthusiasm were lost.[36]

With the fall of the Admiralties, Kavieng on New Ireland and Rabaul on New Britain were the only strongly held Japanese bases remaining in an area fought over since early 1942. Rabaul and Kavieng had been neutralized, and continuing air strikes would ensure that they remained so. The South Pacific, except for such air strikes, was largely bypassed by the war and came under General MacArthur's Southwest Pacific Area command. With his northern flank now secure, MacArthur could move westward down the coast of New Guinea and then northward toward a major objective, the Philippine Islands.

Allied Air Forces were growing stronger by the day. They now included a Dutch detachment, Royal New Zealand Air Force squadrons, a large number of U.S. Navy and Marine Corps fighters and bombers in the Solomons, the Royal Australian Air Force, and two United States Army Air Forces—the Fifth and the smaller but nonetheless potent Thirteenth. By early 1944, many, if not most, of these units had had experience with ground support missions. Although improvement was still possible, successful techniques for delivering true close support of ground troops had been developed, and personnel were available to a greater extent than ever. A second air communications squadron, a source of communications personnel for support air parties, arrived in the theater in late 1943. Another joined the Thirteenth Air Force. Twenty rated air observers, actually glider pilots, arrived in the theater to serve as officers in support air parties. Communications equipment, though far from ideal, proved usable. Immediate communications between air support personnel on the ground and striking aircraft was infrequent and sporadic, but possible. The very high frequency radios (VHF) coming into the theater, however, were to improve significantly those communications. Progress was made in identifying friendly positions and targets, primarily by smoke, and the Australians had even developed a technique employing lead-in, light aircraft to indicate and even mark close support targets. With these developments, close support could have played a much greater role than it did for the remainder of 1944.[37]

In each campaign after March of 1944 and before January of 1945, there were specific reasons for the failure to make the most of close support missions, but there were also some general reasons. Air commanders in the southwest Pacific were more than willing to aid ground forces. Nevertheless, the priority in their thinking and planning went far in defeating Japanese air. The establishment of new air bases, strikes on enemy shipping, and other more glamorous uses of air power would further hasten final victory over enemy air.

It was hard to retain experienced personnel in American combat units in World War II. Obviously, some experience was lost through casualties, as in the case of Capt. Frederick, but aircrews were rotated back to the states after fairly short tours of duty (which might seem very long indeed to a pilot or gunner), and by 1944 the process of rotating ground personnel had begun.

Newspapers carried headlines about strategic bombing attacks on Germany, about heroic fighter defense of Chinese cities, and about low-level skip-bombing attacks on Japanese shipping; but there were few stories about the bombers and fighter-bombers that struck dug-in Japanese in support of American or Australian infantry. Last but not least, ground commanders had vivid recollections of air strikes that had gone astray and inflicted casualties on friendly forces. Successful strikes had not left such strong memories.

In April 1944, General Headquarters of the Southwest Pacific Area issued a comprehensive operating procedure for aerial cooperation with naval surface forces. As a result, SWPA procedures came to parallel those developed in the Central Pacific, but with some exceptions: the air units involved were to be land-based Army Air Forces units, and the officers controlling them were to be Army Air Forces officers. On the other hand, Army Air Forces officers controlling aircraft during the amphibious phase were to be controlled by of the commander of the amphibious force until the commander of the landing force took command ashore.

The main center of Japanese strength in New Guinea was Wewak; and since this base was, by mid–1944, in range of land- based fighters, it seemed the likely objective of southwest Pacific forces after the Admiralties. In reality, General MacArthur's objective was Hollandia (now Djajapura), much farther up the coast, and a landing there would require support by carrier-based aircraft. Central Pacific naval headquarters agreed to supply both fast carriers and escort carriers in support of Hollandia landings. Since three separate landings were scheduled, the Seventh Fleet was divided into three corresponding attack forces. The United States Pacific Fleet provided a commander of support aircraft for the flagship of each attack force to control supporting aircraft during the amphibious phase of the operation. Also aboard each flagship was an air support party provided by the Allied Air Forces, the senior officer of each being designated Allied Air Forces controller. So long as he remained aboard ship, the Allied Air Forces controller advised the Commander Support Aircraft concerning land-based air. Other support air parties went ashore with the ground troops. On air matters, the attack force commander was advised by the commander support aircraft and the Allied Air Forces controller.[38]

During the amphibious phase of the operation, requests for air support went from the support air parties ashore to the commander support aircraft aboard ship. The commander support aircraft could use air alert planes to perform the mission or, he could transmit the request to the carriers. He also could speak with strike aircraft over another communications net and issue strike instructions directly. The operations plan additionally called for an "air coordinator" airborne over the landing area. If it seemed appropriate, the commander support aircraft could turn control of strike aircraft over to the air coordinator.

After control of the operation had passed to the landing force commander and after land-based planes had begun to supply air support for the operation, requests for air support went from one of the support air parties* to one of three operational air headquarters, Advanced Echelon Fifth Air Force, and Sixth Army. Operational air headquarters consisted of the 308th, 309th, and 310th Bomb Wings of the Fifth Air Force, formerly the First, Second, and Third Air Task Forces. Requests for support could be rejected by Advanced Echelon Fifth Air Force, Sixth Army, or these bombardment wings.

The support air direction net continued as it was during the amphibious phase, except that the commander support aircraft and the air coordinator no longer existed. Communication with planes overhead improved, and each air support party was now equipped with a powerful SCR–299 radio for long-distance communication, two less powerful HF SCR–193s mounted on a weapons carrier, one jeep-mounted SCR–193, and a VHF SCR–634. The last radio, remarkably free from interference, but with only line-of-sight range, was supposedly superior for communicating with planes overhead. At any rate, it was essential at Hollandia, because Navy aircraft used only VHF equipment.[39]

Despite all these elaborate arrangements, very little air support was rendered at Hollandia and Aitape during and after the landings on April 22, 1944. The Japanese had obviously expected an attack at Wewak, and the troops at Hollandia and Aitape were service troops, not infantry. They seem to have been completely demoralized by the sustained preparatory bombing by the Allied Air Forces and to have taken to the jungle when the amphibious attack came. The 1st Battalion of the 21st Regiment, 24th Division asked for a strike against dug-in Japanese in their front on D + 1, and three Navy fighters appeared in little more than two minutes to strafe the enemy. Unfortunately the attack was not effective, and not until the next morning, following a night-long bombardment by artillery and mortars, could the Americans dislodge those in the entrenchments.[40]

Australian and American engineers had Tadji Airfield at Aitape ready for light planes forty-one hours after they had begun work on D–day afternoon. On the morning of April 25, Royal Australian Air Force P–40s began patrolling the beachhead. The fast carriers and half of the escort carriers departed on that day, and the remaining escort carriers set sail on May 5. A

---

*Six were involved: one with the 163d Regimental Combat Team at Aitape, one with I Corps at Hollandia, one with each of the two divisions operating at Hollandia, one in the Admiralty Islands to serve as a relay if needed, and one in reserve.

mainly Australian force of P–40s, Beaufighters, and Beauforts flew some one thousand six hundred sorties in May and even more in June, although few if any of these were close support missions. During the Battle of the Driniumor in July, when the Japanese attempted to recapture Aitape, many more strikes were launched against the attacking Japanese, but not for close support. In fact, the jungle cover was so heavy in the area that it would have been extremely difficult to fly close support had it been requested. Before the end of the war, Australian troops relieved the Americans in the Aitape area, but the Japanese still held Wewak when the war ended.[41]

Southwest Pacific forces moved rapidly west from Hollandia down the coast of New Guinea. This involved four amphibious operations, the objectives being Wakde-Sarmi (May 17, 1944), Biak (May 27, 1944), Noemfoor (July 2, 1944), Sansapor (July 30, 1944), and then northward to Morotai (September 15, 1944). The pace of these movements, as compared to those of the previous year, gives evidence of the growing strength of the Allies and the declining capabilities of the Japanese, although the individual Japanese infantryman continued to fight competently, bravely, and to the death.

Land-based air provided by the Allied Air Forces (Far East Air Forces after June 14, 1944) supported all these operations. However, the Far East Air Forces (FEAF) adopted most of the measures for air support that had been used in the Hollandia operation. After all, these methods had been developed by consultation between air, ground, and naval forces. All of the personnel were air personnel (actually, all seem to have been Fifth Air Force personnel), but the Army Air Forces' commander of support aircraft aboard the headquarters ship directed air support during the landing phase, using naval communications equipment. He could temporarily pass control to an airborne coordinator over the beaches, or to a commander of support aircraft ashore. When command passed from the commander of the amphibious force to the commander of the landing force, the commander of support aircraft ashore, who was the head of an air support party, took control. One new feature was an airborne ground officer, usually referred to as "air observer," whose main function was to keep up with the position of the ground forces.

For communications, the support air request net included the support air party ashore, the 310th Bombardment Wing at Hollandia, the commander of support aircraft afloat so long as he functioned, the air coordinator, and the air observer. The support air direction net included the support air party ashore, the commander of support aircraft afloat, the air coordinator, and the support aircraft. This, with minor modifications, would be the basic machinery for controlling air support of ground troops in the southwest Pacific until the invasion of Leyte.[42]

Sarmi was believed to be strongly garrisoned, so landings were made at Arare, just opposite Wakde. The Japanese counterattacked strongly on May 19, and Royal Australian Air Force P–40s from Hollandia bombed and strafed at intervals all that day and some of the next, hitting areas marked by smoke shells. Apparently they halted the counterattack. The P–40s were alert planes carrying 500–pound bombs as well as machinegun ammunition. On May 18, heavy strikes were mounted on Wakde, including B–24s, P–40s, and A–20s. The 8th Bombardment Squadron at Hollandia, with only 14 planes assigned, put five 6–plane strikes over Wakde during the day. Apparently none of the Wakde strikes was directed from the ground, but some were led to the target by the air coordinator. Although the Japanese fought well, they suffered 759 dead and 4 captured, compared with 40 Americans killed and 107 wounded.[43]

On the main island of New Guinea the fighting would last much longer than at Wakde. Adm. Chester W. Nimitz used this as evidence in favor of island warfare when possible. Opposition to the landings at Wakde was strong, but the fighting lasted only two days at a cost of 40 American lives. The landing was almost unopposed at Arare, but in the Japanese counterattacks that followed, usually called the Battle of Lone Tree Hill, almost four hundred American lives were lost. This battle was the occasion of strong air support, provided in the main by Republic P–47s (Thunderbolts) based on Wakde. For short ranges, the aircraft could carry two one-thousand-pound bombs, exceeding the maximum load of an A–20. Many of these were close support strikes, in that the planes were assigned targets by the support air party, and in some instances the targets were marked by smoke. Some of the fighter pilots who had time to become reasonably familiar with the area were talked in to their targets by ground controllers. On one occasion the P–47s dropped full belly tanks, then set the gasoline afire with machineguns.[44]

Biak, the next southwest Pacific invasion target, was 190 miles west of Wakde. The air support arrangements for the amphibious phase were practically identical to those for Wakde, but weather prevented the delivery of many of the strikes that had been planned, especially those by heavy bombers. Even so, the 41st Division was able to get ashore without too much difficulty. The Japanese garrison, however, was larger than expected. It received some reinforcement during the battle, was well led, and took full advantage of a terrain—featuring jungle and limestone caves—that was ideal for a Japanese-type defense. The troops landed on May 27, 1944; organized resistance did not end until July 22, 1944. No planes could be stationed on airfields at Biak until June 22.

Weather interfered greatly with the air effort, but even so, Biak received more ground support missions than any invaded area yet attacked by the southwest Pacific forces. Air commanders were so eager to help that Brig. Gen. Ennis Whitehead, Commander of Fifth Air Force, planned to send two or three squadrons of B–24s from Nadzab to bomb ground support targets on Biak. These planes were then to land at Wakde, and the next day fly two missions against Biak from there. The third morning, they were to hit targets on

Biak and then return to Nadzab. This plan was preempted by Japanese fleet activity, but it demonstrated the willingness of the air arm to cooperate when the acquisition of needed airfields was the objective.[45]

The above is an example of the trend toward innovative use of all sorts of bombers for ground support. Long after D–day, A–20s and B–25s were on air alert when weather permitted. Even P–40s, P–39s, and P–38s participated. Most missions were assigned, but they were not easy. For example, B–25s and P–40s attacked cave openings with 500–pound bombs in the face of 500–foot cliffs. But the Japanese were well-protected. Their last stronghold, the Ibdi Pocket, did not interfere with airfield operation, so it was bombarded for a long time before the infantry moved in. Forty thousand mortar and artillery shells were fired between June 21 and July 10 into an area less than 600 yards square, and then the pocket was bombed and strafed by P–39s. The Japanese, nevertheless, repulsed the infantry attack that followed the intensive preparation. During the next ten days, more than 6,000 additional shells were fired into the pocket. On July 22, 1,275 rounds of 105–mm and 155–mm artillery shells were fired, and B–24s dropped sixty-four 1,000–pound bombs. The infantry attack that day did succeed. As late as September 7, however, it was estimated that 1,600 Japanese continued to resist on Biak and a neighboring island.[46]

Allied ground forces on Biak were not satisfied with the air support they received, and ground commanders tended to consider poor liaison responsible. The support air party on Biak did have some trouble communicating with planes seeking a secondary or tertiary target; but on the other hand, communications with the 308th and 310th Bomb Wings remained open at all times, and these air units were eager to participate in assaulting the Biak airdromes. There were three major problems: (1) weather, which turned back many sorties during June, (2) a threat of Japanese naval action in early June that made it necessary to use many aircraft for search missions that otherwise would have been available for ground support, and (3) insufficient air support that failed to break Japanese resistance and caused some ground commanders to believe that they had received less than their due. In reality, Allied forces on Biak received more air support than any other comparable campaign in the southwest Pacific until Luzon. Air support contributed much to the victory, though less than the infantry, and probably less than the artillery.[47]

The invasion of Noemfoor deserves attention only because of the effectiveness of the prelanding bombardment. This was carried out by destroyers and 2 cruisers and by 33 B–24s that dropped 300 bombs weighing 1,000 pounds each on the Japanese defensive positions just behind or beyond the beach. The B–25s and A–20s were on air alert, and fighter bombers were on call, but there was little need for them. Japanese defenders were so dazed by the bombardment that they neither fought nor fled, but simply milled about in confusion until they were killed. General Kenney reported this incident in his memoirs but neglected to mention the naval bombardment. Samuel Eliot Morison, the distinguished naval historian, also described it, but he ignored the participation of the heavy bombers. Actually this was as good an example of ground, naval, and air cooperation as the New Guinea campaigns could afford.[48]

Air support by Far East Air Forces improved only modestly during the period from April to September 1944. Both air and ground units had gained experience, and in some respects, particularly target identification, there were advances. On the north coast of New Guinea, gridded oblique photographs, smoke shells, lead-in aircraft, and oral direction by means of air-ground radio were used. Communication also improved both in concept and in equipment, but one meaningful feature of close support that was not exploited nearly as much as it probably should have been was the direction of close support strikes from the front lines. The example that Captain Frederick set in the Admiralties was not followed.

Air Commanders learned that all types of aircraft could be used for direct support of ground forces, and medium and light bombers, B–25s, A–20s, and Beauforts were used from the beginning. At Biak, heavy bombers, B–24s, played a significant part, though more as siege artillery than as air power. Most important was the increasing use of fighters. P–40s and P–39s had long been used in support of ground troops, but now P–38s and P–47s became fighter-bombers. With napalm added to their armament they were a fearful threat to dug-in enemy troops.

The next southwest Pacific target after Morotai was Leyte, invaded on October 20, 1944. Originally plans had called for the first assault on the Philippines to strike Mindanao, the southernmost of the main islands, but a lightly opposed carrier strike into the central Philippines persuaded Adm. William Halsey, and through him, General MacArthur and the Joint Chiefs of Staff, that the Japanese were weak enough for a successful landing on Leyte. In September, with experience gained in the Hollandia operation and in subsequent southwest Pacific landings as well as in Central Pacific operations, Headquarters Southwest Pacific issued a standard operating procedure for air support of amphibious operations when both naval and land-based planes were to be used. This procedure formalized the role of the commander of support aircraft afloat and ashore, the air coordinator, and the air observer. It called for a support air request net and a support air direction net such as had been used in New Guinea and Morotai. This standard operating procedure also designated the air liaison party (a term occasionally used in the southwest Pacific to refer to the support air party) as a communications team that informed the commander of support aircraft as to the position of friendly troops, the location of good targets, and the results of close support missions.

Once land-based planes took responsibility for air support, a support aircraft party would assume the responsibility previously exercised by the commander of support aircraft afloat or ashore. Although there were some differences in nomenclature, this was basically the same system for supporting amphibious operations by carrier aircraft as that developed in the Central Pacific campaigns from the Gilberts through the Marianas.[49]

The planning for Leyte was in every sense a cooperative activity, even though the operation was hurriedly conceived and executed. The X Corps, an infantry corps provided by the Southwest Pacific Area, and Seventh Fleet were to train air liaison parties from the corps at Hollandia. Central Pacific Command provided the XXIV Corps, then en route to invade Yap Island but recalled for the new assignment. Its air liaison parties came from the 2d and 3d Joint Assault Signal Companies, which were Marine Corps organizations. Finally, the Fifth Air Force provided support air parties to accompany corps and division headquarters. Thus the support air parties for the Leyte operation consisted of Air Forces personnel, air liaison parties from the X Corps came from Army personnel trained by the Navy, and air liaison parties for the XXIV Corps were Marines from another theater. Plans for the operation called for three naval task forces, each task force to have a commander of support aircraft and the remainder of the customary air support machinery. Fast carriers were to contribute to air support during the first few days of the operation, and no less that eighteen escort carriers were assigned.[50]

The air support plans for the assault on Leyte were, for the most part, unnecessary. Resistance on the beaches was light, so the D–day bombardment and air alert played only a minor role. Following the bombardment the Japanese Navy came out for its last major battle of the war, and naval air was of necessity directed against the enemy afloat. The escort carriers suffered heavy losses and were never again able to offer the amount of air support that they had afforded before the battle. The construction of airfields on Leyte was much more difficult than assumed in the planning, and considerably fewer Army Air Forces planes could be brought forward than programmed. These planes and some Marine fighters that arrived before the battle was over were fully occupied with defense and with strikes at ships bringing Japanese reinforcements to Leyte. But most important of all, the Japanese threw a new weapon into the struggle, the *kamikaze* pilot.

Using suicide tactics, these remaining Japanese pilots were a far more potent weapon than they had been with conventional tactics. It was increasingly important to destroy Japanese planes on their bases, and if they got into the air to shoot them down before they reached a target. Thus U.S. fighters had to deploy forward, leaving bombers behind, while aboard the carriers the number of fighters increased and the number of bombers declined. Most of the time, these fighters abandoned the role of fighter-bomber to combat the suddenly far more dangerous Japanese air arm.[51]

Leyte presented a problem to engineers responsible for airfield construction, and the Leyte campaign convincingly demonstrated the need for land-based aircraft in general and land-based fighters in particular. Allied commanders therefore felt it was essential to acquire another site for airfields, a site where construction would be easier than on Leyte and that would be closer to Luzon when that main Philippine Island was invaded. Mindoro island met these requirements.

The *kamikaze* threat was now so great that Vice Adm. Thomas C. Kinkaid, Commander of the Seventh Fleet, was reluctant to risk his escort carriers, but General MacArthur ordered the invasion forward, though he did consent to delay it for a week. The landing was made almost without resistance, but the *kamikazes* did swarm over the invading fleet, and air reaction to the landings was strong for that stage of the war. Our troops ashore did not require a great deal of support, and fighters from defensive patrols overhead were normally able to provide what was needed.[52]

Luzon would see the most extensive close support in the Pacific. This was appropriate, since it was the largest land battle of that war, but other factors contributed to bringing about this state of affairs. For the landings, no fewer than eighteen escort carriers were assigned to support two corps of infantry on the shores of Lingayen Bay. In addition, thirteen fast carriers provided indirect support with strikes at Luzon airfields, Formosa, and Vietnam. Finally, by D–day, January 9, 1945, the 310th Bombardment Wing of Fifth Air Force provided three groups of fighters, one squadron of Northrop P–61 (Black Widow) night fighters, and two tactical reconnaissance squadrons flying specially equipped fighter planes from airfields on Mindoro. This proved to be far more aviation firepower than was needed. General Tomoyuki Yamashita, the Japanese commander, had decided not to fight for the beaches. The real opposition to the landings came from *kamikaze* planes, and most of that before D–day.[53]

In the southwest Pacific, plans for close air support following the amphibious phase were elaborate. No less than twelve air support parties were called for: one for Sixth Army, one for each corps (I and XIV), and one for each division and independent regimental combat team. Personnel were provided from the three tactical air communications squadrons in the theater, and ten more rated officers (both pilots and observers) were added to the squadrons. Each party included two rated officers and twenty enlisted men, the latter including radio operators, cryptographers, radio technicians, and drivers. Thus the support air parties were much larger than they had been in New Guinea, and each had adequate radio equipment and transportation. From the beginning these parties were equipped with radios that could be used to direct close support missions from the ground. Thus forward air observer teams, an officer with necessary communications specialists and a radio jeep, could go to the front and direct such ground missions.[54]

As in previous operations, some divisions contained AAF air liaison parties made up of ground communications personnel with fewer men and less equipment than a support air party. The support air parties supplied the forward observers. Communications employed the same radio techniques that had been used since Hollandia, made more elaborate, as required for the larger operation.

Approximately 85 percent of the sorties flown over Luzon between January 9, 1945 and the end of the war supported ground forces. This is a staggering total of 47,000 out of 55,000 sorties. This commitment to the infantry was possible because the other tasks of the air arm had been accomplished. The Japanese air forces no longer posed a threat in the Philippines, and air superiority was complete. For all practical purposes, the Philippine Islands were completely isolated from other Japanese-held areas. Very few aircraft were able to sneak in at night, but most that tried were lost. Japan's sea communications with the East Indies, Singapore, and Burma were also under attack by submarines and aircraft, although the Japanese Navy and merchant marine had been so reduced there was not much traffic to interdict. As the demand for air operations declined, lower loss rates and the incredible productivity of American factories and training facilities entered the picture to make Allied Air Forces stronger than ever. With Manila Bay under control early in March, the troops on Luzon were in a position of reduced pressure. Commanders could depend more on artillery shells and air strikes, less on manpower, to dispose of the Japanese on their front.[55]

Two Marine Corps dive-bomber groups equipped with SBDs played an important role in Luzon close support until April, when they were transferred to Mindanao. These groups were left behind in the Solomons as the war swept westward and northward, and before the Luzon invasion they were instructed to prepare themselves to provide ground support in the Philippines. There is little more they could have done with their outmoded planes. In fact, in 1942 General Kenney had removed the A–24, the Army Air Forces version of the SBD, from combat in New Guinea.

These Marines had no experience in close support since Bougainville. Therefore, largely under the guidance of Col. Keith McCutcheon, they drew up a training program, practiced with the 37th Infantry Division, and prepared for operations. As his personal papers indicate, Colonel McCutcheon was fully aware that the achievement of air superiority and the destruction of enemy communications took priority over ground support, but his assigned mission was ground support, and he believed that such missions should be directed from the ground. Consequently, he created what he called air liaison parties, basically a stripped down version of the Army Air Forces' support air party. But a support air party officer could be any rated officer, and most of them seem to have been rated observers. Apparently the officer heading a Marine air liaison party was always a pilot. A pilot, and especially one accustomed to the type of aircraft giving support, obviously was better equipped to advise a ground force commander and to direct an air strike from the ground than was an officer trained as a glider pilot, as were some support air party officers.

The Marine dive-bomber groups, which were controlled by the Fifth Air Force command and in the same command and control communications net as Army Air Forces units, rendered superb close support, including an air alert for the 1st Cavalry Division's famed dash to Manila. Actually their planes executed very few close support missions during the Manila drive, but they kept a steady flow of up-to-the-minute intelligence to the advancing ground forces, and their presence overhead seemed to have intimidated Japanese who might otherwise have tried to contest the advance. They also gave good close support to the guerrilla forces that played a larger and larger role in the Luzon campaign.

What particularly endeared these Marines to the ground forces was their obvious desire to give support. They did not get on station any quicker than the Army Air Forces aircraft, and their communications followed the same route as those of other air units. But it was not unusual for some of the pilots to show up in the front lines on the afternoon before the next morning's mission to view the situation and assess the targets. The achievements of the Marine Corps' close support effort were appreciated at the time, and the fact that their exploits were celebrated in a number of well-written books has kept this appreciation alive. There are probably some U.S. Air Force officers who believe the concept of close air support began with the Marine Corps.[56]

Every type of aircraft that the Allies had in the Philippines except PBYs (Navy flying boats used for overwater reconnaissance, rescue work, and antisubmarine patrol) seems to have been used for ground support in Luzon. Heavy bombers (B–24s) were not used in close proximity to ground troops, but they attacked many ground support targets in response to ground force requests. They flew as low as, and on a few occasions below, 4,000 ft, resulting in much more accurate bombing than from high altitudes. The B–25s and A–20s had been the ground support workhorses in New Guinea, and they continued to fly such missions in the Philippines. Usually they bombed in line abreast from treetop level, strafing as they went, using delay-fused demolition bombs or parachute-rigged fragmentation bombs. The SBDs, of course, dive-bombed and seldom if ever dropped anything other than demolition bombs.

Fighters flew nine-tenths of the ground support sorties on Luzon. The P–39 had finally been phased out by the beginning of the Luzon campaign, and the P–40 was rapidly being replaced by the North American P–51 (Mustang). The P–40 and the P–51 could each carry two 500–pound bombs. This load was equal to that carried by the SBD. The single-engine P–47 and the twin-engine P–38 normally could each deliver two 1,000–pound bombs. Thus they had a carrying capacity superior to the SBD, equal to the A–20, and not much less than that of the B–25. In New Guinea, fighters had normally approached their bombing target in a glide, but in the battle of Luzon they ordinarily bombed from level flight at low altitude (this was always the case when they were delivering napalm) or dive-bombed. Accuracy was believed to be greater when general purpose bombs were delivered from a dive, and strafing from a dive was more effective against enemy troops in open foxholes.[57]

The close air support arsenal on Luzon introduced napalm as a weapon. A mixture of gasoline and a jelling agent, napalm was dropped in a container with an igniter to set it off when it hit the ground and ruptured. It was dropped in light bomb casings, in 55–gallon oil drums, and, most effectively, in external wing tanks—containing 165 gallons originally designed to extend the range of fighter aircraft. One tank in open terrain created an intensely hot fire lasting more than a minute over a tear-shaped area 100 yards long and 50 yards wide at the widest point. Post-strike observations by infantry indicate that it was dangerous against troops exposed or in shallow shelters. In addition, it drove enemy troops from their shelters and thus made them vulnerable to strafing, artillery, mortars, fragmentation bombs, and fire from ground troops.

Most demolition bombs were 500–pounders, but many 1,000–pounders and some 2,000–pounders were dropped on close support targets. High explosives did not kill many men in well prepared positions, but left them dazed and disorganized. The closer that the attacking infantry followed up a bomb strike, the less organized resistance the defenders were able to offer. If the enemy had much more than five minutes to recover, however, his power to resist was likely to be restored.[58]

As stated earlier, the use of forward air observers to direct close support strikes and even assigned strikes at some distance from friendly ground troops was very common during the Luzon campaign. Very seldom, if at all, was an air coordinator designated; however, the leader of a flight of aircraft often acted as an air coordinator, getting instructions from the forward air observer or Marine air liaison party on the ground and then directing aircraft in to the strike. With B–25s or A–20s, which usually bombed and strafed as a unit, a flight leader might actually lead his flight to the target, and this could also be done with fighters dropping napalm. Dive-bombing differed, since only one aircraft bombed at any given time.

The strength available for close support was so great that strikes could be requested at frequent intervals the next day. These requests would specify a target, but if the ground commander felt the bombs would do more good elsewhere when the planes arrived overhead, the forward air observer could direct the planes to the new target. Thus a ground commander who planned ahead could obtain air support practically on demand. In an emergency, a skillful air liaison or forward observer officer could often call in single planes or even flights of planes to hit targets for which missions had not been formally requested.[59]

Close air support on Luzon was not perfect. Planes at times missed their targets, and a few bombed and strafed friendly troops. Some junior air party officers had difficulties with the higher-ranking infantry officers in headquarters, with whom they worked, while the high volume of radio traffic led to much interference and some lost tempers. During the amphibious phase, Navy Grumman F6Fs (Hellcats) erroneously attacked and even shot down one of the P–47s, and in a few instances the Japanese were able to break into the support air direction circuits and direct planes to profitless targets. Additionally, the jeeps which were used for directing strikes wore out rapidly because the engines idled almost constantly, and these breakdowns interfered with communications. Even so, the ground forces on Luzon had as much close support as they could use. Much of it was wasted, but much was invaluable. Messages from ground units made it clear that ground units were delighted with the support they received. Their greatest complaint was that it could not be delivered at night as well as during the day.[60]

Fighting on Luzon continued until the end of the war, although at a declining pace. While it continued, other Allied forces were busy liberating the central and southern Philippines, Borneo, Bougainville, and mopping up those parts of New Guinea still occupied by Japanese troops. Close support of these operations fell largely upon the Thirteenth Air Force, the Royal Australian Air Force, and the Royal New Zealand Air Force. As was the case on Luzon, aircraft were available but distances sometimes reduced their effectiveness. Amphibious operations absorbed most to this support. Ten major and dozens of lesser landings were executed in the central and southern Philippines and Borneo.

The task of air support of these operations was put under the control of Thirteenth Air Force, a much smaller command than Fifth Air Force. Thirteenth Air Force executed many of the strikes with its own planes, and it could call on the Fifth Air Force for help when necessary. However, two Marine Corps fighter groups with F4Us were already under Thirteenth Air Force control at Leyte, and the two Marine SBD groups on Luzon would be transferred south in April. Operating from airfields seized on the Zamboanga Peninsula, reinforced with a PBJ (B–25) squadron and designated MAGSZAMBO, these Marine units delivered more close support sorties in the southern Philippines than any other command. Far to the rear, the Royal New Zealand Air Force P–40s gave excellent close support to Australian troops on Bougainville, and the fighters of the Royal Australian Air Force supported troops closing in on Wewak in New Guinea. Royal Australian Air Force B–24s would support operations in Borneo, as would Beauforts and P–40s. Finally, three escort carriers would provide support for the invasion of Balikpapan, in Borneo.[61]

No less than seven different types of ground parties controlled strikes during these southern campaigns. The Seventh Air Communications Squadron, assigned to Thirteenth Air Force, had been "borrowed" by Fifth Air Force for the Luzon operation. It was broken up into support air parties and forward observer teams, but enough of it was recovered to form support air parties for the operations in the central and southern Philippines. For directing air support for guerrillas, a number of guerrilla air support teams were formed, each composed of a pilot and a number of enlisted communications specialists. Marine units on Luzon brought their air liaison parties south with them and may have formed others. A Marine joint assault signal company was either formed or came from the central Pacific where the joint air assault company had become the equivalent of the southwest Pacific air support party and more, and its personnel were attached to ground units to direct close air support. Air coordinators continued to direct strikes from the air over targets, but in these campaigns the coordinator was often called the air observer. The officer directing air strikes was never a ground officer, however, and he was usually an officer of the service delivering the strike.

During amphibious operations, the commander of support aircraft and his party directed strikes as had been the practice since Hollandia. The commander of support aircraft was always an air officer, sometimes a Marine, sometimes a rated officer of the Army Air Forces. Finally, in the Borneo campaign and presumably on Bougainville, the Royal Australian Air Force had an air support section very similar to a support air party but not so large. Each of these established radio communications with the supporting aircraft and talked them to the target. They often led airborne aircraft to the target. During these campaigns, a ground officer attached to each air unit aided in the briefing of crews delivering strikes.[62]

Special note must be given to air support of guerillas. Guerillas had remained active in the Philippines throughout the Japanese occupation, but after the liberation of the islands began, their numbers and activity grew rapidly. The Allies encouraged them, and when it became possible, supported them with aircraft attacks upon the Japanese. The Marines sent air liaison parties to the guerrillas on Luzon while they remained on that island, and, as has been noted, the Thirteenth Air Force created special guerrilla air support teams for the central and southern Philippines. Guerrillas received support almost everywhere they were active, but this was especially the case in the liberation of Mindanao, where the guerrillas maintained an airfield that pilots could use for emergency landings, as they did on Cebu. When it became necessary to transport a guerrilla air support team and its jeep across the roadless center of Cebu so that it could control attacks near Cebu City, hundreds of Filipinos dragged the jeep across the island, against the grain of the razorback mountains, up some slopes so steep they had to cut steps to gain mechanical advantage in pulling. In going downhill, they sat down and let the friction between their bodies and the hillside break the descent of the jeep. When tactical considerations demanded it, they returned the jeep to the west side of the island by the same methods.[63]

Allies used many types of aircraft in supporting these southern operations, and one PBY crew even dropped its bombload on a target that a guerrilla air support team had located. In New Guinea and Bougainville, Australians used Boomerangs and Wirraways to lead strike planes to targets, and there were a few instances in Mindanao when L–5s (a very light tactical reconnaissance aircraft normally used for spotting artillery fire) dropped smoke grenades on enemy targets. Fighters including P–38s, F4Us, and Royal Australian Air Force and Royal New Zealand Air Force P–40s and Spitfires, dive-bombed, strafed, and delivered attacks with napalm at minimum altitude. Of the bombers, usually B–25s and A–20s delivered close support strikes and provided air alert planes for amphibious operations. On several occasions a B–25 housed the air coordinator. The SBDs of the Marine Corps units played a major role in this area as they had on Luzon.

The most unusual feature of close support in the south was the frequent use of B–24s, especially in the Borneo operations. Because of their long range, the heavy bombers flown by Thirteenth Air Force pilots, and some by the Royal Australian Air Force, were especially useful in Borneo before local fields had been captured and put in condition. In some instances, air alert B–24s remained over a beachhead for as long as two hours. These heavy bombers were also used by air coordinators and led strike planes in to their targets. The B–24s operated at low altitudes; three were shot down by Japanese ground fire while providing support. Some bombed within five hundred yards of friendly troops. One support strike was made by fighters and bombers from an escort carrier at Balikpapan. The pilots, who had no previous experience at close support, inflicted casualties upon Australian troops. The liberation of the central and southern Philippines and Borneo was almost complete when the war ended.[64]

Certain conclusions emerge from the southwest Pacific experience in close air support operations. These conclusions are not necessarily universal, but they apply to the time and to the equipment in the southwest Pacific, and to some extent to the enemy in that theater. The experience acquired in the war against Japan must be evaluated most carefully if applied to current operational environment. The speed of aircraft in the 1980s, weapons available to friendly and hostile forces, improved communications, and electronic navigation equipment available in modern air war tend to diminish what had been learned in close air operations during World War II. Nevertheless, the experience can still be useful.

Air superiority, at least of a local nature, was an absolute requirement. Planes under attack by enemy aircraft could not render effective support to ground troops. Even when it was possible to make air support strikes without day-long air superiority (for example, early in the morning or late in the afternoon when Japanese aircraft were based so far away that they could not operate over the front lines except at mid-day, as at Guadalcanal), commanders chose to use their planes against the enemy air force. Fighter aircraft flying cover on bombing missions, shipping, or strafing airfields were not available for close support.

Other factors played a part, but diversion for other assignments was the main reason that the ground troops on Leyte got so little direct air support. The greatly weakened Japanese air arm suddenly became far more dangerous and required far more attention when it began using suicide tactics. Thus the few aircraft based on Leyte and the fast carrier forces were busy striking *kamikaze* bases and providing air defense.

Aircraft could generally be more profitably used against lines of communication targets, as long as they existed, than against close support targets. The planes employed in the Battle of the Bismarck Sea, which essentially severed sea communications between Rabaul and eastern New Guinea, accomplished far more than if they had delivered the same amount of munitions against ground support targets. Also when the Japanese high command decided to fight the decisive battle of the Philippines on Leyte, bombers and fighter bombers were much more effective in attacks on enemy shipping bringing reinforcements than they would have been attacking Japanese ground positions. On the other hand, by the time American troops were ashore on Luzon, only a fraction of the aircraft available were needed for communications targets, so almost all missions there, and in the southern Philippines, could be directed at targets chosen by the ground forces.

Ideal battle conditions for close air support did not assure that such missions could be flown. Many extraneous factors could prevent them, and did, especially early in the war. It meant little to have perfect conditions if no aircraft crews were available to fly the missions. The crews for the southwest Pacific had to be trained in the United States, in the main, and early in the war pilots and other crewmen were not available. This was demonstrated by the fact that aviation cadets were sent into combat in early 1942. If aircraft were useless without trained aircrew personnel, both planes and flying personnel were useless without trained maintenance men who could keep the aircraft flying. Lack of maintenance personnel was a great handicap to the Allied Air Forces in Australia in 1942 and almost certainly played a major role in making the Japanese air force ineffective after early 1944. Thousands of highly trained Japanese maintenance personnel, if they survived, finished out the war at Wewak, in the jungles around Hollandia, and in the mountains of the Philippines. Last, but not least, machines, crews, and maintenance personnel could not keep aircraft functioning unless there were airfields from which they could operate. Leyte is an example. Because the soil was not suited to airfield construction, land-based aircraft could not be brought forward as rapidly as planned, and although there were aircraft to the south, too few of them were within striking distance of Japanese targets on Luzon and in the central Philippines.

The attitude of the air commander was a major factor in determining how much air support the ground forces would receive. General Kenney and other air commanders in the southwest Pacific were willing to extend all possible air support to the ground forces, subject to the restraints already mentioned. The only truly strategic targets within range of southwest Pacific bombers were oil refineries in Indonesia; and once Japanese communications had been interrupted, it was no longer essential that they be totally destroyed, though they were destroyed anyway. Thus the air units under Kenney's command were, from the beginning, a tactical air force. After other tactical targets, enemy air and communications, had been attacked, southwest Pacific aircraft had to fly ground support missions or remain idle. If the Allied aircraft in the theater were devoted to ground support in 1945, commanders

In the island war, even long-range B-24 Liberators appeared over beachheads in support of engaged troops.

would have had to concede that they had no mission, an admission that few commanders were ever willing to make.

None of the above would have had great significance for close support, if the aircrew delivering munitions had not been able to identify the targets they were expected to hit. In the 1940s, this was not a minor problem. It is never easy to identify visually any terrain feature from the air at high speed, and when such features were jungle-covered, as they usually were in the southwest Pacific, the difficulty was magnified. Even in hilly terrain, aircrew discovered that one jungle-clad ridge looked exactly like the next one and the one before. Gridded oblique photographs helped, but a World War II camera could see no more than the human eye. Sometimes target identification could be accomplished by reference to a coastline, a river, or on Luzon's plains, a road or railroad, but usually the crew on a close support mission saw only jungle. If an area was fought over for some time, then the results of shelling and bombing might make target identification simpler, though never easy.

There was no single complete solution to this target identification problem. The more time pilots had to become familiar with the local terrain, the better they could do. This was a factor on Guadalcanal and on Biak, and with Australian pilots on the Ramu Valley of New Guinea. In the late stages of the war, it was their intimate familiarity with their battle area that explains the highly successful operations of Royal New Zealand Air Force pilots on Bougainville and Royal Australian Air Force pilots in the Wewak area of New Guinea. Additionally, these strike pilots had the services of tactical reconnaissance pilots, men far more familiar with the terrain than they were, to lead them in to close support targets and even to mark those targets by tracer fire or with smoke grenades.

Probably artificial marking of targets, nearly always with smoke, was overall the most effective means of making identification possible. Panels and other similar markings were seldom successful, but smoke did work. The most satisfactory system seems to have been to mark friendly front lines with colored smoke and to mark the targets, sometimes the four corners of the target, with white smoke. There were very few, if any, instances of the Japanese firing smoke shells to mislead Allied pilots or bombardiers. One gains the impression that usually by the time the Japanese were brought to bay in an infantry battle, they had become too disorganized to carry out such countermeasures effectively. They would still fight to the death and inflict casualties on Allied infantry, but their communications almost ceased to exist.

There were apparently no successful attempts to "talk" planes in to their targets during 1943. During 1944, however, commanders and air coordinators of support aircraft in amphibious operations occasionally performed this function. It was an idea whose time had come. The *ad hoc* forward air observer team, which often directed strikes by voice radio, was an accepted part of the support air party by the end of the year. At the beginning, however, the only role of the support air party was to provide communications, mainly for requests for air strikes, between the ground forces and air head-quarters. The Marine Corps in the southwest Pacific and the Solomon Islands long advocated control of close support aircraft by an air liaison party on the ground, and when Marine planes were given an air support mission, ground control was a feature from the beginning. For the campaign in the central and southern Philippines and Borneo, Thirteenth Air Force devised some sort of air liaison party for every need.

In the southwest Pacific, ground commanders were never given opera-tional control of aircraft. Ground commanders *requested* strikes, but these requests were transmitted to air headquarters through air communications channels, and they could be rejected by air headquarters. If the strike was directed from the ground, it was directed by air personnel who accompanied the ground forces. By the end of the war, ground commanders could, in effect, get air strikes at regular intervals, strikes they could assign to targets as they developed, by selecting targets other than those for which strikes had been requested. These requests had to be approved by air headquarters how-ever, and changes in targets had to be approved by the air party with the ground forces. Close support procedures used in the Southwest Pacific never threatened the integrity of air force command.

A final word needs to be said concerning communications. The radio communications available to the Army Air Forces in 1942 and 1943 were primitive by modern standard and by any standards unreliable. Poor commu-nications, probably some overemphasis on security, and the many demands on the air power available in the southwest Pacific, resulted in an excessive time gap between the ground force request for close support and the air force's delivery of the strike. This, and the nature of tropical weather, which tended to grow worse as the day wore on, led to "day after" strikes being acceptable, even though more rapid reaction might have been prefered. Later, when an abundant supply of close support aircraft was available, as on Luzon, a ground commander could obtain air strikes against targets located in the past few hours or even minutes. The same service could be provided by air alert planes during an amphibious operation.

Taking into consideration aircraft and personnel supply, the nature of the campaign, the weather, the enemy, and the strategy and tactics employed in the southwest Pacific, the air arm developed a system of close air support for that theater that was, by 1945, probably as effective as any system could be under those conditions.

Notes

1. Riley Sunderland, *Evolution of Command and Control Doctrine for Close Air Support* (Washington, 1973), pp 21–25.
2. Thomas H. Greer, *The Development of Air Doctrine in the Army Air Arm, 1917–1954* (USAF Hist Study 89, Maxwell AFB, Ala., 1955), pp 4, 32; *Characteristics of an Air Force of the Army to Provide Immediate Support for Ground Forces* (Air Corps Tactical School, Maxwell AFB, Ala., 1936), pp 6–12; Claire Lee Chennault, *Way of a Fighter: The Memoirs of Claire Lee Chennault* (New York, 1949), pp 18–19.
3. *The Air Force to Support and to Operate Beyond the Sphere of Influence of the Ground Forces* (Air Corps Tactical School, Maxwell AFB, Ala., 1936), pp 4, 10; *Characteristics of an Air Force of the Army*, pp 7–8; Sunderland, *Evolution of Command and Control Doctrine*, pp 9–10; Thomas J. Maycock, "Notes on the Development of AAF Tactical Air Doctrine," *Military Affairs*, 14 (Winter 1950), p 187; Wesley Frank Craven and James Lea Cate, eds., *The Army Air Forces in World War II*, 7 Vols (Chicago, 1948–1958), Vol I, *Plans and Early Operations, Jan 1939 to Aug 1942*, pp 17–33; James A. Huston, "Tactical Use of Air Power in World War II: the Army Experience," *Military Affairs*, 14 (Winter 1950), p 172.
4. Quoted in Joe Gray Taylor, "They Taught Tactics," *Aerospace History*, 13 (Summer 1966), p 69; see also Craven and Cate, *AAF in WW II*, I, pp 33–71.
5. Taylor, "They Taught Tactics," pp 67–72; Greer, *Development of Air Doctrine*, p 66; Lewis H. Brereton, *The Brereton Diaries: War in the Pacific, Middle East and Europe, Oct 3, 1941–May 8, 1945* (New York, 1976), p 143; Robert Frank Futrell, *Command of Observation Aviation: A Study in Control of Tactical Air Power* (Maxwell AFB, Ala., 1976), p 25; Intvw, Maj Gen Donald Wilson, transcript undated: U. S. Air Force Hist Research Center, Maxwell AFB, Ala., hereafter cited as USAFHRC, pp 66–67; intvw, citation forbidden, USAFHRC.
6. Charles W. Dickens, *A Survey of Air–Ground Doctrine* (TAC Hist Study 34, Langley AFB, Va., 1958), p 5; Greer, *Development of Air Doctrine*, pp 115, 122; Huston, "Tactical Use of Air Power," pp 167–68.
7. John A. De Chant, *Devilbirds: The Story of United States Marine Corps Aviation in World War II* (Washington, 1947), pp 15–16.
8. Henry M. Dater, "Tactical Use of Air Power in World War II: The Navy Experience," *Military History*, 14 (Winter 1950), p 193.
9. George C. Kenney, *General Kenney Reports: A Personal History of the Pacific War* (New York, 1949), pp 101–2; Wesley Frank Craven and James Lea Cate, eds, *The Army Air Forces in World War II*, 7 Vols (Chicago, 1948–1958), Vol IV, *The Pacific: Guadalcanal to Saipan, Aug 1942 to Jul 1944*, pp 25, 93–98, 101–2; Samuel Milner, *Victory in Papua* [US Army in World War II The War in the Pacific] (Washington, 1957), pp 56–100; intvw with Capt Charles L. Marburg, Aide de Camp to Gen Scanlon, Oct 6, 1942: USAFHRC; Douglas Gillison, *Royal Australian Air Force, 1939–1942* (Canberra, 1962), p 603, *passim*; Ltr, Lt Gen S. L. Bowell, CG New Guinea Force to CG Allied Air Forces, Aug 31, 1942: Kenney Papers, 1941–1945, currently located at Office of Air Force History, Bolling AFB, Washington, D. C.
10. Osmar White, *Green Armor* (New York, 1945), pp 209–10; George H. Johnston, *Toughest Fighting in the World* (New York, 1943), pp 122–127; Milner, *Victory in Papua*, pp 74–88; Samuel Eliot Morison, *History of United States Naval Operations in World War II*, 15 Vols (Boston, 1947–1962). Vol VI, *Breaking the Bismarcks Barrier, 22 Jul 1942–1 May 1944*, pp 34–40.
11. Air Support of Pacific Amphibious Operations: A Report for Naval Analysis Div, United States Strategic Bombing Survey (Pacific), Prepared by Commander AIS Support Control Units, Amphibious Forces, US Pacific Fleet: Navy Department Library, Washington Navy Yard, hereafter cited as NDL, pp 4–5, 59; Vice Adm George Carroll Dyer, *The Amphibians Came to Conquer: The Story of Adm Richmond Kelly Turner*, 2 Vols, I (Washington, c. 1970), pp 346–48; An Evening with Adm H. D. Felt, Mar 4, 1968: Operational Archives, US Navy History Div, Washington Navy Yard, hereafter cited as USNHD: Robert Sherrod, *History of*

Marine Corps Aviation in World War II (Washington, 1952), p 76; intvw with Maj Gen A. A. Vandegrift, USMC, on Air Operations on Guadalcanal: Intelligence Services, AAF, Feb 5, 1943, USAFHRC, p 7.

12. John Miller, Jr, *Guadalcanal: The First Offensive* [US Army in World War II: The War in the Pacific] (Washington, 1949), pp 86–87; Craven and Cate, *AAF in WW II*, IV, pp 40–41.

13. Intvw, Gen Dean C. Strother, Aug 21–24, 1978: USAFHRC, p 67; Sherrod, *History of Marine Corps Aviation*, p 80; Air Support Comparative Analysis, US vs. Foreign Systems, Mar 10, 1943: USAFHRC, p 5; An Evaluation of Air Operations Affecting the US Marine Corps During World War II, 1945; Gen Keith B. McCutcheon Papers, Box 2, Personal Papers Collection, Marine Corps Hist Center, Washington Navy Yard, hereafter cited as USMCHC: Maj Charles W. Boggs, Jr, USMC, *Marine Aviation in the Philippines* (Washington, 1951), p 59; Air Support of Pacific Amphibious Operations, p 64; Miller, *Guadalcanal*, pp 265, 270, 309; Joe Gray Taylor, *Close Air Support in the War Against Japan* (USAF Hist Study 86, Maxwell AFB, Ala, 1955), pp 21–30.

14. Gillison, *Royal Australian Air Force*, p 603, Kenney Papers, Nov 30, 1942.

15. Comments by Col Harry I.T. Creswell and Maj Charles W. Walson: Observers Reports, Air Support Branch, G–3 Section, Army Ground Forces, 3d Phase Tactical Air Operations, Jan 26, 1944, USAFHRC; Taylor, *Close Air Support*, pp 13–14.

16. Robert L. Eichelberger in collaboration with Milton MacKaye, *Our Jungle Road to Tokyo* (New York, 1950), pp 40, 43, 53; Kenney Papers, 11, 14, Nov 25, 1942; Milner, *Victory in Papua*, 169–321; Craven and Cate, *AAF in WW II*, Vol IV, pp 123–28.

17. Capt Walter Karig and Comdr Eric Purdon, *Battle Report: Pacific War: Middle Phase* (New York, 1947), pp 208–12; Jeter A. Isely and Philip A. Crowl, *The US Marines and Amphibious War: Its Theory and Practice in the Pacific* (Princeton, 1951), pp 172–73; CTF 31 Opn Plans A8–43, Annex "D": Operations Plans and Orders, Thirteenth AF, 1942–43, USAFHRC; Sherrod, *History of Marine Corps Aviation*, pp 145–48; John Miller, Jr, *Cartwheel: The Reduction of Rabaul* [US Army in World War II The War in the Pacific] (Washington, 1959), pp 65–96; Dyer, *Amphibians Came to Conquer*, I, p 527.

18. Miller, *Cartwheel*, pp 141–42; Maj John N. Rentz, *Marines in the Central Solomons* (Washington, 1952), p 144; Craven and Cate, *AAF in WW II*, IV, pp 229–37.

19. Greer, *Development of Air Doctrine*, p 122; Richard L. Watson, Jr, *The Fifth Air Force in the Huon Peninsula Campaign* (Washington, 1946), p 59; Ltr, Kenney to Burdette 42; S. Wright, Dec 8, 1942: Kenney Papers, Dec 16, 1942; Craven and Cate, *AAF in WW II*, IV, pp 231–34; Miller, *Cartwheel*, p 142.

20. Ltr, Kenney to Arnold, Jan 1, 1943: Activation and History, Fifth AF, 1941–1943, USAFHRC.

21. Corps Opn Order Nr 1, Hq I MAC, Guadalcanal, BSI, Oct 15, 1943, Annex "B": Opns Plans and Orders, Thirteenth AF, 1942–1943; Dyer, *Amphibians Came to Conquer*, II, p 1058; Sherrod, *History of Marine Corps Aviation*, pp 189–90; De Chant, *Devilbirds*, pp 122–23; US Fleet, Hq CINC, Apr 22, 1944, COMINCH P–001, USAFHRC; An Evaluation of Air Operations Affecting the US Marine Corps; Isely and Crowl, *Marines and Amphibious War*, 180–81.

22. Army Ground Forces Observers Bd, SWPA, Rprt Nr 9 (Air Support of Ground Troops Before, During and After the Landing at Arawe, Feb 11, 1944); 7th Amphibious Force, Command File, World War II, USNHD; Admin History, Commander, United States Naval Forces Southwest Pacific, Chap VI, p 6, Chap VII, pp 6, 24, Chap X, pp 85–86, NDL; Harris G. Warren, *The Fifth Air Force in the Conquest of the Bismarck Archipelago, Nov 1943 to Mar 1944* (AAF Hist Study 43, Washington, 1945), pp 33–34, 55, 83–84; Kenney Papers, Dec 24, 1943, Jan 2, 1944; Miller, *Cartwheel*, p 286; Watson, *Fifth Air Force in the Huon Peninsula Campaign*, pp 184–85, 212.

23. Craven and Cate, *AAF in WW II*, IV, 328–37; Warren, *Fifth Air Force in the Bismarck Archipelago*, pp 31, 36–37; Boggs, *US Marine Aviation in the Philippines*, p 59; Ltr, Kenney to Arnold, Nov 14, 1944: Kenney Papers; Air Support of Pacific Amphibious Operations, pp 16–17, 104–5; Taylor, *Close Air Support*, pp 78–82.

24. Signal Plan for Dexterity: Air Force Unit and Supply Movements—Backhander—Signal Plan, Fifth AF, Dec 3, 1943–Jan 2, 1944, USAFHRC; Warren, *Fifth Air Force in the Bismarck Archipelago*, pp 50–55, 58; Taylor, *Close Air Support*, pp 83–84.

25. Signal Plan for Dexterity; Chronology, Fifth AF, 1942–1944, USAFHRC; Krueger [Lt Gen Walter] Report on Saidor Arawe, Cape Gloucester, May 17, 1944: General Consolidated Files, Fifth AF, USAFHRC; Report of Investigation—B–25s Shot Down by LST Crews, Hq ADVON Fifth AF, Mar 30, 1944: General Consolidated Files, Fifth AF.

26. Daily Intelligence Summary, ComAirSols, 1943, USAFHRC; Evaluation of Air Operations Affecting the US Marine Corps; *The Bougainville Operation, Prepared by the Hist Div, United States Marine Corps* (Washington, undated), pp 16, 25, Miller, *Cartwheel*, p 265; De Chant, *Devilbirds*, pp 122–24, 188; Frank O. Hough, *The Island War: The United States Marine Corps in the Pacific* (Philadelphia, 1947), p 121; Sherrod, *History of Marine Corps Aviation*, p 181; Isely and Crowl, *Marines and Amphibious War*, pp 180–81.

27. Daily Intelligence Summary, ComAirSols, Jan–Mar 1944; Supporting Documents, History, 7th Air Support Communications Squadron, Jun 1942–Sept 1944, USAFHRC; Report on Lessons Learned in the Bougainville Operation, Prepared by CG XIV Corps, undated, p 19, USAFHRC; Taylor, *Close Air Support*, pp 44–51.

28. Watson, *Fifth Air Force in the Huon Peninsula Campaign*, pp 19, 114; Dickens, *A Survey of Air–Ground Doctrine*, pp 6–7; Intvw, Gen George C. Kenney, 10–21 Aug 1974, p 6, USAFHRC.

29. Miller, *Cartwheel*, p 189; Kenney Papers, Jan 11, Feb 23, Aug 21, 1943; Taylor, *Close Air Support*, pp 57–63.

30. Air Support in New Guinea (undated, but probably early 1944. unattributed), pp 87–89, USAFHRC; Army Ground Forces Observers Report, SWPA, Nr 9; Close Air Support SOP Nr 6, General Headquarters, SWPA, Jun 24, 1943: McCutcheon Papers, Box 2; Msg AG452.9, Kenney to Arnold, Feb 1, 1943: Kenney Papers; Memo, Brig. Gen George C. Whitehead to Gen Sir Thomas Blamey, Apr 8, 1943: Kenney Papers; Col Henry P. Dexter, Air Support in Southwest Pacific Area—Nov 1, 1943 to Feb 1, 1944, Hq AGF, *passim*.

31. Dexter, Air Support in SWPA, pp 1–20.

32. *Ibid*; George Odgers, *Air War Against Japan, 1943–1945* (Canberra, 1957), pp 182–98; Miller, *Cartwheel*, p 300; Air Support in New Guinea, p 89; Watson, *Fifth Air Force in the Huon Peninsula Campaign*, pp 131–33, 200–1.

33. Air Support in New Guinea, p 89.

34. Dexter, Air Support in SWPA, pp 10–11; Weekly Intelligence Reviews, Nos. 8–10, ADVON Fifth AF, Jan 17–Feb 6, 1944, USAFHRC: Taylor, *Close Air Support*, pp 73–75.

35. Warren, *Fifth Air Force in the Bismarck Archipelago*, pp 11, 34, 37, 59–72; Taylor, *Close Air Support*, pp 78–88.

36. History, Fifth AF, Part III, Feb 1–Jun 15, 1944, Vol I, App II, Docs 10, 13, USAFHRC: *The Admiralties: Operations of the 1st Cavalry Div (Feb 29–May 18 1944)* (Armed Forces in Action Series, Washington, 1945), *passim*; History, Fifth Air Support Communications Squadron, 1944, App 40, USAFHRC: Miller, *Cartwheel*, pp 315–50; Craven and Cate, *AAF in WW II*, IV, pp 555–70; Morison, *Breaking the Bismarcks Barrier*, pp 331–48; Taylor, *Close Air Support*, pp 89–99.

37. Dexter, Air Support in SWPA, *passim*; Taylor, *Close Air Support*, p 90.

38. Admin History, Commander US Naval Forces, SWPA, pp 87–88; Ops Instructions Nr 49, Hq. AAFSWPA, Mar 21, 1944: Hist Fifth AF, Part III, Feb 1–Jun 15, 1944, Vol II, App II, Doc 162.

39. Air Support Communications Plan for Operations "G," Hq. ADVON Fifth AF, Apr 9, 1944: Hist Fifth AF, Part III, Feb 1–Jun 15, 1944, Vol II, App II, Doc 162; History of the Hollandia Operation, Reckless Task Force, 1944, USAFHRC; Hist 5th ASC Sq, pp 65–68.

40. Robert Ross Smith, *The Approach to the Philippines* [United States Army in World War II: The War in the Pacific] (Washington, 1953), p 61.

41. *Ibid*, pp 61–73, 103–4, 129–30, 199–200, 295; Eichelberger, *Jungle Road to Tokyo*, pp 161–62; Odgers, *Air War Against Japan*, p 210.

42. Ops Instructions Nr 1, Hq. ADVON Fifth AF, 12 May 1944: Ops Instruction, Fifth AF, 1943–1944, USAFHRC; Annex III/1 to STRAIGHTLINE Air Ops Plan (as Amended): Detailed Plan of AF Communications for Opn. STICKATNAUGHT–TOPHEAVY, Hq, ADVON Fifth AF, May 12, 1944: Ops Instruction, Fifth AF, 1943–1944; Taylor, *Close Air Support*, pp 105–7.

43. Smith, *Approach to the Philippines*, pp 218–31; Hist, Fifth AF, Part III, Feb 1–Jun 15, 1944 (Supplement), p 4; Taylor, *Close Air Support*, pp 106–7.

44. E. B. Potter and Adm Chester W. Nimitz, eds, *The Great Sea War: The Story of Naval Action in World War II* (Englewood Cliffs, N.J., 1960), p 345; Narrative History, 26th Support Air Part: Hist 7th ASC Sq, Jan–Apr 1945; Smith, *Approach to the Philippines*, pp 232–79; Odgers, *Air War Against Japan*, p 223; Taylor, *Close Air Support*, 108–10.

45. Memo, Brig Gen Ennis C. Whitehead to Col David Hutchinson, Jun 1, 1944: Ltrs from Gen Kenney to Gen Whitehead and Other Top Officials, Apr 1944–Sep 1945, USAFHRC.

46. Hist Fifth AF, Part III, Feb 1–Jun 15, 1944 (Supplement), pp 8–10; History of the Biak Operation, 15–27 Jun 1944, I Corps, 6th Army USNHD: Weekly Intelligence Reviews Nrs 28–41, Fifth AF, Jun 4–Sep 9, 1944, USAFHRC; Smith, *Approach to the Philippines*, pp 280–396; Craven and Cate, *AAF in WW II*, IV, pp 631–46.

47. Taylor, *Close Air Support*, p 119.

48. Kenney, *General Kenney Reports*, p 407, Samuel Eliot Morison, *History of United States Naval Operations in World War II*, 15 Vols (Boston, 1947–1962), Vol VIII, *New Guinea and the Marianas, Mar 1944–Aug 1944*, p 82; Smith, *Approach to the Philippines*, p 407; Odgers, *Air War Against Japan*, p 238; Potter and Nimitz, *Great Sea War*, p 346; Craven and Cate, *AAF in WW II*, Vol IV, pp 652–61.

49. Stand Operating Procedure Instructions Nr 16/2, General Headquarters, SWPA, Sep 26, 1944, USAFHRC: Taylor, *Close Air Support*, pp 132–216.

50. Ops Instructions Nr 71, Hq AAFSWPA, Sep 1944: AAFSWPA Ops Instruction Aug 13, 1944–Oct 8, 1944; Enc. (C) to CTG 79.1 Report of Amphibious Ops for the Capture of Leyte, P. I., Comments on Air Support: Div of Naval Records, Office of Naval Operations, cited in Taylor, *Close Air Support*, p 373, fn 3; Lt Gen Walter Krueger, *Down Under to Nippon: The Story of Sixth Army in World War II*, pp 141–51.

51. Wesley Frank Craven and James Lea Cate, eds, *The Army Air Forces in World War II*, 7 Vols (Chicago, 1948–1952), Vol V, *The Pacific: Matterhorn to Nagasaki Jun 1944 to Aug 1945*, pp 355; V. J. Croizat, RAND Corporation, Close Air Support Procedures in the War Against Japan: McCuthcheon Papers, Box 3, Ltr, Kenney to Arnold, Nov 14, 1944: Kenney Papers, Nov 30, 1944; Command History, Seventh Amphibious Force, Jan 10, 1943–Dec 23, 1945, 1, 10, USNHD; Admin History, Commander US Naval Forces, SWPA, pp 79, 88; Army Air Support System: McCutcheon Papers, Box 2, Krueger, *Down Under to Nippon*, pp 194–95; Boggs, *Marine Aviation in the Philippines*, pp 43–44; M. Hamlin Cannon, *Leyte: The Return to the Philippines* [US Army in World War II; The War in the Pacific] (Washington, 1954), pp 88, 369, *passim*.

52. Ltr, Kenney to Arnold, Nov 14, 1944: Kenney Papers, Nov 30, 1944; Weekly Intelligence Review Nr 55, Fifth AF, Dec 1016, 1944; Report on the Mindoro Ops, Dec 15–31, 1944, Hq 6th Army, Apr 22, 1945, p 20, USAFHRC; Memo, Hq Fifth AF to CO 308th Bomb Wing, Nov 29, 1944: Ltrs from Gen Kenney; Craven and Cate, *AAF in WW II*, V, pp 390–401.

53. Samuel Eliot Morison, *History of United States Naval Operations in World War II*, 15 Vols (Boston, 1947–1962), Vol XIII, *The Liberation of the Philippines: Luzon, Mindanao, the Visayas, 1944–1945*, pp 6–16, 93–156, 184–210; Luzon Campaign, Rprt Nr 12, AAF Eval Bd, SWPA, 2 Vols, I, p 218, II, p 60 USAFHRC; Lt Gen Walter Krueger, from *Down Under to Nippon*, pp 220–27; Craven and Cate, *AAF in WW II*, Vol V, pp 413–18.

54. Taylor, *Close Air Support*, pp 259–60; Army Air Support System: McCutcheon Papers, Box 2.

55. Robert Ross Smith, *Triumph in the Philippines* [US Army in World War II: The War in the Pacific] (Washington, 1963), *passim*; Craven and Cate, *AAF in WW II*, V, pp 323–40; Taylor, *Close Air Support*, pp 227–30, 235–38.

56. Marine Dive Bombers in the Philippines: Intelligence Section, Div of Aviation, Hq US Marine Corps, May 5, 1945, USNHD: Training Memo Nr 1–44, Hq Commander Aircraft Northern Solomons, Oct 21, 1944: McCutcheon Papers, Box 2; Ops Training Order, Hq MAG–24, 1st MAW, Fleet Marine Force, Ground Training Program in Close Support, Nov 28, 1944: McCutcheon Papers, Box 2; Close Air Support Aviation: McCutcheon Papers, Box 3; Boggs, *Marine Aviation in the Philippines*, pp 61–101, *passim*, De Chant, *Devilbirds*, pp 56–57, 177–82, *passim*; Sherrod, *History of Marine Corps Aviation*, pp 295–312.

57. Summary Report of Air Liaison Party Attached to 121st Regiment, USAFIP, during the Period from Mar 1 to Mar 14, 1945, Inc 22: Hist 308th Bomb Wing, Jan–May 1945, USAFHRC; Weekly Intelligence Review Nos 61–74, Fifth AF, Jan 21–Apr 28, 1945; Ftr Bombing and Strafing, Rprt Nr 16, AAF Eval Bd, SWPA, *passim*, USAFHRC; Area Bomb Study Four and Supplement, V Ftr Command, Incs 46, 73–76: Hist V Ftr Command, Apr–Sep 1945, Vol II, Chap II; Taylor, *Close Air Support*, pp 273–77.

58. Ftr Bombing and Strafing, Rprt Nr 16, AAF Eval Bd, SWPA, pp 15–16; Area Bomb Study Four and Supplement, Philippine Islands, Prepared by the 34th Statistical Control Unit, Oct 1944–Jun 1945, USAFHRC; The Tactical Employment of Napalm by Fifth Air Force, Hq Fifth AF, May 20, 1945: Correspondence and Messages, Fifth AF, Sep 1942–Sep 1945 [incomplete], USAFHRC; Col Roy R. Brischetto, AC/S V Ftr Command, Napalm Attacks on Ipo Dam and Other Areas: Inc Nr 7, Hist V Ftr Command, Apr–Sep 1945; Krueger, *Down Under to Nippon*, pp 290–97; Ltr, CG 37th Inf Div to CG Fifth AF, Jul 1, 1945: Weekly Intelligence Review Nr 85, Fifth AF, Jul 8–14, 1945.

59. Taylor, *Close Air Support*, pp 259, 265–72.

60. *Ibid*, 227–95; msg, MacArthur to CG FEAF, date obscured c May 1945); msg, Kenney to Krueger, Jan 31, 1945: Adv Hq to Kenney, Feb 5, 1945: Kenney Papers, Jan–May 1945; Smith, *Triumph in the Philippines*, p 235.

61. Daily Intelligence Summaries, Thirteenth AF, Nov 1944–Aug 1945, USAFHRC; Eichelberger, *Jungle Road to Tokyo*, pp 202–2, 250; Lt Col Benjamin E. Lippincott, *From Fiji Through the Philippines With the Thirteenth Air Force* (San Angelo, Tex, 1948), xiii; History Thirteenth AF, Jan–Mar 1945, Chap II, pp 2–3, 31–32, USAFHRC; Report of CG Eighth Army on the Leyte–Samar Operation (Including Clearance of the Visayan Passages), Dec 26, 1944–May 8, 1945, *passim*, USAFHRC; Craven and Cate, *AAF in WW II*, Vol V, pp 448–50; Kenney Papers, Feb 11, 1945.

62. Hist, 7th ASC Sq. May–Jul 1945; Report of CG Eighth Army on Palawan and Zamboanga Operations, Victor III and IV, pp 1–27, USAFHRC; Ops Instructions, Thirteenth AF, May 1944–Jun 25, 1945, USAFHRC; Report of CG Eighth Army on Panay–Negros and Cebu Operation, p 155, USAFHRC; Air–Ground Training Program, Eighth Army, May–Jun 1945, USAFHRC; Air Force Communication, Rprt Nr 19, AAF Eval Bd, SWPA, II, Annex 16, pp 302–3; Taylor, *Close Air Support*, pp 336–41.

63. Joe Gray Taylor, "Air Support of Guerrillas on Cebu," *Military Affairs*, 23 (Fall 1959), pp 149–52.

64. Sherrod, *History of Marine Corps Aviation*, p 322; Potter and Nimitz, *The Great Sea War*, p 437; Boggs, *Marine Aviation in the Philippines*, pp 94–95, 115, 119, 121, 129; Eichelberger, *Our Jungle Road to Tokyo*, p 206; Air Support of Pacific Amphibious Landings, p 54; Kenney Papers, Feb 11, 1945; Lippincott, *Fiji Through the Philippines*, xiii; Odgers, *Air War Against Japan*, pp 318–19, 341, 485; Close Air Support Aviation: McCutcheon Papers; Seventh Amphibious Force, Command File, World War II; Action Report of Tarakan, Borneo, Operation, May 1–3, 1945: Commander Amphibious Force 6, May 5, 1945, USAFHRC, pp 32–35, 43–44, 50–51; Action Report, Amphibious Attack on Brunei, Borneo, Jun 10–17, 1945: Commander Amphibious Gp 6, 19 Jun 1945, pp 43–48, 59, 72–73, USAFHRC; Report of CG Eighth Army on Mindanao Operation, Victor V, p 117, *passim*, USAFHRC .

Bibliographical Essay

Sources dealing with close air support in the Southwest Pacific Area are varied and many. Much information can be extracted from Air Force Communication Report No, 19, AAF Evaluation Board, SWPA (USAF Historical Research Center, Maxwell AFB, Alabama, hereafter cited as USAFHRC); Fighter Bombing and Strafing Report No. 16, AAF Evaluation Board, SWPA (USAFHRC); Luzon Campaign: Report No. 12, AAF Evaluation Board, SWPA, 2 vols. (USAFHRC); and The Occupation of Leyte: Report No.III, AAF Evaluation Board, Pacific Ocean Area (U.S. Navy History Division, Washington Navy Yard, cited hereafter as USNHD). Of much greater value is Col. Henry P. Dexter, Air Support in the Southwest Pacific Area—November 1, 1943 to February 1, 1944: Headquarters Army Ground Forces, April 10, 1944 (provided by U.S. Army Military History Institute, Carlisle Barracks, Pa.). Air Support of Pacific amphibious Operations: A Report for Naval Analysis Division, U.S. Strategic Bombing Survey (Pacific), prepared by Commander Air Support Control Units, Amphibious Forces, U.S. Pacific Fleet (Navy Department Library, Washington Navy Yard, hereafter cited as NDL) is probably the best single source of information on carrier-based air support of ground forces.

The numerous amphibious operations in the southern Philippines are especially well documented. Action Report on Balikpapan, Borneo, June 13–July 2, 1945: Commander Task Group 74.2, July 8, 1945, III (USAFHRC); Action Report of Tarakan Operation, May 1–3, 1945: Commander Amphibious Force 6, May 8, 1945 (USAFHRC); Report of Commanding General Eighth Army on the Leyte-Samar Operation (including clearance of the Visayan passages), December 26, 1944–May 8, 1945 (USAFHRC); Report of Commanding General Eighth Army on Palawan and Zamboanga Operations, May–July 1945 (USAFHRC); and Report of Amphibious Attack on Brunei Borneo, June 10–17, 1945: Commander Amphibious Group 6, June 19, 1945 (USAFHRC) give adequate attention to air support.

Unit histories vary greatly in quality. Too often the added burden of maintaining a record of a unit's activities, whether that unit was a squadron, a group, or a higher headquarters, was assigned to an already overworked clerk or conversely, to some individual who had already demonstrated a lack of capacity for any other work. When this is taken into consideration, it is amazing that so many unit histories are as good as they are. In general the histories of higher headquarters were better written and kept up to date more conscientiously, but it must be remembered that the higher the headquarters, the farther it was removed from actual operations. For this study History,

Fifth Air Force, June 1944–September 1945, 2 vols. (USAFHRC); History, Thirteenth Air Force, 1943–1945 (USAFHRC); History, 7th Air Support Communications Squadron, 1942–1945 (USAFHRC); History 308th Bombardment Wing, Fifth AF, 1943–1945 (USAFHRC); History, 309th Bombardment Wing, Fifth AF, 1943–1945 (USAFHRC) and History 310 Bombardment Wing, Fifth AF, 1943–1945 (USAFHRC) were especially valuable Air Force sources. For naval aspects of air support in the southwest Pacific, Administrative History, Commander, United States Naval Forces Southwest Pacific (NDL) and Command History, Seventh Amphibious Force, January 10, 1943–December 23, 1945 (USNHD) were equally useful.

Fortunately, interviews with a significant number of World War II leaders were recorded and transcribed. Unfortunately, very few of these had anything to do with close air support in the southwest Pacific. Interviews, General George C. Kenney, undated (USAFHRC), and August 10–21, 1974 (USAFHRC); and, An Evening with Admiral [H. D.] Felt, March 4, 1968 (USNHD) have some bearing on close air support. Interview with Major General A. A. Vandergrift, USMC, on Air Operations on Guadalcanal: Intelligence Service, AAF, February 3, 1943 (USAFHRC) and a group of wartime interviews with miscellaneous Fifth Air Force personnel, Fifth Air Force Interviews, 1942–1944 (USAFHRC) are valuable. It is a pity that more of the history of air support in World War II was not preserved in oral form.

Fifth and Thirteenth Air Force files and operations plans of various types, especially Correspondence and Messages, Fifth AF, September 1942–September 1945 [incomplete] (USAFHRC); General Consolidated Files, Fifth AF (USAFHRC); Letters from General Kenney to General Whitehead and other Top Officials, April 1944–September 1945 (USAFHRC); Operations Instructions and Annexes, 13th AF, 1944–1945 (USAFHRC); Operations Plans and Orders, 13th AF, 1942–1943 (USAFHRC); and Seventh Amphibious Force: Command Files, World War II (USNHD) have provided information.

Obviously, daily intelligence summaries, weekly intelligence reviews, chronologies, and similar sources such as Daily Intelligence Summary, ComAirSols, 1943–1944 (USAFHRC), Daily Intelligence Summaries, Thirteenth AF, 1944–1945 (USAFHRC); Chronology, Fifth AF, 1942–1944 (USAFHRC); and An Evaluation of Air Operations Affecting the U.S. Marine Corps During World War II; The Gen. Keith B. McCutcheon Papers (Marine Corps Historical Center, Washington Navy Yard, hereafter cited as MCHC) are not only valuable for what they reveal about this leader in Marine air support efforts, but they contain pertinent documents not easily found elsewhere. Above all, the Kenney Papers, 1941–1945 (currently located at the Office of Air Force History, Bolling AFB, Washington, D.C.) newly available, are a source of tremendous value. These papers were obviously the source for the general's memoirs, but they contain much not found in the memoirs, including significant correspondence; Kenney's comments, added in pencil, are often revealing in themselves.

The Air Force and the Marine Corps have been responsible for the production of a large number of monographs, many of these have some bearing, greater or lesser, on the role of close air support in the Southwest Pacific. *The Bougainville Operation, Prepared by the Historical Division, U.S. Marine Corps* (Washington: Headquarters U.S. Marine Corps, undated) is one such work. Among those produced by the Air Force are Thomas H. Greer, *The Development of Air Doctrine in the Army Air Arm, 1917–1954* (Maxwell AFB, AL: Research Studies Institute, Air University, 1955); Richard L. Watson, Jr., *The Fifth Air Force in the Huon Peninsula Campaign* (Washington: Headquarters Army Air Forces, 1946); Harris G. Warren, *The Fifth Air Force in the Conquest of the Bismarck Archipelago, November 1942 to March 1944* (Washington: AAF Historical Office, 1945); and Joe Gray Taylor, *Close Air Support in the War Against Japan* (Maxwell AFB, Ala.: Research Studies Institute, Air University, 1955).

Any list of service-sponsored books that shed light on close air support in the Southwest Pacific must begin with three volumes of Wesley Frank Craven and James Lea Cate, eds., *The Army Air Forces in World War II*, 7 vols. (Chicago: University of Chicago Press, 1948–1958 and reprinted by Office of Air Force History): Vol. I, *Plans and Early Operations, January 1939 to August 1942*; Vol. IV, *The Pacific: Guadalcanal to Saipan, August 1942 to July 1944*; and Vol. V, *The Pacific: Matterhorn to Nagasaki, June 1944 to August 1945*. This series, thirty and more years after publication, is still a monument to military historical scholarship.

Useful volumes of the official United States Army histories include John Miller, Jr.'s two volumes, *Guadalcanal: The First Offensive* [The United States Army in World War II: The War in the Pacific] (Washington: Office of the Chief of Military History, Department of the Army, 1949), and *Cartwheel: The Reduction of Rabaul* [The United States Army in World War II: The War in the Pacific] (Washington: Office of the Chief of Military History, Department of the Army, 1959). Samuel Milner wrote *Victory in Papua* [The United States Army in World War II: The War in the Pacific] (Washington: Office of the Chief of Military History, Department of the Army, 1957), and Hamlin Cannon produced *Leyte: The Return to the Philippines* [The United States Army in World War II: The War in the Pacific] (Washington: Office of the chief of Military History, Department of the Army, 1954). Robert Ross Smith described the campaign westward along the New Guinea coast in *The Approach to the Philippines* [The United States Army in World War II: The War in the Pacific] (Washington: Office of the Chief of Military History, Department of the Army, 1953), and he described the final victory in Luzon, the Visayans, and the southern islands in *Triumph in the Philippines* [The United States Army in World War II: The War in the Pacific] (Washington: Office of the Chief of Military History, Department of the Army, 1963).

Major Charles W. Boggs, Jr., of the Marine Corps prepared *Marine Aviation in the Philippines* (Washington: Historical Division, Headquarters United States Marine Corps, 1951). Of more recent vintage, applying to Korea and Viet Nam as well as to World War II, is Riley Sunderland's *Evolution of Command and Control Doctrine for Close Air Support* (Washington: Office of Air Force History, Headquarters United States Air Force, 1973).

The appropriate volumes for this study of Samuel Eliot Morison's *History of the United States Naval Actions in World War II*, 15 vols. (Boston: Little, Brown, and Company, 1947–1962) are Vol. V, *The Struggle for Guadalcanal, August 1942–February 1943*; Vol. VI, *Breaking the Bismarcks Barrier, July 11, 1942–May 1, 1944*; Vol. VIII, *New Guinea and the Marianas, March 1944–January 1945*; and Vol. XIII, *The Liberation of the Philippines: Luzon, Mindanao, the Visayans, 1944–1945*. From a literary point of view, this series is undoubtedly the best of the official histories of the war, and it is almost certainly more widely read than either the Army Air Force or the Army series. Unfortunately, these volumes seem to contain more evidence of service bias than the others. All of the official histories, written so soon after the close of the war, and in part during the period of extremely intense service rivalry, demonstrate some bias, but Admiral Morison admits some non-naval air accomplishments grudgingly, denies others, and makes some untenable accusations. Even so, one wishes that other official historians had been able to write even half as well as he did. Despite the flaws they may bear, these volumes are essential for anyone who wishes to understand the war in the Pacific.

Commercially published histories and memoirs are important sources for this study. John A. DeChant, *Devilbirds: The Story of the United States Marine Corps Aviation in World War II* (Washington: Senger Publishing Co., Inc., 1947); Frank O. Hough, *The Island War: The United States Marine Corps in the Pacific* (Philadelphia: J. P. Lippincott Company, 1947); and Robert Sherrod, *History of Marine Corps Aviation in World War II* (Washington: Combat Forces Press, 1952) are necessary for a study of the Marine Corps role. Maj. Gen. Claire Lee Chennault's *Way of a Fighter: The Memoirs of Claire Lee Chennault* (New York: G. P. Putnam's Sons, 1949); Lt. Gen. Robert L. Eichelberger's (in collaboration with Milton MacKaye) *Our Jungle Road to Tokyo* (New York: Viking Press, 1950); and Gen. Walter Krueger's *From Down Under to Nippon: The Story of Sixth Army in World War II* (Washington: Combat Press, 1953) are useful memoirs.

Jeter A. Isely and Phillip A. Crowl, *The U.S. Marines and Amphibious War: Its Theory and Practice in the Pacific* (Princeton: Princeton University

Press, 1951) is an aid to understanding that highly specialized form of warfare, and George Odgers, *Air War Against Japan, 1943–1945* (Canberra: Australian War Memorial, 1957) is the only convenient source on the operations of the Royal Australian Air Force in the Pacific War. Finally, Gen. George C. Kenney's *General Kenney Reports: A Personal History of the Pacific War* (New York: Duell, Sloan & Pearce, 1949) is the best single work on the air war in the Southwest Pacific. General Kenney was not exempt from the human tendency to remember what one wants to remember and to forget what one wants to forget, but for a memoir his work is remarkably free of bias. It is definitely better when dealing with the early years of Allied air operation in this theatre.

8

Korea, 1950–1953

Allan R. Millett

The images of air–ground battle in the Korean War remain in fact and cinematic fantasy: hard-pressed American troops battle hordes of Chinese across rice paddy and ridgeline, but just as the enemy prepares to mount a final rush, a flight of American jet fighter-bombers thunders in to scorch the Communists with cannon-fire and napalm, saving the beleaguered infantry. In fact, close air-support operations—one of many types of missions flown by the aviation units of United Nations Command (UNC)—did provide important fire support for UNC ground troops throughout the war. As North Korean and Chinese prisoners testified, the Communist field armies designed their operations to avoid UNC air strikes. Operating under an umbrella of air superiority established early in the war, UNC air operations deprived the Communists of free movement by day, forced them into a massive program of field engineering, denied them supplies for sustained offensives, and demoralized their troops. Three American air organizations mounted tactical offensive air operations for United Nations Command: the U.S. Air Force's Far East Air Forces (FEAF), principally the Fifth Air Force; the 1st Marine Air Wing; and the U.S. Navy's carrier air groups embarked on the carriers of the Seventh Fleet's Task Force 77. A limited number of South Korean and allied squadrons also flew sorties under the control of Fifth Air Force. These aviation forces, however, had different views on the relative contribution to ground operations of interdiction strikes and close air-support missions views that embodied substantial differences in doctrine, organization, training, equipment, and tactical techniques. The differences between the Air Force on one hand and the Navy and Marine Corps on the other produced a series of interservice disputes that sometimes obscured the overall contribution of UNC air operations to the conduct of the war. The only practical experts on the effectiveness of close air-support operations—the Communist ground forces—could hardly distinguish between interdiction and close air-support strikes. Data that UNC aviators and ground commanders collected for analysis produced limited and often ambiguous conclusions about the effectiveness of both interdiction and close air support. Although

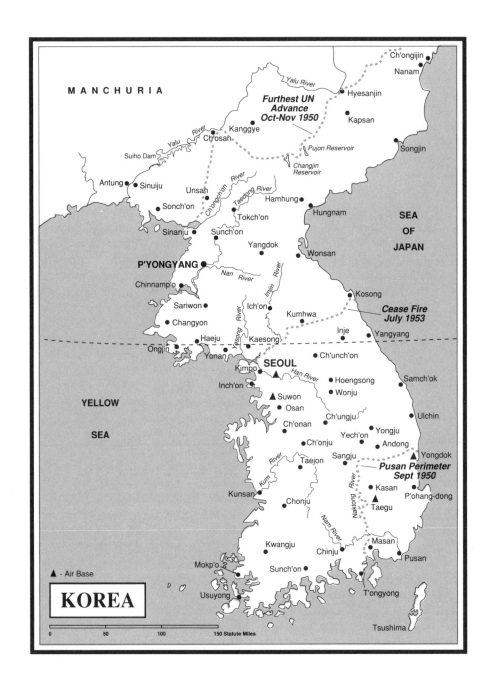

MANCHURIA

Yalu River

Ch'ongijin
Nanam

Furthest UN Advance Oct-Nov 1950

Hyesanjin

Kapsan

Yalu River

Kanggye

Ch'osan

Suiho Dam

Pujon Reservoir

Songjin

Changjin Reservoir

Antung

Sinuiju

Unsan

Sonch'on

Ch'ongch'on River

Taedong River

Hamhung

Hungnam

SEA OF JAPAN

Tokch'on

Sinanju

Sunch'on

Yangdok

Wonsan

P'YONGYANG

Nan River

Imjin River

Chinnamp'o

Kosong

Sariwon

Ich'on

Kumhwa

Cease Fire July 1953

Changyon

Yesong River

Inje

Yangyang

Haeju

Kaesong

Ongjin

Yonan

Ch'unch'on

Kimpo

SEOUL ▲

Han River

Hoengsong

Samch'ok

Inch'on

▲ Suwon

Wonju

YELLOW

Osan

SEA

Ch'ungju

Ulchin

Ch'onan

Yech'on

Yongju

Ch'onju

Andong

Yongdok ▲

Taejon

Sangju

Pusan Perimeter Sept 1950

River

Kum

Naktong River

Kasan

P'ohang-dong

Kunsan

Taegu ▲

Chonju

Nam River

Kwangju

Masan

Chinju

Pusan

Mokp'o

Sunch'on

T'ongyong

Usuyong

Tsushima

▲ - Air Base

KOREA

0   50   100   150 Statute Miles

346

tactical air operations gave United Nations Command an important advantage over its enemies, the value of close air support, as one element of those operations, remained controversial from the beginning to the end of the Korean War.[1]

Rooted in the experiences of World War II, principally in Allied operations in the Mediterranean and northern Europe, the Army Air Forces insisted that air war had become a distinct and potentially decisive type of combat. Although strategic bombardment provided the foundation of this belief and justified the creation of an independent Air Force in 1947, tactical air force commanders insisted that they, too, needed autonomy for their part of the air war, i.e., the destruction of enemy military forces by aviation attack. Tactical air commanders scored their most important doctrinal victory with the publication of FM 100–20, *The Command and Employment of Air Power* (July, 1943). Adopted without concurrence of Headquarters Army Ground Forces, the wartime Army's agency for the organization and training of ground combat forces, FM 100–20 established several important doctrines. First, "land power and air power are coequal and interdependent forces; neither is an auxiliary of the other."

In organizational terms this principle meant that the command of air forces must rest with an air commander who would take orders only from a theater commander. Moreover, FM 100–20 spelled out the kind of air warfare American air officers favored: strategic bombardment; air superiority operations, designed to end any major enemy offensive air threat; interdiction operations, which would destroy an enemy's units and supplies before they reached the ground battlefield; and close air support, air strikes against enemy units and positions on the battlefield itself. The latter task required detailed planning and control to avoid striking friendly troops, to reduce air losses to enemy ground fire, and to ensure that the air attacks hit the intended targets. For maximum effectiveness, close air-support missions required unprecedented integration with the operations of ground forces.

The Army provided doctrinal refinement for tactical aviation in FM 31–35, *Air-Ground Operations* (1946). Based primarily on procedures developed by the U.S. 12th Army Group and the Ninth Air Force in northern Europe 1944–1945, the new manual standardized air–ground operations. The theater air commander retained absolute authority over all tactical air forces, answerable only to the theater commander, but he would assign a tactical air command or air force to support each army group and army. The lowest echelon of decentralization in determining air mission priorities would be the tactical air force, whose commander would cooperate with his ground force counterpart, the army commander. These two would establish a Joint Operations Center (JOC), collocated with the army headquarters, to coordinate air–ground operations. Close air-support missions, therefore, required both air and ground approval before they were flown. The actual conduct of operations remained firmly in the hands of air officers.[2]

Although the JOC contained an army air–ground operations section, it was also an instrument of command for the tactical air force. Basically, the JOC processed tactical air requests and directed tactical air missions through two air force agencies, the Combat Operations Section and the Tactical Air Control Center (TACC). The tactical air request (TAR) system depended upon the ground officers assigned to the Air-Ground Operations System (AGOS), which reached down from ground army through each corps to each division headquarters. Within each tactical headquarters, the ground forces would provide an operations officer, G–3 (Air), who specialized in air-ground operations. Each headquarters also would include a G–2 (Air), who concentrated on employing aircraft for information collecting missions. Air Force liaison officers (ALOs) might be assigned to ground units to advise commanders, but it remained the responsibility of the ground commander to initiate air requests through his chain of command to the senior ground force headquarters. The army G–3 (Air) and G–2 (Air), who headed the air-ground operations section in the JOC, would decide which missions had the highest priority from the perspective of the army commander. Ground forces provided the communications system supporting the request network.

The conduct of air operations remained in the hands of the tactical air commander through the tactical air direction (TAD) system. Within the JOC, the senior air officer, the director of operations, decided which missions would be flown, guided by priorities established by his air force commander. Mission requirements passed from the combat operations section to the Tactical Air Control Center, the air force's command and control agency, to the airfields of the affected air units. At the air wing level the air commanders planned the missions with the assistance of a ground force liaison party, which maintained communications with army headquarters. This liaison party advised the air commander on the ground situation and the integration of the mission into ground forces operations.

The influence of the liaison party ended when the air mission began, for the aircraft flew under the direction of the TACC or a subordinate Tactical Air Direction Center (TADC) that might be collocated with a corps headquarters. The control of air attacks remained the responsibility of air force personnel. Air Force provided two different types of close control agencies: the ground forward air controller (FAC) of the Tactical Air Control Party (TACP) or an airborne Tactical Air Coordinator (TAC) flying in a light observation aircraft or a fighter-bomber. These agencies guided the attacking aircraft onto the target and away from friendly troops through combinations of voice communication, marking rockets, artillery smoke shells, and electronic signals. Officers who directed air strikes were pilots with prior experience in flying close-support sorties.[3]

When the Air Force became an independent service in 1947, the principles and procedures of FM 31–35 remained in effect because the Air Force retained the responsibility for providing tactical air support for the Army. The Tactical Air Command assumed the mission of developing the tactical air operations capability in the new Air Force. In February 1949, Headquarters Tactical Air Command suggested to Headquarters, Army Field Forces that they review FM 31–35 and establish a document to guide future joint training, especially for airborne and amphibious operations. Early in 1950 the two staffs agreed that FM 31–35 needed revision. Essentially, Tactical Air Command and Army Field Forces inherited a running argument that had divided the Air Staff and the Army General Staff for two years, for principal Army leaders like Generals J. Lawton Collins and Mark W. Clark had questioned the coequal status of ground and air commanders in determining tactical priorities.

The strong interest in this subject reflected in part the disheartening results of eight major joint tactical air exercises conducted in 1947–1950. The problem encountered in Operation Swarmer (April–May 1950) dramatized earlier defects in close-support operations. Although the Air Force concluded that jet fighter-bombers could deliver accurate strikes against ground targets, Air Force evaluators worried about fighter-bomber vulnerability to enemy interceptors, their limited time over the target, and their difficulties in identifying targets. The major defects, however, came from the performance of the air request and air control system. Although the Air Force and the Army created an Air–Ground Operations System and Joint Operations Center for all their exercises, neither service could man or equip the system. Headquarters Tactical Air Command had one control agency, the 502d Tactical Control Group, and Air Force inspectors rated it only thirty percent effective. The TACPs showed little skill or interest in their mission, and the Air Force's communications capability appeared good only in comparison with the Army's worst performance. Ironically, Air Force commanders appreciated their units' deficiencies far better than the Army's tactical commanders. Only Maj. Gen. Clovis C. Byers, Commander, 82d Airborne Division, questioned the small number of TACPs, the centralization of all mission-tasking in the JOC, and the long response time for sorties. When Tactical Air Command began its doctrinal review, it found greater interest in Congress than in much of the Army, whose senior commanders appear to have regarded close air support as a lost cause after the Air Force became a separate service.[4]

On June 25, 1950, galvanized by the actual outbreak of war in Korea, Tactical Air Command and Army Field Forces published their doctrinal effort in "Joint Training Directive for Air–Ground Operations" (September 1, 1950) (or JTD). Neither the Army Staff nor the Air Staff accepted the directive as service policy. Neither, however, prevented its application in the war zone despite residual worries in both services. The Air Force thought the guidance endangered its control of mission priorities, and the Army thought the directive failed to give ground commanders any real power over tactical air support. In fact, the Joint Training Directive did not modify the employment and organizational principles established in FM 31–35. The few changes were mere elaborations of established doctrine.

Clarifications in the Tactical Air Request (TAR) and Tactical Air Distribution (TAD) systems placed the burden on the Army to provide communications and staff for one lower echelon of close air-support coordination, since the *Joint Training Directive* now extended the Air–Ground Operations System down to the regimental and armored combat command level. It implied that in special cases even battalions might participate in the Air–Ground Operations System. TACPs and ALOs might also enter the air request system under special circumstances, e.g., in the absence of Army communications, especially in the early phases of an airborne operation. Nevertheless, the air request system, which included extensive, written air request messages, depended upon the Army. In the area of air direction the Joint Training Directive provided more detail. For the control of air strikes, Air Force added a third agency, the radar-equipped Tactical Air Direction Post (TADP). This new agency gave the Air Force a primitive attack capability even when FACs and TACs could not see their targets, for ground radars would then direct the strikes. No change occurred in the policy of assignment of Tactical Air Control Parties (TACP). Although the *JTD* recognized the TACPs might be attached down to the company level to perform air control missions, the division remained the lowest tactical formation that could assume permanent assignment of a TACP. In fact, the *JTD* implied that TACPs would probably be attached as a matter of policy only to lower echelon ground units that were engaged in either airborne or amphibious operations.[5]

Even if the Army had been more influential, it would not have altered the centralized system very much. Reflecting its own experience with coordinating artillery fire support in two European wars, the Army envisioned allowing little initiative below the field army and corps commanders' level. The corps commander had the basic task of working tactical aviation into his plans through his corps fire support coordination center (FSCC), which directed the corps' general support artillery, usually four to six battalions of heavy howitzers and self-propelled guns. Whether the corps G–3 (Air) and G–2 (Air) should operate as part of the FSCC had not been decided in 1950. Although FM 31–35 and the Joint Training Directive used language that allowed artillery and air to strike targets in front of friendly troops, the Army saw artillery as dominant within its range, and air power the principal weapon outside artillery range. In Korea, for example, the "bombline," the geographic limit upon air strikes not under positive close control, tended to coincide with the outer limits of the effective range of corps artillery. Since these limits were normally established by the height of masking mountains, the ranges were shorter than normal for heavy artillery. Nevertheless, the "bombline" normally followed terrain five to eight miles from the front lines. In sum, the Army did not expect integrated close air support, and the Air Force did not intend to deliver it except under carefully circumscribed conditions: clearly marked targets and readily identified friendly troop positions, positive observed direction from Air Force ground or air controllers, near absolute safety from friendly artillery fire, and employment only against targets that could not be attacked with heavy artillery.[6]

As Congressman Carl M. Vinson reminded Air Force officers in Washington, the Navy and the Marine Corps viewed close air support with greater enthusiasm, largely because of their experience in amphibious operations against Japan. In doctrinal terms, naval aviators viewed tactical air warfare in much the same way as did the Air Force. The critical aviation mission was air superiority, i.e., protecting the fleet and the landing force from enemy air operations. In the conduct of ground operations, however, naval aviators viewed interdiction and close air support as equally important, with the enemy's situation and the landing force commander's plan determining factors. Naval doctrine in 1950, published in PHIB 12/NAVMC 4159 "Amphibious Operations: Air Operations" (1948), defined close air support in much the same language as that in FM 31–35.

The Navy–Marine Corps system for both air requests and air direction stressed rapid response and decentralized management of close air-support sorties. After evaluating their wartime experience, principally on Luzon, Iwo Jima, and Okinawa, by centralizing requests and direction in the battalion-level Tactical Air Control Parties (TACP), Marine aviators and ground officers created a system that ensured that close air-support strikes would arrive within minutes. The TACP, composed of two Marine aviators and eight enlisted communicators, maintained a communications net that reached directly to the Tactical Air Control Center (TACC), whether it was afloat or ashore. In emergencies, intermediate air officers worked on the assumption that ground–air liaison at the battalion level had already determined that air was a better source of supporting fire than artillery or naval guns. Upon receiving the tactical air request, the TACC evaluated its available aircraft and competing air missions, but still assumed that the request should be filled as quickly as possible. A request for close air support turned into an order to provide sorties when the TACC contacted an airborne tactical air coordinator (TAC) or a flight of aircraft. The airborne coordinator, in turn, provided the initial link between the flight and the ground FAC of the TACP. All three elements of the air direction system (TAC, FAC, and strike aircraft) were linked by radio. The FAC with the friendly troops controlled the strikes, using the TAC or communicating directly with the flight leader. If the FAC could not see the target, however, he helped the TAC find it through voice direction or marking fires, and the TAC then controlled the strike.[7]

Air Force tactical air experts understood most of the differences between the doctrine established in FM 31–35 and the Joint Training Directive and the Navy–Marine Corps system. Navy–Marine Corps air request and air direction systems did not involve extensive participation of intervening headquarters. The central coordinator was the afloat amphibious task force Tactical Air Control Center or a landing force Tactical Air Direction Center, subordinate to the TACC for air defense but the principal agency for close air-support operations once the landing force had established command ashore. Air Force analysts knew that the naval system depended primarily on the ground FAC to control the actual strikes; the airborne TAC had only a secondary role in strike direction. They also appreciated that naval close air support had been developed for amphibious operations and that the relatively short distances between the landing force and the carriers or expeditionary airfields allowed the Navy and the Marine Corps to keep flights continuously on call in the air. The Air Force thought strip alert was far more economical and allowed pre- strike briefings on the ground. The Air Force, which had ample opportunity to analyze the Navy–Marine Corps system during the roles-and-missions controversies of the 1940s, argued that the naval system might be appropriate for the assault phase of amphibious operations, but that close air support should not substitute for heavy artillery.

As they indicated in their analysis of close air support in the opening months of the Korean War, Air Force officers did not understand some aspects of Navy–Marine Corps close air support. Marine Corps ground commanders did not command Marine aviation units as some Air Force officers thought. Navy and Marine aviation units assigned to an amphibious task force functioned under the direction of a single air officer. During the assault phase, this officer would be a Navy officer, but during extended operations ashore it would be a Marine aviator. Marine aircraft wings were not attached to Marine divisions. Either aircraft wing commanders and division commanders worked on a cooperative basis (as did Army field army commanders and Air Force tactical air commanders) or they functioned under a common superior, the amphibious task force commander or the landing force commander once ashore.

Naval aviation doctrine saw tactical air war in much the same way as did the Air Force: only centralized control under air officers ensured that aviation units performed the full range of tactical missions with maximum effectiveness. The significant difference came in the degree of influence a ground force commander could exercise in requesting and conducting close air-support strikes. The ground commander, however, did not have the authority to order Navy and Marine Corps aviation commanders to allocate more aircraft to close air-support missions. That authority remained with either the task force commander or the senior aviation commander.[8]

After World War II the Navy and Marine Corps, particularly the latter, nurtured their close air-support system in modest amphibious exercises. The Marine Corps had particular incentive to maintain its own system, as it feared it would lose its tactical air units to either the Navy or Air Force. Within the two existing Marine divisions, the signal battalion contained a specialized Air and Naval Gunfire Liaison Company (ANGLICO), which provided the personnel and equipment (but not the aviators) for the TACPs. In addition, other ANGLICO teams had been created in 1949 to support amphibious training with Army divisions on both coasts. Within the two half-strength Marine aircraft wings, each wing headquarters maintained a Marine Tactical Air Control Squadron that was responsible for providing aviators to the TACPs and establishing the Marine portion of the afloat Tactical Air Control Center (TACC) and the landing force Tactical Air Direction Center (TADC).

That Marine squadrons still flew the Chance–Vought F4U–4 Corsair, a prop-driven fighter-bomber that had proven its close air-support capability in World War II, was less important than the fact that the Navy and the Marine Corps had a quick-response close air-support system. By eliminating the requirement that intervening ground force headquarters process requests, and by placing aircraft on station on regular schedules, the naval system ensured that strikes arrived only a few minutes after the FAC made his request. The short response time—supplemented by air direction skill and strike accuracy—constituted effective close air support for Marines.[9]

Close Support in the Extemporized Air War, 1950

From the invasion of South Korea on June 25, 1950 until the end of the year, air operations over the embattled peninsula had all the characteristics of a classic American early war effort. Coordination between the services was minimal; roles and missions became indistinct and overlapping; the lack of preparedness for war ensured confusion, frustration, and inefficiency. Not until January, 1951 did United Nations Command (UNC) air operations show a mature degree of coordination. The first six months of the war also focused attention upon the differences in Air Force and Marine Corps close air-support operations and sparked a serious interservice controversy over which system worked best in Korea and might work best in a major war with the Soviet Union in Europe.

The verbal exchanges about close air support sometimes obscured some important facts about the Korean air war in 1950. First, the U.S. Far East Air Forces, the principal agent of United Nations Command (UNC) air operations, established air superiority over Korea early in the war. Under the umbrella of air superiority, Air Force planes flew some 41,500 interdiction and close air support sorties against the North Korean armed forces. Navy

Maj. Gen. Walton H. Walker, U.S. Eighth Army commander, decorating members of the Turkish Brigade for their valor in the fighting retreat from the Yalu River in late 1950.

and Marine Corps aircraft added another 13,000 sorties to the tactical air offensive. Although the effectiveness of UNC air operations eluded precise calculation, Lt. Gen. Walton H. Walker, Commanding General, U.S. Eighth Army, believed that tactical air support allowed UNC to remain on the peninsula and then march toward the Yalu. Senior officers of the North Korean People's Army (NKPA) who surrendered in 1950 agreed with General Walker. Tactical aviation provided the additional firepower that meant the difference between defeat and victory before the Chinese intervention.[10]

United Nations Command's air success in 1950 stemmed from the characteristics of the opposing air and ground forces. Although it enjoyed clear superiority over the minuscule South Korean Air Force, the North Korean Air Force numbered fewer than two hundred combat aircraft, all propeller-driven Russian planes of World War II vintage. Its pilots' expertise fell far below American standards. Against UNC fighter-bombers and fighter-interceptors, especially the Air Force's jet F–80C Shooting Star and the Navy's jet F9F Panther, the NKAF had little chance of winning the air battle.

The expanding UNC air order-of-battle in 1950 included the following major elements: the B–29s of FEAF Bomber Command (Provisional); B–26 light bombers; F–82 Twin Mustang all-weather fighters; and F–80, F–84, and F–51 fighter-bombers of the U.S. Fifth Air Force; the carrier air groups (each with 4 or 5 squadrons) assigned to the Seventh Fleet's Task Force 77 of 5 large carriers; and the F4Us of the 1st Marine Air Wing, which flew from either 2 escort carriers or land bases. Non-American air units, which flew only 5 percent of all sorties in 1950, provided a small fraction of UNC air assets: the carrier air group embarked on HMS *Triumph*, a Royal Navy carrier; 2 F–51 squadrons from the Royal Australian Air Force and South African Air Force attached to the Fifth Air Force, and 2 South Korean F–51 squadrons. With reinforcements from the United States, American offensive air assets in the Far East increased rapidly from 657 aircraft in July 1950 to more than 1,400 by February 1951. Airfield availability, carrier deployment schedules, and maintenance requirements, resulted in a lower figure for the number of operational aircraft at any particular time. Allied air units fielded superior aircraft and, except for their fields on the Korean peninsula, they flew from secure bases at sea or in Japan. Without overt Russian intervention, the NKAF lacked the capability to menace UNC air bases.

Moreover, the mechanized and motorized ten divisions of the North Korean army made excellent targets for air attack, especially during the day

---

Far East Command Aircraft Strength
(For Offensive Air Missions)

February, 1951

AIR FORCE		NAVY	
Fighter-Bombers:		**Fighter-Bombers:**	
F–51	187	F7F	24*
F–80	252	F9F	66
F–84	75	F4U	259
		AD	73
Air Superiority Fighters:			
F–86	75	**MARINE CORPS**	
Light Bombers:		**Fighter-Bombers:**	
B–26	139	F7F	24*
		F9F	24
Medium Bombers:		F4U	142
B–29	90	*Not carrier-capable	

Workhorses of close air support in Korea *(clockwise beginning below)*: Air Force B–26 Invader's guns being calibrated in night test; F–51 Mustang with 500-pound bombs and 5-inch rockets runs up for a night mission; pilot of Grumman F9F Panther catapults from deck of USS *Boxer*; F–80 Shooting Star with 165-gallon Misawa wing-tip tanks on take-off roll; and F–84 Thunderjets over rugged Korean coastline.

and while on the move. (In 1950 UNC pilots claimed to have destroyed or damaged more than one thousand tanks and more than ten thousand trucks and other vehicles.) Like other mobile armies, the North Korean Army depended on a steady flow of gasoline, ammunition, and supplies to the fighting front, and its logistical trail of truck convoys and trains provided tempting and relatively defenseless targets, for the North Koreans had not formed enough antiaircraft units to defend them.[11]

United Nations Command ground forces' weakness in field artillery, especially heavy artillery, forced UNC air units to concentrate on close air support. The 8 divisions of the ROK Army, organized principally for border patrol and counter-guerrilla operations, had only five 105–mm howitzer battalions of fewer than 100 serviceable guns; most of this artillery force went out of action early in the war. The 4 American infantry divisions in Japan lacked 9 organic 105–mm howitzer batteries, and General Walker estimated that the existing 39 batteries (some 200 guns) had only 60 percent of their personnel and could be rated only 40 percent combat effective. Although the U.S. Army provided the missing divisional artillery battalions by stripping its stateside units, it could not immediately meet Eighth Army's demands for corps heavy artillery. In July 1950, Eighth Army requested 15 battalions of 155–mm howitzers, 8–inch howitzers, and 155–mm self-propelled guns. The Army could provide only 5 heavy artillery battalions. Eighth Army soon increased its requirements by 9 more heavy artillery battalions, but not until 1951 did Eighth Army judge its heavy artillery strength barely adequate.[12]

Despite its relative wealth in air assets, United Nations Command had organizational problems that limited the 1950 tactical air war. At the pinnacle of command stood General of the Army Douglas MacArthur, American Theater and United Nations commander. However highly he regarded tactical aviation—which he did—General MacArthur continued his World War II practice of maintaining a theater staff that was joint and unified only in name, for his principal staff officers were all Army generals. The strongman of MacArthur's staff, Maj. Gen. Edward M. Almond, the FEC/UNC Chief-of-Staff, regarded himself an expert on tactical air.[13] Without any real air planning integration at the UNC level, the command of American aviation in the Far East followed service lines. Far East Air Forces (Lt. Gen. George E. Stratemeyer) controlled three air forces (the Fifth, Thirteenth, and Twentieth). Only the Fifth and Thirteenth Air Forces, however, had real close air-support capabilities, for Twentieth Air Force had a principal mission of strategic bombing. In reality, all three air forces previously had focused on their air defense and air superiority missions. When the Korean War began, the Japan-based Fifth Air Force (Maj. Gen. Earl E. Partridge) assumed major responsibility for offensive tactical air operations, drawing reinforcements from other FEAF forces and stateside commands.[14]

Naval forces in Japan fell under the command of Vice Adm. C. Turner

Joy, Commander Naval Forces Far East (COMNAVFE). Navy's land-based long-range patrol aircraft and the air group on *Valley Forge*, the one attack carrier assigned to the U.S. Seventh Fleet (Vice Adm. Arthur D. Struble), did not belong to COMNAVFE. The Seventh Fleet did not come under MacArthur's operational control until after the war began, and the other carriers in the Pacific belonged to the Commander, U.S. Pacific Fleet (CINCPACFLT) until he assigned them to the Seventh Fleet. CINCPACFLT in June, 1950 was Adm. Arthur W. Radford, an ardent champion of naval aviation. Although assigned to Adm. Radford as part of the Fleet Marine Force Pacific, the 1st Marine Air Wing remained in strategic reserve at its bases in California.

The prospect of three services conducting air operations in Korea alarmed General Stratemeyer, who pressed Maj. Gen. Edward M. Almond to persuade MacArthur to designate the FEAF Commander as the operational commander of the air war. A number of events brought the first effort to integrate tactical air operations. On July 3–4, acting on hurried orders from Far East Command (FEC) Headquarters, *Valley Forge* launched an air strike on NKAF airfields and the North Korean transportation system near Pyongyang. Learning of the carrier air strike, FEAF canceled its own bomber attack on the same targets. On the same day, MacArthur requested that the Joint Chiefs of Staff send FEC a Marine brigade with an attached air group for an amphibious landing, a request approved the next day. Stratemeyer correctly predicted that aerial confusion would soon reign over the peninsula. On July 8 he persuaded MacArthur to issue an order that the FEAF Commander would be the theater air commander. Only MacArthur, however, could define missions for the Seventh Fleet, which meant that Stratemeyer did not have operational control of the carrier air of TF 77.

Unhappy with the remaining ambiguity of the July 8 order, Admiral Joy pressed for a more precise definition of responsibility since he and Admiral Arthur D. Struble also had missions that might take TF 77 out of the war zone. The interservice compromise, finished on July 15 to no one's complete satisfaction, gave FEAF operational control of all land-based aviation in the theater but limited Stratemeyer to "coordination control" of carrier aviation in the war zone. Although the amplification gave the FEAF Commander operational control of any Marine aviation that came ashore, it also meant that Stratemeyer could only veto proposed carrier strikes—if he knew about them. Such knowledge was tenuous. Task Force 77 normally maintained radio silence at sea, and the incompatibility of Navy and Air Force communications procedures and encryption meant that FEAF would learn TF 77's plans only if FEC and U.S. Navy, Far East (NAVFE) chose to inform it. "Coordination control," in fact, was a relationship that did not exist in the lexicon of joint operations.[15]

Although MacArthur remained aloof from the details of close-support operations, General Almond wanted a system that duplicated the one he had

General of the Army Douglas MacArthur with his eventual successor as Commander-in-Chief, United Nations Command, Lt. Gen. Matthew B. Ridgway.

Maj. Gen. Earle Partridge

used as a division commander in Italy during World War II. Almond's expectations closely paralleled the existing doctrine for making air requests and directing strikes, but his preferred system placed special emphasis on two matters that did not match Fifth Air Force's view of its responsibilities. First, Almond had faith in the efficiency of ground-based FACs in locating targets. Although he recognized the utility of airborne controllers, he regarded the ground FAC as essential in ensuring that bombs hit the enemy and not friendly troops. Almond also believed that the Air Force should dispatch fighter-bomber flights to engaged front-line regiments on a regular schedule rather than wait for missions on ground alert; he doubted that air strikes required detailed presortie briefings if the air direction system worked well. Basing his expectations on the mature air support system operating in the closing campaigns of World War II, Almond did not fully appreciate all the difficulties FEAF faced in providing timely and effective close air support in Korea.[16]

Although its fighter-bombers and light bombers (B–26s) carried the burden of the close air-support role in the first two months of the Korean War, Fifth Air force experienced more defects in readiness and effectiveness than did Navy and Marine Corps tactical aviation. The major difficulty stemmed from Fifth Air Force's air defense role; its pilots were not trained for ground

361

attack missions, and their principal aircraft, the Lockheed F–80C Shooting Star, had limitations as a fighter-bomber. Its high airspeed and fuel consumption at low altitudes meant that the F–80C, carrying a normal load of .50–cal ammunition and a mix of bombs and rockets, could not loiter long over the Korean peninsula. Its on-station time was only around 30 minutes. Moreover, the Shooting Star could not be safely deployed to primitive strips in Korea, since it depended on well-constructed fields and a developed base system. Fifth Air Force extended the F–80C's range and loiter time with wing tanks, but the added fuel load reduced the allowable ordnance. The Shooting Star also entered the war with limited ordnance capacity. Without wing pylons, it could carry only 5–inch, high velocity aerial rockets and 100– or 260–pound bombs on its rocket rails. Only after it had pylons installed could the F–80C carry napalm tanks and 500– and 1,000–pound bombs. The effects of napalm, so heartening to American troops, proved critical in Eighth Army's insistence that the Fifth Air Force use other types of fighter-bombers capable of delivering it.

Primarily to use Korean strips and to improve their ordnance-carrying capability, Fifth Air Force fighter-bomber squadrons switched aircraft in the summer of 1950, a difficult adaptation in the heat of battle. Drawing aircraft from storage in Japan and the United States, Fifth Air Force replaced the

Vice Adm. Arthur D. Struble, commander, U.S. Seventh Fleet.

F–80Cs of six squadrons with the propeller-driven North American F–51 Mustang, the all-around workhorse of World War II. The change, which affected all but one of Fifth Air Force's F–80 groups, could have been made only on the assumption that the United States would continue to hold air superiority. When the transition to the F–51 ended, Fifth Air Force had eight squadrons (including two Commonwealth squadrons) of what appeared to be the optimal fighter-bomber for the Korean War. Familiar with the Mustang's performance in World War II, Army officers and war correspondents praised the F–51's introduction to close air-support operations.

Fifth Air Force learned that the Mustang was a mixed blessing and that a jet fighter-bomber, whether a modified F–80C or the more capable F–84E, had substantial advantages over the Mustang. With bomb pylons and wing tanks, the jets closed the gaps in ordnance load and on-station time. In other critical ways they demonstrated their superior capability. The jets proved they could provide twice the sorties of the F–51 per day, with only about half the maintenance time. Jets had a higher operational readiness rate and better parts availability. In combat, the jet's speed reduced its vulnerability to ground fire. In 1950, Fifth Air Force Mustang losses to enemy action in relation to sorties flown were more than twice those of jets. The jets also enjoyed superior radio communications, since they carried the eight-channel VHF AN/ARC–3 and the Mustang had space for only the four-channel VHF SCR 522.[17] Additionally, the Mustang's liquid-cooled engine was particularly vulnerable to ground fire.

The Air Force close air-support effort in the summer of 1950 benefited from the Fifth Air Force's two B–26 squadrons (increased to four by the end of the year) and the five B–29 groups (five operational squadrons), which were rotated in and out of FEAF's Bomber Command (provisional). Understandably, the Air Force preferred to use its bombers for interdiction missions or strikes on Communist transportation installations and military bases. After mid-July B–29s bombed targets near the battlefield only on exceptional occasions, and, learning from a mixed experiment of "carpet bombing" near Waegwan on August 16, the B–29s focused on targets well north of the bombline. The B–26 squadrons flew a larger percentage of close air-support missions than the B–29s, but their relative superiority in night operations and interdiction attacks meant that the fighter-bombers became the principal instrument for close support.[18]

Whatever the operational characteristics of the aircraft that FEAF could throw into the Korean war, effectiveness of close air support depended upon the Eighth Army–Fifth Air Force organization to request and direct ground attack sorties. Both the TAR and TAD systems proved defective, and neither Eighth Army nor Fifth Air Force were prepared for air–ground operations. In the first week of the war, Fifth Air Force sent an extemporized, undermanned, and ill-equipped Joint Operations Center to the peninsula. This exhausted Fifth Air Force's immediate resources.

When the war began, FEAF communications units had only sixty-five percent of their peacetime strength, and their enlisted personnel had even lower levels of skill qualification. From its own internal assets Fifth Air Force created a rump tactical air direction system during the first week of July; its JOC (virtually unmanned on the Army side) established its headquarters with the 24th Infantry Division on July 5. The tactical situation was so chaotic that the Fifth Air Force forward headquarters, headed by Brig. Gen. Edward J. Timberlake, Jr., set up an air direction system and used it as an ad hoc air request system that did not depend upon Army staffs and communication units. Fifth Air Force created a close air-support coordination system that helped save Eighth Army, but it could hardly be called "joint."

General Timberlake's forward headquarters, which created the JOC and TACC (Angelo), put three TACPs in the field with the 24th Infantry Division and ROK I Corps and built this force to ten during July, 1950. Eager to direct air strikes, the TACPs found themselves battered by Communist fire and naked of infantry protection. Portions of two parties died in action, and almost all of the radio jeeps succumbed to enemy fire and rough terrain. The TACPs' man-packed TRC–7 radios proved unreliable. After July 14 the TACPs, by order, did not take positions forward of infantry regimental headquarters, which meant that the FACs served only as air liaison officers, forwarding requests for air strikes back to Angelo. The burden of actually directing air strikes against visible enemy targets shifted to Fifth Air Force's emergency squadron of airborne tactical air coordinators (TACs), who entered the war on July 10. By the end of the month air direction depended almost solely on the 6147th Tactical Control Squadron (Airborne), commanded by Maj. Merrill H. Carlton.[19]

The airborne TACs began the war flying light observation planes ill-equipped for front-line duties, but the 6147th TCS soon switched to the Air Force's 2–place trainer, the North American T–6 Texan. It had limited ground observation but could carry radio equipment that could both handle requests from the ground as well as from direct fighter-bombers. The common link between the TACPs, the T–6, and the fighter-bombers was the 8–channel ARC–3 radio; communications with Army units depended upon the less reliable SCR–300. Communications limitations affected the entire TAR/TAD system. Since strikes within the bombline required positive links between a ground controller—or at least some Army communicator who could identify the American lines—and the TAC, the Air Force preferred to direct strikes at targets well forward of friendly troops. In practice, the T–6 teams, an Air Force pilot and Army air observer, acquired their own targets by visual reconnaissance, radioed the TACC for a strike, and then directed

**Boeing B-29 Superfortresses were used only
briefly in close air-support missions.**

the ground attack without any coordination with friendly artillery and infantry action. Known by their radio call sign, Mosquito, the airborne TACs flew
269 sorties in July, then more than 1,000 sorties a month for the rest of 1950.
By the end of the year, Mosquitoes had directed 90 percent of Air Force close
air-support sorties at a cost of 18 personnel killed or missing and 24 aircraft
lost to ground fire or accidental crashes. The 6147th TCS losses were trivial
compared with the damage it helped inflict on the Communists around the
Pusan perimeter.[20]

Fifth Air Force's emergency system might have satisfied ground commanders if Navy and Marine Corps fighter-bombers had not entered the battle, the Navy in July and the Marines in August. Acutely aware that air
attacks gave it a critical advantage over the Communists, particularly during
the day, Eighth Army called for a maximum air effort. Its calls for help
included a request for carrier air strikes by Corsairs and Douglas AD

Mosquito Attrition Rate

	Aircraft Lost in Action	Fatalities	Sorties per Aircraft Lost	Hours per Aircraft Lost
July	2	0	134.50	335.17
August	5	4	206.40	555.42
September	3	6	471.33	1275.58
October	4	2	289.25	876.15
November	4	4	329.25	943.42
December	2	0	608.00	1612.67
Total	20	16		
Average			320.25	888.89

Source: Farmer/Strumwesser, *Evolution of the Airborne Forward Air Controller*, p. 65.

Skyraiders, both of which carried heavier loads and had longer on-station time than the Japan-based F–80C. Sometimes the JOC did not know the Navy strikes were on the way, and the very level of Navy effort, which could reach two full squadrons from a single carrier launch, overwhelmed the Mosquito system. When the overabundance of aircraft confused the individual TACs, they chose to direct the jets and F–51s to the target first and put the Navy fighter-bombers into high orbit.

Often the mission was accomplished with the Air Force strikes, which meant that Navy aircraft had to switch to targets of opportunity or jettison their ordnance before returning to their carriers. The frustration of TF 77's pilots boiled up through channels to COMNAVFE, whose staff criticized the Air Force system. The conflict inevitably spread from interservice staff conferences on coordination into newspapers in Japan and the United States. Stratemeyer soon countered with personal briefings and letters to sympathetic reporters. He demanded that MacArthur order the Navy to coordinate its air effort through the JOC. Stratemeyer also told Gen. Earl E. Partridge to move Fifth Air Force units onto the peninsula, to reinforce the Air Force communications system and the 6147th TCS, and to press Walker to create the Army air request system dictated by FM 31–35 and the JTD.[21]

In August 1950, the air and ground Marines of the 1st Brigade (Provisional) moved into the Pusan perimeter defense and introduced their own close air-support system. Already overwhelmed with communications problems, the JOC exercised only nominal control over Marine air, accepting the Marines' argument (supported by Walker) that Marine air should primarily support the brigade's ground element, the 5th Marines (Reinforced), a regimental combat team of three infantry battalions and one of artillery. The brigade's air group, MAG–33, committed three Corsair squadrons to the air war. One squadron of radar-equipped night fighters (VMF(N)–513) operated from Japan under Fifth Air Force control, but the other two entered the fray embarked on two escort carriers, the *Sicily* and *Badoeng Strait*. These squadrons could reach the brigade's front in minutes and remain on-station for as much as four hours, which meant that they were available for on-call missions in a matter of ten rather than thirty or more minutes. Furthermore, the Marine pilots, seventy percent of whom were World War II veterans, averaged about one thousand three hundred hours of flight time and had extensive close air-support training. More importantly, the Marines had a ground FAC with each infantry battalion, a TACC alongside the brigade fire support coordination center (FSCC), an aviation general serving as brigade deputy commander, and jeep and man-portable radio systems superior to those of the Air Force.

The result was a four-week virtuoso performance in close air support that impressed the U.S. 25th Infantry Division and the 5th Regimental Combat Team deployed with the Marines along the critical Naktong River line. Marine air strikes arrived quickly and devastated NKPA defensive complexes, mobile formations, and artillery positions. More than half of the Marine sorties came against targets only half a mile from the frontlines. It was the kind of close air support Marines expected, but it came as a revelation to the Army officers who shared the experience.[22]

Originally designed as trainers, North American T-6 Texans flew as tactical air control aircraft throughout the Korean war.

Irritated by the press praise of Marine support, Stratemeyer concluded that the Navy and Marine Corps wanted both to kill North Koreans and to challenge the Air Force doctrine for close air support. Stratemeyer knew the Air Force's war management required help, a view shared by Gen. Hoyt S. Vandenberg, Chief of Staff of the Air Force.

Early in the war, Maj. Gen. Otto P. Weyland, who had commanded XIX Tactical Air Command in Europe in World War II, came to Tokyo to assume the new position of Vice Chief (Operations), FEAF. As his deputy, General Weyland brought Col. James E. Ferguson, another tactical air veteran, who dominated the working level interservice committees at FEC headquarters. At Fifth Air Force Partridge received similar assistance from newly arrived Col. Gilbert L. Meyers, who became Fifth Air Force Deputy Commander (Operations), which meant that he ran the JOC. Weyland, Colonel Ferguson, and Colonel Meyers turned to the task of organizing a doctrinally correct and operationally effective Air Force close air-support system. In October 1950, they received an important reinforcement, the 502d Tactical Control Group, the only unit of its type in the Air Force.

With his JOC (at least its Air Force component) reaching full efficiency, Meyers strengthened the air direction system by reinforcing the 6147th TCS and giving the 502d TCG control of the ground TACPs. Another reform affected the missions of Army liaison aircraft, whose normal reconnaissance and artillery spotting duties had broadened into requesting and directing air strikes. Too many spotters spoiled the sorties. One Army L–19 and a fighter-bomber had a mid-air collision, and others narrowly missed colliding.

Even more seriously, Army light aircraft placed additional strain on airborne communications. Meyers persuaded Eighth Army to issue restrictive orders on the use of Army light aircraft, which meant no more air directed strikes. He also convinced the Army to allow T–6s to range deeper in search of targets, a plan that reduced congestion around the bombline. Although JOC/TACC efficiency did not satisfy him and he still raged at the communications equipment failures and shortages, by November 1950, Meyers began to feel that Fifth Air Force could run the tactical air war without apology.

At the FEAF level, Weyland and Ferguson shared his confidence and tackled the issue of Air Force–Navy air coordination. By November FEAF and TF 77 had a set of agreements that improved the communications links between FEAF, the Fifth Air Force JOC, and the carriers. Task Force 77 agreed to run an average of eighty sorties a day for support operations when the carriers were on station and to use the JOC–Mosquito system. The Air Force agreed to follow doctrine on joint operations, which gave a Navy task force commander control of all air operations within an amphibious operations area, and to assign naval aviation to a specific part of the front. Stratemeyer also thought that he and Admiral Joy had made a truce in the interservice publicity war.[23]

Air Force Chief of Staff General Hoyt S. Vandenberg *(left)* **is greeted by Lt. Gen. George E. Stratemeyer, commander of Far East Air Forces, as Vandenberg visited the theater in January 1951.**

Victory reduced the interservice recrimination. Executing MacArthur's grand vision of an amphibious turning movement against the NKPA, the Navy's Joint Task Force 7 landed the X Corps, spearheaded by the 1st Marine Division, at Inchon on September 15. As X Corps (General Almond) drove toward Seoul, the NKPA divisions around the Pusan perimeter fell back before the Eighth Army. After two days of hard fighting, the Pusan breakout became a rout with Fifth Air Force fighter-bombers hammering at the retreating North Koreans. Profiting from the enemy's confusion, a better understanding of close-support tactics, ordnance effectiveness, and the growing competence of the Mosquitos, the Air Force devastated Communist forces behind the front.

Even the war's worst incident of air strikes on friendly troops did not poison the "era of good feeling." On September 22 a flight of Mustangs bombed and strafed the 1st Battalion, Argyll and Sutherland Highlanders, British 27th Brigade. Attacking during the Mustangs' errant strike, the North Koreans drove the Highlanders from their hill; enemy action and the accidental air strikes killed and wounded seventy-six Scots. Although the F–51s had obtained directions from both a FAC and a Mosquito, they had struck the wrong position. Fortunately, British high commanders in the Far East regarded the mistake as merely regrettable. Stratemeyer and Partridge appreciated the interallied understanding, doubting that the American press would have been so kind had it known that the ground FAC had directed a strike seven miles from his position. They welcomed instead the news that the G–3

(Air) of Eighth Army believed Fifth Air Force's claims for NKPA losses were probably too modest.[24]

As the Fifth Air Force–Eighth Army close air-support system matured during the drive back to the 38th Parallel, carrier air and Marine Corsairs demonstrated the effectiveness of their system in the campaign for Seoul. Task-organized for amphibious operations, X Corps enjoyed an abundance of aircraft and control agencies. Admiral Struble's TACC ran the air effort until the 1st MAW could establish Marine Tactical Air Control Squadron–2 ashore at Kimpo airfield. The 1st Marine Division deployed twenty TACPs, which meant that each infantry battalion had at least one front line FAC. The U.S. 7th Infantry Division used nine TACPs, furnished by both Fifth Air Force and the Marines, and the X Corps commanders could plan air strikes with confidence and call in orbiting Corsairs whenever an emergency arose.

Already a convert to Marine Corps practices with ground FACs and on-station aircraft, Almond ended the Inchon–Seoul campaign as a vocal and unrestrained champion of Marine close air support. As MacArthur's protege and an independent corps-size landing force commander for future amphibious operations, Almond felt no restraints in criticizing the Fifth Air Force system and freely shared his views with the reporters who followed his headquarters. He also did not press 1st MAW to coordinate its efforts with the JOC. In practice the 1st MAW functioned as a tactical air command for X Corps. So close was air-ground integration in X Corps that Air Force commanders mistakenly believed the 1st MAW was commanded by Maj. Gen. Oliver P. Smith, 1st Marine Division Commander, although he and Maj. Gen. Field Harris, Commanding General, 1st Marine Air Wing, had coequal status and shared a common task force commander, General Almond. Even though the Fifth Air Force JOC system had undeniably improved by October 1950, X Corps wanted none of it, and even the Eighth Army corps and division commanders now expected even more destructive results from the Air Force's fighter-bombers.[25]

President Truman's October decision to reunify Korea brought a major redeployment of MacArthur's forces. The continuation of the exploitation campaign into North Korea perpetuated the schism between the Fifth Air Force–Eighth Army close air-support system and the X Corps system, for MacArthur ordered JTF 7 to make another landing at Wonsan on the peninsula's eastern coast. With the prospect of another amphibious operation, Stratemeyer and Partridge did not press Almond to improve his relations with the JOC. Geographic separation and the lack of communications made the continued division a realistic decision. As he deployed X Corps north from Wonsan—with ROK I Corps under his operational control—Almond requested that Fifth Air Force send him thirty-six TACPs, a plan that would have provided every infantry battalion under his control with a TACP.

Stratemeyer pleaded TACP poverty, but sent four TACPs for the ROK

I Corps. Partridge then visited Almond and held a tutorial for him and his chief-of-staff on the *JTD*. Almond remained unmoved on the superiority of the Marine Corps system. The Air Force generals, still embarrassed by the undermanned and poorly equipped Air Force TACPs assigned to X Corps, did not press the issue.

The "Home by Christmas" campaign surged toward the Yalu River with a euphoria so excessive that MacArthur, Walker, and Almond did not blanch when Chinese divisions suddenly appeared on the battlefield at Unsan and Majon-ni, dealt painful blows to units of the 1st Cavalry Division and the 1st Marine Division, and disappeared in early November. In the meantime, Stratemeyer had a political battle on his hands, not just with Almond, but with a coalition of critics who charged that the Air Force had not provided adequate air support for the Army.[26]

Reacting to recommendations and analysis prepared by General Almond and General Clark, Chief of Army Field Forces, In November 1950, Army Chief of Staff General Collins filed a formal criticism of close air-support operations with Air Force Chief of Staff Hoyt Vandenberg. Although the Army had no desire to create another tactical air force, Collins thought that the current system of "cooperation" and the Air Force's apparent lack of interest in ground attack missions had created an unsatisfactory situation. He proposed that a revision of air-ground doctrine provide field army commanders and their corps subordinates operational control of fighter-bombers on a scale of one air group per division. He also insisted that the Air Force enlarge the number of TACPs it provided to tactical units.

Vandenberg responded that the Air Force would not neglect the close air-support mission, but that the issue needed additional study, both by a joint board established by the Joint Chiefs of Staff and by the principal Army and Air Force commands in the Far East. In any event, the Army had now raised the question of close air-support reform at the highest interservice levels, and Collins intended to press the issue.[27]

As the immediate crisis of saving South Korea ebbed, the Air Force, directed by Secretary of the Air Force Thomas K. Finletter and General Vandenberg, reintroduced its plan to create a ninety-five group (wing) force, and it did not relish a doctrinal dispute that might derail its plans in Congress. Aware that Congressman Vinson, a Navy–Marine champion and the House Armed Services Committee Chairman, still favored giving ground force commanders more direct control of tactical aviation, Finletter and Vandenberg pressed Stratemeyer to give them good news on air operations in Korea. They then dispatched a high-level study group to Japan led by Maj. Gen. Glenn O. Barcus, a tactical air expert. Eager to blunt criticism of organizational partisanship, Finletter and Vandenberg recruited Dr. Robert L. Stearns, President of the University of Colorado, to assume the study's chairmanship. They also recruited support from the Department of the Army, which sent Brig. Gen. Gerald J. Higgins, the director of the Army Air Support Center, to Korea to conduct its own investigation.

From inquiries during November and December, the Stearns-Barcus group and Higgins concluded that doctrine in FM 31–35 and the JTD was sound. The basic problem was that the Air Force and the Army had not yet provided the trained staffs, control agencies, and communications systems necessary to make the doctrine work. The two studies identified much that could be done to improve the JTD system: better radio equipment and more vehicles for the TACPs; better training and longer duty tours for FACs; better radios and aircraft for the 6147th TCS(A); a serious effort by the Army to provide the people and equipment to fill the AGOS; improved training for Army commanders in close air-support operations; improved ordnance and training for fighter-bomber squadrons; increased attention to the use of radar to guide tactical air support strikes; and additional staffing of the JOC.

In all particulars that differentiated the Air Force and Marine Corps systems, the investigators favored the Air Force position. For example, jet aircraft could provide accurate air strikes (a position, in fact, acknowledged by Marine aviators): air alert aircraft were uneconomical; ground commanders did not need operational control of a set quota of close air-support sorties. The demands of X Corps for TACPs appeared excessive; in December 1950, the three-division X Corps had thirty-seven TACPs, the five-division Eighth Army only twenty. The study groups could not envision an Air Force that could provide the number of either close-support aircraft or TACPs corresponding to the number per unit serving the Marines, for an Army large enough to fight the Russians in Europe. In sum, the close air-support doctrine required only more aggressive implementation.[28]

As the Korean winter deepened and snow piled up, study groups came and went, but the People's Liberation Army (PLA) came and stayed. In late November, Chinese divisions fell upon the overextended Eighth Army and X Corps, and in an uncommon understatement, MacArthur reported that his command faced a new war. Despite MacArthur's buoyant promise that air power would crush the Chinese armies at the Yalu (an assessment Stratemeyer and Partridge did not share), the PLA employed its proficiency in night operations, its skill with machineguns and mortars, and its profligate use of infantry, to send UNC backward toward the 38th Parallel. Air Force, Navy, and Marine pilots proved what MacArthur and Walker had told the Stearns-Barcus group: tactical air power provided a critical margin of combat power to the American ground forces. In the crisis of December 1950, Fifth Air Force did its best to cover the Eighth Army's withdrawal, but without a sturdy ground control system, the 2d and 25th U.S. Divisions could not coordinate their retrograde with air strikes. The 2d Division particularly suffered in running a Chinese gauntlet of roadblocks south to Sunchon. The 1st Marine Division, on the other hand, withdrew intact from the Chosin Reservoir and destroyed seven Chinese divisions during its own anabasis. This epic "attack in a different direction" tested the Marine close air-support system and found it fully justified in the most demanding of extended ground operations. The December campaign simply reinforced the conviction in X Corps from General Almond to the lowliest rifleman that the Marine system surpassed the Air Force system in every way. If the Chinese intervention had dampened Eighth Army's satisfaction with Fifth Air Force, it sent X Corps' expectations for close air support soaring.[29]

The crisis provided Stratemeyer and Partridge with the opportunity to integrate the 1st Marine Air Wing into the JOC system; for the redeployment of the X Corps to South Korea ended its existence as an independent command. On December 11, 1950, Stratemeyer, citing the July 8 agreement on operational control, announced that 1st MAW would henceforth support the entire United Nations army. Aware that 1st MAW could not operate from Korean land bases without extensive Fifth Air Force logistical support, Stratemeyer did not expect much opposition from General Harris on the new arrangement, and indeed he received none. General Smith protested the change, but he found that Lt. Gen. Matthew B. Ridgway, who had assumed command of the Eighth Army upon Walker's death in a jeep accident, had limited taste for a battle with the Air Force. MacArthur approved the new arrangement by default. Almond did not like the change, but he found himself isolated among UNC's senior commanders. A new era in Korean War close air support dawned with the arrival of 1951.[30]

Close Air Support

The Chinese intervention sent shock waves through United Nations Command that spread quickly to Washington and brought fundamental changes in American policy in the Far East, reshaping UNC operations, as well as the air war. As Eighth Army arose a chilled phoenix from the ashes of its defeat above the 38th Parallel, the Truman administration decided to stay with the war, but to revert to its original war aim: the restoration of the Republic of South Korea along its prewar border. The implications of this change were many. Hoping to avoid a higher level of involvement with both China and Russia, the government limited the war—including air operations—to the Korean peninsula. Since the Chinese Air Force had massed its air interceptor force of MiG–15s at bases just north of the Yalu, this limitation proved especially onerous to Far East Air Forces. It could not assure air superiority unless it eliminated the MiG–15 threat. Another major implication of the changed policy also increased the demands of other air missions. The JCS told MacArthur that he would not receive any more American divisions. Any increase in UNC combat power would have to come from other sources:

stepped-up air attacks, improved combat effectiveness from the deployed American divisions, the introduction of other UN troops, the enlargement and reform of the ROK Army, and the increased use of heavy artillery at the corps level. Tactical aviation clearly remained a major source of UNC's fighting strength, but Far East Air Forces, too, would not receive major additions to its force structure.[31]

Generals Stratemeyer and Partridge agreed with General Weyland, FEAF Vice Commander for Operations, that the time had arrived to change UNC air employment. In early 1951 FEAF Bomber Command and Fifth Air Force, reinforced with air strikes from TF 77, began a systematic attack upon the Communists' supply line throughout Korea. Between January and June 1951, FEAF aircraft flew 54,410 interdiction sorties and 22,800 close air-support sorties. Though the UNC air effort was not inflexible, the change became inexorable, especially after General Weyland became Commander of FEAF in June. (Stratemeyer, who had suffered a heart attack, and Partridge had both returned to the United States.) On the day he assumed command Weyland wrote Vandenberg that Korea offered the Air Force an unparalleled opportunity to show how tactical air power could win a conventional war. The Air Force, therefore, should "fully exploit its first real opportunity to prove the efficacy of air power in more than a supporting role. . . ." The Korean War experience might provide positive guidance for the USAF force structure and help formulate concepts for the defense of Western Europe, but that experience should come in a massive commitment to interdiction, not to close air support.[32]

As FEAF was to learn, the Communist logistics system and field forces could be difficult to destroy. Night, poor weather, and the mountainous terrain gave the Communists ample opportunity to seek concealment and cover from air attacks. After its fearful experiences with American air in 1950, the Chinese proved adept at hiding in caves and tunnels, in using natural and man-made camouflage, and in digging deep defensive positions for their infantry and crew-served weapons. Russian-style mechanized formations and massed artillery positions virtually disappeared from the battlefield in 1951. Major Chinese assaults occurred almost always at night. Even though they would accept casualties that would have staggered a Western army, the Communists shaped their operations to minimize UNC's superiority in indirect fire support. The Communists' tactical adaptations placed new demands on UNC's close air-support target acquisition and air direction system, a challenge that General Partridge fully recognized in early 1951.[33]

In the first six months of 1951 FEAF made several major reforms to improve the efficiency of its close air-support operations. At Stratemeyer's insistence, the Air Force increased its commitment to remotely controlled bombardment by reinforcing the 502d TCG with MPQ-2 ground radar teams and reequipping FEAF's B–29s and B–26s with improved terminal guidance

The MiG-15, standard interceptor of the Chinese Air Force during the Korean conflict.

systems. Far East Air Forces also improved the accuracy of its level bombing on Communist troop and logistics concentrations by using Razon and Tarzon radar-controlled bombs, which could be guided by the bombardier. In short supply and subject to electronic eccentricities as well as to human error, the radar-controlled ordnance did not have as much impact on operations as did the ordnance of greatest use: proximity-fused bombs, which could be dropped by both bombers and fighter-bombers. By May 1951, FEAF was employing MPQ–2 portable radar sets and proximity-fused bombs with increasing effectiveness. The new techniques were a welcome addition to B–26 operations, which had depended primarily on flare-dropping aircraft to reveal nighttime targets. Nevertheless, the indirect bombing required more sophisticated target acquisition from air and ground reconnaissance units, and it did not replace the TACP–Mosquito system.

General Partridge found much room for improvement in every phase of close air-support operations, and in January 1951 he had a special reason to reform the Eighth Army–Fifth Air Force JOC system. Eighth Army had requested thirteen TACPs for every American division. Thirteen was an unlucky number, for it drew its inspiration from the manning levels enjoyed by X Corps. During the winter campaign of 1950–51, X Corps had organized TACPs manned and equipped by Army officers and enlisted men. These *ad hoc* TACPs were actually controlling air strikes through both Mosquito and Army air observers. Almond ensured that every battalion or similar tactical unit in X Corps had a TACP and ground FAC; on January 21, 1951, X Corps had seventeen Air Force TACPs and eighteen Army TACPs. (Almond had no Marines since the 1st Marine Division had joined IX Corps.) Almond pressed Gen. Matthew G. Ridgway to have Fifth Air Force deploy five Mosquitos every day for X Corps since his rich number of TACPs could easily handle an increased number of sorties. Even though Almond had lost the Marines, he intended to retain their system.[34]

General Partridge and his staff regarded with concern the Eighth Army request to increase Air Force TACPs from fifty-three to double that number, because they did not want to divert more pilots and communicators to what they regarded as marginal air operations. Partridge also protested that Almond's Army TACPs should be disestablished, for he did not believe more TACPs would improve air–ground coordination unless both Eighth Army and Fifth Air Force made radical changes in every part of the close air-support system. He and Stratemeyer still believed that the basic problem was that neither Fifth Air Force nor Eighth Army had really created the system dictated by FM 31–35 and the JTD. Both generals also feared that any concession on doctrine, however modest, would increase Army expectations for close air support not only in Korea, but in future wars. They also rejected a proposal that the Army form more TACPs, for they did not think Army officers were competent enough to direct air strikes. Reassured by Ridgway that he would not support Almond's demands for more TACPs, Partridge attacked the defects in the Air Force's part of the JOC system.[35]

Partridge identified defects in communications procedures and equipment as the heart of the close air-support problem. For the TACPs the Air Force developed a better radio jeep, structurally reinforced and cushioned, that used a more powerful generator to run the radios and a homing beacon. The designers changed the radios as well. The eight-channel ARC–3 and four-channel SCR 522 gave the FAC increased VHF capability to talk with aircraft and linked the FAC, any Mosquito, and fighter-bombers with dependable equipment for the first time. TACP ties to division air liaison officers improved when the jeep-mounted SCR 193 gave way to the ARC–27. The man-portable VHF TRC–7 remained the only weak communications link with aircraft until the ten-channel MAW–8 replaced it by the end of 1951.

In practical terms the reforms meant that the tactical air direction nets increased from four to eight while all Air Force aircraft in the system retained four channels for navigation and emergency purposes. In addition, the 6147th TCG changed Mosquito Mellow, its airborne radio-relay plane, from a T–6 to an especially equipped C–47 that carried a twenty-channel VHF radio over which to vector sorties to a Mosquito or FAC. To improve the assignment and training of Air Force TACPs, Fifth Air Force sent the ground personnel to the 6147th TCG. In addition, the tours of pilot-FACs with ground units increased from three to eight weeks to improve FAC efficiency. To help improve coordination between the JOC, Mosquito Mellow, and all the T–6s, Fifth Air Force finally received enough radars and trained personnel to establish a Tactical Air Direction Center with each American corps headquarters and to establish a MPQ–2 radar site in each corps area. Fifth Air

Force now could have decentralized some of the control of close air-support sorties without taking the direction of actual strikes out of Air Force hands. It did not do so, claiming that the Army side of the request system was still too defective to share mission tasking.[36]

Encouraged by Fifth Air Force's reforms, General Ridgway pressed Partridge and Timberlake to find a way to shorten the time between air strike requests and the actual delivery of air strikes, but Air Force generals insisted that Eighth Army needed to examine the problem more carefully. For example, they objected to assigning air liaison officers strike direction, another Army proposal. Ridgway ordered his staff to examine all of the issues that Almond had raised in the X Corps studies. In a study directed by Brig. Gen. John J. Burns, USA, the Eighth Army chief of artillery and acting G–3 (Air) until early 1951, a joint board recommended that the Eighth Army create the full request system dictated by doctrine. Many of the proposed reforms paralleled those of Fifth Air Force: improved radios, comprehensive training and appropriate assignments for Army air-ground personnel (especially photo-interceptors and intelligence officers), and the reinforcement of the 20th Signal Company (Air–Ground Liaison). The Burns Board report, however, made only one major suggestion for reform: an extension of the Army air–ground staff down to the battalion level. It rejected the Almond–Marine Corps proposals: corps and division operational control of sorties, TACPs with every battalion, and on-station aircraft for any battalion engaged with the enemy. Instead, the Eighth Army command decided first to get its own air–ground system in order.[37]

Eighth Army had good reason not to challenge the existing doctrine and practice. It did not know its own mind on the close air-support question. An Army aviator conducted a close examination of Eighth Army's use of air support. He found that only the 25th Infantry Division routinely requested air support as part of its operational planning. The other divisions followed time-honored practices: "Many of our attacks will be supported by a fire plan, which in substance consists of a battalion commander getting into trouble; pushing the old panic button . . . Air Strikes! . . . Artillery!" Unlike the 1st Marine Division, which maintained a fully organized and highly efficient Fire Support Coordination Center (FSCC), Army divisions and corps could not make up their minds whether their FSCCs should be collocated with their operations sections or with their artillery fire direction centers.

The organizational confusion reflected a serious doctrinal question: should tactical air requests and planning flow through the G–2/G–3 staffs or be managed from the battalion upward by artillery forward observers and liaison officers? Finally reinforced with heavy artillery battalions, corps chiefs of artillery felt that they should have complete control of indirect fire support operations, including air. The corps commanders had no unified position on the issue except that they did not want to allow operational control of heavy artillery and air below the corps level. Although the doctrine had no ambiguity—air-ground management was a G–2/G–3 responsibility— the extemporized nature of the war in 1950 had given Eighth Army's artillery control of the air request process when it functioned outside the TACP– Mosquito system created by Fifth Air Force. Not unexpectedly, the organization with the largest number of proficient personnel and the most effective communications had captured AGOS, and in 1951 artillery officers in Eighth Army saw no reason for change.[38]

The Fifth Air Force's new emphasis on interdiction operations and the reassertion of Army–Air Force close air-support doctrine did not go unchallenged in 1951. Ordered to begin extensive interdiction strikes along Korea's east coast, Admiral Struble, Seventh Fleet Commander, questioned his orders: "In my opinion, strong close air support . . . will do more to hurt the enemy potential than any other type of operation in which we can participate at this time."[39] As TF 77 sailed off to bomb bridges and railways, General Almond kept up his criticism of JOC operations and Air Force doctrine. In addition to demanding that X Corps be given operational control of a fighter- bomber wing, Almond maintained a steady correspondence with the Army Staff in Washington about the Air Force's defects. Partridge, who knew of Almond's complaints, made sure that General Ridgway followed Air Force practices when Eighth Army began a limited offensive against the Chinese in February 1951.[40]

Operation Killer, however, brought the 1st Marine Division back into the battle with the Chinese and back into the battle over close air-support practices. With his division now part of IX Corps, General Smith requested, on February 13, that the 1st MAW operate temporarily under his control. Receiving no response from Ridgway, Smith opened his offensive without assurance he would see Marine Corsairs above his assault battalions. In three days of fighting, the 1st Marine Division did not receive the kind of prompt and accurate air support it expected. When Smith became temporary commander of IX Corps, he confronted Ridgway again with a specific request, that the 1st MAW provide one squadron to the 1st Marine Division's operational control. Ridgway said he could not grant the request: "Smith, I am sorry, but I don't command the Air Force."[41]

After Partridge told him that the JOC would stand inviolate and that the interdiction campaign took precedence over close air support—a decision that meant 1st MAW would support the whole Eighth Army—Smith took the problem to Lt. Gen. Lemuel C. Shepherd, the forceful commanding General of Fleet Marine Force Pacific. After seeing the problems 1st Marine Division had with the JOC system, Shepherd took the issue to MacArthur's headquarters, where he enjoyed considerable influence. Partridge knew a political offensive when he saw one, so he quickly worked out an informal agreement that Marine fighter-bombers dispatched on armed reconnaissance sorties would first check in with Devastate Baker, the 1st MAW control station collocated with the 1st Marine Division. Partridge promised to send a four-aircraft flight on such missions every hour, which he did. He also went aloft himself to monitor Marine air radio messages. When General Harris argued that the 1st Marine Division did little air planning and was not using the sorties he had already authorized, Partridge agreed that no portion of 1st MAW should come under ground force operational control. Backed by Lt. Gen. James Van Fleet, who succeeded Ridgway as commanding general of the Eighth Army on April 14, 1951, Partridge insisted that the 1st Marine Division receive no "special treatment."[42]

The battle in Korea did not halt demands for air-ground reform or force any final resolution of the 1st Marine Division's complaints about JOC close air-support practices. In March 1951, General Ridgway mounted another successful limited offensive, Operation Ripper, but halted the advance upon evidence that the PLA would soon mount its spring offensive. On April 22, the Chinese struck the II ROK Corps and IX U.S. Corps, punching an extended salient through the South Koreans. Van Fleet ordered a retrograde movement that brought the Eighth Army back below the 38th Parallel in a week of hard fighting, especially for the 1st Marine Division, which stopped the major Chinese effort against the IX Corps' left flank. In the crisis, Fifth Air Force fighter-bombers flew almost 400 close-support sorties a day, the heaviest effort of the war. Throughout May, the Bomber Command disrupted the Chinese attacks, classifying as close support sorties almost half of its B–26 and B–29 strikes, particularly radar-directed night sorties. About half of all the close air-support sorties flown for Eighth Army came from Marine aviation, and additional strikes came from the carrier aviation of TF 77. As Communist generals testified later in the year, close air support ruined their offensive, and Chinese prisoners taken in the spring of 1951 blamed their defeat on the continual air strikes they had to endure. When the Chinese made one last offensive effort (May 16–20, 1951), close air support again made a major contribution to defeating the Communists. When Eighth Army returned to the offensive in late May, the Chinese armies in front disintegrated as they fell back across the 38th Parallel.[43]

By the time the Communists agreed to truce talks in June 1951, the pace of the Eighth Army's advance northward had slackened, but as the battle continued, so did the issue of close air support. Complaints about the Air Force system again came from General Almond and his X Corps staff, seconded by the 1st Marine Division, which rejoined X Corps on April 30. With the 1st Marine Division and 2d U.S. Infantry Division carrying the burden, X Corps entered the Eighth Army's critical objective area, "The Iron Triangle," where mountains dominated the line General Van Fleet intended to hold north of the 38th Parallel. For infantry, the battle around "The Punchbowl" and other unhappy terrain features in May and June combined all the horrors of rain, mud, steep slopes, and determined, dug-in defenders. Almond complained that the JOC did not send close air-support sorties when his battalions needed them and again urged that corps commanders have some control over their supporting tactical air. Although the number of incoming flights appeared adequate, their time on station was too short, and their direction to targets was erratic. Almond felt especially unhappy because he could not learn from the JOC which of his requests would be honored and which would not.[44]

The Marines voiced even sharper criticism. The 1st MAW charged that Mosquitos and Air Force TACPs were careless. In three weeks (April 1–21, 1951) sixteen Marine aircraft fell to enemy ground fire, killing nine pilots and sending another into captivity. Although the JOC filled ninety-five percent of the 1st Marine Division's emergency requests, the Marine FACs judged that the missions contained only forty percent of the aircraft required. The average delay in receiving emergency sorties was an hour and a half. Although the division could calculate with accuracy the level of air effort it required on the basis of the type of operation it planned, it found that its preplanned strikes received approval only about half the time. The division abandoned requesting preplanned strikes in June, relying instead on emergency requests, however slow the JOC might be in responding. Most of the delay, the Marines charged, came from the tactical air request system, which required clearance by X Corps and Eighth Army. Again, General Shepherd saw General Ridgway about the JOC system, and once again Partridge persuaded Ridgway not to let the Marines deviate from the Air Force system. He did, however, promise to reevaluate the tactical air request system.[45]

The doctrinal dispute temporarily ebbed, however, for several reasons. At the operating level, Fifth Air Force approved a plan to allow the 1st Marine Division to work directly with the Corsairs of MAG–12, which moved to a strip close to the division. The physical position of the fighter-bombers and a gentlemen's agreement on tactical air requests cut response time in half. The old controversy about Air Force jets *vs.* Marine Corsairs as the optimum aircraft for ground attack faded as Marine squadrons began to shift to the more versatile jet F9F Panther. About to receive Congressional approval of a permanent three-division, three wing FMF, Headquarters Marine Corps did not seek a confrontation with the Air Force. Although Navy and Marine Corps leaders still doubted the value of the Air Force close air-support system, they had little taste for another battle with the Air Force while the Congress was in a generous mood.[46]

Changes in the major commanders in Far East Command/United Nations Command also isolated criticism of the Air Force system. When Stratemeyer and Partridge returned to the United States, General Weyland became FEAF Commander and one of his disciples, Maj. Gen. Frank Everest, took command of Fifth Air Force. Generals Weyland and Everest had no disposition to humor the Marine Corps or the Army on close air support operations. On the

Army side, Ridgway and Van Fleet showed some interest in the dispute, but Almond's departure from Korea, in July 1951, removed the only Army corps commander who championed radical reform.

In September 1951 truce talks had stalled, and the air interdiction campaign intensified when General Van Fleet ordered a limited advance to capture the mountains beyond "the punchbowl." Shaping his ground operations to secure a defensible line across the peninsula, Van Fleet called the 1st Marine Division from X Corps reserve and assigned it the ridges at the northeastern rim of the "the Punchbowl." In three weeks of heavy fighting (September 3–21), the 1st Marine Division took its objectives but found its foe, two NKPA divisions, amply supplied with artillery, mortars, machineguns, in fortified positions. Division FACs called for 182 close air-support strikes, but received only 127, and only 24 of the missions came quickly enough to contribute to the ground battle in an optimal way. Delay time for strikes averaged nearly 2 hours, and for some nearly 4. Only about half of the sorties for the 1st Marine Division came from the 1st MAW, although Marine fighter-bombers flew more missions for the division than any other division in Eighth Army. Since 1st MAW supported all UNC—as well as the interdiction campaign—one-quarter of its total sorties assisted the 1st Marine Division.[47]

Convinced that more close air support would have reduced his one thousand seven hundred casualties, Commanding General Maj. Gen. Gerald C. Thomas of the 1st Marine Division challenged the Fifth Air Force close air-support system. Outraged by an accidental attack by Commonwealth F–51s upon one of his battalions, General Thomas told the JOC that he wanted either Marine aircraft over his division or no close air support at all. General Everest said he would honor the request when possible, but he warned Van Fleet that Eighth Army should quash Thomas's rebellion before it infected Army divisions. Everest argued that the Marines called for four times more air support than other divisions and probably didn't need so much air assistance. In the meantime, Thomas discussed his complaint directly with General Ridgway during one of Ridgway's trips to the front. Ridgway supported Thomas's request that he (Thomas) negotiate with Everest on the assignment of 40 sorties a day from 1st MAW to the operational control of the 1st Marine Division. Already in touch with CINCPACFLT on the issue, Thomas again went to Ridgway with his complaint when Everest refused the 40-sortie program. Sensitive to Ridgway's interest, Van Fleet warned Everest that Thomas' complaints were, in fact, common throughout Eighth Army. The two generals decided they would take one more look at the close air support problem.[48]

Although he had discouraged his corps commanders from requesting too much air support, Van Fleet thought Fifth Air Force might modify its tight control of all air missions, even shifting some sorties from the interdiction campaign to the frontline battle. Given Weyland's dogged commitment to

Maj. Gen. Gerald C. Thomas, USMC, 1st Marine Division Commander in 1951. *(Photo dates from 1952)*

transportation attacks, Everest had little room for maneuver, and he suspected correctly that Van Fleet's new lack of cooperation had been encouraged by Generals Collins and Clark. Everest had no objection to Army TACPs and would make other local experiments, but told Van Fleet that Fifth Air Force would not permit local changes to doctrine without FEAF approval. Unsatisfied, Van Fleet approached Ridgway with a proposal that each U.S. corps in Korea have operational control of one Marine fighter-bomber squadron. In fact, Van Fleet argued that he had been converted to the Marine Corps system: ground FACs ran better strikes closer to troops than Mosquitos; the Marines' simplified request system produced prompt strikes; and the use of on-station aircraft produced much faster results. Van Fleet recognized that such a system required more TACPs, but he could see no reason Army officers could not direct air strikes if properly trained. He also accepted the Marines' argument that the manpower and communications requirements of their system were no more profligate than the elaborate Army-manned air request system and produced far better results. In essence, Van Fleet's analysis of Eighth Army's 1951 operations had made him a convert, and he decided to press the issue with Ridgway, the theater commander.[49]

Caught in a changing war, the Thomas–Van Fleet challenge to the Air Force died in infancy. Under direction from the JCS to shift to the defensive with his ground forces, Ridgway accepted Weyland's argument that air interdiction had become Far East Command's only significant offensive weapon. Even Van Fleet admitted that Fifth Air Force need not change its policies if Eighth Army remained in a static posture. Ironically, the *coup de grace* to

Van Fleet's operational control plan came from the Army staff. After months of review of a comprehensive study of close air support by the Army-funded Operations Research Office, the Assistant Chief of Staff (G–3) issued an *ex cathedra* opinion that the JTD was indeed sound. The Army officially agreed with the Air Force that interdiction took priority over close air support. Furthermore, G–3 thought the Marine Corps had probably used poor statistical analysis to make its case and had a different mission (amphibious warfare) that warped its understanding of close air support. In any event, the Air Force and Army could not wage tactical air war Marine-style since the Air Force could not provide sufficient TACPs and fighter-bombers for a mass army. In all likelihood, almost all targets within a mile of troops should be attacked with heavy artillery, not air. Certainly, the Army did not need operational control of dedicated air sorties or require on-station fighter-bombers.

Ridgway found himself caught between Eighth Army and the positions defended by General Weyland and the Army Staff. To avoid interservice conflict at the theater level, Ridgway and his staff decided that the close air-support question—especially the issue of Army operational control of fighter-bombers—could only be decided by the Joint Chiefs of Staff.[50]

In October 1951, the end of Eighth Army's major offensive operations marked another turning point in UNC close air support. The Joint Operations Center remained firmly in control of the close air-support system, and Fifth Air Force had not allowed the 1st Marine Air Wing out of its grasp. Both the Air Force and Army had made major improvements in the air operations system dictated by FM 31–35 and the JTD. The Air Force system had been challenged by Van Fleet and Thomas, but Ridgway and the Army Staff had dampened the revolt by establishing a theater and Army position that favored the Air Force. With Eighth Army digging in to defend its new Main Line of Resistance across the Korean peninsula, a position it intended to hold until the Communists came to terms, the close air-support controversy should also have diminished. Rooted, however, in contrasting perspectives on the nature of warfare, the close air-support issue remained as alive as the Korean War.

Close Air Support and Siege Warfare
Along the Main Line of Resistance, 1951–1953

From the late autumn of 1951 until a negotiated disengagement brought the war to a close in July 1953, United Nations Command ground forces, numbering roughly seven hundred thousand men, faced a million or more soldiers of the People's Liberation Army and the North Korean People's Army along a one hundred twenty-mile front across the middle of the Korean peninsula. After 1951, Eighth Army did not again take the strategic offensive, and its corps and division operations responded to Communist attacks upon the

Combat Outpost Line or thinly manned Main Line of Resistance (MLR). In fact, battles for advantage in the two armies' outpost zone characterized much of the ground action except those occasions (October 1952 and June–July 1953) when the Communists mounted a "big push" in classic World War I style. In many ways the war resembled operations along the Western Front in France, 1915–1917. Both armies took to the earth, erecting mazes of trenches, bunkers, barbed-wire systems, minefields, and crew-served weapons positions. The Communists dug deeper and bigger fortifications, driven in part by their fear of air attacks. They also proved far more adept at camouflage than Eighth Army. As they had demonstrated in the fluid war, the Communists preferred to fight at night when darkness concealed their infantry.

Eighth Army's commitment to the strategic defense imposed new importance upon its indirect fire capabilities. As truce negotiations ebbed and flowed, United Nations Command tried to hold down infantry casualties. General Ridgway and his successor, General Clark, understood that the United States and those other nations contributing troops to Eighth Army might lose their political will if casualties reached 1950–1951 proportions. In addition, they did not want to endanger the growing and improving ROK Army with crippling losses, for the South Koreans would eventually have to bear the major burden of their own defense. As a general operational concept, UNC hoped that its indirect firepower—heavy artillery ashore and at sea and tactical aviation—would mete out crippling destruction and demoralization to the Communist armies. At a minimum, UNC firepower would prevent any sustained Communist offensive and protect Eighth Army's ground positions. Bombs and shells would offset Communist numbers.[51]

For Far East Air Forces the best way to end the war remained air attacks upon the North Korean transportation system, supplemented by strikes upon a mix of economic and military targets between the MLR and the Yalu River. Until the end of the war, the weight of the FEAF's effort remained interdiction operations. Between July 1951 and July 1953 the Air Force flew 155,000 interdiction sorties and approximately 47,000 close air-support sorties. The same relative emphasis applied to Navy carrier missions and strikes by the 1st Marine Air Wing. In October 1952, for example, FEAF flew as close air support only 3,000 of 24,000 sorties. In the same month, 1st MAW sent out 1,300 close air-support sorties of 3,600 sorties flown. Even in the month of its most intense close air-support effort (June 1953), FEAF's attacks for Eighth Army still fell below half of its total sorties.

As a matter of policy, the Fifth Air Force allocated to the Eighth Army 96 close air-support sorties a day or about 13 percent of its total effort. Fifth Air Force's effort reflected doubts about the relative effectiveness of close air-support missions against the Communists' heavily fortified front, which in 1952 also started to bristle with strong concentrations of antiaircraft artillery. Communist flak often drove Mosquito flights above 6,000 feet, which

FEAF's Combat-Ready Bombers and Fighter-Bombers, Monthly Averages of Numbers Available Daily

Month for Which Average Calculated	Bombers			Fighter-Bombers			Total Fighter-Bombers	Total Bombers and Fighter-Bombers
	B-26	B-29	Total Bombers	F-51	F-80	F-84		
Jul 1950	30	49	79	14	69	None	83	162
Dec 1950	65	63	128	71	118	27	216	344
Jun 1951	58	68	126	66	94	50	210	336
Dec 1951	73	57	130	38	47	70	155	285
Jun 1952	69	64	133	28	54	80	162	295
Dec 1952	98	54	152	34	74	159	267	419
Jun 1953	107	76	183	None	5	195	200	383

Source: United States Air Force, Historical Division Liaison Office, USAF Tactical Operations—World War II and Korean War, 1962.

limited visual reconnaissance and strike direction. To reduce its own losses, Fifth Air Force warned its pilots to avoid heavy flak concentrations, which meant also avoiding attractive targets. Its statistical analyses of its bombing accuracy and its rough damage assessments showed little return for close air-support sorties. Army-sponsored studies provided somewhat more optimistic statistics, but, as a 1951 Operations Research Office study concluded, post-strike analysis did not produce definitive results. Unless UNC aircraft caught Communist troops and vehicles in the open, close air support seemed an inefficient use of air power.[52]

At the Air Force fighter-bomber wing level the war along the MLR had few satisfactions and surprises. Close air support requests produced a hurried ground briefing, sometimes using terrain models and aerial photographs but seldom very detailed information on the ground situation. The actual control of the strikes came from a Mosquito TAC. The pilots might be able to tell whether they had hit their targets but could seldom see whether they had done much damage, unless their bullets and bombs set off secondary explosions. Few strikes came against positions near friendly lines, and even fewer had any relation to infantry maneuver. By 1953, Air Force FACs controlled about one sortie a month per TACP, for most of the pilots attached to UNC ground units worked miles from the front in regimental fire support coordination

Selected Statistics, Fifth Air Force, 1952

	Interdiction Sorties	CAS Sorties	CAS Damage*
Day: 7 June	849	156	86 positions; 39 troops
8 June	703	119	64 positions; 40 troops
9 June	851	140	187 positions; 33 troops
10 June	135	4	Unknown
11 June	335	86	35 positions; 7 troops
12 June	393	97	37 positions; 7 troops
13 June	328	107	108 positions; 125 troops
29 November	801	148	53 positions; 16 troops
30 November	169	19	Unknown
1 December	169	17	Unknown
2 December	396	11	Unknown
3 December	914	152	41 positions; troops unknown
4 December	1002	232	55 positions; troops unknown
5 December	1011	191	43 positions; 5 troops

*Positions destroyed or damaged; troops killed.

Sources:
FEAF, "Intelligence Roundup, 7–13 June 1952," No. 92 and "Intelligence Roundup and Operational Summary, 29 Nov–5 Dec 1952," No. 118, File K720.607A, HRC

centers. Communist flak took its toll. Aircraft combat losses per wing normally ran about four a month; pilot losses per squadron average two a month.[53]

Heavy artillery might have made close air support less important in 1952–1953, and Eighth Army did enjoy increased heavy artillery support. In

Eighth Army Corps Artillery

(October 1952)

	U.S. Army Battalions	ROK Army Battalions
I U.S. Corps	6	6
IX U.S. Corps	6	7
X U.S. Corps	6	5
I ROK Corps	0	5
II ROK Corps	3	12

Source: U.S. Army, "Historical Survey of Army Fire Support," II-A-112.

1952 the three U.S. corps each had six U.S. Army heavy artillery battalions to supplement the guns of each division. In fact, UNC's heavy artillery proved a great equalizer along the MLR, but it faced many limitations. By the standards of the world wars, a force of around nine hundred guns for one hundred twenty miles of front was not generous; seldom could more than three battalions mass their fires on one target without moving their firing positions. Moreover, the mountainous terrain masked many targets and limited all the standard methods of target acquisition and spotting. Airborne artillery observers, flash-sound detection units, radar operators, and forward observers all reported operational difficulties. Communist field engineering, especially the use of caves and reverse slope positions, baffled UNC artillerists. Eighth Army also watched Communist artillery strength grow along the front until enemy barrages—fired from well-built and concealed positions— became a greater menace than nighttime infantry attacks. Even when located, many of the Communist artillery positions could not be successfully attacked except by aircraft.[54]

In the summer of 1952, United Nations Command and Far East Air Force evaluated the progress of the air war, especially the interdiction campaign, and decided the time had come for a change. Despite the damage to their lines of communications, the Communist armies appeared to have increased in combat power. General Weyland and his operations staff believed the target list should extend beyond the transportation system. The new UNC commander, General Clark, USA, approved the change. Vice Adm. Joseph J. "Jocko" Clark, USN, the new Commander, Seventh Fleet,

and an ardent naval aviator, also wanted a different approach to the air campaign. When the two Clarks arrived in the Far East in May 1952, they
received appeals from Van Fleet and Maj. Gen. John T. Selden, the new commander of the 1st Marine Division, to reevaluate the close air-support system
and to redesign the interdiction campaign. Admiral Clark proved especially
easy to persuade: "My own opinion was that the *best* place for our naval air
power to destroy enemy supplies was at the front, not somewhere back in
North Korea. At the front, every bullet, every round of artillery, every pound
of supplies was twice as expensive to the Reds as it was crossing the Yalu. In
my opinion, we could do more harm in a stalemated war by destroying the
enemy's logistics at the battleline."[55] In another era of aerial good feeling, the
Clarks and Weyland, assisted by General Barcus, the new commander of
Fifth Air Force, brought a higher level of interservice integration to their
staffs and designed a more varied "air pressure" strategy. Close air support
again became an open issue.[56]

When he reviewed Eighth Army's plan to take operational control of 1st
Marine Air Wing, General Clark warned Van Fleet that he had not come to
Tokyo to set off a major interservice controversy, but nevertheless he thought
the doctrine of the JTD needed more aggressive implementation.

Clark's known interest in close air support, especially the question of
ground force operational control, heartened those Army, Navy, and Marine
Corps officers who still found Air Force close air support suspect. In July
1952, Clark announced a three-phase program to improve close air support,
a program that in some respects worried Weyland. Much of the Clark program (e.g. more formal air–ground operations training for Army and Air
Force officers) did not alarm Weyland, but several aspects of the "experiment" posed doctrinal challenges. Clark, for example, wanted to have a set
number of daily sorties dedicated to Eighth Army's use for training purposes,
principally battalion-sized operations. Although he did not demand that these
sorties come from on-station aircraft, Clark wanted to see if Fifth Air Force
aircraft could go from strip-alert to their targets in thirty minutes using the
JTD request system. Clark also thought that Fifth Air Force and Eighth
Army should develop a plan to create a JOC for each corps, which meant that
each corps commander might exercise operational control of a set number of
sorties assigned his JOC by Fifth Air Force. Although Clark dodged the
request that Fifth Air Force provide a TACP for every battalion, he thought
that Army officers might eventually control air strikes under the direction of
regimental Air Force liaison officers. Whatever his intent, Clark challenged
some basic parts of Air Force doctrine.[57]

Suspecting that Clark had more than an "experiment" in mind, Weyland
agreed to all the training proposals he found operationally and doctrinally
acceptable. He insisted that any battalion exercises include real ground force
attacks since he warned Clark that Fifth Air Force was losing 1 aircraft for

every 382 close air-support sorties and that Communist ground fire was damaging 1 aircraft per 26 sorties. Such dangers already insured "realistic training" for pilots, and he thought the risks justified his demand that the Army work out antiflak artillery procedures as well as choose meaningful objectives for ground attack.

Weyland also conducted a briefing for Clark on the question of centralized air mission control, and he insisted that there be no transfer of sorties that the JOC could not revoke. In addition, he would not agree to transfer TACP functions to Army control, but he did admit that he could provide infantry battalions with TACPs "when and if required." Weyland also reminded Clark that Dwight D. Eisenhower, whom Weyland assumed would be the next president, approved of the current doctrine and harbored a well-known distaste for interservice conflict. In other words, Clark could accept FEAF's conditions for the air-ground "experiment" or be ready to make his case in Washington. Clark ordered Eighth Army and Fifth Air Force to begin his program within the limits defined by Weyland.[58]

In the meantime, Admiral Clark on his own initiative worked on a plan with Generals Barcus and Van Fleet to send carrier aircraft against Communist front line positions, especially artillery concentrations. Clark's planners designed the attacks, labeled Cherokee Strikes, in order to avoid any doctrinal issues, but the Cherokee plan whetted Eighth Army's appetite for more air support.

Douglas AD Skyraider and F4U Corsair *(foreground)* **on deck of USS** *Valley Forge***, May 1951.**

In concept, Cherokee provided that Navy jets would first suppress enemy flak. The AD Skyraiders and F4U Corsairs would then destroy Communist positions with a rain of 1,000-pound and 2,000-pound bombs, using their slower speeds to achieve greater bombing accuracy. To mollify Fifth Air Force, the mass flights checked in with Mellow, which then passed the mission to a corps TACP, which assigned the mission to a Mosquito. When the airborne controllers again proved they could not handle so much business, Fifth Air Force and Eighth Army moved the bombline closer to the MLR, thus ending the need to control Cherokee strikes with any measure other than radar vectoring. Navy air planners, who used Cherokee strikes until the war's end, believed that TF 77 had vindicated the Navy's concept of tactical air operations against enemy ground forces, but damage assessment remained vague. The TF 77 campaign, however welcome to Eighth Army, did not test the critical features of the JOC system and did not provide any identified clear improvement in close support.[59]

The 1st Marine Division and the 1st Marine Air Wing also looked for ways to demonstrate that their air-ground partnership provided combat power the rest of Eighth Army lacked. In early 1952, the division moved to a critical position along the MLR just north of Seoul. For the next eighteen months the division fought a series of hard outpost battles to keep the PLA off the hills that dominated the Imjin River and the approaches to Seoul. Concerned about the relative inaction of their own tactical air request and control system, the Marines wrested an agreement from Fifth Air Force in May 1952 that MAG–12, a Skyraider and Corsair group, could send twelve sorties a day to the division for "training purposes." The allocation of sorties then rose to twenty. When Eighth Army protested that the 1st Marine Division had secretly captured part of 1st MAW, General Barcus ended the quota system in December, but senior Marine air officers found Barcus willing to allow 1st MAW the first priority in answering the 1st Marine Division's air requests. The JOC sanctioned direct communications between the division and the 1st MAW.

Facing the same enemy and terrain problems that confronted the rest of Eighth Army, the Marines deployed a new radar, MPQ–14, to direct bad-weather and night strikes and used their own spotter aircraft. The Marines also pioneered in using Variable Time (VT) fuzed air-bursting artillery shells (as opposed to proximity fuzed shells) to suppress Communist flak, a practice that produced fewer air casualties. With firm Navy support, by war's end the 1st MAW commanders believed they had worked out a solid arrangement with Fifth Air Force, but the 1st Marine Division still did not like the time delays the JOC imposed by eliminating on-station sorties. The 1st MAW had ample opportunity to see the differences in the two systems, for in February–July 1953 it flew about one of every five close air-support sorties assigned by Fifth Air Force, a sortie share out of proportion to Marine fighter-bomber numbers. The Marines ended the war as they began it, dedicated to their own air support system.[60]

At the same time the Marines struggled to reunite their air–ground team with some JOC assistance, the rest of Eighth Army and Fifth Air Force worked on General Clark's program to improve air–ground operations. In the areas of Army–Air Force planning and the Eighth Army's request system, the participants saw some improvement, especially in terms of intelligence and target analysis. The request system particularly profited from the deployment of the AN/GRC–26 radio-teletype, which replaced the SCR 399 radio. Within approved JTD doctrine, Eighth Army and Fifth Air Force refined their operations and even produced some heartening successes in directing B–29s and B–26s with radar to Chinese troop concentrations.

None of the refinements produced any real change in the close air support system, and two episodes dampened command interest in further reform. First, Generals Clark and Weyland, sensitive to critical press reports, decided that UNC aviators had become too careless about whom they bombed and strafed. Indeed, between June 1950 and April 1953, UNC aircraft dropped ordnance 108 times on friendly positions. Although there had been few casualties, the short bombings had attracted press attention. An investigation Clark ordered determined that Fifth Air Force in 1952 had made 39 errant strikes, the 1st MAW 18, and Navy aviators probably the remaining 6. Instead of changing the air control system, Fifth Air Force insisted on more detailed ground briefings and positive Mosquito control. Target-of-opportunity strikes required TACC and TADC clearance. General Barcus also announced that he would court-martial those pilots who bombed friendly positions and would relieve their wing commanders.[61]

If the issue of misdirected air strikes strained air-ground operations, the results of Operation Smack (January 25, 1953) killed General Clark's reform program. As a prelude to a company-sized raid by the U.S. 7th Infantry Division on a Chinese position called "T–Bone Hill," Fifth Air Force ran a series of strikes on the objective area. Eighth Army artillery deluged the same positions with tons of shells. On the day of the ground attack, a group of military VIPs and newsmen arrived to watch the final assault by the tank-infantry task force, whose sole mission was to assault the position and bring out a prisoner for interrogation.

On the morning of the final attack, ninety-two Air Force and Marine fighter-bombers worked over the ground objective with bombs and napalm for two hours. When the assault force moved forward, however, some fifteen minutes after the last air strike and artillery concentration, the surviving Chinese emerged from their bunkers and stopped the attack with grenades and automatic weapons fire. When the disorganized company withdrew, it had lost seventy-seven men and had not taken a single POW. The reporters present filed stories that Operation Smack had been a flop. Less fairly, they also said that the whole operation had been mounted only to impress them. Once again, they wrote, American troops had died as part of a military ballet inexpertly orchestrated by their generals. Understandably, Clark, Weyland, and Barcus allowed the air–ground "experiments" to die quietly.[62]

By the spring of 1953, close air-support operations along the MLR had again became routine, although incremental improvements in the existing system continued. Artillery flak suppression operations developed to a new level of effectiveness, and in April 1953 UNC aircraft flew four thousand close air-support sorties with the loss of only one aircraft to groundfire. Both the Air Force and Marine Corps air–ground controllers worked on refining radar-guided missions, especially for night operations, and 1st MAW developed a system of providing direct and indirect searchlight illumination for strikes by nightfighters of VMF–513(N). Interservice integration of the JOC system continued, so that in June Navy and Marine Corps liaison parties at the JOC had full communications ties with carrier-based aviation. The Army's development of its side of the joint air operations organization reached the point where Eighth Army willingly assumed the task of providing the equipment and enlisted personnel for the TACPs. Although Air Force ground FACs directed few strikes, the airborne controllers of the 6147th TCG remained active above the MLR and conducted missions much as they had for the past three years.

As part of their eleventh-hour effort to demoralize the South Koreans and seize critical terrain in the "Iron Triangle" area, Communist armies launched a major offensive against the II ROK Corps after fixing Eighth Army's attention to the west with attacks against the U.S. I Corps. In a week's heavy fighting (June 10–18, 1953), the Chinese ruptured the front and forced the defending ROK divisions as much as 4 miles to the rear of the MLR. In the crisis Fifth Air Force and FEAF Bomber Command mounted their most intensive air effort of the war against Communist supply lines and frontline forces. On June 15, UNC pilots flew a one-day record of 3,153 sorties. In the 9–day maximum air effort they flew 810 close air-support sorties. No one questioned the intensity of the air effort in terms of sorties flown and tons of ordnance dropped, but Navy and Marine air commanders believed that the Army–Air Force request and strike control system had again proved to be unsound in fluid operations.

The complaints were familiar and justified. The quota of four TACPs per division effectively eliminated the ground FAC as a source of air control, and Mosquito controllers could not handle the sortie load and target acquisition role without ground assistance. Friendly front lines and enemy flak positions proved nearly impossible to locate, and although Fifth Air Force waived its 3,000-foot minimum altitude for fighter-bombers in order to improve bombing accuracy, this adjustment also brought new risks. During the Chinese offensive UNC lost 18 aircraft to groundfire, eleven of which (9 pilots KIA)

F-84F Thunderjet puts a barrage of 5-inch rockets on a North Korean target.

fell during close air-support runs. In addition, the JOC–AGOS system of processing all missions insured that sorties often arrived too late to provide timely support to beleaguered ground troops. The JOC communications system again proved too centralized and slow, and not one air request from II ROK Corps came through normal channels. In addition, the principal Eighth Army officers in the JOC found themselves ill-informed of the tactical situation by both their Air Force counterparts and their own subordinates. The difficulties of 1950 still applied in 1953.[63]

After the armistice of July 27, 1953, the major participants in UNC's close air-support operations sent representatives to Fifth Air Force headquarters at Seoul to examine the lessons of the war. The Air–Ground Operations Conference (August 8–22, 1953) focused especially on the conduct of close airsupport operations in the war's closing months. In some areas the officers of the four services agreed: the JOC had become truly a joint activity and functioned better than it had in 1951; flak suppression artillery enhanced aircraft survivability; electronic indirect guidance systems had great potential for all-hour, all-weather operations; jet aircraft could make strikes as accurately as propeller-driven fighter-bombers and could function better in contested air space; aviation and ground personnel needed far greater training in air-ground operations; the improvement of all types of communications equipment would pay additional dividends; and all participants needed to pay more attention to target acquisition and poststrike damage assessment.

Army, Navy, and Marine Corps representatives, however, indicted one central feature of the JTD doctrine, a position that brought determined Air Force opposition. The critique did not challenge the central doctrinal foundation for air operations (air superiority first) or even attack the assumption that interdiction strikes paid far greater dividends than close air-support operations. It did not deny that theater air operations required a single air commander during a period of extended land warfare. What the critics did propose were changes in the air request and air control system:

1. Once the theater air commander had decided on the relative importance of all air missions, the JOC should allocate a set number of sorties to ground corps commanders and pass control of the sorties to a subordinate TADC run by an air officer. The corps could communicate directly through the AGOS to the supporting aviation units. In an emergency the JOC could override corps-determined sorties.

2. The corps TADC/FSCC could manage its sorties so that aircraft checked in on a pre-determined time-table for pre-planned strikes, but would be predictably available for emergency missions. The existence of pre-planned missions ensured that the corps would not make up trivial sorties just to use its aircraft.

3. The air request system had to be decentralized and simplified, especially for emergency missions. Whether the request came from a ground officer or air officer, it should go directly to the corps TADC/FSCC. Intervening echelons of command should monitor the TAR net, but not intervene except in emergencies.

4. Because airborne controllers had severe limitations in spotting targets and friendly lines, they could not carry the responsibility alone for directing accurate strikes, especially within a mile of troops. An effective close air-support system demanded a FAC and TACP at the front, which meant an allocation of TACPs on an establishment of four per infantry regiment or armored combat command. Four TACPs per division meant that the FAC would function only as an ALO. Only a ground FAC with each battalion could prevent accidents and reduce the risk to aircraft from enemy or friendly fire.

The Air Force representatives at the Air–Ground Operations Conference refused to endorse any deviation from the existing doctrine in the JTD, even though they often admitted that the Navy–Marine Corps analysis of the 1953 problems was accurate. At the heart of Air Force opposition to any change remained its commitment to interdiction as the principal instrument of air war upon enemy ground forces. The question of increasing the number of TACPs per division from four to thirteen crystallized Air Force opposition to any reform that would increase the relative effectiveness and importance of close air support.

Although the Air Force doubted that any future war, especially one with the Soviet Union, would allow airborne controllers to operate above the battlefield, Air Force officers argued that Mosquito operations reduced the need for FACs. In Korea the Air Force TACPs had directed few strikes, particularly after 1951, so they did not appear to be required. In addition, the Air Force insisted that it could not be expected to provide 364 FACs for a force the size of Eighth Army, let alone a larger army for operations in Europe. Battalion FACs simply generated air requests for targets that could be more economically attacked with heavy artillery. The Army and the Air Force could not afford the wealth of sorties that characterized the Navy–Marine Corps system, which might be necessary for amphibious warfare but had little value in an extended land campaign. Not surprisingly, representatives at the Air–Ground Operations Conference reported that the question of joint all-service doctrine for air-ground operations had not been settled by the war.[64]

United Nations Close Air Support in Korea

Tactical offensive air operations—flown by three American services and token aviation units from five other nations—played a critical role in the campaigns of United Nations Command on the Korean peninsula, 1950–1953. In the course of the war, UNC aircraft flew over a million sorties, about three-quarters of them by the U.S. Air Force. Of the total sorties flown, close air support, defined as strikes within the bombline that received some positive direction from a ground or airborne controller, represented roughly 10 to 15 percent of the air effort. Navy and Marine Corps aircraft probably flew more close air-support sorties than Air Force and allied squadrons. The cost of close air support is more elusive since none of the services divided their aircraft losses to groundfire (816 for the Air Force; 559 for the Navy and Marine Corps) between interdiction and close air-support sorties. Given the complex variables that may affect loss rates, estimates for the Korean War are difficult and comparison with other wars specious. The same condition applies to measuring effectiveness by effort, since sorties flown and tonnages dropped do not necessarily produce damage equivalent to the aerial activity, let alone persuade an enemy to give up a war.[65]

United Nations Command
Air War Sorties, 1950–1953

	Total	Interdiction	CAS
U.S. Air Force	720,980	192,581	57,665
U.S. Navy (TF 77)	167,552	82,100*	35,185*
U.S. Marine Corps	107,303	47,873	32,482
Allied	44,873	15,359	6,063

*TF 77 categorized 70 percent of its sorties as "offensive air," but did not differentiate between interdiction and close air support. These estimates are based upon a further estimate that 70 percent of offensive air sorties were flown as interdiction missions.

Sources: Futrell, *Air War in Korea*, p. 690; Manson and Cagle, *Sea War in Korea*, p. 523.

The effect of close air support cannot be judged outside the perceptions of those who requested the strikes, those who delivered them, and those who received them. In Eighth Army the ground units who used close air support the most, especially from the 1st Marine Air Wing, and who employed a greater number of ground FACs (the divisions in the X Corps) believed that close air support was essential and complemented artillery fire. At the troop level, prompt and accurate air strikes not only destroyed Communist tanks, guns, and infantry, but often heartened UNC ground troops. During the fluid stages of the war, particularly the campaigns of 1950 and 1951, Eighth Army units could see, smell, and count the results of air strikes. On the enemy side North Korean and Chinese soldiers attested to the damage and demoralization that UNC air strikes wrought. Although the Communist armies reached rough parity in artillery, they never broke UNC's grip on the skies over the battlefield and, therefore, had to conduct ground operations with extra attention to cover, concealment, troop and logistical dispersion, and night infiltration tactics. When Eighth Army altered its own operations in 1951 to checkmate their tactics, the Communists found little advantage in their larger numbers of fighting troops. If Eighth Army had continued offensive operations after 1951, tactical aviation would have been the major source of UNC's edge in combat power.

Air Force commitment to interdiction in Korea, while producing some positive results, weakened the potential contribution of close air support. The service's close air support thinking extended beyond the mere allocation of total offensive sorties. The air–ground system created by the Joint Training Directive insured that Fifth Air Force would determine the close air-support request and direction practices used by United Nations Command. By preventing any decentralization of operational control after 1950 and by limiting the number of ground FACs, the Air Force ensured that the alternative close air-support system championed by the Navy and Marine Corps did not operate outside of X Corps and the 1st Marine Division.

In terms of interservice politics, Air Force unanimity on doctrine prevailed because the Army generals who led United Nations Command and Eighth Army did not choose to press the doctrinal issue, accepting instead reforms and refinements within the JTD system. In essence, Army generals may have had differing opinions about close air support, but only Almond mounted a determined effort to change the existing doctrine. After Almond left Korea, only the senior officers of the Navy and Marine Corps in the Far East remained to challenge Air Force doctrine, and they received scant encouragement from their superiors.

Still smarting from the public battle over roles and missions that poisoned interservice relations between 1945 and 1950, the Joint Chiefs of Staff sought no renewal of their doctrinal battles as they directed the general wartime expansion and modernization of their services. The Marine Corps, for example, ended the war with legislative protection for a Fleet Marine Force of three active divisions and three aircraft wings, and the Navy successfully enlarged its number of carriers, carrier aircraft wings, and land-based aviation squadrons. Regarding preparedness for a conventional war with the Soviet Union as their most important contribution to a national strategy of nuclear deterrence and forward, collective defense, the Navy and Marine Corps avoided a pitched political battle over close air support. Such a doctrinal conflict would have been the wrong war at the wrong time.

The doctrinal truce did not represent Army satisfaction with the JTD outside the war zone. In five major exercises in the United States in 1951–1954, the same defects so familiar in Korea appeared in every evaluation. Army commanders did not like the requirement to send air requests through the chronically undermanned, undertrained, and marginally equipped air–ground operations system. Experiments with bypassing intervening echelons of command did indeed provide more timely strikes. Division commanders supported the proposal to assign one TACP to each maneuver battalion and to fuse the air request and air direction functions in the TACP, which would communicate requests directly to the JOC or only through a division FSCC. Air Force commanders resisted the move to multiply the TACPs and enlarge their functions. They experimented with putting FACs in helicopters, but decided the groundfire risk was too great. They also argued that the Army's use of air support was so wasteful that the Air Force should make no special concessions until ground commanders became more competent in planning air support. Even though the Army now supplied all the equipment and enlisted personnel of the TACP, the Air Force saw no profit in providing experienced fighter-bomber pilots for FACs if the Army did not use their skills well.[66]

After the Korean War ended, however, and the services faced the economies of President Eisenhower's "New Look" the Army and Air Force repudiated even the arrangements prescribed by the Joint Training Directive of 1950. The Air Force took the lead in demanding that a series of joint boards writing doctrine be canceled, which was done in 1955. One of these boards had recommended a change in doctrine that would have modified the theater

Wrecked North Korean T-34 tanks cleared from a roadway during UN advance.

air commander's absolute control of air assets. In the meantime, the Air Force published Air Force Manual 1–2, United States Air Force Basic Doctrine (1953), which restated the principle of centralized air war. The supporting manual on theater air war, published in 1954, went so far as to make the Joint Operations Center an all-Air Force agency to which the other services would provide only liaison officers. At the operational level, the Air Force disestablished the 6147th Tactical Control Group on June 23, 1956, thus eliminating the Mosquito system of air direction. The Air Force's declining interest in close air support did not escape the Army. After the failure to draft a joint statement on close air-support operations, the Army announced in January 1955 that the principles of the Joint Training Directive had already been repudiated by the Air Force and therefore did not bind the Army. The final irony was that the Army Chief of Staff who found the doctrine so defective was none other than General Ridgway. Perhaps it was especially appropriate that Eighth Army's most famous commanding general would declare void the Korean War's doctrine for close air-support. For all practical purposes the Army and Air Force had finally found a consensus by agreeing not to agree on what part close air support would play in future war.[67]

Notes

1. The basic history of air–ground operations in Korea is contained in official and semiofficial books published by the armed forces historical agencies: Robert Frank Futrell, *The United States Air Force in Korea, 1950–1953*, rev ed, (Washington, 1983): Lynn Montross, *et. al, US Marine Operations in Korea, 1950–1953*, 5 Vols, (Washington, 1954–1972); James A. Field, Jr, *History of United States Naval Operations: Korea* (Washington, 1962); Cmdr Malcolm W. Cagle, USN, and Cmdr Frank A. Manson, USN, *The Sea War in Korea* (Annapolis, 1957); and three published volumes in the Office of the Chief of Military History, US Army series "The US Army in the Korean War." These books are Col James F. Schnabel, USA, *Policy and Direction: The First Year* (Washington, 1972); Col Roy E. Appleman, USAR, *South to the Naktong, North to the Yalu* (Washington, 1961); and Walter G. Hermes, *Truce Tent and Fighting Front* (Washington, 1967).

2. Will A. Jacobs, "Tactical Air Doctrine and AAF Close Air Support in the European Theater, 1944–1945," *Aerospace Historian* 27 (Spring, 1980), pp 35–49; Charles W. Dickens's *A Survey of Air–Ground Doctrine* (1958), Hq TAC, Hist Study Nr 34, pp 7–25, File 417.041–34, Hist Research Center, Air University, Maxwell AFB, Alabama, hereafter cited as USAFHRC. See also Robert Frank Futrell, *Ideas, Concepts, Doctrine, A History of Basic Thinking in the United States Air Force, 1907–1964* (Maxwell AFB, Ala., 1971), pp 90–93; Alfred Goldberg and Lt Col Donald Smith, USAF, *Army Air Force Relations: The Close Air Support Issue*, (R–906–PR, Santa Monica, Calif., 1971), pp 2–13; Joint Staff Task Force, Phase II: Close Air Support Study, Vol III: "Command and Control," pp A–6 to A–22, File 160.041, USAFHRC; Thomas A. Mayock, "Notes on the Development of AAF Tactical Air Doctrine," *Military Affairs* 14 (Summer, 1950), pp 186–191.

3. US War Department, Field Manual 31–35, *Air–Ground Operations* (Washington, 1946); Riley Sunderland, *Evolution of Command and Control Doctrine for Close Air Support* (Washington, Hq USAF, 1973), pp 21–25.

4. Futrell, *Ideas, Concepts, Doctrine*, pp 187–190; Hq TAC, records and routing sheet, Joint Training Directive, Vol II, historical documents file for 1950, TAC, File 417.01, USAFHRC; Hq Fourteenth AF, "History of Fourteenth Air Force, Jul 1, 1949–Jun 30, 1950," App V: Reports of Special Exercises, File 862.01–8, USAFHRC; Ralph D. Bald, Jr, *Air Force Participation in Joint Army-Air Force Training Exercises, 1947–1950* (USAF Hist Studies Nr 80, Air University, 1955), pp 5, 6, 11–12, 16–31, 67–72. The Congressional view is reported and analyzed in Maj. Gen. T.D. White to Secretary of the Air Force (SecAF). May 4, 1950, encl 2 to Hq USAF, Korean Evaluation Project, "Report of Air Operations," Jan 16, 1951, File K168.041–2, USAFHRC. The above study, variously called the Stearns or Barcus Report, is hereafter cited as Korean Eval Report.

5. Office, Chief of Army Field Forces, and Headquarters, Tactical Air Command, *Joint Training Directive for Air–Ground Operations*, Sep 1, 1950.

6. Futrell, *Ideas, Concepts, Doctrine*, pp 182–203; Hist Branch, Programs Div, Combat Developments Command, US Army, "Hist Survey of Army Fire Support," Mar 18, 1963, Section I, copy in US Army Center of Military History (CMH), Washington.

7. PHIB 12/NAVMC 4159, *Amphibious Operations: Air Operations* (1948), Hist Amphibious Files, Breckinridge Library, Marine Corps Education Center, Quantico, Virginia. (Hereafter cited as HAF.) The quotation is from p 31, Section 4, "Close Air Support"; Air and Naval Gunfire Liaison Company, Signal Battalion, Marine Div, T/O Number K–1853, Jul 16, 1951, Reference Section, History and Museums Div (H&MD), HQMC.

8. Marine Corps Schools, *The Defense of Advanced Naval Bases–Air Operations*, NAVMC 4542 (1948), HAF. For the development of close air support in the naval services in World War II, see Jeter A. Isely and Philip A. Crowl, *The US Marines and Amphibious War* (Princeton, NJ, 1951) and Robert Sherrod, *History of Marine Corps Aviation in World War II* (Washington, 1952). See also report, Hq FEAF to CINCFE, "A General Review of United States Tactical Air Support in Korea, 28 Jun–8 Sep 1950," 1950, File 720–4501A, USAFHRC, and Vol III, Chap 1, "Korea Eval Report," pp 15–23.

9. On interwar Marine Corps aviation, see Lt Col Kenneth J. Clifford, USMCR, *Progress and Purpose: A Developmental History of the US Marine Corps, 1900–1970* (Washington, 1973), 70–82; Lt Col Eugene W. Rawlins, USMC, *Marines and Helicopters, 1946–1962* (Washington, 1976), pp 11–39; Peter B. Mersky, *US Marine Corps Aviation 1912 to the Present* (Annapolis, 1983), pp 120–128; Unit historical summaries for 1st and 2d ANGLICO, FMF, and Marine Tactical Control Squadron Two, Reference Section, H&MD. The general development of interwar navy aviation may be studied in Deputy Chief of Naval Operations (Air) and Commander, Naval Air Systems Command, *United States Naval Aviation, 1910–1970* NAVAIR 00–80P–1, (Washington, 1970), pp 157–178.

10. The best blends of detailed statistics and analysis for 1950 are Operations Research Office, Hq FEC, "Close Air Support Operations in Korea: Preliminary Evaluation," ORO–R–3 (FEC) memo, Feb 1, 1951, USAFHRC; Hq FEAF, *Report on the Korean War*, 2 Vols, 1953, I, pp 10–12, 62–63, File K720.04D, USAFHRC; AC/S, Hq USAF, "A Quantitative Comparison between Land-Based and Carrier-Based Air during the Early Days of the Korean War," Jun 1972, File K–143.044–61, USAFHRC; Sections I–L, Interim Eval Rprt Nr 1, Jun 25–Nov 5, 1950, CINCPACFLT, *Korean War: US Pacific Fleet Operations*, Operational Archives, Naval Hist Center, Washington Navy Yard (hereafter cited as OA/NHC); Hist Office, Hq FEAF, "History of the Far East Air Forces, 25 June–31 Dec 1950," 2 Vols, I, pp 1–12, File K720.01, USAFHRC; Richard C. Kugler, "Air Force Statistical Data on Missions Flown in Support of the Army," OCMH monograph, 1965, CMH.

11. Appleman, *South to the Naktong, North to the Yalu*, pp 8–12; Futrell, *Air Force in Korea*, pp 14–20. Hq FEAF, "Weekly Intelligence Roundups," Sept 3–Oct 28, 1950, File K720.607A, USAFHRC.

12. Appleman, *South to the Naktong, North to the Yalu*, p 119; Schnabel, *Korea: Policy and Direction*, pp 90–92, 96–97, 230; Montross and Canzona, *The Inchon-Seoul Operation*, Vol II: *US Marine Operations in Korea* (Washington, 1955), pp 305–310.

13. Oral memoir, Gen E. E. Partridge, USAF (1974), pp 601–602, K239–0512–729, USAFHRC; entry, Jul 25, 1950, Partridge diaries, Gen E. E. Partridge Papers, USAFHRC.

14. Futrell, *Air Force in Korea*, pp 1–5.

15. CINCFE to COMNAVFE and COMFRAF, Jul 8, 1950, Encl 8 to Col J. Ferguson USAF to VCO FEAF, "Outline of Korean Campaign," Nov 9, 1950, File K417.01, USAFHRC; Cagle and Manson, *Sea War in Korea*, pp 30–47; Futrell, *Air Force in Korea*, pp 44–55; Stephen Jurika, Jr, ed., *From Pearl Harbor to Vietnam: The Memoirs of Admiral Arthur W. Radford* (Stanford, Calif., 1980), pp 228–240.

16. Memo, C/S, GHq, FEC, "Control of Tactical Air Support," Jun 9, 1950, Far East Command, Correspondence: Korean War Miscellaneous, RG 6, MacArthur Memorial Archives, Norfolk, Virginia.

17. Korean Eval Report, Vol III: "Operations and Tactics," pp 24–39; Marcelle Size Knaack, comp, *Encyclopedia of US Air Force Aircraft and Missile Systems*, Vol I: *Post–World War II Fighters* (Washington, 1978).

18. Korean Eval Report, Vol III: "Operations and Tactics," pp 51–69.

19. Hq FEAF to CINCFE, memo, "A General Review of United States Tactical Air Support in Korea, Jun 28–Sept 8, 1950," 1950, File 720–4501A, USAFHRC, Korean Eval Report, Vol II, "The Air–Ground Team"; FEAF, *Report on the Korean War*, Vol II: "The Tactical Air Control System," pp 81–91; Col J. Ferguson to V/CO FEAF, "Outline of Korean Campaign," pp 5–7, 25–26.

20. J. Farmer and M. J. Strumwasser, *The Evolution of the Airborne Forward Air Controller: An Analysis of Mosquito Operations in Korea*. Memo RM–5430–PR, Oct 1967 (Santa Monica, 1967); W. M. Cleveland, comp, *Mosquitos in Korea, 1950–1953*, privately published by the 6147th TCG Association, 1983; 6147th TCG Association, "Mosquitoes: 30th Anniversary Korean Armistice Reunion," 1983, a compilation of historical materials provided by Mr. W. M. Cleveland, group historian, Portsmouth, NH: Maj Tim Cline, USAF, "Forward Air Control in the Korean War," *Journal of American Aviation Hist Society* 21 (Winter, 1976), pp 257–262.

21. CG Ninth AF to CG TAC, "A Review of Tactical Air in Joint Operations," Sep 1950, File K417.01, USAFHRC; entries, Aug 4–18, 1950, Stratemeyer diaries; Maj Gen O. P. Weyland VC/O to C/S, USAF "Some Lessons of the Korean War and Conclusions and Recommenda-

tions Concerning USAF Tactical Air Responsibilities," Oct 10, 1950, File K417.01, USAFHRC.; "Close Air Support Operations," Vol III, Interim Eval Rprt Nr 1, CINCPAC-FLT, *Korean War: US Pacific Fleet Operations.*

22. "Marine Air," Vol IV, Interim Eval Rprt Nr 1, CINCPACFLT, *Korean War: US Fleet Operations;* ORO Hq FEC, "A Comparison of Air Force and Marine Air Support, App B. "Close Air Support Operations in Korea," 1951; and "Operations of the 1st Marine Air Wing, FMF in Korea, Jun 25–Nov 15, 1950," Annex CC, both in Interim Eval Rprt Nr 1. For the role of air support in the ground war in the Pusan perimeter, see Appleman, *South to the Naktong, North to the Yalu,* pp 255–257, 314, 376–397, 467, 473, 480–481, and Montross and Canzona, *The Pusan Perimeter, passim.* On Marine air operations, see also Lt Col C. A. Phillips and Maj H. D. Kuokka, "1st MAW in Korea," *Marine Corps Gazette* 41 (May, 1957), pp 42–47 and (June, 1957), pp 20–26; VADM John S. Thach, USN, "Right on the Button: Marine Close Air Support in Korea," *US Naval Institute Proceedings* 101 (November, 1975), pp 54–56, and oral memoir, ADM John S. Thach, USN, Vol II, pp 532–551, OA/NHD. One of the Navy's most famous fighter "aces" of World War II, Thach commanded *Sicily* (CVE–118) in 1950. Comments by Army commanders in Korea are included in "Commanders' quotes: CAS," File K110.8–33, USAFHRC. Gen Stratemeyer's views on the USAF–USMC controversy and the shortcomings of the Army AGOS are included in entries, Aug 18–23, 1950, Stratemeyer diaries, and CG FEAF to CINCFE, Aug 14, 1950, encl 1, Col J. Ferguson, "Outline of Korean Campaign." See also summary of remarks. Col Paul B. Freeman, CO, 23d Infantry to JCS, Mar 2, 1951, File K239.0291–1, USAFHRC.

23. FEAF, *Report on the Korean War,* Vol II, "The Tactical Air Control System," pp 81–91; Hq FEAF memo, "Conference on Tactical Air Control Procedures in Korea," Sep 22, 1950, and memo, proceedings of conference, Hq Fifth AF and TF 77, Nov 5, 1950, enclosures 2 and 21; Col J. E. Ferguson, "Outline of Korean Campaign;" oral memoir, Maj Gen G. L. Meyers, USAF (1970), pp 137–145, File K239.0512–282, USAFHRC; entries, Sep 4 and Oct 6, 1950, Stratemeyer diaries.

24. Entries, Sep 17–19 and 24–25, 1950, Stratemeyer diaries; entry, Sep 24, 1950, Partridge diaries; Appleman, *South to the Naktong, North to the Yalu,* pp 579, 582–583, 623; Hq Fifth AF, operations analysis memo, "Weapons Selection for Close Support Tactical Operations in Korea," 30 Nov 1951, File K730.3103–24, USAFHRC; Futrell, *Air Force in Korea,* pp 161–175; Brig C. N. Barclay, *The First Commonwealth Div* (Aldershot, 1954) p 20.

25. Entries, Oct 29–Nov 5, 1950, Partridge diaries; entry, Oct 17, 1950, Stratemeyer diary. On the role of air operations in the Inchon–Seoul campaign, see Lynn Montross and Capt Nicholas A. Canzona, USMCR, *US Marine Corps Operations in Korea.* Vol II: *The Inchon–Seoul Campaign* (Washington, 1955): Col Robert D. Heinl, Jr, USMC (Ret.), *Victory at High Tide: The Inchon–Seoul Campaign* (Philadelphia, 1968); Field, *US Naval Operations–Korea,* pp 171–218; oral memoir, Gen Lemuel C. Shepherd, USMC (1967), pp 449–454, Oral History Collection, History and Museums Div, HqMC (OHC/HMD).

26. Col J.E. Ferguson, "Outline of Korean Campaign," pp 20–26; COMFEAF to CG X Corps, Nov 3, 1950, encl 14D to "Outline of Korean Campaign"; entries, Oct 17 and Dec 1, 1950, Partridge diaries; Ltr, CG Fifth AF to CG FEAF, Nov 19, 1950, Stratemeyer diary; entry, Nov 17, 1950, Partridge diaries; Futrell, *Air Force in Korea,* pp 199–237. Almond's position is explained in X Corps, *Army Tactical Air Support Requirements* (1950–51), Gen E. H. Almond Papers, US Army Military History Institute, (USAMHI), Carlisle Barracks, Pa.

27. Office, Chief of Army Field Forces to C/S, USA, memorandum: "Army Requirements for Close Tactical Air Support," Oct 24, 1950; C/S USA to C/S USAF, memorandum: "Close Air Support of Ground Operations," Nov 21, 1950; Ltr, Gen J. L. Collins to Maj Gen E. M. Almond, Feb 1, 1951, all in "Tactical Air Support Files," Almond Papers, USAMHI.

28. Hq USAF, Korean Eval Project, "Report on Air Operations," Jan 16, 1951, File K168.041–2, USAFHRC; Director, Army Air Support Center, to Chief, Army Field Forces, "Air Support in the Korean Campaign," Dec 1, 1950, File K720.4501B, USAFHRC; Futrell, *Ideas, Concepts, Doctrine,* pp 153–154. The political context of the studies is described in Ltr, Col K. S. Axtater to Sec AF, Oct 30, 1950; Memo, DEPTAR (GS USA) to CINCFE, Nov 16, 1950; and Ltr, Dr W. Barton Leach (Maj Gen, USAFR) to Sec AF, "Status of Korean Eval Report," Jan 9, 1951, all enclosures to the basic Stearns–Barcus Report.

29. Futrell, *Air Force in Korea,* pp 254–284; Lynn Montross and Capt Nicholas A. Canzona,

USMC, *US Marines Operations in Korea*, Vol III, *The Chosin Reservoir Campaign* (Washington, 1957); Field, *United States Naval Operations–Korea*, pp 263–305; "Conclusions and Recommendations: Close Air Support," Vol I, pp 175–177; and "Naval Air–Close Air Support," Vol II, pp 465–476, in Interim Eval Rprt Nr 2, Nov 16, 1950–Apr 30, 1951, CINCPACFLT, *US Pacific Fleet Operations: Korean War:* S.L.A. Marshall, *The River and the Gauntlet* (New York, 1953) pp 119,172, 235, 261, 279, 314.

30. Entries, Dec 18, 1950, Jan 14, and Feb 18, 1951, Stratemeyer diaries; entries, Nov 25 and Dec 11, 1950 and Jan 9 and 22, 1951, Partridge diaries; Hq X Corps, "Infantry Battalion TACPs," 1951, M–36670–2–S, and "Army Tactical Air Support Requirements," Dec 25, 1950, M–36670–2–S, both in the Air University Library, Maxwell AFB; oral memoir of Maj Gen O.P. Smith, USMC (1969) pp 285–286, OHC/HMD.

31. Futrell, *Ideas, Concepts, Doctrine*, pp 153–167; Gen Matthew B. Ridgway, USA (Ret.), *The Korean War* (Garden City, N.Y., 1967), pp 79–183; Schnabel, *Policy and Direction: The First Year*, pp 378–396. For the Air Force position of American defense policy, 1951, see testimony of Gen Hoyt S. Vandenberg USAF, May 28 and 29, 1951, US Senate, Committees on Armed Forces and Foreign Relations. Hearings: "Military Situation in the Far East," 82d Cong, 1st sess, (Washington: GPO, 1951), Part 2, pp 1375–1506.

32. Memo, CG FEAF to C/S USAF, memo, "Requirements for Increased Combat Effectiveness," Jun 10, 1951, File K720.161–5, USAFHRC; Hq FEAF, *Report on the Korean War*. I, pp 82–83; Hq FEAF "Weekly Intelligence Roundups" for Apr–May 1951, File K720.607A, HRC; Futrell, *Air Force in Korea*, pp 313–372.

33. Entries, Jan, 1951, Partridge diaries.

34. Entry, Jan 10, 1951, Partridge diaries; Ltrs, Maj Gen E.M. Almond to Lt Gen Matthew B. Ridgway, Jan 21, 1951 and to Gen J. L. Collins, Jan 23, 1951, Almond Papers; "Infantry Battalion TACP's," Jan 26, 1951, X Corps, *Army Tactical Air Support Requirements*, "Tactical Air Support Files," Almond Papers.

35. Entries, Feb 2 and 14, 1951, Partridge diaries; entry, Mar 23, 1951, Stratemeyer diaries.

36. FEAF, "The Tactical Air Control System," *Report on the Korean War*, II, pp 81–91; entry Feb 14, 1951, Partridge diaries; enclosure, "Air Support Annex" to Ltr, Lt Col A. C. Miller II, USA, to DO, Fifth AF, Apr 26, 1951, File K720.4501B, HRC. The latter document is a comprehensive, detailed study of the air support system in 1951.

The organization of the TACPs and airborne TACs changed constantly until 1951. The personnel and equipment of the TACPs, less pilots, were originally pooled in the 6132d Tactical Air Control Gp (Provisional) in July, 1950, but then became the 4th Squadron of the 502d Tactical Control Gp in October, 1950. The TACPs and their supporting establishment then became the 6164th Tactical Control Squadron and then the 6150th Tactical Reconnaissance Squadron when it joined the 6147th Tactical Control Gp, formed Apr 25, 1951. The airborne FACs—"Mosquito"—also started as part of the 6132d TACG. They began their independent life as the 6147th Tactical Control Squadron (Airborne) and then became the 6147th Tactical Control Gp, which included two flying squadrons (the 6148th TCS and the 6149th TCS) as well as support squadrons.

37. Ltrs, Lt Gen M. B. Ridgway to Maj Gen E. M. Almond, Mar 2 and 6, 1951, and entry, Mar 6, 1951 on meeting with Partridge and Timberlake, Eighth Army Correspondence Files, Gen Matthew B. Ridgway Papers, US Army Military History Institute; Report, Joint Air–Ground Operations (Burns) Bd, "Analysis of Air–Ground Operations in Korea," Mar 26, 1951, File K239–04291–1, USAFHRC.

38. Enclosure, "Air Support Annex," to Miller Report, previously cited. See also "Hist Survey of Army Fire Support," previously cited, Chap II.

39. Quoted in Cagle and Manson, *Sea War in Korea*, p 230.

40. Entries, Feb 2 and 14 and Mar 3 and 15, 1951, Partridge diaries.

41. Oral memoir, Lt Gen O. P. Smith USMC (1969), pp 285–286, OHC/HMD; Lynn Montross, Maj Hubard D. Kuokka, and Maj Norman W. Hicks, USMC, *US Marine Corps Operations in Korea*, Vol IV, *The East–Central Front* (Washington, 1962), pp 59–78.

42. Memo, CG FEF to CINCPACFLT, memo with enclosures, "Observations of Close Air Support in Korea," Apr 27, 1951, in Interim Eval Rprt Nr 2, Nov 16, 1950–Apr 30, 1951, CINCPACFLT *US Pacific Fleet Operations: Korean War*, Vol II, pp 477–479; entries, Apr 15, 16, and 18, 1951, Partridge diaries.

In fact, the Marines did receive "special treatment," for the observation aircraft of VMO–6 could still direct air strikes while Army pilots could not.

43. Ridgway, *The Korean War*, pp 150–183; Futrell, *Air War Force in Korea*, pp 335–372; Montross, Kuokka, and Hicks, *The East–Central Front*, pp 79–126; Alexander L. George, *The Chinese Communist Army in Action* (New York, 1967), pp 163–189.

44. Montross, Kuokka, and Hicks, *The East–Central Front*, pp 127–152; Hermes, *Truce Tent and Fighting Front*, pp 73–111; Hq X Corps, memo, "Tactical Air Support X Corps, May 10–Jun 5, 1951," Jul, 1951, File K239–04291–1,USAFHRC.

45. Memorandum, Pacific Fleet Eval Gp, "An Analysis of the Close Air Support Supplied the US 1st Marine Div in Korea during May–Jun 1951," Sept 25, 1951, App 10, Interim Eval Rprt Nr 2, CINCPACFLT, *US Pacific Fleet Operations: Korean War*: entries, May 24 and 26, 1951, Partridge diaries.

46. Policy Analysis Div, HqMC, memo, "S677–Douglass Bill," Apr 7, 1951, "Unification" File, H&MD; memo, Div of Aviation, HqMC, AAT–1737, Apr 13, 1951, "Close Air Support" File, H&MD; memo, OP–003, "Increase Naval Forces," Adm Forrest Sherman Papers, NHD; CMC to SecNav, annual report, 1 Sep 1951, Command File, OA/NHD: Report, Maj Gen F. Harris to CMC, "Report of Bd to Study and Make Recommendations on Air–Ground and Aviation Matters," Aug 27, 1951, HAF.

For the air war from the perspective of Marine squadrons, see Lt Col Gary W. Parker and Maj. Frank M. Batha, Jr, USMC, *A History of Marine Observation Squadron Six* (Washington, 1978) and *A History of Marine Ftr Attack Squadron 312* (Washington, 1978).

47. "Close Air Support," Chap 9 in Interim Eval Report, Nr 3 May 1–Dec 31, 1951, CINCPACFLT, *US Pacific Fleet Operations: Korean War*; Montross, Kuokka, and Hicks, *The East–Central Front*, pp 173–198.

48. Ltr, CG 1st MarDiv to CG Fifth AF, Oct 3, 1951; Ltr, CG Fifth AF to CINCFE, Oct 5 1951; Ltr, CG Eighth Army to CINCFE, Oct 6 1951; Ltr, CINCFE to CG 1st MarDiv, Oct 15 1951; Ltr, CG 1st MarDiv to CINCFE, Oct 18 1951; all in Evaluation Staff, Doctrinal Div, Air War College, "Close Air Support Operations (1950–1953)," File K239.04291–1, HRC. See also oral memoir, Lt Gen G. C. Thomas, USMC (1966), pp 886–907, OHC/H&MD.

49. Memo, Van Fleet–Everest conference on close air support, Nov 17, 1951, and Ltr, CG Eighth Army to CINCFE, Dec 20, 1951, both File K239.04291–1, HRC; Ltr, Maj R. G. Currie, USAF, ALO, 1st Cavalry Div, to CG Fifth Air Force, "Report of Misuse and Criticism of Close Air Support," Nov 25, 1951, File K730.4501A, HRC; Ltr, CG Eighth Army to CINCFE, Dec 19 and 20, 1951, Van Fleet–Ridgway Correspondence, Ridgway Papers; Office, Chief of Army Field Forces, Memorandum, "Tactical Air Support of Ground Forces," Sept 13, 1951, Almond Papers.

50. Office of the AC/S (G–3), Hq US Army, evaluation of ORO–R–3 (FEC), Nov 26, 1951, appended to the original report, previously cited; memo of Ridgway–Weyland conversation, Jan 13, 1952, and Ltr, G–3 to CINCFE, Jan 15, 1952, with Ridgway notations, Jan 2, 1952, CINCFE correspondence, Ridgway Papers.

51. James F. Schnabel and Robert J. Watson, *The History of the Joint Chiefs of Staff*, Vol III, *The Korean War*, 2 parts (Wilmington, Del., 1979), pt. 2, pp 711–909.

52. Hq FEAF, *Report on the Korean War*, I, pp 96–97; Operations Analysis Office, Fifth AF, "An Assessment of Combat Accuracy of Fifth Air Force Ftr Bombers," 1952 and 1953, Studies Nr 57, 68, and 69, File M–35606–C, Air University Library Classified Files; Operations Research Office (FEC), Johns Hopkins University. "Estimates of Effectiveness of UN Close Support Weapons in Use in Korea," 1952, Nr 32, File M–35044–2–C, Air University Library Classified Files; Department of Combat Developments, USAC&GSC, "Effectiveness of Tactical Air Support in World War II and Korea," 1961, and memo, Hq USACONARC ATTNG–THG 461/6 (S), "Lessons Learned from Korea," Feb 17, 1955, copies in Reference Section, H&MD; Operations Research Office, Hq FEC, "Close Air Support Operations in Korea: Preliminary Evaluation," 1951, previously cited.

53. This assessment is based upon 18th Fighter-Bmbr Wing, "Hist Report," Oct 1951–Jul 1953, File K–WG–18–HI, HRC, and 136th Fighter-Bmbr Gp, "History," Jul 1951–Mar 1942, File K–GP–136–HI, USAFHRC.

54. "Hist Survey of Army Fire Support," Chap 2, previously cited. For combat conditions along the MLR, see especially S.L.A. Marshall, *Pork Chop Hill* (New York, 1956).

55. Quoted in Cagle and Manson, *Sea War in Korea*, p 462.

56. Futrell, *Air Force in Korea*, pp 471–504; Cagle and Manson, *Sea War in Korea*, pp 460–464; Hermes, *Truce Tent and Fighting Front*, pp 319–329.

57. CINCFE, memo, "Air Ground Operations," Jul 1, 1952, and Hq FEC letter. "Air Ground Operations," Aug 11, 1952, File K720–4501B, USAFHRC.

58. Hq FEAF, memo AG 373.21, "Air Ground Operations," Sept 12, 1952, with enclosures, File K239–04291–1, HRG; oral memoir, Gen O. P. Weyland, USAF (1974), pp 107–109, 111, 192, File 239.0512–813, USAFHRC; Futrell, *Air Force in Korea*, pp 541–544.

59. "Carrier Operations," Chap 3 in Interim Eval Reports Nr 5, Jul 1, 1952–Jan 31, 1953, and Nr 6 Feb 1–Jul 27, 1953, CINCPACLFLT, *US Pacific Fleet Operations: Korean War*: Cagle and Manson, *Sea War in Korea*, pp 461–469; Field, *US Naval Operations: Korea*, p 443.

60. "Fleet Marine Force–Air," Chap 10 in Interim Eval Reports Nrs 4 to 6, Jan 1 1952–Jul 27, 1953, cited above; oral memoir of Gen. Christian F. Schildt, USMC (1969), pp 124–126; oral memoir of Maj Gen John P. Condon, USMC (1970), pp 112–116; oral memoir of Maj Gen Samuel S. Jack, USMC (1970), pp 64–66; oral memoir of Lt Gen Vernon E. Megee, USMC (1967), pp 178–187; oral memoir of Gen E. A. Pollock, USMC (1971), pp 232–238, all of the above in the Oral History Collection, H&MD. See also Lt Col Pat Meid, USMCR, and Maj James M. Yingling, USMC, *Operations in West Korea*, Vol V in *US Marine Operations in Korea* (Washington, HqMC, 1972).

61. Cagle and Manson, *Sea War in Korea*, pp 467–468; "Fleet Marine Force–Air," Chap 10, *Interim Eval Report*, Nr 6, p 10–90, previously cited; FEAF, Command Hist Report, Jul 1953, Vol I, pp 18–21, with appended memos, D/O, FEAF to D/O, Hq, USAF, Jul 8, 1953 and CG Fifth AF to COs, all Fighter-Bmbr Wings, nd, File 720.02 1953, USAFHRC.

62. Hermes, *Truce Tent and Fighting Front*, pp 385–388; Futrell, *Air Force in Korea*, p 544; Gen Mark W. Clark, USA (Ret), *From the Danube to the Yalu* (New York, 1954), pp 234–236; Ltr, Col T. M. Crawford, USAF (Ret) to author, Jul 26, 1984. Colonel Crawford was the TAC(A) for "Smack."

63. For 1953 close air-support operations, see Futrell, *Air Force in Korea*, pp 672–679; Hermes, *Truce Tent and Fighting Front*, pp 459–478; Meid and Yingling, *Operations in West Korea*, pp 344–353. The critical analysis of the close airsupport effort is from "Fleet Marine Force–Air," Chap 10, *Interim Eval Report*, Nr 6, pp 10–80 to 10–92.

64. My summary is based on, "Fleet Marine Force–Air," Chap 10, cited above; Hq Fifth AF, "Report on Joint Air-Ground Conference, 8–22 Aug 1953," Aug 23, 1953, HRC; Futrell, *Air Force in Korea*, pp 704–708; Meid and Yingling, *Operations in West Korea*, pp 485–493.

65. Futrell, *Air Force in Korea*, pp 689–693.

66. Ralph D. Bald, Jr, *Air Force Participation in Joint Army–Air Force Training Exercises, 1951–1954* (USAF Hist Study Nr 129, Research Studies Institute, Air University, 1957).

67. Sunderland, *Evolution of Command and Control Doctrine for Close Air Support*, p 31–33; Futrell, *Ideas, Concepts, Doctrine*, pp 203–207; Gen Otto P. Weyland, USAF, "The Air Campaign in Korea," *Air University Quarterly Review* 6 (Fall, 1953) pp 3–28.

Bibliographical Essay

All the armed forces have published histories of their Korean War service. For all air operations from the Air Force perspective, see Robert Frank Futrell, *The United States Air Force in Korea, 1950–1953* (rev. ed., Washington, D.C.: Office of Air Force History. 1983). Futrell puts the Air Force experience into a broader perspective in *Ideas, Concepts, Doctrine: A History of Basic Thinking in the United States Air Force, 1907–1964* (Maxwell AFB, Alabama: Air University, 1971), Chapters 6 and 7. The 1st Marine Division––1st Marine Air Wing experience is described in Lynn Montross *et. al.*, *U.S. Marine Corps Operations in Korea, 1950–1953* (5 Vols., Washington, D.C.: Headquarters U.S. Marine Corps, 1954–1972). James A. Field, Jr., *History of United States Naval Operations: Korea* (Washington, D.C.: Office of Naval History, 1962) is the Navy's official history, but see also the semi-official Malcolm W. Cagle and Frank A. Manson, *The Sea War in Korea* (Annapolis, Md.: U.S. Naval Institute, 1957), which contains important interviews and air operations accounts. Three books have thus far appeared in the U.S. Army's series, "The U.S. Army in the Korean War." Two cover the war primarily from the U.S. Army's operational perspective; they are: Roy E. Appleman, *South to the Naktong, North to the Yalu* (Washington, D.C.: Office of the Chief of Military History, 1961) and Walter G. Hermes, *Truce Tent and Fighting Front* (Washington, D.C.: Office of the Chief of Military History, 1967). James F. Schnabel, *Policy and Direction: The First Year* (Washington, D.C.: Office of the Chief of Military History) discusses the war from the varied—and often conflicting-perspectives of the Department of the Army and Headquarters Far East Command. James F. Schnabel and Robert J. Watson, *The History of the Joint Chiefs of Staff*, Vol. III, *The Korean War*, in two parts (Wilmington, Del.: Michael Glazier, 1979) analyzes the war and rearmament policies as viewed by the JCS.

The Air Force archives of the USAF Historical Research Center, Air University, Maxwell Air Force Base, Alabama, contain the single most imposrtant set of documents on the Korean air war. Among the most significant records are: Headquarters, U.S. Air Force, Korean Evaluation Project, "Report of Air Operations," January 16, 1951, File K168.041–2, which includes many supporting documents collected by Far East Air Forces and Fifth Air Force; Headquarters, Far East Air Forces, to Commander-in-Chief, Far East, "A General Review of the United States Tactical Air Support in Korea, 28 June–8 September 1950," File 720–4501A; Headquarters, Far East Air Forces, *Report on the Korean War*, 2 Vols., 1953, File K720.04D; Headquarters Far East Air Forces, "Weekly Intelligence Round-ups," 1950–1953, File K720.607A; Col. J. Ferguson USAF to VCO FEAF, "Outline of the

Korean Campaign," November 9, 1950, File K417.01; "Commanders' Quotes: Close Air Support," File Kll–.8–33; Report, Joint Air–Ground Operations Board, "Analysis of Air–Ground Operations in Korea," March 26, 1951, File K239–04291–1; Evaluation Staff, Doctrinal Division, Air War College, "Close Air-Support Operations (1950–1953)," K239.04291–1, with enclosures; Headquarters, Far East Air Forces, "History of the Far East Air Forces," 2 vols., 1953, File K720.01; and Headquarters Fifth Air Force, "Report on Joint Air-Ground Conference, 8–22 August 1953," August 23, 1953.

Headquarters U.S. Air Force, Far East Command, Far East Air Forces, and Fifth Air Force organized studies during and after the Korean war that provide a core of data and analysis (however often conflicting) on close air-support operations. Most of them are now part of the individual command records stored at the Historical Research Center. See especially Headquarters U.S. Air Force, "A Quantitative Comparison between Land-Based and Carrier-Based Air during the Early Days of the Korean War;" Operations Research Office, Headquarters Far East Command, "Close Air-Support Operations in Korea: Preliminary Evaluation," 1 February 1951; Headquarters Fifth Air Force, "Weapons Selection for Close Air-Support Operations," November 30, 1951; Headquarters Fifth Air Force, "An Assessment of Combat Accuracy of Fifth Air Force Fighter Bombers," 1952 and 1953; Operations Research Office, Far East Command, "Estimates of Effectiveness of UN Close-Support Weapons in Use in Korea," 1952; and Operations Analysis Office, Fifth Air Force, Memorandum No. 69, "History of Bombing Accuracy during the Korean War, Part I: Fighter-Bombers," September 9, 1950.

Among the Air Force records held by the National Archives and Records Agency in either Washington, D.C. or Suitland, Maryland, the most relevant are the records of the Office of the Secretary of the Air Force (Record Group 340), the records of the Office of the Chief of Staff, U.S. Air Force (Record Group 341), and archives of Headquarters, Tactical Air Command in the records of Air Force Commands, Activities, and Organizations (Record Group 342), all of the above administered by the Modern Military Branch of the National Archives. Official organizational histories and supporting documents, however, are managed by the U.S. Air Force Historical Research Center at Maxwell AFB. For example, an important memo by Gen. O.P. Weyland, "Some Lessons of the Korean War and Conclusions and Recommendations Concerning Air Force Tactical Air Responsibilities," October 12, 1950, is appended to the Tactical Air Command history, July–November 1950, Vol. IV.

The private papers of many of the senior officers of Far East Command/ United Nations Command provide important information and personal attitudes towards the close air-support question. For the U.S. Air Force, see the collections at the Historical Research Center for Gen. Earle E. Partridge, Commanding General of Fifth Air Force (1950–1951); Lt. Gen. George E. Stratemeyer, Commanding General of Far East Air Forces (1950–1951); and Gen. Otto P. Weyland, Vice Commander and Commanding General, Far Eastern Air Forces (1950–1954). The oral memoirs of Generals Partridge and Weyland add detail to their diaries and correspondence while the memoirs of Gen. Frank F. Everest, Commanding General, Fifth Air Force (1951–1952) and Maj. Gen. Gilbert L. Meyers, Director of Operations, Fifth Air Force (1950–1952) provide additional insights into air operations. The papers of General Hoyt S. Vandenberg, Chief of Staff of the U.S. Air Force (1948–1953) are held by the Manuscript Division of the Library of Congress.

The Douglas MacArthur Papers in the MacArthur Museum and Archives, Norfolk, Virginia, contain scattered air support documents in "General Correspondence" and "Correspondence: Korean War Miscellaneous," Far East Command, 1950–1951, Record Group 6.

The operations of the Air Force's tactical air controllers (airborne) are described and analyzed in a number of sources. Of particular value are William M. Cleveland, comp., "Mosquitoes in Korea, 1950–1953," 1983, privately published by the Association of the 6147th Tactical Control Group (Airborne) as supplemented by Mr. Cleveland's collection of personal memoirs, "Mosquito Questionnaires," 1983, and the 1984 supplement to the original Association booklet. Two other important studies are J. Farmer and M.J. Sturmwasser, *The Evolution of the Airborne Forward Air Controller: An Analysis of Mosquito Operations in Korea*, Memorandum RM–5430–PR, October, 1967 (Santa Monica, Calif.: The RAND Corporation, 1967) and Timothy E. Kline, "Forward Air Control in the Korean War," *Journal of American Aviation Historical Society* 21 (Winter, 1976), 257–262.

Personal and institutional documents and internal studies for the U.S. Army's experiences with close air support may be found in the Air Force archives already cited and at two principal repositories, the Center of Military History, Department of the Army, Washington, D.C. and the U.S. Army Military History Institute, Carlisle Barracks, Pennsylvania. The papers of Gen. Matthew B. Ridgway, Commanding General of the U.S. Eighth Army and Far East Command (1950–1952), and Lt. Gen. Edward M. Almond, Commanding General, X Corps (1950–1951) are held by the Military History Institute. Almond's "Tactical Air Support" files are especially complete, and both Ridgway and Almond conducted extensive correspondence with Gen. J. Lawton Collins, Army Chief of Staff (1949–1953), and Gen. Mark W. Clark, Commanding General of Army Field Forces (1949–1952), on close air support questions.

The doctrinal context for Air Force–Army air–ground operations is established in a number of critical studies: William A. Jacobs, "Tactical Air

Doctrine and AAF Close Air Support in the European Theater, 1944–1945," *Aerospace Historian* 27 (Spring, 1980). 350 35–49; Charles W. Dickens, *A Survey of Air-Ground Doctrine*, Headquarters Tactical Air Command, Historical Study No. 34, 1958; Alfred Goldberg and Donald Smith, *Army-Air Force Relations: The Close Air-Support Issue*, Memorandum R–906–PR (Santa Monica, Calif.: The RAND Corporation, 1971); Riley Sunderland, *Evolution of Command and Control Doctrine for Close Air Support* (Washington, D.C.: Office of Air Force History, 1973); Historical Branch, Programs Division, Combat Developments Command, U.S. Army, "Historical Survey of Army Fire Support," 18 March 1963; and Joint Staff Task Force, Joint Staff, JCS, "Close Air-Support Study," 1972; Department of Combat Developments, U.S. Army Command and General Staff College, "Effectiveness of Tactical Air Support in World War II and Korea," 1961. The relevant doctrinal publications that shaped close airsupport operations in the Korean War are U.S. War Department, Field Manual 31–35, *Air–Ground Operations* (Washington, D.C.: GPO, 1946) and Office, Chief of Army Field Forces, and Headquarters Tactical Air Command, *Joint Training Directive for Air–Ground Operations*, September 1, 1950. Doctrinal application outside the war zone may be found in Ralph D. Bald, Jr., *Air Force Participation in Joint Army–Air Force Training Exercises, 1947–1950*, Historical Study No. 80, (Maxwell AFB, Ala.: Air University, 1955) and *Air Force Participation in Joint Army–Air Force Training Exercises, 1951–1954*, Historical Study No. 129 (Maxwell AFB, Ala.: Air University, 1957).

Documents on the Marine Corps experience with the close air-support mission may be found in the archives of the Reference Section and the Archives Branch of the History and Museums Division, Marine Corps Historical Center, Washington Navy Yard as well as the "Historical Amphibious Files," James C. Breckinridge Library, Education Center, Marine Corps Combat Development and Education Command, Quantico, Virginia. The former location holds material on the 1st Air and Naval Gunfire Liaison Company, FMF, and Marine Tactical Air Control Squadron 2, the principal air control and air request agencies. See also Maj. Gen. F. Harris to Commandant Marine Corps, "Report of Board to Study and Make Recommendations on Air–Ground and Aviation Matters," August 27, 1951, HAF. Among senior Marine commanders who left opinions about close air support were Gen. O. P. Smith, Commander of the 1st Marine Division (1950–1951), who left a diary, papers, and an oral memoir in the MCHC; oral memoir of Gen. Gerald C. Thomas, Commanding General of the 1st Marine Division (1951–1952); oral memoir of Gen. Edward A. Pollock, Commanding General of the 1st Marine Division (1952–1953); oral memoir of Gen. Christian F. Schildt, Commanding General, 1st Marine Air Wing (1951–1952); oral memoir of Gen. Vernon Megee, Commanding General, 1st Marine Air Wing (1953);

oral memoir of Maj. Gen. Samuel S. Jack, Chief of Staff, 1st Marine Air Wing (1952–1953); and oral memoir of Maj. Gen. John P. Condon, Commanding Officer, Marine Air Groups 33 and 12 (1952–1953).

The close air-support doctrine of Navy and Marine Corps aviation on the eve of the Korean War may be found in PHIB 12/NAVMC 4159, *Amphibious Operations: Air Operations* (1948) and NAVMC 4542, *The Defense of Advanced Naval Bases—Air Operations* (1948), both of which may be found in the Historical Amphibious Files, Breckinridge Library. The key source for the Korean air war for the carrier-based naval aviation of Task Force 77, Seventh Fleet, and the 1st Marine Air Wing, Fleet Marine Forces Pacific, is the series of "Evaluation Reports," 1950–1953, Commander-in-Chief Pacific Fleet, *Korean War: U.S. Pacific Operations*, Operational Archives, Naval Historical Center, Washington Navy Yard, Washington, D.C. These reports contain supporting documents of both doctrinal importance and operational assessment.

9

Southeast Asia

John J. Sbrega

In the aftermath of the Korean War, President Dwight D. Eisenhower resolved that never again would the United States become bogged down in a war like the one in Korea, where the full brunt of American power could not, or would not, be applied. Consequently, American strategists during the 1950's tailored the armed forces to meet an all-out nuclear exchange (including "massive retaliation") and only secondarily a general conventional war. As a result, until about 1960 the Air Force emphasized general nuclear-war capabilities in the belief that these capabilities would meet the requirements of any limited war.[1] Looking back at the 1950s, Gen. T. R. Milton, former Commander of Thirteenth Air Force, lamented the efforts of theater air forces "all trying to be little SACs with the primary and almost the only mission being the nuclear one."[2] Another Air Force leader, Chief of Staff Gen. John P. McConnell, recalled in 1968, "We [USAF] did not even start doing anything about tactical aviation until about 1961 or 1962."[3] In a classic case of understatement, one post–Vietnam Air Force study suggested, "It is quite possible that many of the programs that appeared neglected in the light of our subsequent experiences in Vietnam were logically viewed as less essential during the 1950s."[4]

Tailoring air power to meet the worst possible cases, with the idea that it could then handle all lesser situations, contained certain flaws. As General McConnell pointed out later, the Air Force was quite unprepared for unconventional war. To support this contention, McConnell cited tactical fighter aircraft designed for nuclear delivery or air superiority missions, reconnaissance aircraft sensors and navigation systems ill-suited for the type of warfare found in Southeast Asia, aircrews and weapons loading and armament personnel deficient in training for conventional warfare, and available munitions ineffective for conventional operations.[5] One Air Force officer complained that pilots had to be "many splendored things."[6] Moreover, the careful attention required to develop limited conventional warfare and counterinsurgency doctrine, especially with regard to close air support, lapsed in the all-encompassing strategy of nuclear deterrence.[7]

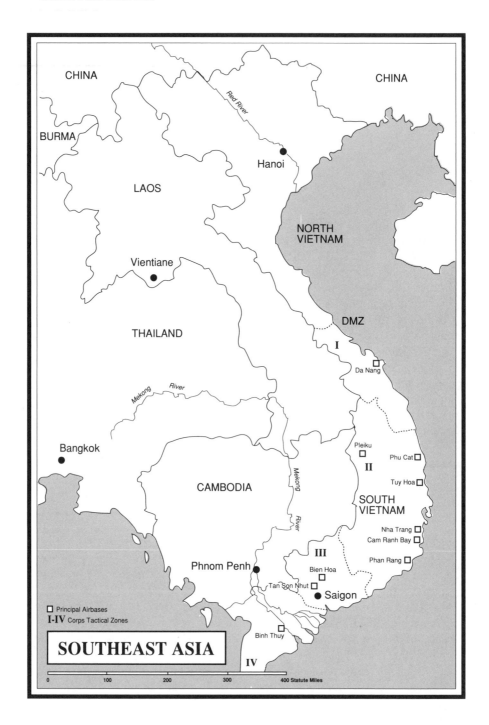

SOUTHEAST ASIA

During the 1950s, Air Force views also created friction with the Army. While the Air Force concentrated on large-scale nuclear conflict, the Army continued to advocate preparation for conventional warfare. In particular, Army strategists argued that a major confrontation with the Soviet Union would involve a land war in Europe. This premise, in turn, led the Army to develop its structure and strength accordingly.[8] For example, between 1955 and 1959, the Army added almost 2,000 air vehicles (3,495 to 5,475).[9] The Air Force inferred from this approach that the Army saw a sharply reduced role for the Air Force. (One Air Force commentator wrote that the Army only wanted the Air Force to deliver airlift and support ground-forces.[10]) Consequently, the strategic perspectives of the two services as shaped in the years immediately following the Korean War seemed destined to clash.

By 1958, with the crises in Quemoy and Lebanon, the Air Force began to think more about the lower levels of the combat spectrum.[11] Army studies from 1959 to 1961 called particular attention to the need for adequate close air support from the Air Force in limited operations.[12] For example, Joint Army–Air Force plans in 1960 fixed the expected Air Force close air support at five sorties per day for each maneuvering Army battalion.[13] A concept of flexible response that emphasized readiness to meet the full range of combat possibilities emerged under Eisenhower.[14]

During the succeeding administration, John F. Kennedy, guided by his influential Defense Secretary, Robert S. McNamara, strengthened the concept of flexible response by promoting development of general purpose forces and by taking other steps to redress the imbalance between nuclear and conventional capabilities. This major shift in U.S. strategic thinking was underscored by the fact that the very ideas Eisenhower had so vigorously opposed—limited wars and implied restrictions on American power—once again became acceptable topics for high-level discussions.

In the early 1960s the Air Force and the Army struggled to reach some accommodation concerning close air support within this general strategic context. Although some voices in the Air Force advocated the creation of special counterinsurgency air units, the predominant view of the Air Force continued to be that high-performance tactical fighter-bombers could satisfy multiple roles, ranging from nuclear strikes in all-out wars to close air support in limited engagements. More specifically, the Air Force doctrine for tactical air power centered on three missions: (1) counterair (gaining supremacy of the air over the battlefield), (2) interdiction (preventing enemy forces and supplies from reaching the battlefield), and (3) close air support (attacking the enemy in contact with friendly forces on a specific part of the battlefield). Air Force leaders expected to set priorities for these missions according to each situation as it arose. For example, interdiction strikes might prevent or retard the buildup of enemy forces massing to attack friendly forces, but the presence of an enemy force, however small, engaged in combat operations with friendly troops could temporarily outweigh the importance of interdicting larger enemy targets behind the battlefield. Always, however, the Air Force argued for centralized Air Force control of these tactical air resources, mainly to assure success in achieving air superiority, the primary mission of air power.[15]

In 1960 and 1961, Army studies on close air support underlined a different perspective. For example, a Continental Army Command (CONARC) study in 1960 maintained that the ground commander should designate the location and the types of specific attacks to be made against the enemy forces he faced. According to this study, the Army had either to be assured that immediate close air support would be provided by the Air Force or develop its own.[16] In 1961 the Army Command and General Staff College examined close air support and recommended (1) Army–Air Force joint operational planning should be decentralized to the level of field army and tactical air force; (2) allocated resources for close air support should be adequate for the actual need; (3) close air support should be under the operational control of the ground commander; and (4) Air Force units designated for close air support "must be equipped with aircraft designed for ground attack as a primary mission."[17] In addition to calling for designated close air-support units and special close air-support aircraft, the Army wanted decentralized operational control under local ground commanders. As Army Chief of Staff Gen. George H. Decker wrote in May 1961: "The Army's requirement is to have close air support where we need it, when we need it, and under a system of operational control that makes it responsive to Army needs."[18] To provide a quantitative and organizational gauge of General Decker's requirement, the Army suggested that three Air Force squadrons designated solely for the close airsupport mission be assigned to each Army division.[19]

To the extent that the Department of Defense entered various parts of this debate, Secretary of Defense McNamara favored development of an aircraft designed especially for close air support. In fact, on October 9, 1961, he put that proposal directly to the Army and Air Force Chiefs of Staff.[20] Two other key points advanced by the Department of Defense that seemed to rebut the Air Force position, were: (1) that operational equipment should not be too sophisticated to allow for possible use by indigenous forces; and (2) multi-purpose, sophisticated equipment might contribute to raising the level of violence in a localized, limited war.[21] Nevertheless, in September 1961 the Department of Defense established the U.S. Strike Command, which coincided with the concept of general purpose forces.[22]

On the eve of the American buildup in Southeast Asia, joint Army–Air Force doctrine—the fundamental principles by which military forces guide their actions—on close air support was virtually nonexistent. The concept of close air support itself was difficult to clarify. How close was close? By the early 1960s, the Joint Chiefs of Staff shaped a working definition of close air support: "Air action against hostile targets . . . in close proximity to friendly forces and which requires detailed integration of each air mission with the fire and movement of those forces."[23] Although interservice differences concerning close air support (such as command and control issues or specially designed air units and aircraft) seemed somewhat remote and abstract in the early 1960s, they would erupt in full force with the rapid buildup of American forces in Southeast Asia.

In April 1962, in accord with the Kennedy policy of flexible response, McNamara asked Secretary of the Army Elvis J. Stahr, Jr., to take a bold new look at land-warfare mobility, especially its aviation support. McNamara wanted an innovative inquiry "conducted in an atmosphere divorced from traditional viewpoints and past policies."[24] The Army set up a Tactical Mobility Requirements Board, better known as the Howze Board (named after its chairman, Lt. Gen. Hamilton H. Howze). The Board's final report, submitted in August 1962, recommended that the Army develop new air assault divisions with their own airsupport capabilities, including organic armed helicopters and fixed-wing assault transports. Although its primary concern focused on air-assault capabilities, the Howze Board did address some important close air-support issues. For example, the board recommended (1) commanders of field armies (or independent corps) possess operational control over all their air support, (2) certain key functions performed by Army organic air vehicles (including some close air support as well as command and control) come directly under division, battalion, or company commanders operating in and supported from a front line environment, (3) the Air Force develop an aircraft designed especially for close air support, and (4) the Air Force adopt quantitative requirements for close air support (e.g., 35–40 sorties made available for each Army division per combat day in a conventional war with the Soviet Union during the period 1965–1970; 25–30 corresponding sorties in a war with Communist China).[25]

Within one month, the Air Force created its own study group to examine the findings and implications of the work of the Army's Howze Board. The Tactical Air Support Requirements Board (or Disosway Board, named after its chairman, Lt. Gen. Gabriel P. Disosway, USAF), reaffirmed the existing system of command and control for close air support, which lay in the hands of the Air Force. Rather than try to divide responsibility (as the Howze Board had done) at various levels for certain key combat functions, like command and control or close air support, the Disosway Board advocated a joint concept wherein all combat-aviation functions would continue to be fulfilled by air vehicles under the command and control of the Air Force. In turn, the Air Force would respond to battle area requirements as directed by the joint task force commander. Once again the traditional Air Force arguments—that the three tactical air functions of close air support, counterair, and interdiction were interrelated and best performed by forces trained and equipped in all

415

three areas—were supported by the Disosway report. Moreover, the Disosway Board not only upheld the idea of designing a multipurpose force to meet the full range of possibilities in conventional warfare but also pointed out that limited funds would not allow a special air assault force of such limited use as that envisioned by the Howze Board. In addition, the Disosway group argued that armed assault helicopters simply could not function in a high threat environment. Although the members of the Disosway Board made clear in their final report of September 1962 that the Air Force was not opposed to the Army becoming more mobile, they felt that the Army did not take into consideration "the full capabilities of the Air Force."[26]

Faced with these differing viewpoints, in February 1963 McNamara ordered a joint Army–Air Force examination of close air support. Two months later, Army and Air Force Close Air Support Boards were organized at the CONARC/Tactical Air Command level. The joint investigation covered five close air-support topics: (1) procedures, tactics, and techniques; (2) training and indoctrination; (3) resources; (4) command relationships; and (5) type of aircraft. Despite some agreement on issues in the first three categories (for example, the use of both Army and Air Force personnel in the air-ground communications system, the need for an Army–Air Force close air-support center, improved munitions, improved target acquisition techniques, and modifications in the pilot training curriculum), the joint group could not reach accord either on command and control issues or on the type of aircraft to be employed. No consensus emerged, and decisions were deferred pending further study.[27]

The deliberations of the Howze Board, the Disosway Board and the Army and Air Force Close Air Support Boards underscored disagreement over a few significant issues that blocked a joint consensus on close air support. One issue was contained in the broad category of command and control. For the Army this meant a decentralized system in which the local groundforce commander received close air support adequate to eliminate the targets he chose at the time he desired. The Army, in fact, wanted the ground commander—perhaps even down to the company level, depending on the situation—to hold operational control over all supporting aircraft once those aircraft entered his area of responsibility (or reported to him). In particular, the Army wanted the ground commander to be able to rely on the supporting aircraft he received without worrying whether the aircraft might be ordered elsewhere without notice just at a time when he needed them. The Air Force, on the other hand, adopted the approach that close air support was a joint venture. According to the Air Force view, a joint task force commander would enjoy operational control over all resources. For instance, he would decide on the allocation of tactical air resources from the general (centralized) pool of Air Force operationally ready aircraft. His jurisdiction would include not only the designation of target priorities but also the scheduling of strikes down to the desired times over targets.

Discussion of this issue, sometimes referred to as the "single manager for air" concept, touched, in turn, on another source of interservice controversy: the setting of quantitative measures to determine "adequate" close air support. The Army desired that each division be allocated a certain number of close air support sorties for each combat day, enabling the division commander to develop operational plans on a reliable basis. Even more important to him: he could be certain of not losing that air support in the midst of an engagement, as he would hold operational control over the aircraft assigned to him each day. In contrast, the Air Force argued that in the fluid, rapidly changing circumstances of combat, battlefield priorities could shift quickly and unexpectedly, and this could necessitate concentrating close air-support resources in a particular area at the expense of denying support to ground units less heavily engaged. Therefore, according to the Air Force, assigning the overriding authority to a joint task-force commander is a method valuable not only for meeting an unforeseen turn of events but also for parceling out tactical air resources to the best advantage. Requests—and problems—of commanders in local parts of the broad battle area must be weighed against the overall tactical situation. Although Air Force leaders remained skeptical about assigning a certain number of close air-support sorties to each Army division in a combat day, they did not absolutely oppose this proposal. Rather, the Air Force called for joint testing and war gaming to determine if the Army's recommendation had merit. Until such time as the merit of the Army's view was proved decisive, however, the Air Force would not agree to the idea.

A third close air-support issue that separated the two services was the new concept of a highly mobile Army assault division. The importance of quick reaction and movement in this concept obviously affected close air support. This discussion, in turn, further fueled the debate of service roles and missions. The Air Force maintained that it could provide whatever air support the Army needed; in addition to the low probability of survival for helicopters in a hostile environment, the arming of Army helicopters appeared not only to impinge on the Air Force mission of providing close air support but also to represent an unnecessary drain on limited budget resources.

Army leaders viewed the helicopters as an integral component of new, highly mobile assault divisions. These divisions, according to the Army, would meet challenges at the lower ends of the combat spectrum—challenges that would be numerous and scattered around the globe, if predictions of future wars of national liberation were to prove true. In addition, the Army wanted its armed helicopters to complement rather than replace Air Force close air support. As Army Chief of Staff Gen. Earle Wheeler explained in

October 1963: "Units of other Services will conduct *close air support* with aircraft that can deliver large volumes of ordnance on call of the ground commander. Aerial vehicles of the Army will conduct *aerial fire support* with aerial vehicles capable of discriminatory firepower in close proximity to ground combat elements."[28] While denying any intent to build a separate air arm, the Army did affirm its intention to use all possible firepower on the modern battlefield.

A fourth major source of interservice friction over close air support stemmed from the question of the need for an aircraft designed especially for close air support. The Air Force remained reluctant to develop specific aircraft for each of its three tactical air missions: counterair, interdiction, and close air support. With air resources centralized in the hands of the task force commander, and with overall tactical priorities, especially between close air support and interdiction, likely to shift as the combat situation dictated, the Air Force preferred the type of aircraft that could handle all three tactical air missions. This meant high-performance jet fighter-bombers. To devote money and other resources to a special aircraft designed only for the close air-support mission seemed inappropriate to Air Force leaders. Nevertheless, Army leaders advocated the development of such an aircraft by the Air Force. They were not at all certain that the high-performance, multimission jets could throttle down sufficiently to deliver effective close air support. The Army wanted slower aircraft to locate and destroy small, hidden, or fleeting targets and longer loiter time over the target than that of the sophisticated jets. The Air Force argued in favor of the faster response times and heavier ordnance loads of the jets.

In short, the positions of the two services on close air support seemed irreconcilable. The Air Force maintained that the system was fundamentally sound but in need of certain improvements—improvements that would come about as the result of joint testing and war gaming. Conversely, the Army argued for organizational and structural changes to improve the responsiveness—both in terms of firepower and timeliness—to the needs of ground commanders for direct fire support.[29] What must be kept in mind is that while these interservice disagreements persisted through the early 1960s, at the time of increasing American involvement in Southeast Asia, McNamara was encouraging the Army, Air Force, and especially Strike Command to sponsor joint training exercises to field-test the contested issues concerning close air support.

Vietnam—The Early Years

Early close air-support operations in South Vietnam were plagued with problems. The Vietnamese Air Force (VNAF) had emerged in 1951 as part of the French Air Force in Indochina. From 1950 to 1957 American contributions (mainly financial) to the VNAF were channeled through the French. This meant that the methods and procedures used by the French Air Force—those that had proved so ineffective in the First Indochina War (1946–1954)—shaped the development of the VNAF.[30] In 1957, when the French departed, and when American influence over the VNAF grew dramatically—Gen. William W. Momyer, commander of Tactical Air Command, 1968–1973, described it as "de facto control"—the complete VNAF inventory amounted to one squadron of F–8Fs and RF–8Fs, two squadrons of L–19s, and two squadrons of C–47s.[31] The primary emphasis for the VNAF lay in reconnaissance rather than tactical combat operations, and the decentralized control of VNAF units, while troublesome later, did not represent an organizational flaw in view of the small size of the total force.[32]

In addition to aircraft shortages, the VNAF lacked trained pilots (especially for close air-support operations at night) and technically qualified support personnel.[33] The U.S. Military Assistance Program (MAP) in South Vietnam was not always helpful. For example, during the late 1950s the Air Force canceled a replacement program to supply T–28s to the VNAF, and the Navy reversed its decision to send AD–4s.[34] In 1959, President Ngo Dinh Diem grounded the worn-out, unsafe F–8Fs, which were the only strike aircraft in the VNAF inventory. The following year, President Eisenhower sent six Navy AD–6s (designated A–1Hs by USAF) and eleven H–34 helicopters, but these aircraft soon ran out of parts. In 1961, the Kennedy administration considerably increased U.S. assistance to South Vietnam, including more AD–6s as well as armed T–28s for the VNAF.[35]

Command and control arrangements for VNAF tactical air operations were woefully inadequate. Although the VNAF established an Air Tactical Command in 1956, no tactical air strikes were flown until 1961.[36] A preplanned request for tactical air support first had to be approved at the division level of the Army of the Republic of Vietnam (ARVN). Next it went to the Tactical Operations Center at the corps level where, if approved (not only by the corps commander but also by the civilian province chief[s] involved), it passed on to Saigon for consideration at the Joint Operations Center (JOC) by the Joint General Staff—and by President Diem. For an approved request, the JOC determined the specifics of the operation (e.g., number of aircraft, armament, time, target, etc.) and sent that information to the Air Support Operations Center (ASOC) in the appropriate corps area to execute the mission. The requesting ARVN unit received separate notice of the approval and strike information from the JOC through the ARVN corps commander. The system for handling emergency requests (for immediate tactical air support) was to divert strike aircraft from other preplanned missions. The process was extremely slow and not always efficient. Moreover, the VNAF representatives at the corps and JOC levels made some contributions in this request process, but in general, the VNAF remained underrepresented and uninfluentual throughout the war, notwithstanding the powerful political positions of the former commander of the VNAF, Nguyen Cao Ky.[37]

In 1961, at Eglin AFB, Florida, the USAF 4400 Combat Crew Training Squadron (CCTS, code-named Jungle Jim) began training to react to "brush fires" anywhere in the world. In October of that year, the 4400 CCTS dispatched a unit (Detachment 2A, code-named Farm Gate) under Lt. Col. Benjamin H. King to Bien Hoa Air Base in South Vietnam. Farm Gate included 154 men and 16 aircraft: 8 T–28s, 4 SC–47s, and 4 RB–26s.[38]

In November 1961, Thirteenth Air Force activated an advanced echelon, 2d ADVON (a meaningless designation), under Brig. Gen. Rollen Anthis (USAF) in Saigon to oversee Farm Gate operations. Because Thirteenth Air Force held no responsibility for air operations in South Vietnam, control of 2d ADVON passed to Military Assistance Advisory Group, Vietnam (MAAG,V). The primary mission for Farm Gate was to train the VNAF in tactical air operations. All Farm Gate aircraft carried VNAF markings and a VNAF trainee-observer. The first armed mission by Farm Gate came in November 1961, when four T–28s reconnoitered the railroad line that ran northeast out of Bien Hoa. A month later saw the first joint operation with Farm Gate and VNAF aircraft supporting the Army of the Republic of Vietnam in War Zone D. The Kennedy administration strictly limited the Farm Gate mission to training and advising the VNAF—although American airmen sometimes exceeded this mandate. Thus, the official reporting of sorties, regardless of their actual nature reflected those innocuous missions.[39]

In the early efforts, Americans learned of the difficulties in conducting close air-support operations in South Vietnam. Political considerations dominated the conduct of the war. Very few ARVN officers—usually only the corps commander, his chief of staff, and the deputy chief of staff—could even so much as forward a request to Saigon. In fact, for a time the President had to approve every air strike in the country. As previously noted, all strike requests were coordinated through civilian as well as military channels. By 1962, South Vietnam was divided into nine tactical zones. The boundaries of the provinces did not coincide with the military zones; consequently, the military commanders and province chiefs, each of whom held veto power over air strikes within his area of responsibility, had to reach mutual agreement on the need for an air strike. As General Milton commented, a potential target in 1961 could become "a subject for protracted negotiations."[40]

That same year, a visiting U.S. Air Force team reported, "The high-level approval required for on-call fighter strikes, along with poor communications and/or procedures for requesting strikes, builds in excessive delays for efficient uses of the tactical air effort."[41] A personal visit to South Vietnam in April 1962 confirmed that grim conclusion for Air Force Chief of Staff Gen. Curtis Lemay.[42]

Brig. Gen. Rollen Anthis

One of the most frequent findings in investigations of excessive delays was that requests for air support never reached the corps-level Air Support Operations Centers. Attempts to determine the cause proved fruitless.[43] Some ARVN commanders either did not know how to submit a request for air support or refused to make one for fear of losing face should it be disapproved. One American advisor complained; "In a lot of cases we found that we had to ask [the ARVN commander] if he wanted air before he would ask for it."[44] A random check of response times for nine VNAF close air-support operations in the period December 16, 1961, to March 2, 1962, revealed that six took fifty minutes or longer and only one arrived under forty minutes.[45]

While Vietnamese civil-military procedures were complicated, the U.S. system of command and control was less than efficient. One distinguished commentator, Professor Russell F. Weigley, characterized the chain of command for Farm Gate as "chaotic." Weigley noted that General Anthis reported on operational matters to Pacific Air Forces Command (PACAF) and the Commander-in-Chief, Pacific (CINCPAC), but he dealt with Thirteenth Air Force on administrative matters. General Anthis also served as Commander of 2d ADVON and Air Force section chief of MAAG. Attempting to sort out these layers, Weigley believed that MAAG,V commanded Farm Gate—a situation, apparently in contravention of United States law, which forbade MAAGs from commanding operational forces.[46]

If command arrangements and the tactical air control system in South Vietnam posed problems, communications also inhibited close air-support operations. For example, in early 1962 one planned strike was canceled because the radios in the T–28s were incompatible with those of the other friendly forces.[47] The VHF, UHF, FM complex of radios in South Vietnam made air-ground communications difficult, especially between the ground commander and pilots of the strike aircraft.

In early 1962, the U.S. Army supplied the ARVN with over 10,000 PRC–10 FM radios, but neither VNAF nor Farm Gate aircraft were equipped for FM communications. Thus, ground commanders did not always have direct communications with the strike aircraft. In fact, shortly after they arrived in 1961, some American forward air controllers strapped PRC–10 ground packs to the back of the pilot's seat in order to speak directly to ground commanders during strikes (while they spoke with the strike pilots over their UHF and VHF radios).[48] As if to underscore the poor communications network in South Vietnam, the Combined Studies Division of the State Department (located in the basement of the MAAG,V building at the U.S. Embassy) constantly monitored all radio traffic. Division personnel frequently alerted the Farm Gate Command Post of strike requests that were slowly making their way through the official system so that operational preparations could begin.[49]

Steps to improve the tactical air control system occurred at about the time Farm Gate began its operations. As the result of a survey requested by MAAG and by CINCPAC in October 1961, plans for a new tactical air control system in South Vietnam took shape. Even in these first stages, the Pacific Air Forces Command (PACAF) asked that the new system be developed so that it could provide for a rapid U.S. Air Force buildup in South Vietnam.[50] In December 1961, the Joint Chiefs of Staff directed PACAF to deploy a tactical air control system to provide cooperative use of VNAF and USAF strike, reconnaissance, and transport capabilities. Additionally, Secretary McNamara ordered a control radar post activated at Tan Son Nhut Air Base (Saigon) by October 5, 1961. Thus, with the approval of President Diem, a phase-in program for the new tactical air control system (code-named Barn Door) was able to begin operations in January 1962. The terms of reference for Air Force personnel associated with Barn Door made clear that the United States was not a belligerent and that Air Force activities should be confined to advising and assisting VNAF operations and training.[51]

The new tactical air control system for VNAF/USAF operations (and training) included an Air Operations Center (AOC) at Tan Son Nhut, which served as the central command post for the VNAF and 2d ADVON. The position of AOC Director was filled by a VNAF officer, and the Deputy Director was a USAF officer. In practice, the Deputy Director controlled all USAF flights in support of the VNAF. The AOC coordinated VNAF training and joint VNAF–USAF tactical air operations, but it served only as a liaison point for U.S. Army, Navy, and Marine Corps air activities. Eventually the new system included Air Support Operations Centers (ASOCs) in I, II, and IV Corps (the AOC covered III Corps) as well as a "floating" ASOC for special operations. The ASOCs controlled close air-support sorties in specific geographical regions on the basis of daily air sorties made available from the central Air Operations Center. Each ASOC, in turn, allocated its daily quota of sorties according to the course of ground operations in the corps area. In addition, radar centers and reporting posts eventually extended to all of South Vietnam (to train the VNAF and to provide radar coverage) for the tactical air control system.[52]

By 1963, estimated enemy strength was double the 1961 level (about 25,000), and this increase strained Farm Gate resources.[53] The Joint Chiefs of Staff authorized more aircraft in January 1963, raising the inventory of Farm Gate strike aircraft to eighteen B–26s and thirteen T–28s.[54] Nevertheless, until the American buildup in 1965, problems continued to hamper the delivery of timely and effective close air support. For example, in January 1963 an ARVN assault at Ap Bac suffered heavy casualties, including five helicopters lost and nine damaged, primarily because no fixed-wing strike aircraft had been requested to support the operation.[55] Late the following year, a similar catastrophe beset Vietnamese forces—the 33d Ranger and 4th Marine Battalions were virtually wiped out—at Binh Gia, again largely as the result of poor planning for close air support.[56]

One Air Force study found that the response time for close air-support requests prior to 1965 averaged ninety minutes and that only about half of all such requests were met. The study attributed this primarily to lack of aircraft, resources, and personnel but also cited the inability of VNAF to respond because of inadequate training or low motivation.[57]

Other studies identified further weaknesses in the close air-support system in South Vietnam. These failings included (1) cumbersome control procedures ("It required a magician to figure out where planes were flying," according to General Momyer),[58] (2) the ambiguous status of American advisors and the extent to which their advice was either requested or acted upon,[59] (3) the saturation of airspace below 9,000 feet (and this prior to 1965!), and (4) lack of procedures to coordinate artillery and air firepower.[60] Most of the criticism centered on the inadequacy of communications, the shortage of qualified (and motivated) VNAF personnel, and the lack of mobility of Air Force facilities in the field necessary to coordinate and commit close air support to Vietnamese ground-forces.[61]

Restrictive rules of engagement seemed to complicate even further the delivery of effective close air support. The South Vietnamese had their own category of restrictions, and President Diem kept a tight rein on VNAF operations. His caution undoubtedly stemmed from an aborted coup (November

B-26 Invaders *(above)* **deployed to Vietnam in a program code-named Farm Gate. The aging planes were withdrawn in the spring of 1964. T-28 Trojan** *(below)*, **another of many trainer designs pressed into combat duty in Vietnam, is shown here escorting a supply train near Bien Hoa, South Vietnam, in January 1963.**

11, 1960) and the bombing of the presidential palace by two renegade pilots (February 26, 1962).[62] In any event, Diem's conservative use of the VNAF neither inspired general confidence in the VNAF nor instilled an offensive spirit.* Stiff penalties awaited anyone approving an air strike that resulted in friendly casualties. Vietnamese leaders were, therefore, understandably reluctant to delegate the power to approve strike requests.[63] No clear lines of authority existed between ARVN division commanders and province chiefs, who had military forces (Civil Guard and Self-Defense Corps) responsible to them apart from ARVN. A presidential directive granted the division commander complete control over all military affairs in his tactical zone, but a province chief could appeal a division commander's decision, via nonmilitary channels, through regional headquarters to the president. Moreover, a province chief could launch paramilitary operations with his own forces without the approval of the division commander. Personalities, consequently, played a key role in how the system worked from province to province.[64]

Requests for air support had to run up and down parallel military and civilian tracks, which sometimes led to excessive delays and lost opportunities. In 1961, for example, upon arriving over the designated target, one flight of an authorized strike found that the enemy had moved only a short distance—but enough to cross into another province. The flight, and subsequent replacements, loitered in the area all day without expending any ordnance, while attempts to locate the chief of that province in order to obtain the necessary strike clearance failed.[65]

American forces, too, labored under strict rules of engagement. When the first air units deployed to Vietnam in 1961—U.S. Army helicopters with U.S. markings and flown by U.S. crews—the Joint Chiefs of Staff insisted that all flights include a Vietnamese crew member or observer and that all firing be in self-defense only (even if enemy forces were clearly identified).[66] Farm Gate personnel operated under a different set of rules: They could strike while under the control of a Vietnamese officer, but their aircraft had to have VNAF markings. Moreover, they could only attack targets that were marked by Vietnamese, and they were authorized to go on separate strike missions only if the VNAF, for some reason, could not do so.[67]

In November 1962, apparently as a result of charges by the International Control Commission in Indochina that the United States and North Vietnam were both violating the 1954 Geneva Agreements, USAF crews could not fly closer than ten kilometers to the Cambodian border, could not log combat time, and could not initiate fire against a target unless fired upon first. For a brief period they could not even return fire.[68] On January 25, 1963, CINC-

---

*For a time, he insisted on approving all strikes personally, and the VNAF did not fly strikes against the enemy until 1961.

PAC allowed the head of the Military Assistance Command, Vietnam (MACV, which had replaced MAAG,V on February 8, 1962) to have a Vietnamese on board the aircraft in certain grave situations.[69]

Night operations opened a whole new category of regulations. At night all USAF strike aircraft had to be under positive radar plot. If a friendly installation came under attack at night, the requirement for a Vietnamese controller was waived. However, if friendly forces in the field (as opposed to in an installation) came under attack, a Vietnamese controller was required.[70] The elusive barrier to the introduction of jet aircraft into South Vietnam crumbled slowly. In 1959, President Diem requested jet aircraft, but Washington suspended plans to deliver two T–33s and four RT–33s because of sensitivity to the Geneva restrictions. By October 1961, however, at Diem's request U.S. Air Force reconnaissance jets (RF–101s), arrived in South Vietnam and began photographing Mekong flooded areas (as well as suspected Viet Cong encampments). With radar reports of overflights by unidentified aircraft in March 1962, Saigon asked for—and received—assistance from USAF jet interceptors (three F–102s and one TF–102). Four months later, the U.S. Navy assigned some jet interceptors to replace the USAF aircraft. The next year, in May 1963, two RB–57s went to Tan Son Nhut ostensibly for

McDonnell F-101 Voodoo. The reconnaissance configuration of this aircraft began its activities in Vietnam in October 1961.

reconnaissance missions.[71] Although jet aircraft operated in South Vietnam, no officially recognized jet air strikes took place before 1965.

One other impediment to timely and responsive close air support in South Vietnam lay in the existence of separate service air control systems. By late 1963, four separate air organizations were operating in South Vietnam: the U.S. Army, with 325 aircraft; the VNAF, with 228 aircraft; the USAF, with 117 aircraft; and the U.S. Marine Corps, with 20 aircraft. These organizations used 2 separate systems of air control: the joint VNAF–USAF tactical air control system and the U.S. Army's air-ground system, which handled both its own and Marine Corps air vehicles.[72]

From the first, the U.S. Army, following a long-standing policy, refused to permit the VNAF–USAF tactical air control system to manage the Army's organic aviation. Rather, in South Vietnam, the U.S. Army worked with the ARVN (and ARVN trainees) in operating its air/ground system, which had a central Tactical Operations Center in Saigon as well as a regional Tactical Air Support Element in each corps.[73]

The Air Force did not want Army aircraft conducting independent and uncoordinated missions. Two unfortunate by-products of the current state of affairs, according to the Air Force, were (1) the lack of overall air efficiency, with all aircraft not being effectively coordinated (especially with different radio nets) and (2) the flying safety problem, exemplified by Army Mohawks flying through VNAF/USAF strike areas.[74]

This problem came to the attention of the Joint Chiefs of Staff. In 1963, the Air Force Test Unit–Vietnam reported that the USAF–VNAF tactical air control system actually managed only half of the 690 total aircraft in South Vietnam. This study concluded, "It is contrary to accepted principles of unit command to have air forces operating in the same area under separate and unilateral command."[75] Army studies, however, supported the need for separate air control systems, one such study insisting that "the air resources in Vietnam are not an entity" and "[p]lacing all aircraft continuously under such a control system as TACS [USAF–VNAF tactical air control system] would have an adverse effect upon USA [Army] and USMC aviation responsiveness."[76] Faced with these differing views, on February 1, 1964 the Joint Chiefs of Staff queried the CINCPAC, Adm. Harry D. Felt, about the situation. Felt, in turn, asked the Commander of MACV (COMUSMACV), Gen. Paul D. Harkins, for an explanation of the existence of two separate air control systems.

In response, Harkins defended the operational requirement for the dual systems. The COMUSMACV pointed out that the TACS, through the Air Operations Center, provided centralized control and decentralized employment of USAF–VNAF resources throughout South Vietnam. But, Harkins emphasized, most of U.S. Army-Marine Corps air resources were assigned to ARVN corps in a direct supporting role. Thus, in each corps tactical zone,

Army–Marine air resources served within an aviation headquarters that functioned under the operational control of the senior American advisor in each corps. In effect, the aviation headquarters managed all Army–Marine aviation units (and aircraft) operating in direct support of operations within its corps tactical zone. In support of the existing dual system, Harkins offered three main arguments. First, he emphasized that the two systems were compatible and complementary. Second, Harkins pointed out that the TACS fulfilled important training functions as well as operational requirements. "A principal objective," he asserted, "is to ensure, when U.S. forces depart, a smoothly functioning VNAF manned TACS." Third, because the Army–Marine aviation units were "wholly special assistance and have no role in the development of the Vietnamese air structure," Harkins wanted to remain free to employ them as he saw fit. In his view, "The US Army and USMC concepts are peculiarly well suited to the requirements of the counterinsurgency effort here in Vietnam." Harkins concluded by suggesting that the "root causes of the real problems in the air support field are operational, not organizational." Specifically, he pointed to the lack of cooperation between the VNAF and ARVN. "Neither VNAF nor ARVN has come of age," Harkins stated, "and deficiencies in ground–air relationships are but one category of the debit sheet".[77]

Harkins' letter did not settle the interservice dispute. The twin debate in Washington over theoretical structures of close air support in general and the actual delivery in South Vietnam of close air support in particular, persisted into 1965. As previously noted, the Army and the Air Force could not resolve their long-standing differences about close air support, not even through the Joint Chiefs of Staff or the Department of Defense. The disagreements continued to center on four main issues: (1) operational control of tactical strike aircraft, (2) the need for an aircraft designed especially for close air support, (3) the quantification of "adequate" close air support (measured by the guaranteed allotment of a certain number of sorties per day to each combat Army unit), and (4) the role of the Army's armed helicopters.

Under the direction of the Secretary of Defense, Strike Command conducted a series of tests in 1963–1964 to evaluate the conflicting service viewpoints. In March and April 1965, partially as a result of these tests and partially because of the services' desires to resolve at least some of their differences (especially with Americans now serving in combat areas), in March and April 1965 the Army and Air Force Chiefs of Staff signed a "Concept for Improved Joint Air–Ground Coordination." The provisions of this pact are best viewed within the context of the overall tactical air control system, but the agreement essentially formalized procedures for the apportionment and allocation of tactical air resources. Thus the joint commander would decide the daily proportion of tactical air resources for close air support, counterair, and interdiction. While the various component commanders might submit recommendations on this apportionment, only the joint commander could change the daily quotas. In turn, the apportionment for close air support had to be specifically reported each day by the air commander to the ground commander, who could then allocate these close air-support resources among his subcommanders.

The new agreement specified that full authority over close air support remain in the hands of the appropriate commander (for economy of use) and that no arbitrary minimum amount of sorties be established. Also, the Air Force agreed in this pact not only to assume responsibility for the required communications in requesting and delivering close air support but also to provide advisers (forward air controllers and air liaison officers in tactical air control parties) down to the level of Army battalions. In addition, the Joint Concept gave these tactical air control parties direct access to the regional coordinating centers (now called Direct Air Support Centers instead of Air Support Operations Centers) for requesting "immediate" (usually emergency) calls for close air support. In his requests for close air support, ground commanders would specify targets to be attacked, target priorities, desired time over target, and the results expected. Air Force advisers would provide him with information about the capabilities and limitations of tactical air power in each situation. The agreement made clear, too, that responsibility for troop safety remained with the ground-force commander.[78]

Although the "Concept for Improved Joint Air–Ground Coordination" would influence the close air support operations in South Vietnam, some improvements in close air support had been introduced even prior to the 1965 agreement. For example, in 1963 the Air Force Test Unit–Vietnam recommended sending all "immediate" requests over the VNAF–USAF communications system. The recommendation was approved, and this became the accepted procedure.[79] Still other changes incorporated as the result of separate studies in 1963 were to provide additional radar facilities and to improve operation of the Joint Air Operations Center (especially to be more responsive in shifting air resources among the corps areas).[80]

In January 1964, Lt. Gen. Joseph H. Moore succeeded Anthis as head of the 2d Air Division (the 2d ADVON's successor, effective October 8, 1962). Moore offered some changes—most of which reflected the findings of the Strike Command exercises in the United States at the time—for the VNAF–USAF TACS. The slow reaction time and ponderous air control system (as reflected in the disaster at Ap Bac) invited a restructuring of the existing system. Moore proposed additional tactical air control parties for regimental or battalion levels. Also, he recommended establishing a new Direct Air Request Network (DARN) which would enable requests for immediate assistance to go directly to the Air Support Operations Center in the corps area of responsibility.

Cumbersome delays would be avoided by eliminating the need for explicit approval at intervening levels of command between the battalion and the corps. Each of the intervening command posts, continuously monitoring the air request network, had five minutes to disapprove (or satisfy by other means) a request for immediate support. No radio intervention, in Moore's proposed system, signified endorsement of the request. His recommendations earned approval from Vietnamese authorities, and the new system went into effect before the end of 1964. By then, sixty-seven air liaison officers and forward air controllers, all with radio equipment and operators, were working with Vietnamese ground units.[81]

With the changes in South Vietnam, and with the "Concept for Improved Joint Air–Ground Coordination" in early 1965, the Army and Air Force had restructured the tactical air system for more timely and responsive close air support. Even more important, the genesis of the improved system coincided with the beginning of the massive American buildup in Southeast Asia.

At the hub of the revised tactical air control system—as it evolved in South Vietnam—was the Tactical Air Control Center (TACC), formerly called the Air Operations Center. Located at Tan Son Nhut, the TACC, with a combined staff of VNAF and USAF personnel, routinely prepared fragments ("frags") of the theater's daily operations order for all VNAF and USAF tactical (strike) aircraft. B–52s remained under the control of the Strategic Air Command. In practice, USAF and VNAF personnel in the TACC worked with the tactical resources of their respective services. Commensurate with the priorities identified by COMUSMACV, the TACC fragged all preplanned missions for close air support to each of the four ARVN corps and the two United States Army Field Forces.*

The TACC, working with MACV's Tactical Air Support Element, also helped match requests for immediate close air support and monitored the progress of tactical air operations throughout South Vietnam. Each week, the TACC Director (VNAF) and Deputy Director (USAF) helped plan the allocation of strike sorties, under the guidelines set by COMUSMACV, with the Commander of the 2d Air Division (later Seventh Air Force). At the height of the war, a typical week might involve frags for more than 500 available tactical strikes.[82]

Combined VNAF–USAF staffs in the Direct Air Support Centers (DASCs), formerly Air Support Operations Centers, formed the next link in the tactical air control chain. In theory, by being highly mobile, DASCs covered changing areas of responsibility (as the battlefield situation progressed).

---

*U.S. I FFV, originally designated Task Force Alpha, activated on August 1, 1965, with headquarters at Nha Trang, operated in II Corps until its inactivation on April 30, 1971; U.S. II FFV, with headquarters at Bien Hoa, operated in III Corps and IV Corps from March 1966 to May 2, 1971.

430

Lt. Gen. Joseph H. Moore, Seventh Air Force commander.

In South Vietnam, the DASCs remained fixed in specified regions. For example, a DASC, was collocated with the Tactical Operations Center in each of the four ARVN corps: at Danang (I Corps), Pleiku (II Corps), Bien Hoa (III Corps), and Can Tho (IV Corps). In II Corps, a second DASC ("Alpha"), made up entirely of USAF personnel, established operations at Nha Trang to work solely with the U.S. I Field Force, Vietnam. The details of managing an air strike (e.g., call signs, radio frequencies, rendezvous point, target coordinates, time over target) fell within the purview of the DASC. The DASCs served as regional extensions of the TACC, receiving and coordinating requests for close air support within their areas of responsibility, as well as working with the TACC to meet tactical air priorities inside—and outside—their regions.[83]

Tactical air control parties (TACPs) represented the furthest extension of the tactical air control system. The 1965 joint agreement specified that TACPs be assigned directly to Army units at every level from field army down to battalion. Each TACP consisted of at least one air liaison officer (ALO), one forward air controller, and one radio operator (who could use four classes of radios—UHF, VHF, HF, and FM—plus Army communications). Early plans called for FACs to remain on the ground, but conditions in South Vietnam, such as the guerrilla hit-and-run tactics, the rugged terrain, and the dense foliage, led the FACs to avail themselves of a better view from the air in directing support strikes. At the various Army levels, each TACP advised and coordinated the tactical air needs of its host.[84]

431

Thus, by 1965, the tactical air control system provided the means for planning, coordinating, directing, and controlling tactical air operations. Planned requests for close air support tested its basic structure, while immediate (emergency) requests challenged the flexibility of the system. The true measure, of course, was how the tactical air control system responded to combat conditions.

Planned requests for close air support might originate at any level. For example, an Army or ARVN battalion, after determining a requirement (with the help of its tactical air control party), would pass its request upward through Army or ARVN channels. The division would analyze the request and integrate it with all the other requests received by the division for air support. (Some requests could be satisfied by organic firepower.) If the request did not carry a division priority, it would have to be resubmitted, and the proposed operation would be delayed.

If the request were endorsed at division level, it would travel upward for a review process at the Corps Tactical Operations Center (or field force level). If approved at that level it made its way, with the other approved requests in that corps to Saigon, usually to the MACV Tactical Air Support Element (TASE). MACV and ARVN then assembled their daily and weekly lists of requests for all of South Vietnam. These lists were given to the VNAF–USAF Tactical Air Control Center (collocated with the TASE), which coordinated the details of supporting each request through the appropriate Direct Air Support Center.

Each request received a priority identification, and a frag order went to the air unit designated to furnish the required support. In turn, the air unit identified air assets to satisfy the request. When the frag cleared the TACC, the appropriate regional Direct Air Support Center provided information about the planned strike to the air liaison officer at the Army/ARVN division. The division air liaison officer then passed this information to the tactical air control party assigned to the original requester. Thus, both the tactical air strike unit and the forward air controller (in the requesting TACP), who would direct the strike, usually knew the details by the early evening hours of the day before the operation. This advance notice enabled the forward air controller to obtain clearances for ordnance, to confirm the target coordinates, and to learn the positions of friendly forces and civilians in the vicinity of the strike.[85]

A "preplanned mission" in South Vietnam was defined as one involving a requirement for air support that would take place three hours or longer after a request had been initiated. On the other hand, immediate requests required an air strike in less than three hours; usually that meant as soon as possible, and often "right now." Requests for immediate air support simply could not afford the time required for the careful analysis, planning, and coordination that marked the system for preplanned request; hence, immediate requests followed a different path.

Any unit or individual could initiate a request for immediate close air support. All requests from battalion level or above went straight to the regional direct air-support center by way of the nearest tactical air control party or airborne forward air controller. Requests from below battalion level first required verification and approval by the battalion command post. From the DASC, the request passed (next door) to the Corps Tactical Operations Center (Army/ARVN) or U.S. Field Force headquarters for final approval or clearance. In the meantime, the DASC began searching for aircraft to fill the request. Within the corps or field force area, the DASC could divert a forward air controller and strike aircraft from either a lower priority mission or airborne alert status, but only the TACC in Saigon could scramble aircraft on ground alert status or divert air resources from a different corps. Each Army/ARVN level learned of the immediate request through its tactical air control party, which continuously monitored the direct air request network. No radio intervention indicated consent to the request by intermediary levels. Notice of disapproval at any level automatically stopped the DASC search for air resources to fill the request. When the immediate request earned final approval—and only the ground-force commander could approve for the air strike—specific information about the strike passed from the DASC through the tactical air control parties to the requester.[86]

The revised tactical air control system complemented the Army air–ground system. In May 1966, Gen. William C. Westmoreland (USA), the COMUSMACV, who had replaced Harkins in 1964, formally integrated the two systems in May 1966. This new system, known as the Joint Air–Ground Operations System (JAGOS), permitted MACV to supervise close air support at all levels. COMUSMACV, in effect, established priorities for ground operations through its weekly allocations of air recources. Ground commanders could still rely on daily allocations, but there was a flexibility built into the immediate request system to meet sudden threats without disturbing plans in other areas.[87]

At the heart of the close air support system in South Vietnam was the forward air controller (FAC). Although the concept of a forward air controller was not new, the idea of an airborne FAC conducting business from his own airplane seems to have been largely ignored between the Korean War and the American involvement in South Vietnam. After Korea, the Air Force gave all its light spotter planes to the Army, and it was not until 1963 that the Army released three 0–1 aircraft to the Air Force for FAC training as well as twenty-two more for use by the USAF air commando squadrons.[88]

No FACs (USAF or VNAF) operated in South Vietnam prior to the arrival of Farm Gate. According to General Momyer, this was partially due to

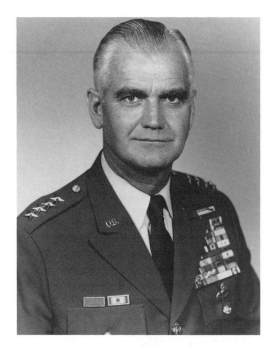

General William C. West-
moreland, commander of
the U.S. Military Assist-
ance Command, Viet-
nam, 1965 to 1968.

the lack of need, early in the war, for precise control of air strikes, since most engagements occurred in unpopulated areas. But perhaps even more important were the continuing shortage of VNAF personnel and the low priority given to the training of FACs.[89] In fact, no formal FAC organization existed in South Vietnam until 1961, when the Air Force provided a five-man FAC pool. These five FACs, on ninety-day tours to South Vietnam, rotated among Vietnamese ground commanders whenever they expected enemy contacts. Initially, the FACs directed air strikes from ground positions, but shortly thereafter they took to the air and remained airborne for the rest of the war.[90]

General Harkins felt it necessary to comment on the lack of teamwork between the VNAF and ARVN. For example, in Harkins' view the ARVN program to train ground liaison officers for VNAF units foundered, principally due to the uncooperative attitude ARVN field commanders had toward the program. Moreover, the VNAF was too strained for pilots to provide air liaison officers for ARVN units.[91] Another example of this troubled ARVN–VNAF relationship arose in April 1962, when the VNAF trained 240 ARVN officers as forward air guides (to "guide" tactical air strikes from ground positions). After the 240 trained guides returned to their ARVN units, not one was ever used, and U.S. Army advisors never heard of Vietnamese forward air guides.[92]

By late 1964, 4 VNAF liaison squadrons, with 38 aircraft, had been formed, and 76 USAF forward air controllers were serving in an advisory capacity. A few months later the total number of FACs from the VNAF increased to 68 and from the USAF to 144.[93] Prior to the American buildup in 1965, the Vietnamese director of each regional Air Support Operations Center established the number of FACs to be assigned to each ground unit. The FAC responsibilities included (1) advising ground unit commanders on tactical air operations, (2) being familiar with radio communications (UHF, VHF, HF, FM) as well as the tactical air control system and the ARVN air–ground system, (3) assisting in the guidance of tactical air strikes against targets in close proximity to friendly forces, and (4) marking the locations of friendly forces, civilians, and enemy targets, and reporting the results of air strikes to the ground commander. Both VNAF and USAF required that their FACs be rated pilots, and USAF regulations called for FACs to have at least one year of experience as fighter pilots.[94]

Only VNAF FACs (or Vietnamese observers flying with U.S. advisors) could mark a target for air attack. As the number and intensity of ground operations increased, pressure mounted to ease this requirement.

Experience quickly taught how difficult it was to acquire and identify small fleeting targets.[95] It took only a short time to rediscover the value of the airborne FAC, as the heavy foliage and the nature of guerrilla warfare contributed to FACs taking to the air. Also, by being able to cover more territory than a surface observer, mobile or not, the airborne FAC helped make up for the shortage of qualified personnel.[96]

FACs arriving with the first U.S. Army deployments to South Vietnam started out by working from ground positions, even though USAF FACs already in-country with ARVN units operated almost exclusively from the air. In time, however, battle experience accelerated the evolution of the air-borne FAC role. One such learning experience was Operation Harvest Moon, a joint ARVN–U.S. Marine Corps operation in December 1965. Radio problems at that time prevented the ground FAC (U.S. Marine Corps) from contacting the air-support center, and USAF airborne FACs were called in to direct the strike.[97]

"Americanization" of the War—1965–1969

Vietnamese markings were removed from U.S. aircraft in March 1965. The introduction of major U.S. forces that year brought a change in rules of engagement that permitted USAF airborne FACs to mark targets and direct strikes. All air strikes still had to have at least the tacit approval of the Vietnamese government through the Joint General Staff and the Tactical Operations Center in Saigon. This modification seemed to suit the VNAF attitude of being willing to let the Americans assume more of the FAC role. Despite a shortage of pilots, the VNAF failed to extend pilot duty hours to provide 24-hour coverage, and weekends were rarely periods of full duty. VNAF liaison units also reduced their hours of operation. In addition, VNAF pilots, having little night or bad weather training or experience, seemed content to let American pilots fly during those conditions. A firefight at Ca Mau in December 1964, when a Vietnamese FAC/observer could not be found to fly with an American FAC in order to mark enemy targets, lent further weight to the perception that the VNAF would be happy to have U.S. pilots operate on their own.[98]

During this phase of the war, three categories of FAC missions developed. One type operated only in support of Free World forces from other countries (e.g., U.S., Korean, Australian, and Thai). A second category either worked with specific Vietnamese contacts (e.g., ARVN units and local officials) or covered a certain geographical area ("Sector FACs"). The third category included all those FACs who supported out-of-country operations (and were usually assigned to a geographical area).

By 1970, more than 800 FACs were operating in Southeast Asia under the administrative control of four tactical air-support squadrons (19th, 20th, 21st, and 22d TASS) and under various operational controls, depending on the assignment of each.[99] The geographical assignments enabled FACs to familiarize themselves with a certain area and to become aware of unusual activity in their areas. This familiarity with a specified region, according to General Momyer, was a key reason why a FAC could bring close air-support strikes within fifty meters of friendly positions.[100]

A proficient FAC had to be, in the words of one historian, "a politician, administrative officer, radio operator, and an effective weapons controller."[101] The best FACs seemed to have four attributes in common: (1) knowledge of standard procedures; (2) an understanding of the capabilities and limitations of the strike aircraft; (3) special techniques, such as briefing methods or marking targets, to ease the task of the strike pilots; and (4) familiarity with the various types of ordnance. Moreover, a variety of verbal interchanges, which ranged from formal briefings to informal "beer bashes," enabled the FACs to develop a rapport with both USAF tactical air units and Army ground-forces. One F–100 wing instituted a "FAC of the Month" award for the FAC who rated highest on the mission debriefing sheets[102]. An Army captain admitted: "Until I really talked to the FAC and found out the effects of 20 Mike–Mike [20–mm ordnance], I really didn't know that you could shoot it as close as, what is it, 50, 75 feet you can bring it in."[103] Army commanders, even platoon leaders, got to know the faces that went with the FAC call signs. FACs, in turn, seemed to take more of a personal interest in their ground-force "charges." A FAC might provide exact fixes for a rifle company or routinely check in with a Special Forces camp.[104]

It became difficult to find suitable aircraft for the FAC. After Korea, no special FAC aircraft appeared because everyone thought the FAC was ground-based. When the value of the airborne FAC became evident, few air frame choices were available. As noted, the Army provided some L–19s (renamed the 0–1) from its air inventory in 1963, but the aircraft was not ideal for FAC operations. It did not have all types of radios; it was restricted in operations at night and in bad weather; it proved highly vulnerable in a hostile environment; it was underpowered; and it had poor capabilities for marking targets. Yet, despite these drawbacks, everyone seemed enamored of the 0–1. Its endurance, easy maintenance, and ability to operate out of primitive strips helped make the 0–1 easy to operate and great fun to fly.[105] Although the replacement 0–2A Super Skymaster brought some improvement, especially in better power performance, it had about the same strengths and weaknesses for FAC operations in South Vietnam as the 0–1.[106] The use of jet aircraft such as the F–100 for the FAC mission (the so-called Fast FAC), while effective in the high-threat environments elsewhere in Southeast Asia, did not work out very well. It was too fast for effective reconnaissance (and to acquire small, fleeting targets), too much of a "gas guzzler" to have any appreciable endurance time, and too inefficient at low altitudes.[107]

The search for an aircraft to fulfill the FAC mission led inevitably to question the development of a specially designed FAC aircraft. This, in turn, touched on the related issue of arming the FACs. Experience in South Vietnam showed that many small enemy groups discovered by FACs disappeared during the interval between the FAC's sighting and the arrival of strike air-

O-2A Super Skymaster.

craft. One Air Force study found that fifty percent of all troops-in-contact incidents ended within twenty minutes and involved fewer than ten enemy soldiers.[108] Another study revealed that in one four-month period during 1970, fifty-four percent of fleeting targets detected by FACs at night were not struck because no firepower was available.[109] But the question was raised: "What if the FACs were armed?"

As early as 1965, 2d Air Division rejected suggestions to arm FAC aircraft. Apparently the deciding factor was the belief—influenced by experiences in World War II—that an armed FAC would be tempted to act like a fighter pilot instead of a FAC.[110] In May 1968, however, USAF Headquarters directed Tactical Air Command to test the concept of the armed FAC. These tests were linked to the theory of "phased response," which sought to give some measure of immediate close air support until strike aircraft could arrive.[111] Neither the 0–1 nor the 0–2A was deemed suitable for these tests, principally because of the vulnerability of both aircraft. Tactical Air Command, with some advice from Seventh Air Force, agreed to test the OV–10 Bronco.[112] Upon careful consideration, including analysis of both the Tactical Air Command tests ("Combat Cover") and its own test ("Misty Bronco"), Seventh Air Force began using armed FACS flying OV–10s in June 1969.[113]

In the form of the OV–10, the theoretical LARA (light armed reconnaissance aircraft) had seen practical application by the Defense Department's Research and Evaluation division as early as 1966.[114] Equipped with four machine guns and four rocket pods, the OV–10 offered limited but highly responsive firepower. During the "Misty Bronco" test period in III Corps (April 4–June 13, 1969), OV–10 pilots handled seventy-eight of ninety-eight requests for close air support by themselves in an average response time of just over seven minutes. Some operational problems developed when the OV–10 was burdened with external fuel tanks in efforts to extend its range for out-of-country operations, but overall, the OV–10 performed the armed FAC role ("Support Opportunity") admirably, especially against small, fleeting targets, in the permissive air environment of South Vietnam. Seventy-four percent of OV–10 responses came in five minutes or less.[115] In the words of one Air Force study, "[a]rming the FAC increases overall tactical air effectiveness."[116]

The special conditions existing in South Vietnam served to intensify the debate over developing a FAC aircraft solely for the mission of close air support. For example, much of the country contained dense jungles so heavily forested that the overlapping foliage produced a canopy often three layers deep. This natural "umbrella" through which little sunlight filtered not only affected plant and animal life on the jungle floor but also presented formidable obstacles to both target acquisition and accurate delivery of ordnance. The terrain also hindered close air-support operations. The low, flat delta region lay in stark contrast to the mountainous jungle areas. Historian Robert

F. Futrell observed, "Mountains and heavy vegetation hampered the ground view, and the flat ground of the delta offered no elevations to help determine range."[117] All of this became apparent to USAF pilots as they arrived in South Vietnam.[118]

In addition, weather patterns made the uneven terrain even more treacherous. Two separate monsoon seasons (beginning roughly in May and December) combined to ensure that either the southern or northern portion of the country was always drenched in heavy rainfall. Thus, strike pilots covering both areas continuously faced adverse weather conditions. Violent thunderstorms, frequently erupting without warning, posed additional air safety hazards. Some tactical aircraft, including FAC, lacked appropriate navigational equipment, and some pilots (especially in the VNAF) in tactical aircraft lacked training in instrument flying necessary for operations in bad weather. Recognizing this deficiency in instrument flying capability, prevailing rules of engagement required FACs to break off the air attack if visual contact with either the target or the strike aircraft were lost.

Taken in combination, the foliage, terrain, and weather characteristics of South Vietnam proved less than ideal for close air-support operations.[119] The nature of the war itself, moreover, was not conducive to these operations. Counterinsurgency operations, unlike conventional warfare, rarely involved the clash of large-size forces. As noted, most of the engagements in South Vietnam consisted of small-size hit-and-run raids by the enemy that rarely exceeded twenty minutes. This set a difficult task for tactical air power. Desirable targets were few, and all too often, small groups of enemy soldiers that had been spotted disappeared before strike aircraft could arrive.

Under the Kennedy administration, the belief that wars of national liberation would become a primary Communist strategy lowered the levels at which armed conflict involving American forces could take place.[120] When no hostile air threat presented itself in counterinsurgency warfare, close air support—together with tactical airlift and aerial reconnaissance—becomes one of the centerpieces of tactical air operations.[121] The United States strategy in Vietnam, developed principally by General Westmoreland, anticipated a wide-ranging war without stable or definable fronts in which highly mobile American ground-forces engaged units of varying sizes throughout the less densely populated interior of South Vietnam.[122] Since large-size enemy units rarely exposed themselves, it became vitally important to knock out the small, fleeting enemy groups that did appear. Although it was more difficult to make close air support a profitable investment, its significance in Vietnam was unquestioned.

The unusual nature of the war and the demanding environment in South Vietnam seemed to call for a special approach. General Harkins stated while still COMUSMACV in 1964: "Bold deviations from past procedures may produce a bloody nose or two, but on the other hand may be the source of truly significant results."[123] From Taiwan, Nationalist Chinese Generalissimo Chiang Kai-shek warned, "If a chariot pulled by four inferior horses were pitted against one pulled by four superior horses, this often [led] to the defeat of the chariot pulled by the superior horses."[124] In other words, American conventional strength, by itself, could prove a disadvantage in Vietnam. In the context of close air support, perhaps sophisticated tactical aircraft and conventional air procedures might not be appropriate for gaining U.S. objectives. One Air Force historian, noting that Farm Gate personnel were not specifically trained for the environment in Vietnam, concluded: "The effort to obtain quick solutions resulted in a de-emphasis of counterinsurgency concepts in favor of more traditional applications of military force. . . . [T]he initial USAF counterinsurgency effort was diverted by expediency."[125] Part of this general issue focused on the debate over the need for an aircraft especially designed for close air support.

Early in the war, before American ground forces were involved, the F8F, B–26, and T–28 constituted the entire close air-support arsenal. All these aircraft reached the end of their useful lives. President Diem grounded the fatigued fleet of VNAF F8Fs because they had become virtually impossible to maintain. Similar problems beset the B–26 and T–28 aircraft, carrying as they did heavy-duty combat operational schedules. For example,

The OV-10 Bronco proved itself a highly capable light armed reconnaissance aircraft.

between January 1962 and January 1963, B–26s flew 1,306 total sorties (14 percent at night), and T–28s flew 2,181 sorties (7 percent at night).[126] All B–26 Invaders were grounded on February 11, 1964, after an investigation prompted by an incidence of wing failure during an air strike revealed extensive structural damage in the wings of other B–26s. Within two months, all B–26s had been withdrawn from South Vietnam.[127]

The 1st Air Commando Squadron (an outgrowth of Farm Gate) borrowed nine T–28 Trojans on an interim basis from the VNAF. The T–28s, which had been sent by Secretary McNamara in late 1961, also suffered, like the B–26s, from the severity of combat operations and old age. During March and April 1964, the wings of two T–28s literally fell off. Faced with the grounding of all his B–26s and T–28s, General Moore declared that "2d Air Division is practically out of business."[128]

A more than satisfactory replacement was found in May 1964, when the Navy provided the VNAF and USAF with the A–1 (both the dual-control "E" and the single-seat "H" models). Pilots praised the capabilities of these Douglas Skyraiders, nicknamed "Spads," which included long loiter times and large ordnance loads (as many as twelve 650–pound bombs). So effective was the performance of this aircraft that the Air Force briefly considered reopening the A–1 production line. The aircraft's only real drawback for close air-support operations was its relatively low airspeed; flying time to the target sometimes led to unacceptably long response times.[129]

American reluctance to introduce jet aircraft to South Vietnam eased in January 1965, when Westmoreland requested and received authority, with the approval of the U.S. Ambassador, to employ jet strike aircraft under emergency conditions. On February 19, 1965, B–57 pilots flew the first jet air strikes in South Vietnam in the central highlands. The previous day the U.S. Embassy had announced that, as the result of a request from the Republic of Vietnam, U.S. aircraft would begin flying attack missions without Vietnamese personnel on board.[130]

Once the ban on jet aircraft had been lifted, F–100 Super Sabres and F–4 Phantoms were also flying strikes in 1965. These two high-performance aircraft carried the close air-support load. Nothing so typified the war in South Vietnam as these streaking jets pounding enemy ground targets pass after pass. The F–100, with multiple combinations of weapon loads, and the F–4, which could carry as many as seventeen 750–pound bombs, brought a formidable increase in firepower to the war.[131]

Modifications of two jet aircraft used in USAF undergraduate training programs eventually made their way to the war. The F–5 (modified T–38) and the YAT/A–37 seemed excellent choices. Each was highly maneuverable, easily maintained, and "forgiving" (i.e. "user friendly"). Moreover, most VNAF trainees went to training bases in the United States, where both unmodified versions were used.[132] Toward the end of the war, the A–7D

Workhorses of close air support in Vietnam *(clockwise beginning below)*: **A1H Skyraider; A7D Corsair II; F-5 Tiger; F-100 Supersabre; B-57 Canberra; F-4 Phantom; and A-37 Dragonfly.**

introduced its impressive capabilities, and even the sophisticated F–111 made a brief appearance.[133]

The high-performance jets proved less than ideal for the delivery of close air support, however. The relatively short loiter time and restricted maneuverability represented major drawbacks in this role. In addition, the high speeds that resulted in expeditious response times turned into certain weaknesses once the jets had arrived in the vicinity of the target. Jet pilots, for instance, encountered the difficulty of acquiring small, fleeting targets in densely canopied jungles while traveling at high rates of speed over a small geographical area. Also, the same engines that produced those high speeds consumed excessive amounts of fuel at lower (strike) altitudes.[134]

In seeking alternatives to high-performance jets for close air support, in addition to the A–37, the Air Force turned to an unlikely source. Transport aircraft were modified as gunships for an unprecedented role of quick-reacting close air support. With longer and relatively less expensive loiter time than the jets, the gunships filled a gap in tactical air capabilities, especially at night, by furnishing airborne alert service.

The AC–47, the first of the "new" gunships, arrived with the 4th Air Commando Squadron in late 1965. It carried its own flares and 3 SUU–11A miniguns on the left fuselage. Each could fire 6,000 rounds per minute. The aircraft lived up to its call sign, "Spooky," and the performance of the SUU–11A prompted its fire-breathing nickname, taken from a popular song, "Puff, the Magic Dragon." The mission of the AC–47s was almost exclusively for close air support at night.[135]

Within the first year of operation, "Spooky" defended 500 outposts; in one 90-day period (July–September 1966), AC–47s claimed to have broken up 166 enemy night attacks.[136] The Tactical Psychological Operations (TAC-PSO) division, within the Tactical Air Control Center at Tan Son Nhut, fragged all of the AC–47s on a monthly basis to cover all four corps. Each outpost kept radio contact with its province headquarters (or sector headquarters). To request air support, an outpost contacted the province chief who, in turn, called the Corps Tactical Operation Center (collocated with the Corps Direct Air Support Center). While the Tactical Operations Center coordinated final approval of the request, usually through ARVN G–3 Air, the duty officer at the Direct Air Support Center diverted an AC–47 on airborne alert to the outpost under attack. In the meantime, an AC–47 on ground alert took off to assume the air alert status of the diverted aircraft. As soon as the original request earned final approval, the AC–47, upon establishing radio contact with the outpost, was cleared to drop flares and fire. In heavy fighting, tactical strike aircraft would be called in, and the AC–47 would act as a flareship. Sometimes the release of the flares alone would cause the enemy to break off the attack.[137] The most 7.62–mm rounds fired in one night by an

AC–47 was 43,500, during the defense of an outpost in Kien Phong Province on October 11, 1966.[138]

Success with the AC–47 led to the development of the Gunboat (later "Gunship II") program, which involved the arming of C–119s and C–130s. In using these larger, faster transports, the Air Force sought to overcome some of the weaknesses of the AC–47, such as slow reaction time, poor cockpit visibility, and aircraft vulnerability.[139]

In early 1966, Operation Shed Light, an Air Force exercise to develop better night attack capabilities, led directly to the Gunboat/Gunship II program. Moreover, a new fire-control system that had been used in small Cessna aircraft ("Little Brother") was adapted to the larger transports in 1967 linking side-firing guns to improved night sensors. That same year, Secretary McNamara approved tests of the AC–119G "Shadow" designed to replace the AC–47.[140] In late 1969, jet-assisted AC–119K "Stingers" began arriving at Phan Rang Air Base.[141] They had more firepower than the "G" model, including two 20–mm multi-barrel guns and improved flares. In 1968, the AC–130 "Spectre," also entered the war, bringing its outstanding capabilities, especially for operations at night or in bad weather.[142]

With their tremendous rate of firepower, the gunships proved highly effective in close airsupport operations. Their vulnerability, due to relatively slow airspeeds and poor maneuverability, with neither armor plating nor self-sealing fuel tanks, rendered the gunships unsuitable for some phases of close air support. Nevertheless, when used appropriately, such as in night or bad weather defense of isolated outposts, the gunships played a key role in the war. One Air Force study calculated a twenty-four minute average response time for gunships as compared with a forty-minute average for jet aircraft.[143] Lt. Gen. Julian J. Ewell (USA), Commander of II Field Force, Vietnam, between April 1969 and April 1970, stressed the reassuring effects the gunships had for an infantryman. He explained: "It gave him a lot of assurance and security to know that if he got in a tight spot, a gunship would be there in fifteen or twenty minutes and start hosing off the countryside."[144]

In addition to the gunship, the Air Force found another unlikely vehicle to participate in the close air-support mission: the B–52. Because all of South Vietnam was considered to be within the bombline, all tactical air operations were considered integral to the scheme of ground maneuver and therefore were classified as close air support.[145] Except for some unusual circumstances, such as the enemy siege at Khe Sanh in 1967–1968, few B–52 sorties could be considered as actually involved in the close air-support mission. For all its value in other roles, nevertheless, the B–52 in South Vietnam unquestionably represented the premier harassment weapon.

American attempts to accommodate new technology led to some odd ploys, such as the use of tactical fighters in the strategic war up north and the use of the B–52 strategic bomber in tactical roles down south. Yet as early as 1943 in World War II, an Army Air Forces field manual had affirmed that strategic air resources should be diverted to tactical air missions at "particularly opportune" moments.[146] With the first deployment of U.S. Marines to Danang in March 1965, Secretary McNamara wanted B–52s to support U.S. ground forces in South Vietnam. As General Momyer, the Commander of USAF units in South Vietnam, 1966–1968, later wrote, "Although most experienced airmen would have chosen to deploy our strategic bombers against the enemy's major target systems and to [use] them for close support only in emergencies, the use of B–52s for in-country missions was in consonance with the Secretary's view that the place to destroy the enemy was in South Vietnam."[147]

By its ability to carpet-bomb a large area within minutes* by its night, all-weather capabilities, by its ability to operate from distant, safe home bases, and—indirectly—by freeing tactical aircraft for urgent close air-support sorties demanding precision attacks, the B–52 contributed significantly to the tactical air mission in the south. Gen. Maxwell D. Taylor† pointed out that "the key was not the vehicle but the weapon."[148] Echoing the near-unanimous praise ground commanders bestowed on B–52s, General Westmoreland called them "the most lethal weapon employed in South Vietnam."[149] According to Maj. Gen. Gordon F. Blood (USAF), Deputy Chief of Staff for Operations, Seventh Air Force, when B–52s averaged approximately 1,800 strikes per month in 1968, more than two-thirds flew to support ground operations.[150] Nevertheless, with their long planning lead times, their flying time to the target from distant bases in Thailand and Guam, their operating altitude restrictions, and their cumbersome procedures for in-flight diversions (SAC insisted on retaining operational control over all B–52 missions), the B–52s could not possibly serve as quick response close airsupport weapons.[151] Rather, their value lay in playing an integral part in General Momyer's concept for marshaling firepower known as SLAM ("Seeking, Locating, Annihilating, and Monitoring").

The close air-support system in South Vietnam generally followed a pattern of gradual development. However, "very often things 'grew like Topsy,' " Col. Allison C. Brooks (Deputy Commander, 2d Air Division) recalled, "and we had to learn the hard way—all over again. . . ."[152] The tactical air control system provided an example of this developmental process—sometimes painful, sometimes uneven. In one 1965 study, the Air Force's Special Air Warfare Board examined this process and concluded:

---

*A modified B–52 could deliver more than seventeen tons of bombs.

†Chairman of the Joint Chiefs of Staff, 1962–64, and Ambassador to South Vietnam, 1964–65.

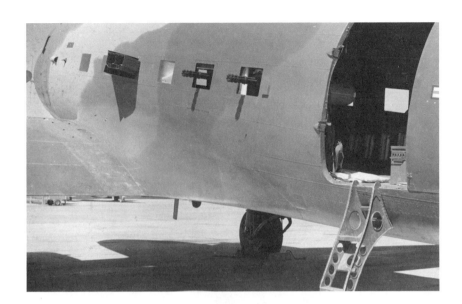

The Air Force converted transport aircraft for close air support missions in Vietnam. The AC-47 (above) displays two miniguns that fired 4,000 rounds per minute. The AC-119K (right) added 20-mm cannon to the array of weaponry. The AC-130 Spectre (below) refined the concept yet again.

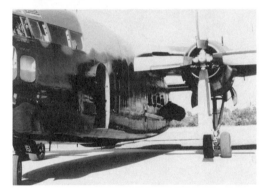

Gen. William W. Momyer.

"The present tactical air control system has grown up in the absence of a framework of doctrine for the conduct of tactical operations."[153] And General Momyer, while admitting that prior to 1965 "it required a magician to figure out where the planes were flying," praised the later tactical air control system "as the real backbone of the high degree of flexibility that was necessary to meet the major offensives in 1968 and in 1972."[154]

In April 1965, the Commander-in-Chief, Pacific (CINCPAC), decreed that the primary air mission in South Vietnam was close air support. Although close air support included several categories, such as preparing landing zone for airborne (helicopter) assaults and escort for road convoys, CINCPAC made clear that the first priority in close air support lay with troops in contact.[155]

Tactical air resources were devoted to that mandate. For example, the number of close air-support sorties jumped dramatically in 1965, the year U.S. ground forces began operations in South Vietnam, from about two thousand sorties in January to more than thirteen thousand in December.[156] Gen.

Bruce Holloway, the Air Force Vice Chief of Staff, reported in 1968 that seventy percent of all tactical air sorties in-country struck enemy troops and locations. He also noted that in one sixty-day period during late 1967, fiftyfive percent of all close air-support sorties supported requests for immediate assistance.[157]

Despite highly complex procedures that involved many communication links, several layers of coordination, and the delivery of ordnance in close proximity to friendly forces and civilians, response times to requests for immediate assistance evolved to produce a general formula of "20/40."

This formula or guideline meant that, on the average, "immediates" would be answered within twenty minutes (by aircraft already airborne being diverted from lower-priority missions) or forty minutes (by scrambling aircraft on the ground). In fact, by 1968, ground commanders incorporated the "20/40" formula in their planning.[158] As a follow up to this process of classifying response times, a joint Army–Air Force study group in 1972 set the general criteria that at least fifty percent of the requests for immediate air support should be answered within fifteen minutes, seventy-five percent within twenty minutes, and one hundred percent within forty minutes.[159]

In addition, changes in the 1966 rules of engagement, such as limiting control of close air support for U.S. Army forces to American FACs only and permitting strikes near villages after inhabitants had been adequately warned to evacuate, had an impact on the close air-support system.[160]

One of the greatest challenges for the close air-support mission in South Vietnam centered on the need for night and all-weather strike capabilities.[161] At night, three principal methods of ordnance delivery evolved. First, the traditional combination of separate flareships, a FAC, and a flight of strike aircraft (with others on ground alert) accounted for about sixty percent of night close air-support sorties.[162] Attempts to arrange proper flare illumination presented a recurring problem. Throughout the war the dud rate for flares averaged about five percent, which was considered high.[163] After 1965, the newer Mark 24 flare, with two-million candlepower, much improved lighting capabilities.[164] In 1966, tests with an Airborne General Illumination Light System, which involved placing twenty eight arc lamps on two rotating pods mounted on the tail ramp of a C–123, showed excellent promise, but technical difficulties in the combat environment rendered the project infeasible.[165]

Self-sufficient gunships represented a second method for delivering close air support at night. These aircraft carried their own flares, communication nets, ordnance, and FAC/Vietnamese observer so that they could work independently (especially, as noted, in defense of remote outposts).[166]

A third method, developed in 1966, was known as Sky Spot. Under Sky Spot procedures, strike aircraft equipped with special radar beacons received radar vectors to a precomputed release point, as much as 150 miles away, and dropped their bombs on command from the radar center. Each of the 5 Sky Spot centers established in 1966 in South Vietnam (Bien Hoa, Pleiku, Dong Ha, Dalat, and Binh Thuy) collected data on the distances and bearing of prominent sites in its area. Specific landmarks, like a bunker or flagpole at the site, served as reference points for these precise measurements. Despite some limitations* ground forces had great confidence in the system. Using 8-digit map coordinates (squares of 10 meters), Sky Spot tests in the United States eventually reduced the circular error probable to within 72 meters of the desired impact point. A MACV directive forbade Sky Spot missions from delivering ordnance within 1,000 meters of friendly positions without the approval of the ground commander, but in June 1966, after benefiting from its use, one Army commander stated that he would not hesitate to use Sky Spot within 500 meters of his troops if the targets were valid and lucrative.[167]

In sum, the development of close air support in South Vietnam brought changes in the tactical air control system, employed imagination in unprecedented use of various aircraft in the tactical air mission, and introduced some innovative methods for delivering ordnance. Speaking in 1968, General Holloway declared, "I believe that when the Vietnam war is concluded, the rapid evolution of close air support will emerge as the outstanding airpower achievement of the war."[168] Holloway cited an Air Force study designed to formulate an "index of effectiveness" for close air support. With the results of an analysis in late 1967 of 15,000 close air-support sorties (and without being too precise in his definitions), Holloway reported that 50 percent of the air strikes had reduced "heavy" enemy fire to "light," while another 23 percent of the sorties had ended the "heavy" fire altogether. In three-quarters of the contacts that involved "moderate" enemy fire and in all contacts with "light" enemy fire, the fire had been reduced to "none" by tactical air power.[169]

Indeed, an overall "index of effectiveness" for close air-support operations in the war was difficult to formulate, largely because of the large number of variables involved. Other sources of firepower, such as artillery and helicopters, often became so intermingled with those of tactical aircraft that it was impossible to isolate and quantify the effects of each. Battle damage assessments were not always accurate for a number of reasons, including poor terrain, bad weather, or the enemy disposition of its casualties.

The nature of guerrilla warfare, too, impeded the evaluation of close air-support operations. In previous wars, progress could be measured in gains made along a recognized front, and the specific contribution of tactical air

---

*These limitations included the fact that a center could handle only one flight at a time and the fact that not all of South Vietnam was covered by the five centers.

operations—even if only in one sector—could be more readily quantified. In South Vietnam, however, no such "front" existed. Progress (or lack thereof) in the war had to be measured in ways other than geographical movement. Thus, the effectiveness of tactical air operations was obscured. Nevertheless, some measure of its effectiveness can be gained by examining specific battles and campaigns.

Early on October 20, 1965, the enemy launched an attack at Plei Me. A flareship arrived within 25 minutes, and strike planes hit their targets at the requested times. Throughout the 7–day Communist attack, tactical aircraft hovered continuously over the beleaguered outpost, delivering more than 830 tons of ordnance in 588 strike sorties; 22 flareship missions dropped more than 3,700 flares. In the end, 326 enemy troops were killed, and captured documents later showed that about 250 of these perished as a result of air power. After the battle, an Army officer working with the Vietnamese defenders affirmed the effectiveness of USAF close air support. He declared:

> If it hadn't been for air, we would have lost this place. The air chopped them up at the wire. My men had about 30 rounds of ammo left per man when the attackers were driven off, never having broken the perimeter. They [USAF strike aircraft] came right down our perimeter with cannon, antipersonnel mines, and then when the enemy began pulling back, they hit them with high explosive stuff.[170]

Throughout 1966, USAF strike planes averaged 5,891 sorties a month in support of ground forces in South Vietnam.[171] An Air Force study of all operations in South Vietnam between mid-March and mid-June of that year showed that 91 percent of all "search and destroy" ground sweeps (985 separate operations) received tactical air support. Of these, 366 involved troops in contact with the enemy (83 were considered "significant" contacts). This study concluded: "For the U.S. operations, it appears that when air support is not used, the operations are primarily those with few contacts."[172]

Ironically, one of the most convincing demonstrations of the effectiveness of close air support was shown in its absence from a battle. In March 1966, the Special Forces camp at A Shau had to be evacuated in the face of enemy attacks. The enemy gained this victory largely because bad weather prevented strike aircraft from supporting the defenders.[173] One of the justifications for the Sky Spot system, therefore, was that it could help prevent any more "A Shaus."[174]

In 1966, during Operation Hawthorne, tactical air support included 124 Sky Spot sorties (85 percent of which were observed by ground units). One air liaison officer reported that ground commanders indicated good target coverage for all ordnance deliveries.[175] Another air liaison officer stated, "I personally would credit Sky Spot for being the prime factor in deterring a full attack on the ARVN outpost of Toumorong."[176] During November 1966, tactical aircraft flew 1,629 strikes in support of Operation Attleboro in Tay Ninh Province. But of the confirmed total of 1,106 enemy killed in Attleboro, no accurate assessment could be made as to which portion of that total was attributable to air strikes.[177]

As a strategy using large ground sweeps continued in 1967, demands for close air support increased. The tactical air control system seemed capable of handling these challenges. For example, throughout 1967 the Direct Air Support Center in III Corps reported average response times of 15 minutes for diversions of airborne aircraft and 30 minutes for the scrambling of ground-alert aircraft.[178] Operation Sam Houston, at the beginning of the year, involved the processing of almost 2,500 close air-support sorties, including more than 400 hundred Sky Spot missions.[179] Other large sweeps, like Thayer II and Junction City, compiled similar impressive totals. In fact, during the lengthy Thayer II, from October 25, 1966, to February 12, 1967, the Air Force responded to every immediate request within 24 minutes.[180]

One of the biggest battles of the war came in early fall 1967 at Hill 875 near Dak To. Flying almost 2,100 close air-support sorties, some of which delivered ordnance within 30 meters of friendly positions, the Air Force accounted for 544 enemy deaths, 117 bunkers destroyed, and 130 secondary explosions or fires. Arc Light (B–52) missions were particularly effective in destroying enemy fortifications and ammunition caches. One after-action report by an Army unit pointed out: "Tac air support was close and continuous regardless of the time or place."[181]

On the night of October 29, 1967, two enemy battalions launched an attack on a camp near Loc Ninh, which forced the defenders to retreat to a command bunker. A lone Spooky gunship, with the help of Army artillery, blunted the enemy attack until daylight and the arrival of reinforcements. As the battle continued, close air support helped repel 5 waves of enemy assaults within the camp perimeter; 452 tactical strikes accounted for most of the 852 dead enemy. An Air Force report concluded, "The battle again illustrated that integrated TAC air, gunships, light fire teams, and artillery can successfully defend fortified positions, particularly when there is a clearly defined perimeter to aid pilots in accurately placing their ordnance."[182]

In retrospect, 1968 was the year of crisis. It opened with North Vietnamese forces besieging the isolated outpost of Khe Sanh. During the 78–day siege 6,000 Marines and South Vietnamese Rangers stood against an enemy force 3 times that number. By the time the siege was broken, tactical aircraft flew almost 25,000 sorties and expended more than 95,000 tons of ordnance. The Air Force contributed about 75 percent of that total in a joint effort with Marine and Navy aircraft. Because of bad weather, most of the strikes had to be delivered under radar control. The after-action estimate of 15,000 enemy killed in action led one State Department official to describe Khe Sanh as "the first major ground action won entirely, or almost entirely, by air power."[183] Historian Roswell Freedman pointed to Khe Sanh as "the episode that publicizes the phenomenal effectiveness of close air support more than perhaps any other in the annals of warfare."[184]

The intensive bombing campaign produced a relatively new category of wartime casualties: "concussion sickness." With no external wounds, some enemy soldiers suffered internal bleeding caused by the incessant pounding of bombs. One enemy soldier, in his 60th day of the siege, confided to his diary the terrifying effects of the air support at Khe Sanh. He wrote:

> If visitors came here, they will say that this is an area where it rains bombs and cartridges. Vegetation and animals, even those who live in deep caves or underground, have been destroyed. One sees nothing but the red dirt removed by bombs.[185]

The crisis of 1968 deepened with the general enemy offensive launched during the Tet holiday. The widespread enemy attacks in Corps I, II, and III, as well as poor weather conditions, strained tactical air capabilities. Nevertheless, Brig. Gen. George W. McLaughlin, who served at Seventh Air Force Headquarters, asserted that no immediate request for air support went unfilled. But he added: "I must admit, however, during the '68 Tet offensive, with various airfields under mortar and rocket as well as ground attack, it was touch-and-go at times, and only due to the inherent flexibility of the system were we able to meet all the requests."[186] Operations during the Tet Offensive also revealed the effectiveness of armed Army helicopters, not only in marginal weather but also in the direct defense of fixed installations, such as Tan Son Nhut and Bien Hoa air bases. Their unique capabilities enabled the armed helicopters to fly almost two thousand air-support sorties during one twenty-four-day period in weather severe enough to ground the fixed-wing fighters.[187]

The Tet Offensive extended the battle area to the cities for the first time. At the occupied city of Hue, for example, General Momyer observed that close air support was used to prevent enemy supplies and reinforcements from getting into the city.[188]

Ironically, the rubble produced by bombing certain cities made it even more difficult for the American and South Vietnamese ground forces to complete their reoccupation and mopping-up chores. Some allegations of excessive and irresponsible Air Force bombings in urban areas led to a special investigation. An Air Force study concluded that "in every instance air was brought in only when it was impossible to root out the enemy or when not to do so would have resulted in unacceptable casualties."[189]

These examples suggest that at times close air support made valuable contributions to the land battle or occasionally, as in the assessments about

Khe Sanh, even influenced the outcome. Close air support, however, did have its problems and even unsatisfactory results, in part because by 1967 enemy tactics had adapted to the extensive use of tactical air power in South Vietnam. Strike pilots experienced difficulty in finding targets as the enemy began using smoke to distort the markings of the intended targets. Furthermore, the enemy commenced stationing antiaircraft units away from the attack site. These units, separated from attacking Communist forces, were equipped with an antiaircraft weapon consisting of four .50-cal machineguns bolted together.[190]

Two significant problems emerged during the battle at Loc Ninh (October 29, 1967), when efforts to coordinate Army artillery with tactical air power produced undue delays. An unexpected amount of time was consumed in shutting down artillery fire in order to obtain sector clearances for strike aircraft, and absence of air-to-air communications between VNAF FACs and USAF FACs hindered the air effort, contributing to the needless loss of 2 VNAF A–1 aircraft.[192] During Operation Irving (October 2–24, 1966), more than 700 tactical sorties produced not a single enemy casualty.[193] Another problem in close air support operations, at least according to the U.S. Air Force, emerged as the tactical air control system was progressively weakening with the gnawing number of other friendly aircraft (such as Army helicopters and Marine or Navy aircraft) outside its control.

Army and Air Force disagreement over certain issues continued to affect close air-support operations during the war. Disputes over the need for a special aircraft designed solely for close air support, over the allocation of close air-support sorties per combat day to each Army combat division, and over the air–ground command relationship were never satisfactorily resolved.[194] However, no close air-support problem seared relations between the two services more than the intrusion of armed Army helicopters. Despite joint service agreements of 1952 (Pace–Finletter Agreement) and 1957 (Department of Defense Directive 5160.22 and CONARC–TAC Agreement), which were to have limited Army aviation's involvement in close air-support operations and to have acknowledged Air Force control over tactical air resources, the Army continued to expand its aviation arm—particularly helicopters—to the Air Force's dismay.[195]

Army leaders considered organic helicopters to be continuously available and immediately responsive to ground commanders. One Army general declared: "The majority of maneuver commanders feel that [helicopter] gunships are more responsive than field artillery."[196] The Army felt that armed helicopters complemented Air Force tactical air power by providing an additional element of firepower between Air Force close air support and Army artillery.[197] Early experiences in South Vietnam, during which unarmed transport helicopters suffered losses in landing zone operations, led Army pilots to mount machineguns on their UH–1A helicopters.[198] Beginning with the 1st Cavalry Division in 1965, introduction of Army air mobile units which possessed little organic artillery served to increase the need for close air support beyond the level required for standard Army divisions. In authorizing these deployments, Secretary McNamara stated his belief that any aircraft in the battle area, including helicopters, should be armed.[199]

Army doctrine introduced new terms, such as "Direct Aerial Fire Support," and drew new distinctions between "direct (or 'shallow') supporting fire" and "heavy (or 'deep') ordnance delivery" close air support. The Army defined "direct aerial fire support Army" as "fire delivered by aerial vehicles organic to ground forces against surface targets and in support of land operations."[200] Army Secretary Stanley R. Resor incorporated the new categories of close air support in his comments on the AH–56A Cheyenne helicopter in February 1968. Resor explained that the Cheyenne was "designed to provide direct fire support to ground forces and when employed as an integral part of the ground combat team to do it better than any other aerial weapons system now in existence."[201]

Air Force leaders could hardly remain unaffected when, between 1960 and 1965, the number of Army helicopters doubled to more than 5,000.[202] In 1968 one Air Force briefing paper set the position of the Air Force: "We are concerned that [Army] overenthusiasm may result in the substitution of armed helicopters for more survivable tactical fighters with a consequent loss in overall combat power."[203] "Overenthusiasm" seemed to be an appropriate description for the Army's use of armed helicopters in South Vietnam.

An Air Force study in 1965 found that Army ground commanders had developed the practice of calling the nearest Army aviation company for immediate support from helicopter gunships. This study also reported that General Westmoreland was urging ground commanders to utilize the VNAF/ USAF tactical air control system in order "to dampen overreliance on helicopters."[204] Another Air Force inquiry discovered that in 1969 "Fire support was provided by armed helicopters in virtually every instance that ground troops of the 25th Infantry Division came in contact with the enemy."[205]

Some in the Air Force suspected that the Army resorted to semantic ploys to camouflage the Army's slicing away of Air Force responsibilities.[206] At least two congressional subcommittees seemed to agree. One of these concluded in 1965: "Present doctrine involves a bit of semantics [that] may satisfy those responsible for keeping the roles and missions of the two services within the agreed limits, but it is obvious to the most casual observer that the Army's armed helicopters have, in fact, been heavily relied upon to provide what is essentially close air support for friendly forces on the ground."[207]

In 1971, the other subcommittee rebuked both services for allowing the debate over helicopters to obstruct "the goal of providing the best possible firepower support for the soldier on the battlefield."[208] From the perspective of the Air Force, however, the stakes were absolutely fundamental, for the debate involved basic questions about roles and missions. As one Air Force study pointed out in that same year, "[T]he logic of Army aviation development could well result in the acquisition of other tactical air functions, ranging from reconnaissance to interdiction and perhaps even some forms of counterair operations."[209] The Air Force maintained, too, that the armed helicopters could not survive in a high-threat environment, and even in a permissive environment, and that close air support remained an Air Force responsibility. Otherwise, the Air Force would ask, what justification was there in the unwarranted duplication of creating another air force?[210]

The issue of armed Army helicopters, furthermore, opened the broader question of command and control of all tactical air resources—whether or not to select a single manager for air.

From the first, *ad hoc* arrangements shaped interservice coordination in South Vietnam. In fact, unity of command in Southeast Asia never materialized because of the parceling out of separate areas of responsibility. The Commander of Seventh Air Force, for example, served essentially as the Air Component Commander—although not always with that title. Yet he had no control over either Navy aircraft, which remained under the Commander-in-Chief, Pacific Fleet, or, until 1968, Marine strike aircraft. Even some Air Force aircraft—those of Strategic Air Command and some of Military Airlift Command—operated outside his jurisdiction. Unity of command and central direction of the war (including management of air resources) failed to materialize in Southeast Asia stemmed because of unique circumstances, which one Air Force study described as "political factors, divergent viewpoints of the armed services, and the gradualism of U.S. involvement."[211] In addition, only about half of the military aircraft in South Vietnam came under the VNAF/USAF tactical air control system. Thus, the command and control of air resources in South Vietnam (prior to March 1968) constituted a system with overlapping and confused responsibilities as well as inadequate controls over separate air forces operating in the same airspace.[212]

Military events in early 1968 altered the situation. Even before the Tet Offensive, Westmoreland told Adm. U.S. Grant Sharp (CINCPAC) that the increased deployment of Army units to I Corps and the impending large-scale battle in that region (indicated by the massing of enemy troops in the Khe Sanh area since late 1967) might require the selection of a single air-manager for fixed-wing, tactical air resources. Sharp urged him to reconsider because the existing system seemed effective.[213] Shortly thereafter, the enemy launched the Tet Offensive. Combat activity escalated dramatically in I Corps, especially with the defense of Khe Sanh—Operation Niagara (January 22–March 31, 1968). The number of maneuver battalions (Army, Marine,

Free World Forces, and ARVN) in I Corps, rose nearly one-third between December 1967 and April 1968, to a total of almost one hundred.[214] Air support for these mixed forces came chiefly from the U.S. Air Force and U.S. Marine Corps, but the two services acted independently. According to one Air Force study, the confusion of separate control systems produced an uneven flow of strike aircraft. Congestion over a target area at times caused aircraft to return to base with unexpended ordnance, and the potential for midair collisions soared. Reports indicated that ground operations were not coordinated with air activities, and tactical airlift aircraft flew through tactical air strikes. Some B–52 and Sky Spot bombings even took place without advance notice to other tactical air units.[215]

A temporary remedy, an Airborne Battlefield Command and Control Center (ABCCC), as an extension of the Seventh Air Force Tactical Air Control Center, was designed to link Air Force and Marine fixed-wing tactical operations in the northern part of I Corps.* These temporary arrangements, however, proved unsatisfactory. Air Force pilots accused Marine pilots of ignoring the ABCCC and proceeding directly to support Marine ground units. Without an overall plan to call upon and coordinate all air resources available throughout I Corps (and elsewhere), the defects of the uneven flow of aircraft—oversaturation at one time and critical shortages at another—continued.[216]

Westmoreland decided to act. He later explained: "I concluded I would be remiss in carrying out the responsibilities of my office if I did not effect arrangements that would most effectively use the total assets available to me, regardless of Service cognizance or past doctrine."[217] On February 20, 1968, under guidance from Westmoreland, General Momyer, as COMUSMACV Deputy for Air Operations, briefed the Commanding General of the III Marine Amphibious Force (MAF), Lt. Gen. Robert E. Cushman, Jr., on plans for Momyer to assume operational control over the 1st Marine Air Wing (excluding helicopters and fixed-wing transports).

Cushman disagreed with the proposed change and argued that it would degrade Marine combat effectiveness. Nevertheless, on February 26, Westmoreland resubmitted his proposal to CINCPAC. Admiral Sharp approved the shift to the single air-manager system subject to the conditions that (1) Marine requests for immediate close air support would not be routed through the Tactical Air Command Center of the Seventh Air Force and (2) all III MAF complaints or suggestions about the new system would go directly to COMUSMACV and CINCPAC. Without objection from the Joint Chiefs of

---

*This center attempted to assign all of the Marine aircraft to the zone nearest Marine ground forces at Khe Sanh.

Staff, Westmoreland appointed Momyer as single manager for air operations on March 8, but delays prevented the system from functioning until April 1, one day after the close of Operation Niagara.[218]

Under the new single-manager system, all Marine strike and reconnaissance aircraft were added to the other aircraft already under the control of Seventh Air Force. The separate Marine tactical air control system would be made available as required. (The Marines had their own direct airsupport centers in I Corps: "Victor" at Hue Phu Bai and special units at Khe Sanh and Dong Ha.) Also in 1968, the VNAF–USAF tactical air control system divided the direct air support center at Da Nang into DASC I (for VNAF–ARVN affairs) and Camp Horn, which was collocated at III Marine Amphibious Force Headquarters (to handle USAF, Navy, Marine, and Korean operations). The single-manager system did not incorporate Marine airlift, Marine helicopters, Army helicopters, or Army fixed-wing reconnaissance aircraft. Although Navy aircraft remained technically outside Momyer's control, the Navy provided a daily number of sorties for the single-manager's use. Strategic Air Command still held responsibility for B–52 strikes (and possible B–52 targets continued to be nominated by MACV), but a SAC representative served at Seventh Air Force Headquarters to assist in the detailed planning of B–52 operations.[219]

The decision to establish a single-manager for air operations sparked further controversy among the services. Describing it as one of his most difficult decisions, Westmoreland stated that some high-ranking officers became "rather emotional" over the question. After the single-manager system was introduced, Westmoreland found that there was "still not a full meeting of the minds."[220]

The traditional Air Force view, which dated back at least to 1942–1943 (when Air Chief Marshal Sir Arthur Tedder, RAF, directed air resources for General Dwight D. Eisenhower in North Africa), held that an air component commander should be appointed to assist the overall theater commander. All air operations, regardless of service affiliations, formed a single air war, despite separate geographical divisions and command arrangements. This centralized control would enable the theater (or joint-force) commander to set various theater priorities by apportioning his total air resources through the air component commander. The single-manager for air operations system would also help prevent costly duplication of expense and effort. For the Air Force, the single-manager system incorporated the fundamental principles of sound organization, such as unity of command, span of control, functional grouping, delegation of authority, and rapid decision making. Valuable air assets should not be weakened by being "penny-packeted" (a phrase dating to World War II) out to low-level units. Also, according to the Air Force view, an air component commander, working with the theater command, would have the flexibility to adjust air resources among the "tactical trinity" of counterair, interdiction, and close air support.[221]

Army voices raised protests against the single air-manager system. This was in keeping with the long-held Army position that the ground commander—not a single air-manager, or anyone else—should have operational control of close air-support resources. According to the Army, the best way to apply combat power lay in a decentralized system of direct allocation of air resources. In this way, each level of ground-force command would hold the means and the directive authority necessary to complete its mission. Under the principle of "habitual availability," each ground commander could count on some minimum number of close air-support sorties at his disposal—sorties that could not be taken away from him and thereby could not disrupt his operational plans. Even more preferable, the Army would like to have had Air Force units placed directly under the operational control of the field army commander.[222]

Ironically, a considerable body of opinion inside Army circles—especially proponents of Army aviation—lobbied for central control of Army air resources. By 1971, over eighty percent of Army aviation was controlled above the division level. As early as 1962, the Howze Board had illustrated this internal contradiction by recommending, on the one hand, decentralized control of highly versatile air systems exercised at lower command levels, while on the other hand giving recognition to just the opposite point of view by affirming the principle that "weapon systems in short supply (as are air weapon systems from a relative basis) must be controlled by higher command level to permit discriminating decisions as to which subordinate echelons have greater requirements."[223] General Momyer himself could not have stated the case for a single air-manager more succinctly. Apparently many people in the Army endorsed at least the spirit of the single air-manager system.[224]

Westmoreland's decision upset the Marines. Their system of close air support had been carefully developed over the years. Unlike the Army–Air Force controversies, the Marine organization experienced no problems about roles and missions. Geared since 1947 to the concept of amphibious operations, Marine and Navy forces launched forty-three amphibious landings in South Vietnam between 1965 and 1967. Marine ground units had only minimal organic firepower and relied heavily on fast-reacting close air support.[225]

In South Vietnam, the 1st Marine Air Wing served as the air arm of the III Marine Amphibious Force. At least two forward air controllers in each marine battalion directed air strikes from ground positions. A tactical air direction center and a direct air-support center (collocated with a tactical operations center) coordinated and controlled Marine aviation. Thus, the Marine system for close air support incorporated central command and supervision of operations at the integrated wing/division level as well as decentralized control and coordination authority through subordinate agencies. Air Support Radar Teams provided all-weather delivery of ordnance similar to the USAF Sky Spot system. The Marine tactical data system was compatible with the Navy system, and in 1969 the Southeast Asia tactical data system, which passed correlated air situation information automatically to Air Force, Navy, and Marine data systems, became operational.[226]

Marine requests for immediate air support went directly to the nearest Marine direct air support center over their tactical air request net. Although silence by intermediate levels normally signified acquiescence, the Marines changed this for operations in South Vietnam to require voice approval at each higher echelon. A Marine officer told the Pike Subcommittee that this was "to ensure no air attack which jeopardizes civilian lives".[227] When the tactical operations center, collocated with the DASC, gave final approval to the request, the DASC could then divert or scramble aircraft to fill the need. Only the tactical air direction center, which monitored all Marine air activity, could shift strike aircraft from another region to answer "immediates." This system, which relied heavily on air alert aircraft, had no other missions, such as interdiction and counterair, as Marine tactical air resources were dedicated to the support of the Marine rifleman. One Marine said: "I think that the Marines down to the so-called lowly rifle-man are very much attuned to this integral close air support and . . . they are looking over their shoulder and they expect it, they don't just anticipate it, they practically are expecting it with demand in their eye."[228]

Consequently, the shift to the single air-manager system reversed a time-honored tradition of responsive close air support by Marine aviation for Marine ground forces. Marines expressed concern to MACV about the possible long-term effects of breaking this air–ground precedent. MACV acknowledged that the single manager for air concept meant, from the Marine commander's point of view, "replacing my aviation commander and control over his assets with one who is not directly under my command; yet my overall operational responsibilities in" I C[orps] T[actical] Z[one] remain the same."[229]

Other Marine complaints focused on the operation of the single air-manager system. They believed that the new system was "producer" rather than "consumer" oriented. Also, because it was inherently more complex (according to the Marines), the new system failed to respond to the needs of the ground commander. They argued that the administrative burdens associated with the single-manager concept represented a "greater layering" with "no countervailing benefits to the front line forces." Something was wrong, in Marine eyes, with a system (a "push system") that filled immediate requests primarily by diverting aircraft assigned to missions previously thought important. Extensive diversions of aircraft led to compromises about type of ordnance load, fuel state, and pilot preparation. And what of the needs of the ground commander who lost his air support through these diversions? Even if the new system performed as designed, Marine spokesmen felt that "it has to remain less effective, for Marine purposes, than the system it replaced."[230]

The Marine Corps carefully documented the performance of tactical air resources under the single air-manager system. Their statistics indicated that, between January 1 and March 10, 1968, only 5 percent of immediate requests by Marine ground commanders were filled by diverting aircraft. In just one week (April 5–11, 1968) under the new system, however, that figure soared to 77 percent.[231] In addition, between April 3 and April 22, 1968, Marines claimed, only 37 percent of preplanned requests for close air support earned final approval in Saigon. But because of many aircraft diversions, only half of the approved were actually struck. On April 20, 1968—"a typical day"—Marine ground commanders submitted 172 planned requests; of these, 64 received approval, but 31 targets were attacked as a result of extensive last-minute diversions.[232] Marines also pointed to errors that occurred under the new command and control arrangements. In one two-day period (April 8–9, 1968), their records showed that (1) Saigon programmed 5 aircraft incorrectly for the direct air support center at Da Nang instead of the air support radar team (ASRT) at Phu Bai, which meant that aircraft on other missions had to be diverted to fill the request; (2) 3 aircraft scheduled for the Phu Bai ASRT should have gone to the Khe Sanh ASRT, as originally requested; and (3) 2 strike aircraft arrived over their target at 0800 instead of 0900 hrs and had insufficient fuel to loiter for the extra hour.[233] Thus, for Marines, the single manager for air resources brought extra burdens without more efficient close air support.

The Navy, too, criticized the decision to establish a single manager for air resources. Although most of the Navy's tactical strike aircraft flew interdiction missions in North Vietnam, the Navy did participate in some close air support operations in the south. In fact Westmoreland, who had been impressed with the capabilities of carrier-based aircraft for close air support, requested the Navy to establish a carrier-based "Dixie" station similar to the "Yankee" station up north. By June 1965, the responsibilities of both the Dixie (100 miles southeast of Cam Ranh Bay) and Yankee stations required 5 carriers.[234] After 1965, however, with the Navy's main attention in North Vietnam, the number of Navy close air support sorties, most of which were either in the Delta (IV Corps) or integrated with Marine ground operations in I Corps, steadily decreased. In December 1966, the Navy flew only 3 close air support missions (compared to 5,120 by the Air Force; 312 by the VNAF; and 265 by the Marine Corps). In December 1967, the totals were 1 by the Navy; 8,526 by the Air Force; 775 by the Marine Corps; 326 by the VNAF; and 142 by the Royal Australian Air Force.[235]

The Navy system of close air support worked through a TACRON (Navy tactical air control squadron), which had overall control of all Navy aircraft in a designated area directing the aircraft through a tactical air control center aboard the naval force flagship.[236] In addition, Navy strike aircraft could enter either the USAF tactical air control system to support Army ground forces, or as was frequently the case, the Marine integrated system.

Apparently the idea of extensive close air support in South Vietnam by carrier-based aircraft appealed to Westmoreland throughout 1965. Late that year, at Westmoreland's request, the 2d Air Division (later replaced by the Seventh Air Force) studied the close air support operations of the Navy, the Marines, and the Air Force. General Moore reported that Navy carrier operations could not provide the type of continuous air support required in South Vietnam.[237]

Although Navy carrier operations were not directly included in the single air-manager system, the Navy provided a number of aircraft to Tactical Air Control Center, Saigon for strikes in I and II Corps on a daily basis. Upon receiving the "frag" from Saigon, the appropriate regional direct air support center scheduled a forward air controller (or radar controller) to work with Navy planes. Carrier aircraft flew only planned sorties and never scrambled for "immediates."[238]

Controversy over the single manager for air concept reached the highest levels. Admiral Sharp (CINCPAC) supported Westmoreland, who as field commander, was in the best position to determine command and control arrangements in the war. The Joint Chiefs of Staff were divided on the issue. Chief of Naval Operations, Adm. Thomas H. Moorer, Army Chief of Staff, General Harold K. Johnson (who fretted that the single air manager would eventually gain control over all Army helicopters), both associated themselves with the arguments of the Marines against the new system.

Westmoreland found support from the Chairman of the Joint Chiefs of Staff, General Earle E. Wheeler (USA), who not only considered it unsound to overrule the on-the-scene commander but chose to interpret the change as a temporary expedient rather than a challenge to traditional service roles. General McConnell, the Air Force Chief of Staff, enthusiastically endorsed the single air-manager concept, and Secretary of Defense Clark Clifford accepted the Westmoreland–Wheeler position, but told the Marine Commandant that the original control system of the III Marine Amphibious Force would be reestablished as soon as the tactical situation eased. Marine leaders managed to put the matter before President Lyndon B. Johnson, but Johnson decided in favor of Westmoreland's decision.[239]

As single air manager, Momyer praised the flexibility of the new system. He said that, by shifting air resources, the centralized system could provide "sustained and massive or brief and highly selective" close air support.[240] A ground commander might start the day with only a dozen or so preplanned sorties, but let him clash with the enemy, and he could have 100 sorties at his disposal within an hour.

Yet the image of the single air-manager shifting and massing tactical air resources throughout the country was not entirely accurate. Controversy about the system persisted, and compromises had to be made. The practice of generating planned sorties deteriorated to virtually a paper exercise. The intention seemed merely to launch a certain number of aircraft into the air, so that they became eligible for diversion to more lucrative targets. Rather than have specific targets, strike pilots received general directions to proceed to rendezvous points to await further instructions.[241]

In May 1968, Westmoreland modified the system to apportion seventy percent of total tactical close air support resources among the ground forces on a weekly basis. He retained the other thirty percent for allocations on a daily basis (as required by the flow of combat). This change greatly reduced the complexity of fragging planned missions. (A Seventh Air Force study showed that all in-country strikes were appearing on one large frag order that incorporated almost six thousand items of information.) Also, the new fragging system reduced the number of daily requests and improved the response to a ground commander's needs by making a weekly commitment of aircraft for use as he wished.[242]

This new (centralized) fragging system seemed to be in line with what the Army–Marine proponents of a decentralized system were advocating. The ground commander now had dedicated air at his disposal. However, the creation of what essentially became an airborne alert pool led in some cases to the misuse of ordnance against certain targets. Moreover, tactical aircraft could not stay airborne waiting for the ideal target, and targets were being assigned regardless of ordnance loads available.[243]

Other problems developed in the single-manager system. Historian Riley Sunderland argued that by 1969, air request procedures had eroded and resembled the conditions of 1962. He pointed out that each major ground force in I Corps handled requests for immediate air support differently.[244] Significantly, the single air-manager system permitted the III Marine Amphibious Force to retain control of the air resources directly supporting its own units. "This exception," stated one Seventh Air Force leader, "left the matter of control of Marine air assets open to interpretation."[245] One Air Force study group concluded, "In reality, single management never deprived the Commanding General, III Amphibious Force, of control over his resources."[246] Moreover, enemy exhaustion after the fighting in 1968, coupled with the initial phases of the withdrawal of American ground forces, contributed to a reduction in the number of large-scale ground operations in South Vietnam. In fact, within a year's time the arguments for a single air-manager system during the crisis of early 1968 scarcely seemed justified.

The extent of the debate over armed Army helicopters and the single air-manager concept reflected the significance that each service attached to the issue. Nevertheless, it was a measure of their professionalism that political or theoretical disagreements could be kept separate from the battlefield. Lt. Gen. Bruce Palmer (USA) emphasized, "You don't see interservice problems at the fighting level."[247] And General Momyer, a central figure in many of these debates, observed, "From 1965 throughout the remainder of the war there were no significant disagreements with the Army about close air support [in South Vietnam]."[248]

Moreover, one Air Force study pointed out, "The divisive factors that have historically caused friction between the services are not encountered in the combat zone at the working level."[249]

Vietnamization of the War, 1969–1973

In early 1969, the new administration of President Richard M. Nixon sought to reduce the overall American commitment to Southeast Asia. A gradual withdrawal of American forces changed the character of the war. At the same time that bombing ceased in North Vietnam, attention turned to the close air-support mission.

In a typical operation, during May 10–20, 1969, tactical aircraft struck around the clock at Dong Ap Bia ("Hamburger Hill"), on the western side of the A Shau Valley. Ordnance delivered during the battle included almost 1,100 tons of bombs, 150 tons of napalm, and 31,000 rounds of 20–mm ammunition.[250] In another 1969 operation (Lancaster II), strike planes flew 424 sorties and expended 750 tons of ordnance. B–52s, in 53 raids, augmented this extended search-and-clear mission conducted by the Marines in Quang Tri Province. An official report on Lancaster II characterized close air support as "both accurate and effective."[251] Also in 1969, the Seventh Air Force logged sortie Number 3,500,000 on November 30. Of this total, 60 percent was close air support.[252]

MACV estimated that the so-called "Vietnamization" of the war would take five years, but in April 1969, Secretary of Defense Melvin Laird directed that the schedule be accelerated to less than three years. Faced with a deadline of December 1971, USAF and VNAF leaders moved to bolster the Vietnamese structure and personnel associated with, among other things, the delivery of close air support. They chose to emphasize four areas: (1) to accelerate VNAF efficiency by early unit activation and transfers; (2) to assign Vietnamese to U.S. units (a MACV suggestion); (3) to move training sites for VNAF personnel from the United States to South Vietnam; and (4) to improve VNAF equipment.[253]

One of the first effects of the American deescalation came on August 26, 1969, when the daily in-country total of preplanned sorties fell almost 20 percent, from 243 to 200 sorties per day. Furthermore, a few days later, on September 1, the total number of U.S. sorties was limited to 14,000 per month.[254] Between August and September 1969, the total number of USAF attack sorties dropped from 5,650 to 4,440; and the monthly USAF total exceeded 4,000 only 6 more times prior to the 1972 Easter Offensive.[255] In 1968, the Air Force had flown nearly 135,000 attack sorties. Thereafter this figure steadily declined (96,524 in 1969; 48,064 in 1970; 11,842 in 1971) until 1972 (40,322). The VNAF flew more attack sorties than any other service in 1971, and in 1972 accounted for about 40 percent of the total for that year.[256] Under American tutelage, the VNAF forward air controller program realized some gains. By May 1971, only VNAF FACs supported ARVN operations, and less than one year later, VNAF FACs controlled over 90 percent of all tactical strikes in-country.[257] The VNAF, too, made some progress, especially in its growing inventory of aircraft. By December 1970, the VNAF had swelled to 9 tactical air wings, 40,000 personnel, and approximately 700 aircraft (A–1Hs, A–37s, F–5s, AC–47s, O–1s, AC–119s). The original plan in 1969 called for building a VNAF force of 45 operational squadrons, but by early 1973 the actual number was 54.[258]

Serious problems nevertheless continued to plague the VNAF. The FACs, for instance, lacked sound training and received less-than-enthusiastic support from the ARVN. Moreover, few VNAF leaders appreciated the importance of FAC roles and the air liaison officer, and few understood the value of aircraft maintenance particularly preventive measures. Perhaps most important, the VNAF was being prepared to operate in a permissive environment, and its pilots had neither the training nor the aircraft to deal with a hostile environment that included SAMs and radar-directed antiaircraft artillery.[259]

Command and control arrangements for close air support—the tactical air control system—increasingly came under Vietnamese control after 1969. To ease the transition, VNAF and USAF personnel were physically collocated at all levels; status boards, displays, and forms were made bilingual; and communications systems were integrated using the English language. Joint USAF–VNAF operation of the Tactical Air Control Center in Saigon terminated in mid-1971, and by the end of that year the VNAF took over all Direct Air Support Centers.[260] Vietnamization of the tactical air control system, however, made the least progress at the level of the tactical air control party. Again, the failure of the Vietnamese to appreciate, and fully support, the FAC and air liaison officer roles degraded the effectiveness of the tactical air control parties.[261]

Despite its problems, the VNAF tactical air control system seemed "workable," in the words of one Air Force study, by the time of the cease-fire in 1973.[262] In the end, however, hope exceeded performance. During the subsequent 1975 debacle leading to ultimate defeat of South Vietnam, General Momyer wrote:

> Much of the difficulty stems from discipline and failure to properly coordinate prior to the operation. Working with the VNAF was a sensitive problem throughout the war. The lack of thorough coordination of activities was apparent on many occasions because of security, lack of radios, experience, national pride, and language. All of these factors make it difficult to achieve the desired coordinated effort when large numbers of sorties are going into a small area under attack.[263]

Three major operations in the period 1970–1972 provided a gauge of the progress of the Vietnamization program. On May 1, 1970, American and South Vietnamese forces crossed into Cambodia. Although ground engagements during the month-long operation proved lighter than expected, the Air Force, with help from the VNAF, averaged about 200 close air-support sorties per day. During the first 10 days, air power accounted for some 300 enemy killed, 1,000 enemy fortifications destroyed, and 250 secondary explosions. In addition to the usual array of tactical aircraft, close air support operations in Cambodia used C–130s to drop 1,500–pound bombs that were specifically designed to clear areas for helicopter landing zones.[264]

VNAF and ARVN performance in Cambodia demonstrated the extensive progress yet required before U.S. withdrawals could be completed. Also, the Cambodian operation disclosed difficulties in coordination between the U.S. Army and U.S. Air Force. An Air Force colonel who worked in the Tactical Air Control Center reported that the Seventh Air Force had to make strenuous efforts to place representatives at appropriate levels in Army–ARVN planning sessions. He added: "The problem is compounded by the Army's continuing attempt to use the helicopter as a substitute for TACAIR."[265]

This operation revealed another lesson—that the typical forward air controller or air liaison officer lacked the background and status to participate effectively at the division level. Preparing for the first day of invasion, the U.S. 1st Cavalry Division submitted a request for a total of eight close air support sorties. Seventh Air Force dispatched an experienced colonel to work with the division commander in straightening out plans for air support. As a result, on the first day of operations the 1st Cavalry actually received one hundred preplanned sorties plus forty immediate "scrambles" (eighty preplanned and thirty "scrambles" on the second day).[266]

One of the purposes of the Cambodian incursion was to destroy enemy sanctuaries, so that the Vietnamization program could continue with a minimum of interruptions. One Air Force study claimed that the operation had obtained 8 months of security for Military Region III, but that statistic seems difficult to substantiate.[267] All tactical sorties in Cambodia after the operation had ended were classified as interdiction missions. The very last days of American involvement in Southeast Asia, however, saw Air Force tactical strikes break a determined enemy effort to seize Phnom Penh. For psychological or propaganda reasons, the North Vietnamese hoped to seize the capital before the exit of U.S. forces on August 15, 1973. Just days before that deadline, American air strikes stopped the enemy attack, producing 16,000 enemy casualties in the process.[268]

The second major operation came in January 1971, when South Vietnamese forces invaded Laos. The purpose of this operation (Lam Son 719) was to cut enemy supply lines, which swung westward out of North Vietnam through Laos and Cambodia and emptied into South Vietnam. Efforts to stop the flow of enemy supplies merged with battles in the civil war between Laotian factions to produce some of the most intense fighting in Southeast Asia.

Lam Son 719 involved only ARVN ground forces supported by USAF tactical air resources.[269] Strictly from the narrow perspective of air–ground coordination, the operations disclosed the progress of ARVN commanders in incorporating close air support in their maneuvers. The overall assessment of Lam Son 719, however, gave cause for concern. The ARVN got its nose bloodied, and the foray further indicated the considerable amount of work still needed in the Vietnamization program. Summarizing the Lam Son 719 operation, Air Force historian Jack S. Ballard wrote: "The operation was but briefly disruptive."[270]

The third critical test of President Nixon's Vietnamization plan unfolded during the North Vietnamese Easter Offensive of 1972. By early 1972, almost all U.S. ground forces had left South Vietnam. Marine strength declined from about 81,000 in 1968 to barely 600 by the end of 1971, and the Air Force total of 28,800 in early 1971 represented less than half the 1968 figure of 58,400.[271] The USAF inventory of tactical fighters in-country stood at just 3 squadrons of F–4s, and 1 of A–37s.[272] In addition, most forward aircontroller responsibilities had shifted to the VNAF, while the few remaining U.S. air liaison officers were redesignated ALO advisors. VNAF personnel controlled most of the tactical air control system.[273]

The enemy offensive, which began in late March 1972, threatened to overwhelm South Vietnam. VNAF tactical strike resources—one F–5 squadron, about 150 other aircraft, and 200 flight crews considered combat ready[274]— could not cope with the powerful enemy thrust, which included tanks and SAMs. It quickly became apparent that U.S. reinforcements would be required. Two Navy carriers, *Constellation* and *Kitty Hawk*, left their stations elsewhere in the Pacific to join the *Hancock* and *Coral Sea* already off the coast of South Vietnam; 2 additional carriers, *Midway* and *Saratoga*, departed from the United States. Marine air units hurried from their Pacific stations to South Vietnam. In a true test of tactical air deployment capabilities, USAF strike forces moved from Korea and the United States during 4 separate stages. They took an average time of 6 days to be in place after receiving first notification.[275]

Evaluating the contribution of tactical air power in the Easter Offensive, one PACAF study declared, "The analysis leaves little doubt that strong relationships did exist between the application of air power and reductions in enemy gains." This study added that because of "the absence of strong resistance on the part of friendly forces," and because of the fact that enemy forces failed in their objective, "it is reasonable to conclude that air power was the determining factor in stopping the enemy's thrust into South Vietnam."[276] Another Air Force study concluded: "Reduction in enemy gains were strongly related to the number of Tacair, gunship, and Arc Light sorties flown. . . . The cumulative effect of air was a powerful influence in blunting the enemy invasion."[277] General Momyer, however, warned that the VNAF strike planes, such as A–1s and A–37s, were too vulnerable to sustain operations in heavily defended areas.[278]

Between March 30 and May 31, 1972, Americans and South Vietnamese launched numerous tactical air strikes in Military Regions I, II, and III, as well as Military Region IV (although it was not involved with the Easter Offensive) in efforts to blunt the widespread enemy assault.[279]

Average Daily Tactical Aircraft Sorties
Mar 30–May 31, 1972

	MR I	MR II	MR III	MR IV
USAF				
(Excluding B–52s)	86	33	78	14
B–52s	23	28	11	1
U.S. Marines/Navy	52	39	52	13
VNAF	46	37	44	33

The defense of An Loc, an important provincial capital, involved 10,000 close air-support sorties. A U.S. Army advisor praised the contribution of tactical air power, saying that some strike planes hit "within 600 meters of the perimeter . . . so close that we took some WIAs [wounded-in-action] getting into bunkers."[280] In another example of "close" air support, a U.S. advisor at besieged Quang Tri City reported: "The tactical situation dictated that normal safe distances . . . be waivered so we could do nothing but watch, wait, and thank God for the U.S. Air Force."[281] Battle damage assessments during the first 2 months of the crisis included 618 North Vietnamese gun positions; 521 AAA pieces; 336 tanks; 1,529 trucks; and possibly as many as 40,000 enemy casualties.[282] Statistics did not indicate how much of this destruction was accounted for by tactical air power but the COMUSMACV, Gen. Frederick C. Weyand, USA, acknowledged "the magnificent job done by our air power."[283] More directly, General Momyer described tactical air power as "decisive" in breaking the enemy offensive.[284]

Conclusions

Assessing the role of close air support in the war remains an elusive task principally because of imprecise standards of evaluation. One measure would be its impact on the way the war in South Vietnam was fought. Within this context, close air support operations seemed to have a profound effect. As General Momyer wrote, "[T]he characteristic engagement was one in which our ground forces located the enemy and kept him in sight while waiting thirty to forty minutes for the fighters to arrive."[285] On this same point, an Air Force study concluded, "Air power was used effectively in its traditional roles as well as in compensating for shortages or as a substitute for ground forces."[286] Of course close air support alone could not guarantee that enemy assaults would always be turned away. Experience in prior wars showed that tactical air units could have only a temporary effect under such conditions.[287] There is some evidence that friendly ground forces did not maintain contact with the enemy as vigorously as in previous wars,[288] but the relevant point for this analysis lies in the fact that close air support played so prominent a role in South Vietnam that it affected the basic assumptions about the conduct of the war. One Army ground force commander illustrated this point when he stated: "I learned after a while that my casualties were tremendously decreased if I used the air power and air strikes and used it [sic] properly. And it was there to use."[289] Similarly, General Momyer observed, "I suppose the significant lesson from Vietnam is the unrealism on the amount of close air support any given ground force commander received regardless of need."[290]

The question of the availability of close air support, in turn, led to the question of its responsiveness in the war. Obviously one of the key measures of close air support lay in whether or not the requests for assistance received timely and effective answers. The "20/40" formula appears to have been a reliable gauge of close air support and, more important, generally sufficient in the war.[291] Thus, virtually every reaction from the "users"—ground force commanders—proved highly favorable. One Army officer, stated: "Actually it's the best [close air support] that I have ever seen, having fought as an enlisted man in World War II, as a Company Commander and a Platoon

Leader in Korea. It was probably the most responsive and finest that I could imagine."[292]

A captain in the Special Forces who had served two tours also reported: "I'd say ninety-nine percent of the time, the time element—the maximum time element—was twenty-two minutes from the time that we requested immediate air until we had it on target."[293]

Similar Army praise for close air-support operations extended to the highest levels. In 1966, the Army Chief of Staff, General Wheeler, said Army officers (some of whom were in their third war) told him that the close air support they received in South Vietnam was better in quality, quantity, and responsiveness than ever before.[294] Westmoreland, at the 1967 Guam Conference, described the close air support in-country as "the finest any Army could hope to get."[295]

In fact, so pervasive and so responsive was close air support that quite an opposite problem arose. Tactical air power may well have been overused in South Vietnam. One Army battalion commander knew of requests for air support "even if you had a two-round sniper contact."[296] Another Army officer told of being pressed by superiors to request air support he did not need. He stated, "I would end up pretty well just picking out of the air an eight-digit coordinate, and sure enough next morning, at ten o'clock I'd hear a tremendous explosion, and we'd think: "Wonderful, the Air Force has hit that eight digit coordinate. . . ."[297] One Air Force forward air controller complained that "every time they run into more than an occasional sniper, they call for all the air we can send them. Oftentimes they don't really need all that air support."[298]

Some of the specific procedures or tactics associated with close airsupport operations helped change the conduct of the war. The development of the tactical air control system, evolution of the gunships, and the arming of the forward air controller's aircraft accelerated the response time to requests for immediate air support by fitting in with the concept of "Phased Response": the theory of providing a certain measure of firepower as soon as possible after a target presented itself, while waiting for the tactical fighters.

Arming Army helicopters appeared to be a forward step. Some FACs and gunships assigned to geographical areas not only acquired target techniques but they also provided an additional source of contacts on a regular basis. In addition, the development of flare operations, gunships, and Sky Spot procedures assisted in close air support at night and in bad weather conditions. B–52 raids, when flown "in the vicinity" of friendly ground forces (and therefore technically close air support), earned general recognition in the war effort, in-country.

Another method of assessing close air-support operations in South Vietnam would be to examine the course of specific battles. But, as noted in the representative cases discussed earlier, in this war where accurate battle damage assessments proved so difficult to obtain and where the results of close air-support operations could rarely be segregated, about the only generalization that could be made is that in some instances close air support seemed to have made a contribution.

Besides the battles previously noted, some other specific examples where close air support apparently affected the outcome were (1) Dan Chi 141 (June 25, 1965), where the Air Support Operations Center in IV Corps had to make extensive reassignments or diversions of strike aircraft to respond to sudden requests by the 21st ARVN Division for a large number of strike aircraft;[299] (2) the report by Maj. Gen. William E. DePuy, Commander of the 1st Infantry Division, that close air support in weather of 200–400-ft ceilings helped him defeat the 3d Battalion, 273d VC Regiment;[300] (3) the crediting to tactical air power for one-half the 326 enemy killed by a unit of 3d Marine Division south of Chu Lai in August 1965;[301] and (4) an engagement on Hill 1338 near Dak To on November 16, 1967, when enemy forces were so close that the ground commander threw smoke grenades to mark the target for strike aircraft, and where a platoon leader subsequently wrote a letter of appreciation to the tactical air unit that had provided him close air support, thanking the pilots for having made Hill 262 "a bare hill where once a forest and NVA stronghold existed."[302] Specific battles, of course, are an unsteady platform for generalizations. Nevertheless, judging from the favorable reports of ground troops throughout the war and in various regions of South Vietnam, it seems that close air support had more than a welcome effect on the course of some battles. Among these reports, few matched the emotion of this unidentified GI:

> You read about this, you see the movies, and everything, but movies are something else, but when you're in real life, you're pinned down under fire, and here comes the Air Force and they just drop the bombs right where they belong and they knock out what they are supposed to knock out and enables us to move around and go to our objective like we're supposed to. It's a fantastic feeling. It's more than thanks. You just can't express it really.[303]

The nature of guerrilla warfare, in posing special challenges for tactical air operations, represented another obstacle in judging the effectiveness of close air support in South Vietnam. "This war is different from any war in which airmen have fought before," one Air Force colonel observed. "No military action takes place without interrelationship between political, economic, psychological, and often, personality factors."[304]

Traditional standards to measure air power, including the number of sorties flown, the amount of ordnance delivered, and battle damage assessments, proved unreliable guidelines in this war. Enemy tactics, especially in launching small attacks that lasted only a short time, seemed designed to avoid prolonged exposure to tactical air power.[305] Rules of engagement were particularly sensitive to political factors, which could make them quite restrictive.

Air Force analysts tried to find out the reasons why damage reports frequently seemed low for the number of sorties flown. In addition to obvious reasons, such as the intermingling of artillery and air power, the fact that certain direct air-support sorties (e.g., escort or harassment) had no fixed targets, and that it was difficult to obtain accurate battle damage assessment at night or in bad weather, the analysis suggested that to substitute air power for ground force led to "overkill," especially when the projected target had not been precisely evaluated beforehand. Also, this Air Force inquiry found not only that ordnance shortages led to sorties flown with partial loads, but also that certain tactical sorties (e.g., clearing helicopter landing zones and continuing air strikes along enemy withdrawal routes after an engagement) would produce little battle damage.[306]

Certain issues about close air support in South Vietnam appeared likely to exacerbate interservice relations long after the war. Such were the concepts of designating a single manager for air resources, arming Army helicopters, and developing aircraft designed solely for close air support. Army leaders still clung to their belief that a certain number of close air-support sorties

Boeing B-52 Stratofortresses had a devastating effect on enemy installations and battlefield units in Vietnam.

should be dedicated to each combat division per combat day.[307] Also, some Air Force leaders wondered about the services drawing the wrong lessons from tactical air resources operating in the highly permissive environment of South Vietnam. General Momyer worried about this, and the Seventh Air Force Handbook warned: "While it is obviously desirable to take full advantage of this freedom, we should not assume that this situation represents a model for the future."[308]

In conclusion, the effectiveness of close air-support operations in South Vietnam remains open to debate. Whether the desired formula was "20/40," or even "5/10," any measure of the effectiveness of close air support is bound to be subjective. Fairly definite conclusions can be reached about such factors as pilot training, ordnance delivery techniques, command and control arrangements, numbers of sorties, and numbers of combat flying hours, but in the end, efforts to arrive at an overall assessment are too judgmental and carry too many variables to be objective. One Air Force study suggested that "for psychological reasons alone," close air support had played a very important role in the war.[309]

The PACAF commander believed that any evaluation of close air support should incorporate its indirect effects as well as the actual damage inflicted. After the 1972 Easter Offensive, he wrote, "Critics often look only at the instantaneous effect and fail to recognize that the cumulative destruction of supplies and personnel has seriously limited the enemy's capability to fulfill his objectives in Southeast Asia."[310] Momyer also touched on this point when he suggested that the fundamental accomplishment of American air power was the restraint it kept on the level of enemy activity in-country. He pointed out: "The combination of the interdiction campaign and close air support prevented the enemy from deploying and maintaining a higher level of effort."[311] Army leaders, especially those expecting tactical air resources to be as responsive as artillery, might disagree with the Air Force perspective.

Despite all variables and extenuating circumstances, in the final analysis the true test of close air-support operations is how well they satisfied the requirements of the ground force commander. Judging from the favorable reactions of ground commanders throughout the war—at least during the "American phase" of the war—close air support met that overriding goal.

Notes

1. USAF, Project Corona Harvest, "USAF Activities in Southeast Asia, 1954–1964," USAF Hist Center, Maxwell AFB, Ala, K239.034–1, 54/00/00–64/00/00, p 4. This study added: "Although both TAC [Tactical Air Command] and PACAF [Pacific Air Command] were developing mobile contingency forces tailored to support a limited war situation, a major expansion of limited war capabilities had to be undertaken during the post–1960 era. The basic concept that general war capabilities would meet limited war requirements contributed to a lag in developing specific Air Force doctrine for limited war and counterinsurgency." Hereafter references to all documents and other archival materials will be by their file numbers. Unless otherwise indicated, all file numbers refer to the USAF Hist Research Center.

2. T. R. Milton, "USAF and the Vietnam Experience," *Air Force Magazine* LVIII (Jun 1975), p 56. Milton believed that higher accident rates in the late 1950s were due in part to pilots performing "unbriefed maneuvers" to relieve their boredom.

3. K239.034–4, 65/01/01–68/03/31, p 33.

4. K239.034–1, 54/00/00–64/00/00, p 10.

5. K239.034–4, 65/01/01–68/03/31, p 33.

6. Stuart E. Kane, "An Examination of the Close Air Support Concept," Thesis, Air War College, Nov 1970, pp 5–7. Hereafter cited as Kane, "Examination."

7. See, for example, Riley Sunderland, *Evolution of Command and Control Doctrine for Close Air Support* (Washington, 1973), p 33 (hereafter cited as Sunderland, *Evolution*); William W. Momyer, *Airpower in Three Wars* (Washington, 1978), pp 6–7 (hereafter cited as Momyer, *Three Wars*); K146.003–14, p 16.

8. K146.003–14, p 41; Momyer, *Three Wars*, pp 6–7.

9. K146.003–14, p 17.

10. Momyer, *Three Wars*, pp 6–7.

11. K146.003–14, p 17.

12. *Ibid.*

13. K168.7085–178.

14. See, for example, K168.7041–144, p 17.

15. The Air Force perspective is described in Momyer, *Three Wars*, p 9ff.

16. US Army, Combat Developments Command, Institute of Special Studies, *A Short History of Close Air Support Issues* (Ft Belvoir, 1968), p 56. Hereafter cited as Army CDC, *Issues*.

17. *Ibid.*

18. *Ibid*, p 57. For more about Army training in close air support, see Hearings before the Special Subcommittee on Tactical Air Support of the Committee on Armed Services, House of Representatives, *Close Air Support*, 89th Cong, 1st sess (Washington, 1966), p 4741 (hereafter cited as Pike, *Hearings*).

19. K146.003–14, pp 18–19. As a counterproposal, the Air Force suggested three air squadrons per Army division to fulfill all tactical air functions.

20. Army CDC, *Issues*, p 57.

21. Momyer, *Three Wars*, p 10.

22. K146.003–14, p 19.

23. Joint Chiefs of Staff, Pub 1.

24. Quoted in Joint Chiefs of Staff, Joint Study Task Force, Phase II, "Close Air Support Study," Oct 11, 1972, I, 48 (hereafter cited as JSTF, "Study"). See also, Army CDC, *Issues*, pp 59–60; K168.06–26, slide 7; K146.003–14, p 20.

25. K177.1511–5; KI46.003–14, p 21; Momyer, *Three Wars*. Sunderland, *Evolution*, pp 42–43; K168.06–26; Myron W. Crowe, "The Development of Close Air Support," Thesis, Air War College, Jun 1968, p 35 (hereafter cited as Crowe, "Development").

26. Army CDC, *Issues*, p 61; K177.1511–5; Momyer, *Three Wars*, p 255; K146.003–14, p 21; K168.06–26, slide 8; K168.06–25: Crowe, "Development," p 35.

27. K177.1511, 5 Vols; USAF, Tactical Air Command, "Cost Effectiveness of Close Air Sup-

port Aircraft," Apr 1965, p 2; Army CDC, *Issues*, p 64; K146.003–14, p 23; James H. Dickinson and Richard H. Kaufman. "Airpower Doctrine: A Case Study in Close Air Support," Research Report, Air War College, Apr 1976, p 7I (hereafter cited as Dickinson and Kaufman, "Airpower Doctrine").

28. Army CDC, *Issues*, p 66.

29. For valuable summaries of the Army–Air Force debate over the four issues, see Army CDC, *Issues*; Momyer, *Three Wars*; Sunderland, *Evolution*.

30. K239.034–1, p 21; United States, Department of State, *Foreign Relations of the United States, 1952–1954*, XIII, Part 2 (Washington, 1982), 2315; United States, Department of State, *Foreign Relations of the United States, 1955–1957*, I (Washington, 1985), pp 9–10, 21–37, 41–49, 58–72, 81–86, 388–90, 633; Momyer, "VNAF History," 1975, M–43227, Air University Library, Maxwell AFB, Ala (hereafter cited as AUL). One Air Force study characterized the French use of air power in Indochina as "inept." See K717.041–3, p 2.

31. Momyer, "VNAF History," p 2.

32. *Ibid*, pp 2–3; M–38245–231, AUL, p 1.

33. Andrew J. Chapman, "How to Increase the Effectiveness of Airpower in Counterguerrilla Warfare," Research Study, Air War College, Jan 1966, p 24; Robert F. Futrell, *The United States Air Force in Southeast Asia: The Advisory Years to 1965* (Washington, 1977), p 54; K239.034–1, p 26. This last-named study emphasized that the VNAF pilot shortage was an important issue because it eventually contributed to the increased use of USAF pilots in combat. Futrell pointed out that the VNAF pilot shortage was exacerbated by the decision in 1959 to replace French civilian aircrews and service technicians in the Air Vietnam commercial airline with VNAF personnel.

34. K239.034–1, p 4, pp 22–24.

35. Futrell, *Advisory Years*, p 55, p 75; Carl Berger, ed, *The United States Air Force In Southeast Asia. 1961–1973* (Washington, 1977), p 11.

36. M–38245–231, AUL, pl.

37. Momyer, "VNAF History," pp v, 10–11, 74–76; Sunderland, *Evolution*, p 38; Futrell, *Advisory Years*, p 49; M–38245–231, AUL, pp 62–71. For an excellent account of the request system in 1962, see 526.3101–2.

38. K168.7041–144, pp 8–9; M–42229–64, AUL, pp 8–11; Momyer, *Three Wars*, p 10. After 1962 the Joint Operations Center was known as the Air Operations Center, then in 1965 the Air Operations Center became the Tactical Air Control Center. See also K168.01–43 (1961–1965), pp 14–15. American interpretation of the 1954 Geneva agreements ruled out jet aircraft and tactical bombers in Vietnam. Consequently US Ambassador Frederick Nolting rejected a separate Air Force offer of one reconnaissance RT/T–33, and the Farm Gate B–26s took on an "R" prefix to imply a reconnaissance role. Intvw, author with Amb Frederick Nolting, Dec 6, 1983.

39. K168.01–43 (1961–1965), pp 14–15; K168.7041–144, pp 8–11; PACAF, Office of History, *Pacific Air Forces, 1957–1981, Hist Highlights: The First Twenty-Five Years* (Hickam AFB, 1982), pp 25, 81 (hereafter cited as Pacaf, *Highlights*); K526.03–12; Berger, *1961–1973*, pp 12–13; Momyer, *Three Wars* pp 65–88.

40. T. R. Milton, "Air Power: Equalizer in Southeast Asia," *Air University Review* XV (Nov–Dec 1963), 4; K526.3101–2, pp 5–9; Sunderland, *Evolution*. p 32; M–38245–231, AUL, pp 11–12; Intvw, Gen Paul D. Harkins, Oral History, MSS Archives, US Military History Institute, Carlisle Barracks, PA (hereafter cited as USMHI), pp 52–61.

41. Quoted in Futrell, *Advisory Years*, p 55.

42. Momyer, *Three Wars*, pp 73–76; Sunderland, *Evolution*. p 40.

43. Sunderland, *Evolution*, p 40. Sunderland described the operation of the air request net as "the outstanding problem of MACV." He attributed the failure of requests to reach the ASOCs to "political, religious, personal or social background, and customs of ARVN and civilian officials."

44. K239.0512–281.

45. K526.03–13. The response times and distances from the air bases in the nine reports were: (1) 55 mins—9 nm [nautical miles]; (2) 60 mins—103 nm; (3) 55 mins—44 nm; (4) 75 mins—124 nm; (5) 55 mins—23 nm; (6) 48 mins—80 nm; (7) 40 mins—no distance available; (8) 70 mins—81 nm; and (9) 30 mins—30 nm.

46. Russell F. Weigley, "Vietnam: What Manner of War?" *Air University Review* XXXIV (Jan–Feb 1983), 114–20. On Nov 1, 1955, MAAG,V had replaced MAG which had been in place since Sep 17, 1950. MACV, a subunified command under CINCPAC, headed by Gen Paul D. Harkins, was formed on Feb 8, 1962.

47. Douglas K. Evans, "Re-Inventing the FAC: Vietnam, 1962," *Air Force Magazine* LXIII (Feb 1980), p 72.

48. K168.7041–144, p 20; K168.01–43 (1961–1965), p 15; K239.034–1, p 17; see also Pike, *Hearings*, pp 4861–62.

49. K168.7041–144.

50. M–38245–110, AUL, p 1; K526.45011–1, p ii.

51. K526.45011–1, p iii; K168.7041–144, pp 9, 13; Futrell, *Advisory Years*, p 74. Also, Futrell pointed out that Kennedy wanted radar installed in South Vietnam to record Soviet over-flights as well as clandestine supply and intelligence missions. Radar centers, of course, were integral parts of the tactical air control system. See also, K168.01–43 (1961–1965), pp 12–14; Momyer,"VNAF History," p 7; PACAF, *Highlights*, p 25; M–42229–64, AUL, p 11.

52. K168.7041–144, pp 11–13, 22; M–38245–231, AUL, pl; K717.0413–67, pp 1–2; Sunderland, *Evolution*. pp 37–38; K160.041–20, Vol I, 21; K526.45011, pp 1–2, 15–19.

53. K168.7041–144, p 14.

54. *Ibid*; PACAF, *Highlights*. p 34.

55. Momyer, *Three Wars,* p 256.

56. K168.7041–144, p 53; M–38245–110, AUL, pp 3–4; K168.01–43 (1965–1970).

57. M–38245–110, AUL, p 2.

58. K740.132.

59. K239.034–1, p 20.

60. K239.034–4, pp 38–39.

61. K526.45011–1, pp iii–iv; K526.45011–2; Thomas A. Siegrist, "Close Air Support," Thesis, Air Command and Staff College, Jun 1967, pp 51–52; Pike, *Hearings,* p 4767; K168.01–43 (1961–1965), pp 62–67. This last-named study noted that, in order to avoid lengthy delays in requesting air support through official channels, Special Forces camps adopted the informal approach of calling in their requests directly to the US Embassy.

62. Futrell, *Advisory Years*, pp 56, 67, 129; K239.0512–522 (Paul Harkins).

63. K526.45011–1, pp 10–12; K168.7041–144, p 23. In all of I Corps, for example, only the Corps Commander, his Chief of Staff, and the Assistant Chief of Staff could approve strike requests.

64. K526.3101–2, p 5. The province chief served as a sector military commander in the corps' chain of command.

65. Futrell, *Advisory Years*. pp 55, 75; Sunderland, *Evolution*, p 36.

66. 178.2152–1, pp 19–20.

67. *Ibid*. The reason for the different sets of rules was that the Army played a direct support role, while Farm Gates's status was merely advisory.

68. K168.01–43 (1961–1965), pp 85–89; Momyer, *Three Wars*. pp 10–11; K168.7041–144, p 11; K717.04I–3, p 3. This study pointed out that until 1965 the United States interpreted the Geneva pact as outlawing jet aircraft, certain categories of munitions, and combat operations by aircraft with only American personnel aboard. Futrell (p 141) linked the restrictions about operations near Cambodia to the possibility of intervention by the Chinese Communists.

69. K168.01–43 (1961–1965), p 89.

70. *Ibid*, K526.45011–1, pp 10–12. One can only wonder about lengthy air-to-air and air-to-ground radio debates as to whether the troops being fired upon below in, say, temporary field camps were to be considered "in the field" (Vietnamese controller required) or in an "installation" (no Vietnamese controller required).

71. Futrell, *Advisory Years*, pp 54, 74–75, 129–31, 168. For more on all the rules of engagement, see K740.131, Blood, Gordon F., E–26; M–42193–248, AUL; K740.131, Aust, Abner M., Jr, p 118; US, MACV Directive 95–4, "Air Operations in RVN," Jul 13, 1965, Marine Corps Hist Center, Washington, (hereafter cited as MCHC); M–35044–39, Vol I; Harkins intvw, USAMHI; J. S. Butz, Jr, "Air Power in Vietnam: The High Price of

Restraint," *Air Force Space/Digest* XLIX (Nov 1966), 40–44; Jac Weller, "American Handicaps in Vietnam," *Army Quarterly* 97 (Jan 1969), 193–202. The restrictive rules continued throughout the war. For example, in Jul 1972 the COMPACAF, Gen John W. Vogt, stated that he had to explain to Washington every crater that appeared in the reconnaissance photos. See K168.06–228.

72. K168.01–43 (1961–1965), p 72. Also, in 1963, this study identified three independent chains of command: (1) for the VNAF, through ARVN to the Joint General Staff; (2) for the USAF, through the 2d Air Div to COMUSMACV: and (3) for the US Navy and Marine Corps, through the senior American advisors of each service to MACV.

73. Dickinson and Kaufman, "Airpower Doctrine," pp 66–67; Sunderland, *Evolution.* p 38; K168.01–43 (1961–1965), pp 73–74; PACAF Manual 55–13, p 36; PACAF Manual 55–17, 7–1.

74. K168.01–43 (1961–1965), p 79.

75. *Ibid.* Another Air Force study observed, "This type of unilateral effort [by the Army] does not contribute to the stated mission of training the VNAF in the conduct and control of RVNAF operations." It cited incidents of US Army advisors to ARVN discouraging requests to the VNAF and urging instead the use of Army Mohawks. See K526.45011–1, App Z.

76. K526.45011–2. This study argued that the ground commander must be able to mass his resources in a minimum amount of time. According to this study, tactical aircraft in South Vietnam were "tools of the battlefield used by ground commanders" and not an independent force. Moreover, the tactical air control system was not responsive to counterinsurgency situations, where most of the engagements involved units less than regimental size.

77. K526.45011–3.

78. K168.06–25; K168.06–26, pp 7–10; Army CDC, *Issues,* pp 61–81; K146.003–14, pp 23–24; K168.01–43 (1965–1970), pp 7–8; M–39080–6, AUL, pp 37–51; K160.041–20, p 24. For more on the Strike Command exercises that led to the basic "Concept" agreement—especially Three Paris, Coulee Crest, Swift Strike III, and Desert Strike—see JSTF, "Study," pp 23–25; John R. Stoner, "The Closer the Better," *Air University Review* XVIII (Sep–Oct 1967), pp 29–41; Joe Wagner, "USAF Tailors Command and Control to Close Air Support," *Armed Forces Management* 11 (Dec 1964), 38–40 (hereafter cited as Wagner, "Tailors"); Sunderland, *Evolution,* p 43; Robert G. Sparkman, "Exercise Gold Fire I," *Air University Review* XVI (Mar–Apr 1965), pp 22–44.

79. Sunderland, *Evolution,* pp 40–42; K168.01–43 (1965–1970), pp 67–70; Air Force Policy Ltr for Commanders, Supp 6, Jun 1965, pp 27–32.

80. K526.45011–1, pp 5–6; K178.2152–1, p 17.

81. JSTF, "Study," p 22; M–38245–110, pp 2–3; K717.0413–56, pp 2–4; K168.01–43 (1965–1970), pp 70–71; Dickinson and Kaufman, "Airpower Doctrine," pp 67–68; K239.034–4, pp 9–10; K526.45011–2; K526.45011–3; K168.7041–144, p 23; Sunderland, *Evolution,* p 44; M–39080–6, AUL, pp 52–55.

82. PACAF Manual 55–13, pp 22–29; K526.45011–1, p 14; K146.003–16, p 17; M–38245–129, AUL, pp x–2; K740.131 McLaughlin, George W., C/D/4–5; M–38245–74, AUL, pp 12–19. Until Aug 4, 1966, TACC managed naval carrier aircraft for in-country strikes as well as a small number of Marine sorties in early 1966. As will be shown, the system expanded dramatically in 1968. See also Momyer, "VNAF History," pp 12–13; USAF, "Effectiveness of Close and Direct Air Support in South Vietnam, 2d Progress Report," 1966; Fleet Marine Force, Pacific, Operations of US Marine Forces, Vietnam, "Hist Summary: Mar 1968," MCHC (hereafter cited as USMC, "Hist Summary"). The primary mission in the close air-support role of the Army's Tactical Air Support Element (division level or higher) and Fire Support Coordination Center (below division level) is to evaluate all requests for close air support (immediate or preplanned), coordinate these with the Fire Support Element, and either approve or disapprove each request for close air support. See K178.2459–1, A–I–a, pp 1–2; PACAF Manual 55–17, pp 5–7.

83. In 1962, Strike Command adopted the concept of a DASC for delivering close air support to corps-sized joint task forces. See K146.003–14, p 19; K160.041–20, p 22. For more on DASCs, see M–38245–110, AUL, p 7; K168.7041–144,

pp 22, 60–61; JSTF, "Study," pp 22–25; K526.45011–1, pp 14–19; K717.0413–58; K717.0413–67, pp 1–5; K717.0413–66; K717.0413–69; Momyer, *Three Wars*, pp 259–61; Sunderland, *Evolution*, pp 51–52; PACAF Manual 55–13, p 31; PACAF Manual 55–17, 6/1; K717.0413–56, p 7; M–38245–231, AUL; M–42210–74, AUL, pp 24–26; M–42728–12, AUL; Wagner, "Tailors," pp 38–40; R.A. Fuller, "The DASC: Nuisance or Necessity?" *Marine Corps Gazette* XLVII (Mar 1963), pp 53–56.

84. K160.041–20, p 22; K168.01–43 (1961–1965), p 14; K168.01–43 (1965–1970), pp 7–9; K168.7041–144, p 22; K717.0413–67, p 5; K178.2459–1, A–I–a–6; US Army, *Army Support for Air Force Tactical Air Control Parties* (Washington, 1967), p 1; M–38245–91, AUL, pp 32–33; M–38245–231, AUL, pp 8–16; K717.0413–67, pp 6–24; William M. Burkett, "The Tactical Air Control Party: Crux of the Tactical Air Control System," Professional Study, Air War College, Apr 1971, pp 2–12; Air Force Policy Ltr for Commanders, Supp 1 (Jan 1967), p 26; Craig Pugh, "They Deal the Aces," *Airman* XXVII (Aug 1983), pp 9–17; Stoner, "Closer," pp 29–41; K239.034–4, p 34; M–42210–74, AUL, p 26; M–38245–129, AUL, pp 27–28; PACAF Manual 55–13, p 31–34, 50. TACPs were collocated with the FSCC or TOC as appropriate. The US Army replaced its regimental structure in the years before the Vietnam war, thus battalions came directly under the division or brigade. Provisions for VNAF TACPs remained unfulfilled because of the shortage of VNAF personnel.

85. K168.01–43 (1965–1970), p 55; K168.7041–144, p 62; K153.054–4, pp 40–48; PACAF Manual 55–13, pp 11, 30; PACAF Manual 55–17, 3/4–7; M–38245–129, p 15; John R. Bode, *Command and Control of Air-Delivered Fire Support in Vietnam* (Washington, 1970), pp 26–31 (hereafter cited as Bode, *Command and Control*); K178.2459–1, A/23–27; Momyer, "VNAF History," pp 12–13; USMC, "Hist Summary," p 63; M–42210–74, AUL, p 31; M–38245–129, AUL, pp 10–15; M–41716–11, AUL, p 4.

86. K740.131, Aust, Abner M., Jr, p 3; K740.131 Smith, Norman G., p 17; K153.054–4, pp 48–51; K168.7041–144, p 62; K717.0413–56, p 9; Sunderland, *Evolution*, pp 51–52; K717.0413–66, pp 10–11; Bode, *Command and Control*, pp 32–34; Wagner, "Tailors," pp 38–40; Dickinson and Kaufman, "Airpower Doctrine," p 76; K160.041–20, p 22; M–38245–110, AUL, p 9.

87. The new JAGOS incorporated not only the Army air–ground system and the USAF/VNAF tactical air control system but also the separate command and control systems of both MACV and the 1st Marine Air Wing (MAW). See K160.041–20, p 25; K239.034–4, pp 5–8; K712.5491–77, C–3; JSTF, "Study," p 25; Sunderland, *Evolution*, p 34; M–38245–74, AUL, pp 18–24; K740.131 McLaughlin, George W., C/D/lO; Jerry Thorius, "CAS: Have Command and Control Kept Up?" *Joint Perspectives* 3 (Winter 1982), 46–55.

88. Pike, *Final Report*, p 4863. The Air Force established a forward air controller school at Hurlburt (part of Eglin AFB, FL) under the Special Air Warfare Center, which in mid–1968 was redesignated the Special Operations Force. See K168.01–43 (1965–1970), p 6; Wagner, "Tailors," pp 38–40.

89. Momyer, "VNAF History," p 15. Momyer wrote that the unimpressive performance of newly graduated VNAF FACs undermined ARVN confidence in the VNAF.

90. K168.7041–144, pp 13, 51; K168.01–43 (1965–1970), pp 12–14.

91. K526.45011–3.

92. K2.0512–281, pp 17–18.

93. M–4780–41, AUL; Sunderland, *Evolution*, p 37; K168.01–43 (1965–1970), pp 4–7, 34.

94. K526.45011–1, p 17; K168.01–43 (1965–1970), pp 12–13.

95. K239.034–1, p 16.

96. K526.45011–1, p 22.

97. K168.01–43 (1965–1970), pp 6–7; Pike, *Hearings*, pp 4820, 4831–34. One Air Force officer wrote, "The evolution of the airborne FAC within the TACS has been bereft of progressive organizational history and clear-cut conception. Putting the FAC in the air was a bright idea, but few military men had the vaguest idea what to do with it." See James C. Moore, *Conflict of Authority: The Tactical Air Control System in South Vietnam* (Norman, OK, 1973), p 3.

98. K168.7041–144, pp 57–58; K168.01–43 (1965–1970), p 33. For an excellent analysis of the problems that beset the VNAF throughout the war—including a lack of influence and

low pay (which forced VNAF personnel to "moonlight" at night and on weekends), see Momyer,"VNAF History."

99. M–38245–91, AUL, p 2; K168.01–43 (1965–1970), pp 12–13; M–39080–6, AUL, pp 52550.
100. K168.7041–71; see also Hearings before the Special Committee on Close Air Support of the Preparedness Investigation Subcommittee of the Committee on Armed Services, Senate, *Close Air Support*, 92d Cong, 1st sess (Washington, 1972), p 29 (hereafter cited as Cannon, *Hearings*).
101. Quoted in Sunderland, *Evolution*, p 53.
102. K740.131 Norman G. Smith, pp 21–22; K740.131 Amber M. Aust, Jr, p 4.
103. K239.0512–11, pp 10–11.
104. K239.0512–103, p 11; K239.0512–127, p 4; K168.7041–144, pp 98–99; J. S. Butz, Jr, "FACs in Vietnam: They Call the Shots," *Air Force and Space Digest* XLIX (May 1966), pp 60–66; M–42370–14, AUL, I, 20; K239.0512–50, pp 5–7; K239.0512–103, p 11; K239.0512–132, p 6; K239.0512–46; Crowe, "Close Air Support," pp 49–52; K168.06–164, pp 4–5; K239.034–4; K717.0413–69, pp 4–10; Sunderland, *Evolution*, p 53; K239.031–123, Tab 4, p 8; K239.031–124, pp 10–11; K178.2459–1, A–I–a–7.
105. K168.7041–144, pp 6–7, 51–52; K168.01–43 (1965–1970), pp 102–107; K740.131 Smith, Norman G., pp 23–26; K526.03–12; K239.031–125, pp 17–18; Pike, *Hearings*, pp 4775–76; K239.0512–124, p 30; Dave S. Johnson, "The Gallant Bird Dog—Oops—0–1," *Army* XVII (Jan 1967), 49–52.
106. K168.01–43 (1965–1970), pp 37, 102–107; K168–7041–144, p 131; K239.031–125, pp 17–18; K740.131 Norman G. Smith, p 27.
107. Stanley M. Mamock, "Use of the Jet Ftr Aircraft as a Forward Air Control Vehicle in a Non-Permissive Environment," Research Study, Air War College, Apr 1976; K168.01–43 (1965–1970), pp 197–198; K239.031–124, p 17.
108. K168.7041–144, r. 130. This study also reported that twenty-four percent of troopsin-contact incidents lasted longer than twenty minutes but still involved small enemy contingents. Strike aircraft arrived in time to attack these targets but often wasted firepower in the "overkill" of small enemy groups. Only 23 percent of troops-in-contact incidents were rated as "large."
109. K717.0414–48, p 26. See also M–30905–2, Nr 70–9, AUL, p 1; K168.01–43 (1965–1970), p 71. This latter study revealed that a FAC devoted 60 percent of his flying time to aerial reconnaissance.
110. K168.7041–144, p 131. This study indicated that many FACs were jerry-rigging grenade launchers and machine guns to their wing struts. Capt Donald R. Hawley created the "Hawley Cocktail" by placing live grenades in peanut butter jars and throwing them out his aircraft window.
111. *Ibid*; K168.01–43 (1965–1970), p 120. The concept of phased response was first suggested in Nov 1966 by the joint Army–Air Force Tactical Air Support Analysis Team.
112. K168.7041–144, p 131.
113. M–30905–2, Nr 70–9, AUL, p 1.
114. K168.06–26, p 19. This study described the OV–10 as a "multi-mission, primitive area, immediate response, 'work horse,' air support system for the low end of the combat spectrum from police work through counterinsurgency."
115. K717.0413–66, pp 30–31; K740.459–2, A/1–A/3; intvw, author with Maj Frank Kricker, Sep 15, 1984. Kricker served in Laos as a "Raven" FAC. See also M–41780–68, AUL, pp 1–2; K168.7041–144, pp 132–133; M–41716–11, AUL, pp 7, 13; K168.01–43 (1965–1970), p 39; K717.0413–98, pp 84–85.
116. M–30905–2, Nr 70–9, p 60. See also, K239.031–124, pp 9, 16; K160.041–20, Tab B, p 8; K740.131 Gordon F. Blood, D/6–D/7; K239.0512–230, p 70; Walter Andrews, "OV–10s 5-Minute Response," *Armed Forces Journal* 107 (Sep 6, 1969), 15.
117. Futrell, *Advisory Years*, p 221.
118. K526.3101–2, p 2.
119. Futrell, Advisory Years, p 169. See also, K740.131 Gordon F. Blood, E/17–18; Keith B. McCutcheon, "Marine Aviation in Vietnam, 1962–1970," in USMC, *The Marines in Vietnam, 1954–1973*, pp 164–165.

120. K239.034–1, p 5.
121. AFM 2–1, p 3/2; M–39080–6, p 26.
122. See, for example, Westmoreland's message dated Jun 24, 1965 to the Joint Chiefs of Staff, *Chronology on COMUSMACV Recommendations-Observations on Use of US Air Power in Vietnam War, 1965–1968*, Navy History Center, Washington, (hereafter cited as NHC).
123. K526.45011–3.
124. Folder "Vietnam: Command of I Field Force, Vietnam," Box "Papers 1970–1981," A.S. Collins Papers, USAMHI.
125. K239.034–1, pp 6–8.
126. M–38245–30, pp 30–31.
127. PACAF, *Highlights*, p 11; Pat D. Johnson, "The Invader Returns," *Air University Review* XV (Nov–Dec 1963), 9–22.
128. PACAF *Highlights*, pp 11, 41; Futrell, *Advisory Years*, p 75; K168.7041–144, p 10.
129. Chapman, "Effectiveness," pp 23–24; James A. Donovan, "The A–1 Aircraft in Southeast Asia," AUL, pp 1–15; A.J.C. Lavalle, ed, *Airpower and the 1972 Spring Invasion* (Washington, 1976), p 12 (hereafter cited as Lavalle, *Spring Invasion*); PACAF *Highlights*, pp 41–42; Pike, *Hearings*, pp 4680–81, 4696; Crowe, "Close Air Support," pp 47–48.
130. M–38245–30, AUL, p 38; *Chronology on COMUSMACV*, NHC, see entries for Jan 26 1965 and Mar 8 1965; PACAF, *Highlights*, p 73; Momyer, *Three Wars*, pp 270–71.
131. Tactical Air Command, *Cost Effectiveness of Close Support Aircraft* (Langley AFB, VA, 1965), p 2; K740.131 Greget, Tony M., pp 1–2; Lavalle, *Spring Invasion*, p 11; M–41780–68, AUL, pp 1–2; Crowe, "Close Air Support," p 48.
132. The F–5A flew its first strike in Oct 1965; the A–37 was introduced in Jul 1967. See K717.0414–17, p 19; K143.054–4, microfilm, roll 31560.
133. K168.06-227; K168.7041-144, pp 139-141. For statistics on the numbers and types of aircraft deployed to Southeast Asia throughout the war, see DOD Statistics, Tables 120 and 121, Book Ia, Jul 25, 1973, Office of Air Force History, Bolling AFB, Washington, D.C. (hereafter cited as AFCHO).
134. Crowe, "Close Air Support," p 45; D.D. Cunningham, "Close Air Support Aircraft," Special Study, May 16, 1960, Air University Command and Staff School. This 1960 study concluded that high performance aircraft were not best suited for the close air-support mission. See also M–41780–68, AUL, pp 1–2.
135. M–38245–30, AUL, pp 23, 55. This study quoted from the Seventh Air Force operations order on the primary purpose of the AC–47: "To respond with flares and firepower in support of hamlets under night attack, supplement strike aircraft in the defense of friendly forces, and provide long endurance escort for convoys." See also Jack S. Ballard, *Development and Employment of Fixed-Wing Ships* (Washington, 1982). Hereafter cited as Ballard, *Gunships*.
136. *Ibid*, p 23.
137. K153.054–4, pp 52–55; K239.042–5588; M–38245–129, AUL, pp 22–23; M–38245–30, AUL, pp 24–28. For examples of AC–47 operations (Special Forces camps at Thuong Duc and Duc Lap), see M–38245–102, AUL.
138. M–38245–30, AUL, p 69.
139. *Ibid*, p 24.
140. K168.2052-2. See also Ballard, *Gunships*.
141. K712.5491-77, C/8–C/26; see also K168.7041–144, p 130; Robert P Everett, "Just a Shadow of Its Former Self," *Airman* XIV (Feb 1970), 11–14; n.a., "The Story of 883," *Airman* XVI (Jan 1972), 35–36. For more on the "Little Brother" program (Cessna Super Sky Master Model 337), see K243.0115–1.
142. K239.0369–3, p 28; K168.7041–144, p 130; Chief of Naval Operations, "Lessons Learned," Jul 15, 1968, I–A–16/17, NHC; George Weiss, "AC-130 Gunships Destroy Trucks and Cargo," *Armed Forces Journal* CIX (Sep 1971), pp 18–19; Ron Fuchs,"The Ghostriders," *Airman* XXVII (Jul 1983), pp 42–47. Ballard, *Gunships*.
143. M–41780–68, AUL, pp 1–2.
144. Oral history, Lt Gen Julian J. Ewell, USAMHI, p 79. One Army officer, however, dismissed the gunships as "eyewash" principally because it was too difficult to pinpoint a target at night under flares. See K239.0512–101, p 34.

145. K153.054–4, p 37. Col Allison C. Brooks (Deputy Commander, 2d Air Div) remarked in 1965: "The enemy is everywhere and nowhere. There is no Bomb Line, and at present, no counterair or interdiction, as we knew it in World War II and Korea." See K526.01, Vol II, Ch. 2, 24.
146. Quoted in Sunderland, *Evolution*, pp 14–15.
147. Momyer, *Three Wars*, p 21.
148. Oral history, Maxwell D. Taylor, #5, USAMHI, p 42. See also John P. McConnell, "Air Power's New Double Role in Vietnam," *Air Force* and *Space Digest* I (Dec 1965), 11; Bennie L. Davis, "Indivisible Airpower," *Air Force Magazine* LXVII (Mar 1984), pp 46–50; Pike, *Report*, p 4870.
149. William C. Westmoreland, *A Soldier Reports* (Garden City, 1976), pp 165–66, 247, 413.
150. K740.131 Gordon F. Blood, E/39.
151. See, for example, K740.132; Intvw, Lt Gen Jonathan O. Seaman Papers, USAMHI, p 42; Momyer, *Three Wars*, pp 99–106; Dana Drenkowski, "The Tragedy of Operation Linebacker II," *Armed Forces Journal International* CXIV (Jul 1977), pp 24–27.
152. K526.01, Vol II, Ch. 2, 24.
153. K168.1518–2, Ch. V, 38.
154. K740.132; Momyer, "VNAF History," p 8.
155. K160.041–20, p 23; K153.054–4, p 37; PACAF Manual 55–13, p 10.
156. M–38245–129, p 1.
157. K168.7031–6, Vol I, Tab 4, 6. For more on close air support reports, see USAF, *Effectiveness of Close and Direct Air Support in South Vietnam, Second Progress Report* (Washington, 1966).
158. K717.0413–66, pp 10–11.
159. JSTF, "Study," p 53. See also M–35044–8, Nr 301, AUL, p 22; K740.131 Norman G. Smith, pp 18–20; K526.45011–1, p 22, App M, p 2, App N, p 2.
160. K168.01–43 (1965–1970), p 71.
161. M–38245–30, AUL; K160.041–35; Crowe, Close Air Support," p 47.
162. M–38245–30, AUL, p 1.
163. *Ibid*, p 7.
164. *Ibid*.
165. *Ibid*, p 65. From an altitude of 5000 feet, the AGILS produced the equivalent of 16 full moons, or 6 million candle power, over an area 1.87 miles in diameter. Rotating the pods enabled the light to stay on a specific target.
166. *Ibid*, p 1.
167. *Ibid*, pp 1, 11–22, 67; K740.132; K712.5491–77, C/33; PACAF Manual 55–13, p 35; JSTF, "Study," p 26.
168. K168.7031–6, Vol I, Tab 4, 3.
169. *Ibid*.
170. Harold Brown, "Air Power in Limited War," *Air University Review* XX (May–Jun 1969), 2–15; K168.06–9, pp 1–3; Howard A. Davis speech, Jan 13, 1966, *Air Force Policy Ltr for Commanders*, Supp 2 (Feb 1966), pp 18–20; Stoner, "Closer," pp 29–41.
171. M–41780–41, AUL, p 11.
172. USAF, *Effectiveness of Close and Direct Air Support in South Vietnam, Second Progress Report* (Washington, 1966), pp 2–3, 13.
173. K717.0413–4.
174. M–38245–30, AUL, p 14.
175. *Ibid*, p 17.
176. *Ibid*.
177. M–41780–41, AUL, pp 12–27. For more information on close air–support activities during 1966, see K168.7041–144 pp 55–56; M–30905–16, AUL, pp 1–3; Col Donald Brown, USAF course outline, Air War College, USAFHRC; K143.054–4, p 40; USAF Management Summary, "SEA Review," Jun 30, 1973, USAFHRC; M–40592–15, AUL; K168.06–136; M–42357–1, AUL; K–Wg–14–HI, Jan–Jun 1966, 2 Vols
178. M–38245–136, AUL, p 21. Recall that DASCs could divert airborne aircraft, but only the TACC could scramble aircraft.
179. M–38245–5, AUL, pp 24–25.

180. *Ibid*, pp 25–27.
181. K239.0369–3, pp 5–7.
182. *Ibid*, pp 7–9. For more on 1967 close air-support operations, see K740.131 Gordon F. Blood, F/6; Seventh Air Force, History, "Chronology of Significant Airpower Events in SEA, 1954–1967," AUL, p 258.
183. *Air Force Policy Ltr for Commanders*, Supp 9, Sep 1973, p 23.
184. Roswell Freedman, "The Evolution of Interdiction and onald Brown, USAF course outline, Air War College, USAFHRC; K143.054–4, p 40; p 57.
185. MACV, "Command History: 1968," Vol I, 425. For more on Khe Sanh, see Momyer, "VNAF History," p 26; K168.01–43 (1965–1970), p 4; US Seventh Fleet, "Monthly Hist Summary: Mar 1968," NHC, p 21; Oral history, Maxwell D. Taylor, # 5, USAMHI, pp 26–28; William C. Westmoreland Papers, History File, #29, USAMHI; Brent W. McLaughlin, "Khe Sanh: Keeping an Outpost Alive," *Air University Review* XX (Nov–Dec 1968), 57–77; William H. Greenhalgh, "AOK Airpower Over Khe Sanh," *Aerospace Historian* XIX (Mar 1972), 2–9.
186. K168.7041–136.
187. K160.041–20, p 27.
188. Momyer, "VNAF History," p 27.
189. *Ibid*, K239.0369–3, pp 10–12.
190. K717.0413–27, pp 15–16.
191. K239.0369–3, pp 5–7.
192. *Ibid*, pp 7–9.
193. M–41780–41, pp 12–27.
194. See, for example, K168.06–25; K168.06–26; Student Research Paper, Walter H. Baxter III, Edward J. Campbell, Fay D. Fulton, James R. Hildreth, William E. Skinner, "An Analysis of Tactical Airpower in Support of the United States Army in South Vietnam," Army War College, Mar 1970, pp 24–25 (hereafter cited as Baxter *et al.*, "Analysis").
195. Army CDC, *Issues*, pp 53–63.
196. Ltr, Maj Gen Roderick Wetherill (USA) to Gen Frederick C. Weyand (USA) Aug 31, 1970, A. S. Collins Papers, folder "Vietnam, Command of I Field Force, Vietnam," Box "Papers, 1970–1981," USAMHI.
197. Max U. Terrien, "Close Air Support: Retrospective and Perspective: Is the Helicopter the Answer?" Thesis, US Army Command and General Staff College, Jun 4, 1982, pp 47–48 (hereafter cited as Terrien, "Helicopter").
198. K160.041–20, pp 21–22.
199. JSTF, "Study," pp 21–26; K168.06–9; K160.06–26, slide 8; Sunderland, *Evolution*, p 33; Terrien, "Helicopter," pp 42–55; Crowe, "Close Air Support," pp 45–47; Baxter *et al.*, "Analysis," p 85.
200. Quoted in Baxter *et al.*, "Analysis," p 85. The definition continued, "Such fire support supplements, is integrated with, and is controlled similarly to Army surface weaponry."
201. M–39080–6, AUL, pp 156–157.
202. K146.003–14, p 27; see also Sunderland, *Evolution*, p 33.
203. K168.06, slide 22.
204. K168.7041–144, p 58.
205. M–42210–74, AUL, pp 5–6.
206. See, for example, General Momyer's views in K239.031–125; also see K168.06–26; Claude Witze, "Close Air Support: The Hardware and the Mission," *Air Force Magazine*, LV (May 1972), pp 17–23 (Hereafter cited as Witze, "Hardware."). Terrien, "Helicopter," p 54.
207. Pike, *Report*, p 4861.
208. Cannon, *Report*, p 18.
209. K146.003–14, p 46. For more on the debate over armed helicopters, including Momyer's view that "the Army had resisted establishing the tactical air control system because of the argument about the control and employment of helicopters," and one Air Force officer's description of the arming of helicopters as "regression in warfare," see Momyer, *Three Wars*, p 254; K239.0512–1.
210. K168.06–26; Army CDC, *Issues*; Witz, "Hardware," p 22.
211. K239.034–4, pp 1–4.

212. *Ibid*; K239.031–123; K239.031–124, p 10; K168.01–43 (1965–1970), p 62; Sunderland, *Evolution*, p 45.
213. USMC, "Hist Summary," p 63.
214. K168.01–43 (1965–1970), p 65. The total of ninety-two battalions included thirty Army, twenty-four USMC, four FWF, and thirty-four ARVN.
215. *Ibid*, p 66.
216. Baxter *et al.*, "Analysis," pp 79–80. For more on the ABCCC, see K153.054–4, pp 55–56; JSTF, "Study," p 23; K717.0413–46. After giving the Marines specific orders to provide close air support to the 1st Cavalry Div (Airmobile), Westmoreland discovered that Nr direct communications had been set up by the Marines (despite their having a DASC about one km. away from the 1st Cav) and that the Commander of the 1st Marine Air Wing (Maj Gen Norman J. Anderson) had not even visited the 1st Cav. Westmoreland recalled, "Needless to say I raised hell about the situation . . .." See Westmoreland Papers, History File, folder Dec 27, 1967–Jan 31, 1968, pp 19–25, file 28, p 13, USAMHI.
217. *Ibid*.
218. K168.06–25; Baxter *et al.*, "Analysis," pp 21–22, 35–36; K740.131 John E. Ralph, p 7; K740.131 Gordon F. Blood, E/37; K740.131 George W. McLaughlin, C/D/1O; K239.0369–3, pp 13–18; Dickinson and Kaufman, "Doctrine," pp 79–84; Westmoreland, *Soldier*, pp 416–19; Sunderland, *Evolution*, pp 45, 48; M–38245–129, AUL, pp 4–6. For Westmoreland's consideration of the single manager for air system in 1965, see K168.01–43 (1965–1970), pp 62–65; JSTF, "Study," p 23; Westmoreland Papers, file 28, p 13, USAMHI.
219. K712.5491–77, C/1–3; McCutcheon, "Marine Aviation," pp 177–79; USMC, "Hist Summary," p 63; K717.0413–67, pp 3–4; K168.7041–144, pp 60–61; Momyer, "VNAF History," p 27; Baxter *et al*, "Analysis," p 81; K717.0413–58.
220. Westmoreland Papers, History File, folder 30, pp 11–13, USAMHI.
221. K168.06–25; K168.01–43 (1965–1970), pp 58–59; Momyer, *Three Wars*, pp 65–66; K239.031–125, p 9; K239.031–123, Tab 15, p 3; Momyer, "VNAF History," p 27; K740.131 Gordon F. Blood, F/9; K168.06–26, slides 1–5.
222. K168.06–25; K168.01–43 (1965–1970), pp 58–59; M–41181–13, AUL, p 39.
223. Quoted in K168.06–25.
224. *Ibid*.; JSTF, "Study," pp 25–26; K168.06–26; M–39080–6, AUL, p 36.
225. USMC, *Marines in Vietnam*; JSTF, "Study," pp 26, 32; Cannon, *Hearings*, p 17; K168.01–43 (1965–1970), p 62; K178.2459–1, A–1–b–a; K146.003–14, p 46.
226. McCutcheon, "Marine Aviation," pp 177–78; M–38245–30, AUL, p 13; M–38245–129, AUL, p 1; JSTF, "Study," pp 22, 26, 28, 32, 39; K712.5491–77, C/3–7; PACAF, *Highlights*, p 44; Sunderland, *Evolution*, p 47; Cannon, *Report*, pp 17–19; Pike, *Hearings*, pp 4744–56; Pike, *Report*, pp 4869–73; Butz, "Open Letter," p 34; Robert M. Fowler, "Close Air Support," *Military Engineer* LII (Nov–Dec 1960), pp 461–62; Robert F. Steinkraus, "Air–Ground Coordination," *Marine Corps Gazette* L (May 1966), 29–31; K.H. Stivers, "Using (and Misusing) the DASC," *Marine Corps Gazette* LXV (May 1981), pp 26–28.
227. Pike, *Hearings*, p 4871.
228. K239.0512–143. For more on the Marine system, see USMC, "Hist Summary," pp 70–71; K717.0414–48, p 9; K168.06–25; K160.041–35; K168.7041–144, p 62; Cannon, *Report*, p 17; K740.131 John E. Ralph, p 6.
229. MACV, "Command History: 1968," Vol I, 436.
230. USMC, "Hist Summary," pp 76–77; MACV, "Command History: 1968," Vol I, 439.
231. USMC, "Hist Summary," p 71.
232. *Ibid*, p 70.
233. *Ibid*. For more on the Marine criticism, see K168.01–43 (1965–1970), pp 4, 65–67; JSTF, "Study," p 27; Sunderland, *Evolution*, pp 47–48.
234. Keith R. Tidman, *The Operations Eval Gp* (Annapolis, 1984), p 272.
235. M–39554–19b, AUL. These figures were for actual "close air-support" sorties. The Department of Defense kept records for "attack" sorties, which were defined as including "strike, armed recce, flak suppression, interdiction, close air support, and direct air support sorties." See DOD, Southeast Asia Statistical Survey, Jan 19, 1972, Book I, Table 312, AFCHO. Under this definition, the statistics for the Navy were: 21,610 in 1966; 443 in

1967; 5,427 in 1968; 8,744 in 1969; 3,895 in 1970; 2,124 in 1971; and 23,505 in 1972. (Book Ia, Nov 21, 1973, Table 304, AFCHO.) The increase in 1972 was due primarily to the recall of American tactical air resources in the Easter Offensive launched by the enemy.

236. Charles R. Pursley, "TACRON," *US Naval Institute Proceedings* XCVI (Aug 1971), 46–51.
237. K526.308–3. A 1972 study by RAND Corporation reached similar conclusions. See K146.003–118. For more on the Navy's system of close air support, see JSTF, "Study," pp 37–38, Tab B, pp 6–8; PACAF Manual 55–13, p 43; Momyer, *Three Wars*, p 88. For a study of the Navy's Enforcer aircraft, see K168.7085–178.
238. M–38245–129, AUL, pp 5–6; see also Seventh Fleet monthly historical summaries in NHC.
239. K168.01–43 (1965–1970), pp 67–68; Westmoreland, *Soldier*, pp 418–19: USMC, "Hist Summary."
240. *Air Force Policy Ltr for Commanders*, Supp 3, Mar 1973, pp 30–32; K239.034–4, p 26; Momyer, "VNAF History," p 27.
241. K740.131 Gordon F. Blood, E/37; K740.131 George W. McLaughlin, C/D/5–6; K740.131 Norman G. Smith, pp 15–16.
242. M–38245–129, AUL, pp 7–9; JSTF, "Study," p 27; K740.131 Gordon F. Blood, E/37; K740.131 George W. McLaughlin, C/D/5–6; K740.131 Norman G. Smith, pp 15–16; USMC, "Hist Summary," p 65.
243. K740.131 Norman G. Smith, pp 15–16.
244. Sunderland, *Evolution*, p 49.
245. K740.131 Gordon F. Blood, F/9.
246. K168.01–43 (1965–1970), pp 67–69. This study added: "The upshot of centralizing air control was that MACV as a whole received more effective air support, III MAF units continued to get responsive air support, and Seventh Air Force benefitted from improved coordination in the employment of airpower." For assessments of the single air-manager system, see McCutcheon, "Marine Aviation," pp 176–78; MACV, "Command History: 1968," Vol I, 439–40; Momyer, *Three Wars*; K239.031–124, p 15.
247. Oral history, Gen Bruce Palmer, P 283, USAMHI.
248. K239.031–125, p 8. But see also K239.031–123, p 3.
249. Baxter *et al.*, "Analysis," p 198.
250. Joint Chiefs of Staff official account, "Battle of Dong Ap Bia," USAMHI.
251. K168.01–40(FY 1969), p 38.
252. Baxter *et al.*, "Analysis," p 161.
253. M–38245–231, AUL, p 12; K168.7041–144, p 128.
254. M–38245–5, AUL, p 47.
255. DOD Statistics, Book Ia, Nov 21, 1973, AFCHO.
256. *Ibid.*
257. M–38245–231, AUL, pp 8–10, 24–28; K168.7041–I44, pp 15, 128–33; K168.01–40 (FY 1970), pp 47–48; Momyer, "VNAF History," pp 55–56.
258. K168.7041–144, pp 128–33.
259. Momyer, "VNAF History," pp 55–57; K168.7041–144, pp 15, 32–33; M–38245–231, AUL, pp 8–10, 29, 72; K712.5491–77, C/26; M–42782–12, AUL, p 124; K717.0414–49, p 30; Harry G. Summers, Jr, *On Strategy* (Novalto, CA, 1982), p 176; A.S. Collins Papers, Jan 7, 1971, pp 9–10, USAMHI; Oral history, Gen J.L. Throckmorton, Mar 15, 1978, pp 2–3.
260. 8245–231, AUL, pp 7–11; M–38245–5, pp 28–32; MACV, "History of USAF Advisory Gp, Jul 1–Sep 30, 1970," Vol I, 18; K168.01–43 (1965–1970), pp 208–210; K168.06–107, pp 1–5; K712.5491–77, C/8; K717.0414–49, pp 41–42; M–38245–137, AUL, pp 8–10; M–38245–143, AUL, p 17.
261. M–38245–231, AUL, pp 15–16.
262. *Ibid*, p 72.
263. K239.031–132, p 5; see also K740.132; Momyer, "VNAF History," p 92.
264. K168.01–40 (FY 1970).
265. K740.131 Ralph, John E., pp 3–4.
266. *Ibid.*
267. K717.0413–98.

268. K168.06–234; K717.0413–84; K168.06–23.
269. K168.7041–I44, p 133.
270. K168.7041–144, p 133; Ballard, *Gunships*, p 165; K717.0413–98; M–42370–47, AUL, I, 40; R.E. Hanser, "The Flight of the Blind Bat," *Air University Review* XXXIII (May–Jun 1982), pp 40–47; K168.06–224; M42193–502, AUL, p 12.
271. DOD Statistics, Book Ia, Table 3, Jun 20, 1973, AFCHO; Momyer, *Three Wars*, p 32.
272. Lavalle, *Spring Invasion*, pp 12–13.
273. K717.0414–49, pp 13–49; K168.06–237, pp 1–2.
274. Lavalle, *Spring Invasion*, pp 12–13.
275. USAF, Project Corona Harvest, Briefing Paper, PACAF, Jul 1972, K717.03–219, 71/07/01–72/06/30.
276. M–39554–60, AUL, p 1.
277. K717.03–219.
278. Momyer, "VNAF History," p 51.
279. K717.03–219.
280. *Ibid*; K168.7041–144, p 1; John D. Howard, "An Loc: A Study of US Power," *Army* XXV (Sep 1975), pp 18–24.
281. M–38245–231, p 94.
282. K717.03–219.
283. K168.7041–144, p 1.
284. Momyer, "VNAF History," p 51. For more on the Easter Offensive, see K168.06–224; M–38245–231, AUL, pp 89–96; Adrian Hill, "Air War Over Vietnam," *Royal United Services Institute Journal* CXXI (Dec 1976), pp 27–31; Edgar Ulsamer, "Airpower Halts an Invasion," *Air Force Magazine* LV (Sep 1972), pp 60–68.
285. Momyer, *Three Wars*, p 338.
286. 239.031–124, p 3. See also K740.131 Norman G. Smith, pp 66–67; Ltr, A.S. Collins to Brig Gen Edward Smith, Nov 15, 1966, A. S. Collins Papers, USAMHI; W. E. Depuy Papers, Sect V, USAMHI.
287. Donald R. Brown, "Guide for Case Study: Tactical Air in Limited Warfare," AUL.
288. See, for example, *Ibid*; also Lt Gen Julian J. Ewell Papers, p 80, USAMHI.
289. K239.0512–111, p 31.
290. K239.031–125, p 9.
291. K7I7.0413–56, p xi.
292. K239.0512–123, p 2.
293. K239.0512–43.
294. Quoted in Crowe, "Close Air Support," pp 44–45.
295. K168.7102–5. For other similar reactions, see M–38245–110, AUL, pp 5–6; K717.0413–67, p 27.
296. K239.0512–111, p 30.
297. K239.0512–50, pp 9–11.
298. M–38245–110, AUL, p 12. For more information, see Pike, *Hearings*, p 4803; K740.131 Blood, Gordon F., E/31; Momyer, "VNAF History," p 54; William H. Rees, "Tac Air—Member of the Team," *Infantry* LXVI (May–Jun 1976), p 17.
299. K526.45011–5, Attachment 3.
300. K168.01–43 (1961–1965), p 1.
301. K168.7041–144, p 55.
302. ʻK168.7031–6, pp 2–3.
303. K239.0512–41, p 6.
304. K526.01, Vol II, Ch. 2, p 24.
305. See, for example, K239.031–124, pp 2–3; K740.131 Alonzo W. Groves, p 2; K740.132; USAF, *Effectiveness of Close and Direct Air Support in South Vietnam* (Washington, 1966), pp 2–3.
306. M–37097–29, Nr 70–19, AUL.
307. See, for example, K170.3–17.
308. K143.054–4, p 61; K239.031–125, pp 10–11; Momyer, *Three Wars*, p 66.
309. K177.1511, p 7.
310. K717.03–219.
311. K239.031–125, p 7.

Bibliographical Essay

This study is based chiefly on documents and papers in the Air Force Historical Research Center (USAFHRC) or Air University Library (AUL), both located at Maxwell AFB, Alabama. Staff members at each of these archives have prepared preliminary bibliographies on close air support (not confined to the war in Southeast Asia), which are useful points of departure. See, for example, the USAFHRC typescript, "Selected Bibliography on Close Air Support" and AUL lists of selected references on close air support, dated September 1965, August 1968, and December 1973.

Two general classifications of Air Force documents are particularly pertinent. "Corona Harvest" collections and Project CHECO [Contemporary Historical Examination of Current Operations] Reports examine the full range of Air Force experiences in Southeast Asia. See the USAFHRC pamphlet prepared by Edward T. Russell, "Research Guide to the Published Project CHECO Reports," August 1977. Also, the different classification numbers for the CHECO Reports used by the USAFHRC and AUL are presented jointly in an AUL bibliographical guide, dated August 1977 (M–27218–8). Some CHECO Reports of particular value to this study include "Night Close Air Support in RVN," "VC Offensive in III Corps," "Fall of A Shau," "Battle of Binh Gia," "VNAF FAC Operations in SVN," "FAC Operations in Close Air Support Role in SVN," "Air Response to Immediate Air Requests in SVN," "TACC Fragging Procedures," "Vietnamization of the Tactical Air Control System," "USAF Quick Reaction Forces," and the separate studies of DASC operations in I, II, and III Corps.

The footnotes in this chapter refer to most of the key documents on close air support in the USAFHRC. Some others, however, are worthy of special mention. For example, the U.S. Army Combat Developments Command produced a special study entitled *A Short History of Close Air Support Issues* (Ft. Belvoir, 1968), which provides a good summary of interservice differences over close airsupport doctrine. Another sound overview of this debate is presented in a study sponsored by the Joint Chiefs of Staff and produced by the Joint Study Task Force in 1972 entitled "Close Air Support Study." For an analysis of the economic side of the question, see Tactical Air Command's study, *Cost Effectiveness of Close-Support Aircraft* (Langley AFB, VA, 1965). Fundamental, too, to an examination of this topic is the study, "Listing of Doctrinal Difficulties in Corona Harvest Reports," K239.031–124.

Some documents are crucial in tracing Army–Air Force differences over close air support. Certain arguments, for instance, made by Gen. Paul D. Harkins (K526.45011–3) and Gen. William C. Westmoreland (K170.3–17) outline the basic perspective of the Army. Air Force views may be found in a position paper/briefing (K160.06–26) and the three-volume study by the USAF Scientific Advisory Board (K168.1518–2).

Gen. William W. Momyer, played a key role in the close air-support story during—and after—the war. Consequently, his memoranda and correspondence are indispensable to any analysis of this topic. See especially files K168.7041–126, K239.031–123, K239.031–125, and K740.132.

File K526.3101–2 offers a good picture of the air request procedures early in the war (1962). Similarly, the report of a Joint Chiefs of Staff visit to South Vietnam in 1963 is contained in K178.2152–1.

In 1968, the Seventh Air Force wrote its "In-County Tactical Air Operations Handbook" (K153.054–4), which describes the various rules, procedures and practices of close air-support operations in South Vietnam. Valuable information, too, is located throughout the Seventh Air Force histories (K526.01).

Finally, two studies by Air Force historian Ralph A. Rowley deserve special mention. Taken together, both comprise an excellent introduction to the general topic. See his "USAF FAC Operations in Southeast Asia," 2 Vols. Jan 1972, K168.01–43; and "Tactics and Techniques of Close Air Support Operations, 1961–1973," 1976, K168.7041–144.

Interviews and End of Tour Reports by the participants in the war proved to be a valuable source of information on close air-support operations. The K239.0512 and K740.131 files contain a number of these reports from both Air Force and Army officers. See especially in K740.131: Abner M. Aust, Jr., Gordon F. Blood, Tony M. Greget, George W. McLaughlin, John E. Ralph, and Norman G. Smith. In addition to the card catalog in the USAFHRC, see the general listings in the Office of Air Force History, "U.S. Air Force Oral History Catalog," 1982.

With the denouement in 1975, Gen. William W. Momyer USAF (Ret), wrote a special study, "VNAF History," which analyzed the development of the VNAF. Momyer's account, deposited in the HRC, while sympathetic, sets forth the problems which beset the development of the VNAF.

Certain research studies (available at the Air University Library) by officers at the professional service schools provide important information about close air support in Southeast Asia. Among the most valuable of these unpublished papers are: Walter H. Baxter III, Edward J. Campbell, Fay D. Fulton, James R. Hildreth, and William E. Skinner, "An Analysis of Tactical Airpower in Support of the United States Army in South Vietnam," Army War College, Mar 1970, Student Research Paper; Andrew J. Chapman, "How to Increase the Effectiveness of Airpower in Counter-guerrilla Warfare," Air War College, Jan 1966, Research Study; Myron W. Crowe, "Development of Close Air Support," Air War College, June 1968, Thesis; James H. Dickinson and Richard H. Kaufman, "Airpower Doctrine: A Case Study in Close Air

Support," Air War College, Apr 1966, Research Study; Stuart E. Kane, "An Examination of the Close Air Support Concept," Air War College, Nov 1970, Thesis; Max U. Terrien, "Close Air Support: Retrospective and Perspective: Is the Helicopter the Answer?" Army Command and General Staff College, June 4, 1982, Thesis.

The archival collections at the U.S. Army Military History Institute, Carlisle Barracks, Pennsylvania, include the papers and oral histories of senior Army officers in the war as well as leaders in Army aviation. Thus, the papers and recollections of Maxwell D. Taylor, Paul D. Harkins, William C. Westmoreland, S.L.A. Marshall, A.S. Collins, W. E. Depuy, Julian J. Ewell, Bruce G. Palmer, Jonathan Seaman, and J. L. Throckmorton are important to the study of virtually any military topic dealing with the Vietnam War. The significance of the Taylor, Harkins, and Westmoreland collections, of course, can hardly be exaggerated. Collections of some officers who influenced the development of Army aviation include Lt. Gen. John J. Tolson III, Col. Delbert Bristol, Lt. Gen. Robert R. Williams, Lt. Gen. George P. Seneff, Brig. Gen. O. Glenn Goodhard, Brig. Gen. Edwin L. Powell, Lt. Gen. H. W. O. Kinnard, and Gen. Hamilton H. Howze. Other pertinent materials from Army sources are located at the Center for Military History in Washington, D.C. and the archives in Suitland, Maryland.

Information about the Marine Corps' perspective on close air support in South Vietnam is available at the Marine Corps Historical Center in Washington, D.C. The best summary of the arguments advanced by the Marine Corps concerning the debate over the single manager for air concept may be found in Fleet Marine Force, Pacific, "Operation of Marine Forces, Vietnam—Monthly Historical Summary: March 1968." For valuable information on Marine operations in-country, see USMC History and Museum Division, *The Marines in Vietnam, 1954–1973: An Anthology and Annotated Bibliography* (Washington, D. C., 1974). Of particular interest in this published collection is the article by Keith B. McCutcheon, "Marine Aviation in Vietnam, 1962–1970," reprinted from *Naval Review 1971* (U.S. Naval Institute).

Although this study does not dwell on the relatively limited, Navy close air-support operations in South Vietnam some worthwhile material, including MACV and CINCPAC command histories, as well as Seventh Fleet historical summaries and COMUSMACV "Recommendations and Observations," is located at the Navy Historical Center in Washington, D.C. For information on general naval air operations, see Keith R. Tidman, *The Operations Evaluation Group* (Annapolis, 1984): Charles R. Pursley, "TACRON," *US Naval Institute Proceedings* XCVI (Aug 1971), pp. 46–51; and Edward J. Marolda and G. Wesley Pryce III, comps., "A Selected Bibliography of the United States Navy and the Southeast Asian Conflict, 1950–1975" rev. ed., (Navy Historical Center, Nov 1983).

No study of close air support in the war is complete without a firm statistical foundation. This study has relied on the Department of Defense statistics, especially the final figures compiled in late 1973, located in the Office of Air Force History, Bolling AFB, D.C.

For an excellent account of Franco–American agreements during the 1950s on the training of South Vietnamese forces as well as crucial background information, see the two studies by the State Department: *Foreign Relations of the United States, 1952–1954*, XIII, Part 2 (Washington, D.C., 1982) and *Foreign Relations of the United States, 1955–1957*, I (Washington, D.C., 1985). Two congressional hearings which shed light on close air-support operations and interservice relations at various points (1965 and 1971) of the war became known as the Pike and Cannon Committees. Respectively, their official titles were: Committee on Armed Services, House of Representatives, *Close Air Support*, 89th Cong., 1st Sess. (Washington, 1955); Hearings before the Special Committee on Close Air Support of the Preparedness Investigation Committee of the Subcommittee on Armed Services, U.S. Senate, *Close Air Support*, 92d Cong., 1st Sess. (Washington, 1972).

Although Guenter Lewy presents some material on close air support in his book, *America in Vietnam* (New York, 1978), most of the published books incorporated in this study were either so-called "official histories" or personal narratives of participants. Two stand out for their analysis of close air-support operations: William W. Momyer, *Airpower in Three Wars* (Washington, D.C., 1978) and Riley Sunderland, *Evolution of Command and Control Doctrine for Close Air Support* (Washington, D. C., 1973). Other recommended books are: Jack S. Ballard, *Development and Employment of Fixed-Wing Gunships* (Washington, D. C., 1982); John R. Bode, *Command and Control of Aerial Delivered Fire Support in Vietnam* (Washington, D. C., 1970); Robert F. Futrell, *The Advisory Years to 1965* (Washington, D. C., 1981); Alfred E. Hurley and Robert C. Ehrhart, eds., *Air Power and Warfare: Proceedings of the Eighth Military History Symposium, US Air Force Academy, 1978* (Washington, D. C., 1979)—see especially Ray L. Bowers, "Air Operations In Southeast Asia: A Tentative Reappraisal"; A. J. C. Lavalle, ed., *Airpower and the 1972 Spring Invasion* (Washington, D. C., 1976); Ronald H. Spector, *Advice and Support: The Early Years, 1941–1960* (Washington, D. C., 1983): William C. Westmoreland, *A Soldier Reports* (Garden City, 1976); Myron J. Smith, *Air War in Southeast Asia, 1961–1973: An Annotated Bibliography and 16-mm Film Guide* (Metuchen, NJ, 1979).

Of the numerous reviews of the literature on the war, a few are worthy of special mention as valuable points of departure for any investigation of the Vietnam War. These are: Joe Dunn, "The Air Force in Vietnam: Official Histories," *Air University Review* XXIV (Jan–Feb 1983), pp. 137–41; Joe Dunn, "In Search of Lessons," *Parameters* IX (Dec 1979), pp. 28–40; Joe Dunn,

"The Vietnam Bookshelf Enters the 80's," *Naval War College Review* XXXIV (Sep–Oct 1981), pp. 107–113; Robin Higham, "Air Power Literature," *National Defense* LX (Sep–Oct 1975), pp. 130–133; Alan Millett, "Lessons Learned From Vietnam: Book Review Essay," *Marine Corps Gazette* LXIV (Sept 1980), pp. 72–76; R. J. Rinaldo, "Vietnam for the Record," *Infantry* LXX (Jan–Feb 1980), pp. 13-16; and Russell F. Weigley, "Vietnam: What Manner of War?" *Air University Review* XXXIV (Jan–Feb 1983), pp. 114–120.

Guides to both civilian and military periodical literature offer hundreds of published articles about close air support in Southeast Asia. Most of these proved to be of only marginal use in this study. Some valuable exceptions were: Harold Brown, "Air Power in Limited War," *Air University Review* XX (May–June 1969), pp. 2–15; J. S. Butz, Jr., "Airpower in Vietnam: The High Price of Restraint," *U.S. Air Force and Space Digest* XLIX (Nov 1966), pp. 40–44; J. S. Butz, Jr., "An Open Letter to Congressman Otis G. Pike, "*Air Force and Space Digest* XLIX (Apr 1966), pp. 34–36; J. S. Butz, Jr., "FACs in Vietnam—They Call the Shots," *Air Force and Space Digest* XLIX (May 1966), pp. 60–66; Sam J. Byerley, "A Concept for Directing Combat Air Operations," *Air University Review* XXI (Mar–Apr 1970), pp. 10–19; T. R. Milton, "USAF and the Vietnam Experience," *Air Force Magazine* LVIII (June 1975), p. 56; Brook Nihart, "Close Air Support: 60 years of Unresolved Problems," *Armed Forces Journal* CVII (Apr 25, 1970), pp. 19–24; William H. Rees, "An Air Force Jet Jockey Tells Us: How Close is Close?" *Infantry* LXII (July–Aug 1972), pp. 32–38; William H. Rees, "TAC Air—Member of the Team," *Infantry* LXVI (May–June 1976), pp. 16–23; Second Air Division, "Air Operations in Vietnam: TAC in the VNAF," *Air University Review* XIV (Sep–Oct 1963), pp. 75–81; John R. Stoner, "The Closer the Better," *Air University Review* XVIII (Sep–Oct 1967), pp. 29–41; Jerry Thorius, "Close Air Support: Have Command and Control Kept Up?" *Joint Perspectives* III (Winter 1982), pp. 46–55; Joe Wagner, "USAF Tailors Command and Control of Close Air Support," *Armed Forces Management* XI (Dec 1964), pp. 38–40; editorial, "With the Wrong Weapons" *Interavia* XX (Apr 1965), p. 497; Claude Witze, "The Case for a Unified Command (in Vietnam): CINCSEA," *Air Force and Space Digest* L (Jan 1967), pp. 23–29.

10

The Israeli Experience

Brereton Greenhous

We don't believe in direct air support in the IAF . . . We have never believed in close support. . . .Instead of using 'close support' we talk of 'participating' in the ground battle, which has a different connotation, and 'participating' means how can we, with airpower, make the ground battle easier, cheaper.

> Major General Mordechai Hod
> commander of *Chel Ha'Avir*
> (the Israeli Air Force), 1966–1973

Israeli strategy and doctrine, both in the air and on the ground, are governed by perilous but immutable socio-geographic facts. The Concise Oxford Dictionary defines an enclave as a "territory surrounded by foreign dominion." Israel is a Jewish enclave in an Arab world, hemmed in on three sides by generally hostile and often politically unstable neighbors (who are able to mobilize between them vastly greater human and material resources than Israel) and on the fourth by the Mediterranean Sea.

Prior to the 1967 Arab–Israeli war, the enclave occupied a mere 8,000 square miles of territory (an area less than that of Massachusetts) consisting mostly of sand and rock, except for a heavily populated, 100–mile coastal strip. North of Tel Aviv the country was no more than 12 miles wide; and at its widest, south of Beersheba, it was just 65 miles from the southern tip of the Dead Sea westward to the base of the Gaza Strip. Moreover, Israel's irregular land boundaries stretched more than 600 miles, and only the 70 miles bordering on Lebanon could be considered somewhat secure.

Two deep salients, one Israeli and one Egyptian, involved special dangers. In 1948 the Israelis established an outpost in west Jerusalem, at the end of a thin line of communication stretching from the coastal plain. Their garrison in the Holy City was something of a hostage to fortune, but a hostage willingly offered for religious and cultural reasons. They were less happy about the other salient in the south, where the Egyptians held the Gaza Strip, a narrow belt of land along the Mediterranean shore thrusting thirty miles north from the Sinai-Negev border. As a prominent Israeli analyst has pointed out, in the past forty-three centuries, Egyptian armies have marched north by that route fifty-five times.[1]

The conquest of the Sinai, the Gaza Strip, and the west bank of the Jordan River in 1967 reduced the length of frontier by almost a third and thickened the 'neck' north of Tel Aviv to 40 miles, but Israel's geostrategic position remains precarious to this day. Although the Camp David accords, signed with Egypt in 1979, eased tensions in the south, they stretched Israeli borders once again by handing most of the Sinai back to the Egyptians, while new threats were developing along the Lebanese frontier in the north. With a current population of only 4 million (3.37 million Jews), the Israelis must maintain armed forces capable of meeting and defeating simultaneous attacks by 2 or more Arab neighbors whose combined populations number well in excess of 120 million.

Poised almost permanently on this ragged edge of war, the Israelis have had to maintain a precarious balance between the demands of military preparation and readiness on the one hand, and the socioeconomic necessities of building a nation-state on the other. Men who are permanently under arms are necessarily unproductive—economic drones—and become, to some extent, alienated from their civilian counterparts. Thus the Israelis have never been able to afford a large standing army like some of their Arab neighbors. Their strategy is predicated on a small cadre of regular soldiers who set the standards for, and train, a citizen army of conscripts and reserves.

They cannot afford to fight a protracted war nor resist aggression within their own narrow boundaries, as the Arabs well realize.[2] The limited depth of Israel does not allow the broad freedom of movement that a doctrine of mobile defense demands. Moreover, the somewhat delicate socio economic structure of Israel has to be protected against the ravages of attrition. Every war the Israelis fight must be a *blitzkrieg*. It must be short, swift, and fought on Arab soil.

Blitzkrieg demands speed, maneuver, violence, and firepower—demands best met by armored ground forces and tactical air power. Neither armor nor aircraft can hold ground; that is still a task for infantry, but they can employ their mobility and firepower to inflict an enormous degree of destruction upon opponents. Moreover, aircraft can do so over a relatively large area, attacking in depth as well as on a broad or narrow front. Their speed and ability to carry the fight deep into hostile territory make them ideal weapons for initiating surprise attacks, and their flexibility is a valuable asset in countering an enemy surprise or in combating simultaneous assaults on more than one front. Thus *Zahal* (an acronym for *Zeva Hsganah LeIsrael*, or the Israeli Defense

Forces) has come to assign a preeminent role—reflected in defense budget allocations—to its air arm, *Chel Ha'Avir*.[3]

Nevertheless, despite general recognition of its special position within the defense structure, *Chel Ha'Avir* has never enjoyed an independent status after the fashion of Britain's Royal Air Force since 1918 or the USAF from 1947. It has always been subordinate to the General Staff, headed by a soldier, in which the highest position yet attained by an airman until recently was head of the Operations Branch. The air force remains theoretically no more than *primus inter pares*—first among equals—with the other arms, such as infantry or armor. In practice, however, their rather different skills and the importance of their role in the strategic scheme of things have given Israeli airmen a high degree of functional autonomy, rather like that enjoyed by the U.S. Army Air Forces in the Second World War.

In Israeli doctrine, tactical air power breaks down into two main categories: interdiction and close air support (CAS); although the effectiveness of both depends entirely upon attaining air superiority at the appropriate time and place. The Israeli Air Staff soon realized that interdiction was to be preferred to CAS. There would be occasions when cost-effectiveness would have to take second place, but interdiction would usually achieve better results for a given expenditure of men and machines, according to Maj. Gen. Dan Tolkovsky, who became *Chel Ha'Avir's* commander in 1953. Moreover, there was, until the 1980s, a technological problem in acquiring and transmitting information about the ground battle quickly enough. Tolkovsky states:

> In all the battles fought by the Israel Defense Forces there has never been real-time intelligence coming up from the ground forces that was adequate . . . .. Interdiction is God's gift to the Middle East. . . . I can give countless specific situations where close support proved effective, but . . . close support, by definition, gives up the basic, inherent capability of air forces to move in depth.[4]

"Real-time intelligence" can be defined as information provided sufficiently soon after the event takes place, or target is identified, to enable the recipient to act on it before the situation changes significantly. In an age of electronic communications, real-time intelligence poses no insuperable technical problem, but the mind-sets of general staff officers (not only Israeli) attuned to the pace of ground operations have frequently failed to mesh with those of air staff members. Interdiction—the suppression of movement to or from the battlefield—is far less demanding in terms of real-time intelligence than is CAS, since its objectives, such as bridges, fuel depots, junctions, etc., are either fixed in time and space or, by their nature, somewhat pinned to a fixed transportation net. Locomotives and rolling stock must stick to railways, trucks to roads, and heavy aircraft to airfields with long concrete runways. Because their transportation routes are often redundant, effective interdiction has been difficult to achieve in more developed parts of the world. But throughout the Middle East road and rail lines are few, and when options are available, they often involve lengthy detours. Thus battlefield interdiction is usually easier to achieve than close air support.

All this had been worked out by Israeli airmen in the very early 1950s but only reluctantly accepted by their General Staff over the next few years. It was clear enough in theory and seemed reasonable in principle, but soldiers (and the politicians) questioned it on two counts. The first was expense. The kind of aircraft required to establish the prerequisite air superiority and serve as fighter-bombers in the interdiction role were inordinately expensive. Though the machines intended simply for ground strikes—at that time Dassault Ouragans, Gloster Meteors, and North American Mustangs, all fitted with bomb racks or rocket pylons as well as 50-cal machineguns—did not need to be as advanced as those providing top cover, they were not cheap.

In the 1948 War of Independence, a hodge-podge of assorted machines, masquerading as a 'balanced' air force of fighters, bombers, and transports, played a slight part in Israeli successes. However, as Edward Luttwak and Dan Horowitz observed in their 1975 study of the Israeli Army:

> [A] majority of [the air arm's] bombing missions were interdiction strikes against targets deep in the enemy rear, or attacks against enemy cities—instead of close support strikes coordinated with the forces on the ground. The IAF had not worked out a set of priorities consistent with Israeli strategy . . . nor developed an operational doctrine suited to local conditions.[5]

The result was that the ground force was always disappointed with the air force," remembered Tolkovsky.[6] Yet both the desert climate and its uncluttered topography favored air power. Good flying weather was the rule; there were, as noted, a limited number of axes for ground operations, and it was often hard to hide anything on the ground from air observation. The potential advantages were obvious, despite the high cost of an air force, and the government was finally persuaded to pay the inevitable price, after Tolkovsky accepted the fact that Israel could not afford a great variety of specialized aircraft. A tactical air force composed of all-purpose fighter-bombers, with a limited number of transport aircraft, was all that *Chel Ha'Avir* needed to defend Israeli air space, provide cover for interdiction and close-support missions, and maintain a very basic lift capability for men or equipment. The newest and best machines would guard the home airspace and provide cover as their first priority. As they aged, they would be relegated to interdiction and then to close support, but all machines should be capable of all functions.

Cost could be kept down, moreover, by emphasizing quality and serviceability. *Chel Ha'Avir* already had an inherent qualitative advantage in the cal-

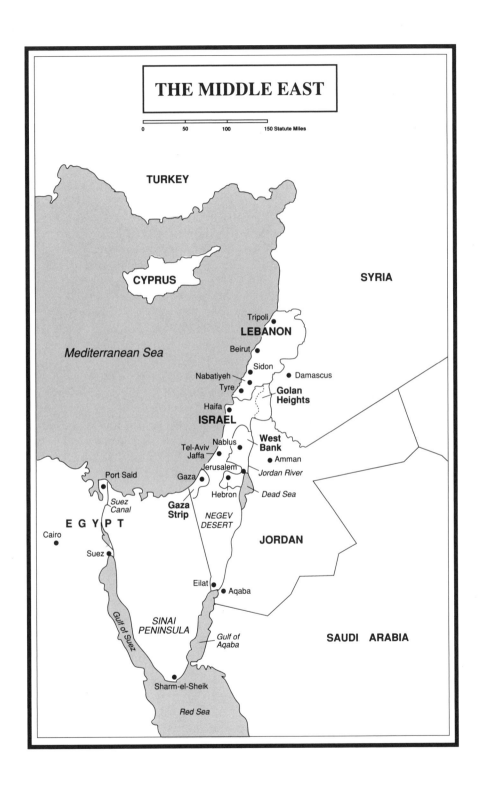

THE MIDDLE EAST

0   50   100   150 Statute Miles

TURKEY

CYPRUS

SYRIA

Mediterranean Sea

Tripoli

LEBANON

Beirut

Sidon

Nabatiyeh

Damascus

Tyre

Golan Heights

Haifa

ISRAEL

Nablus

West Bank

Tel-Aviv
Jaffa

Amman

Jerusalem

Port Said

Gaza

Jordan River

Suez Canal

Gaza Strip

Hebron

Dead Sea

E G Y P T

NEGEV DESERT

JORDAN

Cairo

Suez

Eilat

Aqaba

Gulf of Suez

SINAI PENINSULA

Gulf of Aqaba

SAUDI ARABIA

Sharm-el-Sheik

Red Sea

iber of its human resources. Even this could be improved, so Tolkovsky instituted pilot standards that were, and remain, probably the stiffest in the world. Aircraft maintenance was stressed so that the maximum possible use could be made of every machine. "By the 1967 Six Day War (and again in 1973), from the time a fighter landed after a mission to the time it was ready to take off again with a full fuel and bomb load, only seven to ten minutes had elapsed—this at a time when the United States prided itself on a turn-around time of twenty minutes."[7]

The first test of Tolkovsky's ideas came in the 1956 Suez campaign. During the early part of the year, the Soviet Union delivered large quantities of modern weapons (including MiG–15 fighters) to Egypt. That was followed by an Arab announcement that Egypt, Syria, and Jordan, three of Israel's four immediate neighbors, would place their national forces under a single, unified command in the event of major hostilities with Israel. The Israeli assessment was that hostilities simply awaited their opponents' convenience, and the dangers of coordinated assaults on several fronts were only too obvious. The Arabs could not be allowed to have the initiative, so Israel decided on a preemptive strike in conspiracy with the British and French, who wished to recover the Suez Canal nationalized by the Egyptians in July 1954.

Operation *Kadesh* had limited objectives. By striking the most powerful of their enemies and destroying or severely punishing Egyptian forces massed in the Gaza Strip and the northern Sinai, the Israelis hoped to deter the Arab alliance from the attack they believed it was contemplating. They would take the Gaza Strip, shortening their frontier somewhat, and seize Sharm-el-Sheikh at the southern tip of the Sinai to break the Egyptian blockade of the Gulf of Aqaba. In the center, they would stop short of the Suez Canal and rely upon concurrent British and French operations aimed at reacquiring the Canal Zone on the pretext that freedom of navigation was threatened by the Egyptian–Israeli conflict. Their intent was to discourage the Arabs from escalating the action into a full-scale war.[8]

Since objectives were limited, the Israelis planned to restrict military actions accordingly. Pilots were instructed to stay at least ten miles east of the Canal although most important Egyptian airfields lay west of it. Even though contingency plans existed,[9] there would be no attempt to establish initial air superiority by a counterair strike against the Egyptian Air Force [EAF]. That would be left to British and French allies, while *Chel Ha'Avir* would cover Israeli ground forces but would not intervene until the EAF did, either in the air or on the ground.

The Egyptians mustered some 156 combat aircraft, all jets, but only 84 (30 MiG–15s, 30 De Havilland Vampires, 12 Gloster Meteors, and 12 Il–28 light bombers) were operationally ready. The Israelis, with 53 jets, outnumbered them in aircraft fit to fight, with 16 Dassault Mystere IVAs, 22 Dassault Ouragans, 15 Meteors, 16 De Havilland Mosquitos, 29 North American Mustangs, and 2 B–17 bombers (the last 3 types being obsolescent piston-engine machines of limited value).*[10]

Nevertheless, unless the British and French destroyed or seriously damaged the EAF, air superiority over the Sinai would be difficult to achieve. The Israelis had little radar capability,[11] and standing patrols over the whole battlefield would have required an inordinate proportion of their strength. The eminent American military historian, Brig. Gen. S.L.A. Marshall, noted in his *Sinai Victory* that "by the Air Staff's reckoning, its main decision, in conflict with what is elsewhere considered the controlling principle, came when its forces were committed full-scale to support of the land battle without first achieving air superiority or inflicting any material damage on the enemy Air Force."[12] That was a risk the Israelis chose to take in the cause of inhibiting escalation. They would depend—vainly for the first 48 hours—on their allies to strike down the EAF for them.

Israeli troops crossed the border at 1600 hrs on October 29, 1956, but it was not until the next morning that Egyptian MiGs and Vampires began attacking them. *Chel Ha'Avir* should have been on the scene, providing cover for the ground forces, but according to General Dayan, the Israeli Chief of Staff, "for some reason, during the very hours of the Egyptian attack, none of our planes appeared." Apparently there was a lack of effective liaison between ground and air forces in the initial stages of the conflict. Subsequently, however, "patrols were kept up almost without a break."[13] With the Mysteres providing top cover, the Ouragans, Meteors, and Mustangs began to intervene in the ground battle. Although their intervention was to be significant, much of it was a matter of interdiction (in accordance with General Tolkovsky's ideas) rather than close air support. However, let us look at the CAS element.

On the evening of October 29, an Israeli paratroop battalion, commanded by future Chief of Staff "Raful" Eitan, had been dropped near the east end of the Mitla Pass, a key defile on the southernmost route through the Sinai, some 18 to 20 miles from Suez and about 90 miles west of the Israeli border. During the night this force established a blocking position, and shortly after 0900 the next morning it came into conflict with Egyptian

---

*This seems a good point at which to caution the reader against accepting any set of figures relating to Middle Eastern wars at face value, particularly those relating to strengths or casualties. The "fog of war" and, indeed, of peacetime tensions, is often impenetrable. Security, on the one hand, and propaganda on the other, are both immensely important; and deception is a way of life. "Official" figures are rarely available and, when they are, cannot be trusted. Accordingly, unofficial ones vary widely, even when proffered by the most reputable authors. Those in this essay are more likely to be generally right than specifically so; they represent the author's "educated choice" among the many alternatives available.

troops debouching from the Pass, *en route* to meet the main Israeli forces further east. The paratroopers' heaviest weapons were two 106–mm recoilless rifles and two 120–mm mortars.

Both Israeli and Egyptian commanders promptly called for air support. Egyptian MiGs appeared about an hour later and made a number of strafing runs over the paratroopers. On the ground, "for more than an hour the two forces were engaged in an action of small unit fire and movement with no conclusive result. . . . At noon, when Israeli Air Force jets arrived, Eitan pulled back his maneuvering units to leave the situation to the Air Force."[14] Apparently, it took nearly three hours for the airmen performing CAS to respond, but when they did appear, their work was noticeably more effective than that of Egyptian airmen who were on the scene first.

The balance of the Israeli 202d Para Brigade was moving overland to reinforce the battalion near the Pass. Approaching Nakhl, on the Egyptian supply line to the eastern Sinai, the brigade commander (Ariel Sharon) called for close air support to complement his attack on the village, but before it could be delivered, an Israeli aircraft returning from the Mitla reported "many vehicles moving eastward from the canal towards the passes."[15] Therefore Dov (Sharon's *nom de guerre*) asked that the air strike on Nakhl be diverted to these vehicles. Practice conformed with doctrine. Tactical interdiction of forces approaching the battlefield was considered a better use of limited air power than close air support on the battlefield itself, even by the concerned ground commander. The paratroopers attacked and took Nakhl unaided, then pushed on to link up with their comrades and establish themselves in the pass on the 31st.

It took hard fighting to drive the Egyptians out, and in the course of the battle the enemy was "given air support of four Meteors which were covered by six MiGs from the Kabrit airfield," recorded Moshe Dayan. "The Egyptian planes operated without interference. Actually there were at the time six of our Ouragans in the vicinity of Mitla, but owing to faulty communications our men could not signal them for help."[16] The uncertain nature of ground–air communication in 1956 was manifest in the way in which a passing airman communicated with Sharon at Nakhl, and the latter was able to have aircraft diverted to more important targets, but he was not able to make contact with the Ouragans when he badly needed them, twenty-four hours later.

Further north, Israeli soldiers were battling for control of the vital Abu Ageila crossroads, on the Beersheba–Ismailia road some twenty miles south of El Arish. Abu Ageila itself was occupied by Lt. Col."Bren" Adan's Sherman tank battalion and a mechanized infantry company by 0630 on the 31st, but the Egyptians still held the high ground of Um Shehan and Um Katef, a few miles to the east, which dominated the surrounding desert. In accordance with orders, Israeli ground forces then waited for two and a half hours for an air strike scheduled to hit the defenders of Um Shehan as the soldiers

498

Israeli Super Sherman tanks advance in desert terrain, June 1967.

attacked. But "the aircraft never arrived because the mission was canceled by higher headquarters."[17]

There was still much to be learned about the employment of CAS, most of it relating to the eternal problem of command and control. Israeli air doctrine in the 1980s proclaims that "there is a chain of command and a chain of control . . . control must be vested at the level, and in the instrument, that can read the battle, which may or may not fit the line of command,"[18] but in 1956 that concept had not been fully worked out. Air force headquarters felt entitled to intervene at any level. Although there were forward air controllers (FACs) with the ground forces and "the pilot generally received his target only after he entered the combat area,"[19] there was too little coordination further back.

Pilots were briefed for their missions by the debriefing of returning pilots, a casual procedure that could easily lead to mistakes, (but, in fact, generally seems to have worked very well)[20] and, at the highest levels, all air operations were directed from an air headquarters at Ramle while the ground war was controlled from Tel Aviv, twelve miles away. Subsequent wars would be fought from a combined operations room—"the Pit"—at GHQ in Tel Aviv.

Meanwhile, the Egyptians were planning to retake Abu Ageila with coordinated counterattacks from two directions. A motorized infantry battalion with one company of T–34 tanks and one of selfpropelled seventeen-pounder antitank guns was assigned to attack from the north, while a composite battalion, also with some self-propelled guns, advanced from the east. However, the northern force's approach was stopped by an Israeli air strike, and the possibility of a coordinated assault faded out. The Israelis beat off

499

two separate attacks, but "had the two Egyptian forces coordinated their attacks and converged on Adan," suggested Trevor Dupuy, in *Elusive Victory*,"it is doubtful if [the Israelis] could have held Abu Ageila."[21]

This engagement clearly illustrated both the difficulties and value of close air support. The cancellation of a planned strike and the failure to notify the ground commander concerned of its cancellation brought about a delay in attacking the Um Shehan-Um Katef positions that might have disastrously slowed the pace of the Israeli advance. But the effect of such support, when it did arrive on the scene, may well have been the decisive element in holding Abu Ageila.

Israeli ground forces eventually launched a series of assaults on Um Shehan, not using close air support "because they were afraid of hitting their own troops in the melee"[22]—another classic control problem of CAS. Finally the soldiers pulled back, and throughout the afternoon of November 1 "four Mustangs were kept in the air continuously over the positions, subjecting them [the Egyptians] to bombs, rockets and strafing. . . . When morning came, there seemed to be a strange calm over the whole area."[23] The Egyptian garrison abandoned the position on orders from Cairo and stole silently away into the desert where some of them subsequently perished. Many were picked up by Israeli patrols, to become prisoners of war.

Pressing on toward Bir Gifgafa, the balance of the 7th Armored Brigade had begun a running battle with a retreating battalion of Egyptian tanks, and the air force intervened constantly in that engagement. Israeli air and armor knocked out three T–34s and captured eight, and the Israelis were able to add five of the captured tanks and ten personnel carriers to their own strength. The intact enemy vehicles may have been abandoned because they ran out of fuel, but the 1956 campaign made it clear—as 1967 was to confirm—that the psychological effect of close air support on poorly trained or low-grade troops was a significant one. Especially, "the threat of napalm almost invariably aborted [*sic*] the Egyptian crews from their vehicles or bunkers before it hit," reported S. L. A. Marshall.[24] This may well have been a case of dispirited crewmen abandoning their tanks without good cause.

As Gen. Haim Laskov's Northern Task Force maneuvered to take Rafah, at the base of the Gaza Strip, Israeli air elements assigned to carry out a preliminary night bombardment of the Egyptian defenses found the wrong targets. "Our pilots managed to drop their parachute flares right on our own units, exposed them, and started bombing them," recorded Dayan. "We immediately signalled them to stop. . . ."[25] He did not explain whether this was a visual signal or an electronic one, but it says something about the relatively unsophisticated nature of Operation *Kadesh* that the Israeli Chief of Staff was actually travelling with Laskov's leading armored brigade as it sealed off the Gaza Strip and began to advance westward, through El Arish, on the road towards Kantara and the Canal.

My unit comprised two 6x6 trucks, one a radio truck through which I could maintain constant contact with GHQ command post [in Tel Aviv] and with the Air Force [in Ramle], and the other in which I travelled. With me was the head of the Southern Command Staff, the head of my office, and two signalmen.[26]

Apparently there was no air adviser with him. Perhaps Laskov, the soldier and task force leader, who had preceded Tolkovsky as Commander of *Chel Ha'Avir* four years earlier and established the principles of Israeli air strategy, was considered sufficiently competent without an air adviser.

Large numbers of Egyptian vehicles, armored and soft-skinned, were destroyed or abandoned as the Israeli spearheads drove westwards towards the Canal and the Air Force flew interdiction missions well ahead of them. The only other notable use of CAS came in the capture of Sharm-el-Sheikh, at the southern tip of Sinai. As an Israeli mechanized column raced south along the western shore of the Gulf of Aqaba, *Chel Ha'Avir* bombed, rocketed, and machinegunned the fortifications around the town. The Egyptian commander "lost the battle on the ground before [Col. Avraham] Yoffe's brigade got there," reported S.L.A. Marshall. "Two days of air strafing was more than he could stand; the rockets and the napalm did him in. He said 'I learned about close air support during my schooling in England, or so I thought, until I stood at Sharm-El-Sheikh.' "[27] However, the initial air attack, whatever the Egyptians may have thought, can hardly be classed as *close* air support, since it had occurred before Colonel Yoffe and his men reached the scene. Arriving on November 4, they launched a dawn assault. Israeli aircraft napalmed the Egyptian positions in a genuine close air support operation, and three hours later the last of the garrison surrendered. In the north, the fighting had ended on the 3d, with the Israelis having achieved all their objectives.

During Operation *Kadesh*, the Israelis claimed a sortie rate of better than four per day for their jets and about two and a half per day for their propeller-driven aircraft. It seems unlikely that the Egyptians achieved a rate of one sortie per day even before the Anglo–French attack accounted for nearly two hundred of their aircraft on the ground. Thus, considering their additional advantage in operationally ready aircraft, *Chel Ha'Avir* must have flown many more sorties than its opponents, the vast majority of them on interdiction and close air support missions. Most of the aerial damage inflicted on the Egyptian materiel was undoubtedly the result of interdiction. The damage due to CAS is hard to measure. However, the USAF historian who studied the campaign reported: "Israeli armored force commanders agreed that . . . the IAF proved especially effective against tanks. Other ground commanders believed that the IAF saved the ground forces several days of battle and many casualties."[28]

The Israelis lost fifteen aircraft. Only one of them, a Piper Super Cub, was shot down by Egyptian aircraft; the others, six jets and eight propeller-driven machines, including two more Piper Cubs, fell to ground fire. Another six, all propeller-driven, were severely damaged, but they returned to base. Both sortie and damage rates confirmed that there was no longer any place for propeller-driven aircraft in the Israeli arsenal, either for air combat or tactical air operations.

Under United States and United Nations pressure, the Israelis were compelled to renounce their territorial gains and accept American assurances that the Gulf of Aqaba would be kept open to all shipping. United Nations forces were stationed at Sharm-el-Sheikh and the Gaza strip to ensure that the Egyptians complied.

Taking the apparent lessons of the campaign to heart, the Israeli General Staff set about enlarging the armored component of its ground forces and developing its jet component for the air force. The proportion of the Israeli defense budget allocated to air power—a good measure of importance attached to it by strategic planners—climbed steadily. By 1967 it would account for half of all defense expenditures.[29] Israeli political and military leaders were now convinced that air superiority was the prerequisite for the successful employment of air power, interdiction was its most effective expression, and close air support could, on occasion, contribute significantly to the success of the ground battle.

An uneasy truce extended over the next decade, marked by intermittent (but increasingly frequent) border clashes, and both by the formation of the Palestine Liberation Organization in 1964 and a military coup that put a more extremist anti-Israel government into power in Damascus early in 1966. The Egyptian–Syrian–Jordanian alliance tightened once more and, in May 1967, the Egyptians expelled all UN forces and again closed the Strait of Tiran leading into the Gulf of Aqaba. Arab armies were massing along Israel's southern and eastern frontiers, and in June Tel Aviv directed another preemptive attack against the strongest of their opponents. The Israeli cabinet recognized that this would probably precipitate action by the Egyptians' allies and that they would have to fight the whole Arab alliance.

This time the Israelis were heavily outnumbered in the air. They could call on some 277 combat machines: 92 Dassault Mirage IIIs, 24 Super Mysteres, 82 Mysteres, 55 Ouragans, and 25 Sud-Aviation Vautour II light bombers.[30] There were also 76 Fouga Magister 2-seat jet trainers, destined to play a leading role in close support during the initial hours of the Six Day War. The EAF had about 450 aircraft, including 120 MiG–21s, 80 MiG–19s, 150 MiG–17s and 15s, and 30 Su–7s, plus 70 Il–28 and Tu–16 bombers. If they intervened, Syrians and Jordanians could add another 170 machines, (including 36 MiG–21s and 22 Hawker Hunters). It was also possible for the Iraqis to bring their 100-plus MiGs, Hunters, and light bombers to bear.[31]

There was also the matter of antiaircraft defenses. Most of the losses in Operation *Kadesh* were caused by ground-based small arms fire, with almost all Egyptian antiaircraft guns defending Cairo, Alexandria, and key facilities along the Nile. It was certainly a recognition of the effectiveness of *Chel Ha'Avir* in 1956 that the Egyptians could now muster 950 AA guns of one caliber or another (mostly 57–mm), while the Syrians amassed more than 1,000,[32] together with the radars needed to supply accurate target speeds and ranges. The combination, however, was still not adequate to combat successfully the kind of low-level attacks the Israelis favored. The Arabs lacked computer linkages between gun and radar required to predict "lead" as well as the "power steering" needed to alter the direction and angle of fire quickly enough to keep the gun on target.

In addition, the Egyptians had 160 SA–2 surface-to-air missiles,[33] but this first-generation SAM was designed for use against high-flying bombers. Its initial rate of acceleration was poor, and it did not have the degree of maneuverability needed to hit a fighter or fighter-bomber whose pilot was aware of its approach. In 1967 there was still relatively little to fear from ground-based fire.

The Israelis set about attaining air superiority by destroying the EAF on the ground—using the plan that existed in a more primitive form in 1956 but was not employed for political reasons. Except for a dozen Mirages, held back to defend Israeli cities,[34] virtually all *Chel Ha'Avir*'s first and second-line aircraft, from Mirages to Ouragans, were launched against the Egyptian air bases at breakfast time on June 5, 1967, and subsequently, when the Jordanians and Syrians intervened, against their airfields as well. Surprise was vital in this classic example of counterair operations. By the early afternoon, about 350 Arab aircraft were destroyed and air supremacy assured. Meanwhile, Israeli ground forces, driving into the Sinai, had only the Fouga Magisters to provide close support. However, with Ezer Weizman, a former commander of *Chel Ha'Avir*, as head of *Zahal*'s operations branch, and air headquarters now in the same underground command post as GHQ, there was a better appreciation of what air power could do and far less chance for misunderstanding or error in transmission of orders or requests.

The ground troops started by charging forward in a series of frontal assaults directed at the base of the Gaza Strip. Surprise was on their side, and they gained some ground at first, but the Egyptians soon resisted stubbornly. When the attackers reached the Rafah defenses, resistance had become so strong that the Israeli commander felt compelled to call for an air strike against dug-in artillery, a call that was answered by Fouga Magisters. The Fougas, which could barely reach 300 miles per hour at low level even with their "normal" armament of two 7.62–mm machineguns, had been fitted with rocket pylons and armed with Oerlikon 80–mm rockets for the occasion, which must have reduced their speed considerably. Many of them were flown by aging reservists, the "hot-shot" pilots of 1956.

"While the Israeli aircraft were overhead," recorded British historian

French-built Mysteres

Edgar O'Ballance, "the Egyptian gunners left their guns and took cover, but when the aircraft went away, they returned to their posts and recommenced firing at the Israeli tanks." The armor finally burst through, however, and pressed on to the vicinity of El Jerardi, where virtually the same thing happened. "When the Israeli aircraft disappeared from overhead and the mortar and artillery barrage ceased, the Egyptians returned to their guns. . . ."[35]

The Fougas were not able to carry bombs or napalm tanks, and the weight of fire they were able to bring to bear on a well-entrenched enemy was probably not sufficient to inflict enough physical or psychological damage to demoralize the better-trained and better-commanded enemy troops. Nevertheless, when an Israeli paratroop brigade attacking the Rafah South positions from the east got into difficulty and signaled for help, strikes by these obsolete training aircraft persuaded the Egyptians to desert their guns. Poor command and control by their own leaders and a total lack of air cover soon turned the Egyptian retreat into a rout. Opportunities for interdiction then increased and the need for close support lessened, but higher-performance Israeli aircraft were directed to CAS missions. On the second day of the campaign, Mysteres, Ouragans, and Fougas pounded the Um Katef position from first light until it fell at 0900.[36]

The Fouga Magister trainer doubled as a ground support aircraft.

On the 6th of June, Egyptian armor counterattacked the Yoffe *ugda*, (an all-arms battle group that may vary in size from a brigade to a division) operating between Um Katef and the coast. Israeli air strikes forced the Arabs to scatter but did not stop their advance. Then another Israeli armored force hit the Egyptians from the flank. When the Egyptians broke off and withdrew westwards, "twenty-eight of their tanks were in flames . . . and then our air force went into action and the whole area was covered with burnt vehicles," reported the commander of one of the Israeli armored brigades at a postwar press conference.[37]

A flight commander with a Mystere squadron flew twenty close support missions, and "five were against tanks—new tanks—and the rest of them against artillery or A[rmored] P[ersonnel] C[arrier]s." On one occasion he led his four Mysteres, each armed with two tanks of napalm and a 30–mm DEFA cannon loaded with armor-piercing rounds, against sixteen T–54s that had ambushed Israeli AMX–13 light reconnaissance tanks at the mouth of the Mitla Pass. "We hit all the sixteen tanks, six of them with napalm and the rest of them with the 30–mm . . . we hit all the sixteen and we got contact with another flight that was going the same way and brought them in as well."[38] Israeli operational researchers confirmed twelve air-to-ground kills in their subsequent examination of the battlefield. The others may have been destroyed by ground fire.[39]

For ground attack missions, most Israeli aircraft carried the appropriate combination of 20– or 30–mm cannon (depending on aircraft type), 1,800 pounds of high explosive bombs or napalm tanks, and two pods holding 38

505

68–mm or 72 37–mm rockets. Napalm was effective against men or vehicles in the open and could be somewhat effective against tanks, but "we clobbered tanks with iron bombs and rockets, mostly with rockets," recalls one of the Israeli pilots. "The T–34, T–54, T–55, and even the T–62, [in 1973] had their spare fuel outside, and that was easily lighted with a 30–mm [cannon shell] or with rockets."[40]

On June 8, as the Israeli ground forces closed the Canal, another classic situation developed at the western end of the deep and narrow Giddi Pass, on the road that led down to the Little Bitter Lake. Sixteen Centurions (two with damaged turrets that would no longer rotate) found their way blocked by about thirty T–55s. The Israeli commander called for air support and waited two hours for aircraft to arrive and begin rocketing the Egyptians. When they did arrive, however, "due to the difficulties of maneuvering the aircraft in the narrow valley, only three out of the thirty Egyptian tanks were knocked out by the air force, but Egyptian morale waned," according to Israeli historian Arye Hashavia, another former pilot. "While the Super Mysteres continued firing in the rear, the Centurions opened fire in front of the enemy. . . . The Egyptians fired at the column [debouching from the Pass], but their fear of the air force must have affected their aim. . . . When Aharon's tanks reached the valley, they saw seventeen burning Egyptian tanks."[41]

On the eastern front, where the Jordanians held a large bridgehead on the west bank of the Jordan river and the Dead Sea under the terms of the 1948 armistice, the Jordanian garrison on the West Bank included 2 batteries of 155–mm "Long Tom" cannon. On June 5, 1967, one battery was sited within range of Tel Aviv and the other within range of the principal Israeli air base in northern Israel, Ramat David. Both batteries opened a sporadic fire shortly after breakfast, the second one inflicting damage on installations at Ramat David and cratering some runways. Two Jordanian armored brigades were poised to attack but had not yet begun to move when the Israelis, unwilling to accept the damage to Ramat David, struck first. Israeli troops manning their west Jerusalem outpost and the narrow corridor linking it with the coastal strip attacked Arab-held east Jerusalem and began to push into the hills on the north side of the salient. During the afternoon, after the Jordanian Air Force was destroyed on the ground and the Syrian Air Force crippled, *Chel Ha'Avir* struck hard at Jordanian positions in the hills. In the early evening, Israeli tank columns found the positions "either abandoned or lightly manned."[42]

The Jordanian commander in east Jerusalem radioed for reinforcements, and a battalion of M–48 tanks and an infantry battalion were dispatched from Jericho as soon as darkness fell, presumably in an attempt to avoid the attentions of *Chel Ha'Avir*. If so, the effort was quite unsuccessful. Using flares, in an assault that carried over the uncertain line dividing close air support from the forward edge of tactical interdiction, Israeli airmen

Israeli crews race to their Centurions.

destroyed the whole Jordanian force.[43] Meanwhile, Israeli ground troops pushed into the weakly held northern part of the West Bank, around Jenin, with both air cover (in case of Iraqi or Syrian intervention) and air support, against opponents who entirely lacked both. On the evening of the 6th, an Israeli light tank force in the hills to the east of the Zababida valley was endeavoring to establish a block across the Jenin–Tubas road. "It seemed to them that the entire far side of the valley was covered with well-hidden enemy tanks [but] at 6 pm, six Israeli planes appeared, two Ouragans and two pairs of Mysteres, and began raining down hellfire on the southern end of the valley. The planes scored direct hits on four tanks." Hashavia goes on to claim that "although the actual damage was slight," the movement of Jordanian tanks trying to avoid the air strike exposed their position to the Israeli gunners and enabled them to win the firefight.[44]

The Jordanians withdrew toward Tubas, where they linked up with the forward elements of their 40th Armored Brigade, pushing north "under a hail of Israeli rockets" delivered by air, according to King Hussein.[45] The Arab column was intercepted by Israeli ground troops in the vicinity of Akkaba, three miles north of Tubas and, just after dawn the next morning, the Israelis launched a combined air and armored assault. "Jordanian troops now hastily scattered and withdrew as daylight allowed Israeli aircraft to pick off the Pattons individually. . . . Later some thirty-five Pattons were counted on the battlefield, of which sixteen had been hit by antitank fire and the remainder disabled by air action," according to O'Ballance.[46] The Arabs fell back across the Jordan, still harried from the air.

Further north, two light Syrian probes into the Upper Galilee were easily repulsed by Israeli forces with air support. Then the Syrians returned to their prewar pastime of intermittently shelling Israeli settlements in the valley from the apparent safety of the Golan Heights. It was a policy practically guaranteed to invite Israeli retribution, once the situation in the south came to be stabilized.

By June 9, everything was ready to begin the most technically difficult major operation of war the Israelis had ever attempted. The Syrians had 40,000 men, 250 tanks and self-propelled guns, and 265 artillery pieces on the plateau—all carefully dug in or entrenched to cover the few possible but extremely hazardous routes up the escarpment. The Israelis, with half the number of men, armor, and guns, selected the most difficult (and therefore most unlikely in Syrian eyes) of these, leading up from Kfar Szold towards Banias, at the northern end of the Heights, for their main thrust. There were to be subsidiary thrusts in the center and south, and since the breakthrough was scheduled for daylight, on a single narrow axis that was open to complete observation by the enemy and his artillery, effective air support would be essential.

"I asked 'Dado' [Lt. Gen. David Elazar, commanding the northern front] for a couple of hours to give the plateau a serious work over," recalled the Commander of the Air Force, Maj. Gen. "Motti" Hod. "Back then the planes we had could only carry two [1,000–pound] bombs, so we executed 200 sorties on the Golan . . . attacking tanks and artillery . . . ."[47]

In fact, these attacks employed every available air-to-ground weapon—bombs, napalm, rockets, and cannon and machinegun fire—delivered by Super Mysteres, Mysteres, Ouragans, and Fougas. Mirages flew top cover against any possible intervention by remnants of the Arab air forces (the Iraqis had some planes left and the Jordanians had been partially reequipped by them); and once the ground attack was launched, a continuous succession of Israeli aircraft circled overhead, "on call" by the forward air controllers with the spearheads of the various columns. Communicating directly with pilots who were only twenty or thirty seconds away from the enemy in time, FACs could talk their colleagues right down onto unanticipated or mobile targets—men, guns or tanks—either on the basis of their own judgment or at the behest of a ground commander.

Other aircraft, armed with specific weapon loads, were assigned by the Air/Ground Support Center at Northern Front headquarters to attack predetermined targets in the path of the advance. Real-time intelligence was handled in an irregular fashion. "All air support controllers (forward or rearward) were communicating to the H.Q. A/G Support Center, while all liaison officers in the squadrons listened in to their chatter," recalled senior staff officer "Benny" Peled. "Almost always it was the pilot returning from the FEBA (Forward Edge of the Battle Area) who had better, quicker information on the questions: "Who, where, when and what? . . . That information was supplied to the liaison officers who updated the Center from the pilots, thus completely reversing the flow that the system was supposed to provide."[48]

The Syrians were well dug in, and in material terms, the air attacks seem to have done relatively little damage; but they apparently succeeded in suppressing some Syrian fire, and the psychological effect must have substantially affected the Israelis as well as their opponents. "Each of our aeroplanes gave us new strength," reported one officer. "The scream of jets was like sweet music to the assaulting force, exposed to fire on the slope."[49] Israeli infantry and armor struggled over the crest of the ridge in some of the hardest fighting of the war, and by the next day, when a cease-fire took effect, had reached Al-Kuneitra, 15 miles from the escarpment and only 35 miles from Damascus. Of the 265 Syrian guns on the plateau when the war began, the Israelis claim to have knocked out 150, mainly by aerial action. . . ."[50]

Reviewing the Six-Day War from an air perspective, most of the measurable destruction inflicted on Arab forces by *Chel Ha'Avir* was again the result of interdiction, but there can be little doubt that CAS made the soldier's work easier on a number of occasions. On the Golan it may have been decisive. And, since air superiority had been assured by the destruction of the bulk of Arab air power on the ground and the absence of effective ground-based anti-aircraft fire, the conflict had not been expensive, according to General Hod, speaking after the 1973 war.[51] The Israelis lost forty machines, ten of them on air superiority sorties. Of the remaining thirty, it may be that as many as nineteen (or as few as six)[52] were Fougas, slow enough to be caught by manually operated antiaircraft guns. Arab air defense artillery was still not sophisticated enough to pose a significant threat to faster aircraft.

Nevertheless, the Air Force was not entirely happy when headquarters reviewed the close support aspect of the campaign. "In 1967, except for two staged and prepared A[ir]/ G[round] operations, the flying elements . . . sought out, found, and identified ground enemy forces completely on their own and attacked them on authorization from the control structure, which in turn was vested by the command structure to allow attack," writes Peled. "The formal doctrinal air/ground support organization [that] was manned, equipped and allocated to all major ground . . . formations by the Air Force never succeeded in functioning; they never had information that was valid, important, or timely [enough] to have any effect."[53]

After 1967, the Israelis held their gains, giving themselves distinct 'buffer' zones, deep enough in the Sinai but still relatively shallow on the west bank of the Jordan River and on the Golan Heights, while also shortening their frontiers. The Arabs—at least the Egyptians and the Syrians—were intent on revenge. Their armies and air forces were rebuilt over the next six years, quantitatively and qualitatively stronger than ever, while staff officers plotted new strategies around new technologies. Most notable of these, from an airman's point of view, was the development of vastly improved SAM systems and a quantum jump in the capability of low-level air defense artillery.

The Egyptians and Syrians together could call on 825 fighters and fighter-bombers (270 MiG–21s, 60 MiG–19s, 320 MiG–17s, 130 Su–7s) and 48 bombers by October 1973. There was also the prospect of another 165 such machines being added by Iraq, Libya, and Jordan. The Israelis, who now turned to American aircraft, had 352 fighters and fighter-bombers (140 McDonnell Douglas F–4 Phantoms, 150 A–4 Skyhawks from the same stable, 50 Mirages, 12 Super–Mysteres) and 8 Süd–Aviation Vautour light bombers.[54] The best odds they could expect were less than 2½:1, but most Israeli pilots had logged more than 2,000 hours flying time; most Egyptians and Syrians had less than 1,000. Israeli aircraft, moreover, were better, with longer range and heavier ordnance loads, and more sophisticated electronics. Egyptian Chief of Staff, Lt. Gen. Saad El Shazli, admitted in his memoir of the 1973 campaign, "in their many encounters since 1967 our men had frankly not matched the enemy's."

> In effect the enemy air force was ten years ahead of ours . . . throughout my planning, I was anxious not to bring our air force into direct conflict with the enemy's. From the start I adopted two main principles. First, to avoid chance air encounters. Second, to use our air force for sudden ground-attack strikes where enemy air cover was least likely. Primarily, I wanted the enemy's ground forces and ground targets to taste the psychological impact of our air force, while at the same time I wanted to preserve it from air combat. I was convinced that unless we deployed the air force in a cautious and calculated way, we would merely lose it for the third time, this time in the air.[55]

On the other hand, there was a new, not fully comprehended threat facing the Israelis. As we have noted, prior to the 1970s, ground-based antiaircraft fire had played an insignificant part in deciding the outcome of both the air-to-air battle and the air-ground battle. Ground fire was usually inadequate or inaccurate (often both), and although it could be expected to take a small toll, the technology of air defense had simply not kept up with the technology of air attack. The appearance of a beam-riding SAM linked to radar, the SA–2, had had no impact on the 1967 campaign. It had been designed to counter weapons *Chel Ha'avir* did not have and techniques it did not use— high-flying, relatively unwieldy, heavy bombers. The battery of SA–2s emplaced east of the Canal, at Bir Gifgafa, had been captured intact, and detailed studies had confirmed its limitations.

An improved SA–2, subsequently acquired by the Egyptians, was supplemented by the SA–3, a faster, more maneuverable, still relatively immobile, medium-range missile. The Israelis met both systems during the

Ground attack weapons loads are arrayed before two American aircraft used extensively by the *Chel Ha'Avir*, the A-4 Skyhawk *(above)* and the F-4 Phantom.

so-called "War of Attrition,"—a state of sporadic raiding by Arab forces that nibbled away relentlessly at Israeli resources—between 1967 and August 1970. They found both easy to deal with, at least until the last two days of that war, when they suddenly (and very unexpectedly) lost five Phantoms. General Peled recalled that:

> We took advice from the experts of Vietnam because we lost a couple of aircraft two weeks before that, and we didn't like it. So there was a scramble to find out, what is this magic called ECM pods? . . . They sent over pods and they [Americans] sent over their operational experts to show us how these magical instruments could protect you from the wrath of the missiles—if only you flew the correct formation. You have a pod, it radiates, it spoofs, it jams, and if you're in the right relative positions . . . you're immune, like Superman. That's why we lost those five. We took a recipe. It's the one thing we shouldn't have done—take recipes from another world, another situation where the USAF never had to face anything more complicated than SA–2As and Bs. We were faced with a mix of SA–2As and SA–3s and SA–2s improved. A cocktail.[56]

Chel Ha'Avir had, in fact, come up against an ongoing problem of electronic warfare—the speed at which countermeasures [ECM] and counter-countermeasures [ECCM] may be introduced into the combat equation without any warning—and the way such measures can radically alter the battlefield balance if they are not continually matched and combated by new tactics. In this case, the American system was one step behind. Their ECM pods could neutralize older target-finding and missile guidance systems, but not the newer systems the Egyptians were now using. Yet the need for air superiority over the battlefield, the prerequisite of effective interdiction and close air support, demanded that the missiles be defeated.

Meanwhile, Israeli airmen were trying to solve some of the problems of air-ground coordination on an organizational level. Each of the Army's front commanders had been given an Air Adviser with his own Command and Control Center, and each divisional commander was allocated an Air Coordinator "drawn mainly from the senior aircrew officers of the air force reserves."[57] Ground commanders would plan their battles in close conjunction with their air adviser—likely to be a recently retired and very senior air officer—using the latter's expertise in more or less the same way that they would that of their artillery advisers. Once the plan was settled, the Air Command and Control Center would be responsible for implementing the aspects of it, just as an artillery staff would be responsible for an artillery fire plan. Units and sub-units would use their own commanders or artillery observers as ground-based FACs, with the coordinator assigning aircraft to them in accordance with priorities established by the divisional commander. Front commanders and their air advisers would normally be within speaking distance of each other, divisional commanders and their coordinators would be as close as the operational situation permitted—perhaps in neighboring vehicles—and at every level of command air–ground communications would be monitored by the next higher level, both as a means of "reading" the battle, and for rapid redeployment of aircraft according to the exigencies of the situation.[58]

As Israelis brooded over the missile threat, modified their ECM pods, and experimented with a new ground–air control structure, Egyptians and Syrians continued developing their air defenses with the addition of medium-range, mobile (although it took several hours to recalibrate after a move), and faster SA–6, and also the portable, infrared homing SA–7. Together, these various antiaircraft weapons-systems provided an interlocking coverage over slant ranges to 25 miles, and from nap-of-the-earth up to 50,000 feet. At the very bottom of this spectrum in terms of range, but close to the top in terms of killing power, as events were soon to show, was the radar-predicted and -controlled ZSU–23/4, consisting of four 23–mm automatic guns in combination, effective to 2,000 yards.

The Egyptians were estimated to have 2,880 SAM-launching systems (800 SA–2Bs and –3s, 80 SA–6s, 2,000 of the new SA–7s) and 2,750 antiaircraft guns, including 150 ZSU–23/4s. The Syrians had 2,360 launchers (1,300 SA–2As and –Bs and SA–3s, 60 SA–6s, 1,000 SA–7s) and 1,900 AA guns, including 100 ZSU–23/4s. (The total of SA–7 missiles equated exactly to the number of launchers, but the number of other missiles—those mounted on vehicles in batteries of eight—was considerably larger than the number of their launchers). This missile and gun antiaircraft screen might enable the Arabs to achieve air superiority over the battlefield without engaging in air-to-air combat, a field in which they could not contest the Israelis.

Thus in 1973 *Chel Ha'Avir* was faced with a new threat that it suspected might significantly alter the course of the air war. Had the Israelis decided upon a first strike, as in 1967, Arab missile screens would have been their chosen target. Enemy aircraft were now dispersed and well-protected while on the ground; and there was virtually no hope of causing comparable damage and disruption to Arab airfields, since missiles would grossly complicate attaining air superiority. According to Peled:

> We had well-made, sophisticated, complicated, well orchestrated operational plans to knock out the total missile force along the canal—106 batteries. . . . You could equate it to a huge Cecil DeMille type of spectacle, or a huge musical show. It had an overture, it had a backdrop, it had lighting, it had many other conditions to it. Had all the conditions existed to run the show it would have been a huge success. Within half a day, there would have been no more missiles at all.[59]

A questionable claim, perhaps, but never tested, because for political reasons there could be no first strike. Any repetition of 1967 might inflame public opinion in the West, especially in the United States, then the Israelis' sole source of sophisticated weapon systems. This time the Arabs must be seen as the aggressors; even a precautionary mobilization was delayed as long as possible in order to avoid accusations of provoking an attack. If all went well, the Army would be mobilized in time, but *Chel Ha'Avir*, with its relatively large cadre of regulars, required only a small number of reserves to bring it to a war footing. (They were called up on October 4.) It would have to bear much of the early burden if there were the slightest miscalculation. That, however, was part of the rationale for creating and maintaining a strong air force from the very beginning.

There was such a miscalculation. Early in the morning of October 6—*Yom Kippur* or the Day of Atonement—Israeli intelligence reported that an attack would come at 1800, and partial mobilization was ordered; but at 1405 hrs Egyptians attacked the Bar-Lev line, along the east bank of the Suez Canal, while Syrians struck on the Golan. Initially, the Egyptian assault seemed more dangerous. Most of *Chel Ha'Avir* was armed for a preemptive strike on the Syrian missile screen (since conditions of light and shadow made it advisable to attack Syrian batteries in the early evening, Egyptians in the early morning), and weapon loads had to be changed and new briefings given. The first priority was to secure Israeli air space, the second to deal with Egyptian aircraft attacking targets in the Sinai.[60] Only then could airmen turn their full attention to supporting Bar-Lev line defenders along the Canal. Isolated, sporadic Israeli air attacks began half an hour after the opening of the Egyptian offensive, but strikes in force did not really begin until shortly after 1600 hrs, according to Dupuy.[61] Then, according to Hanoch Bartov, biographer of Israeli Chief of Staff David Elazar, "the air force's experience during the afternoon hours of Yom Kippur had been daunting. Not only had three planes been lost, but the aircraft were forced to keep a safe distance from the missiles, rendering their bombing of the Egyptian forces imprecise and its impact marginal."[62]

All the Egyptian missile batteries and ZSU–23/4s were still on the west bank of the Canal, but SA–7s in the vanguard of the attack struck many of the slower Skyhawks with infrared homing guidance. They went straight for the tailpipes of Israeli planes, but their light, 3½–pound warhead usually only damaged their targets. By nightfall there would be a line of Skyhawks on each Israeli air base waiting for tailpipe repairs or for another twenty-seven inches of pipe to be welded on to narrow the cone of radiation (making hits more difficult to achieve or to minimize the effect of any hits that might be made). A hit by heavier missiles almost always resulted in the loss of the airplane, and soon the SA–7s would be coming in salvos or ripples, making them that much more dangerous.

Israeli strongholds along the Canal "asked for, and got, air strikes, bu. these had little effect," recalled Bren Adan in his account of the southern campaign.[63] The inevitable "pucker factor"—the instinct for survival—meant that Israeli airmen were flying their CAS missions with less than their customary precision. Without effective air support, the Bar-Lev line could not hold, and most of the forward strongpoints had to be abandoned to their fates, the survivors eventually becoming prisoners of war.

There were about 200 Israeli tanks on the 40 miles of the Golan front when the Syrians attacked with more than 1,200 tanks and most of their 300 combat aircraft, backed by "close to 600 artillery pieces, at least 400 antiaircraft guns, and more than 100 batteries of SA-2, SA-3, and SA-6 surface-to-air missiles, with between 400 and 500 launchers."[64] Roughly two-thirds of the Syrian force was directed south of Al-Kuneitra, where the Israelis had only 90 tanks and 44 guns to cover a front of 27 miles.

The Israelis gave little ground until dark. However, they were unable to match the night-fighting effectiveness of superior Syrian materiel and by midnight had lost nearly half of their tanks. By morning of the seventh, three columns of Syrian armor were within nine miles of Lake Kinneret (the Sea of Galilee). Peled, now the Commander of *Chel Ha'Avir*, planned to hit the Egyptian missile screen in the dawn hours:

> [T]he priorities had shifted from midnight Saturday to Sunday morning, to the Golan Heights. The air force was poised to deliver that musical show and actually the first two parts of the overture were delivered, only I had to discontinue that. . . . The Defense Minister phoned me and said, "Benny, leave Sinai, it's of no importance right now, its only sand. It's 200-odd kilometers from Israel. We have a problem right on our doorstep, so just drop everything." So we discontinued the musical show.[65]

The switch presented a marvelous example of the flexibility of air power and its battlefield mobility, but the Israelis were nevertheless still dancing to an Arab tune. Instead of concentrating on the destruction of SAM batteries, which were denying them air superiority where it counted—at low level over the battlefield—the Israeli airmen were compelled to strike Syrian armor, while desperate efforts were made to get more ground forces into the battle. "Motti" Hod, now an Air Force reservist, had been appointed air adviser to the Northern Front Commander. He later reported: "From the first section of airplanes that appeared on the Golan Heights in the Yom Kippur War, I immediately saw that the tactics which we thought could be used there could not be used. And this was because, when the Skyhawks arrived, simultaneously we saw over fifty ground-to-air missiles in the air at one time. Over fifty on a very, very narrow strip of land."[66]

The scale of the missile assault gave Hod an idea.

> The decision that I made, and employed there, was to try and draw out the maximum amount of missiles from their batteries, to drain them dry before air power could be implemented effectively. . . . All the air force could have done—and did—through Sunday and Monday, to lunch time, was to drain dry the air defense system of the Syrians. And they were not clever enough to understand what we did. They kept on shooting and I kept on using tactics just to draw missiles, and threw bombs just to have an effect on the Syrian ground forces by noise, but not doing any damage. Just psychological effect. And by noon Monday they stopped shooting. We did some experiments. No more missiles. Then the air force started to be effective in the ground battle.[67]

On Monday morning, the Egyptians in the south apparently were using their missiles more selectively, but between 1300 and 1600, when GHQ became quite worried about the amount of enemy armor crossing the Canal, *Chel Ha'Avir* managed to break all fourteen floating bridges across it, losing only three aircraft. According to Peled, "The effectiveness of air power against the ground depends on one thing: that you know in real time where the target is and how long it will be there."[68] Consequently, although they could easily be repaired, for General El Shazli "the state of our bridges became of real concern . . . enemy air strikes had damaged so many of our bridge sections that we had [already] lost the equivalent of three complete bridges. We were reduced to three bridges in reserve."[69] Of course the Israelis did not know that at the time, or they would doubtless have continued to attack them relentlessly.

Technically, although they were no more than six or seven miles behind the Egyptian front line, the bridges were targets for tactical interdiction rather than for CAS, and so were the massive traffic jams that occasionally built up at the approaches. They are outside the scope of this study but provide superb examples of the importance and problems of real-time intelligence. The air commander knew that the bridges were there—ground and air forces had reported them—and so ordered his airmen to attack them. He never knew, however, about the traffic jams. His reconnaissance aircraft had photographed them (some of the pictures are reproduced in *Chel Ha'Avir*'s public relations account of the war),[70] but the photographs were passed directly to the army, and communication between air and ground staffs failed dismally in the heat of battle. In Peled's words:

> Who took the pictures? Israeli aircraft. Were they used? No. When did we see them? Two weeks after the war. Now just imagine if I had been entrusted, as a prime contractor, to destroy ground forces as a prime mission, as I am entrusted to destroy air forces; then I would have had to have ways and means to know [about the jams] in time. The whole intelligence structure of the air force was not oriented even to have a look at what belonged to the ground forces.[71]

Even though, as we have noted, the operations staffs of the Army and Air Force had been effectively integrated at the command and control level to the extent that they were housed in one operations room since the later 1950s, apparently there were great gaps on the intelligence side.

Some internal command and control problems also developed under the stresses of battle, despite the reforms of late 1972 and early 1973. "As dawn broke, our airplanes started attacking the enemy in my sector," noted Bren Adan, now commanding a division in the Sinai. "From time to time, unfortunately, they also attacked Natke's brigade. [Col] Natke [Baram] reported seeing enemy tanks two kilometers west of him. I . . . was begging Southern Command to let my own forward air controllers coordinate the air strikes in my sector, since they were with the attacking forces and could handle it the best; but headquarters did not accede to this request."[72] The FACs, well able to "read" the battle on their own small front, were denied control, presumably by the air adviser at Southern Command or even by a decision in Tel Aviv. Theory called for control to be delegated to the level at which it could best be exercised, but in this case at least, principle was abrogated under the pressure of events. Maj. Gen. Shmuel Gonen, GOC Southern Command, was just then being told by Adan that:

> I needed air support very badly. I [Adan] was astonished when he told me that I was *getting* air support. I said I was unaware of this and pointed out that my air support liaison officer [Air Coordinator?] had just been told by his (Gonen's) own staff that my requests could not be complied with. Gonen . . . answered that due to the difficult circumstances, the Israeli Air Force was operating by means of a special technique and therefore would not be able to let my own forward controllers direct the strikes supporting my units.[73]

The nature of this "special technique" has never been revealed, but it seems likely that the expression was simply an excuse to hoard air resources, while senior officers puzzled over the problem of dealing with the Egyptian missile screen. The weight of the EAF was still being held back from the ground battle and interception duties over the battlefield,[74] so that Gonen's cryptic response can best be interpreted as an unwilling tribute to the effectiveness of the ground-based air defenses that were being brought to bear against Israeli air operations three to seven miles east of the Canal. Already, in the first forty-eight hours of fighting the Israelis had lost about forty aircraft, which Armitage and Mason suggest "may be represented either as "approximately three percent of attack sorties flown, or two percent of all sorties flown or, rather more meaningfully, forty percent of all losses throughout the war or fourteen percent of the front-line combat strength of the IAF."[75]

Reputable writers have suggested that the Israelis lost as many as eighty machines in the first three days,[76] thus nearly doubling that loss rate, but that seems unlikely. Nor is it possible to attribute a proportion of losses to any particular weapon system. In any case, "the impact of each weapon was enhanced by its cooperation with others, both of the same kind with complementary field of fire, and of a different kind with a complementary altitude or acquisition system."[77]

There can be no doubt that the Israelis, overconfident, initially underestimated the capabilities of the integrated Arab air defenses. Cockpit warning signals that a missile had been fired became virtually useless when several missiles were in the air at once. There was scarcely time to visually mark and mentally assess each missile threat and then take selective action to avoid them. ECM—chaff, jamming, spoofing, and diversion—could affect a range of radar frequencies, but not always and not all when several types of missiles were in the air simultaneously, some of them "frequency hopping" as they homed on their targets. Heat flares, which were used to deceive infrared homing devices, now failed against "filtered" guidance systems; and close to the ground, where a pilot might be driven to fly in avoiding missiles, there was the threat of ZSU–23/4s. The combination of missile and gun was deadly against low-flying aircraft, and as plane after plane went down, the inevitable "pucker factor" detracted from pilot performance, making for less effective intervention in the ground battle at greater cost.

It was becoming apparent that there were now two kinds of air superiority, one at low and medium altitudes and one at medium and high altitudes. Up in the "wild blue yonder," *Chel Ha'Avir* was still the undisputed master, but it no longer achieved air superiority. It was also questionable whether it could even retain air parity when ground fire entered the equation.

Direct attacks on the missile sites themselves hardly seemed an answer, unless there was an immediate prospect of occupying the ground they stood on. The controlling ground radars of the SA–2s and –3s were in hardened bunkers, with only their antennae exposed, and launchers and antennae could always be replaced under cover of darkness. The mobility of the SA–6 created a significant problem for real-time intelligence, even though when a battery moved it took several hours to set up again and recalibrate its acquisition and tracking radars. Moreover, all the fixed sites were mutually supporting, making even concentrated air attacks very questionable. Assaults on them would have to wait on a combined air–ground offensive, and the Israeli Army was not yet in position to launch a meaningful one. In the meantime, the Egyptian ground forces were only in danger from the air when they moved out from under their air defense umbrella.

They made that mistake on October 9, when their 1st Infantry Brigade started along the lightly held[78] Red Sea shore toward the oil fields of Abu Rudeis. The Egyptian Chief of Staff complained:

> Having captured Ayoun Mousa, the brigade had been ordered to advance through the night of 10/11 to capture [Ras] Sudr, the next stepping stone down the coast. The brigade commander had taken it upon himself to set out a few hours before sunset. The inevitable followed. In open country, outside the protection of our SAMs, the brigade was routed by the enemy air force. Not a single enemy tank or field piece fired a shot. The decisiveness of the encounter was a reminder, if we needed one, of how open our ground forces were to air attack the moment they left our SAM umbrella. . . . The mauling had destroyed it as a fighting unit for several days.[79]

In the north, the battle was turned by a chance application of CAS, in the opinion of General Hod an application that could hardly have been successful if the Syrian missile screen had still been stocked and intact. Some Phantoms assigned to bomb Damascus found their targets clouded over and were diverted to Hod's tactical use on the Golan. "The situation on the ground was stalemate . . . nobody could do anything," but Hod "talked eight of the Phantoms to a pinpoint attack on . . . part of a Syrian armored division . . . and we broke the morale of that Syrian division with those eight Phantoms."[80] Nearly 130,000 pounds of airborne ordnance, carefully applied, can have a dramatic effect on an exhausted armored brigade. Hushniyah, the administrative and logistical center for the Syrians on the Golan, fell the next day.

In the Sinai, the change was slower in coming. The initiative only shifted on October 14, when the Egyptians responded to a Syrian appeal for help to reduce Israeli pressure on the northern front by opening a four-pronged offensive. Although "east of the Canal fourteen surface-to-air batteries were set up, including six batteries of the SAM–6 variety,"[81] not all the Egyptian leaders thought that was a good idea. "The enemy air force can still cripple our ground forces as soon as they poke their noses beyond our SAM umbrella," argued their Chief of Staff El Shazli. "We don't have enough Quadrats (SAM–6) to give mobile protection to our forces in the open. Advance and we destroy our troops without offering any significant relief to our brothers the Syrians."[82]

He was overruled on political grounds, and *Chel Ha'Avir* regained enough air superiority in the absence of a really massive, integrated, antiaircraft screen to pound the Egyptians unmercifully in the largest tank battle since Kursk in 1943. "October 14th was the war's first black day for the Egyptian army," concluded General El Shazli. "It is estimated to have lost between 200 and 250 tanks in armored battles and another few dozen to the Israeli air force."[83] Trevor Dupuy has noted, however, that "the Israelis did not pursue the battered Egyptian columns as they withdrew; the apparent failure was perhaps due to the inability of the IAF to carry its tactical air

Russian-built SA-2 surface-to-air missile

support into the SAM "box," and the unwillingness of the Israelis to expose themselves to Egyptian defensive A[nti] T[ank] fire without such support."[84]

Nevertheless, the Egyptians were left discouraged and somewhat disorganized by the failure of the attack. Most importantly, their Second Army's one armored division, which posed a major threat to any Israeli counterattack designed to carry them across the canal in the vicinity of Deversoir, had been badly damaged. For the moment it was something less than fully effective. Israeli ground forces seized their opportunity and launched a counterattack just before dusk on the fifteenth, when the onset of darkness would enable them to operate effectively without much direct air support. It was split into two thrusts: a diversionary one that hooked north along the east bank of the canal towards the so-called "Chinese Farm," apparently in an attempt to roll up the flank of the Egyptian Second Army, and a main one designed to carry them across the canal.

By first light on the 17th, the Israelis were across the canal in force, and their airmen, at last, could look forward to regaining air superiority achieved for them by the ground forces, which had a whole battalion of 175–mm guns ferried across the canal by noon![85] The bridgehead was no more than 1,400–1,800 yards deep, and the single ferry linking it to the east bank was still far from secure. Heavy artillery of that caliber would normally be at least 6,000 yards behind a firm line, but their need for effective air support and the inability of the Air Force to deliver it until the missile screen was suppressed led the ground forces to take risks. With tanks firing on the closest missile sites—and subsequently overrunning them—the big guns pounded more distant ones out to a range of 20–plus miles, blasting a massive hole in the screen.

By noon on the seventeenth, *Chel Ha'Avir* was "carrying out hundreds of sorties against Egyptian armor, missile batteries, and the Kutmiyeh airfield, as well as providing support for the ground forces," writes General Elazar's biographer, Hanoch Bartov. Reporting to the Israeli Cabinet on the evening of the eighteenth, General Elazar announced that "of the fifty-four surface-to-air missile batteries that were operating there [in the vicinity of Deversoir] a few days ago, only twenty are left."[86] The next morning at a staff conference, "Dado [Elazar] holds that once a fair proportion of the surface-to-air missiles are wiped out, the air force can go into higher gear *and its activity will govern how far the ground forces succeed*."[87] [emphasis added]

As *Chel Ha'Avir* once again intervened in the ground battle, the rate of Egyptian collapse did indeed speed up. General Adan's division, driving south from Deversoir towards Suez, found that:

> Beginning at 0900 [22 Oct] we received artillery and air support. For the first time I was able to allocate planes to each of my brigades at the same time, and, generally, in a continuous manner. . . . At 0904 hours, [the Egyptian] Third Army reported that the enemy was attacking the entire zone of operations of the army as well as its headquarters in strength from the air; the communications systems had been hit and his control

capacity damaged. The 7th [Egyptian] Infantry Division, east of the canal, also reported that it was being hard hit from the air. . . . Over and over again our planes attacked the Egyptian tanks. Their crews could be seen evacuating the tanks, running off, and then returning. The same was the case with the antiaircraft units (23–mm guns) that were deployed near the tanks.[88]

Adan's air liaison officer "operated within the forward command group, alongside the artillery liaison officer. . . . Calmly, efficiently, he requested and distributed squadrons to the brigade, and when things got crowded above us, he sent planes to bomb the greenbelt [along the Sweetwater canal] and even [Egyptian positions] east of the Canal."[89] But Benny Peled concluded:

This better system did not work well, either. Some elements of it started to have some results after we became complete masters of the tactical situation on the ground and we started to dictate to a broken enemy. . . . We beefed up the doctrinal system with the best officers, equipment and detailed procedures. We gave them more authority and still it did not function in the most critical times of the ground battle, which are exactly the times when air blows delivered on time and on real information may reap the most benefit and destroy the most enemy.[90]

Even at the highest levels, the command and control system did not always work, presumably because of a technical "glitch" in communication, or through some genuine misunderstanding, or—given the severity of the missile threat—perhaps because the Air Staff sometimes chose to turn a deaf ear. On October 19, when the bridgehead on the west bank of the Canal was still critically small, *Zahal*'s Chief of Staff complained that his air arm had failed to carry out instructions that would prevent the Egyptian Army from manning a series of positions that dominated the Suez–Cairo road. Elazar was convinced that "they're going to build a disposition around us. . . . But there was only one missile battery there! . . . We might have lost a plane or two, but there wouldn't have been any disposition there. That was the first time I said to the air force people: You didn't do exactly what I asked."[91]

Much has been made of the fact that Israeli "ground soldiers note that not a single Arab tank that came into their possession (more than 1,500) was unequivocally damaged or destroyed by air weapons."[92] Colonel Yoash Tsiddon-Chatto was, by 1973, "in charge of the air force team . . . that looked into the validity of weapons efficiency in the air-to-ground business[:]"

Coming to tank destruction. . . . I found quite a few hits from iron bombs, that I relate mostly to the few Skyhawks with a weapons delivery [navigation] system that was nowhere near what we have today . . . very few rockets and the tremendous efficiency of the Rockeye, the anti-armor C[luster] B[omb] U[nits]. I found penetration even on the slope of the turret in front. . . . A few intelligent bombs were used—Walleye, etc. But all of them [the tanks] had been hit by ground-based fire as well, and which struck first we can not know.[93]

On the evening of October 22, a UN-sponsored cease-fire was scheduled to take effect, but the Israelis were in no hurry to lose the initiative they had so painfully acquired. Moshe Dayan, visiting Adan, announced that he wanted Zidon, eighteen miles away, before agreeing to the cease-fire. Adan was ready and willing to oblige, basing his assessment of the situation on two factors: "First, we were now getting close support from the air force, which was increasing in intensity moment by moment; I assumed that this air support would soon bring about a cumulative effect that would leave its mark on the battlefield. And the second factor was the terrain."[94]

Meanwhile, Maj. Gen. Mohammed Abdul el Moneim Wassel, commanding the Egyptian Third Army, "was constantly complaining to the minister of war that the enemy was making air attacks relentlessly, that he had no more Strela [SA–7] missiles left, and that he urgently needed his own air umbrella."

His words were picked up by Israeli communications intelligence, and *Chel Ha'Avir*, reinforcing success, put more and more effort into CAS. The only hiccough came as Libyan Mirages joined the battle, attacking some of Adan's men on the Havit road, and the Israelis had to turn briefly to the old-fashioned way of achieving air superiority. "We are not getting air support just now," noted Adan, "because they [the Air Force] are busy in a mass air battle with Mirages."[95]

Fighting continued through the 23d, with the airmen flying 354 sorties and "air support playing a decisive role"[96] as the Israelis expanded their west bank bridgehead towards Ismailia in the north, to Suez in the south, and westwards to Kilometer 101 on the Cairo road, building a salient in Africa more than 12 miles deep in places. Eventually a second cease-fire was negotiated—and then a third and a fourth—as the Yom Kippur war slowly wound down. Finally, a cease-fire was held, and at 1015 on October 25, 1973, the Israeli High Command's operations center in Tel Aviv—the Pit—ceased to function.

Air-to-air combat in 1973 demonstrated that despite its numerical inferiority *Chel Ha'Avir* was still capable of establishing traditional air superiority. However, in the initial stages of the campaign the Israelis were not able to suppress ground-based missile fire and therefore could not achieve low-level air superiority over the battlefield, a failure that cost them dearly by seriously inhibiting interdiction and CAS capability through much of the action. The great unanswered question was whether their planned, but never attempted, preemptive strikes on the Arab missile screens would have been successful.

The war divided into three phases from a CAS point of view. During the first three days, about 50 aircraft—13 or 14 percent of *Chel Ha'Avir*'s original combat strength in fighters and fighter-bombers—were lost, and perhaps an equal number damaged, in desperate but probably cost-effective (at least on the Golan) efforts to stem the Arab tide. The next ten or eleven days were marked by different patterns in the north and south, directly related to the handling of missile screens by the enemy. On the Golan, reckless expenditures of missiles created a resupply problem, which the Israelis exacerbated by interdiction bombing of Syrian airfields to hinder the Russian airlift ferrying in new stocks. Before more missiles could be deployed, the Israelis had destroyed enough radars and launchers to make it impossible for the Syrians to re-create the kind of integrated, interlocking system they needed to make good use of the replacements.

In the south, where the Egyptians handled their missile stocks in a more disciplined fashion, the Israelis were compelled to use close air support with great caution and relative ineffectiveness, as long as the enemy stayed under the shield provided by his missile screen. Eventually the crossing of the canal enabled joint air–ground operations to blast a hole in the screen. Losses, in this second phase, were in the "acceptable" range of twenty or twenty-five aircraft. Moreover, once the Egyptian screen had been breached, CAS regained its expected significance on the battlefield, playing a major if not decisive role in the expansion of the bridgehead and the destruction of a large part of the Egyptian Third Army at a cost of no more than fifteen aircraft.

Emphasizing that none of the many published analyses is based on entirely reliable figures—those that follow are an amalgam that owes much to the author's subjective judgments—it seems likely that *Chel Ha'Avir* flew between 10,000 and 11,000 fighter and fighter-bomber sorties during the war and lost about 103 of the aircraft involved for an overall (and mathematically convenient) loss rate of 1 or 1.1 percent compared with .89 percent in the 1967 campaign. Peled, who apparently did not include suppression of missile screens as part of the air-superiority mission, has said that only 5 machines were lost in 4,000 air-superiority sorties. If we deduct another 8 lost through air collision, "friendly" fire, and pilot error (the figure may well have been higher), it follows that overall about 90 were lost in the course of some 7,000 sorties[97] (including missile suppression, interdiction, and close air support) for a loss rate of 1.27 percent. Any further breakdown is impossible, but by comparison in 1967 the loss rate was about 2.0 percent.

A different picture emerges, however, if we look only at the first three days of the 1973 campaign. Fifty machines lost in the course of 1,220 sorties[98] gave a loss rate of 4.1 percent, a rate that no air force—least of all *Chel Ha'Avir*—can afford for very long. Any defense system capable of inflicting such losses must be suppressed quickly or the air arm will be unable to play a part in the land battle.

Breaking down losses by mission-type into losses by cause as well is even more difficult given the limited data. Of the 90-odd fixed-wing machines that fell to ground-based fire of one kind or another, perhaps 70 or more were victims of the combination of SA–6 and –7s and ZSU–23/4s, and a high proportion of them would have been engaged in tactical interdiction or close support. It seems possible that the ZSUs accounted for the majority of these, at least until the missile screens were breached, "because the threat from the SA–6 forced the pilots to fly at low altitudes." After that, the SA–6s were probably more successful, but one authority argues that "the results obtained with the Soviet SA–6 *Gainful* missile in the Yom Kippur War were equally [with the Vietnam experience of SA–2s] unimpressive. . . . As far as can be ascertained from the figures available, an average of 55 [SA–6] missiles was required per kill. SA–6 consumption was therefore of the same order of magnitude as that of the SA–2 in Vietnam. The advantages of the more modern system were obviously counterbalanced by the difficulties involved in hitting a low flying target."[99]

Speed was probably another important survival factor. The bulk, if not all, of CAS sorties were flown by A–4 Skyhawks and the much faster F–4 Phantoms. The IAF lost 53 out of a total of 170 of the former (American resupply added 20 to the original 150 after October 9) and 33 out of a total 177 of the latter (resupply added 37 but probably not all got into action). Of course, the Phantoms also had better built-in ECM.

Three other points seem worth making from the close air support perspective. First, missiles and radar-controlled gun systems depend very heavily upon state-of-the-art electronics rather than human effort, skill, and judgment, and the nature of applied science and technology suggests that the advantage of more sophisticated technology on one side will rarely last long. It will inevitably be matched or surpassed by countermeasures on the other side. Second, ground-based antiaircraft screens are, by definition, pinned in place and therefore relatively immobile and inflexible in air terms. The essence of the Arab antiaircraft defenses in 1973 was their integrated, interlocking, mutually supporting nature. That was also their great weakness. Overall, they lacked mobility, and any ground troops relying on their protection to frustrate Israeli CAS could only advance in very slow, measured bounds. Dupuy quotes an Egyptian divisional commander: "When we tried to move out beyond the SAM umbrella, we took unacceptable losses from the Israeli Air Force."[100]

The last point concerns the long-standing doctrinal relationship between *Chel Ha'Avir* and the ground battle. "The doctrine of the air force supporting in the role of destroying ground forces is false," says Peled. "With the advent of the *Yom Kippur* war we have changed the wording . . . slightly. I changed it from 'supporting the ground forces' to 'participating in the ground battle.'" But he still believes that that is not enough.

The Air Force should have four prime missions: (1) Overcome enemy air forces; (2) defend your own airspace; (3) destroy ground and sea forces; and (4) destroy strategic targets. "These are the basic premises for which an air force exists. And why? Because the atmosphere [air] is spread evenly over ground and over the sea. So if you ask me, 'What is the role of an air force—an atmospheric air force?' I would say very simply to wage warfare within the airspace."[101]

524

Whatever the doctrinal handicaps that *Chel Ha'Avir* may labor under, it can still intervene successfully in the ground battle, and on occasion, engage in close air support, as it did in the June 1982 Lebanon campaign, without incurring losses. The situation then was probably not typical—an "isolated group of missiles in a very, very unfavorable geographic area from the missile point of view, because of the mountains," says "Motti" Hod,[102] but one of his officers has rightly confirmed that *"Chel Ha'Avir* became free when we blasted the missiles away."[103]

The Israelis were still flying Phantoms and Skyhawks for tactical interdiction and close support missions, supplemented by their "home-grown" Kfir C–2 fighter-bomber and Bell AH–1 Huey Cobra and Hughes 5000 Defender attack helicopters, all of them boasting vastly improved Weapons Delivery Navigation Systems (WDNSs) and "black boxes" ("an ounce of ECM is worth a pound of additional aircraft."[104]) They used Remotely Piloted Vehicles (RPVs), Precision Guided Missiles (PGMs), and Improved Conventional Munitions to achieve their objectives. The acquisition of real-time intelligence was finally possible as the air force used RPVs equipped with television cameras and transmitters to locate targets, guide the pilots to them, and monitor the damage inflicted.

Some RPVs carried laser designators to illuminate the target for PGMs. In other cases, information was almost certainly transmitted directly to an aircraft's WDNS by digital data link from air liaison officers in armored vehicles on the ground. At the other end of the command and control spectrum, *Chel Ha'Avir*'s commander at the time, General David Ivry, said that he was able to exercise personal control over every Israeli aircraft in Lebanese air space, presumably from his CP in "the Pit" in Tel Aviv.[105]

It also seems likely that, as in the Suez crossing of 1973, there was a close and effective degree of cooperation between air and ground forces with long-range Israeli artillery—175–mm guns and 290–mm rockets—playing a significant part in destroying the missile screen.

In 1973 the Air Force used helicopters mainly for moving ground troops, casualty evacuation, and resupply. But one of the lessons of *Yom Kippur* was that there was a need for both scout and strike helicopters in the tactical inventory. Particularly, as Col. Tsiddon-Chatto points out: ". . . when you pass to using the topography as your main factor for survivability, you can slow down, you can land, you can coordinate, you can . . . supply your own [real-time] intelligence."[106] Both scout and strike helicopters were used successfully in Lebanon. Altogether, the air force flew about 2,000 close support sorties during the campaign, and only 2 fixed-wing and 6 rotary-wing machines were lost, less than .5 percent of sorties flown.

For their own particular environment—one with climate and terrain well suited to the use of tactical air power—the Israelis have, over the past twenty years, evolved an effective system for command and control of close

A display of the ordnance packages available for the Israeli-designed C-2 Kfir shows its capacity for close air support.

air support. Details of it are still largely classified, and it is a subject that Israeli airmen are reluctant to talk about, but individual comments and analysis permit the outlines of the 1980 system to be sketched in.

The allocation of close air-support resources is determined at the highest level in a combined ground/air operations center at General Headquarters, presumably still in Tel Aviv. This ensures a high degree of synchronization with ground forces operations (although it did break down at least once in 1973). The application of CAS is controlled, initially, through a centralized

Air Force staff carrying out the orders emanating from GHQ by allocating resources to specific theaters or impending operations. In a theater, an air adviser is responsible for advising the front commander where and when it may best be used, and then for implementing the latter's decision. This step may be repeated by an Air Liaison Officer at a divisional level. Control is then decentralized through unit and subunit commanders, or their forward observation officers (artillery), or Forward Air Controllers (air) in order to direct the assignment effectively. The higher the level of command, the greater the flexibility of allocation of resources; the lower the level of control, the greater the flexibility of control over the actual combat missions.

The introduction of better, more reliable, real-time intelligence through RPVs and more complex and precise communication links (which, on the one hand, allow the commander in Tel Aviv to contact each individual pilot in the air and, on the other, can enable the RPV to "talk" by digital data link directly to an individual WDNS) have opened alternative, quicker means of achieving the same ends.

Israeli doctrine is clear. Provided that air superiority can be attained, then the preferred employment of tactical air resources is in interdiction. Speaking at a Tel Aviv symposium in October 1975, the late General David Elazar, *Zahal*'s Chief of Staff, accepted interdiction as his airmen's main task, declaring that "even before 1973 I considered the subject of close air support the last priority task of the Air Force,"[107] and adding that he believed Israeli ground forces, secure from the enemy's air activity, should be able to defeat their enemies unaided.

However, Israeli experience suggests that doctrine can conform and has conformed to circumstance. While interdiction generally pays a greater dividend at lesser risk in a Middle Eastern environment, close support was necessary to maintain the stability of the Syrian front in 1973 and, as Chaim Herzog pointed out in his excellent study of the campaign, "the main element in limiting the scope of the Egyptian operation was the Israeli Air Force. . . . It was the force that dictated the limits of the Egyptian advance, and this dictation would have been valid even if the Israeli Air Force had not made one pass over the battlefield."[108]

Except for reasons of prestige, it does not matter whether close air support comes in the guise of "supporting ground forces" or "participating in the ground battle." These are merely imperfect expressions of the same idea, the success of which depends upon the wholehearted acceptance of it by all the parties concerned. What does matter is that staff officers acquire a flexibility of thought and speed of decisionmaking that will enable them to recognize and seize the moment to pass over from interdiction to close support and back again and that the air force maintain sufficient flexibility in equipment and weapon systems and communications to execute these decisions quickly and effectively.

Notes

1. Mordechai Gichon, "The History of the Gaza Strip: A Geo-Political and Geo-Strategic Perspective," in *The Jerusalem Cathedra*, Nr 2–1982, p 284. On the other hand, Gichon notes that in the last 2,700 years there have been at least 40 attacks launched against Egypt by the same route, while the Egyptians were attacked from other directions only seven times.
2. See, for example, Mohammed H. Haykal, "The Arab War Aims," in *New Outlook*, (October–Nov 1973), p 20.
3. See Lt Col Amnon Gurion, "Israeli Military Strategy Up To The Yom Kippur war," in *Air University Review*, Vol XXXIII, Nr 6 (Sep–Oct, 1982; see also J. L. Wallach, "*Das Wehrkonzept und die Wehrstruktur Israels*," in *Truppenpraxis*, Nr 6 (Jun 1974).
4. Intvw with Maj Gen Dan Tolkovsky taped at Tel Aviv, Jan 13, 1984).
5. Edward Luttwak and Dan Horowitz, *The Israeli Army* (London, 1975), p 119.
6. Tolkovsky tape.
7. Murray Rubinstein and Richard Goldman, *The Israeli Air Force Story*, (London, 1979), pp 67–8.
8. Maj Gen Moshe Dayan, *Diary of the Sinai Campaign* (New York, 1966), p 209.
9. Intvw with Maj Gen Mordechai Hod, taped at Tel Aviv, 16 Jan 1984).
10. Dayan, pp 218 and 221.
11. Tolkovsky tape.
12. S.L.A. Marshall, *Sinai Victory* (New York, 1958), p 262.
13. Dayan, p 88.
14. T. N. Dupuy, *Elusive Victory*, (New York, 1978), p 169.
15. Robert Henriques, *One Hundred Hours to Suez*, (London, 1957), p 108.
16. Dayan, p 101.
17. Henriques, p 147.
18. Tolkovsky tape.
19. Alfred Goldberg, "Air Operations in the Sinai Campaign, 1956," unpublished paper in USAF Hist Div, Nov 1959. p 24.
20. Ltr, Maj Gen B. Peled to auth, 7 Jun 1984.
21. Dupuy, p 166.
22. Goldberg, p 22.
23. Henriques, p 157.
24. Marshall, p 261.
25. Dayan, p 133.
26. *Ibid*, p 143.
27. Marshall, p 262.
28. Goldberg, pp 40–41.
29. Edgar O'Ballance, *The Third Arab–Israeli War* (Hamden, 1972), p 50.
30. Dupuy, p 337.
31. Figures from Rubinstein and Goldman, pp 96–7.
32. Dupuy, p 337.
33. *Ibid*.
34. Tolkovsky tape.
35. O'Ballance, pp 108–9, 115 and 123.
36. *Ibid*, pp 114 and 133–4.
37. Quoted in *Ibid*, p 135 ff.
38. Intvw with Col Avrihu Ben-Nun taped at Hazor Air Base, Israel, 14 Nov 1978.
39. Israeli Operational Research map overlay, in possession of auth.
40. Intvw with Col Yoash Tsiddon-Chatto, taped at Tel Aviv, 14 Jan 1984.
41. Arye Hashavia, *A History of the Six Day War* (Tel Aviv: Ledory, nd), pp 294–5.
42. Dupuy, p 295.
43. *Ibid*, p 296.

44. Hashavia, pp 257–8.
45. King Hussein of Jordan, *My "War" With Israel* (New York, 1969), p 77.
46. O'Ballance, p 214.
47. Hod tape.
48. Peled ltr to auth.
49. Aharon Dolav, "A View from the Mountain," in *Ma'ariv*, 23 Jun 1967 (transl).
50. O'Ballance, p 257.
51. Quoted by R. M. Braybook, "Is it goodbye to Ground Attack?" *Air International* (May 1976), p 243.
52. Rubinstein and Goldman, p 78; O'Ballance, p 79.
53. Peled ltr to auth.
54. Dupuy, p 606.
55. Saad El Shazly, *The Crossing of the Suez* (San Francisco, 1980), pp 19–20 and 25.
56. Intvw with Maj Gen Benjamin Peled taped at Tel Aviv, 13 Jan 1984.
57. Peled ltr to auth.
58. Dupuy, p 608; Hod tape.
59. Peled tape.
60. Hassan El Badry, Taha El Magdoub, and Mohammed Dia El Din Zohdy, *The Ramadan War, 1973* (Dunn Loring, Va, 1978), pp 61–2. Hereafter cited as El Badry.
61. Dupuy, p 418.
62. Hannoch Bartov, *Dado: 48 Years and 20 Days* (Tel Aviv, 1981), p 310.
63. Maj Gen Avraham Adan, *On the Banks of the Suez* (San Rafael, Calif, 1980), p 25.
64. Dupuy, p 441.
65. Peled tape.
66. Hod tape.
67. *Ibid*.
68. Peled tape.
69. El Shazly.
70. Israeli Air Force Hq, *The Israeli Air Force in the Yom Kippur War*, (Israel, 1975), pp 11 and 13; see also El Shazly, p 239.
71. Peled tape.
72. Adan, p 119.
73. *Ibid*.
74. El Shazly, p 25.
75. M. J. Armitage and R. A. Mason, *Air Power In the Nuclear Age* (Urbana, Ill, 1983), p 127.
76. See, for example, Peter Borgart, "The Vulnerability of the Manned Airborne Weapon System—Pt 3, Influence on Tactics and Strategy," in *International Defense Review*, Vol 10, Nr 6 (Dec, 1977), p 1066.
77. Armitage and Mason, pp 127–8.
78. Adan, p 189.
79. El Shazly, pp 241–2.
80. Hod tape, quoted in Bartov, p 382.
81. Bartov, p 460.
82. El Shazli, p 246.
83. *Ibid*, p 461.
84. Dupuy, p 489.
85. Dupuy, p 503.
86. Bartov, p 499.
87. *Ibid*, pp 515 and 519.
88. Adan, pp 385–6.
89. *Ibid*, p 390.
90. Peled tape.
91. Bartov, p 526.
92. Dupuy, p 555.
93. Tsiddon-Chatto tape.
94. Adan, p 387.

95. *Ibid*, pp 390 and 393.
96. Bartov, p 557.
97. Ltr enclosure, Col T. N. Dupuy to auth, 25 Sep 1985.
98. *Ibid*.
99. P. Borgart, p 1064.
100. Dupuy, p 555.
101. Peled tape.
102. Hod tape.
103. Tsiddon-Chatto tape.
104. "Motti" Hod quoted in O'Ballance, *No Victor, No Vanquished*, p 306.
105. Ltr, Col T. N. Dupuy to auth, 25 Sep 1985.
106. Tsiddon-Chatto tape.
107. Quoted in M. J. Armitage and R. A. Mason, p 271.
108. Maj Gen Chaim Herzog, *The War of Atonement, Oct 1973* (Boston and Toronto, 1975), p 276.

Bibliographical Essay

Security is an obsession in the Middle East. Israeli archives are doubtless full of fascinating documents in a language that few gentiles, other than biblical scholars and certain archeologists, can understand. Yet an inability to read them is no handicap, since outsiders cannot obtain access to the documents. Every significant piece of paper generated on military matters since 1947 is still classified. Even such elementary statistics as the number of sorties flown remain profoundly secret.

Since the broad essentials and sequence of events of each campaign are a matter of common knowledge and secrets do not exist in a vacuum, the blanket of official security that envelops everything often serves only to prevent confirmation of certain facts. No doubt there are genuine secrets still to be unearthed, but meanwhile senior Israel officers are often willing to talk unofficially about many matters on which official sources are resolutely silent. It must be accepted that, consciously or unconsciously, these officers may not always be telling the truth, the whole truth, and nothing but the truth, but then, neither do many of the contemporary documents. And after recording such discussions, it is useful to check claims and criticisms against the contemporary public record and the statements of peers in autobiographical publications and such magisterial secondary studies as Trevor N. Dupuy's *Elusive Victory: The Arab–Israeli Wars, 1947–1974* (New York: Harper & Row, 1978).

Dupuy's book is as near as one can get to an official history of the Arab–Israeli wars. There are no truly official histories, either in Hebrew or English (or in Arabic, for that matter), not even of the War of Independence, which was fought more than 35 years ago with Second World War matériel and tactics. The closest that the Israelis have come to such a publication is a 120-page piece of public relations put out by Israeli Air Force Headquarters in February 1975 and entitled *The Air Force in the "Yom Kippur War"* (Israeli Ministry of Defence Publishing House), which is no more than a compendium of daily communiques.

Consequently, taped interviews and correspondence with three former commanders of *Chel Ha'Avir*, Dan Tolkovsky, Mordechai Hod, and Benjamin Peled, formed the basis of this study. A fourth former commander, Ezer Weizman, has also published his memoirs. The flamboyant Weizman, a flyer to his fingertips, did not, however, serve with the Air Force after he became chief of the Operations Branch of the Israeli General Staff in 1958. His *On Eagle's Wings* (London: Weidenfeld and Nicholson, 1976) is most valuable when he writes about the training of his pilots and the ethos he inculcated into them.

There are a number of other published first-person accounts, beginning with then Maj. Gen. Moshe Dayan's *Diary of the Sinai Campaign* (New York: Harper & Row, 1965). Dayan, of course, was not an airman either, but as *Zahal's* Chief of Staff in 1956, *Chel Ha'Avir* came under his command, and he has much to say about its performance. He has also commented on air aspects of the 1967 and 1973 campaigns in *Moshe Dayan: Story of My Life* (New York: William Morrow and Company, Inc., 1976), but understandably, there is little tactical detail. Nor is there much to be learned about air matters from Yitzhak Rabin's *The Rabin Memoirs* (Boston: Little, Brown, and Company, 1979), although Rabin was the Chief of Staff during the 1967 war.

Maj. Gen. Avraham "Bren" Adan gives us his account of the 1973 campaign in *On The Banks of The Suez* (San Rafael, Calif.: Presidio Press, 1980). The emphasis is on his differences with the southern front commander, Lt. Gen. Shmuel Gonen, and with fellow divisional commander Ariel Sharon, but because Adan's concern with applied air power is peripheral to his main thesis, his book is all the more valuable. It goes far toward clarifying *Chel Ha'Avir's* role in breaching the Egyptian missile screen while confirming, from a ground commander's point of view, the value of close air support once the missiles were defeated. In the same vein, Hanoch Bartov's biography of the late General David Elazar, *Dado: 48 Years and 20 Days* (Tel Aviv: Ma'ariv Book Guild, 1981) also looks at *Chel Ha'Avir* from an external perspective, illustrating almost in passing some of its warts as well as its beauty spots.

At a lower level, there are a number of first-person vignettes concerning the employment of close air support to be found in Israeli anthologies of the 1967 war, notably in Mordechai Barkai's *Written in Battle* (Tel Aviv: Le'Dory Publishing House, n.d.), prepared as a supplement to Arye Hashavia's excellent *History of the Six Day War* (Tel Aviv: Le'Dory Publishing House, n.d.). Hashavia is a former Air Force pilot.

On the "other side of the hill" we have nothing at all from the Syrians, but Lt. Gen. Saad El Shazly, who was the Egyptian Chief of Staff in 1973, paints a painfully frank picture of his forces' problems prior to, and during, the *Yom Kippur* War in his *The Crossing of the Suez* (San Francisco: American Mideast Research, 1980). His criticisms of the Egyptian Air Force are harsh but can readily be reconciled with events. The same cannot be said of Maj. Gens. Hassan El Badri, Taha El Magdoub, and Mohammed Zia El Din Zohdy in *The Ramadan War, 1973* (Dunn Loring, Virginia: T. N. Dupuy Associates, Inc., 1974); they carefully ignore facts that do not suit their theories and very often expound too much traditional Arab propaganda to be convincing. All the Egyptian authors are soldiers, not airmen.

King Hussein of Jordan can claim to be soldier, airman, and head of state, giving him an unrivaled perspective from which to write *My "War" With Israel* (New York: William Morrow and Company, Inc., 1969), a transparently honest account of Jordanian participation in the 1967 campaign that emphasizes the fearful damage to his army and air force by *Chel Ha'Avir's* interdiction campaign.

The essential underpinnings of the Israeli air arm are to be found in Edward Luttwak and Dan Horowitz, *The Israeli Army* (London: Allen Lane, 1975) and Gunther Rothenberg, *The Anatomy of the Israeli Army* (London: B.T. Batsford Ltd., 1979). Luttwak and Horowitz concentrate on the political, strategic, and tactical debates that shaped *Zahal* doctrine; Rothenberg is more concerned with structure and organization. Ze'ev Schiff's *A History of the Israeli Army (1870–1974)*, (San Francisco: Straight Arrow Books, 1974) has an interesting chapter on pilot training. Murray Rubinstein and Richard Goldman's *The Israeli Air Force Story* (London: Arms and Armor Press, 1979) emphasizes technology, design, and procurement, as does Bill Gunston's *An Illustrated Guide to the Israeli Air Force* (New York: Salamander Books, 1982).

In addition to Dupuy's excellent single-volume study of the Arab–Israeli wars, the equally prolific British author, Edgar O'Ballance, has produced five separate, slimmer volumes recounting the flow of operations in five separate campaigns. *The Third Arab–Israeli War* (Hamden, Conn.: Archon Books, 1972) deals with the 1967 campaign, while the 1973 fighting is described in *No Victor, No Vanquished: The Yom Kippur War* (San Rafael, California: Presidio Press, 1978). His account of *The Electronic War In The Middle East, 1968–70* (Hamden, Conn.; Archon Books, 1974) deals exclusively with the air aspects of the "War of Attrition" and is virtually the only work in its field outside of the periodical literature.

The doyen of modern military historians, S.L.A. Marshall, wrote perceptively about the 1956 war in *Sinai Victory* (New York: William Morrow & Co., 1958), paying appropriate attention to air aspects of the fighting. Hashavia's *History of the Six-Day War* has already been mentioned. From an air perspective there are really no other satisfactory accounts, although Peter Young's *The Israeli Campaign 1967* (London: William Kimber, 1967) has a few interesting pages outlining the Egyptian Air Force's intentions, had it not been destroyed on the ground before it could act. Ze'ev Schiff's *October Earthquake: Yom Kippur, 1973* (Tel Aviv: University Publishing Projects, 1974) can be balanced by D. K. Palit, *Return to Sinai: The Arab Offensive, 1973* (New Delhi: Palit and Palit, 1973). Palit is an Indian general who has many friends and contacts among the Egyptian and Syrian military and was on the scene soon after the fighting ended.

M. J. Armitage and R. A. Mason put the Middle Eastern experience of air power into a global context in *Air Power In the Nuclear Age* (Urbana, Illinois: University of Illinois Press, 1983), an excellent survey of the field. Lastly, there is a multitude of articles in popular periodicals—*Time*,

Newsweek, etc.—and technical journals such as *Aviation Week and Space Technology* and *International Defense Review*. There is much to be learned from a judicious study of the best of them, but they nearly all need to be read with an intensely critical eye. The paucity of precise information has often led authors to extrapolate from the known to the unknown, basing their arguments on incestuous uses of each other's speculations, until the end product becomes "received knowledge" that is not questioned.

11

A Retrospect on
Close Air Support

I. B. Holley, Jr.

Among military men it is a commonplace that interallied and interservice operations inescapably pose grave difficulties in execution. Differences in equipment, in doctrine, in attitude and outlook stemming from contrasting past experience all inhibit and complicate harmonious interaction. Past successes, however, have shown that these difficulties *can* be overcome where determination is present and effective procedures have been devised and applied by properly trained troops. Experience also shows that armed forces, not only of the United States but of other nations, have been slow to hammer out the necessary procedures. Often corrective steps have been achieved only after many failures in battle. In no area of interservice operations has this phenomenon been more pronounced than in the matter of close air support.

Surprisingly, the processes and procedures by which success was achieved, usually belatedly, in each war in which the United States had been engaged for more than two generations, were largely forgotten by the armed forces by the time they again became actively involved in fighting. This strongly indicates defects in the way the military establishment has provided itself with an institutional memory. More specifically, it indicates a failure to codify the necessary doctrines of close air support properly to pass on the tactics and techniques, the procedures, and indeed the attitudes found essential to support ground forces by Navy, Marine Corps, and Air Force aviation.

The history of close air support since World War I has been marked by tragedy—lives lost, unduly protracted conflict, and victory deferred—because both air and ground officers have too often failed to benefit as they might from history, from experience garnered and recorded by earlier generations of airmen. This repeated pattern of behavior gives credence to the cynical observation that the only thing we learn from history is that we don't. The literature on close air support is extensive, but even if one were to pursue the subject no further than the chapters presented in this book, it should be possible to distill enough insights to lay a solid foundation for a viable system.

Anyone who has carefully read the foregoing chapters should already have more or less reached conclusions comparable to those that follow. Offered here is no prescription, no mandate on "lessons learned" to be followed slavishly and mechanically. Manifestly, differing contexts will require local accommodation and adjustment. The open terrain and sustained good weather in the Middle Eastern theater of operations pose one sort of problem, while the obscuring jungles and long rainy seasons of Southeast Asia pose quite another. Doctrines, which are but generalized statements reflecting past experience, must sometimes be altered or adjusted to fit these local variations. What follows then are insights developed out of hard-bought experience from many wars over many decades as reflected in the historical record. At most, these insights should inform and suggest; they certainly should not rigidly bind tomorrow's commanders.

The Joint Chiefs of Staff define close air support (CAS) as air action against hostile targets that are in close proximity to friendly forces. Such operations require the most meticulous coordination of each air strike with the forces assisted. But close support can better be understood when placed in the broader context of Air Force roles and missions as a whole. Strategic air power seeks to influence *the war* by blows against the enemy's military, political, and economic base for waging war. Tactical air power seeks to influence *the battle*. It does this in two ways, *indirectly* by interdiction, and *directly* by close air support. Interdiction involves strikes at some distance from the point of engagement to prevent or inhibit the flow of men and materiel to the battle site. Close air support, on the other hand, involves direct intervention at the forward edge of battle. In World War I, this could mean strafing a line of trenches with machinegun fire. In World War II, it might mean bombing an enemy gun position on a reverse slope masked from friendly artillery; while in Vietnam it could mean flying cover for a column of trucks to be instantly ready with counterfire against an enemy ambush.

All successful air operations, however, whether strategic or tactical, rest ultimately upon air superiority: freedom to operate, even if only locally and temporarily, without effective interference from the enemy. This requirement, the need to achieve air superiority, constitutes one of the reasons why the delivery of close air support by tactical air units has been so often misunderstood by soldiers on the ground. Combat soldiers, whether infantry or armor, have long been accustomed to calling upon artillery for fire support. Indeed, this is the main function of artillery.

Tactical air, on the other hand, as indicated above, has three functions, rather than just one. It must be ready to fight for air superiority, intercepting and destroying enemy aircraft that seek to drive off friendly air or harass ground units. At the same time, tactical air power must be prepared to try to isolate the battlefield by interdiction strikes. And finally, tactical air must assist, whenever feasible, the ground troops with direct intervention in the battle by rendering close support. Which of these roles it will perform at any given time depends upon the shifting tides of battle.

Planes requested for close support may be diverted on short notice to the air superiority function upon the sudden appearance of enemy fighters. Under such circumstances, ground soldiers, hard-pressed by enemy land forces and unaware of the threat from enemy aircraft, have been inclined to blame the air arm for failing to provide the support to which they felt entitled.

One proposed solution to this difficulty repeatedly proffered by ground officers is to create a specialized force of air units to be used exclusively for close support. Something of this sort was actually tried in Korea when the Air Force took P–51s out of mothballs to repeat their excellent performance of World War II. Flying slower than jets, they could see ground targets more effectively and were therefore expected to excel in this role. Moreover, they were capable of operating from airstrips closer to the forward edge of battle, a decided advantage in cutting response time. But the inexorable advances of technology largely offset these advantages. Propeller-driven planes could not defend themselves against jet interceptors, and as it turned out, friendly jets required far less maintenance; therefore, they generated many more sorties per day then propeller-driven planes. And finally, the principle of economy of force—the ability to shift the same aircraft from one mission area or role to another, depending on the needs of battle—argued in favor of all-purpose, tactical aircraft and against the idea of planes optimized for the close air-support mission alone.

It is evident that there are ample grounds for misunderstanding that arises from the context in which such support is delivered. Just as the forces of two different nations find it difficult to cooperate, so too the different cultures of air and ground units see reality from widely different perspectives. This does not mean, however, that effective cooperation between air and ground is unobtainable. In each major conflict in which the United States has engaged in the twentieth century, procedures have eventually been hammered out to deliver close support with considerable success. So the question is not one of asking if rendering effective support is possible; the real issue is to determine why such procedures are not put into effect much sooner, preferably at the very outset of engagement with the enemy.

What are the particulars, the fundamental elements that make for success in close air support? The advantage of a historical survey such as that presented here becomes evident when one recognizes that there have been, and are, common elements that characterize effective close support, whether one studies the records of 1918, of 1944, or of 1967. A recognition of these elements should make it easier for those commanding air forces to set about their tasks and, what is more, to accommodate all those variations made necessary by differing environments and the continual advances of technology.

Probably no factor colored the performance of close air support more than the attitudes brought to the task by the air and ground personnel involved. Airmen, especially since the U.S. Air Force achieved independence from the U.S. Army, tended to see every bid by ground officers to attain a larger share in the control of close support operations as a threatening encroachment upon their hard-won and long-delayed autonomy. While the airmen's insistence upon retaining ultimate control is certainly valid if the air weapon is to be exploited most effectively, at times it has appeared that this zeal for autonomy has inhibited appropriate accommodations in an enterprise involving mutual interests. Certainly resistance put up by the Air Force when the Army first proposed to arm its helicopters appears to have been inspired more by a desire to protect Air Force roles and missions than by a long-term appraisal of the national interest. Another basic attitude that shapes Air Force practice is the belief that tactical air should give the interdiction mission a higher priority than close support. To hard-pressed infantrymen on the island of Biak in the Southwest Pacific being mauled by a Japanese unit of superior strength during World War II, it was difficult to understand why requested air strikes failed to appear when weather posed no obstacle. However, the planes that could have provided the requested support were diverted to hit a Japanese convoy approaching with reinforcements. Ships at sea with no place to hide make lucrative interdiction targets. In terms of damage imposed weighed against assets risked, the interdiction mission, in the Air Force view, usually outweighs benefits to be derived from close support.

Unfortunately, the effect of an interdiction strike is indirect, delayed, and long-range, and thus difficult to measure against the losses and frustration of the ground commander. To the ground commander who suffered heavy casualties because he failed to get the close support he wanted *when* he wanted it, it counted for little that in the island campaign at Biak the U.S. Army Air Forces mounted more close support sorties than in virtually every other comparable operation in that theater. Given the human dimensions of episodes such as this, one failure to deliver timely succor could easily offset a multitude of successful support operations.

The character of close support operations makes them especially vulnerable to ground fire. To identify an enemy target with assurance and be sure that he is not hitting friendly troops, a pilot is under continuous pressure to come down to ever lower altitudes. The lower he flies, the greater the risk (especially with a P–51, whose cooling system is so vulnerable to ground fire). The increased risk to the plane often makes a dubious trade-off for the damage inflicted, all of which makes interdiction, in Air Force eyes, appear more profitable than close support.

From the perspective of the ground force, the problem presents an entirely different face. Whenever aircraft fail to arrive in response to a request from the ground—whatever the reason, (it is commonly adverse weather)—the reaction is almost certain to be one of irritation. When the air-

538

planes do show up and hit the wrong target, occasionally inflicting casualties on friendly troops, a ground commander whose irritation turns to outrage can scarcely be blamed for this understandably human reaction, even when he is well aware of the difficulties of identifying the target under a jungle canopy of greenery or upon the cratered side of a hill in Korea, where every ridgeline seems to resemble its neighbor.

Fratricidal fire and misplaced bombs were the rare exception when measured against the total number of close support sorties launched. But one such episode creates an aura of mistrust and interservice hostility out of all proportion to the casualties incurred. Even the rumor of such tragedies has been known to induce ground units to fire at anything and everything that flies, hostile or friendly. This reaction exacerbates the mounting level of mutual mistrust. At least one ground commander, severely galled by fire from friendly planes, proposed to court-martial airmen who inflicted casualties on their own troops. But any such disciplinary measure is bound to fail, for the imposition of penalties for honest errors in sighting would inevitably induce pilots to inject such a wide margin of safety into their strikes that they would seldom if ever eliminate the enemy target they were assigned to strike.

Even if there were no other factors present to complicate close air support, the conflicting attitudes engendered by this subject in those involved would almost certainly be sufficient to account for many of the difficulties encountered. However, the sharply differing attitudes of air and ground troops on the subject of close air support are reflected in many other dimensions of the problem, notably the organizations designed to carry out the mission. Army officers have repeatedly sought to have the close support function directly under the control of the ground force commander in the same way that artillery responds to his authority. This yearning reflects a reversion to the time before the Air Force gained its autonomy, when most of the aircraft in the inventory were called corps and division planes and assigned directly to such formations.

The solution begun in World War II and finally hammered out in Korea was to allow the air component to retain control over aviation, subject only to the theater commander. Collocation of headquarters proved decidedly helpful in mitigating difficulties implicit in separate air and ground chains of command. Adjacent headquarters not only facilitated communication between air and ground commanders but encouraged collaboration in planning by their staffs. No less important was the mutual understanding and trust at a personal level which continued association fostered. Each component became aware of each other's problems more fully, and this recognition made for an ever greater sense of common purpose and teamwork.

Vastly improved cooperation at the top did not, however, eliminate all the problems in Korea by any means. The chain of command on both sides was long and cumbersome. An emergency request by a severely pressed battalion commander on the front had to work its way up the echelons through division, corps, and army, then down on the Air Force side in the same fashion until it triggered a scramble at an appropriate airstrip or diverted a pilot already airborne on some other mission of lesser urgency. Inevitably, requests traversing this extended path encountered delays. The experience in Korea was not unique. In the early days of any operation, the communication net has usually left much to be desired, and inexperienced staff at each echelon usually added to the confusion.

Proposals to shorten the lag in response by giving greater authority to lower echelons to call up air assets have met with continued resistance. Each higher echelon encompasses a broader picture of the battle, affording a better basis for making sound decisions on priorities where hard choices have to be made in the assignment of limited resources.

The Israeli experience in the Yom Kippur war clearly illustrates this point. To the evident irritation of ground forces, the Israeli Air Force insisted on retaining control of its aircraft at the top. To a ground commander being overrun by Egyptian forces at the Suez Canal, the failure of the air arm to provide expected support must have seemed nothing short of criminal neglect. But he could not know that the situation at the Golan Heights at the other end of the nation required a massive reassignment of Israeli air assets. In short, whether one considered the Twelfth Air Force moving northward up the Italian peninsula in 1944 or the Israeli Air Force in 1973, air arm insistence upon centralized control was undoubtedly sound, even though it involved an inescapable cost in terms of a longer chain of command and concomitant delays in response times.

Once the fundamental importance of centralized control of air assets is understood by both air and ground officers, the solution lies not in fighting over the control of airplanes used for close support but rather in perfecting both the organization and procedures employed. Experience has shown that by devising effective structures and procedures, it is entirely possible to retain centralized control, which involves a long chain of command, without sacrificing too much in terms of the adequacy and timeliness of the close support desired by the ground units. The tragedy has been that each time the services have, after much delay, constructed a solution, the system has been abandoned and largely forgotten almost as soon as the fighting stops, only to be reconstituted in some form after much suffering and delay when the next war occurs.

Collocation of headquarters has usually made a significant difference in the quality of advanced planning. As the airmen got a better grasp of the expected stages of advance by the ground troops, they were able to plan more realistically.

During World War II, in North Africa, the lack of Allied air bases near the front imposed serious delays, since support aircraft had to spend time "commuting" from distant bases. This experience drove home the importance of including substantial components of engineers with heavy equipment for rapid airbase construction in the initial deployment of tactical aircraft. By late 1943, the engineers were building airstrips just behind the front in less than twenty-four hours and complete air bases within five days. This process had to be repeated again and again as the Allied armies moved up the boot of Italy or across France, driving home the point that the organizational structure needed to ensure adequate close support was not just a matter of facilitating the communication of requests for air strikes through the chain of command but also involved provision for suitable logistical support.

The interaction between fighter doctrine and airstrip construction merits attention. So long as air-arm doctrine envisioned fighter aircraft as almost exclusively weapons for air-to-air combat, with only an occasional strafing run, the engineers could safely specify a 3,500–foot airstrip. But when the fighters became fighter-bombers that had to take off with two 500–pound bombs, this involved extending the runways to at least 5,000 feet, with medium bombers requiring even longer take-off runs. A 5,000–foot runway involved 750 tons of pierced-steel planking used for temporary runway construction. This kind of tonnage had to be secured all over again as the ground troops moved deeper into enemy territory and new airstrips had to be created just behind the front. Finding the trucks needed to transport the pierced steel planking from port cities to forward locations, not to mention the shipping required to get the planking to the port, gives some indication of the way in which prevailing doctrine can influence the quality of the close support rendered, even if by the most indirect set of circumstances.

Improved command at the top of the chain would not have solved the problem of close support without similar developments at the lower end of the chain. The British showed the way with the system they devised in North Africa, which was perfected by the Americans after they moved into Italy. The challenge was how to help the pilot who finally arrived over the target locate it with sufficient precision to make the desired kill without harming friendly troops. This was an information problem with a two-fold solution. Pilots, serving as forward air controllers on the ground in radio-equipped jeeps, could relay requests from the ground troops and talk the aircraft overhead onto the targets. When the nature of the terrain prevented this, airborne controllers in light liaison planes, such as L–5s, performed the same service. Whether ground-based or airborne, the essence of the forward air controller lay in his ability to meld the point of view of the ground troops with a sure knowledge of the capabilities and limitations of airplanes.

By the end of World War II, a reasonably effective system for providing close air support had been worked out. This was codified as official doctrine in FM 31–35 published by the Army in 1946. But doctrine is, or should be, more than a set of manuals on the shelf. Doctrine must be understood and

541

internalized by commanders and by the troop units who are expected to employ it. To be understood, doctrine must be actively inculcated by a regular and repetitious training program. Unfortunately, in the peacetime environment, given the paucity of funds and the lower priority accorded to close support in order to sustain the strategic bomber force, it proved to be fatally easy to downgrade if not totally neglect such training. As a result, hard-won lessons were lost and had to be acquired all over again, as the experience in Korea in 1950 revealed so pointedly.

Many months were to pass before the Air Force was able to rebuild an organization and perfect procedures. Pilots who performed superbly in the battle for air superiority had little if any training in support operations. And it was all very well for the manuals to call for joint operations centers to merge air and ground perspectives, but in the absence of trained staff and suitable communications, these centers remained paper ideals.

Organizational problems in Korea were complicated by the presence of two other air forces—carrier-based Navy units and Marine Corps elements—in addition to the newly autonomous USAF. These three air forces had fought side by side in the Pacific during World War II, but then they went home and wrote separate doctrinal manuals. Each of these separate service manuals reflected only segments of the World War II experience and not the full spectrum. Field Manual 31–35, "Air Ground Operations," issued in 1946, was based largely on the experience of the Ninth Air Force in conjunction with the 12th Army Group in Europe. This was an exceedingly important body of experience but parochial insofar as it failed to provide guidance on collaboration with the Navy and Marine Corps.

Competition in close support from Marine Corps aviation in Korea at first proved painfully embarrassing to the Air Force because of the superior performance of the Marines. Marine flyers were specialists in close support. It was their major mission, they were trained for it, and their equipment was optimized for the role. They were consciously part of a well-honed team, imbued with the Corps traditions; and when they served on the ground as forward air controllers, they usually operated right up at the front with the troops. Pilots assigned to a preplanned mission would frequently visit the ground troops in person the day before a mission to look over the terrain and get the local commander's views on just how he wanted the strike conducted. Little wonder that Marine aviation was almost universally praised by ground troops and almost universally feared by the enemy, according to POW testimony. The net effect of this competition was to induce the Air Force to match the Marine Corps performance or lose credibility. The specific measures, such as building air bases in Korea instead of operating from Japan in order to cut response time, were of less importance than the principle involved; interservice competition can have a decidedly beneficial impact by raising the standard of performance for those who rely on services rendered.

542

By the time the shooting stopped in Korea, the organizations and procedures developed to provide close support, while still less than ideal, nonetheless achieved a high degree of effectiveness. One might reasonably assume
that this would provide a sound basis for the distillation of improved doctrine
and a determination in Air Force circles not to repeat the neglect of close
support that had followed World War II.

Unfortunately, this was not the case. When U.S. forces again went into
action more than a decade later, this time in Southeast Asia, the Air Force
found itself once more unprepared to provide the kind of close support the
ground units required, and the Army was still arguing that ground commanders should have operational control of the aircraft assigned to the close support
mission. It seemed as if a new generation of leaders with little knowledge of
the past was going to fight over the same old issues. And it did. Eventually, of
course, these leaders perfected a workable organization with appropriate procedures, but this involved years of delay and a great deal of friction that might
well have been avoided if the experience of World War II and Korea had been
more successfully internalized. There is a note of pathos in the comment of
the colonel who candidly admitted of the experience in Vietnam: "We had to
learn the hard way all over again." Nor was this an isolated perception. An
official Air Force air warfare board in 1965 clearly identified the difficulty as
a failure to develop sound doctrine. But why?

Many factors doubtlessly entered into the Air Force tendency to back-
slide on the close support role. Preoccupation with the strategic offensive,
even to the point of making fighter aircraft nuclear-capable, is often cited as
a major cause. When funds are scarce in years of retrenchment, roles and
missions perceived to warrant a lower priority are the first to be cut. Then
too, rapid turnover in personnel and short tours in any one specialty contributed to the loss of institutional memory. But probably more important was
the absence of a shooting war to provide actual experience. While many Air
Force roles, such as strategic bombing and fighter tactics, can be practiced
with much benefit in peacetime exercises, it is difficult if not impossible to
attain the realism required to make close support training meaningful.

In Vietnam, dedicated and conscientious individuals ultimately worked
out a viable organization and increasingly sound procedures just as their
predecessors had in the several theaters in World War II and in Korea, belatedly and only after many mistakes and losses. One noteworthy procedural
improvement devised by 1965 was the agreement signed by the air and
ground components, establishing a system of apportionment and allocation.
By this arrangement, the joint task force commander, advised by his air component commander, would decide each day what portion of the available air
assets would be devoted to close support, to interdiction, and to air superiority. When the air component commander received word of this appointment,
he could then allocate his available forces to provide a known number of air-

craft or sorties to the ground commander, who could employ them on specific targets according to the priorities he felt desirable. This system left full authority at the top as the Air Force had desired all along, but gave each ground commander receiving an allocation, substantial advance assurance that he could count on a given number of sorties.

There was much to be said for the scheme of apportionment and allocation. It offered something for everybody. The airmen retained the centralized control they saw as essential, and the ground commanders felt they had some assurance that the air support they asked for would actually be forthcoming. While the arrangement was effective, one should not overlook the fact that it was premised upon the availability of a relatively large inventory of aircraft, normally enough to satisfy the simultaneous needs of all three missions—air superiority, interdiction, and close support. When the aircraft inventory is less than adequate, especially in the opening days of a conflict, there is little doubt that virtually every available aircraft would be devoted to high priority roles to the neglect of close support. In sum, while the system seemed to work well in the mature phase of U.S. intervention in Vietnam, any attempt to perfect close-support doctrine on the basis of experience there should include consideration of the early period of scarcity as well as the later period of plenty.

While the record is replete with instances in which disgruntled ground commanders excoriated the failure of the Air Force to respond to requests for air support, few indeed are the reports of ground commanders who misused or abused the close support to which they were entitled. But such misuse did occur. Sometimes air sorties were called in when fire support from available artillery would have readily served to meet the need at less cost and less risk. Occasionally, some airmen got the impression that a ground unit expected them to decimate a stubborn enemy force before the foot soldiers would continue offensive operations. More common was the practice of calling for a planned sortie for which the ground commanders would give grid coordinates, almost at random, supposedly designating a bothersome target for elimination, but one in which they had little or no real interest. They did this in order to get an airplane in the air with a planned strike simply to give themselves some assurance that, if they filed a short-notice, emergency request, there would be a higher probability of getting a plane diverted to their use. Whether the practice of requesting a dummy planned strike was an abuse or merely an example of individuals learning to work the system to get practical results despite the inherent rigidities is unimportant. What is important is that those who undertake to study the Vietnam experience recognize the practice and take it into account when generalizing on the subject.

When reviewing air arm attempts to devise suitable organizations and procedures for close air support, an effort which had gone on from 1917 to the present, one is struck by the absence of standard or stable terminology. In each new resurgence of interest in close support, those involved seem to have coined virtually a whole new vocabulary of organizational terms. Terms such as air observers, air coordinators, air liaison officers, and air support parties are examples of this practice. In organizations with a high turnover, the absence of standardized terminology can significantly inhibit understanding and complicate training. In the Army, the platoon, company, battalion, or regiment have remained stable, identifiable entities from one generation to another. The numbers involved may change and new weapons may be incorporated, but the organizations persist. This stability simplifies training and facilitates communication. The Air Force has been less sensitive to the value of standardized terminology and notably so with regard to nomenclature relating to organizations and personnel associated with close support.

While devising workable organizational structures and effective procedures to ensure a smoothly functioning close support system has been the principal challenge, other elements and factors have also been involved, notably the equipment required to do the job. Broadly speaking, this included three classes of materiél: aircraft, ordnance, and communications. Each merits discussion.

Ground officers repeatedly urged the development of specialized aircraft to perform the close-support role. The continual development of a high-performance plane increasingly widened the gap between those characteristics best suited to the support function and those appropriate for air superiority. Higher speeds impair the ability of an observer to identify small targets on the ground, and reduced loiter time means longer periods when the ground troops will lack air support. The advocates of specialized aircraft have also argued that lowperformance aircraft suited to the support role would be less costly and therefore could be procured in large numbers. But all these arguments in favor of low-performance aircraft presuppose air superiority. The horrible losses suffered by slow-flying observation planes attacked by fast, maneuverable fighters in World War I demonstrated this beyond question. When virtual air superiority had been achieved, however, low-performance planes could be effective. The ability of unarmed L–5 liaison planes roaming as much as five miles behind the German lines in Italy proved the point.

The high-wing L–5 gave excellent visibility, but when it was used in Korea, its inability to carry adequate communications gear and its lack of defensive armament limited its value as a vehicle for use by forward air controllers guiding close support strikes. At the same time, pilots of high-performance F–80 jets found it difficult to identify ground targets. This led to the use of the sturdy AT–6, slow enough to give pilots time to search the terrain and heavy enough to carry communication gear permitting them to talk with ground commanders *and* with the jets. But the low-wing AT–6 had far less visibility than the high-wing L–5.

In groping for a way to optimize plane performance, there had to be trade-offs. When jets were too fast, P–51s left over from World War II came on the scene. But it turned out that losses to ground fire were twice those of the jets. When the Chinese entered the war and began using Russian jets, the role of maintaining air superiority abruptly resumed top priority.

When U.S. troops became actively engaged in Vietnam, the whole question of finding a suitable aircraft for close support surfaced again and repeated the dialectic of Korea. The L–5 had now become the L–19, rechristened O–1, and the jets were now F–100s and F–4s—yet the story was the same. The O–1 was easy to maintain and afforded good visibility, but it was underpowered, unarmed, and lacked adequate capacity for all-around communication, while the fuel-guzzling jets lacked loiter time and were too fast to see fleeting targets.

In 1969, *four years* after U.S. units began fighting in Vietnam, the Air Force finally came up with a compromise solution: the OV–10. This twin-engine plane carried four machineguns and four rocket pods, which meant that it could provide an immediate response in its forward air controller role. It was designed to pursue a fleeting target that would have disappeared into the jungle long before a jet fighter could be called in for the kill. But the OV–10 could not hope to survive against North Vietnamese jets, so while it proved to be highly effective, it was largely limited to in-country operations in an area made safe by a protective umbrella of friendly jets.

Perhaps the most imaginative and certainly the most unorthodox attempt to resolve the close-support dilemma was the use of the more than 30-year-old C–47 as a gunship. This slow and unmaneuverable cargo plane proved to be a surprisingly effective support vehicle when equipped with illuminating flares and three 6,000-round-a-minute miniguns firing 7.62–mm ammunition. Though highly vulnerable because of its slow speed and lack of self-sealing fuel tanks, the gunship performed yeoman service by virtue of its long loiter time (and thus short response time) and its ability to provide a high volume of fire. Its unique service was in relieving outposts besieged by enemy forces. By operating at night and in bad weather, the C–47, for all its limitations, proved remarkably able to survive. But, like the OV–10, the gunship was a special adaptation to a more or less unique situation. Could it be incorporated into the general doctrine of close air support?

Doctrinal promulgations are generalizations based on what past experience has shown usually works best. As the foregoing chapters clearly show, the Air Force has consistently found it difficult to achieve these generalizations. Doctrine has too often been distilled from fragmentary evidence, from some portion of the totality of experience, to the detriment of sound guidance for those without actual exposure to combat. Will planes with the characteristics of the OV–10 and the gunships be incorporated into the doctrine of close support for general application in the future, or will they be seen as responses to a unique situation?

The dilemmas confronting those who would write sound doctrine are real, for the extended record of past experience presents many seeming contradictions. Manifestly, the proper choice of aircraft for close support is a matter of critical importance. The long lead time required for design and production and the need for extended training make selecting the right equipment essential if the Air Force is to deliver effective close support at the opening of a future conflict, and not months or years later. In view of the fact that equipment ranging from B–52 bombers, such as those bombing close to the defensive perimeter of the besieged Marine base at Khe Sanh, down to the unarmed L–5s of World War II, has proved to be effective under certain conditions and at different periods, choosing the ideal aircraft for close support will in the future undoubtedly prove as difficult as in the past.

Ordnance items constitute another materiel factor influencing the character of close air support. The slow evolution of suitable ordnance during the island-hopping campaign in the Southwest Pacific during World War II offers insights on the relationship between ordnance and aircraft. At the outbreak of war, fighter aircraft lacked suitable shackles and pylons for bombing. When these modifications were finally made, a P–40, the plane available in greatest numbers, could handle two 500–pound bombs. With the arrival of the P–47 this was upgraded to two 1,000–pound bombs, which was more than the bombload of an A–20 and almost as much as the B–25 carried. This maximum bombload was possible, however, only if the aircraft had but a limited distance to the target.

The evolution of the fighter into a fighter-bomber merits careful study for the light it sheds on the difficulties confronting those who hope to develop sound close-support systems for the future. Air Corps officers during the 1920s and 1930s devoted much thought to developing two specialized types of aircraft to perform the support function. These were an observation airplane, which became the O–49 on the eve of World War II, and an attack aircraft, which became the A–20. As soon as the shooting started, it was discovered that the observation plane as conceived and implemented in the O–49 was worthless, because it was utterly vulnerable. Fast, and usually unarmed or modified fighter types took over one part of the observation function, while slow, unarmed "puddle-jumpers", modeled on civilian Piper aircraft and typified by the L–5, took over the remaining portion. While the A–20 did perform well as a light bomber for interdiction missions, much of its attack role was taken over by modified fighter-bombers.

The task of those who must prepare the nation for a future war is, then, a matter of matching the characteristics of the planes selected for support work to the environment created by the prevailing level of technology in ordnance as well as aircraft. Can the A–10 "Warthog" survive in the era of radar-controlled AA and Precision-Guided Munitions, or will it go the way of the O–49 when the shooting starts?

Fighter-bombers such as the P–47 of World War II with their heavier bombs meant greater destruction of installations but proved to be of limited effectiveness against enemy troops well entrenched. Experiments with parafrags met with scarcely more success against such entrenched units. This led resourceful commanders to try burning out the enemy by releasing gasoline-laden drop tanks that were then ignited by tracer fire. This crude beginning eventually led to napalm bombs, horrifying but successful weapons that could sometimes kill even covered troops, not alone by burning but by oxygen deprivation.

In addition to bombs and bullets, ordnance includes pyrotechnic devices. The need for battlefield illumination at night has been recognized since the days of trench warfare in World War I, so the desired characteristics of this particular weapon ought to be well understood: the highest candlepower, the lowest dud rate, and the lowest possible sink rate to protract the period of illumination as long as possible. Obvious or not, suitable illuminants were not available at the start of each new conflict. What is more, ancillary equipment such as flare-launching chutes have repeatedly been left off aircraft in time of peace.

Some pyrotechnic devices lie on the borderline between weaponry and communication devices. For example, gunship pilots sometimes found that they could drive off or discourage the attackers surrounding a besieged outpost in Vietnam merely by launching a two million candlepower illuminating flare, which turned night into day and robbed the enemy of all concealment. Or again, when support aircraft laid smoke over a high hill used as an observation post by enemy fire-control officers, they were certainly using smoke offensively. More commonly, of course, colored smokes have been used as target markers.

Because a whole generation has passed in which the U.S. forces enjoyed substantial air superiority over the battlefront, in Korea and in Vietnam, it is all too easy to perceive the use of colored smoke for target-marking as something *we* do to *them*. Will the doctrinal manuals prepare the U.S. military for a future war in which air superiority over the front is not assured, and the enemy uses smoke to mark targets on *our* side of the front? Will they be prepared to launch comparable markers to confuse enemy support aircraft with deceptive displays at innocuous locations? Doctrine rests on experience, but there is always the danger of viewing experience too narrowly and drawing the wrong inferences from it.

In the use of colored smoke for marking and signalling, prior coordination between air and ground forces is critically important. Incredible as it may seem, bombers supporting advancing ground troops in France shortly after the Normandy invasion relied upon the same color smoke for target-marking as that employed by the ground troops to indicate position. These heavy casualties suffered by friendly forces resulting from the failure to coordinate stand as a vivid reminder for positive confirmation on the agreed-upon smoke signals of the day, a point that doctrine writers must emphasize.

Even the strictest compliance with the requirement for coordinating smoke signals, however, will not ensure against fratricidal strikes. Several such instances, including the one in which Gen. Leslie McNair, the head of the U.S. Army Ground Forces during World War II, was killed, resulted from the practice of having an entire bomber formation follow the action of the bombardier in the lead bomber. When mechanical failure, or enemy antiaircraft fire, causes the lead bomber to drop its ordnance prematurely, and the whole formation follows suit, the tragedy of misplaced bombs is multiplied to catastrophic proportions, in one instance amounting to 400 casualties among friendly troops. Episodes such as these, though few, suggest that heavy bombers in close-support operations should abandon formation bombing keyed to a single plane.

Any consideration of ordnance for close support must take account of the interrelationship between the ordnance and the aircraft that carried it. When U.S. troops went into combat in Korea, 500–pound bombs were available, but the F–80 jets were not equipped with pylons to carry them. Undoubtedly this reflected the higher priority afforded air-superiority mission but also the prevailing mind-set of Air Force officers, indicated by the way the Air Corps, as late as 1941, turned down a proposal to put bomb shackles on fighter aircraft for fear that this would lead to an "improper tactical use" of the fighters.

The built-in reward system of the service designates a man an ace after five kills in air-to-air combat, where high speed and maneuverability are essential. Pylons and ordnance slow down a fighter and limit its maneuverability. The tactical significance of five air-to-ground support operations might well be of crucial importance to the success of the battle on the ground, but they will never make a pilot an ace.

Another interrelationship affecting ordnance was first seen in the appearance of electronically controlled gravity bombs rather late in World War II. By radio control the bombardier could deflect the fins of the bomb to steer it more accurately to the target. This opened new vistas for close support, since even a limited capacity for steering meant that the larger bombs of high-altitude heavy bombers might be used in relative proximity to friendly troops. By the time of the Korean War, advances in electronics made it possible to use ground-based radar units for remotely controlled bombing. Although still crude in the 1950s, this marriage of ordnance and electronics pointed toward a wide development in the future of close air support.

Communications are yet another material factor in close air support. Because coordination of air and ground operations is of vital importance, provision of adequate means of communication is of central concern. Today, at the mention of communications, one automatically thinks of electronics, but the road to the present has involved many alternative modes. In World War I, front-line troops whose phone lines had been cut used pigeons and display panels to request air support. The use of display panels to mark the progress of advancing friendly troops has persisted down to the present even though this practice has never proved to be very satisfactory. Such panels may inform support aircraft, but they also inform the enemy and draw fire. Nervous troops miles behind the forward edge of battle have been known to put out panels to avoid bombing by friendly aircraft, thus unwittingly giving false signals to the pilots overhead as to the location of the front. On the other hand, smoke signals drift away while display panels persist.

Because major weapon systems attract the lion's share of attention, the minutiae of ancillary equipment get short shrift in after-action reports. Yet these minutiae are the raw materials from which doctrine is developed. Experience in World War II revealed that red panels had far better visibility than yellow smoke. What is more, since some types of explosives generated various hues of yellow smoke, it was sometimes difficult for pilots to distinguish shell bursts from signal flares. But unless those who write after-action reports routinely include such minor details, those who try to build on past experience in formulating doctrine will encounter great difficulty in arriving at sound generalizations.

Although radios were installed in a small number of planes during World War I, they were crude and unreliable. Moreover, dependence on code transmissions restricted the flow of information drastically. Sometimes the technical limitations of radio created almost ludicrous conditions. In World War I, radios carried by a tank unit to facilitate communication with support aircraft would not function inside the tank. The radio operator had to dismount, erect an aerial mast and conduct his transmission outside the tank. This was hardly conducive to easy air–ground coordination.

By the outbreak of World War II, radio had made remarkable technical strides, but it is worth recalling that virtually all the combatants suffered from serious defects in their communication systems. *Luftwaffe* radios operated on different frequencies from those of the German Army. German fighters had voice radios, but *Luftwaffe* bombers still had to rely on code transmissions. Not until 1941, two years after the war started, did the Soviets manage to provide radio control over their fighters performing the close air-support function. About the same time, in the United States, Air Corps planes participating in the Louisiana maneuvers had to have their radios converted to Army frequencies to permit air-ground coordination. But in doing this they lost their ability to communicate at long range, and lost or disoriented pilots found themselves unable to communicate with their airbase for guidance. In short, the evidence, foreign and domestic, pointed to surprising delays in recognizing the critical importance of providing means for an easy flow of information among *all* echelons and *all* arms and services that were expected to operate cooperatively.

Lack of money to develop and procure adequate communications equipment was the reason usually offered to explain the shortcomings experienced in this area. There was a good deal of validity to the contention insofar as it applied to the peacetime years. But in wartime, when funds were lavished on the armed forces, it is harder to explain the long delays in devising means to ensure the prompt and unimpeded flow of information. In the Southwest Pacific during World War II, for example, Army units with HF radios could not communicate with Navy fighters equipped with VHF until suitable equipment was obtained late in the war. After the experience in three wars, the problem resurfaced during the *Mayaguez* incident in 1975. When Cambodian Communists attacked the U.S. freighter, rescue operations disclosed that the problem of interservice communication still had not been resolved.

The gridded map has long been a vital adjunct for fast and accurate communication in military operations. In the European Theater the ready availability of superb terrain maps made the problem simply one of supply. In World War II, mobile cartographic units turned out tens of thousands of multicolored maps for tactical commanders. These could be updated periodically using information secured from aerial photography. But in the Pacific Theater there were vast areas of jungle-clad islands for which no terrain maps were available. Without maps, pilots assigned to support missions would often return to base in frustration, unable to find their assigned targets, saying: "It all looks the same." Eventually a technique was devised for preparing photo mosaics that were gridded, providing a practical substitute for conventional terrain maps developed from surveys. In sum, communications for close-support operations required far more than the electronic gear most prominently associated with the term.

One theme that recurs in foregoing chapters is the difficulty of delivering close air support in the early days of any conflict because of a shortage of trained personnel. These shortages seemed most acute in the ancillary fields. If the staff is insufficient, lacking radio operators, aerial photograph interpreters, or cartographic specialists, the quality of close support delivered is bound to suffer until the training command turns out the necessary volume of qualified personnel. In peacetime, when resources are constrained, high-priority functions will, reasonably enough, receive the lion's share of support. If the Air Force is to avoid the chronic shortages encountered by the low priority of the support mission, then it will clearly be necessary to cast about for ways to escape this dilemma. Thus it appears essential to have greater peacetime emphasis on lower-cost reserve units ready for rapid deployment to perform in those ancillary fields, including close air support, where the shortages have been most acute.

The availability of qualified pilots raises another dimension of the personnel problem in close air support. Because the production of trained pilots has always borne a relationship to the number of aircraft on hand, a shortage of pilots has seldom been the weak link in the early days of a conflict when other shortfalls are usually most apparent. When pilots are used as forward air controllers on the ground, however, the situation changes drastically. The argument for this use of pilots is that only a fully qualified pilot will be able to understand the capabilities and limitations of the airplanes he is talking down on a target. With appropriate training however, individuals without pilot wings probably could do the job. Even though the confidence level of the pilot of the strike plane is bound to be raised when he knows that he is being directed by one who may be swapping roles with him in a few days. There is also much to be said for having pilots get to know the ground personnel being supported. The camaraderie developed could positively affect a pilot's determination when he is called on to eliminate a heavily defended enemy target harassing the ground unit he had recently served as a forward air controller.

Although a strong case has long been made for using pilots as ground controllers, a substantial case can also be made for using other trained personnel. With the cost of training a modern jet pilot at somewhere between one and two million dollars, it may not be cost-effective to assign pilots duty as ground controllers. To be fully effective, a controller should operate as closely as possible to the ground unit being served in a risky front-line environment. Would it not be better military economics to risk pilots in fighter-bombers rather than on the ground performing a role that might be performed by a less expensive officer? The British practice in World War II of using army officers rather than pilots as ground controllers suggests a precedent worth investigating.

Another personnel practice that has affected the quality of close support is the controversial World War II policy of setting a fixed quota of combat missions after which a pilot is relieved from further combat duty. Where this was interpreted to authorize rotation back to the United States, commanders were inclined to question the policy because it involved a severe drain of the most experienced pilots, the very individuals whose survival through a full quota of missions indicated superior tactical skill. Such men were desperately needed to break-in the green replacement pilots newly arrived in the theater.

After the invasion of Normandy, when experienced ground forward air controllers were far too few to meet the need, the tac air commander resorted to assigning to this duty pilots who had completed their required quota of combat sorties. Service at the front on the ground was not regarded as a reward for gallantry in the air by those chosen for this assignment, especially when others who completed their combat tours were returned to the United

States. Eventually, a compromise emerged in which each veteran pilot would serve a ninety-day tour as a ground controller. This insured a flow of experienced pilots for ground duty but at the same time preserved the principle of rotation. Despite the experience, the use of pilots as controllers and the principle of rotation are unresolved issues.

The development of electronic warfare is another factor in the close-support equation. Although the roots of electronic warfare date before World War II, it was during that conflict that the field came into its own. The concern here is with electronic measures only insofar as they affect close air support, especially in countering defenses. So long as antiaircraft guns were optically sighted and depended upon the gunner's skill at estimating lead and range, AA fire tended to be ineffectual, posing but limited threat to attacking aircraft. But the advent of radar, computing sights, and proximity fuses made AA fire more lethal than it had ever been before. By the Korean War, defense suppression was regarded as a critical component of close support, and rockets mounted on fighters as a supplement to gunfire proved to be a most effective weapon against AA batteries. As a consequence of the advances in air defense, the bombs, bullets, and rockets that had earlier characterized defense suppression now were supplemented with electronic gear for jamming and spoofing.

The electronic revolution in antiaircraft weaponry and its implications for close air support were probably best illustrated by the Israeli experience. In the Six Day War of 1967, the Israeli Air Force, when attacking the Syrians on the Golan Heights, set up "cab ranks" of fighter-bombers circling aloft a mere thirty seconds away from the decisive ground action. These planes could be quickly summoned by forward air controllers on the ground to support the advancing Israeli tanks by eliminating whatever unexpected enemy obstacle blocked the way. By 1973, in the Yom Kippur War, this kind of support was no longer possible because of the greater range and accuracy of surface-to-air missiles.

The sophisticated surface-to-air missiles supplied to the Arabs by the Russians imposed formidable losses on the Israeli Air Force during the first few days of battle. In desperation the Israelis called upon the United States to share the high technology electronic countermeasure pods developed by the U.S. Air Force to counter the Russians SAMs supplied to the North Vietnamese. These were quickly flown to Israel but proved inadequate. Despite the short lapse of time between the Air Force use of this equipment in Southeast Asia and the Yom Kippur War, the pods were obsolete on arrival because of the fast pace of Soviet technological development, and the Israelis lost several planes in consequence.

This painful experience offers a clear warning to those developing Air Force doctrine. Perfectly sound doctrine of only yesterday, doctrine fully warranted on the basis of extended experience, can become obsolete when the enemy achieves an unexpected technological breakthrough. Penetration of enemy defenses in an environment where SAMs may reach out to a range of 25 miles up to a ceiling of 50,000 feet, and are supplemented with multi-barreled, radar-controlled AA guns for close-in defense, will present a far different tactical problem for close support from what it had been in previous wars. The officer who aspires to make sound decisions reads history for informing insights, hoping to benefit from the experience of others. But only the naive expect to find clear-cut lessons, prescriptions with the precision of a how-to-do-it manual, in an historical account. The educated reader knows that the record is confusing and often contradictory, nonetheless it can be decidedly valuable. If it doesn't give pat formulas for success, it can suggest some of the questions one might usefully ask—and answer, not solely in terms of the past but of the past enlightened by the facts of the present.

Many obstacles beset the road to the past; what purports to be the record of experience often turns out to be but a fragment of the past. And if doctrine is sound generalization from past experience, to rely upon a selected segment of that experience may well be to invite disaster. Even when one is reasonably persuaded that approved doctrine rests on a properly broad base of experience and therefore merits confidence, along comes a technological breakthrough that calls into question portions of that doctrine almost overnight. So one draws conclusions with caution. Nevertheless, the multinational survey of close air support presented in the foregoing chapters suggests a number of continuities and commonalities worth noting.

To begin with, the third place priority—behind air superiority and interdiction—assigned to close support by the U.S. Air Force is not just an arbitrary stance reflecting the struggle of the airmen to achieve independent status. That struggle did indeed influence their attitudes and approaches significantly at various times, but the bottom priority rests mainly on functional realities, not prejudice. The fact that this same precedence of priorities had been established in 1939 by the *Luftwaffe* (a force traditionally more army-oriented), and by the Israeli Air Force in 1973 supports this view.

Further, the insistence by the Air Force on centralized control, often criticized by ground officers as the principal cause of delayed responses to their requests for support in dire emergencies, is supported in the experience of others. Ironically, perhaps the most persuasive argument for centralized control of air assets comes from the Army itself. Since the Army operates more aircraft than the Air Force, managers of those assets find the argument for centralization compelling. Divisional artillerymen may complain that they don't control spotting planes as they once did, but their answer from division headquarters replicates the arguments used for years by the Air Force. The principle of economy of force and the logic of the situation justify centralized control.

Centralized control, however, does not mean license for the Air Force to follow whatever course it pleases. It does mean authorization to employ air power in ways that maximize its effectiveness per POL, aircraft, and manpower expended. On occasion that may involve temporarily giving the highest priority to close support. Nevertheless, the often limited resources must be flexibly assigned in response to the shifting tides of battle.

The other side of the coin of centralization is the obligation to eschew the parochial views and service prejudices in order to achieve unified effort by all arms and all allies. The most recent Israeli experience illuminates this point. The Israeli Air Force lost fifty planes in the first three days during the Yom Kippur War of 1973 when confronted with interlocking batteries of surface-to-air missiles. By skirting Syrian SAM batteries to tempt them into firing and exhausting their supply of missiles, and by interdiction strikes on Syrian airfields to prevent Soviet transports from flying-in replacements, the Israelis gradually reduced the Syrian SAMs to a level permitting close air-support operations with ground troops. This attrition would not have been possible without the continual pressure of Israeli ground units on the Syrians, forcing them to conclude that they *had* to fend off the air attacks.

An episode from the experience of U.S. Army Air Forces in the Southwest Pacific during World War II dramatically illustrates that a spirit of cooperation is probably far more important than the precise structure of the organization designed to do the job or the procedures followed. In 1943, when Army Air Forces headquarters in Washington sent out a full complement of officers to staff a separate Air Support Command, General Kenney would have none of it. He preferred cooperation to formal structure.

Even with thoroughgoing commitment to a spirit of cooperation on the part of both air and ground officers, the inherent problems and intrinsic limitations of close support will undoubtedly persist. Despite such innovations as the gunship, powerful illuminating flares, and infrared sensing, close-support operations at night will probably continue to be difficult; and certainly terrain, foliage, and weather will in varying degrees inhibit effective support operations. And troops on the ground about to be overrun by a strong enemy force, who call for air support and fail to get it immediately, will, understandably, be aggrieved. This irritation will turn to fury, when aircraft finally arrive and mistakenly bomb the wrong target, killing and wounding numbers of the long-suffering ground troops. Finally, in fluid situations, when the ground units are advancing or especially when retreating, air support is going to be less reliable, less accurate, and less frequent than when it is serving a more or less static front.

Perhaps the most important question of all remains to be answered: is close air support by high-performance air force aircraft a viable mission in the era of precision-guided munitions? The historical record cannot answer that question, but it can provide the context within which new experience may produce a solution.

Contributors

BENJAMIN FRANKLIN COOLING served as Chief, Special Histories Branch and Senior Historian for Contract Programs, Office of Air Force History, Washington, D.C. He has previously been associated with the U.S. Army Center of Military History as an historian, and more recently as Assistant Director for Historical Services, U.S. Army Military History Institute, Carlisle Barracks, Pennsylvania. A former National Park Historian, Assistant Professor at PMC Colleges, he has taught also at the University of Pennsylvania and the U.S. Army War College. He was a Naval War College Research Associate in 1973–74, is a Fellow of the Company of Military Historians, and Executive Director of the American Military Institute. He holds the Master of Arts and Doctor of Philosophy degrees in history from the University of Pennsylvania. He has written or edited numerous articles, volumes, and series in the field of military and naval history including: *Benjamin Franklin Tracy, Father of the Modern American Fighting Navy*; *Symbol, Sword, and Shield*; *Defending Washington During the Civil War*; *War, Business, and American Society* (editor); *New American State Papers, Military Affairs*—20 volumes (editor); *Gray Steel and Blue Water Navy*; *Formative Years of America's Military-Industrial Complex*; *War, Business, and International Military-Industrial Complexes* (editor); *Combined Operations in Peace and War* (co-author); *Forts Henry and Donelson, Key to the Southern Heartland*; and *Jubal Early's Raid on Washington, 1864*. In 1989, Dr. Cooling accepted the position of chief historian of the Department of Energy.

BRERETON GREENHOUS is a historian with the Canadian Department of National Defence. His special interest is in tactical aspects of the aircraft/armor interface. Born in the United Kingdom in 1929, his military service has been in the British Army, with the Malayan Police, and in the Canadian Army. Upon leaving the Canadian Army in 1965, he turned to an academic career, taking a B.A. degree at Carleton University, Ottawa and an M.A. at Queen's University, Kingston, and going on to teach at Lakehead University, Thunder Bay, Ontario, before taking his present post in 1971. He is the author of two regimental histories, *Dragoon: the Centennial History of the Royal Canadian Dragoons, 1883-1983* (Belleville, Ont.; Guild of the RCD, 1984) and *Semper Paratus: the History of the Royal Hamilton Light Infantry, 1862–1977* (Hamilton, Ont., RHLI Historical Association, 1977), and co-author of *Out of the Shadows: Canada in the Second World War* (Toronto: Oxford University Press, 1977). He is the editor of *A Rattle of Pebbles: The First World War Diaries of Two Canadian Airmen* (Ottawa: Canadian

Government Publishing Centre, 1987), and his articles on aspects of tactical airpower have been required reading at West Point and the USAF Academy. He is the designated principal author of the forthcoming third volume of the Official History of the Royal Canadian Air Force, which will deal with RCAF operations overseas during the Second World War.

I. B. HOLLEY, JR. is Professor of History at Duke University, Durham, N.C. Born in Connecticut, he received his B.A. from Amherst College in 1940, his M.A. and Ph.D in 1942 and 1947 from Yale University. He served for five years in the U.S. Army Air Forces during World War II and then joined the U.S. Air Force Reserve, retiring as a Major General in 1981. His scholarly works include *Ideas and Weapons*, now in its third edition (New Haven: Yale Press, 1953; Hamden, Conn.: Archon Books, 1971; and Washington [D.C.]: Government Printing Office, 1983); *Buying Aircraft: Materiel Procurement for the Army Air Forces*, a volume in the official history series, *The United States Army in World War II* (Washington [D.C.]: Government Printing Office, 1964) and *General John M. Palmer, Citizen Soldiers, and the Army of a Democracy* (Westport, Conn.: Greenwood Press, 1982). Professor Holley has been Visiting Professor at the U.S. Military Academy, West Point, N.Y., and at the National Defense University in Washington, D.C. He is a regular lecturer at the Air University, Maxwell AFB, Alabama; the Army War College, Carlisle Barracks, Pennsylvania; the Command and General Staff College, Fort Leavenworth, Kansas; and a number of other institutions. Many of his articles and chapters have been assigned as required reading at one or another of the military professional schools. Professor Holley is on the editorial advisory boards of four professional journals and frequent contributes book reviews.

W. A. JACOBS is Professor of History at the University of Alaska, Anchorage, where he has taught Modern European History since 1973. He is a graduate of Wisconsin State University, Eau Claire, and holds M.A. and Ph.D. degrees from the University of Oregon. Originally trained as a social and economic historian, he later turned to the history of warfare. His "Tactical Air Doctrine and AAF Close Air Support in the European Theater, 1944-45," (*Aerospace Historian*, Spring 1980) and "Close Air Support for the British Army, 1939-45," (*Military Affairs*, Winter 1982) shed light on tactical air organization, doctrine, and operations in World War II. His "Strategic Bombing and American National Strategy, 1941-43," (*Military Affairs, summer, 1986*) is an analysis of the process by which an American strategic bombing offensive became part of Allied strategy. His most recent article,

"Allied Air Command in the United Kingdom, 1943–1944," (*Journal of Strategic Studies*, March, 1988), is an analysis of the organizational politics of Allied air commands in the European theater.

LEE KENNETT is Professor of History and lecturer in military science at the University of Georgia. He received his Bachelor of Arts degree in political science at the University of North Carolina in 1952. After two years of service in the United States Navy, he entered graduate school, receiving an M.A. in history from the University of Mississippi and the Ph.D. in the same subject from the University of Virginia. He has been visiting professor at the University of Toulouse and l'Ecole Pratique des Hautes Etudes, Fourth Section, and has given lectures at a number of academic and military institutions in the United States and Europe. He is the author of several books on military history, including *A History of Strategic Bombing*, and has published articles in such journals as *Aerospace Historian*, *Military Affairs*, *Military Review*, *Revue Historique des Armees*, and *U.S. Naval Institute Proceedings*.

ALLAN R. MILLETT is Professor of History and Director of the Program in International Security and Military Affairs, The Mershon Center, The Ohio State University. A 1959 graduate of DePauw University, Dr. Millett's postgraduate degrees (1963, 1966) are from The Ohio State University. Dr. Millett is the author of four books: *The Politics of Intervention: The Military Occupation of Cuba, 1906–1909* (1968); *The General: Robert L. Bullard and Officership in the United States Army, 1881-1925* (1975); and *Semper Fidelis: The History of the United States Marine Corps* (1980). Written in collaboration with Dr. Peter Maslowski, a former student, his latest book, *For the Common Defense: A Military History of the United States, 1607-1983*, was published in 1984. He has contributed essays to books on American historiography, foreign policy, and military history, and he has written articles for *Military Affairs*, *The Americas*, *Armed Forces and Society*, and the *Marine Corps Gazette*. He has also written studies of academic education in national security policy, military professionalism, and American civil-military relations. A two-time trustee and current president of the American Military Institute, he is also a council member of the Inter-University Seminar on Armed Forces and Society, former Chairman, Section on Military Studies, International Studies Association, a trustee of the Marine Corps Historical Foundation, and an associate editor of *Armed Forces and Society*. A colonel in the U.S. Marine Corps Reserve, he is currently assigned to the Advanced Amphibious Study Group, Headquarters U.S. Marine Corps and the Marine Corps Command and Staff College, and commands Mobilization Training Unit DC-7 (Historical).

WILLIAMSON MURRAY is Professor of History at the Ohio State University. After active service in the United States Air Force, he received a Ph.D. from Yale University in 1975. He is the author of two books, *The Change in the European Balance of Power, 1938–1939: the Path to Ruin* (Princeton: Princeton University Press, 1984); and *Luftwaffe* (Baltimore: Nautical and Aviation Press, 1985). He has also authored articles that have appeared in scholarly and military journals. He is co-editor with Professor Allen Millet of *Military Effectiveness*, Vols. I-III published by Unwin Human in 1988. Professor Murray has also been a research associate at the Air War College, and visiting professor at the United States Military Academy and at the Naval War College.

JOHN J. SBREGA is Assistant Dean of Academic Affairs at the Community College of Rhode Island. He received his B.A. from Union College and his M.A. and Ph.D from Georgetown University. From 1963 to 1968, Sbrega served in the Air Force as a pilot acquiring extensive experience in Southeast Asia. His academic awards include a Fulbright Scholarship to the United Kingdom, a fellowship from the Center for Strategic and International Studies, two research grants from the National Endowment for the Humanities, a Beveridge Grant from the American Historical Association, and the Moncado Prize from the American Military Institute. He has published several articles in such journals as *Pacific Historical Review, Political Science Quarterly, Military Affairs, Asian Affairs*, and the *Journal of Southeast Asian Studies*. His book, *Anglo-American Relations and Colonialism in East Asia, 1941–1945*, published by Garland Publishing, was nominated for the 1984 Bernath Prize. Sbrega has also compiled an annotated bibliography, *The War Against Japan, 1941–1945* (Garland, 1989) and co-edited with Constance M. Jones and Derris L. Raper *The American Experience* (Kendall/Hunt, 2d ed., 1986).

DAVID SYRETT was educated at Columbia University and the University of London. Professor Syrett has been a member of the History Department, Queens College, Columbia University of New York (CUNY) since 1966. In 1970, he published *Shipping and the American War* and *The Siege and Capture of Havana, 1762*. In 1975, he co-edited *The Lost War: Letters from British Officers During the American Revolution* and in 1985 his *Neutral Rights and the War in the Narrow Seas, 1778–82* was published. During the academic year 1981–82, he was the John F. Morrison Professor of Military History at the USAC&GSC. Dr. Syrett's articles have appeared in *The William and Mary Quarterly, The Bulletin of the Institute of Historical Research, The Journal of the Society for Army Historical Research, New York History, The*

Mariner's Mirror, Military Review, U.S. Naval Institute Proceedings, Armed Forces and Society, The Naval War College Review, Military Intelligence, The American Neptune, and *Marine-Rundschau.*

JOE GRAY TAYLOR took the M.A. and Ph.D. degrees in history at Louisiana State University upon returning from World War II, during which he had flown seventy combat missions as a bombardier-navigator with the 81st Bomb Squadron, 12th Bomb Group, Tenth Air Force in the China-Burma-India Theater. He is the author of five Air Force Historical Studies, including *Close Air Support in the War Against Japan* and *Air Supply in the Burma Campaigns.* He has published articles in *Air Force History* and *Military Affairs.* Among numerous works on non-military history, he has published *Louisiana: A Bicentennial History* and *Eating, Drinking, and Visiting in the South: An Informal History.* He was Dean of Liberal Arts at McNeese State University, Lake Charles, Louisiana, at his death in 1987.

KENNETH R. WHITING, retired Chief of the Documentary Research Division, Center of Aerospace Doctrine, Research and Education, at the Air University, is a renowned Sovietologist. He received his Ph.D. in Russian history from Harvard University in 1951, and has contributed numerous articles and studies on Soviet and Chinese affairs to a variety of publications. Among works of relevance to his essay in this volume are: *The Chinese Communist Armed Forces* (Maxwell AFB: Aerospace Studies Institute, 1967); *The Development of the Soviet Armed Forces, 1917–1972* (Maxwell AFB: Air University, 1972); *Soviet Air Power, 1917–1976* (Maxwell AFB: Air University, 1980); and "Soviet Aviation and Air Power under Stalin, 1928–1941," Robin Higham and Jacob W. Kipp, editors, in *Soviet Aviation and Air Power: A Historical View* (Boulder, CO: Westview Press, 1977).

ALAN F. WILT is Professor of History at Iowa State University. He received his B.A. from DePauw University and M.A. and Ph.D. from the University of Michigan. In between, he served as an air intelligence officer for three years, with a tour in South Korea. After completing his doctorate, he has been engaged in teaching and research. His teaching duties, in addition to those at Iowa State, have included a year at the Air War College. His research has resulted in two books, *The Atlantic Wall: Hitler's Defenses in the West, 1941–1944,* published by Iowa State University Press, and *The French Riviera Campaign of August 1944,* published by Southern Illinois University Press, plus numerous articles in *Military Affairs,* the *Journal of Strategic Studies,* and *Air University Review.* He is now writing a comparative study of German and British military decisionmaking during World War II.

Index